HISTORY OF
THE SECOND WORLD WAR
UNITED KINGDOM MILITARY SERIES
Edited by Sir James Butler

The authors of the Military Histories have been given full access to official documents. They and the editor are alone responsible for the statements made and the views expressed.

1. Field Marshal Sir Archibald Wavell, Lieut.-General J. W. Stilwell, Lieut.-General H. H. Arnold, Lieut.-General B. B. Somervell, Field Marshal Sir John Dill.

THE WAR AGAINST JAPAN

VOLUME II
India's Most Dangerous Hour

BY

MAJOR-GENERAL S. WOODBURN KIRBY
C.B., C.M.G., C.I.E., O.B.E., M.C.

WITH
CAPTAIN C. T. ADDIS, D.S.O., R.N.
COLONEL J. F. MEIKLEJOHN, C.I.E.
(succeeded by BRIGADIER M. R. ROBERTS, D.S.O.)
COLONEL G. T. WARDS, C.M.G., O.B.E.
AIR VICE-MARSHALL N. L. DESOER, C.B.E.

This edition of The War Against Japan: Volume II
first published in 2004
by The Naval & Military Press Ltd

Published by
The Naval & Military Press Ltd
Unit 10 Ridgewood Industrial Park,
Uckfield, East Sussex,
TN22 5QE England
Tel: +44 (0) 1825 749494
Fax: +44 (0) 1825 765701
www.naval-military-press.com

The War Against Japan: Volume II first published in 1958.
© Crown copyright. Reprinted with the permission of
the Controller of HMSO and Queen's Printer for Scotland.

*In reprinting in facsimile from the original, any imperfections are inevitably reproduced
and the quality may fall short of modern type and cartographic standards.*

CONTENTS

	Page
INTRODUCTION	xv
CHAPTER I. PLANS FOR THE DEFENCE OF BURMA, 1937–1941	1
CHAPTER II. THE JAPANESE INVASION OF SOUTHERN BURMA (December 1941–February 1942)	23
CHAPTER III. INDIA BECOMES THE BASE FOR THE WAR IN THE FAR EAST (December 1941–February 1942)	47
CHAPTER IV. THE BILIN RIVER ACTION AND THE DISASTER AT THE SITTANG (February 1942)	59
CHAPTER V. THE EVACUATION OF RANGOON (February–March 1942)	79
CHAPTER VI. THE DEFENCE OF INDIA AND CEYLON (March 1942)	105
CHAPTER VII. JAPANESE NAVAL RAIDS ON CEYLON (April 1942)	115
CHAPTER VIII. MADAGASCAR (April–November 1942)	133
CHAPTER IX. THE STRUGGLE FOR CENTRAL BURMA BEGINS (March 1942)	145
CHAPTER X. THE LOSS OF CENTRAL BURMA (April 1942)	163
CHAPTER XI. THE DEVELOPMENT OF INDIA AS A BASE (April–May 1942)	187
CHAPTER XII. THE ALLIED WITHDRAWAL FROM BURMA (May 1942)	199

CONTENTS

	Page
Chapter XIII. THE PACIFIC (January–June 1942)	221
Chapter XIV. FRUSTRATIONS DURING THE 1942 MONSOON	235
Chapter XV. THE FIRST ARAKAN OFFENSIVE (September 1942–February 1943)	253
Chapter XVI. THE PACIFIC (June 1942–February 1943)	269
Chapter XVII. PLANS FOR THE REOCCUPATION OF BURMA IN 1944	291
Chapter XVIII. THE FIRST CHINDIT OPERATION (February–April 1943)	309
Chapter XIX. THE JAPANESE OFFENSIVE IN ARAKAN (February–March 1943)	331
Chapter XX. THE END OF THE ARAKAN CAMPAIGN	347
Chapter XXI. PLANS FOR AN OFFENSIVE IN 1944 FRUSTRATED	361
Chapter XXII. THE PACIFIC (February–April 1943)	373
Chapter XXIII. THE TRIDENT CONFERENCE (May–June 1943)	379
Chapter XXIV. THE AFTERMATH OF TRIDENT (May–August 1943)	389
Chapter XXV. THE PACIFIC (May–September 1943)	409
Chapter XXVI. ALLIED AND JAPANESE PLANS FOR THE DRY WEATHER 1943–44	419
Index	523

APPENDICES

	Page
APPENDIX 1. Order of Battle of the Army in Burma, 27th December 1941	439
APPENDIX 2. The State of Training of Brigades forming 17th Indian Infantry Division in December 1941	440
APPENDIX 3. Order of Battle of the Japanese 15th Army, December 1941	442
APPENDIX 4. Dispositions of Brigades of 17th Indian Infantry Division, 8th February 1942	443
APPENDIX 5. Order of Battle of 17th Indian Infantry Division at the Bilin River Action	444
APPENDIX 6. Parade State of the Infantry of 17th Indian Division, 24th February 1942	445
APPENDIX 7. Directive to Vice-Admiral Layton on Appointment as Commander-in-Chief, Ceylon, on the 5th March 1942	446
APPENDIX 8. Order of Battle of Air Forces, Ceylon, 31st March 1942	447
APPENDIX 9. Naval Forces taking Part in Operations off Ceylon, 29th March–10th April 1942	448
APPENDIX 10. Naval Forces and Other Shipping taking Part in the Operation to Capture Diego Suarez	450
APPENDIX 11. Order of Battle of the Japanese 5th Air Division, March 1942	451
APPENDIX 12. Order of Battle of the Chinese Expeditionary Force in Burma	452
APPENDIX 13. Order of Battle of Burcorps on Formation, 19th March 1942	454
APPENDIX 14. Directive to General J. W. Stilwell, February 1942	457
APPENDIX 15. Order of Battle of Fighting Formations in Burcorps, 6th April 1942	459
APPENDIX 16. Order of Battle of Eastern and Southern Armies, 21st April 1942	461

APPENDICES

	Page
APPENDIX 17. Order of Battle of Fighting Formations in Burcorps, 30th April 1942	462
APPENDIX 18. The Administrative Background to the First Burma Campaign, December 1941–May 1942	464
APPENDIX 19. Order of Battle of the Japanese 3rd Air Army, July 1942	476
APPENDIX 20. G.H.Q. Operation Instruction No. 11	477
APPENDIX 21. Order of Battle of Air Forces, India and Ceylon, September 1942	479
APPENDIX 22. Order of Battle of 14th Indian Infantry Division	480
APPENDIX 23. Particulars of British and Enemy Aircraft in use in South East Asia during the Period covered by this Volume	481
APPENDIX 24. Administrative Problems in India Command, 1942–43	489
APPENDIX 25. Supply and Administrative Problems during the First Chindit Expedition	499
APPENDIX 26. The Composition of 77th Indian Infantry Brigade (The Chindits), February 1943	503
APPENDIX 27. Wingate's Order of the Day, 13th February 1943	505
APPENDIX 28. The Organization of the Japanese 55th Division for the Counter-Offensive in Arakan, March–May 1943	506
APPENDIX 29. Eastern Army Operation Instruction No. 31	507
APPENDIX 30. Order of Battle of 26th Indian Infantry Division, 23rd April 1943	509
APPENDIX 31. Administrative Problems during the First Arakan Campaign, September 1942–May 1943	511
APPENDIX 32. Order of Battle of Air Forces, India and Ceylon, June 1943	518
APPENDIX 33. Order of Battle of the Japanese 5th Air Division during the 1943 Monsoon	520

MAPS AND SKETCHES

Forest growth is shown only where it is considered necessary for the purpose of illustrating the text.

Natural jungle is shown in green on the coloured maps and in a neutral tint in black and white sketches. Plantations (mostly rubber) are indicated by the conventional symbol for trees, in black and white.

Conventional topographical symbols have been used on all maps. For economy in printing or for clarity, roads appear in black, red or brown.

MAPS

Facing page

Strategic Map of Burma and Malaya . . *at end of volume*	
1. Moulmein—Rangoon, January–March 1942 . . .	23
2. The Action on the Bilin River, February 1942 . . .	62
3. The Action at the Sittang	78
4. India and Ceylon—showing Boundaries of India Command Areas	105
5. Naval Operations off Ceylon, April 1942	126
6. Indian Ocean	132
7. Madagascar, 1942	142
8. Toungoo—Prome, March–April 1942	145
9. Mandalay—Kalewa, April–May 1942	163
10. New Guinea—Solomon Islands	221
11. Maungdaw—Buthidaung—Rathedaung	253
12. Bhamo—Tamu, February–May 1943	309
13. The Line of Communication for the Arakan Campaign 1942–43	360
14. The North East Frontier 1942–43	434
15. The Pacific showing Command Areas 1942–43 . . .	434

SKETCHES

Facing page

1. Burma superimposed on Part of Europe		2
2. Burma Monthly Rainfall, May–October		3
3. Moulmein		34
4. Sittang Bridge		70
5. Pegu	*Page*	91
6. Yenangyaung		169
7. Monywa		203
8. Shwegyin		211
9. Rathedaung	*Facing page*	268
10. Guadalcanal	*Page*	285
11. Papua	*Facing page*	290

MAPS AND SKETCHES

Facing page

12. Htizwe Bridgehead	338
13. Donbaik	340
14. Atet Nanra—Indin	346
15. Letwedet—Maungdaw	358
16. Tiddim—Tamu . . . . *Page*	407
17. Assam Line of Communications 1943 . . *Facing page*	408
18. Huon Peninsula	412
19. New Georgia Group . . . . . *Page*	415
20. India superimposed on Europe . . . *Facing page*	494

PHOTOGRAPHS

Most of the photographs in this volume are Crown copyright and are reproduced by courtesy of the Imperial War Museum and the Ministries concerned. For permission to reproduce Nos. 2 and 3 the authors are indebted respectively to Lieut-General Hutton and Major-General Smyth.

1. Field Marshal Sir Archibald Wavell, Lieut.-General J. W. Stilwell, Lieut.-General H. H. Arnold, Lieut.-General B. B. Somervell, Field Marshal Sir John Dill . *Frontispiece*
2. Lieut.-General T. J. Hutton . . . . *Facing page* 86
3. Major-General J. G. Smyth 86
4. Moulmein 87
5. The Sittang Bridge 87
6. Admiral Sir Geoffrey Layton 118
7. Admiral Sir James Somerville 118
8. H.M.S. *Hermes* 119
9. H.M.S. *Cornwall* 119
10. Diego Suarez looking west from Antsirane . . . 134
11. Vice-Admiral E. N. Syfret 135
12. Sir Reginald Dorman-Smith and General the Hon. Sir Harold Alexander 158
13. Lieut.-General Shojiro Iida 158
14. Major-General J. Bruce Scott, Sir John Wise, General the Hon. Sir Harold Alexander, General Sir Archibald Wavell, Lieut.-General W. J. Slim, Brigadier H. L. Davies . . . 159
15. Air Chief Marshal Sir Richard Peirse 159
16. Central Burma: dry zone crops 174
17. Central Burma: rice fields in the Prome area . . . 174
18. The Ava Bridge 175
19. The Chindwin north of Kalewa 175
20. Near Taunggyi in the Shan States 190
21. The Burma Road near Wanting 191
22. General Sir Claude Auchinleck 318

PHOTOGRAPHS

23. Major-General O. C. Wingate . . . *Facing page* 318
24. Deciduous forest north of Shweli River 319
25. Supply drop by a Dakota (C. 47) 319
26. Lieut.-General N. M. S. Irwin, Major-General W. L. Lloyd . 334
27. Lieut.-General Takishi Koga 334
28. Animal barge on the Naf River near Tumbru . . . 335
29. Kalapanzin Valley near Buthidaung, looking south-west, Mayu Range in the background 335
30. Maungdaw from the north 350
31. Donbaik. 351
32. Landslide on the Imphal Road 398
33. Jogighopa—Goalpara vehicle ferry 398
34. Loading by hand, Dhubri 399
35. Amingaon—Pandu rail ferry 399

PUBLISHED SOURCES

INDIA AND BURMA

Despatch by General Sir Archibald Wavell (covering reports by Lieut.-General T. J. Hutton and General The Honourable Sir Harold Alexander) on operations in Burma from 15th December 1941 to 20th May 1942.
(Supplement to the *London Gazette* of 5th March 1948, No. 38228).

Despatch by Field Marshal The Viscount Wavell on operations in the Eastern Theatre, based on India, from March 1942 to 31st December 1942.
(Supplement to the *London Gazette* of 17th September 1946, No. 37728).

Despatch by Field Marshal The Viscount Wavell on operations in the India Command from 1st January 1943 to 20th June 1943.
(Supplement to the *London Gazette* of 20th April 1948, No. 38266).

Despatch by Air Vice-Marshal D. F. Stevenson on air operations in Burma and Bay of Bengal from 1st January to 22nd May 1942.
(Supplement to the *London Gazette* of 11th March 1948, No. 38229).

Official History of the Indian Armed Forces in the Second World War: The Retreat from Burma, 1941-1942 (India, 1953), and *The Arakan Operations, 1942-1945* (India, 1954).

ROMANUS and SUNDERLAND, *United States Army in World War II: The China-Burma-India Theater, Stilwell's Mission to China* (Washington, 1953).

CRAVEN and CATE, *The Army Air Forces in World War II: Volume 1, Plans and Early Operations* (Chicago, 1948).

MADAGASCAR

Despatch by Rear-Admiral E. N. Syfret (including a report by Lieut.-General Sir Robert Sturges) on the Capture of Diego Suarez.
(Supplement to the *London Gazette* of 2nd March 1948, No. 38225).

Despatch by Lieut.-General Sir William Platt on operations of East Africa Command, 12th July 1941 to 8th January 1943.
(Supplement to the *London Gazette* of 16th July 1946, No. 37655). .

THE PACIFIC

MORISON, *History of United States Naval Operations in World War II:*
Volume IV, *Coral Sea, Midway and Submarine Actions, May 1942-August 1942* (O.U.P., 1949).
Volume V, *The Struggle for Guadalcanal, August 1942-February 1943* (O.U.P., 1949).

Volume VI, Breaking the Bismarcks Barrier, 22 July 1942–1 May 1944 (O.U.P., 1950).

Volume VII, Aleutians, Gilberts & Marshalls, June 1942–April 1944 (O.U.P., 1952).

ROSKILL, *Official History of the Second World War: The War at Sea, Volume II, The Period of Balance* (H.M.S.O., 1956).

MATLOFF and SNELL, *United States Army in World War II: The War Department, Strategic Planning for Coalition Warfare, 1941–1942* (Washington, 1953).

MILLER, *United States Army in World War II: The War in the Pacific, Guadalcanal: The First Offensive.* (Washington, 1949).

HALSEY and BRYAN, *Admiral Halsey's Story* (New York, 1947).

EICHELBERGER, *Jungle Road to Tokyo* (Odhams Press, 1951).

KENNEY, *General Kenney Reports* (New York, 1949).

INTRODUCTION

VOLUME I of this history, after recounting briefly the events leading up to the outbreak of war with Japan, told of the first three disastrous months in which the Allies, unprepared and outnumbered, vainly tried to halt the Japanese advance. It covered the loss of the Philippines, Hong Kong, Malaya and the Dutch East Indies and ended with the fall of Java in March 1942.

The present volume divides itself into two parts. The first twelve chapters, telling of the loss of Burma, belong chronologically to Volume I. But, for reasons of space and because geographically Burma is more closely connected with India than with the Far East and strategically her defence was bound up with that of India, they have been included in this volume. The remaining chapters tell of the first abortive attempt to reoccupy Akyab, the experiment with a long-range penetration group, the plans for a major counter-offensive and the build-up of India as a base from which to launch it. The volume ends with the decision on the 25th August 1943 to form South-East Asia Command.

The fundamental cause of the loss of Burma as of Malaya was that the British had neither the trained manpower nor the resources to defend it. Many of the newly-formed army formations and much of India's manpower raised in the initial expansion had been sent to Malaya and the Middle East with the result that, when the war with Japan broke out and Burma was placed under India Command, there was little to spare for her defence. To make matters worse, such military formations and equipment as were then available went to reinforce Malaya in the vain hope of saving Singapore. The reinforcements eventually sent to Burma therefore not only contained an unusually high proportion of partly-trained men, but were too few and arrived too late.

The Army in Burma fought under difficult conditions of country and climate, in open plain and thick jungle, in clouds of dust under a burning sun, short of water and tormented by thirst and prickly heat, or soaked to the skin in steamy heat when the first rains of the monsoon brought swarms of mosquitoes and leeches. In the early days of the war there was no mepacrine and anti-malaria discipline could not always be effectively enforced. Tropical disease was often a more deadly foe than the Japanese. There was nothing wrong with the courage of the troops who fought in Burma, but, half-trained as they were, they were no match for the veterans of the Japanese *15th Army*.

An invasion of India's north-east frontier across the grain of the country had never been visualized because of the distance of any possible enemy, the difficulties of the terrain and the fact that such communications as there were in Burma ran north and south. The traditional threat had always been from the north-west and India's defences had been planned to meet it. The capture of Malaya by the Japanese and their invasion of Burma thus necessitated a complete reorientation of India's military organization. This raised vast administrative problems. The complexity of modern war has made sound administration imperative and no apology is therefore made for the space which is devoted to it in this volume.

The story told in the second part of the volume is one of frustration. Two successive theatre commanders did their best to launch a counter-offensive but their plans came to nothing. Owing to the requirements of the war in Europe and the shortage of shipping, the Chiefs of Staff were unable to supply all the men and equipment required. The total engineering resources in India proved insufficient to cope quickly enough with the enormous task of building the many airfields, base installations and roads needed for an invasion of Burma, nor could they in the time available improve the capacity of the rail and river communications to and in Assam. Political and economic factors in India also impeded progress and a particularly severe monsoon seriously interrupted the railway systems in Bengal at a critical period. The delay caused by the combination of all these circumstances, though disappointing to those concerned with the conduct of the war, was perhaps a blessing in disguise, for until the latter part of 1943 the lessons of the earlier campaigns had not been fully absorbed, nor had the newly-raised formations been adequately trained.

In writing of the campaigns in Burma and Arakan we have tried to show, when things went wrong, why they did so. The views expressed are our own: they have been formed after careful sifting of all the available evidence at our disposal, from despatches, war diaries, narratives, demi-official letters and telegrams written at the time as well as from Japanese documents, personal interviews and correspondence with some of those who took part.

The story of the war in the Pacific, which was an American theatre, is given only in sufficient outline to allow the reader to follow its progress and maintain a balanced view of the war as a whole. The reader who wishes to study it in detail is referred to the American, Australian and New Zealand histories.

Tribute has already been paid to the historians, librarians and cartographers who are assisting in the preparation of the Military Histories as a series, but we should also like to thank those who have helped us with this volume in particular. We have had the advantage of using the staff histories written by Commander L. J. Pitcairn-Jones and Major C. S. Goldingham of the Admiralty Historical Section, the narratives written by Brigadier J. A. Blood, Brigadier M. Henry, Lieut.-Colonel J. E. B. Barton and Captain W. Miles of the Cabinet Office Historical Section, and accounts prepared by the Air Historical Branch of the Air Ministry. We should also like to express our thanks to Mr. Gardner, Chief of the U.S. Foreign Histories Division, and his staff for research work carried out in Japan on our behalf and for supplying us with information from Japanese sources.

Many officers who took part in the operations in Burma and in the building up of India as a base have read and commented on the various drafts of this volume. It is impossible to mention them here by name, but we wish to express our gratitude to them for the great help they have given us. Mr Gavin Long, the General Editor of the Australian War History, has kindly assisted us in connection with the New Guinea campaign. We are grateful to Miss M. M. Baird and Mrs H. G. R. Pickthorn for their careful research work which has been of the greatest value to us and to the secretarial assistance given by Miss B. Wallen.

The lines from Kipling's '*Boxing*' are reprinted by kind permission of Mrs. George Bambridge, and the comment from '*Other Men's Flowers*' by kind permission of Lady Wavell.

S.W.K.
C.T.A.
J.F.M.
M.R.R.
G.T.W.
N.L.D.

*"Man cannot tell, but Allah knows
How much the other side was hurt!"*
                                    KIPLING

"The ... two lines illustrate my favourite military maxim, that when things are going badly in battle the best tonic is to take one's mind off one's own troubles by considering what a rotten time one's opponent must be having."
                                    A.P.W.

(Wavell, *Other Men's Flowers*, Jonathan Cape, 1944).

CHAPTER I

PLANS FOR THE DEFENCE OF BURMA 1937–1941

See Strategic Map, Map 15 and Sketches 1 and 2

JAPAN'S object in going to war with the Allies was to become the dominant power in the south-west Pacific by setting up, under her own aegis, a Greater East Asia Co-Prosperity Sphere comprising the Philippines, the Netherlands East Indies and Malaya. For strategic and economic reasons Burma was also to be occupied, to protect the north-western flank of the conquered territories and to procure additional supplies of oil and rice.[1]

The importance of Burma to the Allied cause in general and to the defence of India in particular in a war against Japan is obvious from a glance at the map. In 1941 Burma was bordered on the north-west by the Indian provinces of Bengal and Assam and the State of Manipur; on the north and north-east by China and on the east by China, French Indo-China and Siam. On the west, its coastline on the Bay of Bengal stretched for some twelve hundred miles, from Maungdaw in the Akyab district in the north to Victoria Point at the tip of Tenasserim in the south. From the viewpoint of Allied strategy, it was essential that China should be enabled to continue her struggle against Japan and thus contain large enemy forces. Through Burma lay the only route by which the Chinese armies could be kept supplied, and the American air bases in China maintained. From India's point of view, so long as Burma was held, Calcutta and the great industrial centres of north-east India were practically immune from air attack, and her eastern land frontiers were secure from the threat of invasion.

When considering the geography of Burma, it is important to realize the size of the country. Sandwiched on the map of Asia between the vast sub-continents of India and China, Burma seems to be a small narrow strip of territory, but it has a total area of no less than 240,000 square miles and if superimposed on Europe would cover France and Belgium.[2] It is divided from India on the west and China and Siam on the east by mountain ranges which, like fingers

---

[1] See Volume I, Chapter V.
[2] See Sketch 1.

of a hand, stretch southwards from the eastern end of the great Himalayan chain. Burma (excluding Arakan) is separated from India by the great range of mountains which form the western of these fingers. The range runs in a south-westerly direction from the Himalayas near Fort Hertz for some three hundred miles to Imphal, where it reaches its greatest width of about a hundred miles. It then turns south and continues for another four hundred miles to a point a little north of Bassein on the Bay of Bengal. It is known as the Naga Hills in the north, the Chin Hills in the centre and the Arakan Yomas in the south,[1] but is in fact one continuous tangled and precipitous mountain system normally covered up to a height of 6,000 feet in dense jungle.

In 1941 it was not traversed by any roads, and the few through tracks which existed at the time were tortuous and liable to interruption by floods and landslides. In the Naga Hills the peaks rise to 12,000 feet and in the Chin Hills there are many between 8,000 and 10,000 feet. The Arakan Yomas which run parallel to the Arakan coast are much lower; nevertheless they form an effective barrier between Burma proper and the Arakan coastal regions. The India-Burma border lies along the range from a point seventy miles north of Fort Hertz to the Chin Hills and then continues in a south-westerly direction to the estuary of the Naf River near Maungdaw on the Bay of Bengal. In the Naga Hills and as far south as Tamu the border lies near the Burma or eastern side of the range; it then crosses to the Indian or western side and remains there. Thus so long as military operations took place near the border, the land communications were simpler for the Japanese in the north and for the British in the south.

The coastal province of Arakan is separated from the rest of Burma by the Arakan Yomas. These were pierced by a cart track which ran from Prome to Taungup in the south of the province. There was, however, no road link from Taungup to northern Arakan nor from the latter to eastern Bengal, though the villages along the coast were connected by rough tracks interrupted by unbridged rivers and deep estuaries.

Plans for joining the road system of Burma with that of Assam had often been considered, but the ease and cheapness of sea communications between Burma and India across the Bay of Bengal rendered any such project uneconomical. Land communications between the two countries, apart from some jungle paths which wound through the mountains between Assam and the upper Chindwin, were limited to an unbridged track, impassable in wet weather, from Palel to Tamu (on the frontier) down the Kabaw Valley to Kalemyo.

---

[1] Yoma: range

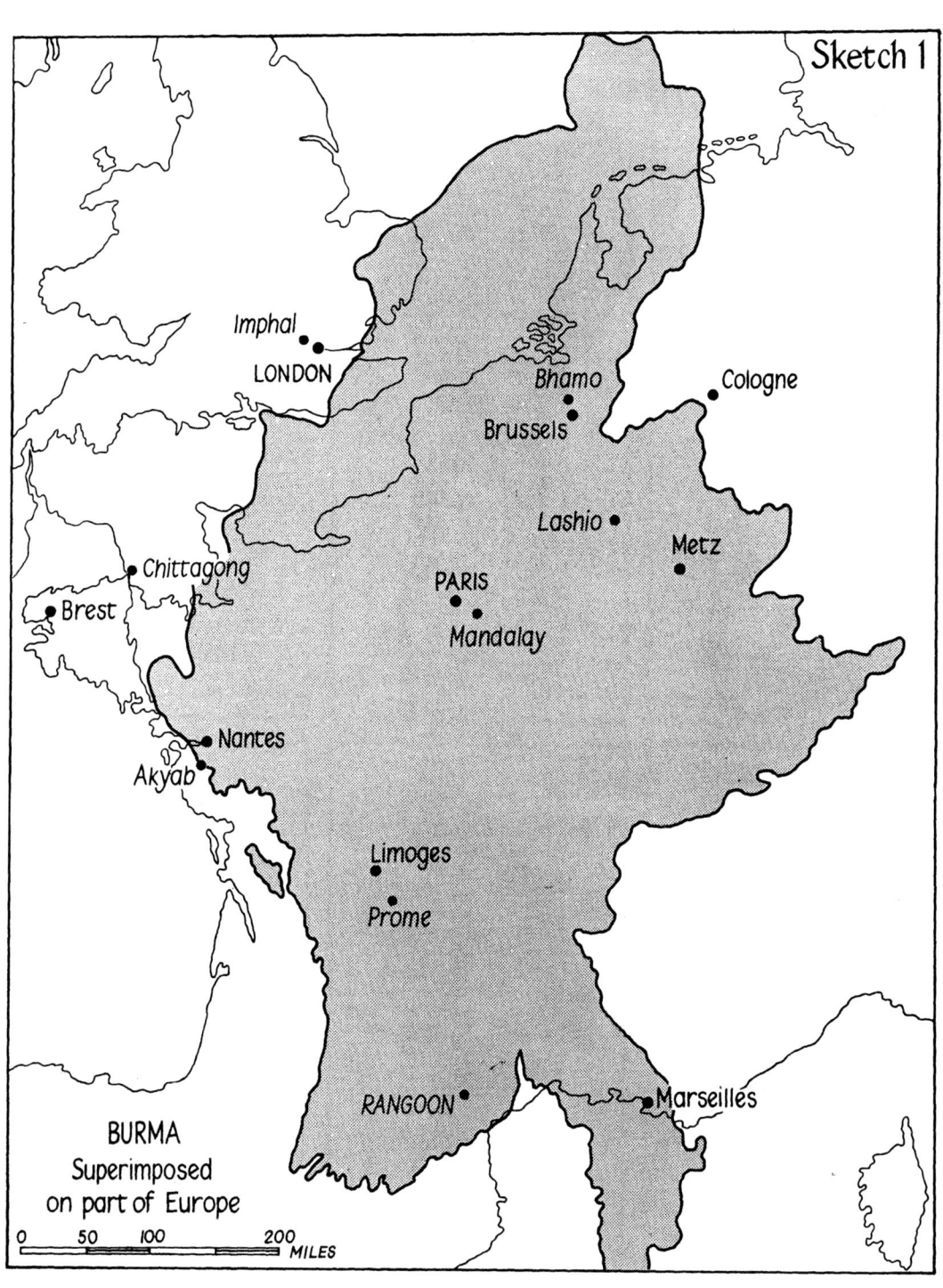

BURMA MONTHLY RAINFALL
May – October

Sketch 2

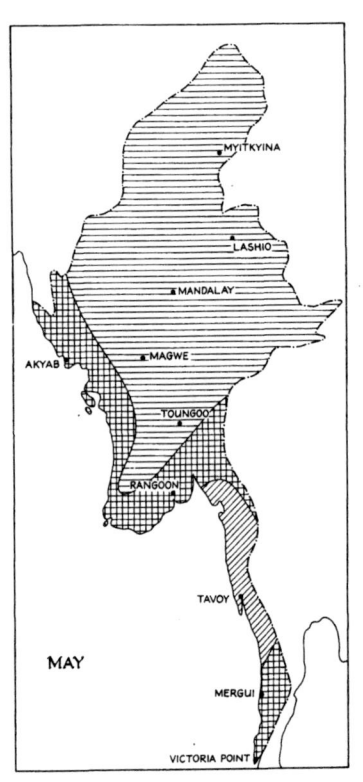
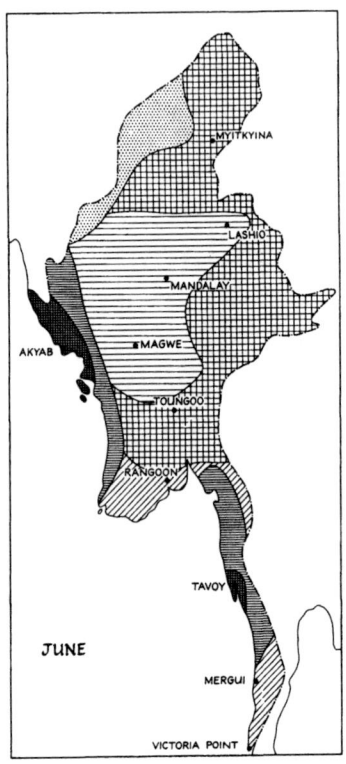
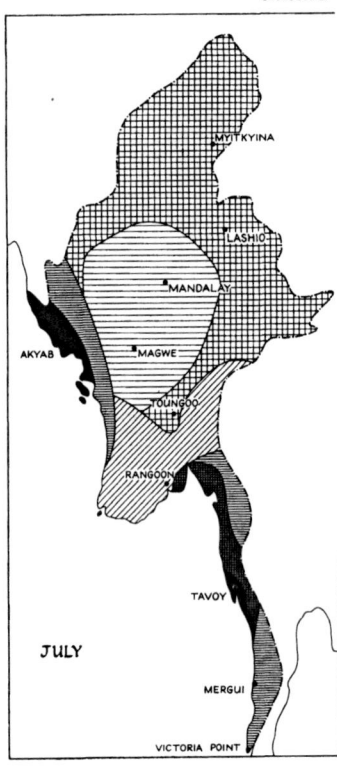
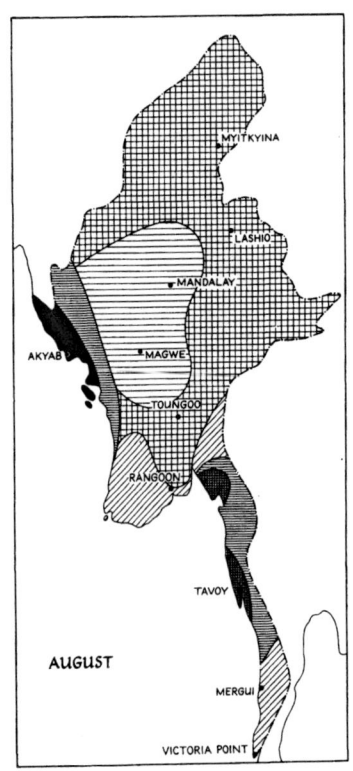
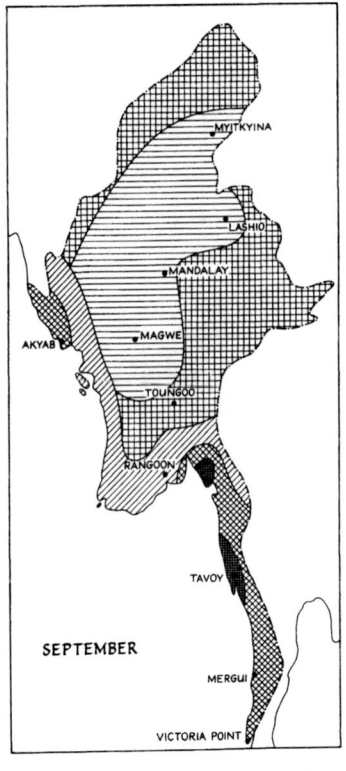
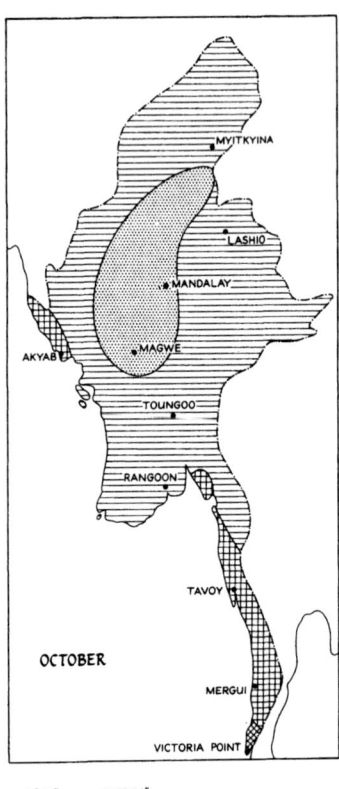

0"–5"   5"–10"   10"–15"   15"–20"   20"–30"   30"–40"   40"–50"   OVER 50"

A short stretch of bridged road led from this village to Kalewa on the Chindwin. On the opposite side of this river a rough unbridged track ran to the railway at Yeu and on to Shwebo. There was also an unbridged track down the Myittha valley connecting Kalemyo with Pakokku on the Irrawaddy.[1]

The Burma-China border lies along the mountains forming the eastern finger, running from the northern end of the India-Burma border, north of Fort Hertz, in a southerly direction for some three hundred miles to Loiwing and thence south-east to the River Mekong where it meets the Indo-China border north of Mong Sing. At this point it turns south-west, separating Burma from first Indo-China and then Siam, running along the south of the Shan States to the Karen Hills until it joins the Salween River south-east of Toungoo. From there it runs south along the eastern side of Tenasserim to Victoria Point on the Isthmus of Kra. As on the western frontier, the mountains are high in the north and gradually diminish till they peter out at the southern end of Tenasserim. The frontier with China was crossed by the Burma Road near Wanting (north-east of Mandalay); that with Siam by a track from Kengtung in the east of the Shan States to Chiengrai, and from Loikaw to Chiengmai. Further south there were two tracks into Siam, the one over the Dawna Range from Moulmein to Raheng and the other from Moulmein through Three Pagodas Pass to Bangkok.

Burma is watered by three rivers. The Irrawaddy rises near Fort Hertz and flows down the centre of the country through Mandalay and Myingyan, where it is joined by its tributary the Chindwin, to the delta at Rangoon; it is navigable up to Myitkyina 1,000 miles from the sea, and the Chindwin to a point some 200 miles north of Kalewa. The Sittang, like the Irrawaddy, also flows from north to south through the central plain from just south of Meiktila to the Gulf of Martaban. The Salween, which rises in China and crosses the border to the east of Wanting, flows through the Shan States, the Karen Hills and Tenasserim into the Gulf of Martaban at Moulmein; it is swift, navigable only to a limited extent near its mouth and was unbridged except where crossed by the Burma Road between Wanting and Paoshan.

Rangoon, the capital city and main port, is situated on the Irrawaddy delta about twenty-five miles from the sea. In 1941 its population of about half a million was cosmopolitan; most of the municipal and dock labourers were Indians, who had no roots in Burma.[2] It was linked by regular shipping services with Calcutta and Madras, and through it passed the greater part of Burma's imports and exports. Moulmein, Bassein and Akyab, the only

---
[1] See Map 14.
[2] The total population of Burma was about seventeen million (1941 census).

other seaports of any size, served a very limited hinterland and were therefore of minor importance. Tavoy and Mergui in the extreme south of Tenasserim were used mainly by local craft and coastal shipping.

In 1941 the main internal communications ran in general north from Rangoon. The main metre gauge railway, passing through Pegu and Toungoo, ran up the valley of the Sittang River to Mandalay. It had branches to the oil-bearing areas on the east bank of the Irrawaddy, to Shwenyaung, nine miles east of Heho in the Shan States and a loop from Thazi, ten miles east of Meiktila, through Myingyan to Mandalay. It then crossed the Irrawaddy by the great Ava bridge and ran north through Indaw to Myitkyina, with a branch to Monywa and Yeu. Three other lines existed, one from Mandalay to Lashio, a second from Rangoon to Prome with a branch to Bassein and Kyangin and a third from Pegu across the Sittang River to Martaban at the mouth of the Salween River, where a railway ferry connected it with Moulmein and the line to Ye in Tenasserim.

The main all-weather road to the north followed the line of the railway up the Sittang valley through Toungoo and Meiktila to Mandalay. From Meiktila a branch road serving the Shan States ran east through Loilem to Takaw on the Salween River and, after crossing the ferry at Takaw, continued as far as Kengtung. A motorable road through the Karen Hills connected Toungoo with Loilem. There was also an all-weather road up the Irrawaddy valley to Prome; this continued through Magwe and Yenangyaung to Myingyan, Meiktila and Mandalay but, as it lacked bridges over the major chaungs, was not always passable after heavy rains. The Burma Road began at Mandalay and ran through Lashio to the Chinese border near Wanting and, crossing the only bridge over the Salween, went on through Paoshan and Kunming to Chungking. The Irrawaddy River and the large fleet of vessels maintained by the Irrawaddy Flotilla Company, which ran regular services throughout its navigable length, as well as on the Chindwin, provided the most important of the internal communications. It will be noted that almost all communications ran north and south: with the exception of the Meiktila-Kengtung road, there was practically none running east and west.

Burma is affected by two monsoons. The north-east monsoon blows from the middle of October to the middle of May. During this season rain is rare and for much of the period the climate is cool and enjoyable. In March the heat increases and, while the north-east winds are dying out, April and the first half of May are intensely hot and damp. Then the south-west monsoon begins, bringing heavy rainfall to the greater part of the country: it exceeds 200 inches in the coastal regions of Arakan and Tenasserim and along the Assam border. In the dry zone in the central plain covering the Mandalay-Magwe-Toungoo area, the rainfall is only between twenty and thirty inches.[1] This monsoon dies out during September and October. During April before it begins, and in October and November at its tail end, small quantities of rain may be expected at intervals, though October and November may be at times very wet on the Arakan coast in the vicinity of Akyab. There are very few areas in Burma where malaria is not endemic.

Burma's chief agricultural product was rice, of which she exported large quantities to India, and her chief industry was timber, particularly teak of which she was the world's main source of supply. From a military point of view her most important products were oil and wolfram. The principal oil-bearing area was at Yenangyaung, the oil being piped direct to the refinery plants around Syriam, southeast of Rangoon.[2] The mines at Mawchi supplied ten per cent. of the world's and thirty-five per cent. of the Commonwealth's wolfram supplies.

With the development of commercial aviation, Burma had become an important link on the Imperial air route from Great Britain to Australia. British, Indian, Dutch and French commercial aircraft used her airfields as ports of call, and in 1941 an air service was operating between Rangoon and Chungking, with an intermediate stop at Lashio.

On her separation from India in April 1937, Burma achieved a considerable measure of self-government. This, however, did not satisfy the politically conscious among the Burmese who, despite their party dissensions and personal jealousies, were united in a demand for greater independence. The extremists—the Thakin Party, composed mainly of young students of whom many looked to Aung San for leadership—formed a minority which, helped by the political immaturity of the country, slowly increased in influence. This party was openly anti-British. After the outbreak of war with Germany in September 1939, the Thakins repeatedly asserted their opposition to Britain and their determination to secure the independence of Burma by force. That this revolutionary movement was viewed with favour by the Japanese there is little doubt; several of the Thakin leaders visited Tokyo and looked to Japan to assist their national aspirations.

In the autumn of 1941 U Saw, the Premier, took advantage of Britain's difficulties to press for full self-government to be granted

---
[1] See Sketch 2.
[2] See Map 1.

immediately after the war. The Governor of Burma (Sir Reginald Dorman-Smith)[1] suggested to the Secretary of State for Burma that U Saw should visit England to enable him to argue his case direct with the British Government. He did so, but his demands were refused. He then left for Burma by way of the United States. The day after he reached Hawaii the attack on Pearl Harbour took place and he turned back with the intention of flying back to Burma by way of Europe. While in Lisbon he contacted the Japanese Embassy. On resuming his journey, he was arrested in Palestine and kept in detention in East Africa for the rest of the war.

The disaffected element of the Burmese population was quite small. The uneducated masses remained largely indifferent—neither pro-British nor pro-Japanese—though later many displayed a tendency to assist the invader when it looked as if he would emerge victorious. This however applied only to the Burmans: with few exceptions, the Karens in the south and the hill peoples of the north remained staunchly loyal. Before the war the Japanese community in Burma was small, but its members worked unobtrusively against British interests and acted as agents for their own Government.

After separation from India, Burma became responsible for her own defence. She had to finance such armed forces as she maintained and obtain military stores and equipment through the War Office. The Committee of Imperial Defence was responsible for telling the Governor what scale of attack to expect, but the Government of Burma was, in peacetime, responsible for assessing the scale of defence necessary. Since Burma was the geographical link between India and Malaya and her security was vital to both countries, it had been a vexed question from 1937 onwards whether the conduct of operations for her defence should be the responsibility of the Commander-in-Chief in India, or of the Chiefs of Staff. Before General Sir Archibald Wavell's appointment as Commander-in-Chief in India in July, 1941, three of his predecessors—Field Marshal Sir Philip Chetwode, General Sir Robert Cassels and General Sir Claude Auchinleck—had repeatedly urged the necessity for placing Burma under India's control for defence purposes.

In August 1940, the Governor-General of India had represented that the defence of the Bay of Bengal and the surrounding territories constituted a single strategical problem for which India should become responsible. The Chiefs of Staff decided that the defence of this area was not an isolated problem: it figured in the general defence of the Far East in which not only India, but Burma, Malaya and Australia were all vitally interested. India's main responsibility was the defence of her North West Frontier and her own internal

---

[1] Sir Reginald Dorman-Smith became Governor of Burma on the 5th May 1941.

security—her interest lay more in the Middle Eastern than the Far Eastern bloc. Australia's primary concern was the defence of her own territory. The defence of Malaya and that of Burma, however, were closely connected and required a carefully co-ordinated plan to meet the threat from Japan. Since Malaya was the focus of British defence against Japan, plans for the defence of Burma had to be co-ordinated by the commanders in the Far East; it therefore would not come under India. The result of this ruling was that, when in November 1940 a unified command was established in the Far East with its headquarters in Singapore[1], Burma was included therein for operational purposes, administration remaining directly under the War Office.

At the same time the Commander-in-Chief in India was told that the defence of Burma was recognized to be of vital concern to India, and that he should therefore co-operate with the Commander-in-Chief, Far East, in measures for the land and air defence of Burma and the Bay of Bengal, furnishing 'as far as may be possible' any necessary men and material which Burma herself could not provide, subject to the general approval in each case of His Majesty's Government.

General Wavell was not satisfied with this arrangement. He visited the United Kingdom in September 1941 and sought to persuade the Chiefs of Staff that the defence of Burma should be transferred from Far East Command to India. But even the fact that the Japanese had by this time occupied Indo-China, thus bringing the danger to Burma much closer, was not held to justify the change. After returning to India, Wavell visited both Malaya and Burma and discussed the question with the Commander-in-Chief, Far East (Air Chief Marshal Sir Robert Brooke-Popham), and with the Governor of Burma as well as with the General Officer Commanding, Burma (Lieut.-General D. K. McLeod). The Governor supported him, and suggested that Burma should come directly under the Commander-in-Chief in India in the same way as Iraq, and not indirectly through the Indian Defence Department. Sir Robert recognized the force of Wavell's arguments in favour of transfer, but considered that, as it would complicate air support to China and the passage of supplies to that country, Burma should remain his responsibility. On the 11th November 1941 Wavell sent a cable to the Chiefs of Staff embodying Sir Reginald's and Sir Robert's views and again strongly recommending that Burma should be transferred to India Command.

The Chiefs of Staff agreed, but on a recommendation of the Defence Committee deferred a decision until after the arrival in

---

[1] See Volume I, page 50.

Singapore of the newly appointed Commander-in-Chief, Far East (Lieut.-General Sir Henry Pownall). On the 11th December, three days after war in the Far East broke out, the Chiefs of Staff raised the matter again. As there was by that time a chance that Singapore might be practically isolated, the arguments in favour of making a change were even stronger than before. That evening, the Prime Minister and the Chiefs of Staff decided that the control of Burma should pass forthwith to the Commander-in-Chief in India.

As Burma had never been regarded as liable to attack by a major power, only very small regular forces had been maintained in the country after her separation from India. These consisted of two British battalions, four battalions of the Burma Rifles, a small engineer works service and, on loan from India, a mountain battery and a field company; these units were mostly located in the Rangoon and Maymyo districts.[1] A demand for a higher proportion of Burmans in the armed forces caused the Governor to form two territorial battalions. But this did not satisfy Burman aspirations and consequently Burman companies were formed and included in the Burma Rifles, hitherto recruited solely from the Chins, Kachins and Karens. The force on which Burma chiefly relied, both for her internal security and for watch and ward on her land frontiers, was the Burma Military Police, consisting of nine battalions. After the separation from India, six of these battalions had been converted into the Burma Frontier Force (B.F.F.) but they remained under civil control. There was also the Burma Auxiliary Force (B.A.F.) composed of volunteers recruited from the European, Anglo-Burmese and Anglo-Indian communities. In view of the size of the defence forces, Army Headquarters, Burma, was very small and in fact no larger than a normal second class district headquarters in India.

On the outbreak of war in Europe the B.F.F. was made responsible for the defence of the principal airfields in addition to its other duties, and the B.A.F. was embodied for the protection of the Syriam oil refineries and to man the examination battery at the mouth of the Rangoon river.[2] Between 1939 and 1941 the forces in Burma were expanded but under grave difficulties, for peacetime defence expenditure had been severely restricted with the result that instructors as well as reserves of arms and equipment were lacking, and the administrative services were inadequate. Further, as there seemed to be no prospect of Burma being exposed to attack, the Government had been unwilling to finance large increases in the armed

---

[1] Maymyo lies in the hills some thirty-five miles to the east of Mandalay. See Map 9.

[2] This battery consisted originally of 18-pounder field guns. When 6-inch coast defence guns were later installed, 5th Field Battery (B.A.F.) was raised and equipped with 18-pounders.

forces, while the War Office, endeavouring to meet the requirements of the active theatres of war and areas of greater strategical importance, had to place the country at the bottom of the order of priority for weapons and equipment.

Nevertheless something had been achieved. The Army in Burma Reserve of Officers formed in 1939 had been expanded; in November 1940 service in the Burma Auxiliary Force had been made obligatory for all European British subjects of military age; a corps of Burma Sappers and Miners consisting of a depot and two field companies had been formed; measures to improve the administrative services had been taken; and the strength of the Burma Rifles doubled—four additional regular battalions, as well as two more territorial battalions, being raised. This expansion had fallen heavily on the only two regular British battalions in Burma, 1st Gloucestershire and 2nd King's Own Yorkshire Light Infantry, which had been drawn upon to provide the necessary British framework for the newly-raised units and services. These battalions had already sent a number of officers and other ranks to India and the United Kingdom and, as a result of this further call on their resources, in December 1941 neither unit could muster more than two companies.

Special units from within the Burma Frontier Force were raised in 1941 to harass and delay any enemy advance in the frontier regions. At first there were only four of these (known as F.F.1 to F.F.4) but later their number was increased.[1] On the 6th November 1941 the Burma Frontier Force was transferred from civil to military control, but its administration was left with the civil government, an arrangement which caused considerable difficulty.

An anti-aircraft unit—1st Heavy Anti-Aircraft Regiment (B.A.F.)—was formed and began to train, though it had no guns until well after the outbreak of war in the Far East. An observer corps was raised and by 1941 was able to man a series of posts along the eastern frontier. Since no wireless sets were available, the location of these posts was dictated by the existing telephone and telegraph systems.

In the autumn of 1941, with a considerable internal security problem on her hands and facing a growing threat from Japan, Burma was practically without the means of defending herself. Such units as she had were only partly trained, were not organized in field formations and were almost without artillery, engineers and mobile medical and administrative units. There were no anti-aircraft guns in the country, no reserves of rifles and machine-guns and the supplies of submachine-guns, mortars, mortar ammunition, grenades, anti-tank mines, steel helmets and web equipment were entirely inadequate.[2]

---

[1] For composition see Appendix 1, footnote.
[2] For details of the administrative organization see Appendix 18.

The air force in Burma, as elsewhere in the Far East, was very weak. 60 (Blenheim) Squadron arrived at Mingaladon airfield (Rangoon) early in 1941 and a small R.A.F. command was established, but the squadron was flown to Malaya later in the year. When war with Japan broke out, the only R.A.F. unit in the country was 67 (Fighter) Squadron with some sixteen Buffalo aircraft.[1] The forward airfields were Victoria Point, Mergui, Tavoy, Moulmein, Rangoon (Mingaladon and Zayatkwin), Toungoo, Heho, Namsang, Lashio and Loiwing. The last was an American-built airfield on the Chinese side of the frontier, north of Lashio. Immediately to the east of most of these airfields came the jungle-clad mountains along the frontier, leaving insufficient space for an effective warning system to be established. Nevertheless the Government of Burma organized a warning system manned by civilians but, except in the case of Rangoon, the approach of enemy aircraft to these airfields could rarely be predicted. There were other airfields at Akyab, Magwe, Meiktila, Shwebo and Myitkyina. Some of these were still under construction but by December 1941 could be used as landing grounds. The airfields at Victoria Point, Moulmein, Tavoy and Mergui were essential links on the air reinforcement route to Malaya, since the distance from Rangoon to Singapore was too great for the aircraft then in commission to cover without refuelling. They were therefore of great strategic importance.

The Chinese had agreed in April 1941 that a number of American air squadrons manned by volunteers (which became known as the American Volunteer Group (A.V.G.)) should be formed for service in China and gave a virtual promise that, if Burma were attacked, a part of this group would be detailed for its defence. In June the first contingent of the A.V.G. arrived in Burma, where it was to assemble and test its aircraft. By November three squadrons of Tomahawk (P.40) fighters had been formed at Toungoo. When war broke out Generalissimo Chiang Kai-shek kept his promise and one squadron was retained in Burma to assist in the air defence of Rangoon, the other two having been moved to Kunming, the Chinese end of the Burma Road.

When Burma became responsible for her own naval defence in 1937, plans were made to form a Burma R.N.V.R. with the function of naval administration and defence of ports and coasts in time of war. There was considerable delay in the formation of this force, mainly owing to the fact that the Government of Burma Act had no clause empowering the Governor to raise naval forces. Without this clause, members of this force would have been liable to be regarded as pirates if they put to sea in an armed ship. By December 1941 the

---

[1] See Appendix 23.

only naval force in Burmese waters was a flotilla of five motor launches of the B.R.N.V.R. and a few auxiliary vessels, under the command of Commander K. S. Lyle, R.N., who was responsible for the whole work of naval administration.

In discussing the forces available for the defence of Burma, mention has been made only of the troops actually in the country, but arrangements existed for military assistance from China in the event of a Japanese attack. Shortly after Far East Command had been set up in November 1940, Major-General L. E. Dennys was appointed Military Attaché in Chungking with a view to his becoming the head of a British military mission in China should war break out.[1] Largely owing to his work and that of Wing Commander J. Warburton (Air Attaché), British relations with the Chinese were satisfactory, and considerable progress was made in plans for mutual co-operation. These included a visit in April 1941 by a Chinese military mission to Burma and Singapore.

British assistance took the form of aid in the preparation of airfield sites in the Kunming area for the protection of the Burma Road and the despatch of stocks of explosives, aviation petrol, bombs and other material to China. In addition, special squads of British and Indian personnel were put under training in Burma for eventual attachment to the fifteen Chinese guerilla companies which were being formed in China. It was proposed ultimately to double the number of these companies and, consequently, that of the special squads. The Chinese on their part promised to send troops into Burma if required, and to threaten the Japanese northern flank should they advance against Burma by way of Chiengrai.

The possibility of an attack on Burma across her eastern frontier had for long been regarded as remote, and in 1939 the General Officer Commanding, Burma, did not consider there was any real danger of invasion from that quarter. In August 1940 the Chiefs of Staff reviewed the situation in the Far East and concluded that, though a Japanese occupation of Siam would bring the threat of air attack on Burma closer, the invasion of Burmese territory would still be a comparatively remote threat. Reinforcements were needed, but since the defence of Malaya had to have precedence, the provision of these could only be a very long-term project.

In October a Defence Conference, held at Singapore, examined in detail the position of Burma in the light of a Japanese threat from Siam. They came to the conclusion that air attacks on the oil refineries and docks at Rangoon and land, seaborne and air attacks on

---

[1] Known as 204 Mission.

the Tenasserim coast to capture or destroy airfields on the Singapore air route might be expected and must be provided against. It was, they thought, unlikely that the Japanese would concentrate all their aircraft based in Siam on Burma since Malaya was 'a vastly more attractive and important objective.' The air forces normally to be stationed in Burma could thus be limited to two bomber squadrons, one fighter squadron, a general reconnaissance squadron and one army co-operation squadron.

Contrary to the opinion expressed a year previously by the General Officer Commanding, the conference though that, while attacks on Burma's eastern territory might in the first instance be confined to raids, a Japanese attack from Chiengrai into the southern Shan States was a feasible proposition for a large force. They therefore recommended that Burma be reinforced at once by seven infantry battalions, a field regiment, a mountain battery, an anti-tank battery, three field companies and a light tank company.

The Chiefs of Staff considered that the conference had overestimated the scale of attack and the strength of the forces required to meet it. They themselves were not able to provide any of the reinforcements asked for, and therefore told India to earmark a brigade group for despatch to Burma in an emergency. India agreed to earmark 13th Indian Infantry Brigade Group (Brigadier A. C. Curtis), and on the 7th February 1941 the Chiefs of Staff decided it should be sent to Burma as soon as possible. It landed in Rangoon in March/April and was sent to Mandalay.[1]

As the attitude of Japan grew more menacing during 1941, units from Maymyo were moved into the southern Shan States for the defence of the eastern frontier, later becoming 1st Burma Brigade (Brigadier G. A. L. Farwell). Further south in Tenasserim, four battalions of the Burma Rifles were allotted to frontier defence, eventually forming 2nd Burma Brigade (Brigadier A. J. H. Bourke). In July 1st Burma Division (Major-General J. Bruce Scott) was formed. Its staff was found from local resources and its headquarters was located at Toungoo. It consisted of 1st and 2nd Burma and 13th Indian Brigades, but was short of artillery, engineers, signals, medical and transport units. None of its brigades had had any collective training and from an operational point of view it was at that time a division in name only.

In August 1941, the Commander-in-Chief, Far East, having reviewed the state of the defence of Burma, told the War Office it was essential that within eleven days of a Japanese attack on the country, Burma should be reinforced by an infantry brigade. In view of the importance of Burma to the defence of India, and the grave risks

---

[1] The 13th Brigade Group consisted of 2/7th Rajput Regiment, 5/1st Punjab Regiment, 1/18th Royal Garhwal Rifles and 12th and 23rd Mountain Batteries.

involved in reinforcing it after war had broken out, General Wavell advised that a brigade should be sent as soon as possible. His advice was accepted and 16th Indian Infantry Brigade (Brigadier J. K. Jones) began the move to Burma at the end of November and was still arriving on the outbreak of war.[1] It was sent to Mandalay, but remained as a general reserve under the command of the General Officer Commanding, Burma.

Despite the steps taken between 1939 and 1941 to improve the defences, and the arrival of two brigades from India, the Army in Burma in December 1941 was unfit for war with a major military power, and the country was unprepared to face invasion. There was, for example, no adequate intelligence staff. Internal intelligence was a civil responsibility and for news of what was happening just over the Siamese border reliance had to be placed on information received from Singapore. As a result, what was known of the enemy in Siam was largely out of date. Army Headquarters had to combine the rôles, at one and the same time, of a war office, a general headquarters, a corps headquarters, and a line of communication area headquarters.

The position was no more satisfactory on the civil side. No arrangements had been made by December 1941 to provide for military control of the railways and inland water transport systems in an emergency.[2] A Civil Defence Commissioner had, however, been appointed in November 1941 and a start had been made in forming an air raid precautions organization in Rangoon, but the nature of the subsoil in the town had prevented the construction of underground shelters and surface shelters were built for only five per cent. of the population. By the time war broke out, owing to the difficulty of obtaining equipment and supplies, very little had been achieved.

When war with Japan became imminent, the Commander-in-Chief, Far East, told General McLeod that he was to protect the airfields in southern Burma in order to maintain the Imperial air route to Singapore and safeguard the Burma Road and communications with China. McLeod thus had to assess the probable weight and direction of a Japanese invasion from Siam.

Road and rail communications in Siam pointed to Chiengrai and Chiengmai in the north as likely concentration areas for an invasion of Burma through the Shan States and along the Kengtung-Meiktila road. An invasion along that route constituted no immediate threat to Rangoon, the main base of the Army in Burma. In Tenasserim,

---

[1] The 16th Indian Infantry Brigade consisted of 1/7th Gurkha Rifles, 1/9th Royal Jat Regiment and 4/12th Frontier Force Regiment. The transport was partly motors and partly pack mules. For its state of training see Appendix 2.

[2] See Appendix 18.

however, an enemy advance along the Raheng-Moulmein track, comparatively easy once the first twenty miles through the precipitous and jungle-clad Dawna Range had been crossed, more directly threatened the Tenasserim airfields and was the shortest way to Rangoon. McLeod estimated that the enemy might concentrate up to eight divisions in Siam, but that, owing to administrative difficulties, only two could be employed against Burma and that these might be supported by eight bomber and four fighter squadrons, a remarkably accurate forecast.

Since operations in both Europe and Africa had shown how dependent modern armies were on motor transport, McLeod decided that the threat of invasion was more serious in the north, i.e. along the road through the Shan States to central Burma. With Brooke-Popham's approval he therefore moved 1st Burma and 13th Indian Brigades into the Shan States, instead of reinforcing 2nd Burma Brigade in Tenasserim. Since he considered it necessary to maintain a force for internal security purposes, he retained 1st Gloucestershire and a Burma Auxiliary Force battalion in Rangoon and units of the Burma Rifles and Burma Frontier Force in central Burma. His plan of defence against a superior invading force was to delay the enemy until he reached the line of the Salween River which was to be held at all costs. Because of their isolated position near the frontier and the lack of communications, the protection of the airfields at Tavoy, Mergui and Victoria Point, which could not be ignored so long as Malaya was held, was peculiarly difficult. In the circumstances McLeod decided that in the event of serious attack the garrison of Victoria Point would be withdrawn by sea, and the garrison of Mergui evacuated to Tavoy, which was to be held.

On the 8th December 1941 the war with Japan broke out. Four days later the Chiefs of Staff transferred the control of Burma from Far East Command to India Command, and General Wavell thus became responsible for her defence. He was told by the Prime Minister that 18th British Division, then at the Cape, would be allotted to him for the defence of India and Burma and that he could retain 17th Indian Division, previously earmarked for Iraq. He was also promised a 'special hamper' of anti-tank and anti-aircraft artillery and told that four squadrons of fighters would be diverted from the Middle East to India.[1] Later he was promised six squadrons of Blenheim bombers for Burma.

He immediately sent a considerable number of staff officers and technical experts to reinforce Army Headquarters, Burma, and pre-

---

[1] See Volume I, pages 254-55.

pared to despatch 45th Brigade of 17th Indian Division.[1] He had asked the Chiefs of Staff in November for some African troops, for the campaign in Italian East Africa had been successfully concluded, and on the 16th December he was told that two brigades of these troops could be made available, the first of which would be ready to embark at the end of January.

On the 21st December Wavell visited Rangoon. By that time he was no longer able to count on having the use of the whole of 18th British and 17th Indian Divisions as reinforcements for Burma, for the Chiefs of Staff had diverted 53rd Brigade of 18th Division to Malaya (and it seemed possible that the remainder of the division might have to follow it), and had ordered him to send 45th Brigade from 17th Division to Singapore. In addition he had received a request from the Commander-in-Chief, Far East, for a second Indian brigade group. Wavell had, however, reason to hope that such reinforcements as would become available for Burma, including the two African brigades, would arrive in time, since Far East Command had informed him that an attack in force against Burma was unlikely until the Japanese had completed their campaigns in Malaya and the Philippines.

The day after his arrival in Rangoon he cabled the Chief of the Imperial General Staff that, since Burma provided the only route for supplies to China and was an integral part of the defence of eastern India, where a large proportion of India's munition factories were sited, its security was absolutely vital to the effective prosecution of the war against Japan. Burma was however far from being secure: the defence forces were insufficient for their task and the fighting qualities of a large proportion of their units were quite unknown; the available staff and administrative services were inadequate both in quantity and quality;[2] and above all the great weakness from the defensive point of view was the need to depend on only one port of entry and that in an exposed position. In his view the primary consideration was the defence of Rangoon against attack by air, sea or land. To render Burma a secure base from which an offensive organization could later be built up, he required immediately two bomber and two modern fighter squadrons, a divisional headquarters and two infantry brigade groups, apparatus for a warning system and anti-aircraft artillery.

Having been informed by the War Office and Far East Command that an attack in force against Burma was not imminent, and

---

[1] The 17th Indian Division had been raised as a War Office Reserve Division and was to be sent to Iraq early in 1942, where it was to receive its full quota of modern arms and equipment and complete its training as a fully mechanized division in desert warfare. In December 1941 its training was far from complete and it was not fit for active operations. See Appendix 2.

[2] See Appendix 18.

C

since an extensive reorganization of the defences of Burma was essential, Wavell decided to replace General McLeod by Lieut.-General T. J. Hutton, his Chief of the General Staff in India, whose ability as an administrator had been amply proved. Hutton arrived in Rangoon on the 27th December and assumed command forthwith.[1] In his directive from Wavell, he was given the task of defending Burma, particularly Rangoon, from external aggression, and of drawing up plans for offensive operations against Siam. He was instructed to organize the military resources of Burma to enable a maximum force of four divisions, supported by fifteen squadrons R.A.F., to be maintained and operated from that country. He was told that it was hoped to send him the following reinforcements: 17th Indian Division (less one brigade group), two African brigades (by March) and various ancillary units.

From Rangoon General Wavell, with Major-General G. H. Brett of the United States Army Air Force, flew to Chungking for consultations with Generalissimo Chiang Kai-Shek.[2] The main object of his visit was to ensure that, as promised, at least one of the three A.V.G. squadrons remained in Burma for the defence of Rangoon, and that some of the lease-lend stores for China, then accumulating in the Rangoon docks and not quickly removable, could be released in order to make good the most serious deficiencies in the Burma Army.

Since this conference was to result in misunderstandings between the Allies, it is necessary to examine the background against which it was held. On the day the war in the Far East broke out, the Generalissimo asked the British Ambassador to China and General Dennys to convey to the British Government and to the Commander-in-Chief, Far East, a message to the effect that all China's manpower, armed forces and resources were unreservedly placed at the disposal of the British and United States Governments for the prosecution of the war; that China was very anxious to give direct assistance to Burma; that one regiment of 93rd Chinese Division which was in the Puerh area could be increased to a full division, if Burma could supply rice; and that troops could be made available for service in northern Burma, if Burma could supply rations.

The Chiefs of Staff replied on the 14th that the British High Command was most grateful for the generous Chinese offer and had instructed Wavell to approach the Generalissimo as soon as possible to arrange for the exchange of senior military officers, so that discussions could take place on how British and Chinese forces could best co-operate in the common cause.

---

[1] For order of battle of the Army in Burma on this date see Appendix 1.

[2] General Brett was on his way to China to investigate the possibility of basing heavy bombers there. The American War Department took advantage of this circumstance to make him its representative at the conferences in Chungking.

The following day, at an interview with the Generalissimo, the British Ambassador and Dennys told him of the early disasters in Malaya and the weakness of Burma without adequate air support. They said the British would welcome any assistance that China could give, so that the crisis could be weathered. Dennys asked the Generalissimo to reconsider a decision he had made earlier that day to withdraw the A.V.G. from Burma altogether.[1] In addition he asked that some of the lease-lend stores in Rangoon which were urgently required for the defence of Burma might be released for the use of the Army in Burma, that the strength of the Chinese troops stationed at Wanting should be brought up to one division to act as a reserve for the southern Shan States and that a second division should be earmarked for use in case it were required. The Generalissimo replied that he would be prepared to leave an A.V.G. squadron in Burma if a proper air raid warning system were established. He regarded the defence of Burma as the defence of China and could make an army corps, 50,000 strong, available to operate under the command of the General Officer Commanding, Burma, while in that country. He made the proviso that Chinese troops should be given a definite area or line of communications to guard and should not be mixed up with Burmese troops. If this were not done, he said he could not accept responsibility for anything that might happen.

At a further interview on the 16th the Chinese Minister for War said he felt that the British requests for assistance were too modest for the existing situation, and that China was prepared to send the whole of her V and VI Armies if Burma required them, but again there was a proviso that they should be given a separate area and neither mixed with nor put in reserve behind Burmese troops. Reports of these three interviews had been cabled, as they occurred, to London, to the Commander-in-Chief, Far East, and to the Commander-in-Chief in India; thus Wavell knew before he flew to Chungking the attitude which Chiang Kai-shek might adopt.

The head of the American Military Mission to China, Brigadier-General J. Magruder, and some of his staff were present at these interviews. Their accounts differed from those of the British. In reporting the conditions under which Chinese troops would enter Burma they said that the Generalissimo insisted that his troops enter *en masse*, occupy a definite sector and operate under a comprehensive plan. They further reported that he had explicitly and forcefully objected to any piecemeal commitment of his troops.[2] The American interpretation was more realistic than the British, for later the Generalissimo said:

---

[1] The squadron of the A.V.G. at Toungoo had been moved to Rangoon on the 12th December.

[2] Romanus & Sunderland, *United States Army in World War II: The China–Burma–India Theater, Stilwell's Mission to China* (Washington, 1953) pages 53–55.

'The way the Chinese Armies acquit themselves in Burma is a matter which touches the honour and pride of China. The eyes of the world will be upon them and they cannot risk defeat. If they are in sufficient numbers they will not be defeated, but if their strength is insufficient I cannot give any guarantee. You must remember that my honour and pride are concerned too and you should listen to my views as to what is best.'

Wavell and Brett arrived in Chungking on the 22nd December, and on the 23rd and 24th had conferences with the Generalissimo at which the British Ambassador, Magruder and Dennys were present. The Generalissimo gave no definite reply to Wavell's requests for the retention of an A.V.G. squadron in Burma or to the release of lease-lend equipment, though he agreed in principle. He repeated his offer to place V and VI Chinese Armies at Wavell's disposal for the defence of Burma. Wavell said he was prepared to accept 93rd Chinese Division (part of which was approaching the Burma border from Szemao) and would like 49th Chinese Division to be moved to Wanting near the frontier to act as a general reserve. Since he had information that 55th Chinese Division (the third division of VI Chinese Army) was very scattered, would take some time to collect and was of poor quality, he did not suggest that it too should be moved with the 49th to Wanting.[1]

The V Chinese Army, reported to be of good quality and comparatively well-equipped, was in the process of assembling near Kunming. Wavell did not for the time being wish it to be moved into Burma, since he was unable to give it the required separate line of communication and hoped to get sufficient reinforcements from India to secure the safety of Burma. He therefore asked that it should be held in reserve in the Kunming area. There he considered it would be well placed either to advance into Burma, to defend Yunnan, if the Japanese were to make an advance north from Indo-China against the Burma Road (a contingency which the Chinese had not long before represented as the enemy's most probable move), or to undertake offensive operations into Indo-China in co-operation with an advance from Burma should the operations progress satisfactorily.

Neither Wavell nor the Generalissimo felt satisfied with the outcome of the conference. Wavell had not been able to obtain a categorical reply to the questions which exercised his mind. He had gained the impression that the Generalissimo was inclined to be unpractical and visionary in discussing military plans, and was mainly interested in the establishment of an inter-allied council at Chungking and in the consideration of his views on world strategy. Buoyed up with hopes of speedy American assistance and a rapid end to the Sino-Japanese War which had lasted so long, the General-

---
[1] For order of battle of the Chinese Expeditionary Force see Appendix 12.

issimo had expected to be given definite dates when such assistance would arrive, and showed no understanding of either the problems connected with its provision or the organization required to get troops and aircraft to China and maintain them after their arrival.

The Chinese representative in Washington (T. V. Soong) later told the British Ambassador and others there that the visit of the two Generals had created 'a very painful impression' in Chungking since they had not been in a position to have 'any real discussions.' The British Ambassador to China declared this to be a great exaggeration, though it was clear that the Generalissimo had been disappointed when he realized that neither Wavell nor Brett was in a position to take with him decisions on broad questions of strategy.

When the conference ended, both Brett and Magruder cabled to Washington that Wavell had refused the offer of Chinese troops for the defence of Burma.[1] They no doubt based their views on their understanding of the Generalissimo's conditions and consequently considered that Wavell, in accepting only part of VI Chinese Army, had made the very limitation to which the Chinese had objected. The Chinese too apparently construed Wavell's reply as a refusal and, as late as the end of January 1942, the British Ambassador reported persistent rumours in China that the British had scorned the Chinese offer of help.

Meanwhile another event occurred which was to strain Sino-British relations even further. On the 18th December an American ship, the s.s. *Tulsa*, had arrived in Rangoon with a valuable cargo of lease-lend military equipment for China. Since air raids were clearly imminent, the Governor of Burma ordered the ship to be unloaded at once and the cargo placed in safe storage under British control away from the dock area. The American officer responsible for lease-lend stores in Burma was notified and concurred in this action. General Yu Fei-peng, the senior Chinese representative in Burma, was also told of the action taken; he was informed that none of the goods had been released for the use of the British forces in Burma, despite the fact that much of the equipment was badly needed to ensure the safety of Rangoon. Yu Fei-peng, who realized the urgent need of equipment in Burma, then suggested that a three-power committee should be set up in Rangoon to decide on the best division of the available stocks among the Allies. Since nothing could be decided without the agreement of Chungking, the American representative in Rangoon informed General Magruder of the position on the 21st.[2]

But as a last resort, in order to enable an ammunition ship to be unloaded, the Governor of Burma gave authority on the 20th for the

---
[1] Romanus & Sunderland, pages 55–56.
[2] Romanus & Sunderland, page 58.

drivers of some lease-lend motor lorries to be borrowed, which temporarily immobilized these vehicles. He failed however to inform General Yu Fei-peng and the committee, which had already met. Despite an explanation by the Governor of his action, Yu Fei-peng telegraphed Chungking accusing the British of having seized the *Tulsa's* cargo. On the 27th the British Ambassador cabled both Delhi and Rangoon saying, 'A report has reached the Generalissimo which has so angered him that he is minded to withdraw all co-operation with Burma. He is persuaded that he has been double-crossed in matters which he had been discussing with General Wavell and in regard to which he was about to meet General Wavell's wishes'. This cable was closely followed by another in which the Ambassador said that, although the Generalissimo's anger remained undiminished, he had been persuaded to authorize the transfer of a quantity of military equipment as detailed in a list drawn up by Wavell. The next day Dennys reported that the Generalissimo had ordered the despatch of a second squadron of the A.V.G. to Rangoon.

The tension nevertheless persisted, for the Generalissimo received further reports from Rangoon saying that the British authorities were removing lease-lend cargoes from two more ships. The facts were that one ship had been returned to Calcutta with its cargo intact because of shortage of dock labour at Rangoon, and the cargo of the other had been unloaded and stored in a place of safety, though the need for much of the equipment was extreme. There is no doubt that some Chinese official in Rangoon deliberately misled the authorities in Chungking.

Meanwhile on his return from Chungking on the 26th Wavell, in view of the necessity of protecting Rangoon which had just suffered a heavy air raid, had authorized the General Officer Commanding, Burma, to make temporary use of some of the lease-lend anti-aircraft and light machine-guns for the protection of the Rangoon airfields. Having done this he cabled Dennys at Chungking instructing him to inform the Generalissimo of the action he had taken saying, 'I am sure that he will approve my action in view of his promise to me that material essential for the defence of Rangoon would at once be placed at my service'. The use of these guns by the British was apparently accepted by the Generalissimo without demur.

On the 5th January, the Prime Minister, then in Washington, himself gave instructions that all lease-lend material under British control was to be transferred to the Chinese. Dennys thereupon flew to Rangoon to discuss the alleged seizure of stores with both Yu Fei-peng and the American lease-lend representative. On the 7th, the Chinese General cabled to the Generalissimo saying that all the *Tulsa's* cargo had been transferred to his control and that the incident was entirely due to the misinterpretation of the ownership of lease-lend cargoes and the lack of proper procedure. Through the good offices of Dennys, both sides had now reached a complete understanding. 'In view,' said Yu Fei-peng, 'of the solidarity of co-operation and relationship between Great Britain and China, especially in face of our present strife against the common enemy, I beg Your Excellency to consider this incident closed'. These incidents and the misunderstandings which arose from them were unfortunate in that they disturbed the harmony between the Allies right at the start of the struggle and created a spirit of mistrust, which was to persist.

Shortly after his return to India, Wavell was told of his appointment as Supreme Commander of the newly constituted South-West Pacific Command, afterwards known as ABDA Command, in which Burma was included. He at once recommended that the defence of that country should remain the responsibility of the Commander-in-Chief in India. On the grounds that Chiang Kai-shek must feel himself connected with the new South-West Pacific Command, the Combined Chiefs of Staff decided that Burma should be included for operational purposes in the ABDA area, while remaining under India for administration, reinforcements and supplies. There is no doubt that, whatever the political advantages, from the military point of view this was a mistake, for experience has shown that it is always wrong to separate operational from administrative responsibility. Furthermore the new command's headquarters in Java were 2,000 miles from Rangoon. There were no reliable means of communication, even by wireless, between Burma and Java, and thus all communications had to be routed through Delhi with the result that, when active operations began, most of Wavell's instructions were based on out-of-date information.

On the 1st January 1942 the Chiefs of Staff informed all commanders in the Far East of their policy regarding the despatch of reinforcements to the various theatres in the Far East—Burma, Malaya and the Netherlands East Indies. Burma was to be reinforced by two divisions, six light bomber squadrons and six fighter squadrons. Headquarters 17th Indian Division with 46th Brigade, and 14th Indian Division, less one brigade group, were definitely allotted to Burma; the finding of the remaining three brigades was however a matter of some difficulty and it was left to the Commander-in-Chief in India to find them at his discretion from 34th Indian Division and the two East African brigades already allotted to India on their arrival.

General Headquarters, India, pointed out that 34th Indian Division (less one brigade) was already providing the garrison for Ceylon and none of its formations could be spared, but that it proposed to send 17th Indian Divisional Headquarters and 46th Brigade Group as soon as possible, 48th Brigade Group (from 19th Indian Division) shortly afterwards and the two East African brigades in February and March. It further proposed to hold 14th Indian Division (less one brigade) as an additional reinforcement to be available in March. These proposals provided the equivalent of the two divisions, which was all that the Chiefs of Staff at that time considered necessary, but not till March-April 1942.

Map 1

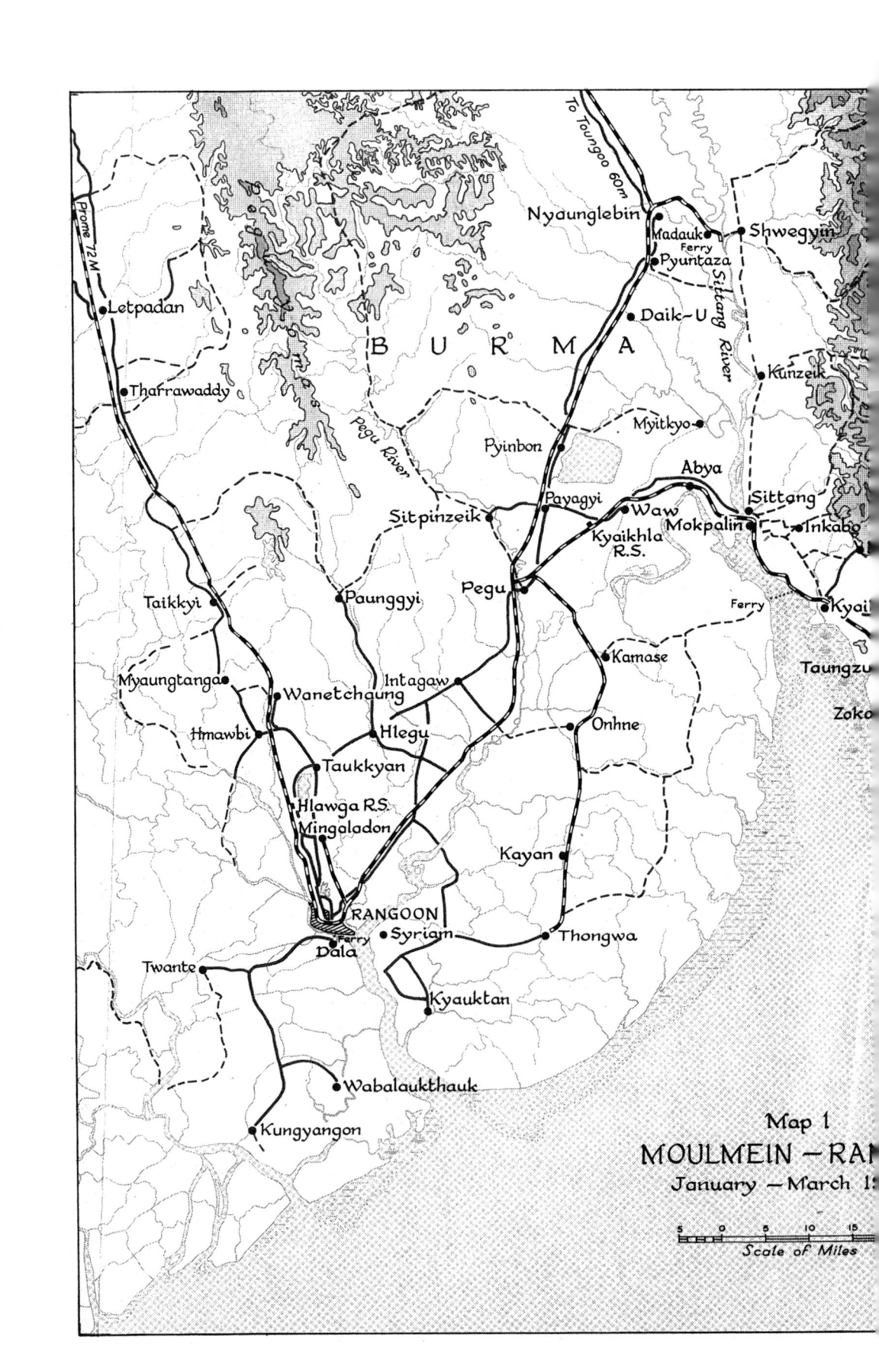

MOULMEIN – RAN
January – March 1942

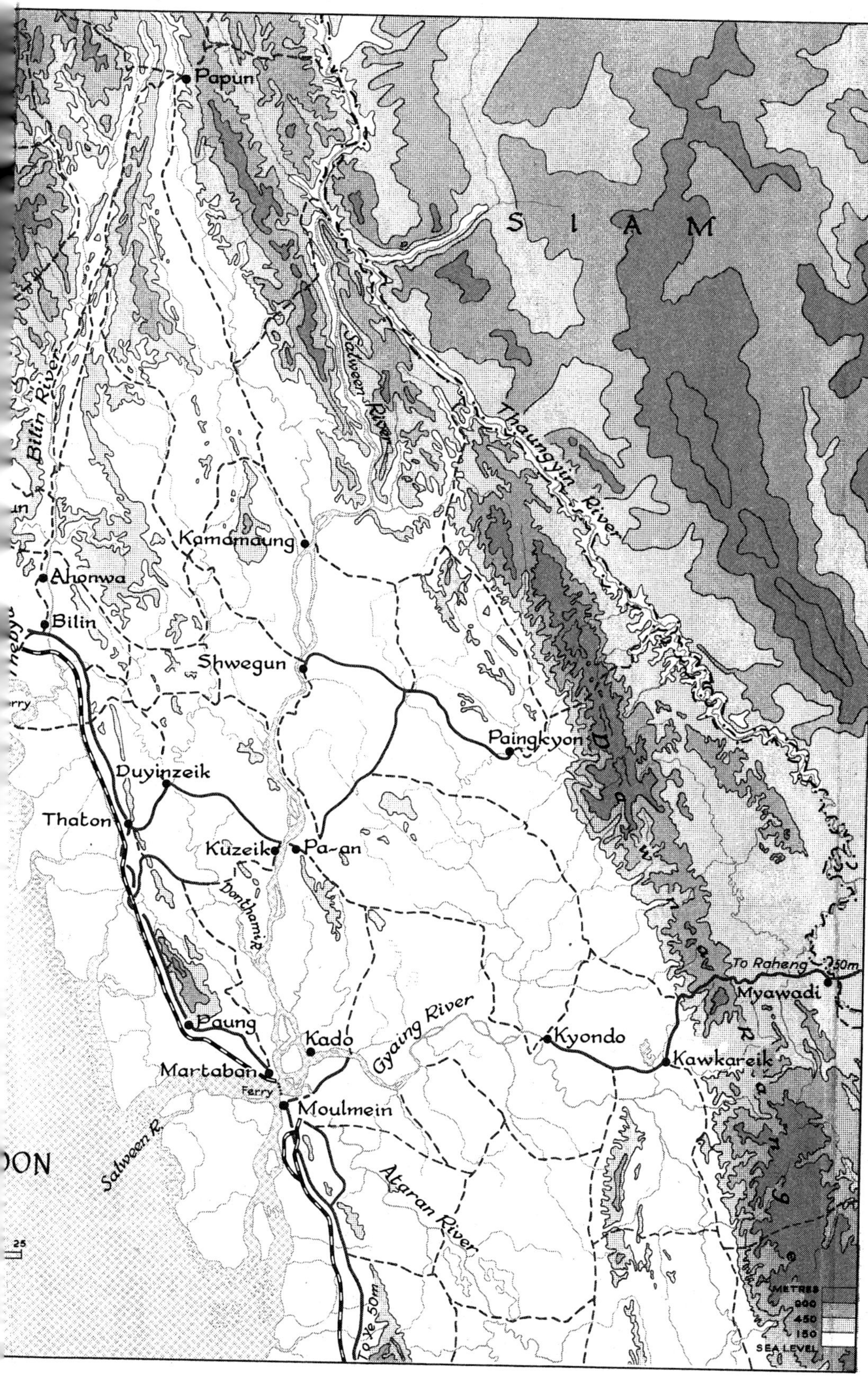

Papun
SIAM
Salween River
Thaungyin River
Bilin River
Kamamaung
Ahonwa
Bilin
Shwegun
Ferry
Paingkyon
Duyinzeik
Thaton
Kuzeik
Pa-an
Donthami R.
To Raheng 250m
Myawadi
Paung
Kado
Gyaing River
Kyondo
Kawkareik
Martaban
Ferry
Moulmein
Salween R.
Ataran River
To Ye 50m
METRES
900
450
150
SEA LEVEL

CHAPTER II

THE JAPANESE INVASION OF SOUTHERN BURMA

(December 1941 – February 1942)

See Strategic Map, Map 1 and Sketch 3

IN the Japanese plans for the capture of the Southern Region, as described in Volume I, Chapter V, the initial rôle of *15th Army*, consisting of *33rd Division* and *55th Division* (less one infantry regiment) and supported by *10th Air Brigade*,[1] was to occupy Siam including the Isthmus of Kra, as far south as Nakhorn. It was then to capture the British airfields in Tenasserim, act as a right flank guard to *Southern Army* and protect the right and rear of *25th Army* during its advance into Malaya.[2] Later, when *Southern Army* was satisfied that *25th Army* operations in Malaya were developing according to plan, *15th Army* was to invade Burma by way of the Raheng-Moulmein route with the immediate object of capturing Rangoon.

The *15th Army*, to which the *Imperial Guards Division* had temporarily been loaned, entered Bangkok on the 8th December 1941 and thereafter was master of Siam with its airfields, railways and assembly areas for the invasion of Burma. The same day, in order to secure the Isthmus of Kra between Bangkok and Singora, *143rd Infantry Regiment* of *55th Division* was landed at Nakhorn, Bandon, Jumbhorn and Prachuab with the first flight of *25th Army*[3]. Its orders were to secure the airfields there and at Victoria Point, provide guards for the Siam-Malaya railway and prepare for the occupation of the Tenasserim coast. Thus when, in accordance with a pre-war plan, two British columns of F.F.2 crossed into Siam from Mergui on the 9th in an endeavour to cut this strategic railway, they encountered strong enemy forces and were repulsed, suffering heavy casualties.

On the 11th one battalion of *143rd Regiment* from Jumbhorn crossed the Burma-Siam frontier and reached Victoria Point on the 16th unopposed, for the small British garrison had been withdrawn. Later in the month the regiment, leaving one battalion as garrison at

---
[1] The *10th Air Brigade* was a part of *3rd Air Division*.
[2] For order of battle of *15th Army* see Appendix 3.
[3] See Volume I, page 178.

Victoria Point, moved to Raheng where *55th Division Headquarters* and *112th Regiment* had already concentrated, and reorganized on a pack transport basis in readiness for the proposed advance into southern Burma.

Information that the Japanese had begun to improve the Raheng-Moulmein route up to the frontier and that both enemy and Siamese formations were concentrating at Raheng soon reached Rangoon. On arrival at Rangoon on the 19th December, 1/7th Gurkha Rifles (16th Brigade) was sent to Moulmein to strengthen the forces defending this region. At the same time 1/18th Royal Garhwal Rifles was sent as a precautionary measure from 13th Brigade to reinforce F.F.5, which was watching the approaches from Siam into the Karen Hills.

In the southern Shan States December passed quietly, but Japanese heavy guns and tanks were reported as being sent by rail to Chiengmai. One regiment of 93rd Division of VI Chinese Army was therefore moved across the frontier to take over the defence of the Mekong River where it formed the boundary between French Indo-China and Burma. The rest of this division remained at Szemao in China, about 100 miles from the frontier. During the month the internal situation in Burma remained quiet. The action of the British Government in detaining the Premier, U Saw, caused excited comment but no repercussions; the arrest of some three hundred fifth columnists probably acted as a check to seditious activity.

Rangoon suffered its first air raid on the 23rd December when about sixty bombers, with fighter escort, raided Mingaladon airfield and the dock area. The defence of the town rested on the R.A.F. and A.V.G. fighter squadrons, for there were no anti-aircraft guns; two aircraft of the A.V.G. were shot down, and a few R.A.F. aircraft were damaged on the ground. The Japanese losses were estimated at the time as nine bombers and one fighter. The military casualties and damage caused were not extensive. The civilians, to whom this was a new experience, flocked into the streets to watch instead of taking cover and their casualties were consequently heavy, being estimated at well over 2,000.

The Government had originally contemplated an evacuation scheme under which one-fifth of the inhabitants—the 'non-essential' elements—were to be moved to camps outside the city, but in September 1941 they abandoned the idea and when war broke out encouraged the population to remain in the city. Nevertheless after this raid there was a general exodus from the city. Most of the dock labour force, which was mainly Indian, fled; a serious matter when important cargoes required handling. The Burmans took refuge in the jungle, but most of the large Indian population set out to try to reach India by the overland routes. The hordes of refugees presented the civil and military authorities with an almost insoluble problem.

The second air raid on Rangoon came on Christmas Day and hastened the flight of Indian dock labourers and others who still wavered. On this occasion two A.V.G. and six R.A.F. fighters (two on the ground) were lost, but it was estimated that the Tomahawks of the A.V.G. and the Buffaloes of 67 Squadron destroyed some twenty Japanese aircraft out of the hundred bombers and fighters which made the raid.

On the 31st December the first reinforcements from India—8th Indian Heavy and 3rd Indian Light Anti-Aircraft Batteries—arrived at Rangoon. The units were quickly disembarked, despite the acute shortage of labour in the port, and placed in position for the protection of airfields and other vital points around the city.

Air Vice-Marshal D. F. Stevenson, who had been appointed Air Officer Commanding, Burma, on the 1st January 1942, calculated that the Japanese had some hundred and fifty fighter and bomber aircraft within striking distance of Rangoon, against which he could at the time muster only some thirty effective Allied aircraft. Information now available shows this to have been a reasonably good estimate. At the beginning of the war, air support for the Japanese *15th Army* had been provided by *10th Air Brigade* under the control of *3rd Air Division* which was in support of *25th Army* in Malaya. Directly after the fall of Manila in January 1942, *5th Air Division* (Lieut.-General H. Obata) with *4th Air Brigade* was moved to Siam from Formosa. This air division took control of *10th Air Brigade* and throughout the campaign in Burma provided air support for *15th Army*. Its strength in January 1942 was some two hundred aircraft.

Japanese air policy at that time was to concentrate more on the destruction of the weak Allied air forces in Burma than on giving close support to the advance of *15th Army*. Early in January therefore General Obata renewed the attacks on Rangoon with combined fighter and bomber squadrons in daylight raids. On the 4th January a force of some thirty Japanese fighters, trying to break through to the city, was intercepted by the A.V.G. and driven off with loss. This raid was followed by night bombing on a limited scale and it was not till the 23rd that General Obata launched his main effort to overwhelm the Allied air force. From the 23rd to the 29th there was continuous day fighting over Rangoon in which some fifty Japanese bombers and fighters were believed destroyed as against ten R.A.F. and two A.V.G. aircraft. The Japanese admit that these attacks caused them heavy loss; on one day a squadron of heavy bombers from *14th Air Regiment* was completely destroyed. As a result of the week's air fighting Obata greatly overestimated the strength of the Allies and, finding that his heavy bombers were vulnerable to the

Allied fighters, abandoned daylight raids and reverted once again to sporadic night attacks, using his air force mainly in support of *15th Army*. But more dock and other labour fled before the air peril, and by the end of January it was more than ever difficult to work the port and keep the city functioning.

Since the grave disparity between the Allied and Japanese air forces increased as the First Burma Campaign progressed, it is of interest here to compare the air strength envisaged by the Air Ministry as being necessary, with the strength that actually became available. The Air Ministry programme for the defence of Burma reckoned on six fighter, seven bomber and two army co-operation squadrons, with one general reconnaissance squadron, a total of sixteen squadrons. In fact only one A.V.G. squadron and three fighter squadrons (17, 67 and 135), three bomber squadrons (45, 60 and 113), two army co-operation squadrons (1 Indian and 28) and part of a general reconnaissance squadron joined action with the enemy in the course of the campaign. Of the seven vital radar stations proposed by the Air Ministry, only one materialized. This campaign was the baptism of fire of the Indian Air Force: the Indian army co-operation squadron and the two general reconnaissance flights proved their gallantry and efficiency on many occasions.

The only naval forces in Burmese waters were five motor launches of the Burmese R.N.V.R. and a few auxiliary vessels. During the Tenasserim operations these launches were chiefly employed in the evacuation of troops, guns and equipment, and their crews in the demolition of any stores which could not be removed. They engaged the enemy whenever opportunity offered, and their wireless sets at times provided the only link between Tenasserim and Rangoon.

Early in January General Hutton prepared a detailed appreciation of the situation in Burma and the steps necessary to meet a Japanese attack, which formed the basis of his policy throughout the period of his command. He realized that the base on which all operations in Burma depended was Rangoon: in the absence of any land link with India no other base was possible, for it was the only port in Burma which had the requisite communications leading into the interior, and the necessary wharf and other facilities. Its security therefore was of prime importance. But the strategical unsuitability of Rangoon as a base, exposed as it was to air, sea and land attack, was obvious and in view of the importance of the target a heavy scale of air attack was to be expected. Hutton consequently decided to stock a series of depots in upper Burma in the area Mandalay–Meiktila–Myingyan by backloading stores from Rangoon. He hoped that these depots would eventually be supplied by a road from Tamu to Kalewa which would have to be built without delay. This would link up with the road from Imphal to Tamu, already being constructed by India, and provide the necessary overland communication.[1]

In December 1941 the maximum scale of enemy attack had been estimated as one division against Moulmein and one division against Kengtung, with possibly brigade groups against Toungoo and Mongpan. Hutton clearly foresaw the advantages to the enemy of an advance through Tenasserim, and made an accurate forecast of the possible strength, mobility and tactical methods of an invading force. He stressed the Japanese methods of deployment on a wide front, their bold enveloping movements which included outflanking landings from the sea, their awareness of the advantages of air superiority and the early seizure of airfields. He saw the advantage of making prompt and full use of V and VI Chinese Armies so as to permit the concentration of the British forces in Tenasserim.[2] At the same time he appreciated the danger of endeavouring to hold the whole of the Shan States east of the Salween, as well as the Tenasserim coast as far south as Mergui.

He reached the conclusion that to defend Burma he would have to concentrate his forces in the areas traversed by the practicable routes from Siam into Burma. These were: Tenasserim between Moulmein and the Sittang, the Karen Hills east of Toungoo and the Shan States in the vicinity of Mongpan and Kengtung. Adequate protection for the communications between Meiktila, Rangoon and Moulmein was, however, clearly essential. His reserves would therefore have to be situated along the Sittang River and in the Toungoo area.

By the 9th January Major-General J. G. Smyth, V.C., commanding 17th Indian Division, and his divisional headquarters had arrived in Rangoon. In view of reliable information that the Japanese were concentrating at Raheng and on the frontier to the west of the town, Hutton ordered 16th Brigade (Brigadier Jones) to move from Mandalay to Moulmein (where one of its battalions, 1/7th Gurkhas, had already been sent) and placed both it and 2nd Burma Brigade (Brigadier Bourke) which was already in Tenasserim, under command of 17th Division. The 16th Brigade arrived in the area on the 14th January. Two days later the partially trained 46th Indian Infantry Brigade (Brigadier R. G. Ekin) arrived in Rangoon from India and was sent to the Bilin area under command of 17th Division.[3] Smyth was given the responsibility for the defence of an area extending from Mergui in the south to Papun in the

---

[1] The details of road communications between India and Burma will be found in Chapter III.

[2] The civil division of Tenasserim comprised six districts: Toungoo, Salween, Thaton, Amherst, Tavoy and Mergui.

[3] The 46th Indian Infantry Brigade consisted of 7/10th Baluch Regiment, 3/7th Gurkha Rifles and 5/17th Dogra Regiment.

north, a distance of some 400 miles. His first action was to order 16th Brigade (less 4/12th Frontier Force Regiment) to Kawkareik, where it was to take under command 4th Burma Rifles already in position on the crest of the Dawna Range, and oppose any Japanese advance across the frontier from Raheng.[1] Brigadier Jones disposed his brigade with 1/7th Gurkhas (less one company) on the frontier, 4th Burma Rifles in the main position on the crest of the range and 1/9th Royal Jats in reserve near Kawkareik. He prepared demolitions along all approaches from the east, and sent one company of 1/7th Gurkhas to watch Three Pagodas Pass.

During the first fortnight of January enemy aircraft had been active. Moulmein with its airfield, Martaban with its ferry and railway yards and the landing stage at Kyondo had all been bombed. On the 17th January fourteen Japanese bombers with fighter escort raided Moulmein, but did comparatively little damage. Tavoy also suffered, and enemy reconnaissance aircraft paid particular attention to the track running east from the town towards the frontier.

British fighters from the advanced bases of Moulmein, Tavoy and Mergui attacked the enemy wherever found. In order to force the Japanese to disperse their fighters, objectives were bombed as far apart as Chiengmai and Chiengrai in the north and Singora and the Siam–Malaya railway in the south, the targets being enemy airfields, motor transport and trains. Bangkok, too, was attacked on the 8th January by bombers of 113 Squadron R.A.F. which had begun to arrive at Rangoon.

At the beginning of January 1942 the Japanese *55th Division*, less the battalion of *143rd Regiment* garrisoning Victoria Point and one battalion of *112th Regiment* retained under command of *Southern Army*, had concentrated at Raheng.[2] By the 10th January *33rd Division*, less *213th Regiment*, had arrived at Bangkok from China and was sent to the Phitsanulok–Raheng area. Both divisions began to prepare for the advance into Burma and, with the aid of local Siamese labour, worked on improving the road to the frontier.

Meanwhile *Southern Army* had ordered *III/112th Battalion* to capture Tavoy. Crossing the frontier on the 15th January it occupied the town on the 19th, overwhelming 6th Burma Rifles and a battery of the Burma Auxiliary Force which formed its garrison. Soon afterwards enemy aircraft began to land on the airfield. With Tavoy in Japanese hands the garrison of Mergui was cut off. Consequently it

---

[1] See Map 1.
[2] The *55th Division* at this time consisted of *112th* and *143rd Infantry Regiments* (each less one battalion), *55th Cavalry Regiment*, *55th Mountain Artillery Regiment*, *55th Engineer Regiment* and *55th Transport Regiment*.

was withdrawn by sea between the 20th and 23rd, after the airfield had been rendered unusable and the tin and wolfram mines in the vicinity put out of action. The operations in southern Tenasserim were on a minor scale but their importance lay in the fact that, by the 24th, the Japanese had secured the three airfields on the Tenasserim coast—Victoria Point, Mergui and Tavoy—from which they could give fighter escort to their bombers attacking Rangoon.

Operations on a larger scale began on the 20th, when the advanced guard of the Japanese *55th Division* attacked and surrounded a company of 1/7th Gurkhas near the frontier[1]. By the 21st it had become apparent that the Japanese were advancing in strength. Hutton had told Smyth that 16th Brigade should not get so involved in the Kawkareik area as to render withdrawal impossible. Thus, when the enemy was found to be working round the right flank of the main position, Jones ordered a withdrawal. Hutton approved this action but said that no more ground than necessary was to be given up.

Contact was broken without difficulty but the withdrawal did not take place in an entirely orderly manner. A sudden burst of firing, for which there was no apparent cause, stampeded the mules and part of brigade headquarters including the signal section, and this together with an unfortunate accident upset the whole plan for the withdrawal. The main line of communication from Kawkareik was by road to Kyondo and thence by boat down the Gyaing River to Moulmein, but all vehicles had to cross the river by vehicle ferry, seven miles south-west of Kawkareik, and move along the poor but motorable track to Moulmein. The brigade motor transport column moved off first, but an overloaded ammunition truck sank the vehicle ferry and all the transport was effectively marooned east of the river. Jones then sent the whole column to Kyondo. There he ordered the vehicles and much of their contents to be destroyed, sent his wounded to Moulmein in the only two boats available and asked for river transport to be sent to meet the brigade which he proposed should move down the left bank of the river.

The Japanese made no attempt to press 16th Brigade during its retreat. It marched down the river for two days until picked up by steamers and conveyed to Martaban. Although its casualties had not been heavy, its morale had been shaken; it had lost all its transport and, with the exception of those of 4th Burma Rifles, most of its supporting weapons. It required time for reorganization and re-equipment before being fit for action. Meanwhile, following a heavy air raid on Moulmein on the 21st, Smyth had ordered the evacuation of all European and Indian women and children and had assumed control of the town.

---

[1] The company later rejoined its battalion without its vehicles, but with all its weapons and equipment.

The situation facing Hutton and Smyth at this time was very disturbing. They had little definite information on the Japanese dispositions but estimated that they were opposed by at least one division. To meet the Japanese advance there was only the hurriedly thrown together and widely dispersed 17th Division. The 2nd Burma Brigade, mainly composed of untried Burma Rifle battalions, was disposed for the defence of Moulmein,[1] 16th Brigade was being withdrawn towards Martaban, while the partly-trained 46th Brigade, which had just arrived from India and was without its transport till the end of the month, was in the Bilin area. On the 23rd Smyth advocated a withdrawal to the Bilin–Kyaikto–Sittang area where all approaches converged. There he wished to concentrate his division and establish a secure base from which a counterstroke would be feasible. Hutton, however, did not think the situation justified a withdrawal on this scale and directed that Moulmein should be held for as long as possible in order to delay the Japanese advance; but, as he did not wish 2nd Burma Brigade to be closely invested, he ordered plans for the backloading of stores and the evacuation of the town to be prepared. He also ordered Smyth to regain contact with the Japanese south and east of Moulmein, and arranged that 2nd K.O.Y.L.I. from 1st Burma Division should reinforce 17th Division as soon as possible.

On the 24th Smyth moved his divisional headquarters from Moulmein to Kyaikto on the Sittang estuary. Next day he gave 16th Brigade the task of protecting the crossings of the Salween from Pa-an to Martaban and 46th Brigade that of protecting the Bilin–Kyaikto area. On the nights of the 24th, 27th and 28th, in an effort to reduce the scale of Japanese air attacks and interrupt their preparations, the R.A.F. with their one Blenheim squadron (the average operational strength was only six aircraft) attacked the Japanese base at Bangkok.

On the night of the 24th/25th General Wavell flew from Java to Rangoon to see for himself the situation in Burma. He found the atmosphere calmer and more confident than the telegrams he had received had led him to expect and, before returning to ABDA Headquarters on the following night, he confirmed Hutton's instructions that Moulmein should be held for as long as possible. When Hutton and Smyth visited Moulmein on the 28th they agreed that, in view of the responsibilities of the local commander in respect of administrative units and the civil population, Brigadier Ekin (46th

---

[1] The 2nd Burma Brigade (Brigadier A. J. H. Bourke) consisted at this time of 4/12th Frontier Force Regiment, 3rd Burma Rifles (less two companies), 7th Burma Rifles, 8th Burma Rifles, 12th Indian Mountain Battery, one troop 3rd Indian Anti-Aircraft Battery, a small detachment of 60th Field Company, Sappers and Miners, and six platoons of the Kokine Battalion. This last was a battalion of the Burma Frontier Force formed in 1940 to provide detachments for airfield protection duties.

Brigade) should be sent to take command if a Japanese attack on the town appeared likely.

On the 26th Lieut.-General Iida (*15th Army*) ordered *55th Division*, which was concentrating west of Kawkareik, to capture Moulmein forthwith, and *33rd Division* to cross the frontier and move to an area north of Kawkareik in preparation for an advance on Pa-an.

The town of Moulmein, lying at the mouth of the Salween River, has a river frontage facing westward for about six thousand yards and northward for over two thousand.[1] It is dominated by a long, steep ridge running north and south. Much of the surrounding country consisted of flat ricefields with patches of jungle, but to the south, where there were rubber plantations, the ground was more broken. Only four battalions were available to defend the perimeter of about twelve miles, whereas at least two infantry brigades were needed for a protracted defence. The 2nd Burma Brigade was disposed with 7th Burma Rifles holding the northern sector, 3rd Burma Rifles the west bank of the Ataran River and 8th Burma Rifles the southern sector. The 4/12th Frontier Force Regiment was in reserve.

Early on the 30th the Japanese attacked the perimeter from the south and east. About midday, having received a report that about a thousand Japanese had entered Kado and were engaged on building rafts, Smyth asked the R.A.F. to bomb the village, but was told that this was impossible as all aircraft were already employed on other duties. At noon Ekin reached Moulmein and assumed command, receiving every assistance from Brigadier Bourke who willingly agreed to serve under him. He found that, although 8th Burma Rifles in the southern sector had repulsed all enemy attacks, the Japanese had succeeded in crossing the Ataran River and had occupied Ngante and Hmyawlin, overrunning the forward posts of 3rd Burma Rifles. After a visit to the headquarters of this battalion at 1 p.m., he ordered it to withdraw to a north-south line through Myenigon and moved his reserve battalion (4/12th F.F. Regiment) into a position along the ridge. During the afternoon 3rd Burma Rifles disintegrated in face of further attacks and, by 5.30 p.m., 4/12th F.F. Regiment was closely engaged with the enemy along the whole length of the ridge and, well supported by 12th Mountain Battery, defied all efforts to break into its position. Just as darkness fell Ekin was told that boats carrying Japanese troops had been seen coming down the river from the direction of Kado and that 8th Burma Rifles in the southern sector was becoming exhausted. He thereupon decided to shorten and strengthen his perimeter, and at 8 p.m. withdrew 8th Burma Rifles to an east-west line running from the southern end of the ridge to the river.

---
[1] See Sketch 3.

During the afternoon Smyth came to the conclusion that the position in Moulmein was becoming serious and reported the situation to Hutton in Rangoon. He said that there were in his opinion only two alternatives: to reinforce the garrison with two battalions drawn from 16th Brigade in Martaban or to withdraw 2nd Burma Brigade. To reinforce at the eleventh hour was, he thought, inadvisable and unlikely to succeed and he therefore advocated the withdrawal of the garrison from the town as soon as it appeared necessary. Hutton agreed and left the decision on the timing to Smyth, but said that after the withdrawal the line of the Salween including Martaban must be held.

The situation in Moulmein began to deteriorate when at about 10 p.m. the Japanese made a landing on the northern end of the perimeter and fighting broke out in the area held by 7th Burma Rifles. This new threat, coupled with increasing pressure against the eastern and southern sides of the perimeter, led Ekin to report about midnight that he doubted whether Moulmein could be held during daylight on the 31st. Smyth told him that he could draw up plans for evacuating the town and put them into action when he thought fit. Ekin immediately ordered the fleet of some fifteen river steamers waiting at Martaban to be brought across to Moulmein (where they arrived at 3 a.m.) and prepared for the withdrawal.

By 2 a.m., 7th Burma Rifles had been driven back to the Police Lines and a troop of Bofors light anti-aircraft guns had been lost. Ekin, realizing that the situation had now become highly dangerous, decided that the time had come to evacuate the town and at 3.30 a.m. on the 31st issued orders for a withdrawal to begin at 8 a.m. The Japanese attacked on all fronts just after the withdrawal had begun but were too late to prevent the forward troops from disengaging. The rearguards were not heavily pressed to start with and by 10 a.m. most of the troops had embarked, with the exception of 4/12th F.F. Regiment holding a shallow bridgehead covering the two southern jetties. Shortly afterwards the battalion and brigade headquarters managed to embark, under heavy pressure, in the last steamer at Mission Street Jetty; as the vessel cast off, enemy troops reached the quayside.

Japanese artillery had by this time been established on the ridge and as the ships moved slowly across the estuary towards Martaban they came under heavy fire, but only one was sunk. At frequent intervals throughout the embarkation formations of enemy bombers passed over Moulmein on their way to bomb Martaban. Each time this happened the civilian crews moved their vessels into midstream, thus delaying the evacuation programme. Had the bombers been given Moulmein jetties as their target, the withdrawal could not have been carried out successfully. As it was, 2nd Burma Brigade reached

Martaban with all its essential equipment including wireless sets, all its guns except four Bofors and some vehicles, but with the loss of about a quarter of its effective strength.

The defence of Moulmein might well have ended in disaster, since the defenders had their backs to a wide river estuary. Many units, however, such as 12th Mountain Battery, 4/12th F.F. Regiment and 8th Burma Rifles, for all of whom it was a first experience of war, put up a stubborn defence and the withdrawal was brilliantly handled in exceptionally difficult circumstances. The Japanese had been made to suffer severely for the possession of the town, their first objective in the invasion of Burma. Their war diaries speak of the 'fierce hand-to-hand fighting on all sides of Moulmein' and 'the resistance of a determined enemy'.

When it had appeared that Moulmein might be isolated and a withdrawal to the Bilin–Sittang area forced on him, Hutton had on the 22nd January issued orders that three-quarters of all the reserve stocks held in Rangoon were to be moved to the Mandalay area, the transfer to be completed in one month. This meant moving to the new depots the main portion of an advanced base which amounted to some 14,000 tons of miscellaneous stores, as well as R.A.F. and civil government stores of petrol, oil and lubricants (P.O.L.).[1]

Although the total tonnage to be moved was within the capacity of the railway and the Irrawaddy Flotilla Company, there were many difficulties. No plans had been made before the outbreak of war for the formation, in an emergency, of military transportation units from the employees of the several transportation agencies, nor had any action been taken to form such units by the time the Japanese invasion began. The army staff had thus to deal with numerous civil departments and transportation agencies who were attempting to meet the urgent requirements of the army, while still organized on a peacetime basis. The employees of these agencies were deserting in large numbers. There was a chronic shortage of mechanical transport and the air raids on Rangoon had upset the normal working of the port. It must be remembered that, during the whole period of the backloading, fighting was in progress in Tenasserim, and the inadequate staffs of the administrative services were often so engaged on meeting urgent demands from the fighting troops that the evacuation programme had to be temporarily suspended. The fact that the great bulk of the stores was successfully moved says much for the ability of the small administrative staffs and services, as well as the civil agencies, to improvise under most adverse circumstances.[2]

---

[1] The transfer of lease-lend stocks was a Sino-American responsibility.
[2] See Appendix 18.

As soon as he knew that the Japanese had crossed the frontier in force on the 20th January, Hutton had cabled Wavell saying, 'It is possible that fate of Rangoon may be decided within the next week entirely owing to lack of infantry. Can you get a brigade, even without transport here in the shortest possible period'. On the 22nd the Governor told the Secretary of State for Burma that 'Hutton is fairly confident that with the dispositions he proposes the worst will not happen, but in view of the possibility and with his complete concurrence, I feel bound to take certain steps'. These included arrangements to enable the Government to function from some centre in upper Burma, the clearance of essential lease-lend stores from Rangoon, the speeding up of the preparation of the Rangoon denial scheme and further efforts to urge the Chinese to hasten the arrival of their armies in Burma. The same day Hutton again cabled Wavell (repeating the message to India Command and the War Office). He stressed how essential it was that sufficient troops and air forces were provided without delay to hold Burma under all circumstances, and said that he would require a total of four divisions at the earliest possible moment (at the time he had the equivalent of one and two-thirds divisions), and that one additional division should be prepared by India for despatch to Burma if necessary. In conclusion he asked that Burma's needs should be given absolute priority over those of both the Middle East and Iraq.

The same day the Chiefs of Staff told the Commander-in-Chief in India that

> 'In view of the situation developing in Burma and of the extreme importance of Burma both to you and to China, we would like you to consider measures to accelerate the arrival of reinforcements. You will appreciate that time is of the essence of the contract. Although loath to do so, we suggest that, in view of the arrival in India shortly of British battalions from the United Kingdom, you might consider the despatch to Burma of a brigade made up of three British battalions. We fully realize what a sacrifice we are asking of you. It is however a time for rapid action . . .'[1]

The Commander-in-Chief in India had already anticipated this suggestion and had speeded up the despatch of 46th and 48th Brigades. He had also made arrangements to send, as unallotted units, three British battalions (1st West Yorkshire, 2nd Duke of Wellington's and 1st Cameronians) between the end of January and the middle of February, and had begun to prepare an additional Indian infantry brigade (63rd) with mainly animal transport, ready for despatch later if required. He told the Chiefs of Staff, however,

---

[1] Three British battalions from the United Kingdom were due at Bombay on the 28th January.

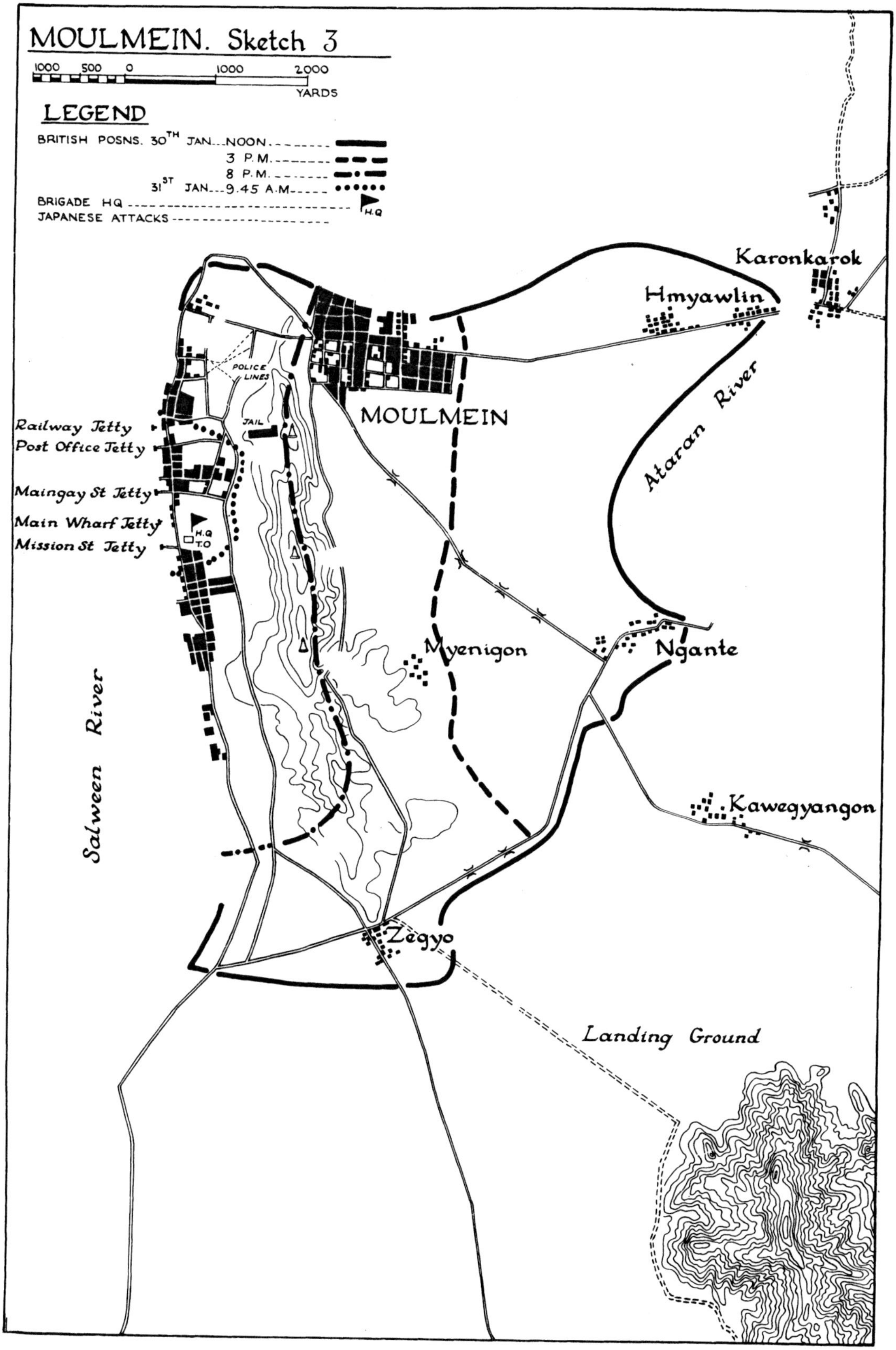

MOULMEIN. Sketch 3
1000 500 0 1000 2000
YARDS
LEGEND
BRITISH POSNS. 30TH JAN. NOON
3 P.M.
8 P.M.
31ST JAN. 9.45 A.M.
BRIGADE HQ
H.Q
JAPANESE ATTACKS
Karonkarok
Hmyawlin
MOULMEIN
POLICE LINES
JAIL
Ataran River
Railway Jetty
Post Office Jetty
Maingay St Jetty
Main Wharf Jetty
Mission St Jetty
H.Q
T.O
Myenigon
Ngante
Salween River
Kawegyangon
Zegyo
Landing Ground

that these additional emergency measures had once again adversely affected the equipment position which was already most unsatisfactory; the dates of readiness of the formations preparing for Burma therefore depended largely on the arrival of equipment from the United Kingdom, and their despatch would retard India's other commitments and her expansion programme.[1]

In reply to Hutton's telegram of the 22nd, the Commander-in-Chief in India said on the 24th that, in addition to 46th and 48th Brigades and three British battalions, he hoped in due course to send 63rd Brigade and 14th Division, less one brigade. He pointed out that these reinforcements together with the troops already in Burma, plus the two East African brigades,[2] would produce the equivalent of four divisions—the maximum for which the base and line of communication organization was being planned. The request for an additional division, however, could be met only as a very long-term project, and even the despatch of 14th Division would be delayed owing to the allotment of equipment to other units being sent to Burma. It was not till three weeks later that the Commander-in-Chief in India was able to give March–April as a firm date for the despatch of 14th Division.

Besides asking for reinforcements from India, Hutton had been looking to the Chinese for assistance. His original instructions had been that no Chinese troops other than 93rd Division of VI Chinese Army were to be brought into Burma without reference to ABDA Command. Early in January one regiment of the division had taken over the Mekong River line, and on the 19th Hutton arranged for the remainder to enter the Shan States. On the 20th he asked Wavell for permission to bring in a second Chinese division to take over the defence of the Siamese north-west frontier. This was granted. On the 29th, therefore, it was arranged that 49th Chinese Division should come into the southern Shan States via Lashio and take over the area east of the Salween about Takaw (where the Kengtung–Meiktila road crossed that river) and where, it will be noted, it would block the invasion route from Chiengrai, via Kengtung. It was also decided to bring forward 55th Chinese Division into reserve at Wanting (the frontier post on the Burma Road, about 100 miles north-east of Lashio) where it would complete its training and equipment.

In pursuance of his policy of concentrating the British forces in southern Burma where a Japanese advance most menaced Rangoon and the communications with China, Hutton ordered General Bruce Scott (1st Burma Division) to send 2nd K.O.Y.L.I., a B.A.F. field

---

[1] The situation greatly improved when in February ships at sea containing equipment for the Singapore garrison were diverted to India.
[2] See page 15.

battery and 1st Burma Rifles from 1st Burma Brigade to reinforce 17th Division and, as the Chinese troops arrived, move 1st Burma Brigade (now reduced to 5th Burma Rifles and F.F.3) to the Heho–Loilem area, and 13th Brigade to the Bawlake area east of Toungoo to gain touch with 17th Division about Papun. On the 31st January 48th Indian Brigade arrived in Rangoon and was temporarily retained there in army reserve awaiting the arrival of its transport.[1]

Chiang Kai-shek had insisted that Chinese troops in Burma should be given their own area of operations.[2] This proved highly desirable for they had their own peculiar system of command and set little store by supply and other administrative services, always expecting to live on the country. A separate operational area helped also to mitigate the language difficulty. The Chinese were in many respects embarrassing allies, not from any lack of goodwill on either side, but from the difference in customs and usages.

Since the Chinese formations had neither transport nor medical units, Hutton took steps to improvise them. He gave Mr. R. J. Holmes, who was operating a civilian transport organization on the Burma Road, the local rank of Colonel and told him to mobilize all available civil transport to supply the Chinese armies. At the same time he took over and expanded an ambulance unit run by Dr. Gordon Seagrave, an American medical missionary, to provide an embryo medical organization. This unit rendered invaluable aid to the Chinese throughout the campaign. He also created a Chinese Liaison Mission, consisting of civil and military officers whose duties were to be threefold: to convey his instructions to the Chinese forces which had entered Burma, to arrange the interchange of information between British and Chinese forces and to make administrative arrangements for the Chinese in Burma. In practice the third rôle assumed such importance that it almost swamped the other two.

It soon became obvious that the control over Chinese formations exercised by the British was little more than nominal. Each Chinese army and divisional commander seemed determined to carry out his own plans within the area allotted to him, and in practice would take orders only from Chungking. And here may be mentioned a weakness of the Chinese system of command: the absolute insistence upon direct personal orders. To carry any weight an order had either to be given personally or be written and signed by the commander with

---

[1] The 48th Indian Infantry Brigade (Brigadier N. Hugh-Jones) consisted of 1/3rd, 1/4th and 2/5th Gurkha Rifles. The brigade transport had been shipped from India separately with the result that it was not fully ready for action when ordered to move from Rangoon on the 3rd.

[2] Generalissimo Chiang Kai-shek assumed supreme command of all the Allied forces in China on the 3rd January 1942.

his own hand. The Chinese were quite unable to understand the system of a staff officer acting for his chief.[1]

By capturing Moulmein and its airfield, the Japanese had taken an important step forward on the road to Rangoon. Their next task was to cross the Salween, which they described as a river greatly hampering military operations, and gain the line of the Sittang River. The area for which 17th Division was now responsible extended from Martaban up the Salween for a distance of some eighty-five miles, then westward to the Sittang River and southward along the eighty miles of coastline between the mouth of the Sittang and Martaban. The line of communication serving this area ran parallel with the coast from Martaban through Thaton and Bilin to Kyaikto and thence to the Sittang. Although the area was open to attack from across the Salween on the east and from the sea on the west, there were two obvious lines of advance open to the enemy, by way of Martaban and Pa-an, both of which involved difficult river crossings.

Smyth advocated giving up part of the large and vulnerable salient at the southern end of which lay Martaban, and proposed that the line Thaton–Kuzeik should be held. Hutton, who had to ensure that there was sufficient time for reinforcements to arrive at Rangoon and for the Chinese divisions to reach their allotted areas in the north, felt unable to allow the enemy to cross the Salween unopposed and ordered the river line as far south as Martaban to be held, and no ground given up. At the same time, in order to prevent the Japanese from moving by sea from Malaya and landing on the vulnerable coast north of Martaban, he appealed to ABDA Command for warships, but none could be spared.

Smyth was in a quandary. He had been ordered to hold both Martaban which, being the allied rail and roadhead, was a likely objective for the Japanese, and the crossing of the Salween at Pa-an, on which strong enemy forces were already converging from the south and east. He also had to watch the western coastline and the crossings of the Salween at Shwegun and Kamamaung, and even Papun, 100 miles to the north, all of which were possible enemy lines of advance. It was obvious that, with the troops available, he could hold only the key points on the main routes and rely on patrols to give warning of enemy advances on the others, while retaining strong reserves in a central position. Since he felt that the Japanese could infiltrate through the forward positions almost anywhere, he deployed his division in great depth. He gave 16th Brigade the task of holding the Thaton–Kamamaung–Pa-an–Martaban area, 46th

---

[1] See Appendix 18, Part II.

Brigade the Bilin–Papun area and placed 2nd Burma Brigade,[1] weakened as a result of the fighting in Moulmein, in the Kyaikto area to guard the coastline and track between Kyaikto and the bridge at Sittang, the sole link with Rangoon.

On the 3rd February, in order to provide Smyth with a divisional reserve, Hutton ordered 48th Indian Infantry Brigade (Brigadier N. Hugh-Jones) to move to Kyaikto to join 17th Division by the 7th. He gave instructions that it was to be kept concentrated and not used till it was complete with its transport. So that the brigade might not be tied to roads—a serious handicap when fighting an enemy trained and equipped for cross-country movement—it had been sent from India equipped on an experimental basis with mixed animal and motor transport, but had had no time to train with its new scale of transport.

Meanwhile on the 30th January, the eve of the fall of Moulmein, General Iida (*15th Army*) had ordered *55th Division* to concentrate at Moulmein after its capture and prepare for the drive northwards, and *33rd Division* to secure the ford across the Salween at Pa-an. The former spent the next three days in bringing up munitions and river-crossing equipment while the latter moved on Pa-an. On the night of the 3rd/4th February, after a brisk engagement with patrols of 1/7th Gurkhas of 16th Brigade, the advanced guard of *215th Regiment* occupied Pa-an. The Japanese then halted to reconnoitre the British position at Kuzeik on the opposite side of the river, and to collect bridging equipment. Further south patrols from *55th Division* made repeated attempts to land at Martaban under cover of darkness, and the town itself was subjected not only to continual air raids, but to heavy artillery bombardment to which no reply could be made as the guns of 27th Mountain Regiment were outranged.

On the night of the 4th/5th February, General Wavell flew from Java to Rangoon where he hoped to meet Chiang Kai-shek who was on his way to Calcutta, but the Generalissimo, lacking any definite news of the date of Wavell's arrival, had flown direct to India from Lashio. On the 6th Wavell, accompanied by Hutton, visited Headquarters 17th Division at Kyaikto where he was told of the general situation. He urged that the Japanese, despite their initial successes, should not be regarded as supermen. Their advance, he said, should be checked and, since offence was the best means of defence, an effort should be made to retake the lost areas of Tenasserim. Key points such as the Sittang Bridge, Kyaikto, Bilin, Thaton, Martaban, Kuzeik and Papun should be strongly held and the Salween River

---

[1] The Burma Rifles, with certain exceptions, had shown that they could not stand up to determined enemy attacks. They had, however, the advantage over British and Indian troops that they could move freely in the jungle and knew the local language. It was therefore decided to brigade them with other troops and the brigades of 17th Division were reconstructed so that each included a Burma Rifles battalion.

line watched. Wavell's visit had one very important result for, impressed with the suitability of the dry ricefields for armoured troops, he decided to propose to the Chiefs of Staff that 7th Armoured Brigade, then on its way from the Middle East to Malaya, should be diverted to Burma.[1]

On the 8th Smyth relieved 16th Brigade, hitherto responsible for the Salween line, by 46th Brigade. Owing to the limited number of troops available, some units of 16th Brigade remained where they were in the forward area and came under orders of 46th Brigade. On completion of the relief 46th Brigade held Martaban, Kuzeik, Duyinzeik and Thaton and patrolled the Salween, while 16th Brigade was located in the Bilin area.[2] The same day Smyth wrote an appreciation of the situation on the southern front. His immediate object, he said, was to prevent the Japanese from making any further advance into Tenasserim and, having accomplished this, to resume the offensive to regain the parts of Tenasserim already lost. His general deductions were that, although his division had of necessity to occupy and watch a very large area and the troops were very dispersed, it was for the first time since the operations began in a position to fight on a co-ordinated plan. He wanted more anti-aircraft guns, and more fully-trained troops. He proposed that 46th Brigade's general scheme of defence should be mobile and offensive based on three bastions, Martaban, Kuzeik and Thaton, which had to be strongly held and, if lost, regained by counter-attack. The Japanese should be worried by mobile columns and by bold and wide patrolling, the maximum number of troops being maintained forward for counter-attack. The 48th Brigade should be kept in hand until the scale and direction of the Japanese offensive was fully disclosed.

On the 9th February an operation instruction issued by *Southern Army* directed *15th Army* to advance to the Rangoon area and, in doing so, to occupy as much ground as possible to the north so as to facilitate subsequent operations for the capture of the Yenangyaung and Mandalay areas. General Iida thereupon ordered *33rd* and *55th Divisions* to take the offensive as early as possible without waiting for the arrival of their rear echelons. Both divisions, acting in co-ordination, were to drive the enemy from the line of the Salween and Sittang Rivers and advance to Pegu. The *55th* was then to move on Toungoo, destroying any Chinese forces opposing it, while the *33rd* made a rapid advance towards Rangoon where the British-Indian forces were to be overcome. The *33rd Division* was then to establish

---

[1] See Volume I, page 350.
[2] For detailed dispositions see Appendix 4.

Rangoon as a base and, at the same time, seize as much ground to the north as possible in preparation for operations in central and northern Burma.

While the relief of 16th Brigade by 46th Brigade (Brigadier Ekin) was taking place, Martaban, Kuzeik and Thaton were bombed. Early on the 9th it was discovered that the Japanese had landed west of Martaban and had established a road block near Paung, eight miles north of the town, and that the telephone line to Thaton had been cut. The first attempt to clear the block failed with the loss of two armoured cars, but in the afternoon two companies of 3/7th Gurkhas cleared the block at the point of the bayonet and drove the enemy into the hills with the loss of some equipment and an infantry gun. When Ekin learnt of the landing he decided, with Smyth's approval, to withdraw the garrison from Martaban. Unable to communicate with its commander by wireless, which as frequently happened had broken down, he sent a liaison officer with orders. The officer was killed and the orders did not get through.

During the afternoon, observation posts in Martaban reported that further large numbers of Japanese were landing west of the town and were moving north across the flat coastal belt towards Paung. It was now obvious that the enemy was in a position to attack Martaban from the north-west. Since no good purpose could be served by holding the town any longer, the garrison commander decided on his own initiative to withdraw. He collected his small force and, after destroying his motor transport, moved north after nightfall by the track running parallel with the Salween. The force, after an exhausting march of about fifty miles, reached Thaton on the 11th without meeting the enemy.

The Japanese *33rd Division* opened its offensive from Pa-an on the 11th and there were clashes between patrols west of the river during the day. In the evening the commanding officer of 7/10th Baluch in Kuzeik, expecting to be attacked that night, asked 5/17th Dogras in position at Duyinzeik to move forward to support him. At about the same time Ekin, aware of the growing danger to the Baluchis, ordered the Dogras to go to their aid. During the night of the 11th/12th two battalions of *215th Regiment* crossed the river near Kuzeik, whilst the third battalion crossed two miles further south. The former advanced due west and then, turning north-east, attacked the rear of the 7/10th Baluch position at Kuzeik in the early hours of the 12th. From 1 a.m. till 9 a.m. the Baluchis were engaged in a fierce hand-to-hand struggle against overwhelming odds, and it was not until three of its companies had been practically annihilated that the remnants of the battalion gave ground. Only five of its platoons which were out on patrol, together with the few survivors of the action, later rejoined 46th Brigade. The Dogras, largely owing to the inadequacy of the ferry over the Donthami River, did not advance till 11 a.m. on the 12th. At a point six miles short of Kuzeik, they met stragglers from the Baluchis who reported that the Japanese had been driven back; the battalion thereupon withdrew to its former position. The failure of the Dogras to advance to the aid of the Baluchis on the 11th was serious, for it gave the Japanese the opportunity to overwhelm the isolated Baluchis quickly and establish themselves west of the Salween.

Smyth had been ordered to hold the Duyinzeik–Thaton line for as long as possible so as to gain time, but the Japanese, once across the Salween, could turn the left flank of 46th Brigade at Duyinzeik and cut its line of communication by moving on Bilin. It was clear that a withdrawal could not be delayed. At this juncture Brigadier D. T. Cowan, formerly Director of Military Training at General Headquarters, India, arrived at Headquarters 17th Division to take over command of a brigade. Smyth considered that Cowan could best be used as a Brigadier General Staff, and sent him back to Rangoon on the 12th with a request to this effect. He told him to impress on Hutton the grave danger in which 17th Division stood of being cut off from the Sittang Bridge, and to urge that he might be allowed to withdraw the division behind the Bilin River immediately and that there should be no delay in the next stage of the withdrawal, which should be behind the Sittang River.

On the afternoon of the 13th the enemy suddenly opened an artillery and mortar bombardment on 5/17th Dogras at Duyinzeik; this lasted for some forty-five minutes and, though no infantry attack was made, it showed that the Japanese had followed up their success at Kuzeik. During the day Smyth had sent Hutton a message pointing out that most of the units of 17th Division consisted of inadequately trained troops with inexperienced officers. They were very tired and shaken by constant air attacks, had little air support, no anti-aircraft guns and very little artillery. Only one battalion (2nd K.O.Y.L.I.) out of 16th and 46th Brigades was fit for offensive action and the remaining battalions would probably not stand in face of heavy attack with dive-bombers and artillery.[1] The 48th Brigade was fresh and ready, but behind it there was at Kyaikto only one battalion of any value (4/12th F.F. Regiment) and, at the Sittang Bridge, 3rd Burma Rifles who would not stand up to a heavy attack.[2] Consequently he suggested a withdrawal and concentration behind the Bilin River, unless heavy reinforcements were due. At 5.40 p.m. that evening Hutton, who by this time had seen Cowan and heard Smyth's views on the situation, replied, 'Situation fully understood.

---

[1] The disposition of 17th Division on the 13th was the same as on the 8th. See Appendix 4.
[2] This battalion had already failed at Moulmein, see page 31.

I wish to fight as far forward as possible but leave you with discretion as indicated by telephone. Reinforcements on the way and a British battalion may be available in a few days. . . .' There is no record of the telephone conversation but it seems possible that Hutton, from his subsequent actions, said that he did not consider any withdrawal from the Thaton–Duyinzeik position was at the time necessary.

The onus of deciding when to withdraw from the Thaton–Duyinzeik position now rested on Smyth but, with the knowledge that Hutton was loath to give up any ground, the decision was difficult to make. During the 14th the Japanese made no attempt to attack at Duyinzeik. Both Smyth and Ekin became more and more concerned, for they suspected that the enemy was by-passing their positions and moving round 46th Brigade's left flank with a view to cutting its communications. Their suspicion was well founded for *214th Regiment of 33rd Division* had been directed to move by tracks east of the Thaton–Kyaikto road to Ahonwa on the Bilin River, while *215th Regiment*, which was reorganizing after its battle at Kuzeik, moved on Thaton. As the day drew to its close, Smyth felt he could wait no longer and at 5.30 p.m. ordered 46th Brigade to withdraw, and his division to take up a position on the general line of the Bilin River.

He told Hutton that evening that he considered an attack on Duyinzeik and Thaton was probable in the very near future and that, as these positions were weak and difficult to support, he was gradually withdrawing 46th Brigade. He was concentrating his division behind the Bilin River and was confident he could hold the new area. At the same time he wrote Hutton a demi-official letter in which he acknowledged the receipt of his communication sent by the hand of Cowan and said,

> 'We have considered very carefully the pros and cons for fighting behind the Bilin River or for supporting 46th Brigade in their forward positions at Duyinzeik and Thaton. I had felt quite decided that the former course was the best and laid on plans and reconnaissance accordingly, but waited to consult Cowan and see what news he had as regards future policy. Having found that his views entirely agreed with mine and bearing in mind your requirements, I had no hesitation in putting the plan into effect.'

A report on the operations leading up to the crossing of the Sittang, written by Smyth on the 26th February, makes it quite clear what Hutton's 'requirements' were. In this he said,

> 'On the 14th February I decided to concentrate behind the Bilin River where I considered the division would have a better chance of putting up a good fight and ensuring for the Army Commander his two main requests, i.e. time and killing Japanese, instead of fighting further forward in small detachments with a long and very vulnerable line of communications.'

Smyth was now in the defensive area, the holding of which he had advocated from the start of the operations. His plan was for 16th Brigade to occupy the river line; 48th Brigade to remain in divisional reserve and be prepared to hold a line on the Thebyu River covering Kyaikto; and 46th Brigade to evacuate Thaton by dawn on the 15th, handing back 2nd K.O.Y.L.I. to 16th Brigade on reaching the Bilin River, leaving 5/17th Dogras to hold an outpost position astride the main road east of Bilin, and then moving back to Kyaikto where it was to rest and reorganize. The retirement of 46th Brigade, which involved the assembly of units and detachments scattered over ten miles of difficult country and the movement of some 400 vehicles along a single road, was effected without incident during the 15th.

Meanwhile to ensure that the line of the Sittang River between Sittang and Shwegyin was adequately patrolled Hutton had, on the 13th, told H.Q. 2nd Burma Brigade to move with 7th Burma Rifles from Mokpalin to Nyaunglebin, where it was to come under command of the L. of C. Area, leaving 3rd Burma Rifles to guard the Sittang Bridge. On the 14th he made 17th Division responsible for the preparation of the bridge for demolition and for destroying it if necessary. The stage was now set for the first major action of the campaign—the defence of the Bilin River by 17th Division, concentrated for the first time, opposed by *33rd* and *55th Japanese Divisions*, each of two regiments.

Towards the end of January, 28 (A.C.) Squadron R.A.F. and 1 (A.C.) Squadron I.A.F. had arrived from India equipped with Lysander aircraft. Although their primary rôle was tactical reconnaissance it was decided to employ both squadrons as light bombers. During the first fortnight of February they were used in conjunction with the few remaining Blenheims in direct support of the army. They attacked river craft and landing stages on the Salween, railway stations, battery positions and dumps, and bombed Kado, Moulmein and Pa-an. Whenever possible these attacks were given fighter escort, but this had to be at the expense of the air defence of Rangoon, which had been given priority in order to ensure the safe arrival of reinforcements by sea. Since the effective air strength at this time averaged only thirty-five fighters and thirty-two bombers,[1] and the enemy was widely dispersed and free to move across country, these attacks could do little to check the Japanese advance.

Before describing the action on the Bilin River, it is necessary to touch on what had been happening behind the battle line while 17th Division was making its fighting withdrawal. When Hutton was

---

[1] 8 Blenheims and 24 Lysanders.

on his way to Lashio to meet Chiang Kai-shek, his aircraft made a forced landing on the night of the 2nd/3rd February alongside the railway south-west of Lashio. The pilot was killed and Hutton himself was badly bruised and shaken. Nevertheless on the 3rd he had an interview with the Generalissimo who made it clear that the Chinese troops were to be under his (Hutton's) command. Chiang Kai-shek agreed that VI Chinese Army (Lieut.-General Kan Li-chu) should take over the defence of the whole of the northern frontier with Siam as soon as possible, thus freeing 1st Burma Division for operations south of Toungoo, and that V Chinese Army (Lieut.-General Tu Yu-ming), comprising 22nd, 96th and 200th Divisions, should move into the Toungoo area for the defence of the Burma Road. They arranged that 49th and 93rd Divisions of VI Army would remain as heretofore in the Shan States, and that 55th Division would move from Wanting to cover the frontier in the Karen Hills north-east of Toungoo.[1] General Kan Li-chu however, averse to the dispersal of his forces, released only one regiment (the equivalent of a British battalion) for this purpose.

By the middle of February a large proportion of the civil population of Rangoon had fled. Numbers of Indians had set out on foot for Prome with the intention of making their way across the Arakan Yomas to Taungup, and thence to Chittagong by country craft; others had gone to upper Burma, preferring to follow the Chindwin routes into Assam. The civil authorities did what they could for them, but supplies and medical facilities were lacking and the long columns of men, women and children suffered great hardships and many died on the way. As the Japanese advanced into Burma, the flood of refugees swelled till it eventually hampered military operations and embarrassed the already overloaded military administrative machine.

Strenuous efforts had been made to keep the port and the oil refineries near Rangoon working in spite of the shortage of dock and other labour caused by this exodus, for it was essential that reinforcements and military stores should be disembarked and the fast accumulating lease-lend supplies for China sent up the Burma Road. An outbreak of looting and arson in the half-deserted city was dealt with by setting the offenders to work under military guard at the docks. This had the dual effect of quickly restoring order and partly solving the labour problem, and the port was kept working.

Hutton's object was to gain time for reinforcements to arrive, especially 7th Armoured Brigade due on the 21st, and for the Chinese to move into Burma. By the 12th February, however, the Japanese were well established across the Salween and he realized that the

---

[1] See page 35.

chance of achieving his object was fading. On the 13th, after having interviewed Brigadier Cowan and seen Smyth's telegram reviewing the state of his troops, he sent the Commander-in-Chief in India an appreciation of the position. He said he had every intention of fighting it out east of the Sittang, but it was possible that the exhaustion of the available troops and continued infiltration might eventually result in 17th Division being driven back to the river. Withdrawal of transport across the river would be very difficult since, except for the vulnerable rail-road bridge, communications consisted of ferries of which only one had a road connection. He would therefore fight hard to retain a bridgehead. West of the Sittang there were large areas of dry open ricefields ideal for the operation of tanks and armoured cars; provided minimum infantry forces were available, he should therefore be able to control this area. At present there were no reserves, but 7th Armoured Brigade was on its way. The situation for the next month, until more infantry arrived and V Chinese Army reached lower Burma, would therefore be critical. A few British battalions, which might perhaps be replaced in India from the Middle East, would be invaluable, since they were more able to sustain casualties without loss of fighting value than the partially trained Indian troops. The most immediate need was for more battalions of any kind.

Evidently fearing that 17th Division might be forced back across the Sittang before adequate reinforcements arrived, Hutton continued,

> 'We shall exert every effort to defend Rangoon but if Pegu were lost its fate would be more or less certain. In this event remnants of our forces will endeavour to withdraw northwards towards Prome covering the bases now being stocked in central Burma and the road to India with a view to subsequent counter-offensive. Toungoo and the upper reaches of river Sittang will be covered by 1st Burma Division and V Chinese Army.'

This appreciation proved to be an extremely accurate forecast.

The same day, finding that his responsibilities were becoming too great, and in order to make the best use of the forces which would eventually be available for the defence of Burma, Hutton asked Wavell to provide a corps headquarters to take command of the British formations in southern Burma and a high level liaison mission to work with the Chinese.[1]

On the 15th Hutton heard that Smyth had withdrawn from the Duyinzeik–Thaton position. From the information available to him at Rangoon at the time there seemed to be no reason for this withdrawal, for there was little indication of the danger to the division's left flank and the line had not been attacked. He therefore wrote to

---

[1] The corps headquarters did not arrive till March.

Smyth expressing his disapproval of this action which he considered to have been premature. The same day, reporting the situation to Wavell, he said: '[I] shall endeavour to stop this [withdrawal], but Thaton has already been evacuated'. It is easy to understand how to Hutton this withdrawal appeared at the time to be unnecessary (though afterwards he agreed it was justified and carried out in the nick of time) and his concern at the effect it had on his timetable, for the arrival of the promised reinforcements could not possibly be accelerated. Some reinforcements had however reached Rangoon—1st West Yorkshire on the 28th January and 2nd Duke of Wellington's on the 14th February. The former was employed to watch the coastline of the Gulf of Martaban east of Rangoon and the latter retained temporarily in army reserve for the protection of the city.

When Wavell heard of the withdrawal to the Bilin River he telegraphed Hutton,

> 'I do not know what considerations caused withdrawal behind Bilin River without further fighting. I have every confidence in judgement and fighting spirit of you and Smyth but bear in mind that continual withdrawal, as experience of Malaya showed, is most damaging to morale of troops, especially Indian troops. Time can often be gained as effectively and less expensively by bold counter-offensive. This especially so against the Japanese.'

CHAPTER III

INDIA BECOMES THE BASE FOR THE WAR IN THE FAR EAST

(December 1941 – February 1942)

See Maps 4, 6 and 14 and Sketch 16

ON the outbreak of war with Japan, India had more or less completed her accelerated 1940 expansion and was busy with the 1941 programme, which involved the raising and training of 14th, 17th, 19th, 20th and 34th Indian Divisions, the reforming of 7th Indian Division and the despatch of the balance of 31st Indian Armoured Division to Iraq.[1] At the same time she was starting on the 1942 programme which involved the raising of four more infantry divisions, one armoured division and a very large number of base, line of communication and non-divisional units, both for her own purposes and to supply the ever-growing requirements of the Middle East and Iraq.[2]

At the end of 1941 India had about 900,000 men under arms. Of these over 300,000 had been sent overseas to the Middle East, Iraq and Malaya. The balance in India included some 150,000 on watch and ward on the North West Frontier and on internal security duty throughout the country, approximately 300,000 undergoing recruit training at training centres and the remainder in field formations and administrative units which were being raised. Recruits were being taken in at the average rate of 50,000 per month.

There was, however, a very great shortage of weapons and equipment of all sorts. The following table gives the percentage allocation by October 1941 of certain weapons to meet the requirements of

---

[1] For details of India's expansion programme see Volume I, pages 36–42. The 1940 programme involved the raising of 6th, 7th, 8th, 9th and 10th Infantry Divisions and 31st Armoured Division. Of these 6th, 8th and 10th Infantry and part of 31st Armoured Divisions had been sent to Iraq and 9th to Malaya. The 7th, which had supplied 13th and 16th Brigades to Burma, remained in India.

[2] The 1942 expansion programme included 23rd, 25th, 26th and 'X' Infantry Divisions and 32nd Indian Armoured Division. 'X' Division was not formed, for the units earmarked for it were used to reform 17th Division and reconstruct 1st Burma Division into 39th Division after the withdrawal of these formations from Burma in May 1942.

48 INDIA BECOMES THE FAR EAST BASE

Home Command, the Middle East and India (against her demands for the 1940 expansion programme).

Weapons	Britain %	Middle East %	India %
25-pounder field artillery guns	81	107	36
2-pounder anti-tank guns	79	93	23
Bren light machine-guns	84	67	19
Mortars (2-inch and 3-inch)	66½	47	11
Anti-tank rifles	50½	42	4

India had been allotted some 25 per cent. of her requirements of heavy anti-aircraft guns, 15 per cent. of light anti-aircraft guns and 82 out of 300 tanks; but only a small proportion of all these had actually been shipped to Indian ports. Signal equipment, particularly wireless, was very short. This lack of weapons and equipment not only prevented field formations from being prepared for active operations, but seriously retarded the training of formations and units which were being raised.

Shortly after the outbreak of war with Japan, 17th Indian Division was broken up and sent piecemeal as reinforcements for Malaya and Burma; 44th and 45th Brigades went to Malaya and 17th Divisional Headquarters, divisional troops and 46th Brigade to Burma. The 48th Brigade from 19th Division had been sent to Burma in January and 63rd Brigade from 14th Division was to follow in February.[1] Thus by mid-February 1942 the only formations left in India were the balance of the 1941 programme—14th Division less one brigade (and this division was earmarked for Burma in April), 7th and 19th Divisions consisting of little except their infantry and 34th Division which, less one brigade, was in Ceylon.

In the air the situation was even worse. In Bengal for the defence of Calcutta there was 5 (Fighter) Squadron equipped with eight Mohawks, while in Assam there was an improvised fighter squadron (146 Squadron) with Audax aircraft, normally used in India for army co-operation. On the North West Frontier there were three squadrons of the Indian Air Force equipped for the most part with obsolete aircraft. There were six coastal defence flights manned by the Indian Air Force Volunteer Reserve, some of their aircraft being of types not less than twelve years old.[2] There was also 31 (Bomber-Transport) Squadron with a few Dakota (D.C.2) aircraft engaged in air transport into upper Burma. In Burma there were two fighter squadrons—67 (Buffalo) Squadron R.A.F. and a (Tomahawk) squadron of the A.V.G.—and one bomber squadron, 60 (Blenheim)

---

[1] See page 35.
[2] These coastal defence flights were disbanded in March 1942.

Squadron R.A.F. In Ceylon under H.Q. 222 Group there were only 273 (Vildebeeste) Torpedo-Bomber Squadron and a detachment of 205 Flying-Boat Squadron with Catalina flying-boats.[1] The only other aircraft in the island were those of visiting units of the Fleet Air Arm. The number and size of the existing airfields, most of which were sited for the defence of the North West Frontier, fell far short of requirements. Apart from this lack of airfields, the air defence was dangerously handicapped by the absence of any warning system covering north-east India and of radar to protect Ceylon and the long length of India's eastern shores.

Perhaps India's most difficult problem, and one which grew in importance as the likelihood of the loss of Singapore and possibly Rangoon loomed nearer, was the reorientation of her defences. The traditional invasion route into India had always been through Afghanistan across the North West Frontier. For generations Indian defence forces had been disposed to defend that frontier, and the necessary strategic roads and railways, administrative installations and airfields had been sited so as to support the military forces deployed in its defence. After the outbreak of war with Germany not only were these defences strengthened but, when the expansion of Indian forces began, new formations were raised and new administrative installations established in areas which were selected for their suitability for the defence of this frontier. An invasion of the east coast had never been contemplated for there was no enemy within striking distance. Nor had a threat to the north-east frontier been seriously envisaged, since the nature of the country itself was considered to give a very considerable measure of security. Thus little thought had been given to the defence of these areas.

A situation was now developing, however, which made the defence of the eastern borders a matter of urgency. It was soon found that the paucity of the transportation services, the lack of roads and the absence of administrative installations and airfields in eastern and especially north-eastern India was such that the deployment and maintenance of the forces required to defend these areas were fraught with greatest difficulties. India had therefore to face the problem of preparing a completely new administrative lay-out facing east, and of siting and constructing a very large number of new airfields so as to enable her to defend her eastern frontiers and support the forces which would eventually be employed to recapture any British territory which had been lost. All this had to be undertaken in areas where the capacity of the existing communications was barely sufficient to maintain the normal requirements of the local inhabitants and their industries, and where nature, in the form of

---

[1] For the performance of these aircraft, see Appendix 23.

rivers which frequently changed their courses and a monsoon of great severity, made the improvement of these communications a task of great magnitude.

At this juncture India Command lost both its Commander-in-Chief and Chief of the General Staff, for early in January 1942 Wavell left India to take up his appointment as Supreme Commander of the ABDA Area,[1] and on the 27th December 1941 his Chief of Staff, Lieut.-General Hutton, had left for Rangoon to be General Officer Commanding, Burma.[2] There was considerable delay in filling these two important posts in India. Eventually General Sir Alan F. Hartley, from Northern Command, was appointed Commander-in-Chief and Lieut.-General E. L. Morris, from the United Kingdom, Chief of the General Staff. Thus for most of the critical month of January, India Command was without either a commander or chief staff officer, which naturally resulted in delays, for there was no one with sufficient authority to take decisions. It would seem that at this time the possibility of India becoming a base for British military effort against Japan was not fully appreciated. General Hartley remained as Commander-in-Chief in India till the 28th February when General Wavell resumed command, after the dissolution of ABDA Command on the 25th[3]; whereupon he became Deputy Commander-in-Chief, a new appointment.

The lines of communication from India to the Assam–Burma and the eastern Bengal–Arakan frontiers were, early in 1942, so poor that they could scarcely support even the minimum land and air forces considered necessary for the defence of these frontiers against an invasion from Burma. The unbridged Brahmaputra River lay across them and provided a difficult obstacle. Its level normally fluctuates during the year by as much as twenty-five feet, and its course constantly changes: an annual variation of half a mile is not unusual. Thus at the ghats (the crossing places or ports of call for river steamers), jetties, roads and railway spurs running to them have to be abandoned usually at least once during the monsoon on the eroded bank, whereas on the opposite bank they have to be lengthened or even rebuilt elsewhere.

The western bank of the river was served by spurs from the broad gauge railway which ran northwards from Calcutta through Santahar and Parbatipur to Siliguri[4], and by a metre gauge railway from Parbatipur along the foothills of the Himalayas through Bongaigaon

---

[1] See Volume I, Chapter XVI.
[2] See page 16.
[3] See Volume I, pages 429–30.
[4] These spurs ran to Khulna, Goalundo and Sirajganj.

COMMUNICATIONS TO THE NORTH-EAST

to the river port of Amingaon, with a spur to the river port of Dhubri.[1] There was an alternative route by means of the low capacity metre gauge line from the main broad gauge system of India at Benares, or across the ferry at Mokameh Ghat, to Parbatipur. In addition, there was a metre gauge connection from the broad gauge system at Santahar, which served the river port of Tistamukh and joined the Parbatipur–Amingaon line at Kaunia. All men, animals, equipment and stores on the way to Assam or eastern Bengal had to be transferred to the metre gauge at Parbatipur or Santahar or, if the alternative route were used, at Benares and Mokameh Ghat.

On the east of the river there were two metre gauge railways. The first, in Assam, ran from Pandu (opposite Amingaon) by way of Lumding and Dimapur to Ledo with branches to the river ports at Silghat (opposite Tezpur) and Donaigaon through Jorhat and from Tinsukia to Dibrugarh.[2] The maximum capacity of this line in December 1941 was 600 tons a day. The second, in eastern Bengal, ran southwards from Bahadurabad (opposite Tistamukh) through Mymensingh (where the branch to Dacca began) to Akhaura. At Akhaura the line divided again, one branch running north-east into Assam through Badarpur to Silchar and Lalaghat, with a branch from Badarpur over the hills to connect with the Assam railway at Lumding; the other branch ran south from Akhaura through Laksam and Feni to the seaport of Chittagong and ended some twenty-five miles further south at Dohazari. There were also spurs from Laksam to Chandpur and Noakhali.

As there was no road link from India to the west bank of the Brahmaputra, all vehicles had to be carried by rail, thus greatly increasing the load on the metre gauge approach railways. East of the river a second-class all-weather road, known as the Assam trunk road, ran from the river port of Goalpara (opposite Jogighopa) through Pandu (opposite Amingaon) and Gauhati to Jorhat and thence through Dibrugarh to Ledo. A spur from this road ran to the hill station at Shillong and thence south to Sylhet. Another connected Jorhat with Golaghat, but Dimapur was inaccessible by road as the river south of Golaghat was unbridged. Thus all traffic to Dimapur, including vehicles, had to be carried by the railway. In addition there was the all-important single-width metalled road from Dimapur on the railway through Kohima to Imphal in Manipur State (referred to from now on as the Imphal Road). There were no roads of any importance in eastern Bengal.

---

[1] See Sketch 17.

[2] The branch to Tezpur, Donaigaon and Jorhat was narrow gauge. It was converted to metre gauge in 1943.

The ports on both sides of the Brahmaputra from its mouth up to Dibrugarh in the north-east of Assam were served in peacetime by a fleet of river steamers and barges. The capacity of this fleet had however been greatly reduced during 1940 and 1941, since many of the steamers and barges had been loaned by India to meet the demands for this type of vessel in Iraq. There were wagon ferries across the river at Amingaon–Pandu (Gauhati) capable of carrying 250 wagons a day, and others at Tistamukh–Bahadurabad.

From the above it will be seen that in January 1942 the lines of communication to the Assam frontier were: firstly, the broad gauge railway running north from Calcutta, supplemented by the metre gauge running east from Benares and Mokameh Ghat to the junction at Parbatipur. From this junction there was but the single line metre gauge railway to Amingaon, where all traffic had to cross the Brahmaputra River by ferry and then proceed either by the single line metre gauge Assam railway to Dimapur and onwards by road to Imphal, or by rail or road to Ledo. Secondly, the Brahmaputra River with its steamer services from river ports in Bengal to those in north-east Assam and onwards by road and rail to Imphal and Ledo. All men, animals, equipment and stores for Imphal had therefore to be transferred several times during their journey from India.

To the eastern Bengal–Arakan frontier the line of communication was firstly by sea from Calcutta to Chittagong, secondly, by broad gauge railway to Goalundo and then by river steamer to Chandpur and onwards by metre gauge to Chittagong and, thirdly, by broad gauge to Santahar and metre gauge to Tistamukh, across the Brahmaputra by ferry to Bahadurabad and thence by metre gauge to Chittagong. It was possible to supply both Dimapur and Ledo by sea to Chittagong, from there by rail through Akhaura and Badarpur to Lumding and thence onwards on the Assam railway. The capacity of this route was, however, extremely limited owing to the steep gradients on the hill section between Badarpur and Lumding.

The lines of communication to the north-eastern frontier were thus not only long and slow, but they had a very limited capacity. The railways lacked adequate crossing places and up-to-date telegraph, telephone and control systems. The capacity of the ferries was small. The roads were second-class, narrow and unable to stand up to continuous heavy traffic during the monsoon.[1] Land-slides and wash-outs were common on parts of the Imphal Road and on the metre gauge railway where it ran parallel with the foothills of the Himalayas and crossed a number of mountain-fed rivers. Both the rail and road systems passed through highly malarious areas.

---

[1] The road from Gauhati to Shillong was however first-class.

In January 1942 General Headquarters, India, took the first steps to overcome these difficulties. Orders were issued for the construction of a reserve supply depot and an engineer depot at Benares, and a reserve ordnance and ammunition depot at Jamalpur, from both of which there was fairly easy access to the metre gauge railway to Assam and to eastern Bengal and the Orissa coast. To supply troops on the Assam frontier, work was begun on a railhead and an advanced base depot at Dimapur (which became known as the Manipur Road Depot) at the northern end of the Imphal Road. This depot was planned to hold thirty days' supplies for three divisions and eventually to be capable of handling 1,000 tons of stores daily.

At the same time a start was made on improving the lines of communication from India to these advanced depots. The capacity of the Amingaon–Pandu ferry was increased, additional crossing places on the single line railway were constructed and the railway telegraph system and the Assam trunk road were improved. But these steps were only the beginning of an enormous programme of work which was to continue until the end of the war.

On the outbreak of war with Japan, General Headquarters, India, realized that the creation of satisfactory land communications between Burma and India would become a matter of prime importance, and came to the conclusion that the most feasible alignment for a road link between the two countries was an extension of the Imphal Road through Palel to Tamu on the India-Burma frontier and thence down the Kabaw Valley to Kalewa on the Chindwin. From there a road could be built to the railhead at Yeu, or the river itself could be used as a means of communication southwards to the railway at Monywa. At the end of 1941 the Imphal Road, 134 miles in length, was a single-way twelve foot wide metalled and partly tarmac road as far as Imphal, and a metalled single track extended it a further twenty-eight miles to Palel. Beyond this point there were only jungle tracks.

In December 1941 General Wavell arranged for the Assam Public Works Department to widen the Imphal Road and extend it to Tamu on the Burmese frontier. Early in January 1942 General Headquarters proposed that an all-weather road twenty feet wide, capable of carrying two hundred fully loaded lorries daily each way, should be built on this alignment. Work to extend it to Tamu was accelerated and at the same time the Government of Burma was asked to construct the Tamu–Kalewa section as a matter of the highest priority. It was planned that the India section, as a single-way road, should reach Tamu by the 15th May.

By the end of February 1942 it had become clear that the Assam Public Works Department was unable to cope with the construction of the road, and that army engineers would have to take over responsibility for it. Its completion was a matter of extreme urgency and something drastic had to be done. A unique administrative post was therefore created. Major-General E. Wood was sent to Assam with plenary powers to ensure that the demands of the engineers were met and the road driven through from the Indian end. A number of specialist Royal Engineer units were hurriedly despatched to Assam, and the Indian Tea Association, which had already undertaken the task of organizing routes and camps for the evacuation of Indian refugees from Burma, was asked to provide the necessary labour. The Association, the Tea Planters of Assam and their Indian employees responded magnificently. The first contingent arrived for work on the 1st March, but, owing to the congestion on the Assam railway, it was not until the 31st March that the full quota of some 28,000 men was at work. Labour found locally and from the Naga Hills brought the total up to about 50,000. As a result of the measures taken, a fair-weather road had reached Tamu by the 28th April, and it was estimated that an all-weather one-way road would be completed to the frontier by the target date.

While on a visit to Delhi during February, Chiang Kai-shek had urged that in addition to the extension of the Imphal Road to the Chindwin, a road should be built from Ledo by way of Fort Hertz to Myitkyina. At a conference at Myitkyina, early in March, representatives from China and Burma agreed that the best alignment would be from Ledo across the Pangsau Pass to Mogaung, and the Governor of Burma asked for India's co-operation in building a road on this alignment. Wavell agreed to start work at once to build a six foot jeep track from Ledo to Shingbwiyang to facilitate the eventual construction of an all-weather road (which became known as the Ledo Road) to carry 2,000 tons a day. Arrangements were immediately made with the Indian Tea Association to recruit an additional 75,000 coolies for work on the road. By the middle of March some 15,000 had been assembled, and by the 9th May it was expected that the first thirty-two miles of the jeep track would be motorable by the end of the month. By that time, however, it had become evident that all the available labour would have to be employed to build and stock camps urgently required along the refugee evacuation routes, and on the 11th May the Ledo jeep road project was abandoned.

When Singapore fell on the 15th February and there was a growing possibility that Rangoon, too, might fall (for by then the British forces in Burma had been forced back to the Bilin River), the speedy expansion of the lines of communication and the solution of India's administrative problems became vital, for India was the only base from which the war in the Far East could be prosecuted and a counter-offensive launched. But the construction of airfields, roads and administrative installations and the improvement of railway and port facilities are by their very nature long-term projects. While they were being carried out, the Commander-in-Chief in India had to accept the limitations which the existing lines of communication imposed, and do the best he could with the troops and aircraft at his disposal to defend not only the frontiers but the coastline of India and Ceylon, all of which were now exposed to attack.[1]

General Hartley at this time estimated that his minimum requirements for defence were: Ceylon, one division; the east coast of southern India, two divisions; the provinces of Bihar and Orissa, one division; Calcutta and the Ganges Delta, one division and the Sundarbans Flotilla;[2] Assam, one division; and a reserve of at least two divisions—a total of eight divisions, against which he had only five as yet incomplete divisions. He knew that no assistance from overseas could reach India for some time, and he therefore took steps to accelerate as much as possible the raising and completion of the formations which remained in India and the administrative units required for their maintenance. By denuding the North West Frontier of all its reserves and reducing the number of troops on internal security duty, 14th Division was brought up to strength and two divisions of the 1942 programme (23rd and 26th) were formed. All these formations were however short of weapons and equipment. They had practically no artillery, and the standard of training they had reached was such that they were still quite unfit to meet an invasion.

We must now consider the steps that Britain took to meet the new dangers which arose in the Far East after the fall of Singapore. The Chiefs of Staff considered that the Japanese would first concentrate on the capture of Java so as to gain control of the Malay Barrier. They would then be in a position to extend the scope of their invasion of Burma, raid the east coast of India and, by seizing Ceylon, threaten the vital communications from the United Kingdom, by way of the Cape, to India, the Middle East and the Persian Gulf. On the 16th February the Defence Committee expressed the view that in the circumstances there was no alternative but to withhold further reinforcements for Java and concentrate everything on the defence of Burma, India, Ceylon and Australia. The Committee decided, however, to defer a decision on the action to be taken until

---

[1] Ceylon had been placed under India Command on the 22nd November 1941.

[2] The Sundarbans Flotilla, raised for reconnaissance and defence purposes in the Ganges Delta, consisted of four companies each operating twenty armed launches.

the meeting of the Pacific War Council the following day,[1] at which the views of the Dutch could be heard.

That day the Chiefs of Staff received a telegram from General Wavell (Supreme Commander, ABDA Command) in which he said, '... Burma and Australia are absolutely vital for war against Japan. The loss of Java, though a severe blow from every point of view, would not be fatal. Efforts should not therefore be made to reinforce Java which might compromise the defence of Burma or Australia'. Wavell went on to recommend that 1st Australian Corps (6th and 7th Divisions), of which 7th Division was already on its way to Java from the Middle East, should not be sent there; if it were decided to divert the corps elsewhere, at least one division should go to Burma, and both if they could be maintained. The presence of such a force in Burma, he said, would have a very great effect on enemy strategy and a heartening effect on China and India, for it was the only theatre in which offensive land operations against the Japanese were possible in the near future.

It was with this background that the Pacific War Council met on the evening of the 17th February. After the Australian, New Zealand and Dutch views had been heard, the Council decided that Java should be defended with the utmost resolution by all the forces then in the island, and that Wavell should have discretion to augment its defence with prospective naval reinforcements and with American aircraft which were being assembled in Australia. Army reinforcements on their way from the west (i.e. the Australian corps) should not, however, proceed to Java, but should be used to augment the defence of points vital to the continuance of the struggle with Japan —Burma, Ceylon and Australia. The Council recommended that all Australian forces serving outside the area affected by the war with Japan should be sent to that area at the earliest opportunity. In view however of the imminent threat to Rangoon, and the vital importance of keeping open the supply route to China, the Australian Government should be asked to allow 7th Australian Division, the leading elements of which were off Colombo and were thus the nearest troops to Rangoon,[2] to go to Burma and assist in its defence until relieved by other forces. They also recommended that 70th British Division (less one brigade to Ceylon) should be moved from the Middle East to Burma, 9th and 6th Australian Divisions sent

---

[1] The Pacific War Council, composed of representatives of the British, Australian, New Zealand and Netherlands Governments and presided over by the Prime Minister, was set up in London in February 1942 to review the broad fundamental policies to be followed in the war against Japan. China was represented at later meetings. A Pacific War Council was also set up in Washington, under the chairmanship of President Roosevelt; the two Councils kept in close touch with each other.

[2] On the 20th February Headquarters 7th Australian Division and 25th Brigade were at Colombo, 18th Brigade at Bombay and 21st Brigade in convoy to the east of Colombo.

to Australia as rapidly as possible and the movement of an Indian division from the Middle East to India considered. Ceylon should be provided with adequate defences, particularly air forces, anti-aircraft guns and radar, at the earliest possible moment. Meanwhile every effort should be made to expedite the despatch of four divisions from the United Kingdom to the Middle East and/or the Far East.

On the 18th, in pursuance of this policy, the Chiefs of Staff ordered 70th Division to embark for Burma by way of India, took steps to send some Catalina flying-boats, and diverted anti-aircraft units and radar sets already at sea, to Ceylon. They arranged that the army capacity of the convoy due to sail round the Cape to the Indian Ocean towards the end of March should be wholly allotted to reinforcements for India or Indian Ocean defence, and not as heretofore to the Middle East; this meant that 5th British Division due to sail in this convoy for the Middle East was allotted to India. The R.A.F. quota in the convoy was to be increased at the expense of army personnel. Two days later the Chiefs of Staff decided to give the despatch of 70th British Division priority over 6th and 9th Australian Divisions; to ask Middle East Command to send 5th Indian Division, less one brigade, from Cyprus to Burma;[1] to ask India Command to send six British battalions and some artillery to Burma at once, on the understanding that they would be returned on the arrival of 70th Division at Rangoon; and to include three Hurricane and two Blenheim squadrons in the convoy.

On the 20th February the Prime Minister telegraphed the Prime Minister of Australia (The Rt. Hon. John Curtin) urging in the strongest terms that 7th Australian Division should be made available for Burma. Assuming a favourable response, he diverted the convoy carrying the leading brigade to Rangoon where it could have arrived about the 27th. On the 22nd Mr. Curtin refused to agree to the diversion of the division on the ground that the movement of Australian forces to this theatre was not a reasonable hazard of war in the light of earlier Australian losses in Greece and Malaya, superior Japanese sea and air power in the Bay of Bengal and the grave effects which adverse results of the move would have on Australian morale. When Mr. Churchill told him that part of the division had already been temporarily diverted, thus allowing an opportunity for reconsideration of the decision, Mr. Curtin replied on the 23rd,

> '... Java faces imminent invasion. Australia's outer defences are now quickly vanishing and our vulnerability is completely exposed. With A.I.F. troops we sought to save Malaya and Singapore, falling back on Netherlands East Indies. All these

---

[1] The 4th and 5th Indian Divisions had been formed in the Middle East in 1939-40.

northern defences are gone or going. Now you contemplate using the A.I.F. to save Burma. All this has been done, as in Greece, without adequate air support. We feel a primary obligation to save Australia not only for itself, but to preserve it as a base for the development of the war against Japan. In the circumstances it is quite impossible to reverse a decision which we made with the utmost care . . . '

The Chiefs of Staff had meanwhile taken steps to safeguard the line of communication across the Indian Ocean, and prepared plans to build up the Eastern Fleet and develop a chain of naval and air bases and refuelling stations between South Africa and Ceylon. Since the ports of Colombo and Trincomalee in Ceylon were too small to hold the Eastern Fleet when it reached its full strength, work was begun on the development, as a fleet base, of Addu Atoll, a barren ring of islets at the southern end of the Maldive Islands.[1] Steps were also taken to provide defences for the Seychelles, Mauritius and Diego Garcia, all of which were required as fuelling and minor operational bases for naval craft and for flying-boats to enable air reconnaissance to be extended to areas out of range of Ceylon.

The fact that the island of Madagascar, controlled by the Vichy French Government, themselves under German domination, lay across these communications had given rise to some anxiety at the time of the fall of France. Plans to seize control of the island had been discussed in December 1940 but, in view of the difficulty at that time of finding the forces required for the operation, it had been decided that no attempt would be made to occupy the island unless the use of its bases by enemy raiders made such action imperative. When in November 1941 information had been received that the Vichy Government had agreed, under German pressure, to Japanese occupation of the island, plans were prepared for the capture of Diego Suarez, the principal port at its northern end. Owing however to other commitments, it had been found impossible to make shipping and naval escorts available and the proposed operation had been cancelled. After the fall of Singapore, the threat to the security of the lines of communication in the Indian Ocean once more focused attention on the strategic importance of Madagascar. The Chiefs of Staff decided that at all costs a possible Japanese descent on the island had to be forestalled.[2] Plans had therefore been put in hand to mount an expedition to capture and hold the naval and air base at Diego Suarez. This operation was given the code name of 'Ironclad'.

---
[1] See Map 6.
[2] The occupation of Madagascar was never considered by the Japanese.

CHAPTER IV

THE BILIN RIVER ACTION AND THE DISASTER AT THE SITTANG
(February 1942)

See Maps 1, 2 and 3 and Sketch 4

TO revert to events in Burma: early on the 15th February, 17th Indian Division had withdrawn from the Duyinzeik–Thaton area to take up its new position on the Bilin River. This position was not naturally strong for the river was fordable practically anywhere and both flanks were liable to be turned, the one by landings from the sea and the other by movement along the many jungle tracks to the north. General Smyth disposed his division in depth: 16th Brigade on the river line itself, 48th Brigade in divisional reserve behind the Thebyu River with orders to be ready to hold the line of the river from Taungzun to Thebyuchaung and 46th Brigade manning the defences of Kyaikto.[1] Both flanks were watched by columns from F.F.2.

Brigadier Jones (16th Brigade) was instructed to hold the general line of the Bilin River from the railway bridge south of Bilin to Paya. He gave 1/9th Royal Jats the right sector covering the main road and railway, 8th Burma Rifles the centre covering Bilin village and 2nd K.O.Y.L.I. the left covering Danyingon and Paya, with a detached company at Yinon. He kept 1/7th Gurkhas in reserve and left 5/17th Dogras in an outpost position on the Bilin–Thaton road some four miles south-east of Bilin.[2]

The Japanese lost little time in following up the retirement from Thaton. After the occupation of Kuzeik, *33rd Division* had ordered *214th Regiment* to move on Ahonwa, using tracks to the east of the Thaton–Bilin road, and *215th Regiment* to advance along the Duyinzeik–Thaton road and, after capturing Thaton, to move on Bilin. On reaching Thaton, *55th Division* was to wait until *33rd Division* had cleared the town and then cross the Bilin River estuary to Zokali and advance on Taungzun and Kyaikto, so as to turn the right flank of any

---
[1] For order of battle of 17th Division at the Bilin River action see Appendix 5.
[2] See Map 2.

British position on the Bilin River. The *214th Regiment* had reached the Bilin before 16th Brigade and portions of its two leading battalions had crossed the river to Danyingon. Thus when early on the 16th February 2nd K.O.Y.L.I. (the left battalion of 16th Brigade) was moving into position, it found that it had been forestalled. The battalion was unable to clear the village, but its detached company sent to protect the left flank was able to occupy Yinon without opposition. At 9 p.m. that night Jones ordered his reserve battalion (1/7th Gurkhas) to counter-attack and occupy Danyingon next day.

During the 16th, General Hutton visited Kyaikto and accompanied Smyth on an inspection of some of the units in the area. Before returning to Rangoon, Hutton reminded him that the Bilin River position was to be held for as long as possible and that there was to be no withdrawal without his permission.

At about 8 a.m. on the 17th the counter-attack by 1/7th Gurkhas went in. Fierce fighting at close quarters ensued but the Japanese held firm and no progress could be made. Smyth then ordered 48th Brigade to send forward 1/4th Gurkhas in motor transport. At 5.30 p.m. that evening the 1/4th, supported by 5th Mountain Battery and all the brigade mortars, successfully attacked Danyingon and Point 313. Although the southern half of the village and the hill were occupied, the enemy held on to a shallow bridgehead on the west bank. At 6 p.m. it was discovered that the Japanese had established a road block on the Yinon road immediately south of Paya and an attempt by 2nd K.O.Y.L.I. to clear it failed.[1]

Meanwhile, at 1 p.m., having already used his reserve, Jones had ordered 5/17th Dogras to withdraw during the afternoon from its outpost position east of the river into reserve. The movement began at 2.15 p.m., but troops of *215th Regiment* had already interposed between the outpost position and the road bridge over the river near Bilin, and when the battalion attempted to cross near the railway bridge it came under accurate mortar and machine-gun fire and disintegrated. By 3.30 p.m. most of the men were across the river, having suffered surprisingly few casualties, but without many of their weapons; for the time being the battalion was of little value as a fighting unit. Meanwhile the outpost company of 8th Burma Rifles to the east of the river opposite Bilin had been forced back to the west bank.

By this time Smyth had come to the conclusion that the front, extending for fifteen miles from the mouth of the Bilin to Yinon, was far too wide for the exercise of a single brigade command. He therefore sent forward Brigadier Hugh-Jones (48th Brigade) with one of his two remaining battalions (2/5th Gurkhas) to take over from 16th

---

[1] This block was established by the advanced guard of *III/214th Battalion* which had crossed the river between Yinon and Ahonwa during the 17th.

Brigade the command of 8th Burma Rifles, 1/9th Royal Jats and the remnants of 5/17th Dogras and the responsibility for the southern part of the position from Bilin to the mouth of the river,[1] leaving Jones (16th Brigade) with 2nd K.O.Y.L.I., 1/4th and 1/7th Gurkhas to secure the left flank. During the day he wrote to Hutton stressing the importance of 2nd Burma Brigade having a really good battalion to look after Mokpalin and the Sittang Bridge.

During the night of the 17th/18th the enemy crossed the river near Bilin and attacked 8th Burma Rifles. The battalion gave ground and left a gap in the line on the left flank of the Jats. Early on the 18th, information was received at divisional headquarters of a large concentration of Japanese troops on the eastern side of the Bilin River estuary south-east of Zokali,[2] and of enemy troops moving west through Paya. During the morning Smyth visited his forward brigades which were both in close contact with the enemy west of the Bilin River. He found that a counter-attack by 2/5th Gurkhas had closed the gap near Bilin, a further attempt by 2nd K.O.Y.L.I. to clear the block near Paya had failed and there had also been considerable activity in the Danyingon area, where a Japanese attempt to counter-attack had been broken up by artillery fire and bombing by the R.A.F. On his return to Kyaikto he sent Hutton a situation report, timed 4.45 p.m. but not received till 11.30 p.m. Having described the situation as he had found it, he said that 16th Brigade, which had done most of the fighting, had been 'fought to a standstill' and that the enemy was far more numerous than he had previously thought.[3] He ended, 'Am taking chances on coastal landings and defence Kyaikto. Putting my last battalion (4/12th F.F. Regiment) into counter-attack against concentration threatening left of 16th Brigade'.

Shortly afterwards, hearing of Japanese being seen in the Zokali area, he ordered 48th Brigade to send a company of 2/5th Gurkhas to Zothok to watch the right flank. In a demi-official letter to Hutton that evening he wrote,

> 'As I have told you I have put in my last battalion which is really capable of active operations, i.e. 4/12th. Having done so I hear of a party of enemy approaching along the coast, which we shall have to try and deal with as best we can. I know you will realize the situation and send me something more as soon as you can spare it.'

---

[1] The 1/3rd Gurkhas remained at Thebyuchaung to protect the Thebyu River.

[2] The Japanese *55th Division*.

[3] Smyth included in this situation report the approximate strengths of the battalions in 16th Brigade. These were: 1/7th Gurkhas, 400; 2nd K.O.Y.L.I. (less the detached company at Yinon), 350; 1/4th Gurkhas, nearly full strength.

Meanwhile at Rangoon Hutton had during the day ordered one company of 2nd Duke of Wellington's to move to the Sittang Bridge for its protection, under command of 2nd Burma Brigade. He also sent Wavell a report saying that 17th Division had checked the enemy on the Bilin River, but the troops were tired and had suffered a good many casualties. In the event of an enemy offensive with fresh troops, which appeared possible in the near future, he could not be certain of holding the position on the Bilin River though every effort would be made to do so. If such an offensive took place the enemy might penetrate the line of the Sittang River without difficulty. 'Probably the best that can be hoped for is that it will be possible to hold the line of the Sittang River possibly with bridgeheads on the east bank'.

Realizing that with his last reserve committed Smyth's position was becoming critical, Hutton decided to go to Kyaikto early on the 19th to discuss the position with him. When he arrived he found the situation was much the same as it had been on the afternoon of the 18th, with the exception that enemy detachments had been discovered early that day at Taungale in rear of the right of 48th Brigade's position. There was no news of the progress of the counter-attack by 4/12th F.F. Regiment. With the enemy well established across the river in the centre of the position, with indications that they were bringing up reinforcements against the left flank and with the new and probably growing threat to the right flank, Hutton came to the conclusion that there was a grave risk of not being able to disengage the troops unless a further withdrawal was ordered. He had gained the time he wanted. To continue the fight on the Bilin with the obstacle of the Sittang River only thirty miles to the rear had now nothing to recommend it, and it was essential to get 17th Division behind the Sittang as soon as possible where it could be supported by 7th Armoured Brigade in country suitable for armour. He therefore told Smyth to make all preparations for a withdrawal and to judge for himself when it was necessary to carry it out.

Between 1 and 2 p.m. Army Headquarters, on Hutton's instructions, issued orders for 2nd Duke of Wellington's, then in Rangoon less its detached company at the Sittang Bridge, to come under command of 17th Division, for 7/10th Baluch (now reorganized and guarding a supply dump at Mokpalin Quarries) to relieve the Duke's company at Sittang, which was then to rejoin its battalion,[1] and for a detachment of 2nd Indian Anti-Tank Regiment to come under orders of 2nd Burma Brigade and move to Sittang for the defence of the bridge. That evening Army Headquarters sent Smyth a confirmatory telegram which read, 'G.O.C. gives permission to with-

---

[1] By this order 3rd Burma Rifles and 7/10th Baluch were entrusted with the close defence of the Sittang Bridge under orders of 2nd Burma Brigade, itself under the L. of C. Area.

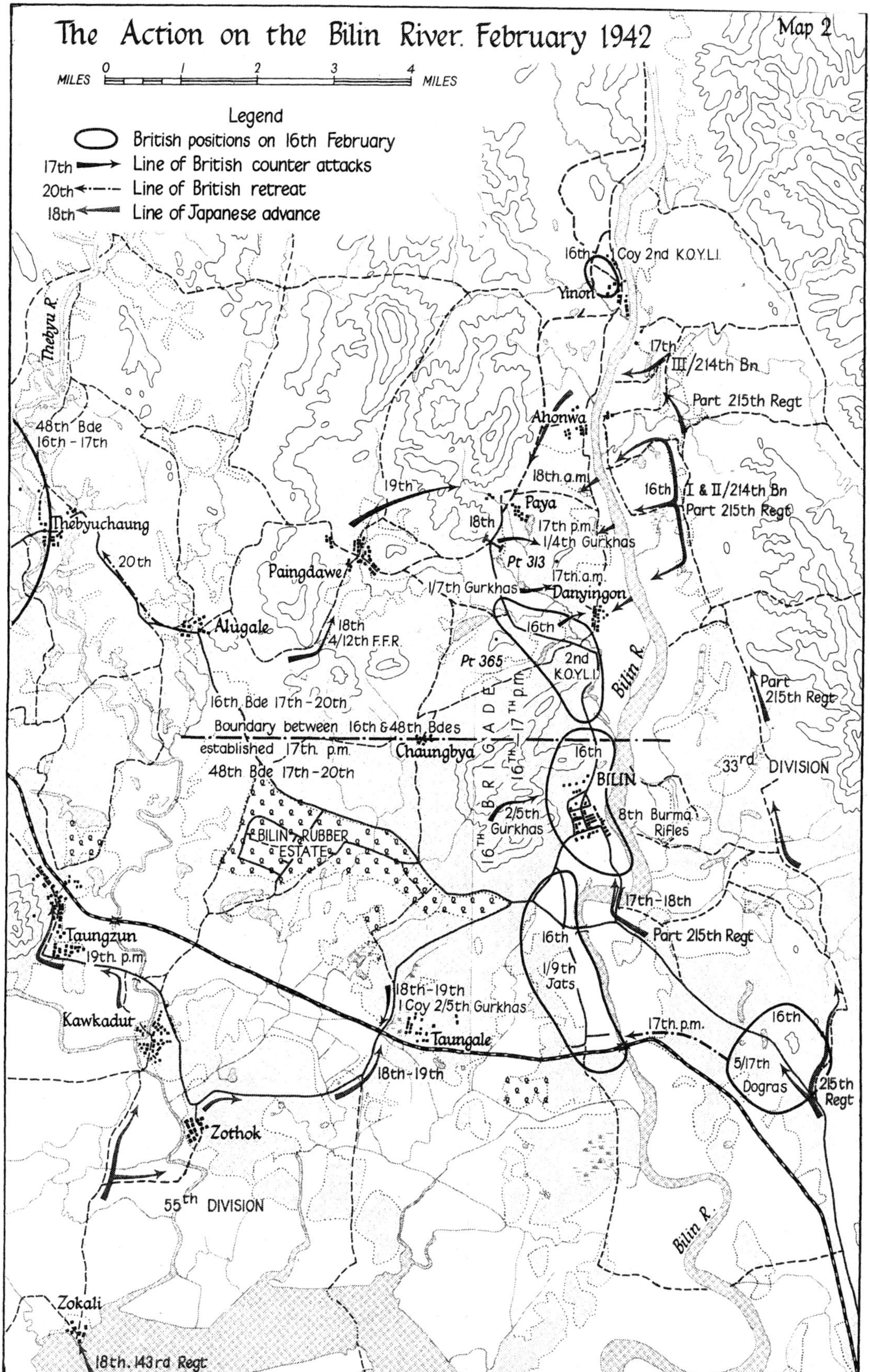
The Action on the Bilin River. February 1942
Map 2
MILES 0 1 2 3 4 MILES
Legend
British positions on 16th February
17th Line of British counter attacks
20th Line of British retreat
18th Line of Japanese advance
16th Coy 2nd K.O.Y.L.I.
Yinon
Thebyu R.
17th III/214th Bn
Part 215th Regt
Ahonwa
48th Bde 16th - 17th
18th a.m.
19th
16th I & II/214th Bn Part 215th Regt
Paya
18th
17th p.m.
1/4th Gurkhas
Thebyuchaung
20th
Pt 313
Paingdawe
17th a.m.
1/7th Gurkhas
Danyingon
Alugale
18th 4/12th F.F.R.
16th
Pt 365
2nd K.O.Y.L.I.
Bilin R.
16th - 17th p.m.
16th BRIGADE
Part 215th Regt
16th Bde 17th - 20th
Boundary between 16th & 48th Bdes established 17th p.m.
Chaungbya
48th Bde 17th - 20th
16th
BILIN
33rd DIVISION
2/5th Gurkhas
8th Burma Rifles
BILIN RUBBER ESTATE
17th - 18th
Part 215th Regt
Taungzun
19th p.m.
16th
1/9th Jats
Kawkadut
18th - 19th 1 Coy 2/5th Gurkhas
Taungale
17th p.m.
16th
5/17th Dogras
215th Regt
18th - 19th
Zothok
55th DIVISION
Bilin R.
Zokali
18th 143rd Regt

draw if necessary to keep the force intact. Heavy A.A. [anti-aircraft] if still east of the Sittang is to be moved to west bank immediately'.

Leaving one company at Kyaikto to watch the coast, 4/12th F.F. Regiment, in preparation for its counter-attack, had meanwhile moved by motor transport to Alugale and thence on foot to Paingdawe, arriving there at first light on the 19th. It then advanced towards Paya and by early afternoon had succeeded in driving the enemy from the hills overlooking the village from the west. No further progress could be made and repeated enemy counter-attacks eventually forced it to give ground. After dark Jones ordered it to withdraw to Chaungbya. On the southern flank the Japanese were encountered during the afternoon near Taungzun railway station, and by 4 p.m. all attempts by a company of 2/5th Gurkhas to drive them from Taungale had failed. Air reconnaissance during the day had reported enemy landings on the coast in the Bilin River area and the arrival of enemy reinforcements in the Bilin–Ahonwa area.

The danger to his division was rapidly growing, and after dark Smyth issued an operation order outlining his plan for a withdrawal from the Bilin position. All concerned were to carry out reconnaissances and be ready to put the plan into effect if necessary. The withdrawal was to start either on receipt of a code word issued by divisional headquarters, or at the discretion of both 16th and 48th Brigade commanders who were to form a combined headquarters. The 48th Brigade was to cover the withdrawal of 16th Brigade and then, reconstituted with its own battalions and supported by 12th Mountain Battery, act as rearguard on the line of the Thebyu River. All other troops in the forward area were, under orders of 16th Brigade, to take up a position alongside 46th Brigade behind the Kadat Chaung.[1] When 16th and 46th Brigades were in position, 48th Brigade, having blown up all the bridges east of the Kadat Chaung, was to withdraw into divisional reserve near Kyaikto. This order was received by the forward brigades at 7.30 p.m. Later that evening Smyth, realizing from the information he had that it might be impossible to extricate his troops unless he acted at once, issued the code word for the withdrawal; this was received by the forward brigades at 11.30 p.m.

The Japanese had been held up on the Bilin River for four days and their leading division had been forced to deploy almost all its strength, thus temporarily breaking the momentum of its advance. The time gained now made it certain that 7th Armoured Brigade, due at Rangoon on the 21st, would be in action on the Sittang River ready to oppose any attempts by the enemy to establish bridgeheads west of it. To get 17th Division to the west bank of the Sittang as quickly as possible was now a matter of urgency.

---
[1] See Map 3.

Before describing the retreat to the Sittang, we must pause for a moment and view the Bilin River action through Japanese eyes. By the morning of the 19th the situation of *33rd Division* was that the whole of *214th Regiment* was engaged in the Paya–Point 313–Danyingon area and its outflanking movement had not succeeded in dislodging the British. The *215th Regiment* had one battalion west of the river near Bilin and the other two in reserve. Further south, *143rd Regiment* of *55th Division* had begun to land at Zokali and its leading troops had entered Taungale and Taungzun. With his left flank covered by *55th Division*, which was moving direct on Kyaikto to turn the British right, General Sakurai (*33rd Division*) decided to make what he described as 'a double enveloping movement' and ordered *215th Regiment* less one battalion to move to Ahonwa and, having crossed the river on the night of the 19th/20th, to turn the British left flank. That evening orders for the withdrawal were sent out in clear by some formation or unit of 17th Division and were intercepted by the Japanese. Sakurai saw the opportunity and ordered *215th Regiment*, less one battalion, which was poised for its advance round the British left flank, to move at once on the Sittang Bridge using cross-country tracks already marked by forward patrols; the remainder of the division was to follow as rapidly as possible with *214th Regiment* directed on Mokpalin. Thus it was that on the night of the 19th/20th February, as the forward brigades of 17th Division began to withdraw from the Bilin River, the Japanese started to move at top speed across country to the Sittang Bridge.

The 16th Brigade, aided by a heavy mist, broke contact during the early hours of the 20th and, having dropped 1/3rd and 1/4th Gurkhas at Thebyuchaung to rejoin their own brigade, had by evening reached the Boyagyi Rubber Estate north-west of Kyaikto where it was joined later by 8th Burma Rifles and 1/9th Royal Jats. The withdrawal of 48th Brigade proved more difficult, for the enemy had attacked and penetrated the position held by the Jats before they could begin their rearward movement. During the morning it was decided that the battalion would have to break out by itself at noon on the 20th, under cover of bombing by the R.A.F. The break-out was successfully accomplished, though the battalion suffered casualties through some British aircraft mistaking it for the enemy. At about 6.30 p.m., as 48th Brigade reached the Thebyu River crossing, Hugh-Jones received a letter from Smyth which read,

> 'You know best the condition of your troops and the local situation. I leave you therefore a free hand to harbour for the night wherever you wish. I think however you should make a big effort to get west of the Thebyuchaung River before dark if you

can. I have sent you some M.T. to assist. The sooner you get into Kyaikto the better I shall be pleased, as we have still unlocated parties of Japanese in the coastal area and there may of course be other parties working round the flanks. When we do get you right back, I hope very much to be able to give you a little rest.'

Hugh-Jones destroyed the bridge over the Thebyu River and after a short halt moved his three battalions, by the motor transport sent by Smyth, to Kyaikto where they arrived about 10.30 p.m. Thus in less than twenty-four hours Smyth had succeeded in breaking contact and withdrawing his whole division some seventeen miles to Kyaikto, only some fifteen miles from the Sittang Bridge itself.

During the 20th there were no signs of any enemy attempt to follow up the retreat, though a column with elephant transport had been seen on the railway some three miles north-west of Taungzun. The 2nd Duke of Wellington's (less its company at the Sittang Bridge which had not yet been relieved by 7/10th Baluch) on reaching Kyaikto during the day was placed under command of 46th Brigade. In the afternoon Smyth sent Hutton a message saying that he had 'decided to withdraw from Kyaikto as otherwise probably impossible to extricate force intact'. The same day Hutton placed 2nd Burma Brigade under command of 17th Division.

It was on the 20th that Smyth began to plan the withdrawal of his formation behind the Sittang River. The all-weather road which had so far served as the main line of communication for the division came to an end at Kyaikto. Between there and the Sittang Bridge there was only an unmetalled road, already much cut up by motor traffic, full of bomb craters and deep in dust, which, after skirting the eastern boundary of the Boyagyi Rubber Estate, ran through dense jungle to Mokpalin and thence to the bridge.[1] The railway which ran between it and the river afforded an alternative route for marching troops, though the bridge over the Kalun Chaung had not been decked. The road and the railway converged at Mokpalin and continued in close proximity for a mile until the railway turned westward to the bridge and the road swung north-eastwards before approaching Sittang village. Here the road and railway enclosed a ridge, its western part crowned by a pagoda and known as Pagoda Hill and its eastern extremity bearing a great image of Buddha and named Buddha Hill. The railway emerged on to the bridge by way of a cutting through a bluff overlooking the river. The bridge of eleven spans, each of 150 feet, had been decked over and could thus take road traffic. On its upstream side a ferry service operated by three power-driven vessels had been established. The river was a formidable obstacle since it widened above and below the bridge, the current was swift and the stream subject to a strong tidal bore.

---

[1] See Sketch 4.

Smyth's problem was to get his three brigades and all his transport as quickly as possible over the Sittang Bridge, which could take traffic only in single line. The main factors were: the vital bridge itself was covered only by 3rd Burma Rifles (some 250 strong), a battalion which Smyth knew could not stand a heavy attack,[1] and one company of the Duke of Wellington's—an inadequate force to man an effective bridgehead; the whole division would be concentrated by about midnight in the Boyagyi Rubber Estate–Kyaikto area, but its two forward brigades would be tired for they would have broken contact and withdrawn some distance after a four-day battle; although the distance from Kyaikto to Sittang was only some fifteen miles, the one motorable road would be subjected to air attack by day; and lastly there were indications that the enemy might be moving across country direct on the bridge round the northern flank of the division, as well as advancing on Kyaikto along the railway.

During the Bilin action Brigadier Ekin (46th Brigade) had been warned that he might have to act as rearguard to the division when it withdrew across the Sittang, and had therefore studied the problem. He believed that the Japanese would by-pass Kyaikto (as they had the Thaton–Duyinzeik line) and make direct for the bridge, and during the day suggested to his divisional commander that his brigade should at once go back to the Sittang Bridge to forestall any such move, and that all except essential fighting transport should be sent across the river on the 21st. Smyth was not, however, prepared to uncover the Kyaikto area until he had more definite information about the direction and strength of the Japanese advance and whether or not his forward brigades were being closely followed up. Furthermore he thought it inadvisable to send back so large an amount of transport without a formation to control traffic at the bridge.[2]

Later that day he issued orders for the further withdrawal of the division after it had concentrated at Kyaikto. Early on the 21st the Malerkotla Field Company and 4/12th F.F. Regiment were to move to the bridge: the former to complete its preparations for demolition and the latter to strengthen its defences. Divisional headquarters was to lead the withdrawal, followed by 48th and 16th Brigades, and 46th Brigade was to act as rearguard. Each brigade was to be accompanied by its transport. Divisional headquarters, together with Headquarters 48th Brigade and one battalion, were to halt for the night of the 21st/22nd at Mokpalin Quarries and the remaining battalions of 48th Brigade on the track at camps four and seven miles

---

[1] See page 41.

[2] Throughout the operations east of the Sittang, 17th Division suffered severely from the lack of provost personnel.

respectively in rear of their brigade headquarters.[1] This order meant that only one battalion and a field company would reach the bridge on the 21st, that the head of the divisional column would move only nine out of the fifteen miles towards the bridge during the day and that neither 16th nor 46th Brigades would move at all.

At about 5 a.m. on the 21st a Japanese raiding party attacked Smyth's advanced headquarters in Kyaikto. Beyond creating some confusion the raid achieved little and the party apparently withdrew at daybreak. The 4/12th F.F. Regiment and the Malerkotla Field Company moved off early in the morning and were followed by divisional headquarters at about 10 a.m. The 48th Brigade which was to move in rear of divisional headquarters did not begin its march till late in the morning.

The 21st was very dry and hot, and dense clouds of thick red dust and a shortage of water added to the trials of man and beast alike. During the day the columns on the main track and the troops in the Boyagyi Rubber Estate were repeatedly bombed and machine-gunned, first by Japanese aircraft and later by aircraft carrying Allied markings. As a result vehicles, including ambulances full of wounded, were ditched or destroyed; mules, carrying weapons and wireless sets, broke loose and vanished with their loads into the jungle; casualties were numerous; the march was delayed; considerable disorganization was caused and morale suffered. Most of the persistent attacks which caused this havoc were, owing to a grievous error, made by British and A.V.G. aircraft. Air reconnaissance in the morning had falsely reported an enemy column of three hundred vehicles moving through Kyaikto to Kinmun. All available aircraft at Rangoon were ordered to attack and were given the Kyaikto–Mokpalin road instead of the Kyaikto–Kinmun road as the western limit for the bombing operations.

By evening 4/12th F.F. Regiment and the Malerkotla Field Company had reached the bridge, where they found little had been done to prepare a bridgehead position and only one span of the bridge had been partially prepared for demolition. Divisional headquarters, 7/10th Baluch and 1/4th Gurkhas had reached Mokpalin Quarries, 2/5th and 1/3rd Gurkhas had halted on the track and 16th Brigade was still in the Boyagyi Rubber Estate covered by 46th Brigade holding a rearguard position west of Kyaikto. About 2.30 p.m. both the F.F.2 columns guarding the left flank had been heavily engaged and had fallen back along jungle tracks leading to the river north of Sittang. The news of their contact with the enemy and subsequent withdrawal did not, however, reach Headquarters 17th Division till evening.

---

[1] The reason for the spreading out of 48th Brigade was that water was obtainable only at these points.

During the day, divisional headquarters was for some time out of touch by wireless either with Rangoon or with 16th and 46th Brigades. About midnight on the 21st/22nd, however, a message was received from Rangoon that the Japanese might try to capture the bridge by parachute attack. To deal with this threat Smyth ordered 1/4th Gurkhas to move to the bridge at 4 a.m., cross it and, taking the company of the Duke of Wellington's under command, watch for an attack by paratroops at first light. At 1 a.m. on the 22nd he warned 16th and 46th Brigades that a strong Japanese force was probably moving round the division's left flank and suggested that they should move towards the river as early as possible.[1]

Six hours before the receipt of this message Ekin had visited Jones at his headquarters in the Boyagyi Rubber Estate to decide on a starting time and the order of march for the 22nd, for neither of them had received any definite orders and they were bound to conform with the movements of 48th Brigade. Ekin's rearguard troops were already in touch with enemy patrols and, convinced that the enemy was outflanking the division from the north, he was anxious to march during the night since it appeared to him that the enemy might reach the bridge first. But the track was blocked by 48th Brigade and an immediate move was out of the question. The two Brigadiers decided that the transport of 16th and 46th Brigades (in that order) should move at 3 a.m. followed by 16th Brigade at 6 a.m. The rearguard (46th Brigade), with the exception of 4th Burma Rifles which would withdraw along the railway line, would follow immediately behind 16th Brigade. The receipt of Smyth's message at about 1 a.m. did not affect these times since everything was dependent on the progress of 48th Brigade.

The divisional column began to move towards the bridge from Mokpalin Quarries at 4 a.m. preceded by some of divisional headquarters' transport. At this juncture, when every minute was precious, all traffic across the bridge was held up by a vehicle running off the decking on the bridge and becoming jammed in the girders. It was not till 6.30 a.m. that the bridge was cleared and movement restarted. As a result the road right back to Mokpalin and beyond was blocked by stationary vehicles, often double-banked. To add to the congestion, the transport of the two rear brigades had begun to arrive.

The 1/4th Gurkhas, followed by the headquarters of both the division and 48th Brigade, had safely crossed the bridge when, just as 7/10th Baluch was marching through the railway cutting on to the bridge at about 8.30 a.m., there was a burst of firing and the enemy

---

[1] It is not known when this information reached 17th Divisional Headquarters, but 48th Brigade Headquarters learnt of the enemy's outflanking movement (presumably from F.F.2) by 6.30 p.m. on the 21st.

FIGHTING AT THE SITTANG BRIDGEHEAD

attacked from the jungle north-east of the bridgehead. The detachment of 3rd Burma Rifles holding this area gave way at once and it seemed for the moment that the Japanese might capture the bridge intact. The Malerkotla Field Company had just completed the preparations for destroying one span of the bridge and was ordered to stand by to blow it up. An immediate counter-attack by two companies of 4/12th F.F. Regiment, supported by the weak 7/10th Baluch, succeeded however in recapturing the lost ground east of the cutting at the cost of fifty casualties, and the immediate danger passed.

At about 10 a.m. Smyth ordered Hugh-Jones (48th Brigade) to take command of all troops holding the bridgehead.[1] Hugh-Jones immediately extended it to the general line Bungalow Hill–the railway cutting–Pagoda Hill. During the morning the C.R.E. 17th Division ordered 24th Field Company to destroy all the power-driven craft which could not be manned and most of the three hundred small country boats which, on payment to their owners, had been collected at Sittang to prevent them from falling into enemy hands. A power ferry had been located near the bridge and ramps built on either side of the river at Hutton's orders, in case the bridge were damaged by enemy air action, and to help the division to cross the river. The ferry was destroyed by enemy action during the day.

Simultaneously with their assault on the bridgehead, the Japanese had attacked the column of transport, protected only by weak baggage guards, which packed the route immediately south of Mokpalin. The 2/5th Gurkhas, the next battalion in the line of march, soon arrived and was at once ordered to clear the high ground on the eastern side of the road, with a view to piqueting it until all transport had crossed the bridge. The battalion, with little mortar and no artillery support (the mules carrying the mortars had stampeded and the artillery had not come up) went in with great resolution. It suffered severely from mortar fire, but reached Mokpalin Railway Station at the third attempt.

The next battalion (1/3rd Gurkhas) then arrived on the scene and the two commanding officers conferred. Having no knowledge of events at the bridgehead they assumed that the enemy held both Buddha and Pagoda Hills, and decided that the 1/3rd should attack both under cover of an artillery bombardment, while the 2/5th held the high ground on the eastern outskirts of Mokpalin. Unfortunately they were unaware that bridgehead troops were holding Bungalow Hill. Had they made contact with them, a co-ordinated attack controlled by Brigadier Hugh-Jones could have been launched which might well have opened the way to the bridge.

---

[1] These included 4/12th F.F. Regiment, 7/10th Baluch, one company 2nd Duke of Wellington's and 3rd Burma Rifles.

The artillery bombardment began at about 2 p.m. and forced the bridgehead troops from Pagoda Hill. Despite strong opposition, 1/3rd Gurkhas occupied Buddha Hill. The Japanese lost no time in hitting back. Bitter fighting ensued in which the commanding officer of the 1/3rd was killed, but the troops, with no British officers left, maintained their position though losses were heavy. At about 4 p.m. Hugh-Jones' bridgehead troops reoccupied their position from Bungalow Hill to Pagoda Hill. Buddha Hill was still held by the remnants of 1/3rd Gurkhas but there was a gap between them and 2/5th Gurkhas at Mokpalin.

Meanwhile an entirely separate action was being fought further south. At about 9.30 a.m., 46th Brigade halted just south of Meyun Chaung to allow the rearguard—the Duke of Wellington's—to catch up. The 16th Brigade, unaware of this halt, continued its march and a gap of about one mile developed between the two brigades. The Japanese reached the road between them at this moment and established a road block. While 3/7th Gurkhas, the leading battalion of 46th Brigade, was trying vainly to clear the way forward, the rest of the brigade was suddenly and heavily attacked from the east, the enemy pouring in a deadly fire with light automatics and mortars. In the confused hand-to-hand fighting which ensued, units got mixed up and no progress towards Mokpalin could be made.

Ekin then decided to clear the road by moving through the jungle to the west and collected a mixed force of about 500 rifles for this purpose. The jungle was dense and the force, losing direction, split up. It was not till after dark that he and some 300 men reached the railway at Tawgon, two and a half miles south of Mokpalin. His action had, however, enabled the remnants of the Duke's and 3/7th Gurkhas to work round the block. They eventually reached the Mokpalin Quarries where they rejoined 4th Burma Rifles which had arrived there at about 1 p.m. by way of the railway. About 8 p.m. Ekin and his detachment at Tawgon encountered an enemy column moving up the railway, and in avoiding it became further split up.

When Jones (16th Brigade) arrived at Mokpalin late in the afternoon of the 22nd, he found a most confused situation and, taking command of all troops in the area, organized a perimeter defence round the village for the night. It was well that he did so, for, as darkness fell, the Japanese attacked from north, east and south. The enemy mortar and artillery fire set alight many of the vehicles in the long lines of transport still crowding the road. So close was the fighting that the three mountain batteries (5th, 12th and 28th) were continuously engaging targets over open sights in the moonlight.[1] But the defence held firm. During the night, unable to get reliable

---

[1] The 28th Mountain Battery arrived from India on the 14th February and joined 17th Division on the 17th.

Sketch 4 — SITTANG BRIDGE

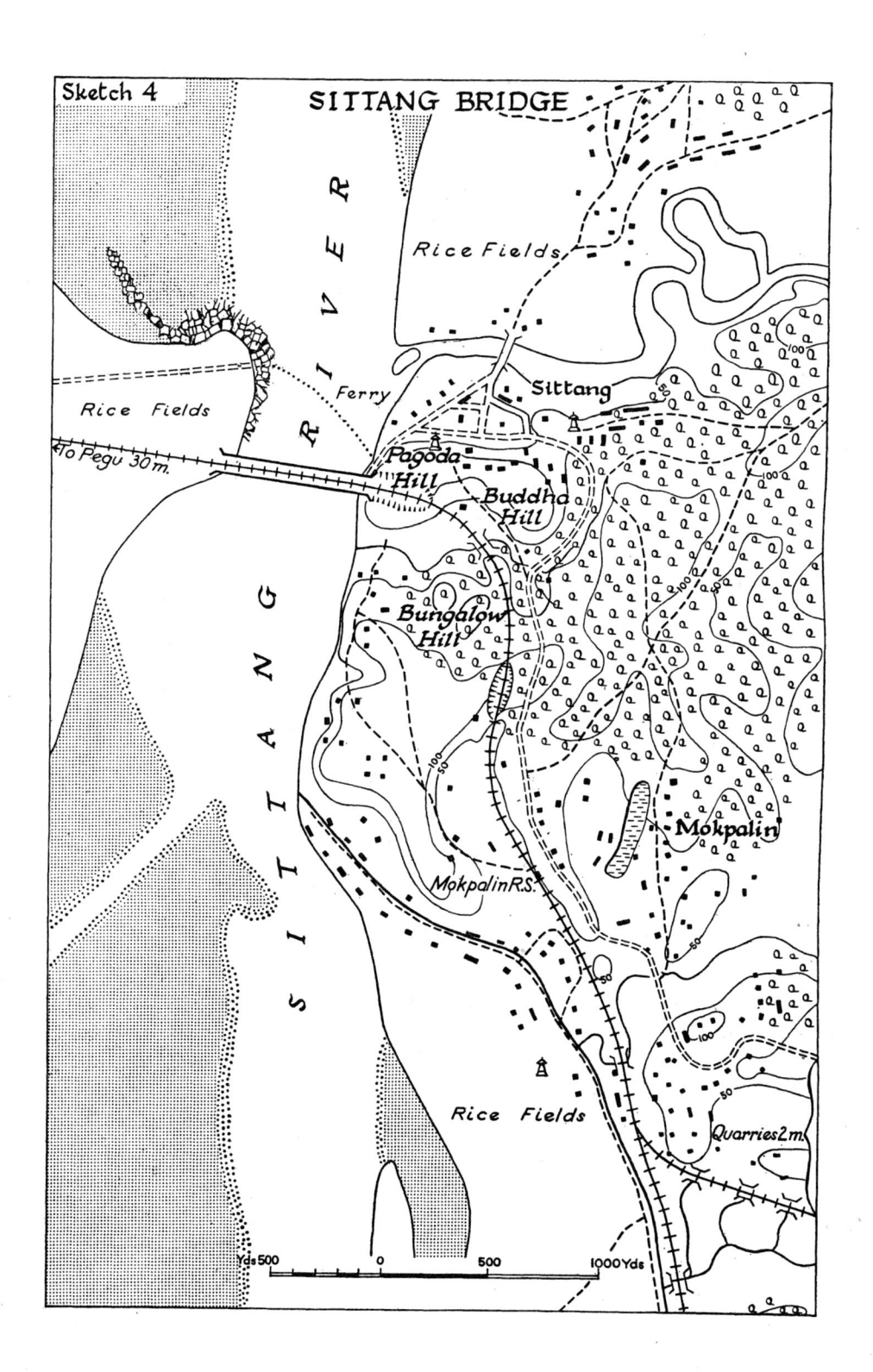

information of the situation at the bridge, Jones tried to get in touch by wireless with Smyth, but owing to atmospheric interruptions was unable to do so. Believing, as had the Gurkha battalions on the previous day, that Buddha and Pagoda Hills were in enemy hands, he decided to attack them at dawn on the 23rd to gain access to the bridge and move his troops across.

We must now return to the bridgehead itself and describe the events of the night of the 22nd/23rd February. By 6 p.m. the Malerkotla Field Company had completed its preparations for the demolition of the three centre spans of the bridge but, owing to the shortage of fuse and electric cable, had had to locate the firing point for the demolition on the bridge itself, some way from the western bank. Hugh-Jones did his best to communicate by wireless with his two battalions on the eastern bank and with 16th and 46th Brigades, but was unable to make contact with anyone. After darkness fell stragglers began to enter the bridgehead from the south along the river bank; all had the same story to tell of battalions ambushed, cut up and scattered and transport wrecked, so that Hugh-Jones gathered that there was scarcely a unit of the division intact and that the enemy was advancing steadily towards the southern flank of the bridgehead. In the bridgehead area there was much firing and it appeared at times that the bridge itself was under observed fire. At about 2 a.m. on the 23rd Hugh-Jones asked Captain R. C. Orgill (Malerkotla Field Company) whether, if the bridge were not demolished during the night, he could guarantee that it could be successfully blown up during daylight with the enemy holding the far bank and the bridge consequently under observed fire. Orgill could give no such guarantee.

As the night wore on, enemy pressure increased and the situation within the bridgehead appeared to be getting rapidly worse. After consulting the battalion commanders, Hugh-Jones came to the conclusion that, if the Japanese were to launch an attack before dawn, the bridgehead could not be held. He was faced with a most difficult decision for, if the bridge were to fall to the Japanese intact, the road to Rangoon would lie open to them; yet to blow it would mean abandoning all the troops on the east bank—the greater part of 17th Division. If he waited till dawn he might be unable to demolish it, and from the information available to him it seemed improbable that 16th and 46th Brigades would be able to break through.

At about 4.30 a.m. on the 23rd a staff officer of 48th Brigade spoke on the telephone over a very bad line to Brigadier Cowan who was at divisional headquarters in Abya. He said that his Brigadier could not guarantee to hold the bridge for more than another hour and wanted a definite order whether he should blow the bridge or not. When asked by Cowan whether 'Jonah' (the nickname for the commander of 16th Brigade) was across, the staff officer said that he was, possibly muddling Jones with Hugh-Jones. Cowan reported the conversation to Smyth who, thinking that most of the division was on the western bank, gave authority to the brigade commander to destroy the bridge, leaving it to his discretion to select the best moment. Hugh-Jones made his decision at 5.30 a.m. When the covering troops were all across he gave Orgill the order to demolish the bridge.[1] The Malerkotla Field Company had done its work well—two spans fell into the river and a third was badly damaged. At the sound of the great explosion all firing ceased and for a brief period complete silence reigned.

To the British and Indian troops still on the eastern side of the river the explosion was a shattering announcement that their line of retreat no longer existed. At Mokpalin Jones cancelled his proposed dawn counter-attack and decided to maintain his position during the hours of daylight, but gradually thin out so that a withdrawal across the river could be completed by dawn on the 24th. All men who could be spared from the defence were immediately put on to building rafts. During the morning of the 23rd the Japanese, supported by artillery and mortar fire, made repeated attempts to break into the Mokpalin position but the defence held firm, even though 4th Burma Rifles broke and was driven back to the river in some disorder. At about 11.15 a.m. twenty-seven enemy bombers attacked the defences; some gun ammunition caught fire and the surrounding jungle began to burn. Enemy pressure had now eased, but his troops were exhausted and Jones knew that the position could not be held much longer. Shortly after 2 p.m. he ordered a general withdrawal. Although fighting occurred at some points, the Japanese showed considerable reluctance to follow up, perhaps because of exhaustion.

From the western side of the Sittang, the artillery gave such covering fire as was possible. The scene on the eastern bank, which fortunately was protected by a cliff, was thus described by Ekin, who had reached Mokpalin only after the bridge had been blown:

> 'Here there was chaos and confusion; hundreds of men throwing down their arms, equipment and clothing and taking to the water . . . some bringing their arms with them on improvised rafts. . . As we crossed, the river was a mass of bobbing heads. We were attacked from the air and sniped at continuously from the east bank. Although it was a disastrous situation there were many stout hearts and parties shouted to each other egging on others to swim faster with jokes about the boat race.'

---

[1] Shortly before dawn on the 23rd the two companies of 1/3rd Gurkhas on Buddha Hill, having exhausted their ammunition, were finally overrun.

Most units maintained their cohesion until the men received the order to enter the water; groups then endeavoured to keep together, swimmers helping the non-swimmers. Men were seen to cross and recross two or three times to bring over the wounded. But many were drowned in the swift-flowing river, which was over a mile wide. Others who could not face the ordeal went back into the jungle and, working their way north, crossed the river higher up. Some withdrew after dark to the bridge itself and constructed a lifeline across the gap. Although it was under fire, at least 300 who could not swim were saved in this way.

The order to withdraw failed to reach the troops holding the southern side of the Mokpalin perimeter and they held on throughout the afternoon, thereby containing a large number of Japanese who would otherwise undoubtedly have closed the river.[1] At 7.30 p.m. a retirement was ordered. Some reached the river and swam to safety, others were captured; but their stubborn defence had certainly enabled many of their comrades to cross the river successfully.

The remnants of 17th Division withdrew to the Pegu area. As a fighting force the division had, for the time being, almost ceased to exist; it had lost some guns, most of its transport and the greater part of its equipment. On the 24th February the infantry of the division mustered only 80 officers and 3,404 other ranks, of whom only 1,420 still had their rifles.[2] At Pegu the troops, most of whom were without boots and possessed nothing but what they stood up in, were reclothed, partly re-equipped and rearmed.

Throughout the fighting on the Bilin River and the withdrawal to the Sittang the Allied air forces, despite the unfortunate mistake on the 21st, had given considerable support to 17th Division. Fighters and bombers, operating from the main base at Rangoon— for with the loss of Moulmein no forward airfield remained—carried out daily reconnaissances and attacks on troop concentrations, motor transport, river traffic and enemy-occupied airfields.[3] Though this effort was of much assistance to the division during the actual fighting on the Bilin River, the air forces were unable to locate or interfere with the Japanese advancing from Ahonwa to the Sittang through thick jungle.

Since the action at Sittang ended the first phase of the campaign, this is a convenient moment to review the conduct of the retreat from the

---

[1] They included 8th Burma Rifles, two companies of 2nd K.O.Y.L.I., the headquarters company of 3/7th Gurkhas and the remnants of 5/17th Dogras.

[2] See Appendix 6.

[3] From the 16th to the 23rd February a total of 103 bomber sorties was flown during which some 39 tons of bombs were dropped.

Dawna Range. Hutton and Smyth each had an extremely difficult task in January 1942. The only division available to meet the experienced and well-trained Japanese forces was the 17th (Indian) and it was a division in name only. It was deficient in artillery and signals and had not trained as a formation. Its three Indian brigades had been hastily assembled, and as they had done no brigade training their commanders had had no practice in handling their formations. The units composing them contained a high proportion of young and partly-trained soldiers. The division was not concentrated when the Japanese invasion began and two of its brigades on arrival had to wait for their transport before they could be employed. The Burma brigade added to the division consisted mainly of untried and partly trained Burma Rifle battalions.

The strategical object was to hold as much of Burma as possible and, in particular, keep open the line of communication from Rangoon to Mandalay and China. This route ran for some distance close to the west bank of the Sittang River. Its defence therefore demanded that the battle should be fought as far as possible to the south and east of the Sittang. The fact that Rangoon, the only available port, was vulnerable to air attack also made it desirable that the Japanese should be kept at a distance and denied the use of airfields in Burma within fighter range. Time too had to be gained to enable reinforcements to be brought into Rangoon, and the slow-moving Chinese armies to be concentrated in central Burma. In such circumstances Hutton had no alternative but to fight for Tenasserim as far south as possible and for as long as possible. Thus, with Wavell's full approval, he had to insist that Smyth should use his division piecemeal as it became available to keep the Japanese away from the Sittang, and that ground should be given up only when absolutely necessary. Smyth, on the other hand, was unwilling to commit his untrained formation to battle piecemeal in an area which required a wide measure of dispersion. He therefore at the very start of the campaign urged that he might be allowed to withdraw his division back to the Bilin–Kyaikto–Sittang area, on which all approaches converged, where he felt he could concentrate it and eventually launch a counter-offensive. Although for a time after Wavell's visit on the 6th February Smyth was clearly influenced by the Supreme Commander's views, he later reverted to his original idea which he continued to press throughout the rest of the retreat. Strategic and tactical considerations conflicted. The former had to prevail.

The reader will have noted that after the fall of Moulmein Wavell, during a brief visit from Java where he had the colossal task of trying to hold Malaya and the Netherlands East Indies, advocated that the Army in Burma should take the offensive to regain the lost ground in south Tenasserim. It seems that Wavell failed at this time to grasp the difference in calibre between the British and Japanese troops. A counter-offensive was never a feasible proposition.

On the 10th February Hutton was told that 7th Armoured Brigade would reach Rangoon by the 21st, and he knew by that time that two additional British battalions would have arrived. He could expect to get the armoured formation into action in the Sittang area by about the 24th. His immediate object therefore was to delay the Japanese for a fortnight east of the Sittang.

For the first ten days of February, 17th Division had two brigades (one of four and one of five battalions) with which to dispute the crossings of the Salween, since 48th Brigade, although at Kyaikto from the 3rd, was not ready for action. One enemy division was known to be in Moulmein and there was every indication that another enemy force was concentrating in the Pa-an area. Martaban and Kuzeik were therefore the most probable lines of the Japanese advance. Smyth gave one brigade the task of holding the Thaton and Duyinzeik area with three battalions, and Martaban (which he had been ordered to hold) and Kuzeik each with one battalion. He placed the other brigade with three of its battalions at Bilin and the fourth at Papun. Martaban, which without command of the sea was indefensible, had to be hurriedly evacuated on the 9th, and it then became a question of delaying the enemy for as long as possible on the Thaton–Kuzeik line. If this line were to be held the Japanese had to be prevented from establishing themselves west of the Salween in the Kuzeik area, from where they could with ease cut the communications with Kyaikto. The isolated battalion at Kuzeik, fifteen miles from the nearest support, was quite inadequate for the task and was quickly overwhelmed. Smyth thus found himself outflanked and, despite Hutton's wishes, had to withdraw his forward brigade hurriedly. Had the division been more concentrated early in February, and a complete formation given the task of defending the crossings of the Salween in the Kuzeik area, 48th Brigade being brought forward in reserve as soon as it was ready to move, several days might have been gained without grave risk.

The decision to fight on the line of the Bilin River, thirty miles in front of the Sittang with its single bridge, might appear to be open to criticism. It is clear however that, to ensure the line of the Sittang being held until the expected reinforcements arrived, the Japanese could not be allowed to get to the river unhindered. After the failure to delay them at Thaton and Kuzeik, the Bilin was the only possible position on which to offer battle. Hutton could hardly do other than try to impose the maximum delay on that line, more especially as on the 14th Smyth had written to him saying, 'I had felt quite decided that the former course [a stand on the Bilin River] was the best and laid on plans and reconnaissance accordingly' and had also said that he was confident that he could hold the position.[1]

The 17th Division, for the first time more or less concentrated, put up an excellent defence and brought *33rd Division* to a standstill, but successive enemy attempts to turn the left and the arrival of *55th Division* behind the right flank made withdrawal during the night of the 19th/20th imperative. Smyth had carried out Hutton's instructions: he had gained time and had inflicted considerable losses on the Japanese. It was now a matter of getting his division across the Sittang River as quickly as possible.

By the afternoon of the 18th, 17th Division, except for 1/3rd Gurkhas holding the Thebyu River crossings and the weak 46th Brigade holding the Kyaikto defences, was closely engaged and the enemy had been checked and forced to deploy. An invaluable three days' delay had been imposed on the enemy, and to stay longer was to take a great risk. There is no doubt that a withdrawal on the night of the 18th/19th would have been the safer course to take.

The decision to withdraw had, however, been taken out of Smyth's hands. When the Bilin position was occupied Hutton, anxious to gain as much time as possible, took upon himself the responsibility for making the decision when to withdraw. This was a case when the existence of a corps headquarters close to the scene of operations would have been invaluable. Communication with Kyaikto was at the time unreliable and with his multifarious duties, which necessitated his spending most of his time in Rangoon and visiting places as far away as Lashio, Hutton could not give his full attention to the conduct of operations. In view of the great importance of getting 17th Division safely across the Sittang, Hutton might have been wiser, once action had been joined on the Bilin, to leave Smyth a free hand.

When reporting the situation on the afternoon of the 18th, Smyth however did not press for an immediate withdrawal as he might have done or, as he had done at Thaton, decide on a withdrawal on his own responsibility. Implicitly obeying his instructions not to withdraw without permission, he threw in his last available reserve in an attempt to gain further time. It was not till late that night that news of his action reached Rangoon. Early next day Hutton went to Smyth's headquarters at Kyaikto and gave him permission to withdraw when he thought fit. Smyth decided to break contact that night.

The withdrawal on the night of the 19th/20th was not necessarily too late, for it is now known that both sides began their move towards the bridge at the same time; but the margin for error had by this time become so small that any mistake might prove fatal. The 17th

---

[1] See page 42.

Division had a good metalled road as far as Kyaikto and an unmetalled but motorable road from there to the Sittang Bridge, while the Japanese could use only jungle tracks. Smyth therefore had an advantage.

That very evening, however, the first seeds of the eventual disaster at the bridge were sown. Some unit or units sent out the withdrawal orders in clear, which gave the Japanese knowledge for which they would normally have had to fight. They had thus no need to follow up the withdrawal. The *33rd Division* was free to move across country —a typical Japanese manoeuvre for which preparations had already been made—direct on Sittang and Mokpalin. Moving by hilly tracks through the jungle the division accomplished the journey by forced marches in fifty-six hours. The 17th Division on the other hand, having successfully carried out the difficult task of breaking contact and withdrawing to within fifteen miles of the Sittang Bridge in twenty-four hours, then remained more or less stationary for a complete day. There seems to have been little sense of urgency either on the 20th or the 21st.[1] In view of the undefended state of the vital bridge, neither the weariness of the troops nor the lack of water should have been allowed to stand in the way of the despatch before dawn on the 21st of one of the brigades in the available motor transport, closely followed by the rest of the division.

---

[1] See pages 64–68.

Map 3
THE ACTION at the SITTANG

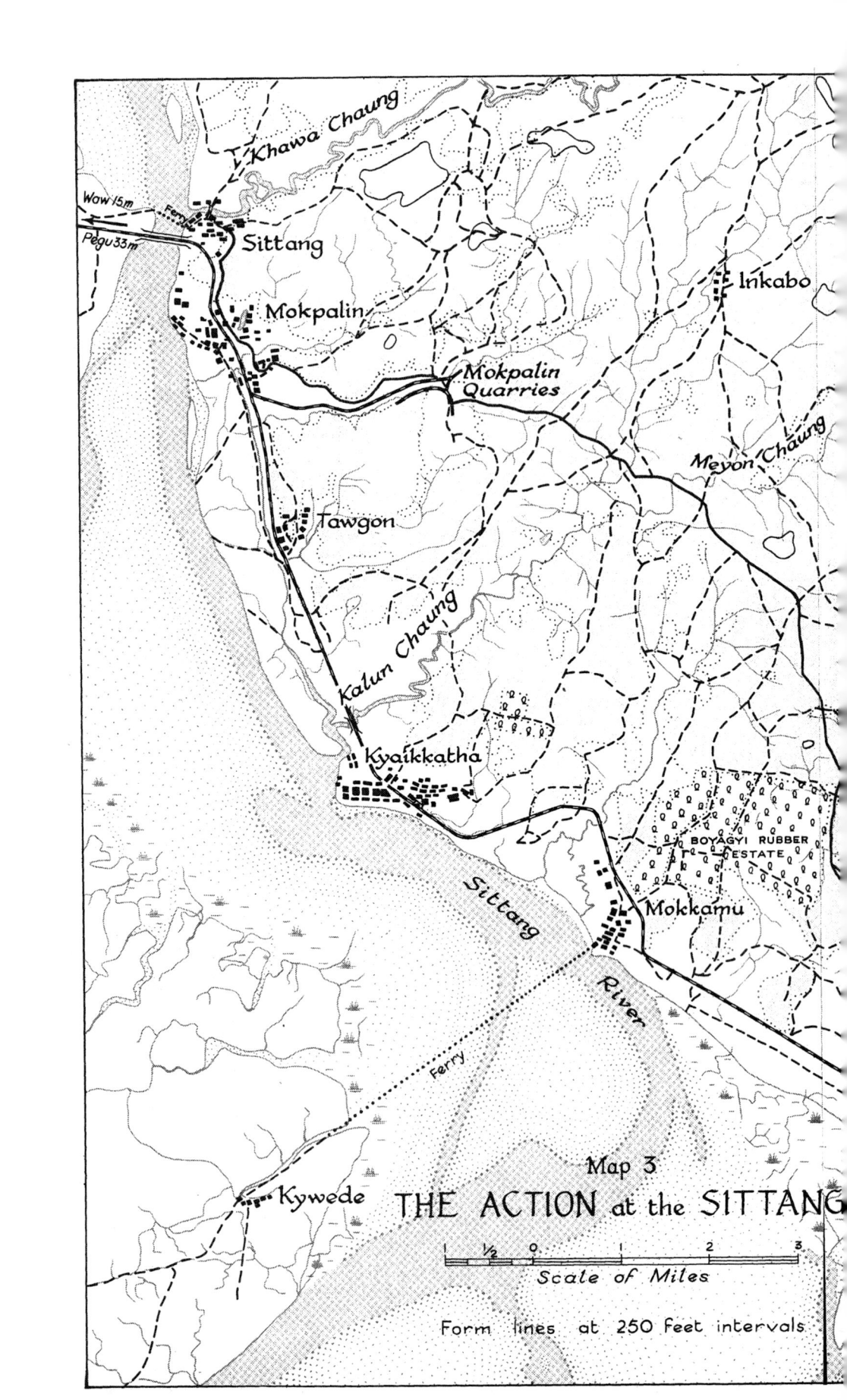

Scale of Miles

Form lines at 250 feet intervals

Map 3

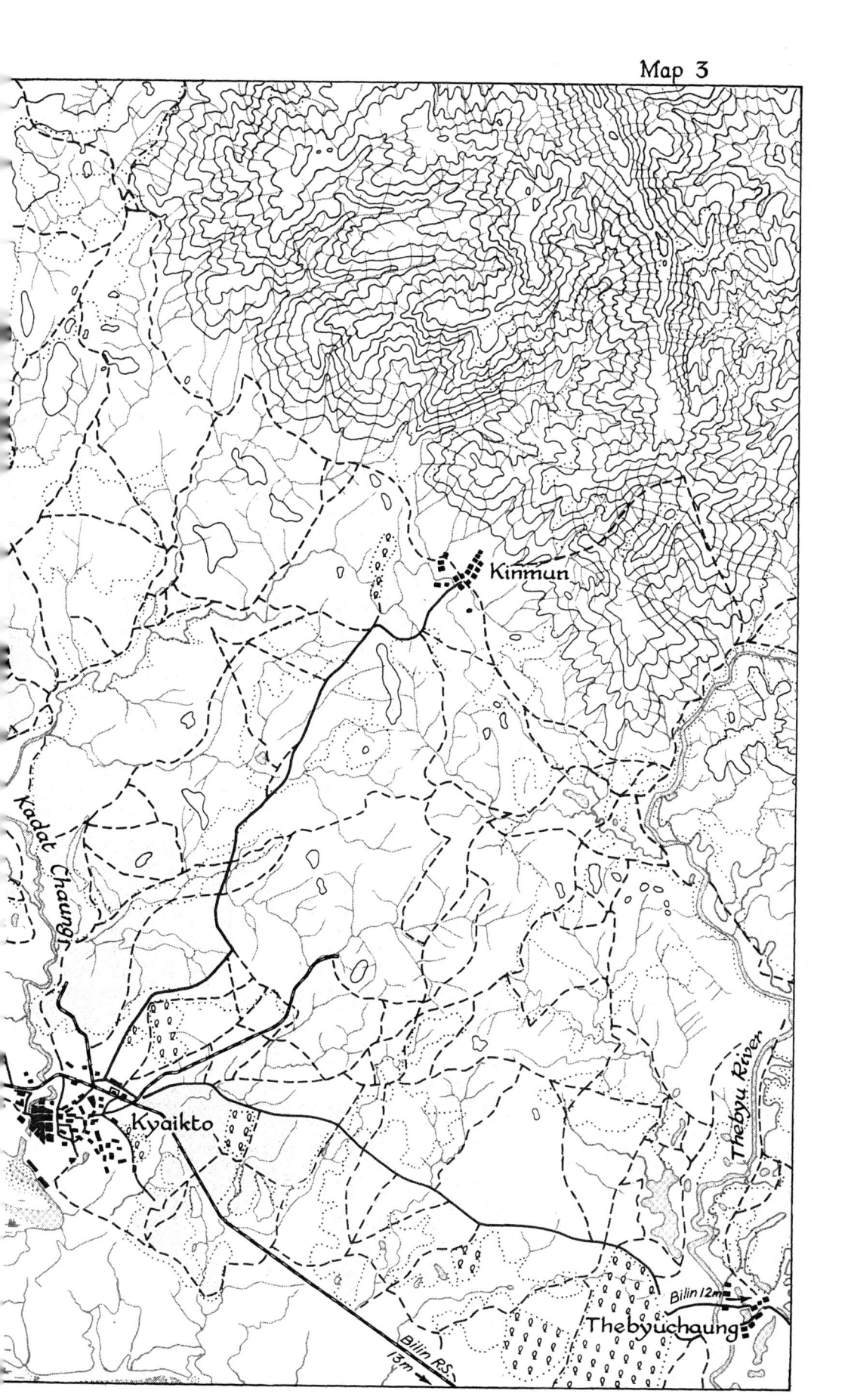

Kinmun

Kadat Chaung

Kyaikto

Thebyu River

Bilin 12m
Thebyuchaung

Billin R.S.
13m

CHAPTER V

THE EVACUATION OF RANGOON
(February–March 1942)

See Strategic Map, Maps 1 and 8 and Sketch 5

ON the 18th February, while the fighting on the Bilin River was still in progress, General Hutton sent ABDA Command and the War Office his appreciation of the position in Burma. He said that in the event of a fresh enemy offensive in the near future he could not be certain of holding the position on the Bilin River. Should he fail to do so, the enemy might penetrate the line of the Sittang River without much difficulty and the evacuation of Rangoon might become an imminent necessity. The best he could hope for was that the line of the Sittang River could be held, possibly with bridgeheads on the eastern bank. A withdrawal to the river would, however, seriously interfere with the use of the railway to the north and thus with the movement of men and supplies to Mandalay, and on to China. To hold the line of the river permanently and to undertake the offensive, he would want the additional division (14th) which had already been promised him from India but was not scheduled to arrive until April. Meanwhile he could only hope that V Chinese Army would fill the gap. To defend Rangoon against a seaborne attack on the scale which had now become possible, he would require a second additional division, while to provide for a reserve and for internal security a third was desirable. He therefore needed three divisions over and above the two he already had. The main question was whether the prospects of holding Rangoon and denying the oilfields justified the efforts to find these reinforcements, which could be despatched only at the expense of India. He himself thought that, provided reinforcements could be sent earlier than at that time envisaged, the effort would be justified but, without an acceleration of the reinforcement programme, the risk of losing Rangoon was considerable.

On the 20th, while the withdrawal of 17th Division to the Sittang River was in progress, General Hutton held a conference at which the Governor and Air Marshal Stevenson were present. He told them that the troops of the Burma Frontier Force and the Burma

Rifles were not fighting well, that the armed police were deserting their posts without warning and that 17th Division was very tired. There was therefore a possibility that, in the event of a renewed enemy offensive, the defence might break. He did not expect 7th Armoured Brigade, which would be without the backing of solid infantry support, to do more than temporarily stabilize the situation. In the circumstances the conference decided that only that part of the convoy arriving on the 21st which carried fighting units—7th Armoured Brigade, 1st Cameronians and a pioneer battalion— would be accepted at Rangoon and the remainder—administrative units which at this juncture would have been but a liability—should be turned back.

The future conduct of air operations was also reviewed. With the Japanese on the Sittang it was obvious that the retention of Rangoon as an air base had become highly dangerous, since adequate warning of enemy air attack could no longer be provided. Stevenson stated that the only course open to the R.A.F. in Burma was to establish their main base in eastern India, to station mixed operational wings at airfields at Magwe and Akyab, where reasonable warning could be expected, and to use the airfields in the Rangoon area only as advanced landing grounds. He cabled the gist of this to ABDA Command and the Air Ministry, and immediately took steps to improve the facilities of the airfield at Magwe and to evacuate all surplus stores and reserves by sea to Akyab.

The same day Hutton told General Wavell and the War Office that, in view of the possibility of collapse of resistance on the Sittang River and landings in the Gulf of Martaban, the consequences of the loss of Rangoon in the very near future must be faced. He went on to say that, as the arrival of a large convoy at that moment might result in heavy loss of men and stores, he had asked the naval authorities to return all ships except those carrying 7th Armoured Brigade and other fighting units. Later in the day he sent messages to Wavell and Hartley giving his views on the state of the troops and warning them that, although the arrival of the armoured brigade could completely change the situation, it might arrive too late, and that there were strong indications of another Japanese offensive towards the northern Shan States. He had begun the evacuation scheme, had closed down the Syriam refineries, had brought the demolition scheme to a state of readiness, and was sending back to India those ships which did not contain units likely to affect the outcome of operations in the immediate future.

Wavell, some 2,000 miles away in Java and therefore out of touch with the actual state of affairs in Burma, was puzzled by Hutton's cable of the 20th, and asked him early on the 21st 'why on earth should resistance on the Sittang River collapse . . . What is the matter

BURMA TRANSFERRED TO INDIA COMMAND 81

that these sudden pessimistic reports are given'. Later in the morning, after he had received Hutton's appreciation of the 18th and Stevenson's message of the 20th, he told Hutton,

> 'There seems on surface no reason whatever for decision practically to abandon fight for Rangoon and continue retrograde movement. You have checked enemy and he must be tired and have suffered heavy casualties. No sign that he is in superior strength. You must stop all further withdrawal and counter-attack whenever possible. Whole fate of war in Far East depends on most resolute and determined action. You have little air opposition at present and should attack enemy with all air forces available.'

That evening Wavell ordered Hutton to draw up immediately plans for a counter-attack with 7th Armoured Brigade and all available troops, if at all possible east of the Sittang River. 'In any event', he said, 'plans must be made to hit enemy, and hit him hard, if he ever succeeds in crossing. He will go back quick in face of determined attack'.

The same day the Chiefs of Staff, having reviewed the position disclosed by Hutton's telegrams of the 18th and 20th, defined their policy with particular reference to whether Rangoon should or should not be held. Their view was that the port should be held so long as its retention contributed to the keeping open of the supply route to China but that, should the Japanese cut the Burma Road, any attempt to hold the port, once it had been isolated, merely to impose delay on the enemy was risking the loss of the garrison and would not be justified. They reminded Wavell and Hutton that, if the use of the port were lost, the capacity of the overland supply route would limit the size of the forces which could operate in Burma. They asked Wavell whether in the circumstances he still wished 7th Australian Division to be diverted to Rangoon.[1] The same day, with Wavell practically isolated in Java and unable to exercise effective control, they ordered that Burma should revert to the operational command of the Commander-in-Chief in India as from the 22nd February. The responsibility for its defence then fell on General Hartley's shoulders.

On the 18th February when events in Burma were reaching their most critical stage, the Viceroy of India (the Marquess of Linlithgow) sent a wire which led to a change in command in Burma. Actuated by reports of constant retreats and of the poor fighting value of the troops, and influenced by the advice of senior military officers in Delhi, he cabled London that he had not the least doubt that the fact that the troops in Burma were 'not fighting with proper

---
[1] See page 56.

relish' was in great part due to the lack of drive and inspiration from the top. The Prime Minister repeated the Viceroy's telegram to Wavell the same day, adding, 'the Chief of the Imperial General Staff wants to know what you think. If you concur with the Viceroy, he will send [General] Alexander at once'.[1]

Wavell replied immediately that he too was very much distressed at the lack of real fighting spirit in the troops which had been evident in Malaya and, so far, in Burma. He had considered, when he selected him, that Hutton would make a resolute and skilful commander, and he had no reason now to think otherwise. He agreed that Alexander's forceful personality might act as a stimulus to the troops, but he was reluctant to make a change. Before giving a decision, however, he wished to know whether all or part of the Australian corps was being sent to Burma.

When he received Hutton's appreciation of the 18th and cable of the 20th, Wavell lost confidence in him and on the 21st recommended that Alexander should be sent to Burma as early as possible. His cable crossed one from the C.I.G.S. announcing that Alexander was leaving for Burma at once. On the 22nd Hutton was informed that the War Cabinet had decided, in view of the proposed increase in the army in Burma, that General Alexander should be appointed General Officer Commanding, Burma, and that he was to remain as Alexander's Chief of Staff.

Hutton had flown to Lashio on the 21st, where he expected to meet the Generalissimo who was on his way back to China after a visit to India, with the object of hastening the arrival of V Chinese Army so as to free 1st Burma Division to concentrate further south. The meeting did not take place because the Generalissimo decided at the last moment not to land at Lashio. Hutton returned to Rangoon on the evening of the 22nd to find awaiting him the Chiefs of Staff's views on the retention of Rangoon, the information that Burma had been transferred to India Command, Wavell's cables and orders of the 21st, the news that he was to be superseded in command and a report showing that the very serious situation on the Sittang, which he had feared might arise, had in fact arisen. He immediately replied to Wavell's cables saying that he had no intention of abandoning Rangoon and no one was panicking, but it was his considered opinion that, since the enemy appeared to have two divisions on the Sittang, the prospects of holding the port were not good.

Although no longer responsible for Burma, Wavell told the Chiefs of Staff and Hutton on the 22nd that he saw no reason why air action

---

[1] General The Honourable Sir Harold Alexander was at this time General Officer Commanding, Southern Command, in the United Kingdom.

should close Rangoon port; he thought that neither Rangoon nor Burma would be held by defensive methods and by maintaining a front, and that the only prospect of success lay in a vigorous counter-offensive at an early date, for which 7th Armoured Brigade and one Australian division would be necessary. Despite the dangers of bringing large convoys into Rangoon with the enemy air force established in Moulmein, and the fact that, without regular shipment of supplies from India, he could maintain it for some twelve days only, Hutton agreed on the 23rd to accept 7th Australian Division, always provided that it arrived in time. He said, however, that a final decision as to whether the convoys carrying it should or should not enter the port would have to be made twenty-four hours before their arrival.

The following morning he held a conference with Smyth at Pegu to ascertain for himself the state of 17th Division and to co-ordinate arrangements for the defence of the Waw–Pegu area. He had already ordered a special effort to be made to speed up the disembarkation of 7th Armoured Brigade,[1] so that 17th Division could be reinforced on the line of the Sittang River. As a result of this order, a squadron of 2nd Royal Tank Regiment reached Pegu twenty-seven hours after disembarkation started—a very fine piece of organization.

Having been apprised of the situation he ordered 7th Armoured Brigade (Brigadier J. H. Anstice) to occupy and hold the Payagyi–Waw area, while 17th Division concentrated at Pegu and was reorganized. He was unable to move his armour further east since the tanks could not cross the canal bridge at Waw. Owing to the heavy losses suffered by the division during the fighting on the Bilin River and at the crossing of the Sittang, Hutton ordered a number of battalions to be amalgamated, 46th Brigade to be broken up and the division reconstituted with 16th and 48th Brigades only.

On relief by VI Chinese Army, 1st Burma Division, now consisting of three weak brigades, had moved out of the Shan States and by the 23rd was in the Sittang valley north of Pegu, less 13th Brigade which remained in the Karen Hills covering the crossing of the Salween at Kemapyu and the wolfram and tin mines at Mawchi.[2] The 2nd Burma Brigade was holding Nyaunglebin and 1st Burma Brigade Kyauktaga, fifteen miles further north. Thus between 2nd Burma Brigade at Nyaunglebin and 7th Armoured Brigade at Payagyi there was a gap of some thirty-five miles. In the event of a further withdrawal, which with the small forces available appeared inevitable, Hutton ordered 17th Division, supported by 7th Armoured Brigade, to cover Rangoon for as long as possible and then retire on Prome to cover the oilfields, while 1st Burma Division retired northwards to

---
[1] The 7th Armoured Brigade consisted of 7th Hussars, 2nd Royal Tank Regiment and 414th Battery, R.H.A.; 1st Cameronians was attached on arrival in Burma.
[2] See Map 8.

cover the deployment of V Chinese Army at Toungoo and the newly-formed supply bases in central Burma.

The following day (24th) Hutton, referring to Wavell's telegrams of the 21st, cabled to Hartley saying,

> 'I have never given you or anyone else the slightest indication of any intention to abandon Rangoon and protest most strongly at this implication. I have said, quite correctly, that I did not feel certain Rangoon could be held. This now appears to be realized and action is in consequence being taken to send 7th Australian Division which may just save the situation.... The possibility of offensive action has always been in my mind but it is impossible to ignore the realities of the situation.... Practically everything I have said has been actually borne out by events, but the unpleasant truth is never popular.'

When the Australian Government refused to agree to the diversion of 7th Australian Division to Burma,[1] the whole situation changed. The only reinforcements for Burma immediately in sight were the partially trained 63rd Indian Brigade,[2] an Indian field regiment due on the 2nd March, three British battalions due on the 8th and a further three at some unspecified date as soon as possible after the 8th.[3]

On the 25th and 26th February the Japanese made what proved to be their last attempt to gain air superiority over Rangoon. On the afternoon of the 25th formations of enemy bombers, armed with light fragmentation bombs and escorted by fighters, attacked the airfield at Mingaladon. Radar warning had, however, been received and British and American fighters were able to intercept them. Many enemy aircraft, mostly fighters, were believed destroyed in the action which ensued, for the loss of only one Hurricane. Early the following morning a small formation of Blenheims, escorted by Hurricanes, raided the airfield at Moulmein which the Japanese had occupied. This stirred up a hornets' nest and throughout the day enemy formations attempted to penetrate the Rangoon defence zone; they paid dearly in the many interceptions which took place.

During the two days, the enemy force of some 170 bombers and fighters lost in all about one-fifth of their strength, mostly to the A.V.G. Against this the Allied losses totalled only two aircraft shot down, though many were damaged either in the air or on the ground. The combined fighter strength of the R.A.F. and A.V.G., which at the start of these operations totalled forty-four Hurricanes and Toma-

---
[1] See pages 57–58.
[2] The 63rd Brigade (Brigadier J. Wickham) consisted of 1/11th Sikhs, 2/13th Frontier Force Rifles and 1/10th Gurkha Rifles.
[3] Provided by India in answer to the request of the Chiefs of Staff, see page 57.

hawks, fell on the 27th to as low as ten, owing chiefly to the number which had been damaged and were temporarily unserviceable because of lack of spares with which to repair them. All three of the R.A.F. fighter squadrons (67, 17 and 135) and the A.V.G. received the personal congratulations of the Secretary of State for Air and General Wavell for the part that they had played in the air defence of Rangoon. The heavy loss inflicted on the Japanese air force in these two days was more than it could face with equanimity. Enemy formations never again entered the Rangoon air defence zone until after the city had been evacuated. This air victory enabled the convoys bringing in the last reinforcements for the Burma Army to arrive, and the evacuation by land, sea and air to be carried out, without any interference from enemy aircraft.

On the 26th February Hutton who, having been Chief of the General Staff in India, knew only too well the state of training of the expanding Indian Army, informed Hartley that he did not consider the arrival of the partially trained 63rd Brigade, or even of the three British battalions, would materially affect the fate of Rangoon. All indications showed that the enemy was preparing a big scale attack, and to endeavour to hold on till these reinforcements arrived would prejudice the evacuation of administrative units, postpone the execution of the denial scheme to a dangerous degree and risk the destruction of fighter aircraft by forcing them to remain on airfields which were no longer covered by an adequate warning net.

By the 27th it was clear that Japanese patrols were across the Sittang; clashes occurred with renegade Burmans supported by the Japanese at Waw, and the enemy was reported to be concentrating at Myitkyo.[1] It looked as if the enemy were intending to move through the gap between 1st Burma Division and 7th Armoured Brigade. To counter the danger of enemy infiltration across the Pegu Yomas into the Irrawaddy valley, Hutton sent a squadron of 7th Hussars and a company of the West Yorkshire Regiment to Tharrawaddy on the Rangoon–Prome road. He ordered Headquarters 17th Division and 16th Brigade to move back from Pegu to Hlegu and 2nd Royal Tank Regiment, which was covering Pegu on the line Waw–Payagyi, to withdraw to Pegu, for he had come to the conclusion that, in the event of an enemy offensive, the line of withdrawal could not be covered for more than a brief period with the forces available.

That evening he told Wavell and Hartley that, unless instructions to the contrary were received on the following day, he intended to

---

[1] These encounters were the first indication that the Japanese had raised, armed and organized a Burman force (later known as the Burma Independent Army).

carry out the demolitions in Rangoon and evacuate the city. He proposed that the convoy carrying 63rd Brigade should be turned back to Calcutta or directed to Akyab. Hartley agreed and the convoy was ordered to return to Calcutta. The Governor informed London at the same time that he was in full agreement with Hutton's decision, since the arrival of further brigades at that juncture was of little value. What was required, he said, was an army corps.

On the 28th Wavell, who had resumed his appointment as Commander-in-Chief in India that day,[1] told Hutton that, if possible, no action should be taken until his arrival in Burma. On the 1st March he met the Governor, Hutton and Stevenson at Magwe. The situation, as Wavell saw it, was that there was at that time no evidence of any great enemy strength west of the Sittang, 7th Armoured Brigade was still intact and Chinese troops were moving down towards Toungoo. He considered that, if Rangoon had to be evacuated, the largest possible force would be needed to establish a front across the lower Irrawaddy and to link up with the Chinese further east. He therefore decided that Rangoon should continue to be held, at least for long enough to enable the reinforcements then at sea—an Indian field artillery regiment and 63rd Brigade, now due on the 3rd and 5th respectively—to be landed. The convoy carrying 63rd Brigade was then once again routed to Rangoon.

Immediately after the Magwe conference Wavell flew to Rangoon, whence he motored to 17th Divisional Headquarters at Hlegu. Finding Smyth a sick man, he instructed Hutton to appoint Brigadier Cowan to the command of the division. The following day (2nd March), after visiting the troops on the Pegu front, he flew to Lashio and had what he described as two satisfactory interviews with Chiang Kai-shek. The Generalissimo was pleased that Rangoon was still being held, and promised to send V Chinese Army towards Toungoo as rapidly as possible. On his return to India on the 3rd, General Wavell met General Sir Harold Alexander, who was on his way to take over command of the Burma Army, at Calcutta, and gave him a verbal directive to the following effect:

> 'The retention of Rangoon is a matter of vital importance to our position in the Far East and every effort must be made to hold it. If however that is not possible, the British force must not be allowed to be cut off and destroyed, but must be withdrawn from the Rangoon area for the defence of upper Burma. This must be held as long as possible in order to safeguard the oilfields at Yenangyaung, keep contact with the Chinese and protect the construction of the road from Assam to Burma.'

---

[1] See page 50.

2. Lieut.-General T. J. Hutton.

3. Major-General J. G. Smyth.

4. Moulmein looking north-north-west towards Martaban.

5. The Sittang Bridge
(Taken in 1944 after the Japanese had carried out repairs).

ENEMY PLAN FOR CAPTURE OF RANGOON

General Iida had received information that British reinforcements had been arriving in Rangoon and that Chinese armies were moving into Burma, both of which facts emphasized the need for speed in the capture of Rangoon; but his supply position had become so parlous by the time his divisions reached the Sittang River that he was forced to make a prolonged pause in the operations. Before launching its offensive from Siam on the 20th January, *15th Army* had repaired the road from Raheng to the Burmese frontier. Once it had crossed the frontier, it had had to rely on what it could carry or obtain locally in Burma until the damage caused by the demolitions in the Dawna Range had been repaired and the road extended to Moulmein and made fit for motor transport. Despite great efforts the road did not reach Moulmein till the 15th February. In these circumstances the advance of *33rd* and *55th Divisions* from the frontier to the Sittang River in some thirty-four days, which included a number of days of fierce battle, without receiving any supplies from the rear, was a remarkable feat of endurance and improvisation.

Although the Sittang River had been reached on the 23rd February, the crossing could not be made in force till the 3rd March, for the equipment to enable this formidable obstacle to be crossed could not be brought up till the end of the month. During the interval a difference of opinion arose between *Headquarters Southern Army* and General Iida. On the 9th February the former had directed *15th Army* first to capture Rangoon and then later to move north on the oilfields and Mandalay. On the 26th they proposed that, rather than make an early capture of Rangoon, *15th Army* should turn north and deal first with the Chinese armies entering Burma. Iida did not agree, for his supply position was so precarious that he considered the early capture of Rangoon was essential. With the port in its hands, *15th Army* could be reinforced and better able to defeat the Chinese in northern Burma. His view prevailed and *Headquarters Southern Army* allowed the original order to stand.

On the 27th, Iida ordered *33rd* and *55th Divisions* to cross the Sittang on the 3rd March and capture Rangoon by a rapid advance. He directed that a detachment from *55th Division* (the *Kawashima Detachment*), comprising *II/143rd Battalion, 55th Cavalry Regiment* and a battery of mountain artillery, was to occupy Daik-U and protect the flank and rear of the main body of the army from any interference from the direction of Toungoo; *33rd Division* was to advance across country to the line Hmawbi–Hlegu, and at the same time guard against any interference from the direction of Tharrawaddy; *55th Division* (less the *Kawashima Detachment*), supported by a light tank company and an anti-tank company, was to advance on Pegu, while one battalion moving east of the Pegu River was to occupy the oil installations at Syriam. The boundary line between the two divisions was to be the line Sittang Bridge–Sitpinzeik–Hlegu, inclusive to *55th Division*.

The *Kawashima Detachment* crossed the Sittang at Kunzeik on the evening of the 2nd March, and by the 4th had occupied Daik-U and established a road block at Pyuntaza seven miles to the north. The *33rd Division* crossed on the evening of the 3rd near Myitkyo, with *215th Regiment* on the right and *214th Regiment* on the left, and by the morning of the 4th reached the line of the main road and railway near Pyinbon. By the 5th it had crossed the Pegu River near Sitpinzeik and reached a point some miles south-west of the river. Further south *55th Division* had sent one battalion from *112th Regiment* across the Sittang at the ferry west of Kyaikto on the 26th February, to move by way of Kamase and Onhne on the refineries at Syriam, and an advanced guard of one battalion on the 1st March with orders to occupy Waw. The rest of the division crossed on the 3rd with *112th Regiment* on the right directed on Payagyi and *143rd Regiment* on the left directed on Pegu. With the idea of surrounding and destroying the British forces in the Pegu area, *55th Division* then ordered *112th Regiment* (less one battalion) to cross the Pegu River at Sitpinzeik and move south along its west bank to cut the railway and road to Rangoon some four miles south of Pegu, while *143rd Regiment* (less one battalion) attacked the town from the north and east.

Following the decision taken at Magwe on the 1st March, General Hutton ordered 7th Armoured Brigade to reoccupy Waw. The Japanese were found to be in occupation of the village, and an attack by a company of the Cameronians on the afternoon of the 2nd failed to dislodge them. Next day units of the brigade encountered Japanese on the main road south of Pyinbon, and also at Kyaikhla, where once again an attack by a company of Cameronians failed to drive them back. During the 4th there were confused encounters around Payagyi, and that night the village was occupied by the enemy. Japanese patrols were also encountered west of the Pegu River well north of Pegu itself. It was evident that the expected outflanking movement on Pegu from the north-west was in progress.

On the morning of the 5th Hutton, when he arrived at Hlegu on his way to visit 48th Brigade, found that the road had been cut by the enemy near Payathonzu south of Pegu.[1] He also learnt that an enemy column, believed to include tanks, had already passed westwards through Paunggyi presumably making for the Prome road. The withdrawal of the force from Rangoon was now

---

[1] See Sketch 5.

likely to be much more hazardous. After consulting General Cowan (17th Division) he ordered 48th Brigade, which was not considered at that time fit for offensive operations, to withdraw from Pegu to Hlegu, and 16th Brigade from Hlegu to Taukkyan.

At noon on the 5th General Alexander arrived in Rangoon and assumed command. During the afternoon he went forward to Headquarters 17th Division at Hlegu where he met Hutton and Cowan. A very unpromising situation confronted the new commander. Reinforcements had indeed arrived: 1st Indian Field Regiment had landed on the 3rd, and 63rd Brigade (but not its transport) had just disembarked and was being concentrated at Hlawga, twelve miles north of Rangoon.[1] But 7th Armoured Brigade and 48th Brigade were actively engaged with an aggressive enemy in the vicinity of Pegu; the Japanese appeared to be moving through the gap between 17th Division and 1st Burma Division and across the Pegu Yomas with the obvious intention of cutting the Rangoon–Prome road; and air reconnaissance had discovered the approach of eight powerdriven river craft along the coast from the mouth of the Salween. Although one had been intercepted by the B.R.N.V.R. and found to contain a party of renegade Burmans commanded by a Japanese officer, the others had succeeded in landing their parties, thus threatening the Syriam oil refineries.[2]

Between the 3rd, when Alexander had been briefed by Wavell in Calcutta, and the 5th, the situation had deteriorated so rapidly that it had become very doubtful whether Rangoon could be held. Alexander saw that there were only two courses open: to close the gap between 1st Burma and 17th Divisions, or to accept defeat and abandon the city. He was not prepared to take the latter course without first trying to restore the situation. He accordingly cancelled the orders already issued by Hutton and instructed 17th Division, reinforced by 63rd Brigade, and 7th Armoured Brigade to take the offensive in the Waw area, and 1st Burma Division to advance southwards from Nyaunglebin. While these new orders were being issued at Hlegu on the 5th, the road forward from Hlegu had been reopened and that evening a reconnaissance party consisting of Brigadier Wickham (63rd Brigade) and his three battalion commanders was able to reach Pegu, which had been heavily bombed during the afternoon, many fires being started.

The troops defending Pegu were disposed as follows: 48th Brigade (Hugh-Jones) covered the town from the east;[3] 1st West Yorkshire

---

[1] The transport joined the brigade twenty-four hours later.
[2] At this time the B.R.N.V.R. motor launches were engaged on inshore work, with sloops of the Royal Indian Navy (*Hindustan, Ratmagiri* and *Indus*) patrolling to seaward.
[3] The 48th Brigade now consisted of 1/4th Gurkha Rifles, 5/3rd Gurkha Rifles, a composite battalion formed from the 1/3rd and 2/5th, and a composite battalion of 1/7th (originally 16th Brigade) and 3/7th Gurkha Rifles (from 46th Brigade which had been broken up).

(less two companies) covered the area north-west of the town;[1] 1st Cameronians (less two companies) was in Pegu itself guarding the road bridges across the river and railway, while its remaining companies were holding a position at Shanywagyi on the railway five miles north-east of the town, but with orders to withdraw early on the 6th; and 7th Hussars with 414th Battery R.H.A. and a company of 1st West Yorkshire were at the northern exits of Pegu east of the river.[2]

The *143rd Regiment*, which had moved through Payagyi after the action at Kyaikhla on the 3rd and crossed to the west of the Pegu River, advanced down the railway from the north at dawn on the 6th under cover of a heavy mist. Despite the gallant defence put up by the greatly outnumbered Yorkshiremen, the Japanese reached the railway station during the morning and occupied the jungle-covered hills west of the town. Repeated attacks on the bridges followed, but the Cameronians, reinforced by their two companies from Shanywagyi, held firm.

Meanwhile 63rd Brigade, advancing from Hlegu to reinforce 48th Brigade, found that the enemy had again established a road block south of Payathonzu, and at about 9.30 a.m. took up a position covering the road junction at Intagaw. The 2nd Royal Tank Regiment was then ordered to send a detachment to break through and bring back the Brigadier and battalion commanders of 63rd Brigade who had gone forward to Pegu on the 5th. The tanks forced their way through the block and returned with the officers in two carriers, but Japanese snipers in trees overlooking the road killed or wounded all the occupants of the carriers. For any brigade suddenly to lose its Brigadier and all its battalion commanders would be serious, but it was particularly so for 63rd Brigade which was about to go into action for the first time.

In Pegu, a counter-attack was launched at noon against the railway station by a composite force of three companies. It was completely successful, the enemy suffering severely as he withdrew northwards out of the town. Enemy aircraft retaliated by bombing, causing several casualties among the staff of 48th Brigade Headquarters. For the rest of the day fighting, sometimes hand-to-hand, continued on the western side of the town but the defenders maintained their positions.

While this bitter fighting was taking place in Pegu, 7th Hussars was fighting a separate action further north. At first light on the 6th it had advanced towards Payagyi, but soon came under fire from

---

[1] One company 1st West Yorkshire was operating in support of 7th Hussars and a second was with the detachment of 7th Hussars at Tharrawaddy.

[2] The 7th Armoured Brigade Headquarters and 2nd Royal Tank Regiment had been withdrawn to Hlegu on the 5th.

Sketch 5
PEGU

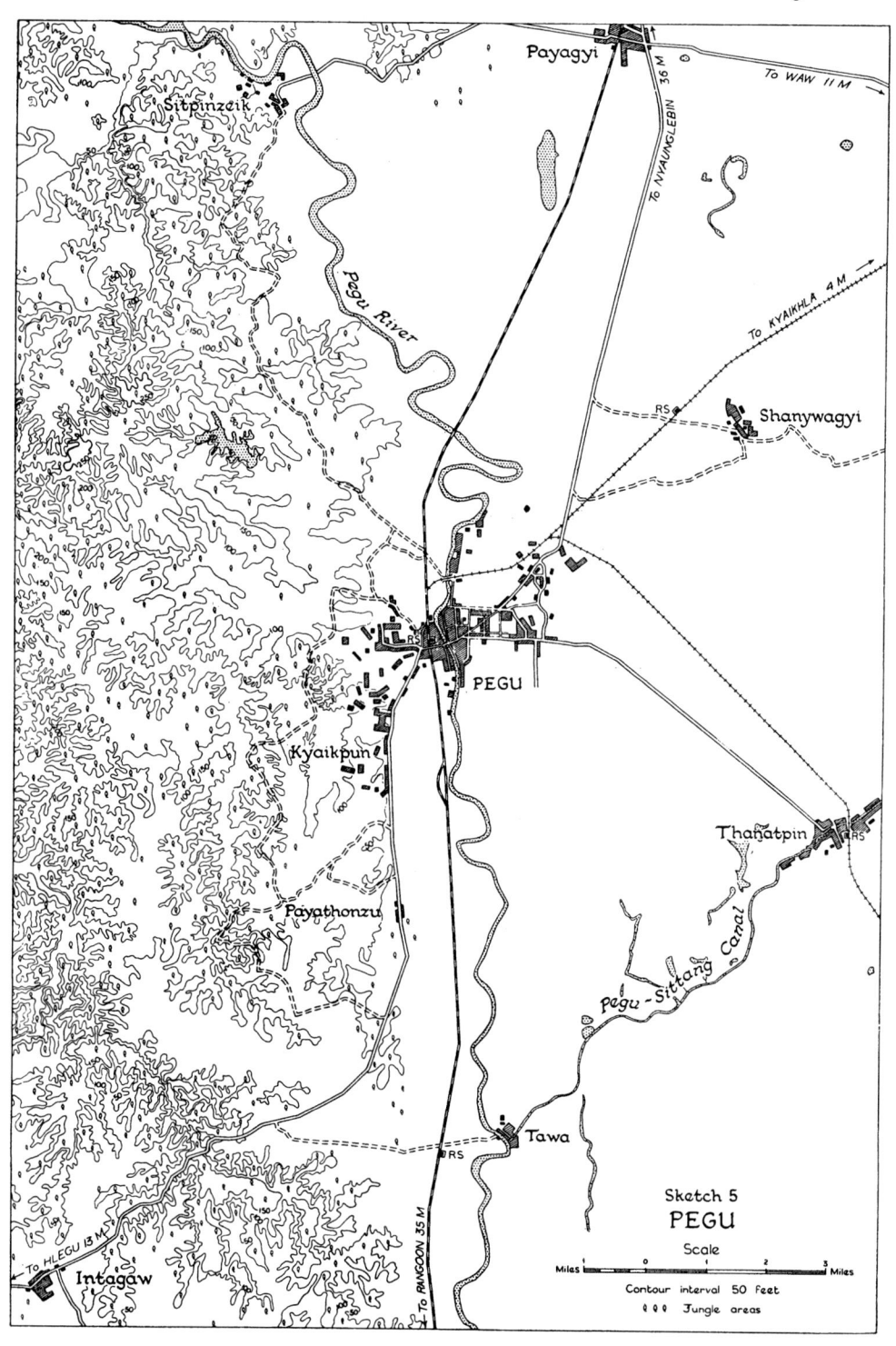

anti-tank guns. A successful action followed in which the enemy lost some tanks and guns. The Japanese force encountered was *55th Divisional Headquarters* which, with an escort of all arms, had arrived in Payagyi the previous day. At 3.40 p.m., 7th Hussars was ordered to pull back and concentrate in Pegu where it was to come under orders of 48th Brigade. That evening Hugh-Jones was again ordered to withdraw. At a conference summoned at once, he issued orders for 7th Hussars to cross the Pegu River after dark that night followed by 48th Brigade with all the transport. While the brigade closed up behind them, the Hussars were to break the road block near Payathonzu and the whole column was to pass through as soon as it was cleared. The 1st West Yorkshire and 1st Cameronians, less detachments, already in position west of the river near the railway station, were to blow the road and railway bridges as soon as the tail of 48th Brigade was across, and then act as rearguard to the column.

The Hussars moved off at 8.10 p.m. and, finding the road block still held, harboured for the night with a view to attacking it next morning. The 48th Brigade followed in the early hours of the 7th with 1/7th Gurkhas as advanced guard. After passing through the position held by the West Yorkshires and Cameronians, 1/4th Gurkhas on the right and 5/3rd Gurkhas on the left formed a box with the transport on the road between them. When the advanced guard made contact with the Hussars the column halted, the transport closed up on the road 'double banked' and the flank battalions were disposed on each side of and close to the road. Both bridges over the Pegu River were blown at about 6.30 a.m. on the 7th. The blowing of the bridges was the signal for an enemy attack on the rearguard, which was driven off. At the same time enemy mortars and machine-guns opened up on the crowded road and, before being forced to desist, inflicted much damage and casualties.

After overcoming strong opposition, 7th Hussars cleared the road block by 10 a.m. and then went through, but failed to leave piquets to keep it open. Thus when 1/7th Gurkhas arrived, the enemy was once again back in position. The 48th Brigade's transport column had to halt while it was cleared. The Gurkhas drove the enemy off and opened the road and, leaving one company and headquarters as piquets, went straight on to Intagaw. The bulk of the transport now moved through, but by 2 p.m. the enemy had once more infiltrated into the area. The block was again cleared and the road piqueted with a post every fifty yards. The remaining transport then got through without difficulty and reached Hlegu.

Once all the vehicles were clear, the rest of the infantry of the brigade moved south-east to the railway, along it to Tawa Railway Station and thence by the track back to the main road. They finally arrived at Hlegu at midday on the following day (8th). Losses, especially in senior officers, had been severe, but the force had fought its way out of a trap with considerable skill and determination and had inflicted severe loss on the enemy, who did not follow up.

We must now turn to events as seen by General Iida. By the morning of the 5th the *Kawashima Detachment* had occupied Daik-U without opposition, *33rd Division* had crossed the Pegu River (its leading troops had reached Paunggyi) and *55th Division* was in the process of preparing for its attack on Pegu the following morning. Iida considered that this progress was so satisfactory that he could attempt to capture Rangoon by a *coup-de-main*. Accordingly during the day he issued a further operation instruction: *33rd Division* was, firstly, to effect the early capture of Rangoon and, secondly, to destroy the enemy forces round the city; *55th Division*, after the capture of Pegu, was to send one infantry regiment to pursue the British towards Rangoon, while the other concentrated in Pegu in preparation for a northward drive. On receiving these instructions Lieut.-General Sakurai (*33rd Division*) decided that instead of moving directly south from the general line Hmawbi–Hlegu he would cross the Prome road near Wanetchaung and, moving through Hmawbi and Hlawga, attempt to enter Rangoon from the north-west.

Conditions in Rangoon had been growing steadily worse since the end of December. After the first air raids there had been a general dispersal of the population. Thousands of Indians had left by the road to Prome, bringing the life of the city almost to a standstill, but when they found the raids were not repeated large numbers had been persuaded to return. A second mass exodus had taken place in the middle of January as a result of rumours, which proved to be false, that Rangoon was to be subjected to fifteen days' concentrated bombing. But all the time there had been a steady egress of evacuees and by the end of the month the population of half a million had been more than halved. The transfer of Government departments to upper Burma had started at the end of January, and by the third week in February all but essential skeleton staffs and certain administrative sections of Army Headquarters had left.

The evacuation of the civil population had been planned in three stages. The first stage (Signal E) began on the 20th February after the withdrawal from the Bilin, when all civilians not employed on essential work were advised to leave, and the Syriam refineries were closed down in order to ensure the timely withdrawal of civilians and to enable preparations for demolitions to be completed. The following day patients from the hospital were sent by train to Mandalay, orders were given to release the inmates of the mental home, which included a number of criminal lunatics, and prisons were thrown open. From the time that Signal E was given law and order broke down in Rangoon. Nearly all the police had left. A wave of incendiarism swept the city and large areas were burnt out. Looting of shops and private houses took place on a large scale. The imposition of a curfew and orders to military patrols and such police as remained to shoot looters on sight stopped the worst of the looting and checked, but did not stop, incendiarism. Living conditions, as can be imagined, were not easy for those who remained to carry on essential work.

This phase did not last long however. On the afternoon of the 28th February, General Hutton ordered the second stage to begin. All, except those required for the final denial of the city and a few other 'indispensables', were instructed to leave, and orders were issued for the withdrawal of the civil administration throughout the delta. Only what were known as 'last-ditchers' remained in the deserted city. It had been intended to begin the third and final stage on the following day but it was postponed on the orders of General Wavell until reinforcements, then at sea, had arrived. This was the situation when Alexander assumed command. He had at first refused to abandon hope of saving the city but with Pegu encircled, the Syriam oil refineries threatened and reports coming in of strong enemy forces passing west through Paunggyi, he decided late on the afternoon of the 6th March that the retention of Rangoon was no longer possible and that the right course was to carry out the demolitions, evacuate the city and regroup his forces further north in the Irrawaddy valley. At midnight he gave orders for the denial scheme to be put into operation and that demolitions were to begin at 2 p.m. on the 7th.

The important refinery and storage tanks, the power station and many other public buildings were either blown up or set on fire. Machinery not already moved up-country from the railway workshops was rendered useless, locomotives were immobilized and motor vehicles which could not be moved destroyed. Only partial measures could, however, be taken to deny the use of the port, for the jetties and warehouses extended over several miles of waterfront. Shipping berths with their storage sheds were blown up or fired, wharf equipment smashed and power-driven vessels scuttled, but in the short time, and with the few engineer troops available, it was impossible to do more.

Many warehouses, wharves and jetties remained undamaged; hundreds of river craft were still afloat and numerous undamaged workshops were still to be found in rice and timber mills. In spite of the large quantities of valuable goods despatched to India by sea during January and February and the strenuous efforts made to remove military stores and lease-lend material to northern Burma, very large stocks of various kinds, including timber, coal, steel rails and bridging material had to be left behind. The port when evacuated was still capable of maintaining more divisions than the Japanese were ever likely to use in Burma. When all that could be done was accomplished, the 'last-ditchers' took their leave of the burning city. Launches left the jetty for the three ships waiting downstream to take them to Calcutta, and at 7.30 p.m. on the 7th March the last train drew out of Rangoon. The following description of the passage of the launches down river is given in the Governor's report on the Burma campaign:

> 'As the launches passed down Rangoon River against a strong flood-tide a strange spectacle was presented to the eyes of the weary passengers. A heavy pall of smoke hung over the town but a light southerly wind kept the smoke off the foreshore and it could be distinguished that the electric power station was ablaze, there were fires at Sule Pagoda Wharf where the port warehouses were blackening skeletons of what they had once been; on the docks the cranes, damaged by dynamite leant over at a drunken angle and the columns of smoke rising behind the wharves indicated the end of the principal buildings of a city of half a million inhabitants. . . . All along the normally thronged foreshore not a sign of human life was to be seen. By the time that Syriam was abeam it was almost dark and the flames, topped by columns of dense black smoke rising thousands of feet into the air from the oil refineries presented an awe-inspiring sight and as the night fell the whole sky was lurid with the glare of that inferno.'

The Navy as always played an important part in the evacuation. Commodore C. M. Graham (Senior Naval Officer, Persian Gulf) had arrived on the 14th February to co-ordinate the activities of all local defence craft and take command of all naval shore establishments. When evacuation was ordered, he sent all seaworthy motor launches and local naval defence vessels to Akyab for the protection of that port and its airfield from seaborne attack. He dismantled the naval wireless station and formed part of it into a mobile station to accompany Army Headquarters during its withdrawal into upper Burma. He arranged for two motor launches and six minesweepers to be towed to India, and destroyed the remainder. Early on the 8th March the *Heinrich Jensen*,[1] having embarked the demolition parties, weighed anchor and steamed down the Rangoon river. Two ships of the Royal Navy had formed the spearhead of the attack when the British captured Rangoon in 1824. One hundred and eighteen years later the Navy was the last to leave the port.

---

[1] The *Heinrich Jensen* (a requisitioned Danish ship) had escaped from Hong Kong and Singapore and was the last vessel to leave Rangoon.

A flotilla, known as Force Viper, had been formed of four government launches and three motor boats armed with machine-guns and mortars and manned by a detachment of about a hundred Royal Marines, which had arrived from Colombo on the 11th February. On the 7th March, having covered the embarkation of the demolition parties, the flotilla moved up the Irrawaddy and reached Prome on the 13th. Force Viper was then attached to 17th Division with the duty of protecting its right flank against any enemy coming up the river.

Air Marshal Stevenson meanwhile had been putting into effect the plans for the withdrawal of the R.A.F.[1] About 3,000 airmen had been transferred to India, airstrips had been cut in the dry paddy fields at intervals along the Prome road, the best of which was at Zigon some 120 miles north of Rangoon, and an improvised headquarters known as 'X' Wing had been formed to control air operations in the Rangoon area during the withdrawal from the city. On the 7th March 'X' Wing, together with the few remaining fighter aircraft, was established at Zigon; there it continued to function till the 11th when, its task accomplished, it was disbanded.

Meanwhile at Magwe 'Burwing' had been formed from 17 (Fighter) Squadron, 45 (Bomber) Squadron, a detachment of 28 (Army Co-operation) Squadron and an A.V.G. (fighter) squadron. At Akyab 'Akwing' had been formed from 135 (Fighter) Squadron, 67 (Fighter) Squadron, a detachment of 139 (General Reconnaissance) Squadron and a few light aircraft for communication duties.

When General Alexander made his decision on the 6th March to evacuate Rangoon, he ordered the garrison of the city to move by way of the Prome road to Tharrawaddy, covered by an advanced guard consisting of a squadron of 7th Hussars (called back from Tharrawaddy),[2] a battery of 1st Indian Field Regiment and two companies of 2nd K.O.Y.L.I. The 17th Division, with 7th Armoured Brigade under command, was meanwhile to hold Hlegu till the garrison column had cleared Taukkyan and then form the rearguard.[3] The advanced guard moved off at dawn on the 7th from Taukkyan and, leaving a small detachment near Wanetchaung to watch the dangerous eastern flank, reached Tharrawaddy without incident.

---

[1] See page 80.
[2] See page 85.
[3] The Rangoon garrison consisted of 1st Heavy A.A. Regiment B.A.F., Rangoon Field Brigade B.A.F., detachment Royal Engineers, detachment Burma Sappers and Miners, 1st Gloucestershire, 12th Burma Rifles, one company 1/9th Royal Jat, two garrison companies and F.F.4.

The Rangoon garrison set out from Rangoon at the same time but on reaching Taukkyan learnt that the Japanese had established a road block a few miles up the road. A rapidly organized attack by 1st Gloucesters, supported by tanks, failed; a second attack by 2/13th F.F. Rifles, brought up from 63rd Brigade and also supported by tanks, fared no better and, with night approaching, the 2/13th dug in along the south side of the block. Meanwhile from the direction of Pegu, 17th Division with 16th Brigade as rearguard was also falling back on Taukkyan and, in the words of one unit's war diary, the Taukkyan cross roads area by the evening of the 7th presented a spectacle in comparison with which 'Piccadilly Circus on Coronation night would have appeared deserted'. To the south, the whole sky was dark with smoke from burning Rangoon and its oil stores and refinery.

When the advanced guard commander arrived at Tharrawaddy soon after midday, he heard of the road block south of his detachment at Wanetchaung and immediately took his force back there. He decided to attack the block, but the attack made by 1st Gloucesters from the south had begun and the 'overs' from it fell among his troops just as they were forming up north of the block. His wireless had failed and, unable to get in touch with the forces attacking from the south, he cancelled the attack and, leaving the Wanetchaung detachment in position, ordered the bulk of the advanced guard to return to Tharrawaddy.

By the evening of the 7th the situation was desperate and Alexander ordered 63rd Brigade, supported by all the available armour and artillery, to clear the block at all costs in the morning. The plan of attack was for 1/11th Sikhs and 1/10th Gurkhas to attack the block on the east and west of the road respectively, while the tanks and 2/13th F.F. Rifles broke through on its axis. The attack was to be preceded by an artillery concentration starting at 8.35 a.m.

The 1/10th Gurkhas had great difficulty in getting to its forming-up place as it had to pass through the congested area at Taukkyan, and did not reach it till the small hours of the morning, very tired and hungry. The Sikhs reached their rendezvous somewhat earlier and soon became aware that the enemy was quite close to them. There now followed a night of surprises. Soon after dark the detachment of the advanced guard at Wanetchaung discovered that a large enemy force was crossing the Prome road from east to west; the movement went on for three hours, but it could not pass the information to the main body. In the early hours of the 8th, 1/10th Gurkhas, in position to the west of the road block, saw a large force of enemy to its left moving south—i.e. towards Rangoon, and sent a message to 63rd Brigade on the main road, but it was treated with scepticism. Thus Alexander did not learn what was happening. The next surprise was when, shortly before the attack by 63rd Brigade and 7th Armoured Brigade was due to begin, 2nd Royal Tank Regiment reported that the road block was unoccupied. The artillery concentration was cancelled and the armour and infantry on the road began to piquet the road block area for the Rangoon garrison to pass through.

Meanwhile the flank battalions, unaware of these events, fared badly. The 1/11th Sikhs on the right was in the open and soon after the morning mist lifted was severely bombed and machine-gunned by low-flying Japanese aircraft. It eventually made its way against some opposition to Hmawbi, arriving in the small hours of the 9th to find that the main body had gone through towards Tharrawaddy during the 8th.[1] The Gurkhas on the left, uncertain of their position but expecting to be guided by the artillery concentrations due to begin at 8.35 a.m., were completely nonplussed when the only bombardment they heard was far to the east and south-east.[2] Soon after this they made contact with men of the Sikhs, who during the air attack on the battalion had taken refuge in the jungle near the road block, and were told by them that their battalion had been driven back. Believing that to move back to the main road might land them in a trap, for they knew a very large force of Japanese was now behind them, the Gurkhas made a detour to the west and eventually reached the Prome road much further north.

At 10 a.m. on the 8th the Rangoon garrison, followed by 17th Division, less 1/11th Sikhs and 1/10th Gurkha Rifles, with 16th Brigade as rearguard, began to pass through the road block area and withdraw northwards. There was no interference from the enemy except for a few high-level bombing attacks which did little damage. Thanks largely to the measure of local air superiority established in the preceding fortnight, the column was not subjected to heavy low-flying air attacks, and by 11 p.m. on the 8th the last of the marching troops were clear of Hmawbi. During the 9th and 10th, covered by 7th Armoured Brigade, they were moved in motor transport to the Tharrawaddy area.

It is interesting to examine how, by evacuating the road block north of Taukkyan, the Japanese lost their opportunity of preventing the British forces from breaking out of Rangoon. The *33rd Division* had planned to cross the Prome road after dark on the 7th and then turn south and advance on Rangoon from the north-west. On the morning of the 7th the advanced guard (*III/214th Battalion*) reached the Prome

---

[1] The Sikhs during their advance captured or found many documents identifying the Japanese *33rd Division*.

[2] What they had heard was the Japanese air bombardment of the Sikhs.

road some five miles north of Taukkyan to find that British troops in considerable numbers were moving north. In order to protect the flank of the division as it crossed the road, the advanced guard commander cut the road and by about noon had established a strong road block. Colonel Sakuma (*214th Regiment*), to whom this action had been reported, left his headquarters at about 1.30 p.m. to visit his divisional commander. He suggested that, as the fighting on the road might give away the plan, he should carry out the operation as planned without delay, and that his advanced guard should be withdrawn from the block and move with the regiment on Rangoon.

Assuming that the British intended to hold Rangoon, and fearing that this encounter on the Prome road would cause them to strengthen their defences against an attack from the north-west and thus might jeopardize the success of the operations of his division, General Sakurai agreed with his regimental commander's suggestion. At 7 p.m. on his return to his headquarters, Sakuma ordered his regiment to continue its encircling movement on Rangoon and, finding that *III/214th Battalion* was under heavy pressure at the road block, ordered it to disengage as soon as it could after dark and follow up the main body of the regiment. It was thus that during the hours of darkness Japanese troops and transport were seen to be crossing the Prome road and to be moving south within 200 yards of 1/10th Gurkha Rifles.

About midday on the 8th, *215th Regiment* entered Rangoon to find to its surprise that the city was unoccupied and deserted. General Sakurai immediately ordered it to pursue the British column which he now realized was the whole of the British forces from the Rangoon area. It was too late, and the golden opportunity of hemming in and destroying the British garrison had been lost. The regiment reached Taukkyan after the British rearguard had moved north and, having covered over thirty miles in some seventeen hours, it was then forced to halt through lack of supplies and ammunition.

One of the repercussions of the loss of Rangoon was the evacuation of the Andaman Islands.[1] These islands had considerable strategic importance, for they flanked the approaches to Rangoon. Port Blair had an airstrip suitable for fighters, and its harbour provided an excellent potential base for flying-boats and submarines. The original garrison of one British company had been replaced in January 1942 by a battalion of Gurkhas. When however it became obvious that Rangoon could no longer be held, General Wavell decided to withdraw the whole garrison, and this was done on the 12th March.

---

[1] See Strategic Map.

The Japanese appreciated the importance of the Andamans and as early as the 7th February *Imperial General Headquarters* had issued orders for their capture. The opportunity to do so occurred when reinforcements were being sent to Burma by sea after the occupation of Rangoon.[1] A battalion of *18th Division* which was en route to Rangoon from Malaya, together with a naval component consisting of detachments from *9th* and *12th Special Base Forces*, sailed from Penang on the 20th March and three days later Port Blair was occupied and an air base quickly established.

Looked at from every angle the loss of Rangoon was a serious setback to the Allied cause. China was now cut off from her Allies, for the only seaport through which it had been possible to supply her was in the hands of her enemy, and the question now arose whether she could survive and fight on. The Allies were deprived of Burma's valuable exports—rice, oil, timber and minerals—a loss which was particularly serious to India since it would be difficult indeed to find other sources from which to feed her teeming millions and keep the wheels of her industry turning. The fall of Rangoon was to mean the eventual loss of Burma and determined for Britain the future course of the war in the Far East.

The Army in Burma had now to fight facing its former base. It was virtually cut off from outside assistance, for only a trickle of reinforcements and supplies could be brought in by air, and there was no through road from India in existence. Although base and line of communication installations, with a considerable reserve of commodities, had already been moved north of Rangoon, the army could subsist and fight on these for a limited time only. The loss of the Rangoon oil refineries meant that, once the reserves of petrol and aviation spirit were exhausted, recourse had to be made to improvised refining methods at the oilfields themselves. With the loss of the Rangoon airfields and their comparatively efficient warning system, air defence had now to be based largely on India, and the R.A.F. and A.V.G. squadrons remaining in Burma were exposed to the possibility of destruction. Finally the Japanese were freed to reinforce Burma from Malaya by sea instead of by the difficult land line of communications through Raheng and Moulmein, and they could reinforce *15th Army* with as many divisions and aircraft as they wished.

The effect that the loss of Rangoon would have on the British war effort was well known to the War Cabinet, the Chiefs of Staff and to all commanders in the Far East. Yet, despite the breathing space of

---

[1] For details of these reinforcements see pages 145–46.

six weeks between the outbreak of war and the start of the Japanese drive into southern Burma, no adequate steps were taken to build up the forces required to repel the comparatively small force the Japanese could maintain across the Siamese frontier, and an enemy force, equivalent to about one and two-thirds British divisions at war strength, was able to capture this vital port in a campaign of only seven weeks. The causes of this third successive disaster to British arms in the Far East are clear.

The refusal of the responsible authorities in London to place the defence of Burma in the hands of the Commander-in-Chief in India during those fateful years of 1940 and 1941, when war with Japan loomed ever nearer, deprived the country, already at the very bottom of the priority list for men and warlike stores, of the aid which India Command could have given to her effort to prepare for war. She was thus almost defenceless in December 1941. It was not till then that the immediate need for military forces to defend her frontiers was recognized. On the 12th December 1941 the Prime Minister, when informing the Commander-in-Chief in India (General Wavell) that reinforcements were being sent to him, said:

> 'You must now look East. Burma is now placed under your command. You must resist the Japanese advance towards Burma and India and try to cut their communications down the Malay Peninsula. . . . Marry these forces as you think best and work them into the Eastern fighting front to the highest advantage. . . .'[1]

—and this front could only be in Burma.

But at that time few imagined that the Japanese advance into Malaya would not be halted. When in northern Malaya the air force was overwhelmed and ten days later the defence of that area collapsed, it was still thought that Singapore could be held and all the reinforcements which could be made available in time were diverted there, only to be swallowed up in the maelstrom of disaster. Thus, despite the time which elapsed before the opening of the Japanese offensive, Burma still remained practically defenceless. General Hutton, when appointed to command in Burma at the end of December, was given the task of making bricks without straw. As in Malaya the attempt to reinforce Burma after the Japanese invasion had begun was doomed to failure, for there was insufficient time to enable reinforcements to be brought from those distant bases from which alone they could be found. Once 18th British and part of 17th Indian Division had been committed to Malaya, the only hope of providing an adequate force for Burma lay in the diversion there of 7th Armoured Brigade and, if it could arrive in time, 7th

---

[1] Churchill, *The Second World War*, Volume III (Cassell, 1950) page 564.

Australian Division. The armoured brigade arrived just in time but, even if the Australian Government had agreed to the diversion of 7th Australian Division, only one brigade could have reached Rangoon before the port had to be abandoned.

General Wavell's hesitation to accept the Chinese offer of assistance also appears to have been based on the assumption that the defences of Malaya would stand firm. At that time, as he later wrote, he saw no immediate danger to Burma and it appeared to him that British and Indian reinforcements would be arriving in ample time. After it became clear towards the end of December that all the reinforcements which Wavell had envisaged as available for Burma were being diverted to Malaya, there appears to have been an unnecessary delay in bringing Chinese troops into Burma. It was not till the 29th January—nine days after the start of the Japanese offensive—that a second Chinese division (equivalent in fighting strength to a British brigade) was brought in, and not till the 4th February that the third division of VI Chinese Army was moved into Burma and it was agreed that V Chinese Army should be concentrated at Toungoo. As a result of this delay, made worse by the appalling time-lag within the Chinese military organization between the taking of a decision and executive action, the exiguous British forces were spread over large areas of Burma in an attempt to defend all the possible lines along which the Japanese, who held the initiative, might launch an invasion, instead of being concentrated to meet them when they invaded Tenasserim.

Once the enemy had committed his forces to the Raheng–Moulmein line of approach, the move of the whole of 1st Burma Division to Tenasserim would appear to have been preferable to its remaining in the Shan States and Karen Hills until relieved by the Chinese. Hutton did in fact send all but four battalions to reinforce 17th Division. One of these four battalions remained in the Shan States and 13th Brigade was placed in the Mawchi area covering the Bawlake–Toungoo road.[1] He felt on political grounds that he could not at that time denude the Shan States of troops and that, as there was always the possibility of a Japanese advance through the Karen Hills on to the railway at Toungoo, he could not uncover this strategically important town. It is profitless to consider what might have been the outcome had the Chinese come in earlier, and all British forces been concentrated to meet the Japanese invading force in the Bilin–Sittang area. At least the defence would have been given a better chance of holding the enemy east of the Sittang till reinforcements arrived.

But Wavell in Java, overwhelmed with the vast problem of defending the whole of the Malay Barrier with inadequate forces,

---
[1] See Map 8.

could not be expected to give his full attention to Burma, especially as without direct wireless communication he could not be up to date with events in that theatre of war. It was asking too much of any man. He had protested at the inclusion of Burma in his command but had been overruled. Despite the load on his shoulders, he had twice found the time to fly from Java to Rangoon and back. Hutton, who was at one and the same time acting as Chief of the General Staff of a Burma War Office trying to organize the country for defence, and as both an army and a corps commander trying to conduct operations with an inadequate staff, cannot be held responsible that major strategical decisions were not always taken in time.

The whole situation changed after the disaster at the Sittang. Hutton then saw clearly that Rangoon was as good as lost. Having the courage of his convictions, he informed his superiors of the facts as he saw them, and set about taking the preparatory steps necessary to ensure a smooth evacuation and the demolition of the port. But again the disadvantage appeared of placing the command of Burma in the hands of a man controlling a vast theatre of war, provided with poor communications and heavily involved in other pressing problems. Wavell's continued insistence on an immediate offensive, which to anyone on the spot was clearly out of the question, shows how remote he still was from the hard practical facts of the situation in Burma.[1]

The authorities in London and India, blaming the local commander for a course of events for which they themselves were largely responsible, decided to swop horses in mid-stream. Burma, which had been thrown from Far East Command to India Command, from India Command to ABDA Command, but with India remaining responsible for administration, and finally back to India Command, was to suffer the added complication of a change in local command at the most critical stage in the campaign. We see first Wavell in charge, then Wavell and Hartley, then Hartley alone and then a few days later Wavell once again; we see Hutton superseded by Alexander. In such circumstances it was almost impossible for any plan or policy to remain consistent.

When the diversion of 7th Australian Division was mooted, Hutton refused to indulge in wishful thinking. He warned the authorities that to send large convoys to Rangoon at that late hour was to incur a very considerable risk, for the enemy air force was well established at short range and the air defence, even before the air battles of the 25th/26th February, was slender. Nevertheless he signified that he was prepared to hold Rangoon till their arrival, though he could not promise that the presence of part or all of the

---

[1] See pages 38–39, 74 and 81.

Australian division would in fact change the course of events at the last moment, for he was certain that Rangoon could not be held. In this he was correct, for the last-minute arrival of an Australian division could have affected the situation no more than the arrival of 18th Division did at Singapore.[1]

But once again the whole situation changed when the Australian Government could not agree to the diversion of this battle-trained formation to Burma. Hutton knew the value of the only reinforcements which could then reach him. He knew that 63rd Brigade was not in a fit state to meet a first-class enemy, since its units had very few experienced officers and contained a high proportion of recruits, it had recently been issued with weapons with which it had not been trained and its transport mules were unfit. The newly-raised 1st Indian Field Artillery Regiment was an unknown quantity. He therefore felt that to risk being invested in Rangoon, which would not save Burma and would mean the eventual loss of his own force, in order to await the arrival of reinforcements of such doubtful calibre, was not justified. On the other hand Wavell who, despite his experience in ABDA Command, still underestimated the ascendancy gained by the enemy and the speed with which Japanese troops could move across country, decided to delay the inevitable withdrawal from Rangoon in order to bring in these reinforcements, and accepted the risk of losing most of the Army in Burma. His gamble came off and the reinforcements were safely landed in time.

With the Japanese rapidly encircling Rangoon, Hutton realized on the 5th March the danger of the greater part of his army being cut off from upper Burma perhaps within a few hours, and not being permitted to evacuate Rangoon, took the only reasonable steps he could pending the arrival of his successor. Believing that a battle is never lost until it is won and mindful of Wavell's directive, Alexander immediately countermanded Hutton's orders and made a final effort to retrieve the situation and hold Rangoon. He took a far greater risk than he realized at the time, for he had had no opportunity to assess the calibre of his opponent or the state of his own forces. The consequent thirty-hour delay in the issue of orders to withdraw the army to upper Burma should have resulted in the loss of the greater part of the Army in Burma as well as Rangoon, but, as so often occurs in war, the enemy committed a serious error of judgment. The British forces were thus able to escape and dispute the control of Burma for another two and a half months.

---

[1] See Volume I.

Map 4

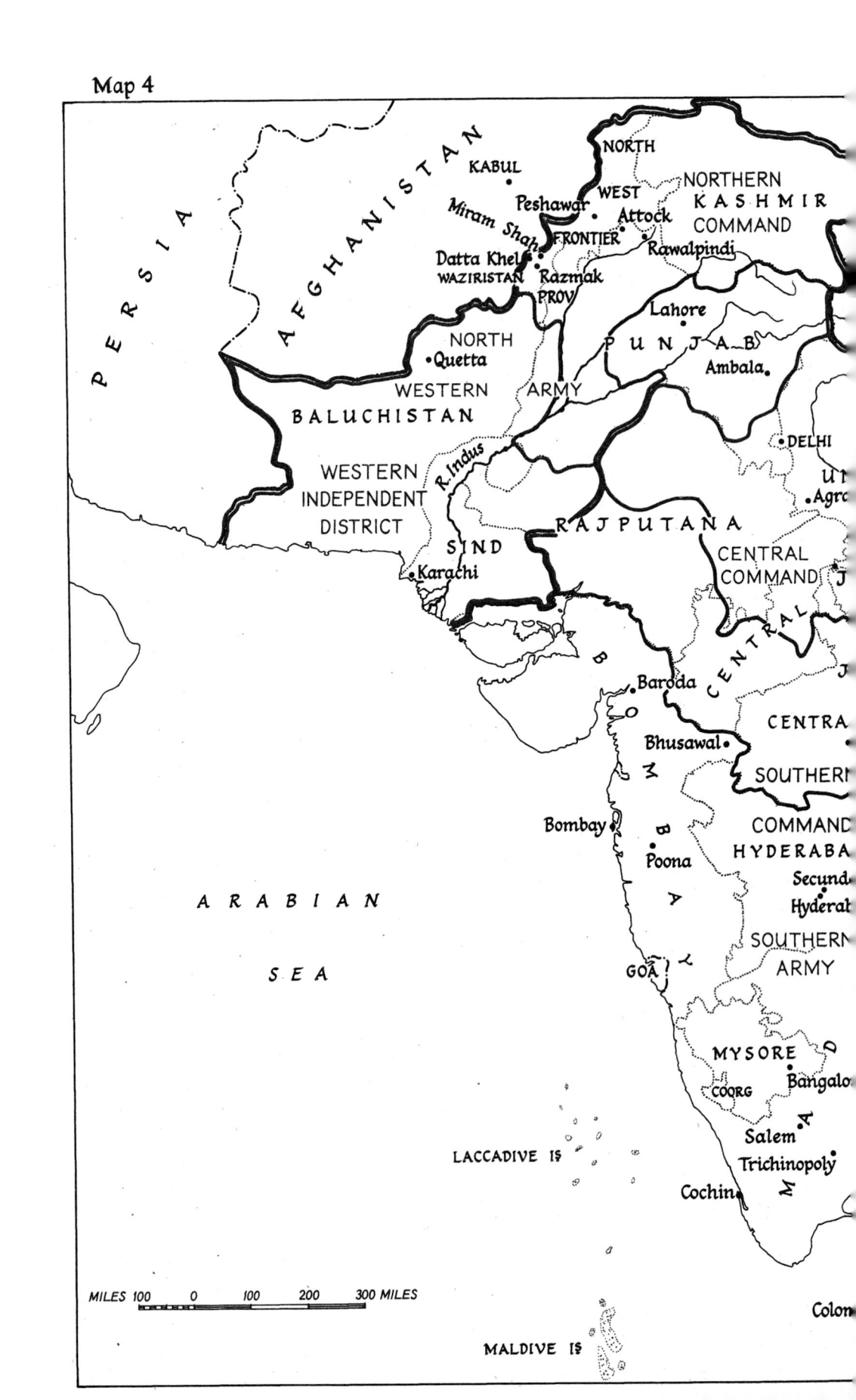

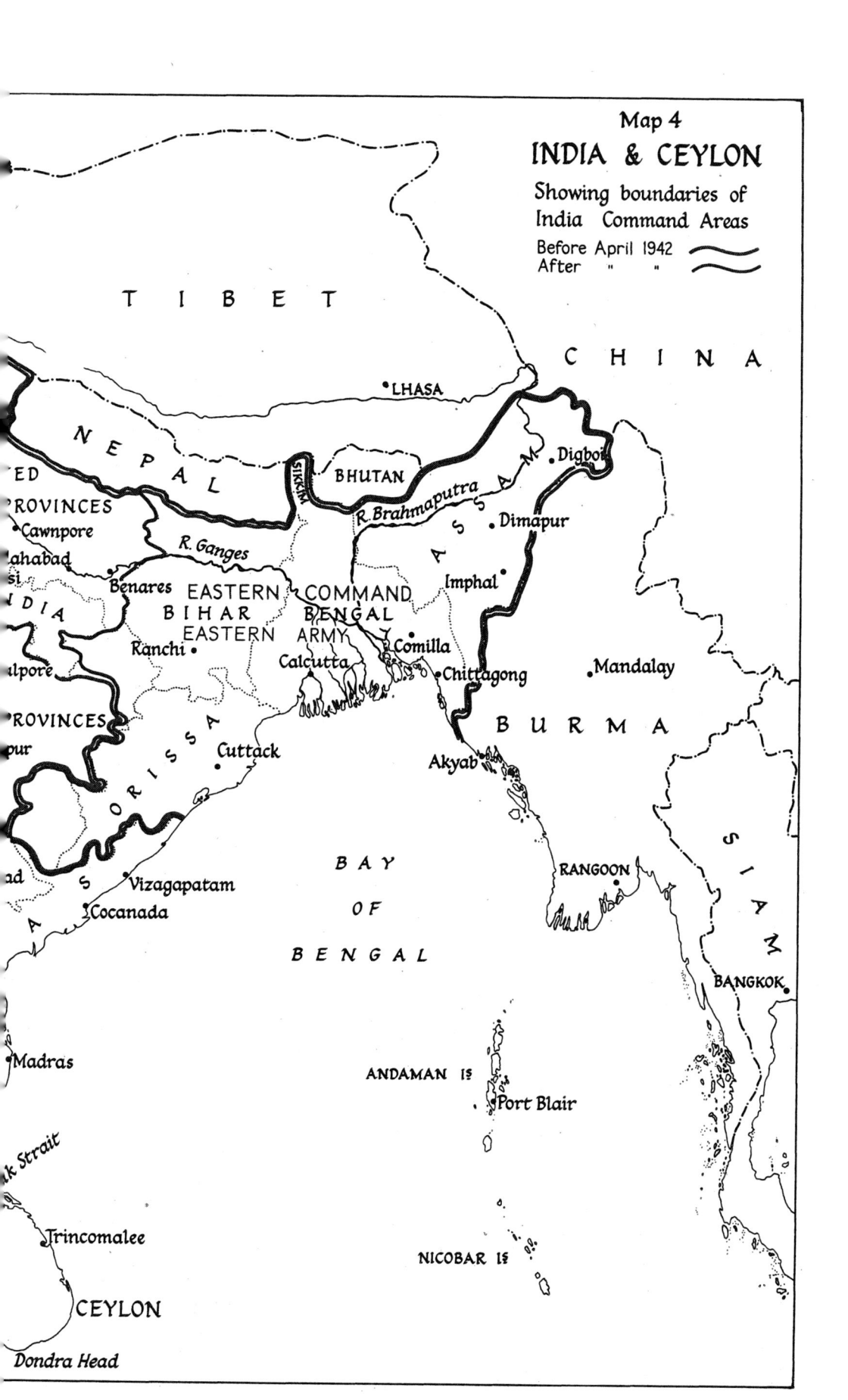

Map 4
INDIA & CEYLON
Showing boundaries of India Command Areas
Before April 1942
After " "

CHAPTER VI

THE DEFENCE OF INDIA AND CEYLON
(March 1942)

See Maps 4 and 14

THE early months of 1942 were some of the most critical and anxious periods in the war. In the west the Battle of the Atlantic was at its height, and with the American entry into the war the toll of merchant ship tonnage sunk by U-boats had reached new and unprecedented proportions. Naval losses of heavy ships in the Mediterranean had been severe. In the last two months of 1941, a battleship and a large aircraft carrier had been sunk and two more battleships damaged and disabled for long periods. At the beginning of 1942 there was not one battleship left in the eastern Mediterranean, and supplies escorted by the Italian battle fleet were reaching the German armies in North Africa. The British advance in North Africa had been brought to a halt, and General Auchinleck's army had been forced back to a line some forty miles west of Tobruk and only a hundred and forty miles west of the Egyptian frontier. Malta was under frequent and increasingly heavy air attacks. The Levant–Caspian front was for the time being secure owing to the gallant and unexpected resistance of the Russian armies, but with the melting of the snows a determined German offensive against Russia was to be expected.

In the Far East the fall of Singapore on the 15th February had brought new dangers and difficulties. The Chiefs of Staff were well aware that once the Japanese effectively breached the Malay Barrier the Indian Ocean lay open to them, and by capturing Ceylon they could imperil the vital line of sea communications to the Middle East, India and Australia. To defend these communications, the Eastern Fleet would have to be built up and Ceylon made safe as its main base.

On the 17th the Pacific War Council decided that 16th British Brigade (part of 70th British Division which was to go to Burma) should be sent to strengthen the weak garrison in the island.[1] On the

---
[1] See page 56.

3rd March the Australian Government, fully alive to the importance of Ceylon, offered, for its temporary defence, two brigades of 6th Australian Division, then embarking at Suez for Australia. This offer was gratefully accepted, and on the same day the Pacific War Council decided that two Hurricane squadrons (30 and 261), already embarked in the *Indomitable* and destined for Java, were to be diverted to Ceylon.

Becoming increasingly anxious about the safety of India, General Wavell told the Chiefs of Staff and Prime Minister on the 5th March that, since the defence of Ceylon was mainly a naval and air problem, large numbers of troops which could be better employed elsewhere should not be locked up there. He therefore proposed to send an East African brigade to Ceylon and keep 70th Division intact for India or Burma. The Chiefs of Staff agreed that the defence of Ceylon was mainly a sea and air problem but, since neither sufficient naval nor air forces could be found in time, thought an increased garrison was the only immediate insurance of its safety. Not only therefore was 16th Brigade still to go to Ceylon, but the East African brigade should be sent as well.

With the loss of Rangoon on the 8th March, followed by the evacuation of the Andaman Islands on the 12th, the danger to Ceylon and the whole of the eastern and north-eastern coastline of India—a coastline as long as that from Hamburg to Gibraltar—became incomparably greater. India's situation at that period was in many ways similar to that of Great Britain after Dunkirk: well-trained troops were scarce and equipment scarcer still. It was obvious that only a small part of this long line could be protected. There were three areas of great strategic importance: Ceylon, with its naval bases at Trincomalee and Colombo; Bengal, with the port of Calcutta and its industrial area; and the frontiers of India in eastern Bengal and Assam, though these were for the time being protected by the presence of the Army in Burma.

On the day that Rangoon was abandoned, Wavell sent the Chiefs of Staff his forecast of the future course of the war in South-East Asia. He thought that the Japanese would concentrate firstly on establishing submarine and air bases in Rangoon, the Andaman Islands and northern Sumatra, and secondly on the capture of central and northern Burma in order to cut the communications between India and China, and to establish air bases for use against India. He believed that they would make these their objectives rather than either Ceylon or Australia. Upper Burma could not be held indefinitely, and if the army had to retreat into India the Japanese would probably attack north-east India by land, sea and air. He therefore emphasized the importance of forming that area into a bastion. He gave a warning, however, that his available resources were very slender and the difficulties of communication in that area extreme. With the danger to India's north-east frontier increasing, he again asked the Chiefs of Staff two days later to reconsider their decision to place 16th Brigade in Ceylon. They sympathized with his difficulties but, in view of the weak naval and air position in Ceylon during the next critical weeks, were not prepared to change their decision; once the Indian Ocean and Ceylon had been strengthened, they said, the brigade might then go on to India. On the 11th Wavell again stressed the need to concentrate the available forces to strengthen north-east India. Since its defence was primarily an air problem, a powerful well-balanced air force was needed both to check aggression and to provide a means of hitting back at the Japanese.

On the 13th the Chiefs of Staff told Wavell that they agreed with his conception of forming a bastion in north-east India, but the security of India depended, in the last resort, on the ability to control sea communications in the Indian Ocean. Secure naval bases were needed for this, and Colombo and Trincomalee were the only ones. For these reasons, the defence requirements of Ceylon must be given priority over those of north-east India. Wavell dissented. He said that in his view any Japanese attack on India would be made from Burma along the Burmese coast under cover of shore-based aircraft, and Ceylon, although it would be threatened and raided, would not be attacked in force. He thought the Chiefs of Staff were allotting an undue proportion of the slender land and air resources to Ceylon, to the detriment of the defence of north-east India. He recommended that the defences of Ceylon should be sufficient only to prevent surprise air raids of the type made on Pearl Harbour and Darwin and to repel hit-and-run landing parties. The main strength of the British air forces should, he contended, be concentrated on the task of securing air superiority in north-east India, and as large land forces as possible should be assembled for the defence of that area where India's main war industries were situated. He therefore again asked for the release of 16th Brigade from Ceylon, the provision of a torpedo-bomber squadron to increase the offensive power of the air forces in Ceylon and the concentration, as a matter of urgency, of the largest possible air force (British and American) in north-east India.

The Chiefs of Staff replied that by the end of March the Eastern Fleet, under the command of Admiral Sir James Somerville, would consist of five battleships, two aircraft carriers and fourteen destroyers concentrated in the Ceylon area, with eleven cruisers in the Indian Ocean. The function of this fleet would be to maintain control of sea communications in the Indian Ocean on which both the Middle East and India depended. It was to act as 'a fleet in being', avoiding unnecessary attrition and the risk of crippling losses. They accepted the fact that the Japanese might move along the Burmese coast towards India and make a raid of the Pearl Harbour type on Ceylon. Their policy of retaining strong fighter forces in Ceylon, even at the expense of north-east India (though they accepted the urgent need for a strong air force in that area), was necessary to prevent loss to the fleet from such a raid. The strong land forces which were being assembled in Ceylon were intended as a deterrent to any attempt on the part of the Japanese to land there until the air forces in the island and naval forces in the Indian Ocean had been built up. They reminded Wavell that the two Australian brigades were only a temporary garrison, for Australia required their return at an early date.

Meanwhile radical changes had taken place in Ceylon. On the 5th March Vice-Admiral Sir Geoffrey Layton, who had transferred his flag as Commander-in-Chief, Eastern Fleet, to Colombo after the formation of ABDA Command, was appointed Commander-in-Chief, Ceylon. The Governor (Sir Andrew Caldecot) and the civil administration, and all naval, military, air and civil authorities in the area, which included the Maldive Islands, were made subject to his direction. On military matters the Commander-in-Chief in India was to be his immediate superior and on civil matters the Secretary of State for the Colonies. The Government was to continue to exercise its normal functions but only so long as it could do so effectively.[1] If in the opinion of the Commander-in-Chief the situation required it, he was authorized to assume himself all the functions of the Government and to substitute military for civil courts of law.

The appointment was unique. It was made at the suggestion of the Prime Minister, who was determined that there should be no repetition of the failures which had occurred at Singapore owing to divided control. Admiral Layton was equally determined. He had been profoundly shocked by the general state of lethargy and ineffectiveness in every aspect of defence which he had found on his arrival in the island. Go-slow strikes in the busy port of Colombo were of frequent occurrence, with the consequence that sometimes as many as fifty valuable ships were lying in the exposed outer anchorage waiting to discharge their cargoes; the A.R.P. organization in the island was woefully inefficient; there was no radar warning system, the fire-fighting arrangements were rudimentary and there were no gas masks.

Admiral Layton had done what he could in the six weeks since his arrival, but his hands had been tied by lack of authority. He now had

---

[1] For the directive to Admiral Layton see Appendix 7.

almost dictatorial powers and the full backing of the Government of the United Kingdom and the Chiefs of Staff. 'Do not ask permission to do things. Do them and report afterwards what you have done', he was told by the First Sea Lord. He wasted no time. He re-formed the existing War Council so as to include himself and the commanders of the three fighting Services, as well as the Governor and his Ministers. To these he later added the Civil Defence Commissioner, when that official took over responsibility for the control of food supplies as well as A.R.P. duties. Apart from these changes he used the existing machinery of government, reinforced by the emergency powers of the Governor, to carry out the reforms he thought necessary to bring the island into a proper state of defence. Much naturally depended on the close and cordial co-operation of Sir Andrew Caldecot, and this he received in full measure.

As regards the Services, Admiral Layton had the able assistance of Lieut.-General Sir Henry Pownall, appointed Force Commander on the 7th March, and Air Vice-Marshal J. H. D'Albiac, who became Air Officer Commanding, Ceylon, four days later. For administrative purposes both these officers were under India Command. This had the advantage that the Commander-in-Chief did not need the large extra staff which would have been required had he been made responsible for the administration of all three Services. Nevertheless it created the anomaly that, although everything and everybody in the island had been made fully subject to his direction, the fighting Services under his jurisdiction also owed allegiance elsewhere.

The Admiral's personality and tireless energy soon made themselves felt. The working of the port was reorganized and a very marked improvement in the scale and speed of the handling of cargoes resulted. The arrangements for the import of food and essential commodities were revised. Efforts were made to increase the export of rubber, of which Ceylon was now almost the sole remaining source for the Allies. Civil Defence was reorganized and an improvised air raid warning system was installed at Colombo. Before the end of the month, an airstrip on the racecourse was completed, and was to prove its value in a matter of days.

Meanwhile reinforcements were arriving fast. The 34th Indian Division (less one brigade) was already there; 16th British Infantry Brigade disembarked on the 14th March, 21st East African Brigade on the 21st and 16th and 17th Australian Brigades on the 23rd. Thus by the end of the month the garrison was equivalent to two divisions. With the arrival of reinforcing aircraft from the Middle East and India during the month, there were in Ceylon four fighter squadrons, one bomber squadron and detachments of two Catalina flying-boat squadrons.[1] In addition there were three Fleet Air Arm squadrons

---
[1] For order of battle of the air forces in Ceylon see Appendix 8.

ashore at Trincomalee. Although this combined force was strong in defence, it had no real striking power against a Japanese expedition approaching the island.

In India Wavell, whose intention was to fight for Assam and eastern Bengal as far forward as possible, had decided by the middle of March to move 1st Indian Infantry Brigade (the reserve for the North West Frontier) to Imphal to protect the new Manipur Road base depot at Dimapur; 14th Indian Division (less one brigade) to Comilla in eastern Bengal to defend the line of the Feni river and the coast from its mouth to Chandpur; 109th Indian Infantry Brigade (less one battalion) to Akyab, which was required by the Navy for the use of light naval forces and by the air force for the defence of Burma; and to concentrate Headquarters IV Corps, 70th British Division (less one brigade)[1] and 23rd Indian Division, at Ranchi, as a mobile reserve.[2] When informing the Chiefs of Staff on the 19th of these dispositions he reiterated that, to compensate for weakness on the ground, he required in north-east India a strong air force and he gave as a minimum a figure of thirty-six squadrons.

By the 26th March, with the enemy in control of Rangoon and most of southern Burma and in enjoyment of air superiority on the Arakan coastline, Wavell appreciated that the garrison of Akyab might be isolated and lost. The 109th Brigade was therefore withdrawn to Calcutta, where it came under command of 26th Indian Division, leaving the original garrison (14/7th Rajput) with some anti-aircraft guns to defend the island.

On the 27th Wavell sent the Chiefs of Staff an estimate of his air requirements. He pointed out that he had to provide for the air defence of Calcutta and the industrial areas of Bengal, for the defence of eastern Bengal and southern India against seaborne attack, for the defence of Ceylon, for air support of the troops operating in Burma and/or India's eastern frontiers, and in addition for a striking force with which to hit back at the enemy. For this he estimated that he would need a total of sixty-four squadrons, a figure which the Chiefs of Staff later amended to sixty-six squadrons.[3] All he had on that date was one general reconnaissance and three fighter squadrons in north-east India and seven squadrons in Ceylon.

The Chiefs of Staff had already started a flow of reinforcing aircraft to India. Since all tropicalized aircraft available had been allotted to the Middle East or were on their way there, this command

---

[1] Headquarters IV Corps and 70th Division reached Bombay on the 10th March.

[2] See Map 14.

[3] The 66 squadrons were made up as follows: 18 fighter, 4 fighter/reconnaissance, 4 bomber/reconnaissance, 11 light bomber, 4 medium bomber, 2 heavy bomber, 7 general reconnaissance (land), 4 general reconnaissance (flying-boats), 4 bomber transport, 6 torpedo-bomber, 1 transport and 1 photographic reconnaissance unit—a total of approximately 1,060 aircraft exclusive of reserves.

was the only immediate source of supply. By the end of March fifty-seven crated Hurricanes had been delivered to Karachi, and forty Hurricanes, forty Blenheims and ten Wellington medium bombers (which had been offered by Middle East Command) were on their way to India. The Chiefs of Staff estimated that the operational strength in India and Ceylon would reach 182 aircraft by the middle of April and 268 by the end of the month.

No matter how quickly aircraft could be sent to meet Wavell's requirements, the air force in India could not expand faster than an organization could be built up to control and administer it. The expansion involved the provision of essential maintenance facilities, and the construction of airfields for the reinforcing squadrons. But in March 1942 Air Headquarters, India, was still on its pre-war establishment of some thirty officers and was quite unable to deal with the many complicated problems which arose with bewildering rapidity. It had to control air operations in Burma, the air defence of India's long coastline and of Ceylon and the policing of the North West Frontier, in addition to dealing with the vast administrative problems involved in the expansion.

On the 2nd March Air Marshal Sir Richard Peirse arrived in Delhi from Java to assume command of the air forces in India and Ceylon, and at once began to reorganize the air command. There were only two group headquarters in India and Ceylon at that time: 1 (Indian) Group at Peshawar to control air operations on the North West Frontier, and 222 Group at Colombo responsible for air force units in Ceylon and the flying-boat bases in the Indian Ocean. A nucleus group existed at Lahore to supervise training. These were increased and adjusted as under:

> 221 Group (from Rangoon) at Calcutta, responsible for bombing and reconnaissance on the Burma front and over the Bay of Bengal.
>
> 222 Group in Ceylon, responsible for the defence of the island.
>
> 223 Group (from 1 Indian Group) at Peshawar, responsible for the North West Frontier.
>
> 224 Group at Calcutta, to control fighter operations in Bengal and Assam.
>
> 225 Group at Bangalore, responsible for the defence of southern India and the whole coastline from Bengal round to Karachi—probably the largest land area covered by any group in the world.
>
> 226 (Maintenance) Group at Karachi, the principal port and air terminal through which reinforcing aircraft for India Command were to flow.
>
> 227 (Training) Group at Lahore, responsible for all training in India.

Early in this period of reorganization it became evident that the control of operational groups in north-east India from Air Headquarters in Delhi, 850 miles from Calcutta (a distance similar to that from London to Warsaw), would be practically impossible, particularly as the telegraph and telephone communications would be inadequate to carry increased traffic in the event of sustained operations. A new headquarters known as Bengal Command was therefore established at Barrackpore (Calcutta) which not only served as an advanced headquarters of the Air Officer Commanding-in-Chief, but was in direct control of 221 and 224 Groups. At the same time it was realized that arrangements would have to be made for aircraft to be transferred quickly from north-east India to Ceylon and vice versa, a distance of some 1,500 miles. These involved the selection and construction of airfields with adequate facilities, the provision of operations rooms for the control of any aircraft using the route and the completion of an extensive and intricate system of communications.

The next problem which Air Headquarters had to solve was that of maintaining the expanding force in India at the end of long lines of communications stretching for thousands of miles from Britain and America. The small maintenance organization which existed in March 1942 at Karachi, and combined the functions of a depot for aircraft erection, engine repairs and the supply of equipment, was quite inadequate for the task. In 1942 the standard of technical development and engineering ability in India was relatively low, and there were comparatively few semi-skilled and fewer skilled industrial technicians on whom to draw when building up a large maintenance organization. Base repair units had to be located where industrial facilities existed, and the fact that these were at great distances from the squadrons they served had to be accepted. A main supply unit for aircraft was established at Allahabad. Base repair facilities were created at first in existing R.A.F. workshops at Lahore and Ambala, and later in railway workshops taken over for the purpose near Calcutta, Cawnpore and Trichinopoly. The Hindustan Aircraft Company's factory at Bangalore was set aside for the repair of flying-boats.[1]

Finally there was the colossal problem of constructing new airfields for the expanding air force. In March 1942 there were only sixteen airfields in India and Ceylon with all-weather runways, none of which was completed to the standards recognized at that time. In order to deploy sixty-six squadrons it was found necessary to construct 215 airfields in all. These included forward operational airfields, complete to the full scale of two runways and accommoda-

---

[1] See Volume I, pages 40–41.

tion for two squadrons; rear airfields for two squadrons, but with reduced accommodation; and others throughout India to provide for internal movement of aircraft as well as for training, maintenance and storage. The construction of these at an estimated cost of some £50,000,000 constituted so great an engineering project that it would not only affect the expansion of the army installations and the line of communications to the north-eastern frontier, but would have serious repercussions on India's internal economy. The problem of how the work could be carried out without disrupting the civil economy and the defence requirements of India taken as a whole was discussed by General Headquarters, Air Headquarters and the Government of India. While these discussions were taking place, reconnaissance, planning and preliminary engineer and administrative arrangements were put in hand. In the search for suitable sites the Governors of Provinces and the Rulers of Indian States gave valuable assistance. Nevertheless, the completion of these preliminaries was a matter of great difficulty, owing to the shortage of skilled engineers. There were, too, no road or rail communications to some of the areas where for tactical reasons airfields were required, nor were there telephone and telegraphic services. Moreover there was often insufficient time to study adequately the conflicting demands of the geological and strategic aspects of the sites inspected.

Meanwhile the nucleus of an American air force had begun to assemble in India. The 10th U.S.A.A.F., formed in America on the 12th February, was assigned to the China–Burma–India theatre. On the 5th March, Major-General L. H. Brereton, U.S.A.A.F., who had been Deputy Air Commander, ABDA Command, assumed command of all American air forces in India and established his headquarters at New Delhi. The organization which he took over existed largely on paper: he had eight heavy bombers (six of which had flown from Java), ten fighters from Australia and a handful of men to form the nucleus of the new air force. Aircraft reinforcements began to arrive in April from America, but losses and delays on the long journey were heavy; supply and base depots, barracks and lines of communication had to be built up, and for months the American air formation laboured under the drawbacks of shortage of equipment and inadequate facilities. Despite this it played an important part in the battle for Burma.

The main function of the 10th U.S.A.A.F. was to keep open an air supply route from India to China so that the Chinese forces could be kept in the field, and American lease-lend commitments to China met. With the loss of Rangoon, the India–Burma–China air route became the only link with China and therefore assumed considerable importance. On the 21st March, the Assam–Burma–China Ferry Command was formed. Dinjan, the one suitable airfield in Assam, was chosen as the Indian terminus of the route; from there it was planned to fly supplies to Myitkyina and take them on into China by road and river. At the same time a possible direct air route over the mountains between Assam and China was surveyed for use in emergency. Because of the complexity and inadequacy of the Indian transport system, an air lift was also planned to connect Karachi, the American port of entry, to Dinjan. Nevertheless much equipment still had to be sent by road and rail across India. In order to begin the air lift on these routes thirty-five transport aircraft were sent from American commercial air lines and the first of these began to arrive in April.[1]

The build-up of India as a base for large Allied land and air forces, the preliminary steps towards which have been described in this chapter, was to continue until the end of the war, and will be referred to from time to time in the course of this and subsequent volumes. The basic plan as described was developed in February and March 1942 as soon as the danger was realized. Meanwhile those responsible for the defence of India and Ceylon, well aware of the weakness of the forces at their disposal, had done their utmost to hasten their expansion and training, and had disposed them as they thought best to counter the enemy's next move.

---

[1] Craven and Cate, *The Army Air Forces in World War II: Volume I, Plans and Early Operations* (Chicago, 1948) Chapter XIV.

CHAPTER VII

JAPANESE NAVAL RAIDS ON CEYLON

(April 1942)

See Maps 4, 5 and 6

THE surrender of Java on the 8th and the occupation of north Sumatra on the 12th March 1942 completed the conquest of the whole of the rich southern area for which Japan had gone to war. It brought to an end the first of the three periods into which her basic war plan was divided.[1] The period of consolidation by the creation of a defensive ring round her conquests had already begun. In the west, the advance into Burma by which China was to be isolated was progressing well. Rangoon had been occupied on the 8th March, which made it possible for the Japanese *15th Army* in Burma to be supplied and reinforced by sea instead of by the long and difficult route through Siam and Tenasserim. But while the Eastern Fleet was based on Ceylon any Japanese convoy entering the Bay of Bengal would be exposed to grave danger. Vice-Admiral Kondo (Commander-in-Chief, *2nd Fleet*) was therefore ordered on the 9th to prepare plans for raids on the two naval bases in the island. At the same time he was to attack shipping in the Bay of Bengal. These attacks had a dual purpose, firstly, to ensure the safe passage of the convoys to Rangoon and secondly, to impress the people of India with Japanese might and foment trouble in India at a time when Anglo-Indian political relations were particularly delicate. The Lord Privy Seal, Sir Stafford Cripps, had recently arrived on a special mission to discuss with the Indian party leaders the question of the future status of their country. No agreement had been arrived at and matters were reaching a deadlock.[2]

Vice-Admiral Nagumo's *First Air Fleet*, which had attacked Pearl Harbour, was chosen for the attacks on Ceylon. As before, a Sunday (the 5th April) was chosen as the provisional date for the first strike, in the hope of finding the fleet in harbour either at Colombo or Trincomalee. If the fleet were found to be divided between the two, first one port and then the other would be attacked. If it were at

---
[1] See Volume I, Chapters V and XXVI.
[2] The Cripps proposals were rejected on the 10th April.

neither, Nagumo's orders were to concentrate on the airfields, dockyards and shipping in the harbours. The *Malaya Force* under Vice-Admiral Ozawa was to make raids on shipping in the Bay of Bengal, but was not to cross the meridian of 85° east until the carriers had made their first attack.

Vice-Admiral Nagumo's striking force of five fleet carriers left Celebes on the 28th and entered the Indian Ocean between Timor and the eastern end of the chain of Dutch islands.[1] The carriers were supported by the *3rd Battle Squadron* (four battleships) and the *8th Cruiser Squadron* (two heavy cruisers) and screened by the light cruiser *Abukuma* and eleven destroyers. Oilers and supply ships were sailed to meet the force at a rendezvous south of Java, and seven submarines already on patrol in the Bay of Bengal were ordered to co-operate with the force.

Admiral Ozawa's *Malaya Force*, consisting of the cruiser *Chokai* and the *7th Cruiser Squadron* (four heavy cruisers) with the light fleet carrier *Ryujo*, the light cruiser *Yura* and the *3rd Destroyer Flotilla* (the light cruiser *Sendai* with eleven destroyers), which had been cruising to the south of the Andamans in support of the invasion of these islands, left Mergui on the 1st April for the attack on shipping.

Admiral Sir James Somerville, Commander-in-Chief, Eastern Fleet, arrived at Colombo on the 24th March and on the 27th relieved Admiral Layton who had temporarily assumed command in December 1941 when the *Prince of Wales* and the *Repulse* had been sunk.[2] The fleet had been gradually assembling in the Indian Ocean as ships became available; it consisted at this time of the battleship *Warspite*, which had just arrived from America by way of Australia after completing repairs to damage sustained in the battle of Crete, the four old 'R' Class battleships (3rd Battle Squadron), the fleet carriers *Indomitable* (flying the flag of Rear-Admiral D. W. Boyd) and *Formidable*, the light fleet carrier *Hermes*, seven cruisers, sixteen destroyers and three submarines. On paper this was a formidable fleet but the 'R' Class battleships were old, slow and of short endurance, four of the cruisers had been laid down in the First World War and most of the destroyers were badly in need of refit. The ships had been gathered from all over the world and had had no opportunity to work and train together as a fleet.

Within forty-eight hours of assuming command, Admiral Somerville received a report that a Japanese force of two or more carriers, several cruisers and a large number of destroyers, possibly supported by battleships of the *Kongo* class, might make an attack on Ceylon about the 1st April. His fleet at that time was scattered. The 3rd Battle Squadron with the carrier *Indomitable* and eight destroyers was

---
[1] See Map 15.
[2] See Volume I, pages 193–99.

at Addu Atoll where the ships had been exercising under Vice-Admiral A. V. Willis, the Second-in-Command.[1] The remaining ships were divided between Colombo and Trincomalee. The Admiral appreciated that the enemy probably intended to make simultaneous air attacks on Colombo and Trincomalee, which he thought would be timed for just before dawn so that the aircraft could land on their carriers in daylight. He expected that the approach would be made from the south-east. He decided therefore to concentrate his fleet on the evening of the 31st March in a position from which he could launch an air attack on the enemy force during the night. Catalina patrols were arranged to a distance of 420 miles from Colombo between the bearings of 110° and 154°, but as there were only six of these aircraft available not more than three could be on patrol at the same time.

The ships at the three ports sailed so as to rendezvous at a selected position at 4 p.m. on the 31st March, the *Warspite* calling at Colombo to embark the Commander-in-Chief and his staff. The Admiral formed his fleet into two forces: Force 'A', a fast division consisting of the *Warspite*, the two fleet carriers, the four larger cruisers and six destroyers, which he kept under his immediate command; and Force 'B', a supporting force consisting of the four 'R' Class battleships, the *Hermes*, the two smaller cruisers and the Dutch cruiser *Heemskerk* and eight destroyers, under command of Admiral Willis. On the 1st April the *Dorsetshire* (Captain A. W. S. Agar, V.C.), which had stopped her refit at Colombo to take part in the operation, joined Force 'A'.[2]

For three days and two nights Admiral Somerville manoeuvred his fleet to the south of Ceylon so as to keep clear of the enemy's probable search area during daylight and to be at a convenient distance at night from the enemy's probable flying-off position. By dusk on the 2nd April there was nothing further to indicate that an attack on Ceylon was likely to take place in the near future, and the Admiral judged that his information regarding the Japanese timing was at fault, or that the enemy might be aware of the presence of his fleet and waiting until it returned to harbour. The possibility of his being detected by Japanese submarines was increasing, and the ships of the 3rd Battle Squadron were running short of water. For these reasons he decided at 9 p.m. to abandon the operation and shaped course for Addu Atoll. During the morning of the 3rd he detached the *Dorsetshire* and *Cornwall* (Captain P. C. W. Manwaring) to Colombo, the former to carry on with her interrupted refit and the latter to escort a convoy. The *Hermes* (Captain R. F. J. Onslow) and *Vampire* (Commander W. T. A. Moran, R.A.N.) were sent to

---
[1] See Map 5.
[2] See Appendix 9.

Trincomalee to prepare for operation 'Ironclad' in which they were to take part.[1]

Force 'A' arrived at Addu Atoll at noon on the 4th followed by Force 'B' at 3 p.m. An hour later a Catalina reported large enemy forces steering to the north-west about 360 miles on a bearing of 155° from Dondra Head. Before it could report their strength the Catalina was shot down. It was clear now that the original information as to the Japanese intentions had been correct, except in the matter of timing, and that Ceylon would be heavily attacked the next day. When the report was received, Force 'A' had only half completed fuelling and Force 'B' had not yet begun. The former, except for the cruisers *Emerald* and *Enterprise* which could not be ready until about midnight, had sufficient fuel to sail at once, but the latter could not leave before 7 a.m. on the 5th at the earliest.

In deciding what to do Admiral Somerville was guided by three considerations. Firstly, the Admiralty policy of keeping the fleet 'in being' was paramount, for the whole defence of the Indian Ocean and its vital lines of communication depended on the existence of the Eastern Fleet. Secondly, to operate the carriers escorted by the *Warspite* within range of enemy battleships and beyond supporting distance of the 3rd Battle Squadron was an unjustifiable risk; his only hope of dealing the enemy an effective blow was therefore by means of his carrier-borne striking force, preferably at night. Lastly, no matter what he did he could not intercept the enemy if they attacked on the 5th; shore-based aircraft from Ceylon might however cripple some of the enemy ships, which could be attacked later, or something might occur to postpone the Japanese raid for twenty-four hours. He decided therefore to wait until the *Emerald* and *Enterprise* were ready and then to sail with Force 'A' for a position 250 miles south of Ceylon, leaving Admiral Willis to follow him with Force 'B' as early as possible the next morning.

The force reported by the Catalina was Admiral Nagumo's striking force. He had met his oilers south of Java and the whole force had fuelled on the way north. At about dawn on the 5th April, when some three hundred miles south of Colombo, fifty-three bombers and thirty-eight dive-bombers escorted by thirty-six fighters took off to attack the port.

The news of the approach of the Japanese force left Admiral Layton at Colombo in no doubt that the port would be heavily attacked the next day. The position given by the Catalina at 4 p.m. on the 4th was 600 miles from Addu Atoll and he realized that there was no possibility of intervention by the Eastern Fleet. He expected the attack to be made in moonlight, and gave orders that all defences

---

[1] See page 58.

6. (*Above*) Admiral Sir Geoffrey Layton.

7. Admiral Sir James Somerville.

8. H.M.S. *Hermes*.

9. H.M.S. *Cornwall*.

were to be at instant readiness from 3 a.m. on the 5th. The Commander-in-Chief, East Indies (Vice-Admiral G. F. Arbuthnot), had already taken steps to reduce the number of ships in the port after the first warning on the 28th. He now cleared the harbour of all ships that could put to sea. He sailed the *Dorsetshire* and *Cornwall* for Addu Atoll at 10 p.m. and ordered the *Hermes* and *Vampire* to leave Trincomalee and steam north-east as soon as they had finished fuelling.

Throughout the night various reports of battleships and cruisers were received from Catalinas on reconnaissance, but no report was received of the aircraft carriers which may have been to the south of their covering force. The expected attack came just before 8 a.m. on Easter Sunday the 5th April. Thunder clouds hung over the harbour and intermittent showers of heavy rain were falling, accompanied by strong gusts of wind. The approaching aircraft were picked up by the incomplete radar system at Colombo, but owing to an error no warning was received until 7.40 a.m. when large formations of aircraft were seen approaching from the south-west. The raiders passed over Ratmalana airfield at about 7,000 feet and then turned and dived on the harbour, bombing and machine-gunning shipping in and outside the breakwater. Other formations attacked the airfield and railway workshops, coming down as low as fifty feet and using their machine-guns. These were followed by high-level bombing attacks on the harbour, but, owing to the timely dispersal of shipping, losses were light. A destroyer (the *Tenedos*), which was refitting, and an armed merchant cruiser were sunk and the submarine depot ship *Lucia* holed by a bomb which penetrated her decks and burst just below the waterline. One merchant ship was hit but the fire caused was quickly extinguished. Severe damage was done to the workshops and quays in the harbour, but damage at the airfield was slight.

Despite the short warning, pilots of fighter aircraft were already in their cockpits when the enemy arrived and forty-two fighters (twenty-two Hurricanes of 30 Squadron, six Fleet Air Arm Fulmars of 803 and 806 Squadrons from Ratmalana and fourteen Hurricanes of 258 Squadron from the racecourse) took off. The Hurricanes of 30 Squadron and the Fulmars were at once engaged by Japanese fighters. Presumably because the Japanese did not know of the newly-constructed airstrip on the racecourse, aircraft of 258 Squadron took off unmolested but, when they attacked the Japanese bombers over the harbour, were in their turn heavily attacked by fighters acting as top cover. By 8.35 a.m. all enemy aircraft had disappeared. Half an hour later a striking force of fourteen Blenheims took off to attack the Japanese Fleet, but was unable to find it.

British losses were two Catalinas, fifteen Hurricanes (five of whose pilots were saved) and four Fulmars. In addition to these, six Swordfish of 788 Squadron, which were on their way from Trincomalee to Ratmalana armed with torpedoes, ran into the enemy fighters over the harbour and were all shot down. The enemy losses are, as always, hard to assess. The Hurricanes and Fulmars of the R.A.F. and Fleet Air Arm claimed nineteen certains and several probables, and the anti-aircraft guns five, of the enemy. The Japanese, on the other hand, admit to the loss of only seven aircraft and claim to have shot down forty-one British aircraft.

Loss of life in Colombo was small, for as it was Easter Sunday offices and shops were shut, streets empty, and the thousands of clerkly 'commuters' absent. Nevertheless after the raid large numbers of the population left the town for the hill country, and some even for India, causing a serious shortage of labour.

Admiral Somerville had left Addu Atoll with Force 'A' at 12.15 a.m. on the day of the raid and had set course and speed so as to reach a position 250 miles south of Ceylon at dawn on the 6th April, ordering the *Dorsetshire* and *Cornwall* to join him in latitude 0° 58' north longitude 77° 36' east at 4 p.m. on the 5th. The two cruisers were already at sea when they received the Commander-in-Chief's signal, and at about 7 a.m. altered course for the rendezvous. About an hour later a report of strong enemy forces sighted at 6.48 a.m. about 150 miles to the eastward was received in the *Dorsetshire*, and Captain Agar increased speed to $27\frac{1}{2}$ knots (the *Cornwall's* maximum) in order to join Force 'A' as soon as possible.

Sky conditions were unlike those over Colombo; there was little or no cloud and visibility was extreme. The sea was calm. At about 11 a.m. the cruisers sighted a single aircraft on the horizon, which disappeared before it could be identified. At 1 p.m. two more aircraft, one of which was judged to be hostile, were sighted and a shadowing report was made. Aircraft from the Japanese cruiser *Tone* were on patrol and at some time during the morning sighted and reported the two cruisers on a southerly course. In little over an hour from the time of sighting, fifty-three bombers from the carrier force took off to attack.

At about 1.40 p.m. the *Dorsetshire* opened fire on aircraft which were sighted overhead. Almost immediately both ships were attacked by waves of formations of three aircraft which came in down sun and from right ahead—the cruisers' blind spot—dropping their bombs from about 1,000 feet. In the first attack the *Dorsetshire* received three direct hits which put half of her anti-aircraft armament out of action, wrecked both wireless offices and disabled the steering gear. Unable to manoeuvre, the ship was hit by at least six more bombs and soon took on a heavy list. When she was slowly turning over on her beam ends, Captain Agar gave the order to abandon ship. About eight minutes after the first bomb had dropped the ship capsized and sank, stern first.

Meanwhile the *Cornwall* though still afloat had fared little better. Bombs fell almost continuously round her, some scoring direct hits, but the majority were very near misses which lifted the ship bodily and caused heavy underwater damage. Shortly before 2 p.m. Captain Manwaring gave the order to abandon ship. Four minutes later the *Cornwall* heeled over and went down by the bows.

A surprisingly large number of officers and men survived these devastating attacks. In five of the ships' boats which, although leaking badly, remained afloat, on rafts and clinging to wreckage, they drifted that evening and throughout the night in shark-infested waters, and during most of the following day under a burning tropical sun; 1,122 officers and men out of a total of 1,546 survived this terrible ordeal. In the late afternoon of the 6th they were picked up by the *Enterprise* and two destroyers which had been sent to their rescue.

When the *Dorsetshire* and *Cornwall* sank, Force 'A' was about eighty-four miles to the south-south-west making for the rendezvous at eighteen knots. Reports from Colombo of the enemy's movements had come in during the night. From daylight on the 5th, four Fulmars from the *Indomitable* searched to a depth of 215 miles to the eastward but reported nothing except one enemy seaplane. Between 7 a.m. and 11 a.m. reports received from Colombo indicated that the enemy battleships were 'marking time' about 120 miles south of Dondra Head while the carriers recovered their aircraft after the raid. At about 1.30 p.m. the signal from the *Dorsetshire* that she was being shadowed was relayed from Colombo, and just before 4 p.m. a reconnaissance aircraft from Force 'A' reported wreckage near the position in which the *Dorsetshire* and *Cornwall* should have been at the time the report was made. A destroyer was sent to investigate, but was recalled an hour later when an aircraft reported five unknown ships only thirty miles from the wreckage. Later reports of the position of the ships varied, but the final assessment received at 6.17 p.m. from Admiral Boyd placed a force of two aircraft carriers and three other vessels about 140 miles to the north of Force 'A' steering north-west.

Admiral Somerville, who had altered the course of the fleet to the southward on the first report, now altered to the north-west to keep within striking distance of the enemy during the night. Air searches to the northward were carried out throughout the hours of darkness but nothing further was seen of the enemy. At daylight on the 6th, Force 'B' joined Force 'A' and, as soon as the fleet was formed up, course was altered to the eastward. From earlier reports of the enemy's movements, Somerville thought it possible that the Japanese

Fleet might be in the vicinity of Addu Atoll, intending either to attack it by air or to await the return of the Eastern Fleet. Acting on this assumption, and adhering to his policy of keeping clear of superior forces by day and attacking them by air at night, he manoeuvred his fleet so as to be in a position from which to intercept the enemy fleet as it came back from the Addu Atoll area. At 11.15 a.m. he altered course to the south-east towards the wreckage reported the previous day, and at 1 p.m. sent the *Enterprise* and two destroyers on ahead to search for survivors.

About an hour later he received a signal from the Commander-in-Chief, Ceylon, giving his belief that a strong Japanese fleet was still between Addu Atoll and Colombo. He decided accordingly to keep clear of the Addu Atoll area until after daylight on the 7th. He continued to the south-east until just before sunset and at 6 p.m., his aircraft having found no trace of any enemy, reversed the course of the fleet and retired to the north-west. At 2 a.m. he altered course to the westward. Shortly afterwards an aircraft reported two submarines to the southward of the fleet and, suspecting that these might be part of a patrol line to the east of Addu Atoll, he decided to make an unexpected approach to the anchorage from the westward. Course was altered accordingly at 7 a.m. on the 7th to return by way of the Veimandu Channel. After aircraft had made a careful search of the area, the fleet entered Addu Atoll at 11 a.m. on the 8th.

As a result of the raid on Colombo, the Admiralty had suggested to Admiral Somerville that he might be finding the presence of the 'R' Class battleships more of a liability than an asset, and had given him full discretion to withdraw them to the east coast of Africa. The experience of the past few days had left the Admiral in no doubt that the time had come to do so. The enemy had complete control of the Bay of Bengal and could obtain local command of the waters south and south-west of Ceylon at will. The British naval and land-based aircraft in the island were quite inadequate to offer sustained resistance. The battle fleet was slow, outgunned and of short endurance, and its carrier-borne air protection of small use against air attacks of the scale used against the *Dorsetshire* and *Cornwall*. There was little security against air or surface attacks at either of the Ceylon naval bases and none at all at Addu Atoll. After discussing the situation with his Flag and Commanding Officers, he informed the Admiralty that for these reasons he intended to send Force 'B' to Kilindini where it could protect the reinforcement route to the Middle East and the Persian Gulf and do some collective training.[1] Force 'A' would remain in Indian waters in order to deter the Japanese from using light forces to attack shipping in the Indian Ocean but for the immediate future would avoid Ceylon.

---
[1] See Map 6.

Vice-Admiral Willis with Force 'B' sailed for Kilindini at 2 a.m. on the 9th April. Four hours later the Commander-in-Chief with Force 'A' sailed for Bombay. As the *Warspite* and the aircraft carriers left Addu Atoll, 91 bombers escorted by 38 fighters took off from the Japanese carriers to attack Trincomalee.

Admiral Nagumo had sighted British reconnaissance aircraft during the afternoon of the 5th and, suspecting the presence of an aircraft carrier, had turned his force to the south-east and from the 6th to the 8th kept outside a 500-mile circle from Dondra Head. On the morning of the 8th he altered course to his flying-off position east of Trincomalee, which he reached at daylight on the 9th.

The first warning of the impending attack was received on the afternoon of the 8th, when a Catalina patrol reported three battleships and a carrier about 470 miles south-east of Trincomalee steering a north-westerly course. The Commander-in-Chief, East Indies, ordered the harbour to be cleared and all ships to sail to the southward keeping close inshore, and to be at least forty miles from the port by dawn on the 9th. Among those which left that night were the *Hermes* and *Vampire*, the tanker *British Sergeant* and the corvette *Hollyhock*, escorting the fleet auxiliary *Athelstane*.

Shortly after daylight on the 9th the enemy force was again sighted by a Catalina, whose signals stopped abruptly before it had given the position or composition of the force. Ten minutes before this, however, the radar had picked up a group of aircraft ninety miles off, approaching the harbour from the eastward. At 7.20 a.m. aircraft in large numbers were sighted coming in at a height of about 15,000 feet and five minutes later the bombs started to fall. The principal targets at Trincomalee were the dockyard, and the airfield at China Bay where considerable damage was done. Thanks to the radar warning, seventeen Hurricanes and six Fulmars—every available aircraft—were airborne when the raid started. Though hopelessly outnumbered they brought down several of the enemy, but eight Hurricanes and a Fulmar were themselves lost.

The signal from the Catalina that morning, though incomplete, enabled the position of the enemy ships to be estimated with reasonable accuracy, and at 8.40 a.m. Blenheims of 11 Squadron were sent to attack the carriers. At 10.25 a.m. they sighted the enemy force, which they reported as consisting of three battleships and four or five carriers screened by destroyers, and were hardly over it before they became involved with Zero fighters at a height of 11,000 feet. Their bombing in consequence was erratic, only three near misses being observed. On the way home they were again attacked by Japanese fighters, and of the nine Blenheims which set out only four returned, all of them damaged.

The *Hermes* and *Vampire*, which had sailed from Trincomalee at

1 a.m., were at the time of the air raid some sixty-five miles to the southward and about five miles off the coast. At 9 a.m. they turned to the northward in order to return to Trincomalee by 4 p.m. The weather was fine, the sea smooth and visibility good. About seven miles to the south-east the *Athelstane* with the *Hollyhock* ahead was in sight, while to the northward the *British Sergeant* had just altered course for Trincomalee.

Half an hour later an intercepted message in clear from a Japanese aircraft was found on translation to be a report that the *Hermes* had been sighted. She was at once ordered to proceed at full speed (24 knots) to Trincomalee, in the hope that she would have time to come under the air umbrella of the port before she was attacked. China Bay and Ratmalana airfields were told to send fighters to her assistance. Owing to a breakdown in communications these orders failed to reach the airfields, and the Hurricanes at China Bay remained in ignorance of the peril to the ships only sixty miles away from them. For the second time in a week surface craft were left to rely upon their guns alone to repel a devastating air attack, with the inevitable result.

The British ships had been reported by enemy reconnaissance aircraft at about 8 a.m. and an hour later a combined force of some ninety bombers and fighters was despatched from the Japanese carriers. At 10.35 a.m. aircraft were sighted by the *Hermes* at about 10,000 feet. Diving at an angle of about 65° they attacked the carrier, which opened fire with every gun that could be brought to bear. In the words of one of the ship's officers, 'the attack was carried out perfectly, relentlessly and quite fearlessly, and was exactly like a highly organized deck display. The aircraft peeled off in threes diving straight down on the ship out of the sun'. In the next ten minutes a rain of bombs fell on or near the ship. By 10.50 a.m. she was stopped and listing heavily to port; the flight deck was awash, but one of the foremost guns was still firing. Suddenly the heel increased and Captain Onslow gave the order to abandon ship. A few minutes later the *Hermes* turned over and sank—only twenty minutes after the bombers had been first sighted. The Japanese then turned their attention to the *Vampire* which was attacked by fifteen or twenty bombers. In ten minutes she broke in half and sank. The hospital ship *Vita* which was on passage to Colombo had witnessed the attacks and picked up 600 survivors from the two ships. Others were rescued by local craft or swam to the shore. Nineteen officers and 283 ratings from the *Hermes* and one officer and seven ratings from the *Vampire* were lost. Neither Captain Onslow nor Commander Moran survived his ship.

Simultaneously with the attack on the *Hermes* and *Vampire*, six bombers attacked the *British Sergeant*, then about twelve miles to the northward, and soon left her in a sinking condition. About an hour later the *Hollyhock* and *Athelstane* met the same fate. As the *Athelstane* sank, eight Fulmars, sent from Ratmalana to patrol over the *Hermes*, appeared on the scene and at once engaged the Japanese bombers, shooting down at least three of them but losing two of their number in doing so.

These sinkings marked the end of the attacks on Ceylon. That afternoon a Catalina reported a fleet of three carriers and nine large vessels accompanied by destroyers 170 miles east of Trincomalee sailing south. It was the last seen of the Japanese Fleet. After the attack on Trincomalee, Admiral Nagumo had steered to the southward during the day and at dusk withdrew the striking force to the eastward making for the Malacca Strait.

Nagumo had good reason to be satisfied. In the past four months his carrier aircraft had shattered the U.S. Fleet at Pearl Harbour, made strikes on Rabaul, Amboina, Timor and Darwin and played a part in the invasion of Java. In all these operations not one of his ships had been damaged. Once again he had struck and retired with his ships unscathed having sunk one aircraft carrier, two heavy cruisers, two destroyers, a corvette and half a dozen merchant ships, and for the loss of proportionately few of his own aircraft had shot down thirty-nine British aircraft.

He had been unaware of the existence of the fleet base at Addu Atoll and had hoped to find the Eastern Fleet at Trincomalee or Colombo. It was merely fortuitous that his strikes on the two ports were each made on the morning after the British Fleet had returned to Addu Atoll. His air searches never found the main body of the Eastern Fleet. Had they done so an air or even surface battle must have taken place and, with the overwhelming preponderance of Admiral Nagumo's aircraft and the greater speed, gunpower and co-ordinated training of his ships, it might have gone hard indeed with the newly assembled and untried Eastern Fleet. Despite his serious losses Admiral Somerville could count himself fortunate.

While Admiral Nagumo and Admiral Somerville had been playing cat and mouse with each other in the waters round Ceylon, Admiral Ozawa's *Malaya Force* had been taking a heavy toll of shipping in the Bay of Bengal. After leaving Mergui on the 1st April, the force had delayed for twenty-four hours in the channel between the Andamans and Nicobars in order to synchronize its attacks with Nagumo's striking force, and on the 4th steered north-west towards the Indian coast. Just before dusk on the 5th, the Admiral split his force into three detachments which diverged in the direction of the coast between Cocanada and Vizagapatam.

In conformity with the emergency measures taken at Colombo at the end of March, shipping at the east coast ports, and at Calcutta

Map 5
NAVAL OPERATIONS OFF CEYLON
April 1942

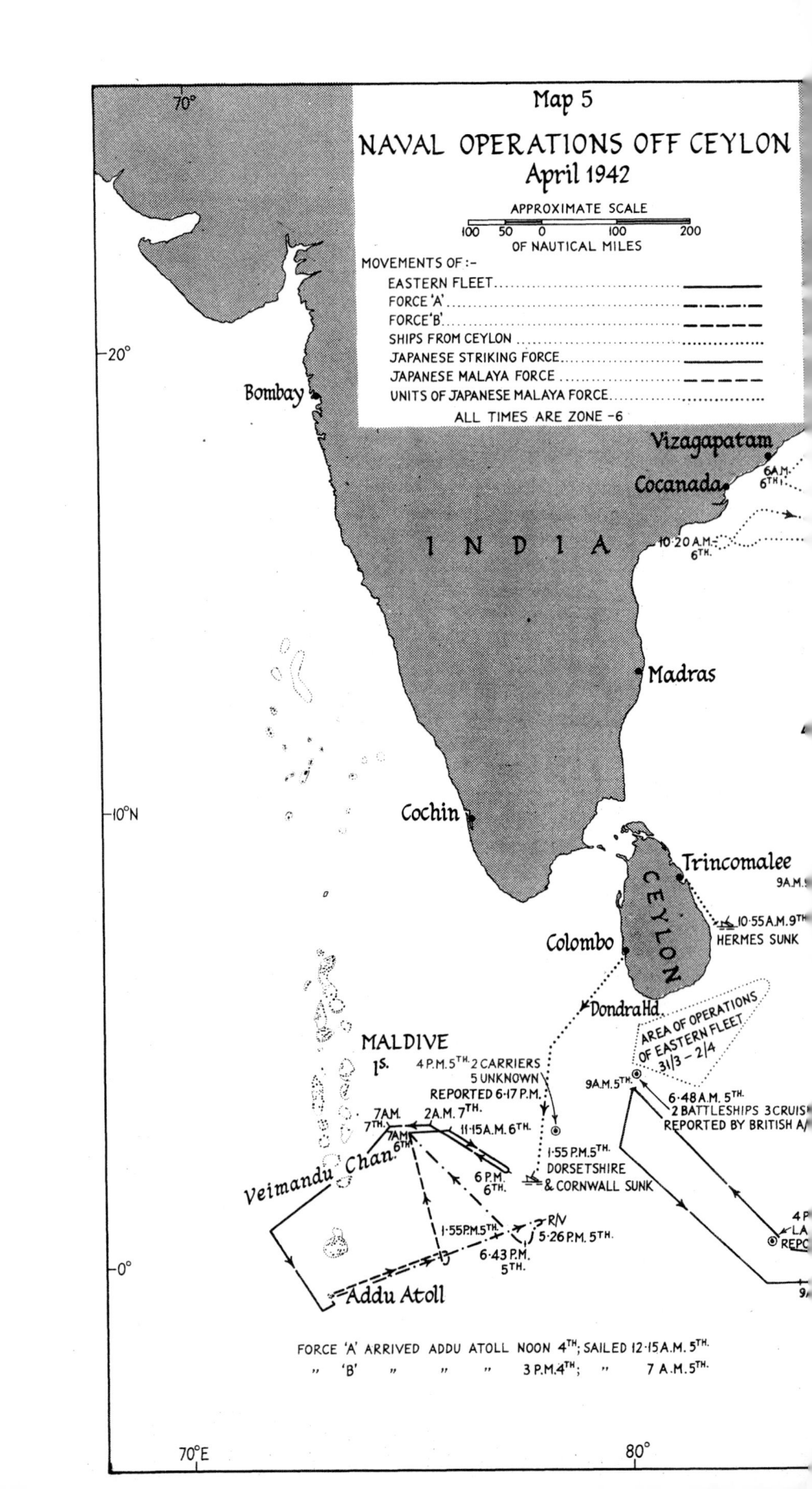

APPROXIMATE SCALE
100 50 0 100 200
OF NAUTICAL MILES

MOVEMENTS OF :-
- EASTERN FLEET .... ———
- FORCE 'A' .... —·—·—
- FORCE 'B' .... — — —
- SHIPS FROM CEYLON .... ·········
- JAPANESE STRIKING FORCE .... ———
- JAPANESE MALAYA FORCE .... — — —
- UNITS OF JAPANESE MALAYA FORCE ..... ·········

ALL TIMES ARE ZONE -6

Bombay
Vizagapatam
Cocanada
6 A.M. 6TH
10·20 A.M. 6TH
INDIA
Madras
Cochin
Trincomalee
9 A.M.
10·55 A.M. 9TH HERMES SUNK
CEYLON
Colombo
Dondra Hd.
AREA OF OPERATIONS OF EASTERN FLEET 31/3 – 2/4

MALDIVE IS.
4 P.M. 5TH 2 CARRIERS 5 UNKNOWN REPORTED 6·17 P.M.
7 A.M. 7TH
2 A.M. 7TH
7 A.M. 7TH
11·15 A.M. 6TH
9 A.M. 5TH
6·48 A.M. 5TH 2 BATTLESHIPS 3 CRUIS REPORTED BY BRITISH A/
Veimandu Chan.
6 P.M. 6TH
1·55 P.M. 5TH DORSETSHIRE & CORNWALL SUNK
1·55 P.M. 5TH
R/V 5·26 P.M. 5TH
6·43 P.M. 5TH
4 P
LA
REPO
Addu Atoll

FORCE 'A' ARRIVED ADDU ATOLL NOON 4TH; SAILED 12·15 A.M. 5TH.
" 'B' " " " 3 P.M. 4TH; " 7 A.M. 5TH.

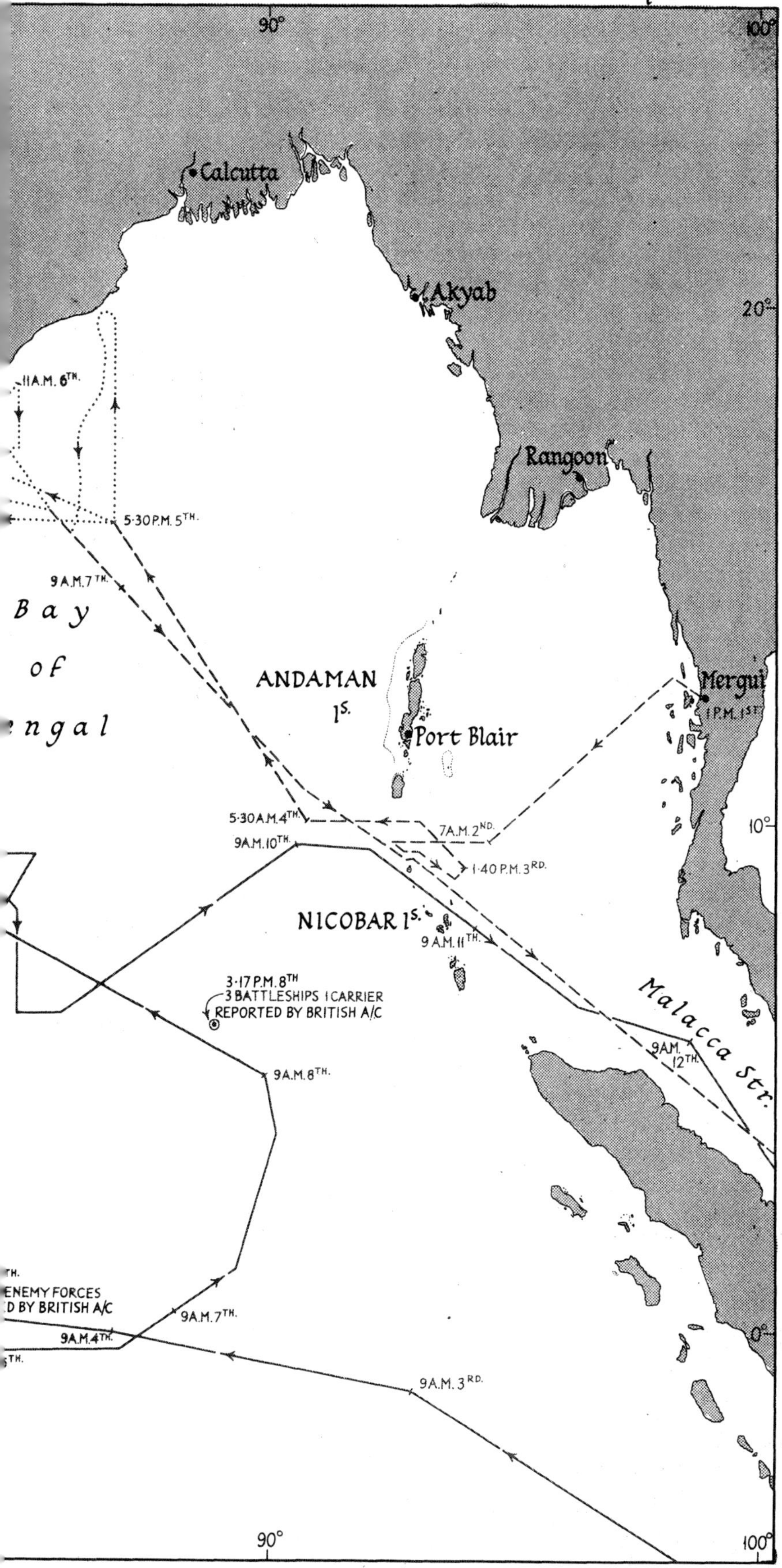

90°
100°
Calcutta
Akyab
20°
11 A.M. 6TH.
Rangoon
5·30 P.M. 5TH.
9 A.M. 7TH.
Bay
of
engal
ANDAMAN
Is.
Port Blair
Mergui
1 P.M. 1ST
5·30 A.M. 4TH.
7 A.M. 2ND.
10°
9 A.M. 10TH.
1·40 P.M. 3RD.
NICOBAR Is.
9 A.M. 11TH.
3·17 P.M. 8TH
3 BATTLESHIPS 1 CARRIER
REPORTED BY BRITISH A/C
Malacca Str.
9 A.M. 12TH.
9 A.M. 8TH.
ENEMY FORCES
D BY BRITISH A/C
9 A.M. 7TH.
9 A.M. 4TH.
0°
9 A.M. 3RD.
90°
100°

in particular, was being reduced. As there were no escorts available, ships were sailing in small unescorted convoys routed as close inshore as practicable. Admiral Ozawa's ships and aircraft wrought havoc among these defenceless ships. In the course of a few hours on the 6th April they sank nineteen of them, a total of over 92,000 tons. The Admiral concentrated his forces on the 7th and then withdrew to Singapore. Sailings from Calcutta were immediately stopped and at the end of April traffic in this once busy port had come almost to a standstill, and for some time the other east coast ports were virtually closed down. Meanwhile, over on the west coast of India, Japanese submarines had accounted for about 32,000 tons of merchant shipping.

The sinking of so many ships close to the coast and the arrival of survivors at all sorts of out-of-the-way places gave rise to much alarm, and when on the 6th bombs were dropped on Cocanada and Vizagapatam—the first to fall on Indian soil—alarm developed into panic. The raids, though light and causing little damage, practically cleared both towns. The panic quickly spread to Madras where, after an air raid warning on the 7th, a heavy exodus began. On the 10th April, the Governor was informed by Southern Command that a large Japanese force was on its way to south India and that the spearhead might be expected to arrive any day after the 15th.[1] The Governor, in fulfilment of a promise given to the people that he would tell them if serious danger were near, issued a communiqué saying that the Government had reason to believe that the threat to Madras was now more serious and advising all non-essential persons to leave within a few days. The Secretariat was withdrawn inland, leaving only the Governor and his principal officers with a skeleton staff in Madras. Southern Command ordered 19th Division to concentrate for the immediate defence of Madras, and the military and civil authorities began to immobilize the port and dislocate the railways. These steps were hardly calculated to engender confidence and for some time panic reigned. Tension spread throughout southern India and did not relax till long after the apparent danger had passed.

On the 11th April a Hudson reconnaissance aircraft from Akyab reported nine flying-boats moored in the harbour at Port Blair. In order to hamper enemy reconnaissance over the Bay of Bengal, a surprise attack by two Hudsons from Akyab was made on the 14th on the harbour. Two twin-engined flying-boats were left burning, one four-engined boat was sunk and the remainder were machine-gunned from a low height. At daylight on the 18th the attack was repeated. This time there were twelve four-engined flying-boats in

---

[1] The information given by Southern Command was due to a misinterpretation of facts.

the port. Two were destroyed and three others seriously damaged in attacks made at masthead height. On that occasion, however, the Japanese were prepared. Navy Zero fighters quickly took off from the small landing ground at Port Blair and in the ensuing action one Hudson was lost. These two small raids, however, did much to reduce the scale of enemy air reconnaissance over the Bay of Bengal.

The threat of invasion did not materialize. Expansion of their fields of conquest westward had never been seriously considered by the Japanese Imperial Staff. The incursion of Admiral Kondo's *Southern Fleet* was no more than a raid and a demonstration timed so as to cover the movements of convoys carrying reinforcements to Rangoon. Nevertheless the appearance of so large a part of the Japanese Fleet in the Indian Ocean had spread a wave of alarm in Britain as well as in India. The immediate reaction of the Chiefs of Staff had been anxiety for the safety of Ceylon which, in the absence of the fleet, would have to depend on aircraft and anti-aircraft guns for its defence. The only source from which they could be got without dangerous delay was the Middle East and, despite the possible effect on his projected offensive in Libya, General Auchinleck was asked to send thirty Hurricanes, twenty bombers and a fully-equipped squadron of torpedo-bombers to the island. General Wavell, too, sent twelve Hurricanes from north-east India and 'mortgaged' ten more from the normal flow to replace recent losses.

At a conference at Bombay on the 13th April, Admiral Somerville drew Wavell's attention to the powerlessness of his ships in the existing crisis. Wavell thereupon taxed the Chiefs of Staff with misleading him with regard to the ability of the Eastern Fleet to protect Ceylon and southern India, and said that the danger of invasion was greater than he had thought. Counting on protection by the fleet for southern India, he had disposed the majority of his troops in north-east India and, although he could not in any case have provided adequate cover for both, he wished London to realize how completely undefended southern India was.

On the 19th he left Bombay in the *Warspite* for discussions with the Commander-in-Chief, Ceylon. While on passage he was again able to discuss the situation with Somerville, who confirmed that he could do nothing at present to prevent the invasion of southern India or Ceylon, and told him that in May practically the whole of his fleet would be engaged in covering the attack on Madagascar ('Ironclad').[1] The Admiral added that he had received no firm information as to what ships were being sent to him or when they would join, but that he hoped by the end of May or early June to be

---
[1] See page 58.

in a position to challenge anything short of a major fleet concentration approaching India.

Before reaching Ceylon, Wavell received a telegram from the Prime Minister telling him of the steps being taken to supply him with aircraft and the policy as regards the fleet. The Prime Minister said that he was trying to build up a fleet in the Indian Ocean strong enough to meet any detachment of their main fleet that the Japanese could afford to send. With this end in view he had asked the President of the United States to transfer an American battleship to the Home Fleet at Scapa Flow, in order to free British ships for the Indian Ocean. Thus in eight or ten weeks Admiral Somerville's fleet should become powerful with three fast capital ships and three large aircraft carriers. He pointed out that if in the meantime Ceylon were lost all this gathering of naval strength would be futile. The defence of the island by anti-aircraft guns and aircraft must be considered as an object more urgent and not less important than the defence of Calcutta. He recognized that it was impossible to provide aircraft to defend the long Indian coastline between Calcutta and Ceylon but, he asked, 'do you really think that it is likely that Japan would consider it worth while to send four or five divisions roaming about the Madras Presidency?'[1]

On the 23rd April, in a review of the situation in the Indian Ocean, the Chiefs of Staff enlarged on the Prime Minister's views. They said the problem was primarily naval, for the eventual security of India and the ability to return to the attack were dependent on regaining control at sea. They believed that for the present Japan would be chiefly concerned with consolidation of her gains and would limit further immediate conquests. On the other hand, although there was no evidence of linked strategy with Germany, it was always possible that Japan, realizing that British defeat was essential for her own survival, might press westwards without a halt. In that case she would try to interrupt the supply route to the Middle East and the oil route from the Persian Gulf, and for this the occupation of Ceylon was an essential prerequisite. Japan's boldest move and her greatest strategic prize would be the capture of Ceylon, but the Chiefs of Staff believed that she was more likely to make a step-by-step coastwise advance to north-east India from Burma under cover of shore-based aircraft.

They realized that the land forces in India lacked at least one armoured division, one army tank brigade and four infantry divisions and that, in a situation which depended fundamentally on adequate air forces, the deficiencies in aircraft were great. These deficiencies could not be made good for some time. Their conclusions were that if Japan pressed boldly westward without a pause for consolidation,

---
[1] Churchill, *The Second World War*, Volume IV (Cassell, 1951) page 164.

undeterred by offensive activities or threats by the Eastern Fleet, by the American Fleet or by the rapid reinforcement of Allied air forces in north-east India, then India was in grave danger and the eventual security of the Middle East and its essential supplies was threatened. Finally they pointed out that the Middle East and India were strategically interdependent, and assured Wavell that the allocation of reinforcements between the two theatres was being kept constantly under review.

This was cold comfort to Wavell, but he could, he thought, at least count on having the protection of the fleet by the end of May or early June. It came as a shock to him therefore when he learnt from Middle East Command that early in May the Chiefs of Staff proposed to move the major units of Somerville's fleet temporarily into the Mediterranean to escort a convoy bringing supplies to Malta. This meant that the Eastern Fleet could not reassemble before the end of June. He was to receive a further shock when on the 29th he was told that the Australian Government were asking for the return of their two brigades from Ceylon, that two brigades of 5th British Division destined for India were being used for 'Ironclad' and would not be available for some considerable time, and that 22nd East African Brigade, which had been earmarked for Ceylon, would probably be retained to garrison Diego Suarez after its capture. Wavell exploded in vehement protest. 'The War Cabinet must really make up their minds whether or not they propose to defend India and Ceylon seriously', he cabled. 'At present we are getting continual messages stressing the vital importance of Ceylon and at the same time our means of defending it are being removed'. All effective naval forces were being removed from the Indian Ocean, although the Chiefs of Staff recognized that the air forces being provided were quite inadequate to stop a seaborne invasion, and at this crisis it was now proposed to reduce by five brigades the land forces which he hoped would be available. 'This seems to me sheer madness if it is really intended to hold Ceylon and India'.

He pointed out that he had but three incomplete divisions to defend Assam, Bengal and Orissa, the threat to which was increasing, seven brigades (including local troops) to defend Ceylon, and for the remainder of India one partially trained division. By taking risks with internal security he had been able to form a reserve brigade of three British battalions, but these he could not send out of the country. If the Australians were to be removed from Ceylon he could not replace them. He added that the political aspect also had to be considered. At the request of the British Government, India had sent overseas the equivalent of seven divisions, a much larger and better trained force than was available in India for her own defence. He had so far succeeded in resisting pressure from within for the return of Indian formations, and in maintaining the sinking Indian morale by being able to give assurances that Britain was determined to render every possible assistance in the defence of India and that large reinforcements were on their way. He could no longer honourably give such an assurance. In the circumstances he requested that a firm policy should be formulated and adhered to.

The Chiefs of Staff did what they could to meet Wavell's needs. Plans for the extension of operations in Madagascar were abandoned for the time being, and the Prime Minister himself informed Wavell that the two Australian brigades would not be moved until they were relieved by two brigades of 5th British Division; the remainder of the division would move direct to India as well as 29th Independent Brigade, as soon as the latter could be relieved in Madagascar by East African troops. These formations would be followed by 2nd British Division. As a result of this plan he should be stronger than he had been led to expect, although there would be a delay in the arrival of 5th Division.

Wavell agreed that eventually he would be stronger, provided that the Madagascar operation did not expand and absorb more troops, but maintained that during the critical months of May and June he would be even weaker than he had expected. He represented that he had not been consulted on 'Ironclad' and though ignorant of the arguments in favour of it suggested that, in view of present weakness, concentration was a better policy than dispersion. The Prime Minister was sympathetic but adamant. He pointed out that the occupation of Diego Suarez was of the highest importance to India, and British communications with the Middle East. The risks during the months of May and June had to be accepted but, subject to the incalculable hazards of war, 5th Division would reach India in May and 2nd Division in June.

In the interim Wavell proposed to relieve the Australian brigades in Ceylon by one Indian brigade (thus bringing 34th Indian Division up to its full strength) and the reserve British brigade which had just been formed. This he said would enable 5th British Division to come to India as a complete formation and would save shipping. The proposal was accepted. He estimated that 5th Division Headquarters and one brigade would arrive on the 17th May, 17th Brigade in mid-June, 13th Brigade the third week in June, 2nd Division the first half of June and 29th Independent Brigade late July or early August.

Wavell's differences of opinion with the Chiefs of Staff and his struggle for the security of India were natural. The Prime Minister and the War Cabinet had, of course, had to view the picture from a broader angle. They had to balance risks, decide priorities and assign reinforcements among urgent claims from all theatres. The security of the United Kingdom had to take precedence, and the needs of India to be related to those of the Middle East. Events were to prove the soundness of their judgment.

A Japanese fleet never again ventured into the Indian Ocean. The sequel to its solitary incursion is curious. Both fleets withdrew from the scene of operations—the British to the coast of Africa and the Japanese to its home ports. But it could not, of course, be known at the time that the danger in the Indian Ocean was in fact over. To all appearances it was greater than ever. The Eastern Fleet was powerless to protect Ceylon or southern India; air strength was practically negligible; the small army in Burma, it soon became obvious, would be unable to hold the enemy since it could not be reinforced by sea nor, owing to lack of communications between Assam and upper Burma, could reinforcements reach it by land. This, as General Wavell records in his despatch, was 'India's most dangerous hour'.

PALESTINE
TRANS-JORDAN
40°E
IRAQ
60°
AFGHANISTAN
Abadan
PERSIA
Aqaba
Kuwait
Persian Gulf
EGYPT
Bahrein
Karachi
Red Sea
SAUDI ARABIA
20°N
Port Sudan
Arabian Sea
Massawa
Khartoum
ERITREA
ADEN
Aden
Gulf of Aden
Socotra
SUDAN
FRENCH SOMALILAND
Djibouti
BRITISH SOMALILAND
Addis Ababa
ETHIOPIA
ITALIAN SOMALILAND
Mogadishu
UGANDA
KENYA
0°
Nairobi
Kilindini
Mombasa
Seychelles Is
TANGANYIKA
Zanzibar
Dar-es-Salaam
N. RHODESIA
NYASALAND
Channel
Diego Suarez
Mozambique
Majunga
INDIA
MOZAMBIQUE
Tamatave
S. RHODESIA
MADAGASCAR
Tananarive
Rodriguez
Beira
Mozambique
Mauritius
Reunion
S. AFRICA
Lourenço Marques
Durban
40°E
60°

Map 6

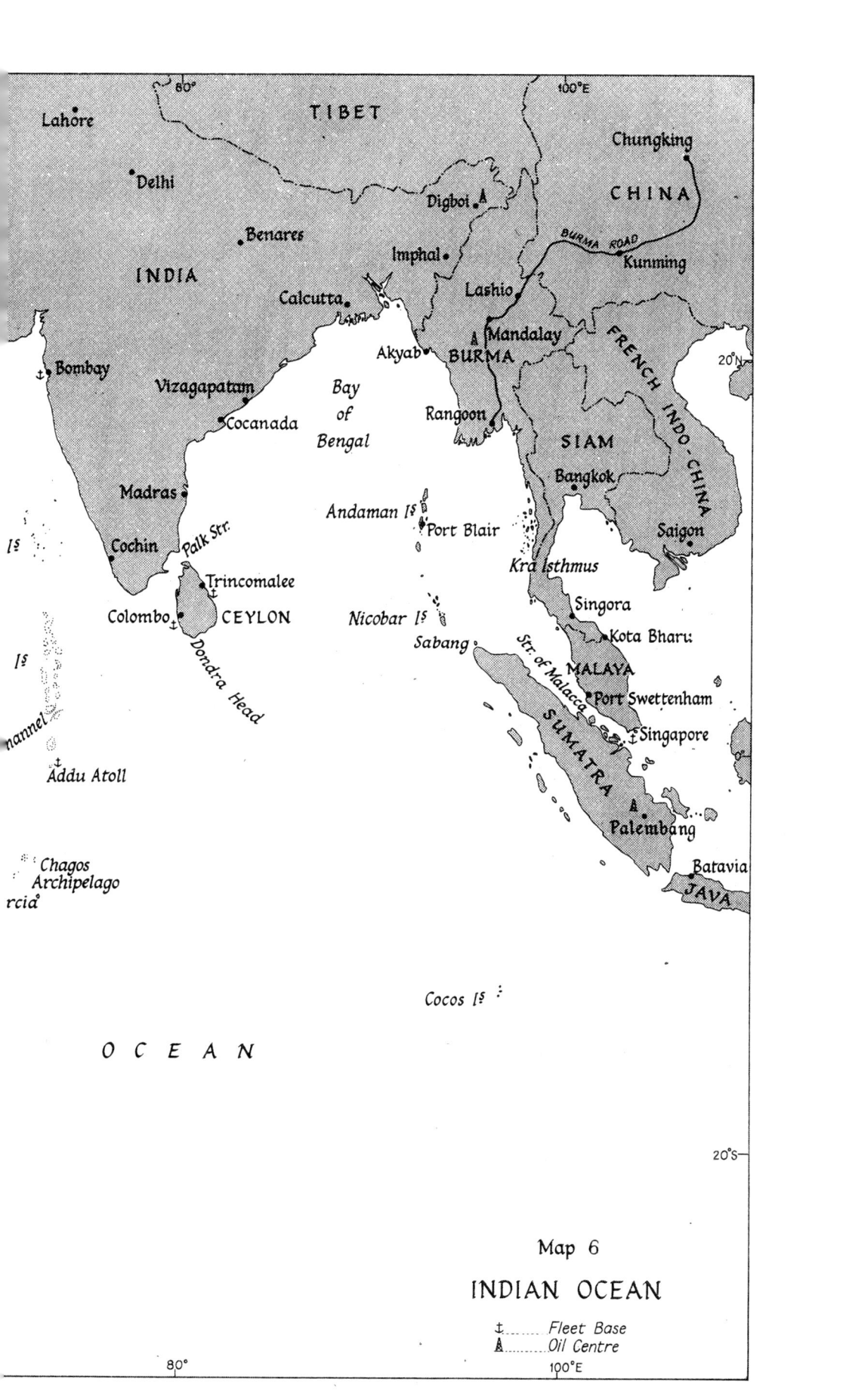

INDIAN OCEAN

☨ Fleet Base
⛭ Oil Centre

CHAPTER VIII

MADAGASCAR

(April–November 1942)

See Map 7

THE Chiefs of Staff had decided early in March 1942 that operation 'Ironclad'—to seize and hold the Vichy French naval and air base at Diego Suarez at the northern tip of Madagascar—was to be undertaken so as to forestall a possible Japanese descent on the island, and to protect the vital lines of communication in the Indian Ocean.[1] The date fixed for the operation was the most convenient day between the 4th and 8th May, when conditions of tide and moon would be most favourable. The port of assembly was to be Durban.

To find shipping and warships was, as always, the difficulty. With the growing threat to India and Ceylon it was clearly inexpedient to weaken the Eastern Fleet, which was then forming in the Indian Ocean. In order to free British naval forces for the operation, the Prime Minister appealed to the President of the United States to provide, as a temporary measure, American naval reinforcements for the Atlantic. The President agreed, and it thus became possible to use the bulk of Force 'H' (the squadron normally guarding the western Mediterranean) as the nucleus of the naval force (Force 'F') for 'Ironclad'. Rear-Admiral E. N. Syfret was appointed as Combined Commander-in-Chief, with Major-General R. C. Sturges, Royal Marines, as Military Force Commander.

The land forces selected (Force 121) included 29th Independent Brigade Group of four battalions (Brigadier F. W. Festing), No. 5 Commando (both of which had reached an advanced stage of training in amphibious operations) and 17th Infantry Brigade Group (Brigadier G. W. B. Tarleton) of 5th Division, which was under orders to sail in convoy for India.[2] This last formation had no experience or training in amphibious operations, but it was convenient

---

[1] See page 58.

[2] The 29th Independent Brigade Group consisted of 1st Royal Scots Fusiliers, 2nd Royal Welch Fusiliers, 2nd East Lancashire Regiment, 2nd South Lancashire Regiment, 455th Light Battery, R.A. (four 3·7-inch and two 25-pounders) and 236th Field Company, R.E. (less one section).

The 17th Brigade Group consisted of 2nd Royal Scots Fusiliers, 6th Seaforth Highlanders, 2nd Northamptonshire Regiment, 9th Field Regiment, R.A., 38th Field Company, R.E. and 141st Field Ambulance, R.A.M.C.

to use it, for its stores and vehicles had already sailed on the 13th March in a convoy bound for the Cape.

Force 121 left the United Kingdom on the 23rd March in a large convoy carrying 5th Division and reinforcements for India and the Middle East, and arrived at Freetown (Sierra Leone) on the 6th April. Admiral Syfret in the battleship *Malaya* accompanied by the cruiser *Hermione* and five destroyers arrived there from Gibraltar on the same day, and later the aircraft carrier *Illustrious*, the cruiser *Devonshire* and four destroyers joined him there. It was at Freetown that the naval and military commanders of the operation met for the first time. They held preliminary discussions with Captain G. A. Garnons-Williams, R.N., who had been appointed Naval Assault Commander at Diego Suarez, and Brigadier Festing, the Military Assault Commander.

The whole force sailed from Freetown on the 9th April. On the way south a message was received that a second infantry brigade group of 5th Division, the 13th (Brigadier V. C. Russell), would join the expedition at Durban as a floating reserve. On the 19th Admiral Syfret, leaving the *Devonshire* to look after the convoy, took the remainder of his force to Capetown, where he transferred his flag to the *Illustrious*, the *Malaya* having been ordered by the Admiralty to return to Freetown. The Admiral was received by the Prime Minister of the Union of South Africa, Field Marshal J. C. Smuts, who took the keenest interest in the expedition. The Field Marshal advocated the capture of two other ports in Madagascar, Tamatave and Majunga, as well as Diego Suarez, and expressed his intention of informing London of his views on the following day.

Admiral Syfret left Capetown on the morning of the 20th in the *Illustrious* with the destroyers, and arrived two days later at Durban where he again transferred his flag, this time to the *Ramillies* which had been detached from the Eastern Fleet at Kilindini to take the place of the *Malaya*. Here he received information from the Commander-in-Chief, Eastern Fleet, of his intended movements to cover operation 'Ironclad' and a rendezvous was fixed for the aircraft carrier *Indomitable*, which was to replace the *Hermes*, originally allotted.[1]

Service representatives had been flown from Freetown to Durban to make preparations for the reception of the convoy. Thus, when the vessels carrying Force 121, augmented by the *Bachaquero* (a new type of tank landing ship), arrived at Durban, all ships were berthed alongside and within a few hours of arrival, work on restowing them began. For the next few days the port was a hive of activity. There was much to be done. The vehicles, guns and equipment of the formations of 5th Division allotted to 'Ironclad' had not been loaded for an

---

[1] Sunk off Ceylon, see page 124.

10. Diego Suarez looking west from Antsirane. (The assault landings were made beyond the dark ridge in the top right hand corner. Diego Suarez town is off to the right.)

11. Vice-Admiral E. N. Syfret.

amphibious operation and thus had to be unloaded and restowed, motor transport had to be serviced, waterproofed and examined, tanks retracked and landing craft refuelled, tested and transferred to their respective assault ships. In addition stocks of petrol and bombs had to be loaded for the South African Air Force, which was to take over when Diego Suarez was secured. Final orders were issued and discussed, and the troops exercised to harden them and get them fit after their long voyage. All this meant a great deal of work for the commanders and their staffs. To add to their burden, early on the morning of the 26th a cable was received from London asking for a report on the possibility of widening the scope of the operation to include the capture of Tamatave and Majunga, either simultaneously with or shortly after the capture of Diego Suarez. The two commanders considered that this could be done provided that 13th Brigade could be retained, and that opposition at Diego Suarez ceased by the evening of the day of the landing. Two days before the day of the assault, however, they were told that because of the extreme importance of the earliest possible arrival in India of 5th Division, this additional commitment was to be held in abeyance.

On the 25th April a slow convoy carrying the stores and equipment left Durban with the *Devonshire*, two destroyers and the corvettes and minesweepers. It was followed three days later by a fast convoy containing the assault and troop ships escorted by the *Ramillies*, *Illustrious*, *Hermione* and six destroyers.[1] Major-General Sturges was with Admiral Syfret in the *Ramillies*.

The harbour at Diego Suarez, roughly the shape and size of Scapa Flow, pierces deeply into the east coast of Madagascar at its northern end and is separated from Courrier Bay and Ambararata Bay on the west coast by a narrow isthmus which varies in width from two and a half to six miles. The Andrakaka Peninsula projects into the southern end of the main harbour of Diego Suarez to within about 1,200 yards of the naval base of Antsirane. The harbour is approached from the eastwards by a channel known as the Oronjia Pass, three-quarters of a mile wide, the entrance to which is seventeen miles from Cape Amber, the northernmost point in the island. The pass was known to be strongly defended by coast defence batteries sited on the Oronjia Peninsula. The bays on the west coast, only ten or twelve miles from Antsirane as the crow flies, were believed to be protected by two batteries only and possibly by a minefield. There was good anchorage in both these bays but they were difficult of access.

The object of the operation was to storm and capture the naval base at Antsirane and the airfield five miles to the southwards. The general plan was to assault from the west across the isthmus, the main

---

[1] For names of the assault and troop ships see Appendix 10.

landing being made by 29th Independent Brigade at three beaches in Ambararata Bay. The brigade was on a light scale of transport and had under its command, among other units, six medium and six light tanks and 455th Light Battery (four 3·7-inch howitzers and two 25-pounders). As soon as it had secured the beaches, it was to advance and capture Antsirane about twenty-one miles by road to the eastward. Concurrently with the main landing, No. 5 Commando and one company of 2nd East Lancashire Regiment were to land in Courrier Bay, silence the batteries and advance east to secure the Andrakaka Peninsula. The 17th Infantry Brigade, followed if necessary by 13th Infantry Brigade, was to land as soon as 29th Brigade was ashore and come into action to complete the capture of Antsirane and the Oronjia Peninsula. Zero hour was to be 4.30 a.m. on the 5th May, an hour and twenty minutes before sunrise.

The passage of the two convoys up the Mozambique Channel was made in good weather, and by dusk on the 3rd the fast convoy had closed to within four miles of the slow convoy. Early that morning Force 'F' had been joined by the *Indomitable*, flying the flag of Rear-Admiral Boyd, and two destroyers. At noon on the 4th the *Ramillies*, *Indomitable*, *Illustrious* and six destroyers set course for their covering position west of Cape Amber. The *Hermione* was detached to carry out a diversion to the eastward of Diego Suarez.

The channel to the selected preliminary anchorage was tortuous and narrow and, it was believed, mined. Scattered islets and reefs lay on either side. The French had extinguished all navigational lights and so hazardous was the passage that they had discounted any possibility of an attempt to make it in darkness. At dusk on the 4th the destroyers *Laforey* (Captain R. M. S. Hutton), *Lightning* and *Anthony* were sent ahead of the convoy, to mark and buoy the difficult channel. Meanwhile the convoy, with the minesweepers ahead, cautiously made its approach through the treacherous currents in darkness. At 9.22 p.m. the moon rose in a clear sky and the high land of the coast could be seen. Shortly after midnight the convoy entered the buoyed channel and, at 1.54 a.m. on the 5th, anchored as noiselessly as possible outside the range of the shore batteries. Captain R. D. Oliver of the *Devonshire* must have heaved a sigh of relief. Had he but known that the minesweepers ahead of him had parted their sweeps on a shoal at the entrance to the channel and that none of it had been swept his relief might have been greater. Fortunately no mines had been laid so far to seaward.

While the assault craft were being lowered and manned, the minesweepers, having repaired their sweep wires, swept the eight-mile channel to the dispersal point in Courrier Bay. They were closely followed by the *Laforey* leading the assault craft carrying No. 5 Commando and a company of the East Lancashires, with the

Lightning and *Royal Ulsterman* astern. Seventeen mines were swept in the channel, two of which were exploded by the sweeps. All waited for the batteries ashore to open fire but, to the great surprise of everyone, the quiet of the summer night was undisturbed and at 3.30 a.m. the landing craft left the dispersal point for their beaches in Courrier Bay in silence.

Despite the explosion of the mines, complete surprise was achieved. No. 5 Commando with one company and two carriers of 2nd East Lancashires landed on their beaches unopposed, captured the shore battery and advanced across the Andrakaka Peninsula. They met slight opposition at the start but quickly overcame it, and at 2.30 p.m. reached Diego Suarez at the easternmost end of the peninsula. They intended to cross to Antsirane but were unable to find any boats.

Meanwhile 29th Independent Brigade was coming ashore in Ambararata Bay. The 1st Royal Scots Fusiliers and 2nd Royal Welch Fusiliers were landed punctually and accurately and met no opposition. The remainder of 2nd East Lancashires from the *Royal Ulsterman* then landed at Basse Point in the landing craft which had been used for the landings on the Courrier Bay beaches. Here a machine-gun post manned by Senegalese opened fire but was soon silenced by return fire from the landing craft. At 6.30 a.m. all the beaches were in British hands and the assault floating reserve, 2nd South Lancashires (less one company), was ordered in.

Over on the east coast of the island, the *Hermione* had been carrying out her diversion south-east of Antsirane. At 4.40 a.m. she opened fire with starshell and rockets and laid smoke floats. At first light the Fleet Air Arm came into action. Aircraft from the *Illustrious* dropped parachutes with dummies to support the *Hermione*'s feint landing. At the same time eighteen aircraft armed with torpedoes, bombs and depth charges attacked shipping in Diego Suarez Bay. An armed merchant cruiser was hit by a torpedo, a submarine sunk by depth charge and the sloop *d'Entrecasteaux* set on fire and forced to beach herself. Fighters demonstrated over the town during the attack. The *Indomitable*'s aircraft meanwhile had been carrying out a low-level bombing attack on the airfield south of Antsirane. Here again surprise was complete. The hangars were full of aircraft which were left in flames. Before the attacks, leaflets were dropped on the town calling on the defenders to surrender. The demand, as was expected, was rejected by the Military Commander who, at 7 a.m., broadcast a statement that he intended to defend his position to the last.

By this time 29th Brigade had started its march to Antsirane. The Welch Fusiliers were the first to move off, led by Bren gun carriers and a motor cycle platoon, followed by the Scots Fusiliers and a light battery. In the sweltering heat of the tropical day the brigade advanced along the single dusty road without meeting any opposition. At 8.15 a.m. a French naval officer was captured and sent back to the town in his car with a letter to the Military Commander demanding surrender. The sending of this message was afterwards recognized as a grave error, for it revealed to the enemy the direction of the advance and gave time for dispositions to be made to meet it. French troops were at once hurried forward in lorries to man an outpost position facing west at a bend in the road about five miles south of the town, somewhat ironically called the Col de Bonne Nouvelle. Here at 11 a.m. the leading carriers and the Welch Fusiliers met machine-gun fire from trenches and pillboxes on high ground commanding the road. Brigadier Festing, who was up with his forward troops, ordered the infantry to attack, supported by the light guns. While they were deploying, three tanks arrived, broke through the position and, leaving the infantry behind, continued their advance along the road. When they were within about three miles of the centre of Antsirane they were joined by two more tanks. Almost immediately they came under heavy and accurate fire from the enemy's main defences. Four tanks were quickly disabled and the fifth was ordered to withdraw. The survivors of the tank crews, armed with light automatics and pistols, fought hard to save their vehicles, but were eventually taken prisoner.

Back at the beaches, the disembarkation of troops had been going on all day. The south-east wind had been rising during the night and by daylight on the 5th was blowing at gale force. To speed up the turn-round of the landing craft, the transports were ordered to leave the preliminary anchorage for the main anchorage off the entrance to Ambararata Bay as soon as the success signal from the beaches in Courrier Bay was received. There was some delay owing to the presence of more mines, but by 8 a.m. these had been swept and the ships began to take up their new berths. By 11 a.m. all troops of 29th Brigade had been landed, but it was midnight before all their transport was ashore. Brigadier Tarleton's 17th Brigade began to come ashore at 11.15 a.m. and continued to do so until nightfall when, in order to avoid damage to the landing craft and to rest their crews, a halt was called until sunrise. The loading and handling of these craft in the heavy seas which had been running all day showed a high standard of seamanship. Owing to the success of the Fleet Air Arm's initial attack on Antsirane airfield little interference was experienced from the French air force, except for a few sporadic machine-gun attacks on the beaches.

Difficulty had been experienced in finding a suitable beach at which the *Bachaquero* could land the field artillery, and it was nearly dark before one was discovered in Courrier Bay and 9th Field Regiment began to disembark. Unfortunately there was no road from

Courrier Bay to the main road from Ambararata Bay to Antsirane, and thus throughout the attacks on the French defences the main part of the artillery could operate only from the Andrakaka Peninsula, separated from the infantry, with the result that 29th Brigade had inadequate fire support throughout.

Meanwhile at the Col de Bonne Nouvelle the enemy defences came to life after the tanks had passed through and held up the infantry, and it was not until 3 p.m., after seven more tanks had arrived, that the position was finally captured and the advance resumed. The tanks were sent forward to locate the field guns which had wrought such havoc, but were forced to withdraw under heavy fire with the loss of two of their number. Shortly afterwards, at 5 p.m., the leading battalions of 29th Brigade, now reorganized, came under fire from the main position. With darkness approaching, Brigadier Festing felt that he could ask no more of his tired troops and ordered his four battalions to take up close perimeter positions for the night.

At 11 p.m. Festing issued his orders for an attack on the main enemy position at dawn on the 6th. This position consisted of two solid and well-concealed forts on the narrowest part of the Antsirane peninsula joined by a line of trenches about a mile long. Two roads ran between the forts and another skirted the bay on the east. His intention was to attack on a three-battalion front. The 2nd South Lancashire was to advance in the moonlight by the easterly road and try to get behind the enemy lines. The 1st Royal Scots Fusiliers in the centre and 2nd East Lancashire on the left were to attack frontally at dawn, supported by the light battery of six guns.

The 2nd South Lancashire moved off at 2 a.m. and, aided by the darkness, penetrated the enemy lines, took many prisoners and eventually got detachments into position about 200 yards behind the enemy trenches. Despite this, the frontal attack failed. When General Sturges reached brigade headquarters at 7 a.m. things looked black. Nothing had been heard from the South Lancashires and he feared that the leading troops were prisoners or casualties. There were insufficient guns and tanks (only five were left) available for a daylight assault. The 17th Brigade was still marching up the road and could not reach the forward area until about 6 p.m. The 13th Brigade had begun landing only at daybreak. The General decided that 17th Brigade, as soon as it was in position, should make a night attack before the moon rose, assisted as necessary by 29th Brigade. Leaving his Brigadiers to carry on with the detailed planning, he went back to ask Admiral Syfret to send a destroyer into the harbour and land a party of marines to create a diversion in the enemy's rear. The two attacks were to take place simultaneously at 8 p.m.

The General reached the Flagship at 2.30 p.m. Just over an hour later fifty marines had embarked in the *Anthony* and were on their way at high speed to Diego Suarez. At 8 p.m. the *Anthony* was off the entrance to the harbour, and increasing speed to 22 knots, set course to pass through Oronjia Pass. She was apparently unobserved until half a mile inside the pass, when the batteries opened up. But their fire soon ceased when the *Devonshire*, which with the *Hermione* had closed to within six miles to give support, opened up with her 8-inch guns. In the darkness the *Anthony* overshot the landing place, but Lieut.-Commander J. M. Hodges skilfully turned his ship and held his stern against the jetty long enough for the marines to get ashore. He then once again ran the gauntlet of the French batteries and escaped unscathed. The marines, groping their way in the darkness, missed the entrance to the town but eventually found a gap in a high wall and, making their way through it, found and captured the artillery headquarters and the naval barracks against slight opposition.

Meanwhile 17th and 29th Brigades had started their attack from the south. When the success signal from the town showed that the marines had landed, 2nd Royal Scots Fusiliers and 2nd Royal Welch Fusiliers pressed home their attack and, by 3 a.m. on the 7th, Festing was able to report that the town and its defences were in his hands.

Shortly afterwards, Admiral Syfret in the *Ramillies* received a message from Sturges asking for all available air and ship support at 9 a.m. when 29th Brigade would assault the Oronjia Peninsula, if negotiations for its surrender broke down. He accordingly shaped course with the *Ramillies* and destroyers to join the *Devonshire* and *Hermione* to the eastward. The French were slow in making up their minds and at 10.40 a.m. the Admiral, 'tired of keeping the fleet steaming up and down in dangerous waters', ordered his ships to open fire 'to encourage the enemy to surrender'. This had the desired effect. In ten minutes a white flag was hoisted.

By 4.20 p.m. the minesweepers had swept the channel and harbour and at 5 p.m. the *Ramillies*, followed by the *Hermione* and two destroyers, entered the harbour. They were joined the following day by the two convoys and the rest of Force 'F'. On the 8th May, in the Residency at Antsirane, the final terms of surrender were accepted by the French Military Commander. Diego Suarez, and with it the Cape route to the east, had been secured.

'Ironclad' was the first large amphibious assault made by British forces since the attempt to storm the Dardanelles in the First World War. In the twenty-seven years which had passed a new technique had developed. That it had to be tested against a former ally was a melancholy turn in the fortunes of war, but happily the fighting was short-lived. Diego Suarez fell in only three days, but over a hundred British lives were lost and nearly three hundred wounded. The French state that their losses were over 150 killed and some 500 wounded.

Meanwhile Field Marshal Smuts had been pressing for the extension of control by the capture of Tamatave and Majunga. This, it will be recalled, had already been considered and held in abeyance. On the 16th May the operation was cancelled. The capture of Diego Suarez was but a means to an end—the securing of the Cape route to the Middle East and India—and General Wavell, with Burma lost and the threat of a Japanese invasion of India after the monsoon, was already protesting against the retention in Madagascar of troops promised to him.

The 13th Brigade sailed for Bombay on the 20th May. A great number of the troops had fallen victim to malaria and dengue fever and it was some time after their arrival in India before they were fit for service. The 17th Brigade followed them on the 12th June, after relief by 22nd East African Brigade under the command of Brigadier W. A. Dimoline.

On the 27th May an unofficial emissary from the Vichy French Governor of Madagascar arrived at Diego Suarez with instructions to seek a basis for an agreement with the British forces which would 'safeguard the honour, sovereignty and neutrality of the Madagascar Government and put an end to the bloodshed'. Negotiations began in the hope that a *modus vivendi* would be reached which would permit the reduction of the British garrison in the island; these negotiations were, as will be seen, to be protracted and unsatisfactory.

By the end of May, the *Indomitable*, *Illustrious* and *Devonshire* had rejoined the Eastern Fleet and the *Hermione* the Mediterranean Fleet, leaving only the *Ramillies*, three destroyers and two corvettes at Diego Suarez. During the course of the operations, Force 'F' had sunk three Vichy submarines, and its aircraft had destroyed about twenty Vichy fighters and bombers. Its own losses had been slight—one minesweeper which had struck a mine in Courrier Bay and five aircraft. It was to suffer a further loss but this time at the hands of a different enemy.

At about 10.30 p.m. on the 29th May an aircraft arrived over the harbour and flew off without being identified. Precautions against a possible dawn submarine or air attack were at once taken. The *Ramillies* got under way at 5 a.m. on the 30th and steamed round the bay until after sunrise, and dawn and dusk patrols were flown by the Fleet Air Arm. At 8.25 p.m. that evening the *Ramillies* and a tanker were torpedoed. The tanker sank almost immediately but the *Ramillies*, which had settled by the bows, was able, by discharging ammunition and oil, to regain her trim and sailed for Durban the following afternoon. The two corvettes searched the harbour throughout the night, dropping depth charges on suspected contacts, but nothing was seen. A few days later two Japanese were rounded up by a commando patrol north of Diego Suarez and, refusing to surrender, were shot. Papers found on them indicated that they were the crew of a Japanese midget submarine.

Five submarines of the *4th Submarine Flotilla* had assembled at Penang at the end of April and had crossed the Indian Ocean, refuelling at sea from two supply ships which accompanied them. Aircraft carried by these submarines reconnoitred East African ports, including Durban on the 2nd May, in search of warships. Drawing a blank they converged on Diego Suarez. Two of the submarines launched their midgets when about ten miles off the entrance to the harbour. The attack was gallantly and skilfully carried out and, as we have seen, with success.

On the 28th May Field Marshal Smuts again urged that Majunga and Tamatave should be occupied, and proposed that 22nd East African Brigade, and 7th South African Brigade which was to provide the eventual garrison of the island, should be used. At a conference in Pretoria on the 20th June presided over by the Field Marshal, at which Lieut.-General Sir William Platt and General Sturges were present,[1] it was agreed that negotiations for a peaceful solution should continue but that, in event of a deadlock, Majunga should be captured and negotiations then resumed. If these renewed negotiations failed, then Tananarive should be threatened. This plan, which involved a seaborne assault on the two ports, necessitated the retention in Madagascar of 29th Brigade Group which had been promised to India, and the return by the end of July of the assault shipping which had already been sent to India to enable General Wavell to begin training for amphibious operations. Owing to reverses in the Middle East and the possibilities of a Japanese invasion of India, the Chiefs of Staff again decided at the end of June that no further operations in Madagascar would be undertaken, and that every effort should be made instead to bring the negotiations with the Madagascar Government to a satisfactory conclusion.

On the 1st July Madagascar was placed under the command of General Platt. The island of Mayotte in the Mozambique Channel was occupied next day, and an airstrip built. By mid-July, it had become clear that the French were attempting to spin out the negotiations until the advent of the rainy season in October, which would make operations in the central part of the island virtually impossible. Platt reported that, if Tananarive were to be occupied before the rains, a decision had become a matter of urgency. On the 19th the Prime Minister told the Chiefs of Staff that, since the situation in India had become less dangerous, it should now be possible to 'tidy up' in Madagascar.

The problem as usual was to find the naval forces, assault shipping and landing craft. Naval forces would be available by the 21st

---

[1] General Platt was General Officer Commanding-in-Chief, East African Command.

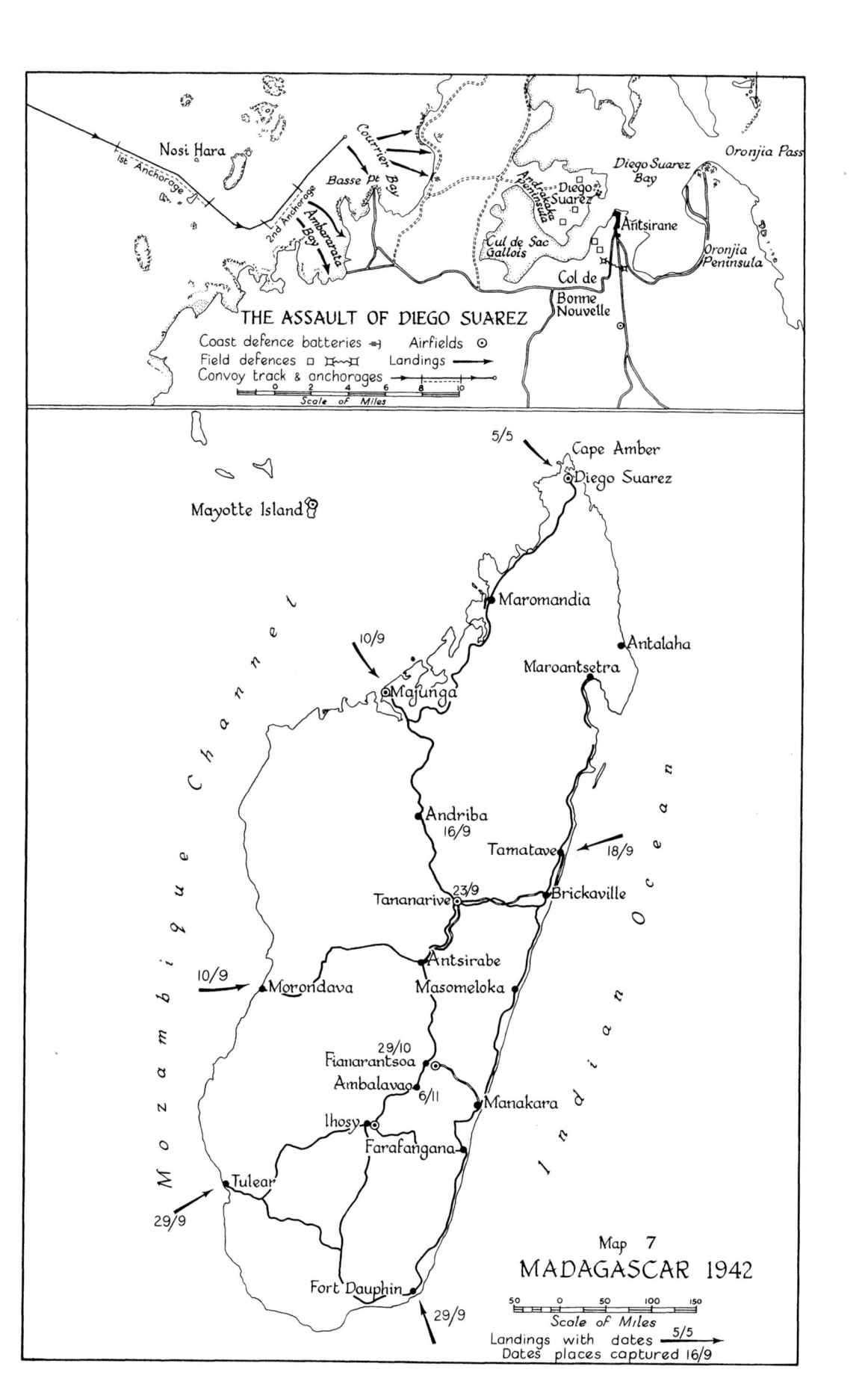

THE ASSAULT OF DIEGO SUAREZ

Coast defence batteries
Field defences
Convoy track & anchorages
Airfields
Landings

Scale of Miles 0 2 4 6 8 10

Nosi Hara — 1st Anchorage — 2nd Anchorage — Basse Pt — Courrier Bay — Ambararata Bay — Andrakaka Peninsula — Diego Suarez — Cul de Sac Gallois — Diego Suarez Bay — Antsirane — Col de Bonne Nouvelle — Oronjia Pass — Oronjia Peninsula

Map 7
MADAGASCAR 1942

Scale of Miles 50 0 50 100 150
Landings with dates 5/5
Dates places captured 16/9

- 5/5 Cape Amber
- Diego Suarez
- Mayotte Island
- Maromandia
- Antalaha
- 10/9 Majunga
- Maroantsetra
- Andriba 16/9
- Tamatave 18/9
- Tananarive 23/9
- Brickaville
- Antsirabe
- 10/9 Morondava
- Masomeloka
- Fianarantsoa 29/10
- Ambalavao 6/11
- Manakara
- Ihosy
- Farafangana
- Tulear 29/9
- Fort Dauphin 29/9

Mozambique Channel — Indian Ocean

August, but it was clear that the scope of the operations would not permit the assault shipping being released before mid-September and possibly not before early October. Since much of this shipping would be required for the proposed Allied landing in North Africa, then timed to take place about 15th October, it appeared once again that further operations in Madagascar would have to be abandoned. But on the 30th July Platt told the Chiefs of Staff that, unless strong action were taken, the situation in Madagascar, which had already deteriorated as a result of inaction, would go from bad to worse. As a result the clearance of Madagascar was again reviewed in London. On the 11th August the War Cabinet approved landings at Majunga and Tamatave and an advance to occupy the capital, Tananarive. The necessary assault and landing craft were to be found from India. Since they could not be returned under two and a half months, Wavell's plans for offensive action in Burma would be adversely affected.[1]

Platt planned that 22nd East African Brigade would be put ashore on the 10th September at Majunga, after 29th Brigade had secured the port, and would advance on Tananarive assisted by a South African armoured car unit. A commando unit would make a diversionary landing at Morondava, and 29th Brigade, withdrawn from Majunga as soon as the East African brigade was ashore, would land on the 18th at Tamatave and also advance on Tananarive. At the same time 7th South African Brigade, which was to take over the duties of garrison at Diego Suarez, was to make a limited advance southwards as far as Maromandia on the west coast and Antalaha on the east coast. It was expected that, with the occupation of the capital, the Vichy French Governor would capitulate and that 29th Brigade, with the assault shipping and landing craft, could be released for return to India by the latter half of October.

The 22nd East African Brigade was landed with little opposition at Majunga on the 10th September and on the 16th had reached Andriba, only 100 miles from the capital. The Governor then asked for an armistice. The terms, which were similar to those presented during the protracted negotiations, were immediately submitted but were rejected on the 17th. The operations were therefore continued. On the 18th, 29th Brigade landed at Tamatave and advanced along the road to the capital. On the 23rd the French declared Tananarive an open town and it was occupied by the East African brigade that afternoon.[2]

The following day Platt issued a proclamation which clarified the British attitude towards French sovereignty, and declared that, pending the establishment of a friendly French régime, the

---

[1] See Chapter XI.
[2] The progress of the various columns converging on the capital is shown on Map 7.

island would be subject to military jurisdiction. The Governor still refused to capitulate and it soon became clear that operations to occupy the south of the island, and particularly Fianarantsoa to which he had retired, would have to be undertaken. Accordingly on the 29th September troops were landed at Tulear and Fort Dauphin at the southern end of the island, and on the 9th October 22nd East African Brigade moved south from the capital. The rains made progress slow and it was not until the 29th October that Fianarantsoa was occupied. Still the Governor would not capitulate. Eventually on the 5th November, completely isolated in Ambalavao, he asked for the British terms of surrender. These were substantially the same as announced when the negotiations started at Diego Suarez in May. They were accepted, and the Governor signed an instrument of capitulation early on the 6th November. Thus the campaign ended eight weeks after the landing at Majunga.

Throughout the second part of the campaign there had been little serious fighting and battle casualties were only 107 all ranks, but both the British and South African troops had suffered severely from malaria. So great was the incidence in 29th Brigade that, on the 18th October, it had to be sent to Durban for a period of convalescence. The prolonged retention in Madagascar of 29th Brigade and 22nd East African Brigade, both urgently needed in India, and the subsequent delays due to sickness which retarded their arrival there, were to have a considerable effect on Wavell's plans.

Map 8

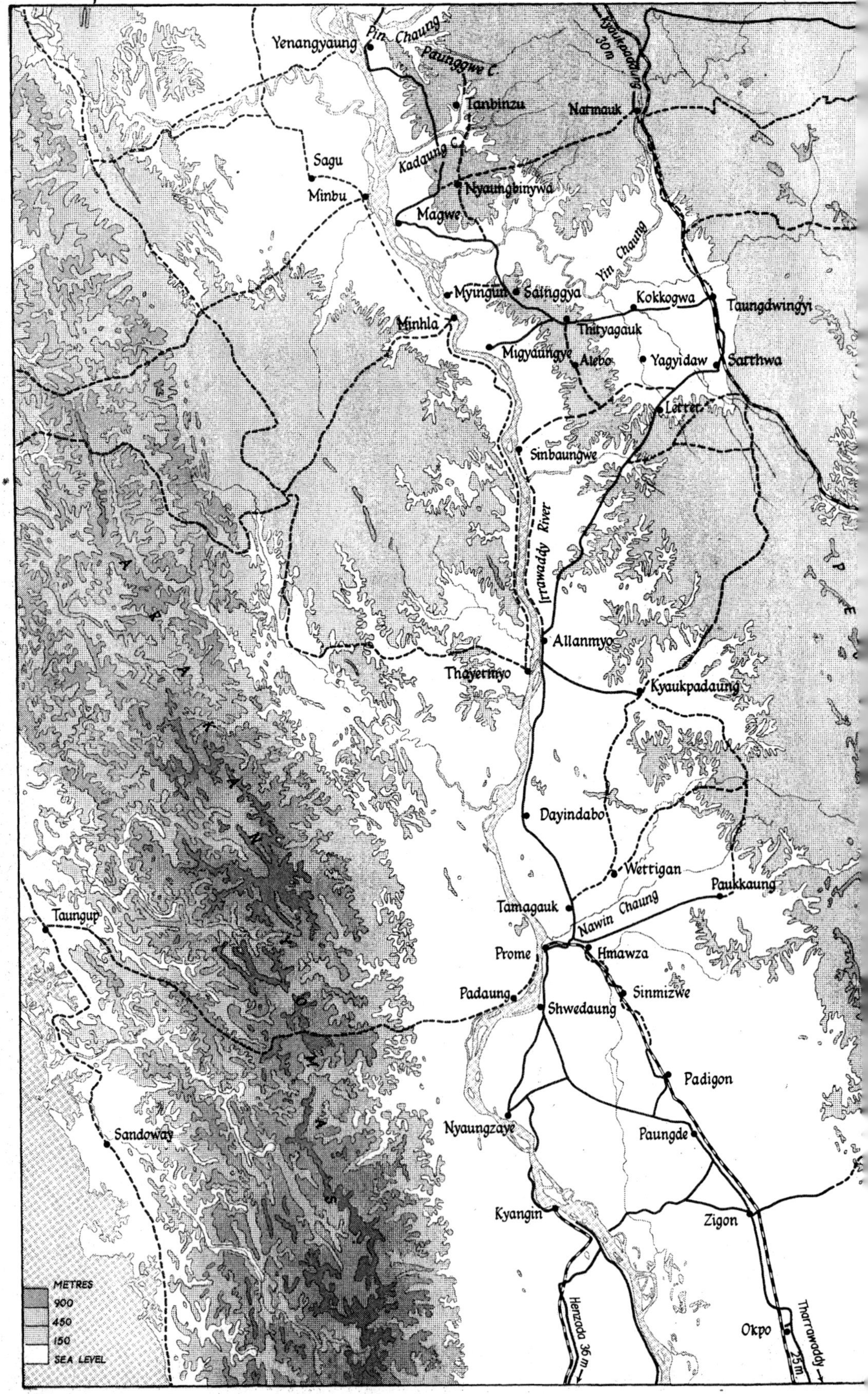
Yenangyaung
Pin Chaung
Paunggwe C.
Kyaukpadaung 30m
Tanbinzu
Natmauk
Sagu
Kadaung C.
Minbu
Nyaungbinywa
Magwe
Yin Chaung
Myingun
Sainggya
Kokkogwa
Taungdwingyi
Minhla
Thityagauk
Migyaungye
Alebo
Yagyidaw
Satthwa
Lettret
Sinbaungwe
Irrawaddy River
ARAKAN YOMA
Allanmyo
Thayetmyo
Kyaukpadaung
Dayindabo
Wettigan
Paukkaung
Tamagauk
Nawin Chaung
Taungup
Prome
Hmawza
Sinmizwe
Padaung
Shwedaung
Padigon
Nyaungzaye
Paungde
Sandoway
Kyangin
Zigon
Henzada 36 m
Okpo
Tharrawaddy 25 m.
METRES
900
450
150
SEA LEVEL

Map 8
TOUNGOO - PROME
March - April 1942

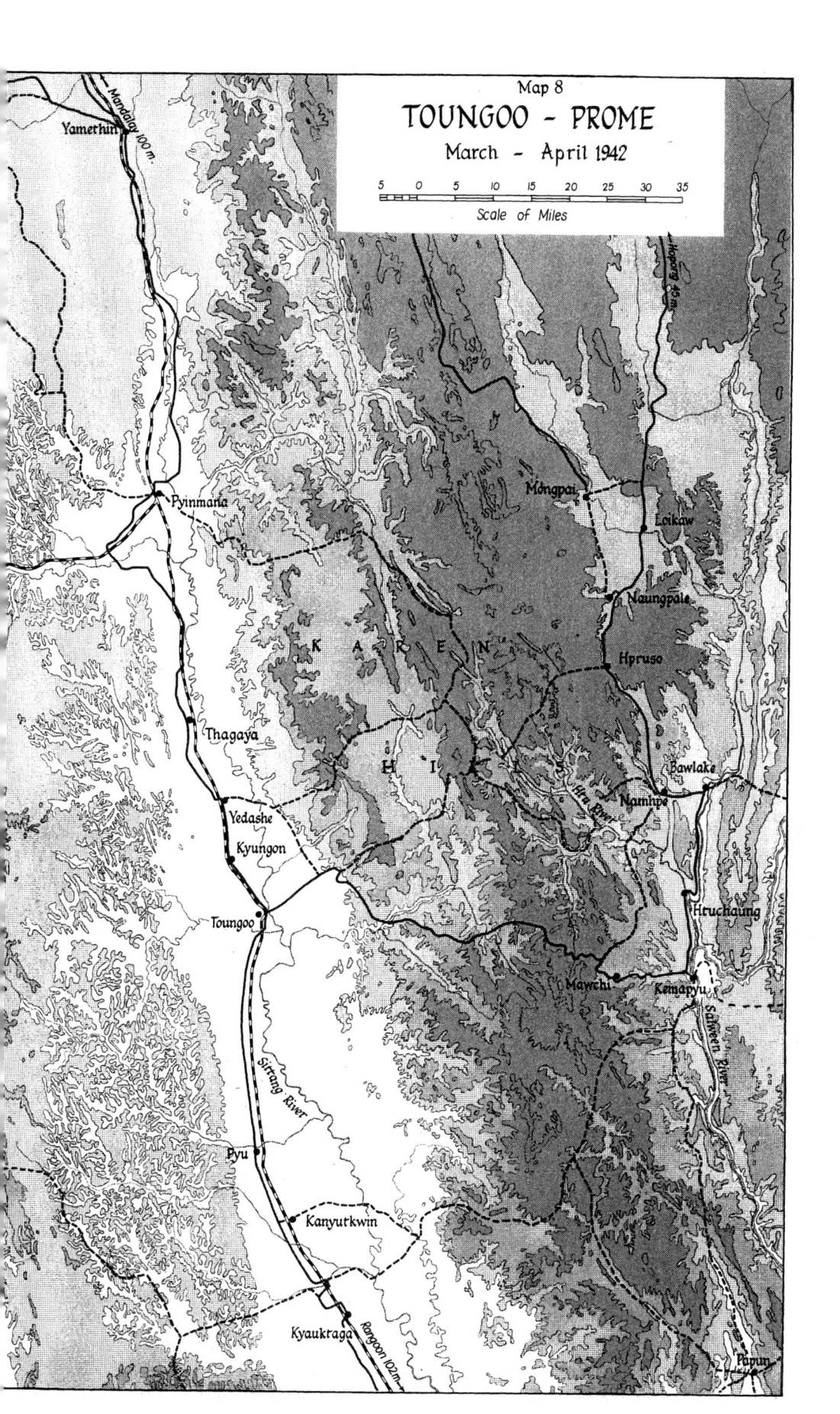

CHAPTER IX

THE STRUGGLE FOR CENTRAL BURMA BEGINS

(March 1942)

See Strategic Map and Maps 1 and 8

THE evacuation of Rangoon completely transformed the campaign in Burma, since all the advantages of sea communications, previously held by the Allies, were now transferred to the Japanese. Cut off from its main base in India, the Army in Burma was now dependent for reinforcements on what could be sent by air and for supplies on the stocks that General Hutton had been able to backload to the Mandalay area, whereas the Japanese, with Malaya and Rangoon in their possession, could pour troops into Burma at will. There was little doubt that the British and Chinese forces would soon be subjected to a heavy scale of attack. It was a question of how long the small British force, aided by V and VI Chinese Armies, could hold central and upper Burma.

On the 7th March, the day before Rangoon fell, *15th Army* received a directive from *Southern Army*. General Iida was instructed to seek out and attack the Allied forces, especially the Chinese armies, bring about a decisive battle in the Mandalay area, and destroy them if possible by the latter part of May. The defeated enemy was then to be pursued to the Sino-Burmese frontier. The advance was to begin without waiting for reinforcements, so as not to lose the opportunity of crushing any enemy forces met south of Mandalay. During the initial operations *15th Army* was to seize the Yenangyaung oilfields and Bassein and, if conditions permitted, the airfield at Akyab.

In order to enable the army to carry out its task it was to be greatly strengthened. On the 18th March, *5th Air Division* was reinforced by the transfer of *7th* and *12th Air Brigades* from Malaya and the Netherlands East Indies, bringing its strength to some 420 aircraft.[1] The *213th Regiment* of *33rd Division* and a mountain artillery regiment, which had reached Bangkok in the latter part of February after the main body of the division had moved into Burma, were sent by sea from Siam to rejoin it and arrived at Rangoon shortly afterwards. A

---

[1] See Appendix 11.

large convoy from Japan carrying the major part of *56th Division* was expected to reach Rangoon on the 25th March,[1] and another carrying *18th Division* from Singapore, less a battalion which was to occupy Port Blair, on the 7th April.[2] Finally two other convoys carrying important reinforcements, which included *1st* and *14th Tank Regiments*, two heavy field artillery regiments, two independent engineer regiments, together with anti-tank, anti-aircraft, signal and line of communication units, were to reach Rangoon early in April.

By the 15th March General Iida had decided on his outline plan of operations. His intention was to begin the advance towards Mandalay as soon as possible along both the Sittang and Irrawaddy valleys and, as his reinforcing formations arrived, deploy them on his right with a view to carrying out a wide enveloping movement, thereby cutting the Allies' line of retreat into China. The *55th Division* was to begin its advance in the middle of March from Pegu northwards along the Rangoon–Mandalay road, and by early April was to be in the Meiktila area so as to protect the assembly of the main body of the army. If circumstances permitted, this division was to detail a detachment to cut the enemy's line of retreat from Yenangyaung. Since the airfield at Toungoo was urgently required to augment the airfields available to *5th Air Division*, it was to be captured in an undamaged condition by a surprise attack. If, during the course of the advance to Meiktila, Allied forces were met advancing southwards, they were to be prevented from interfering with the operations of the rest of the army.

The *33rd Division* was to advance from Rangoon towards the end of March and occupy the Prome–Yenangyaung area by the middle of April. On arrival *56th Division* was to advance to Taunggyi by way of Toungoo and Meiktila. The group of airfields in the vicinity of Taunggyi was to be seized by the middle of April and preparations then made for an advance to the north or north-east. The *18th Division* on arrival was either to move to Taunggyi in preparation for an advance north or north-east, or to be retained in reserve, depending on how the plan developed. Iida expected that the decisive battle for Mandalay would take place on or north of the line Taunggyi–Meiktila–Yenangyaung, that it would be over by the middle of May, and that it would be followed by a drive to complete the occupation of Burma. He proposed to occupy Akyab as soon as the success of the Mandalay operation was assured.

---

[1] The *56th Division* (Lieut.-General Watanabe) was one of the youngest in the Japanese Army, having been raised late in 1941. It consisted of *113th*, *146th* and *148th Infantry Regiments*, but the *146th* had been employed in the operations to capture the Netherlands East Indies (see Volume I, Appendix 23) and did not reach Burma until the 19th April.

[2] The *18th Division* (Lieut.-General Mutaguchi) comprised *55th*, *56th* and *114th Infantry Regiments*.

To meet the expected Japanese offensive, the Allies had in Burma only two weak British divisions—17th Indian (16th, 48th and 63rd Indian Brigades) and 1st Burma (13th Indian, 1st and 2nd Burma Brigades)—7th Armoured Brigade and V and VI Chinese Armies (each equivalent to a division), supported by an Allied air force which could muster only some 150 aircraft. General Alexander had to defend the vital Yenangyaung oilfields and the new base area near Mandalay with three-quarters of these forces, since VI Chinese Army was in the Shan States protecting the left flank and guarding against any Japanese advance northwards from Indo-China. It could thus take no part in the main battle for central Burma which was clearly about to take place.[1] Alexander knew that the length of time he could retain control of central and upper Burma was dependent on the size of the force which the Japanese decided to deploy in the theatre: all he could hope to do was to impose the maximum delay and make them expend resources which they could otherwise use elsewhere.

In order to defend the two routes leading to the vital areas, he decided to concentrate the British forces in the Irrawaddy valley to cover the oilfields, and V Chinese Army in the Sittang valley to cover the direct road and railway leading to Mandalay. The Chinese however were unwilling to move south of Toungoo, and in order to conform with them he had no alternative but to move the British formations in the Irrawaddy valley back to the Prome area. This meant not only sacrificing depth in the defensive zone in front of the oilfields and uncovering the Toungoo–Bawlake road, which gave the enemy easy access to the Karen Hills and Shan States, but abandoning an area which contained large stocks of rice, of which the Chinese were already desperately short.

Alexander therefore decided to withdraw 1st Burma Division, which was in the Sittang valley, and 17th Division, which was reforming at Tharrawaddy, to the Prome area,[2] as soon as 200th Chinese Division (the leading division of V Chinese Army) was in position at Toungoo.[3] This regrouping would result in two British divisions and an armoured brigade concentrating in the Irrawaddy valley, and V Chinese Army under Stilwell's command south of Mandalay. Since Alexander felt he could not satisfactorily undertake the dual rôle of Commander-in-Chief, Burma, and commander of the British forces, he asked, as Hutton had done earlier, for a corps headquarters. Wavell agreed and a skeleton corps headquarters was quickly improvised but, owing to the limitations of air transport from

---

[1] For order of battle of the Chinese Expeditionary Force see Appendix 12.

[2] See Map 1.

[3] This division was the best of the Chinese divisions. Its strength was about 8,500, it was fully mechanized and had a small armoured unit.

India, most of the staff and signals and corps troops had to be found from the forces already in Burma. It was thus deficient in equipment and signal facilities throughout the campaign and was never fully staffed. On the 19th March Lieut.-General W. J. Slim flew in from India to Magwe and assumed command of Burcorps which comprised 1st Burma Division, 17th Indian Division and 7th Armoured Brigade.[1] At the same time 1st Royal Inniskilling Fusiliers was flown into Burma from India.

Although in the Irrawaddy valley there had been no contact with the enemy, there had been considerable fighting in the Sittang valley. On the afternoon of his arrival at Rangoon (5th March) Alexander had given 1st Burma Division orders to attack southwards from Nyaunglebin in co-operation with the attack northwards from Pegu by 17th Division which did not take place.[2] Accordingly on the 11th March, General Bruce Scott advanced on a two-brigade front: 1st Burma Brigade on the right, with Pyuntaza and Daik-U as its objectives; and 2nd Burma Brigade on the left directed on Madauk and, east of the river, on Shwegyin. Pyuntaza was captured, but an immediate Japanese counter-attack by the *Kawashima Detachment* assisted by *I/143rd Battalion* (less one company) and attached troops, which had been sent up from Pegu by *55th Division* and had arrived just in time, forced the evacuation of the village. The 2nd Burma Brigade on the left captured Madauk and Shwegyin, though the attack on the latter met with strong resistance. The division then consolidated on a line astride the main road and railway about three miles south of Nyaunglebin and extending east across the Sittang to Shwegyin.

The following day Alexander ordered the regrouping to begin. The 17th Division was to start withdrawing from the Tharrawaddy area on the 13th and concentrate at Okpo by the 15th, and 1st Burma Division was to move back on the 15th through the Chinese, who by that time would be established in a position covering Toungoo, to Yedashe where it was to entrain for Taungdwingyi.[3] The retirement of 17th Division was practically unmolested; indeed it was the British who showed the offensive spirit by carrying out two successful raids, the first down the river on Henzada on the 17th and the second two days later on Letpadan, both well behind the Japanese lines.[4] The surprise attack on Letpadan, made by the motorized 1st Gloucestershire, drove the enemy out of the town.

The withdrawal of 1st Burma Division did not proceed so smoothly. The Japanese *55th Division* had advanced from Pegu and by the

---

[1] For order of battle of Burcorps on the 19th March 1942 see Appendix 13.
[2] See page 89.
[3] See Map 8.
[4] For Henzada see Strategic Map.

13th March was concentrated at Daik-U, with orders to capture Toungoo and its airfield. The British withdrawal on the 15th upset the Japanese plan to attack 1st Burma Division in its position just south of Nyaunglebin on the night of the 15th/16th. They therefore sent forward two hastily-organized motorized columns, one from each regiment, which gained contact with 1st Burma Brigade on the evening of the 16th at Kyauktaga. Throughout the 17th there was severe fighting near the village. During the night the brigade withdrew and early on the 18th passed through 2nd Burma Brigade in position just south of Kanyutkwin. The latter repulsed a number of Japanese attacks during the day and in turn withdrew in the evening. On the 19th both brigades passed through the advanced posts of 200th Chinese Division about Pyu (with which the enemy made contact that evening) and moved north through Toungoo.[1] By the 21st, 1st Burma Division (less 13th Brigade) had assembled at Yedashe and had begun to entrain for Taungdwingyi, while 13th Brigade had moved from the Mawchi area to Meiktila, leaving a Chinese regiment and Karen Levies to protect the left flank.

Air support for Burcorps was based on the Magwe airfield, a civil airport which had been improved to make it a suitable base for 'Burwing' in the event of the Rangoon airfields becoming unusable except as advanced landing grounds. So long as Rangoon was held, Magwe was covered by an adequate warning system, but when the city was evacuated the whole situation changed. The Japanese air force, likely to be heavily reinforced and with Mingaladon and its satellites at its disposal, was in a position to launch a surprise attack on Magwe where not only was the warning system inadequate but the fighter defence weak. In the circumstances it might have been wiser to concentrate the Allied air forces at Akyab and Loiwing, where they would have been much less exposed to attack, and to make use of Magwe solely as an advanced landing ground to refuel and rearm. The decision to base air forces as far forward as Magwe was influenced largely by the desire to give the fullest close support to the army during this critical period in the land operations, but it had the effect of exposing the weak air forces to the danger of being overwhelmed.

On the 20th March air reconnaissance disclosed a concentration of about a hundred Japanese aircraft in the Rangoon area. Early on the 21st, nine Blenheims escorted by ten Hurricanes made a surprise

---

[1] The withdrawal was greatly complicated by the almost complete lack of Chinese interpreters. General Bruce Scott had to rely on interpreters whose knowledge of English was rudimentary. This lack of competent interpreters continued throughout the campaign.

attack on Mingaladon airfield and destroyed or damaged many aircraft on the ground for the loss of only one Hurricane. Retaliation was immediate: during the day and early the following morning waves of some twenty-seven bombers with the usual fighter escort wrought havoc among the small British force inadequately dispersed on the airfield. Although reinforcements were flown in, only six Blenheims, three Tomahawks and eleven Hurricanes remained by the afternoon of the 22nd, and most of these were unfit for operations. To avoid further losses all aircraft were then withdrawn, the R.A.F. to Akyab and the A.V.G. to Loiwing and Lashio.

The following day Group Captain S. Broughall asked permission to transfer Headquarters 'Burwing' to Lashio and Loiwing which were covered by a more efficient warning system. His request was approved. Road convoys carrying ground staffs moved off that morning, leaving small parties behind to salvage valuable equipment and to refuel any aircraft landing after the departure of 'Burwing'. Later that day Alexander and Stevenson met at Maymyo and decided that an attempt should be made to repair the damage at Magwe. Some of the road convoy comprising repair and salvage parties and defence units were therefore ordered back, and for the next few weeks aircraft operating from India were able to use it as a landing ground.

The enemy air force then set out to neutralize Akyab. The airfield was attacked several times during the 23rd and 24th by forces of up to twenty-seven bombers and fifty fighters and, although the Hurricanes shot down four and probably destroyed two more aircraft, their own loss of six was proportionately far greater. When on the 27th twelve low-flying fighters destroyed seven Hurricanes on the ground and one in the air in a surprise attack, the remnants of 'Akwing' were withdrawn to Chittagong, and Akyab like Magwe was thereafter used only as an advanced landing ground.

Why the weak air forces in Burma, although thrown largely on the defensive, survived the first three months of the war and were able to inflict serious losses on the enemy whenever he attempted to raid Rangoon, while the stronger air force in Malaya was unable to prevent the Japanese from raiding Singapore almost with impunity, and why, after their early successes, the air forces in Burma were suddenly overtaken by disaster, needs some explanation.

The air defence in both countries had been provided with the best warning system which could be produced in the circumstances to guard the most likely lines of approach of enemy aircraft—from Siam and southern Burma in the case of Rangoon and from seawards and from the east coast in Malaya. In northern Malaya there was no fighter control organization and the warning system was ineffective, for the air defence was centred on Singapore. Such was the intensity of enemy air attack on the northern airfields that the advanced British air forces were overwhelmed within the first two days of the war. The subsequent loss of central Malaya destroyed the warning system on the mainland. Moreover, the Japanese concentrated overwhelming strength in the air against Malaya whereas in Burma they used a much smaller air strength at first. As a result the fighter defence of Singapore, which in the early and most decisive stage rested on a fighter aircraft of inferior quality (the Buffalo), was largely swamped. In Burma the Buffaloes were reinforced by Hurricanes sooner and much more easily than was possible in Malaya.[1] Besides, the R.A.F. were supported by the A.V.G. with their Tomahawks, some of whose pilots had met the Japanese air force in China. Finally, the loss of Johore in Malaya not only completed the destruction of the warning system on which the defence depended, but resulted in the three airfields on the north of Singapore Island coming under artillery fire from the mainland. It was this lack of secure airfields which compelled the withdrawal of the defending fighters from Singapore to Sumatra, whereas in Burma, so long as the air defence remained centred on Rangoon, both the Mingaladon airfield (with its satellites) and the warning system protecting it remained inviolate.

But when Rangoon was evacuated, the warning system covering lower Burma largely disintegrated. At Magwe (and Akyab), to which the Allied air force was withdrawn, a warning system of a sort existed but in contrast to that covering Rangoon it was rudimentary, for the observer posts from Mandalay to Prome provided only incomplete cover. Once they had the use of the airfields at Rangoon, the Japanese were able to move their air forces from Malaya, where the fighting had ceased, and bring overwhelming strength to bear on Burma. The conditions which had ruled in Malaya between December 1941 and February 1942 were then reproduced in Burma. The weak Allied air forces, based in areas where they could not get sufficient warning and where they could be attacked by Japanese bombers with fighter escort, were then doomed.

After the destruction of the Allied air force at Magwe and Akyab, the Japanese, instead of using all their air strength to harass the retreating Burma Army, concentrated the greater part of it against traffic on the Irrawaddy and the chief centres of road and rail communication in rear of the Allies. Constant low-flying attacks were made against vessels using the river, and heavy bombing raids were made on Meiktila, Mandalay, Thazi, Pyinmana, Maymyo, Lashio and Taunggyi; some of these towns being almost completely destroyed. After a heavy raid the inhabitants invariably moved out *en masse* to the jungle, and many railway employees and crews of the Irrawaddy Flotilla Company left their posts. Under these attacks the

---
[1] For particulars of British and enemy aircraft see Appendix 23.

police force began to disintegrate, power supplies broke down, disease (especially cholera) became rampant and outbreaks of lawlessness were of frequent occurrence. The dislocation of the public utility services and the growing disorder became a serious embarrassment to the army.

By this time Wavell had realized that he could not count on holding central and upper Burma for long against a determined attack, and that a stage might soon be reached when he would have to decide whether the forces in Burma should withdraw north-east into China, thereby uncovering the Indian frontier, or north-west into Assam, thereby losing touch with China. On the 19th March he told the Prime Minister why he thought the Allied forces would be driven out of Burma, and that he proposed to instruct Alexander that, in the event of a withdrawal, Burcorps should maintain touch with the Chinese at all costs. The Chief of the Imperial General Staff then asked if his desire to maintain touch with the Chinese were based on political or military reasons; what rôle he intended for Burcorps in China; how he proposed to maintain it; if it would include an air detachment; and, finally, whether he could ensure the security of the Assam frontier if Burcorps retreated into China.

Wavell replied that for the time being communications and the location of reserve supplies in the Meiktila–Mandalay area were the ruling factors. If Burcorps were forced back from Prome, the line of withdrawal would have to cover this area. From Mandalay the line of withdrawal towards India was either to Kalewa by river transport up the Chindwin or by tracks from Yeu, or alternatively by rail to Mogaung and thence, when it was constructed, by the Hukawng Valley road to Ledo.[1] Transport was, however, very limited on both the Irrawaddy and Chindwin Rivers. There were no reserves of supplies along the route to India and the roads from the Indian border could not be completed for a long time. The only alternative to falling back towards India by one of these routes was to withdraw with the Chinese on to Lashio. From the political standpoint of keeping China in the war, the presence there of a British-Indian force would presumably have considerable value. The rôle of such a force would be generally to threaten or attack the communications of any enemy advancing on India, and to co-operate in Chinese resistance. Partial, if not total, maintenance would have to be by air once reserves were finished. Whether an air detachment would accompany the force would depend on the general air situation in north-east India at the time. Arrangements for the defence of the Assam frontier would be made independently of the force then in Burma.

[1] See Map 14.

RETREAT TO INDIA OR CHINA PLANNED

When asked for his views, Alexander said he expected the Japanese to advance simultaneously by the Prome and Toungoo routes with the object of occupying the oilfield area and cutting the communications between China and India. Their first objective, after gaining the oilfields, would be the Mandalay area. They would then probably advance to Lashio and Bhamo and finally to Myitkyina. He therefore considered that a gradual withdrawal northwards by the Allied forces was inevitable, for they were weak and without air support whereas the enemy could reinforce through Rangoon.

He proposed to cover Mandalay as long as possible but, if further retirement were necessary, he was considering a plan whereby Burcorps Headquarters, 7th Armoured Brigade and one infantry brigade of four battalions withdrew on Lashio, acting as rearguard to the Chinese armies, while the remainder of the force withdrew to the Monywa–Shwebo area to cover the Kalewa approach to India and to operate on the flank of any Japanese advance on Lashio. The former force might withdraw into China, which would involve supplying it by air, or alternatively to the Bhamo area, where it would constitute a threat to any Japanese advance into China. A part of the latter force might also withdraw to Bhamo or alternatively the whole force might withdraw by way of Kalewa into India. Any forces which retired on Bhamo would have to rely for their communications to India on the road which he understood was likely to be constructed from Ledo down the Hukawng Valley. In forwarding Alexander's views to the Chiefs of Staff, Wavell said he had accepted them and had instructed him to make his administrative preparations accordingly, but the eventual decision would naturally have to depend on the situation at the time.

While the regrouping of the Allied forces on the general line Prome–Toungoo was taking place, the problem of the command of the Chinese armies entering Burma became a live issue. When General Chiang Kai-shek had offered in December to send Chinese troops to Burma, he had agreed that they should be placed under British command.[1] In January he had accepted the President's proposal that he become Supreme Commander of the China theatre of war and had asked for a high-ranking American officer to be sent to China to be his Chief of Staff. The British and American Chiefs of Staff agreed that this officer should also command all American forces in China and any Chinese forces assigned to him; but, if any of these forces had to operate in Burma, they would come under the

---

[1] See page 17.

command of the Supreme Commander, ABDA Area,[1] who would issue the necessary instructions for their co-operation with the troops in Burma under British commanders.

In February Lieut.-General J. W. Stilwell was chosen to fill the post of the Generalissimo's Chief of Staff and appointed Commanding General of the United States Army Forces in the China–Burma–India (CBI) theatre of operations.[2] He arrived in Chungking on the 4th March. Stilwell, who knew the Chinese well and spoke their language, was an unconventional man of fifty-eight but with the mental and physical toughness of a much younger man. He was outspoken to the point of rudeness, his criticisms were often unjustified and he could be utterly uncompromising. These traits made him many enemies and earned for him from his compatriots the nickname 'Vinegar Joe', but those who knew him in action testified to his great courage and determination, and his powers of leadership in the field.

The Generalissimo at once gave him to understand that he would be in command of the Chinese armies in Burma, and on the 9th cabled Washington that he wished Stilwell to command both the British and Chinese troops. His desire appears to have sprung from his mistrust of the British after the misunderstandings which had arisen at the December conference in Chungking[3], and the disasters in Malaya and southern Burma. The attempt to reverse the original decision on the question of command caused some alarm in both Washington and London. Pending a settlement of the problem, the Generalissimo told Stilwell that 200th Chinese Division would stay at Toungoo as long as the British held Prome but that the remaining divisions of V Chinese Army (22nd and 96th) would move only as far south as Mandalay.[4] This would leave only one division to hold the vital Toungoo area.

General Wavell first heard of this on the 14th March when he was told of the Generalissimo's cable to the President. The same day Stilwell, who had flown to Burma, told Alexander that the Generalissimo had placed him in independent command of the Chinese armies in Burma. To both Wavell and Alexander this appeared to be most unsatisfactory, for they considered that not only had Stilwell insufficient staff and local knowledge to take command, but that his other duties in China would inevitably distract his attention from the conduct of operations. Moreover the British had built up a supply organization for the Chinese, who had no supply units, and had

---

[1] See Volume I, pages 266-67. When the control of Burma passed to India Command, this was changed to Commander-in-Chief in India.

[2] Romanus and Sunderland, page 74. For Stilwell's directive as cabled to Wavell see Appendix 14.

[3] See pages 16-19.

[4] Romanus and Sunderland, pages 94-97.

PROBLEM OF ALLIED COMMAND, BURMA 155

provided a complete system of liaison, down to divisions, which Stilwell could not replace.

Stilwell, together with General Lin Wei (Chinese General Staff Mission), had meanwhile seen the commanders of both V and VI Chinese Armies and obtained their agreement to a plan under which V Army was to be concentrated as quickly as possible at Toungoo, and 22nd and 96th Chinese Divisions moved into Burma at once. Stilwell then flew back to Chungking to get the Generalissimo's agreement to his plans. After some persuasion Chiang Kai-shek agreed that 22nd Chinese Division could be used in emergency to assist 200th Division at Toungoo, but he would not permit 96th Division to go beyond Mandalay. He insisted that Stilwell was to adopt a strictly defensive attitude and was not to assist Alexander except in an emergency. Nevertheless he agreed to one division (38th) of LXVI Chinese Army moving to Maymyo while the rest of the army concentrated near the frontier as a reserve to V and VI Armies.[1]

On the the 17th Wavell received a message from Stilwell which read,

> 'I have assumed command of Chinese V and VI Armies by direction of Chiang Kai-shek who has released 22nd and 96th Divisions, now on Chinese border. I have ordered them to positions [in the] vicinity [of] Pyinmana, and will expedite movement as much as possible—will have liaison group at Maymyo from now on. My rear echelon will be [at] Lashio, and forward echelon [at] Pyawbwe alongside V Army Headquarters.'[2]

On the 19th Wavell told the Chiefs of Staff that, although the best solution was unity of command under Alexander, he would be prepared to accept a compromise on the understanding that Alexander would be charged with the co-ordination of both the British and Chinese forces in Burma on his, Wavell's, behalf.

On the 21st Stilwell established his headquarters in Burma and the following day met Alexander at Maymyo. Later Alexander told Wavell that, after further consideration and practical experience, he thought it would be a mistake to alter the arrangements whereby the Chinese armies in Burma had been placed under Stilwell's command. He added that Stilwell had his entire confidence and was likely to obtain more co-operation from the Chinese than anyone else.

The situation changed on the 24th when Alexander went to Chungking to pay his respects to the Generalissimo. Chiang Kai-shek, who had already shown that he was unable to follow a constant policy, once again changed his ground and stated that, in order to

---
[1] Romanus and Sunderland, page 99.
[2] For Pyawbwe see Map 9.

ensure unity of command, and pending a decision in London and Washington, all Chinese forces in Burma would be under Alexander's command. On his return to Maymyo, Alexander informed Stilwell of the Generalissimo's latest wishes. Stilwell, who was in favour of Alexander commanding in Burma, readily agreed to serve under him, while remaining himself in command of the Chinese armies under Alexander's general direction. From that time the two men co-operated with each other loyally until the end of the campaign.

But the system of command of the Chinese forces in Burma was never entirely satisfactory. The Generalissimo, despite his repeated statements that Stilwell was in command of the Chinese armies in Burma, did not give him the Kwan-fang (seal) as Commander-in-Chief but only as Chief of Staff. As a result, the Chinese commanders were not prepared to accept his orders. All orders issued by Stilwell had to pass through General Lin Wei and no orders of a major nature issued by either Alexander, Stilwell or Lin Wei could be carried out unless they had the sanction of the Generalissimo, who constantly changed his mind. Quick decisions for the employment of the Chinese forces were therefore impossible to obtain and this, together with the almost total lack of knowledge of staff duties in the Chinese Army, often caused fatal delay in the execution of urgent movements.

By the 19th March, Japanese forces had gained touch with the forward troops of 200th Chinese Division near Pyu south of Toungoo. The Chinese, fighting stubbornly, fell back slowly to their main perimeter defences around Toungoo. On the morning of the 23rd a motorized column from *143rd Regiment*, making a wide enveloping movement west of the town, occupied the airfield at Kyungon between Toungoo and Yedashe and cut off 200th Division from the rest of V Chinese Army. On the 22nd Stilwell had ordered 55th Chinese Division of VI Army from the Karen Hills to move to the aid of 200th Division, while 22nd Division moved forward to the Pyinmana–Taungdwingyi area and 96th Division to Mandalay. By the 25th, 1st and 2nd Reserve Regiments from the training depot of V Chinese Army had reached the area north of Toungoo, and were ordered to counter-attack and recapture the airfield; but the order was not obeyed.

The Chinese resistance at Toungoo forced the Japanese to reinforce *55th Division* by bringing forward advanced elements of *56th Division* which had arrived in Rangoon on the 25th. At the same time Stilwell, who saw the possibility of inflicting a severe defeat on the Japanese if he could but counter-attack in strength southwards, did his utmost to hurry forward 22nd and 96th Chinese Divisions. The former division had arrived at Pyinmana by the 26th and Stilwell ordered it to attack in order to relieve 200th Division.[1] To his chagrin he found that his command of the Chinese armies was more illusory than real, for the division made no attempt to obey his orders. Despite promises from the Chinese commanders that an attack would be launched on the 28th, again nothing happened. In desperation Stilwell sent a message to Burma Army Headquarters and to Chungking asking that the British take the offensive in the Irrawaddy valley to relieve the pressure on Toungoo, and sent two of his staff officers to Burcorps with the same request. On the 30th, in the face of ever-increasing enemy pressure, 200th Division was forced to abandon its positions in Toungoo and, cutting its way out of the town, passed through 22nd Division, whose advanced troops were at Yedashe, and went into reserve north of Pyinmana.

At Toungoo, 200th Division had put up a most stubborn defence and at the cost of heavy casualties had held numerically superior Japanese forces, closely supported by the Japanese air force, for nearly a fortnight. When forced to withdraw northwards it failed, however, to blow the bridge over the Sittang River which carried the Toungoo–Mawchi–Bawlake road. The Japanese thus gained immediate use of this road, which led into the heart of the Karen Hills and Shan States. The loss of Toungoo and of the control of the Mawchi–Bawlake road were to have a serious effect on the future of the campaign.

We must now turn to events in the Irrawaddy valley. By the 27th March, 17th Division (Cowan) and 7th Armoured Brigade (Anstice) had been concentrated in the Prome area; divisional headquarters, 48th Brigade and 7th Armoured Brigade in the Tamagauk–Wettigan area, 63rd Brigade at Prome and 16th Brigade between Sinmizwe and Prome, while 1st Gloucestershire (which had been organized as the divisional reconnaissance battalion) covered the divisional front in the vicinity of Paungde. The left flank was protected by F.F. units, while Force Viper and an infantry detachment watched the river and right flank.[2] Further north 1st Burma Division was concentrating in the area Thayetmyo–Allanmyo–Kyaukpadaung. Alexander's intention was to base the defence of the valley on two brigade groups holding Prome and Allanmyo respectively, which were to be prepared for all-round defence and held to the last; the rest of Burcorps was to remain mobile and be prepared to take offensive action.

---

[1] Owing to a local government official giving a premature order for the evacuation of Pyinmana without reference to the military, the railway staff was evacuated. Consequently 22nd Chinese Division was compelled to detrain north of Pyinmana some sixty miles from Toungoo. This evacuation also immobilized the branch line to Kyaukpadaung.
[2] See page 96 for Force Viper.

On the 26th, Slim (Burcorps) received a message from Headquarters, Burma Army, asking him to stage a demonstration on the Prome front to coincide with an attack by 22nd Chinese Division at Toungoo. He gave the task to 17th Division. Cowan thereupon formed a striking force, under command of Brigadier Anstice, consisting of 7th Hussars, 414th Battery, R.H.A., 14th Field Company, 1st Cameronians, 2nd Duke of Wellington's, 1st Gloucestershire and one company of 1st West Yorkshire.[1] Two days later Slim received a telegram from Alexander, then in Chungking, instructing him to act offensively to relieve pressure on the Chinese. Accordingly he directed Cowan to launch a local offensive immediately, with the object of securing Paungde on the 29th and Okpo (some fifty miles to the south) on the 30th and destroying any enemy encountered. Nyaungzaye was to be occupied to protect the west flank against a mixed force of Burmans and Japanese, estimated at over 4,000 strong and reported to be advancing up the right bank of the river.

On the 25th, however, the Japanese had begun their advance northwards from the Letpadan–Henzada area, *33rd Division* moving with *214th Regiment* along the main road to Prome and *215th Regiment*, accompanied by a force of rebel Burmans, west of the Irrawaddy River; and on the 28th a clash occurred between the Gloucesters and the advanced elements of *214th Regiment* at Paungde. To prevent the Gloucesters from being isolated, Anstice withdrew them during the day and ordered Paungde to be attacked the following day as a prelude to the proposed advance on Okpo.

During the 29th the striking force became involved in two separate actions: one at Padigon and the other at Paungde. All attempts to clear Padigon failed but a footing in Paungde was gained by 11 a.m. Later in the day, however, it was discovered that an enemy force had entered Shwedaung behind the British striking force, and Cowan immediately ordered Anstice to break off the actions at Padigon and Paungde and concentrate his force to fight its way back to Prome. At the same time he ordered 4/12th F.F. Regiment and 2/13th F.F.Rifles, supported by a battery of Indian field artillery, to retake Shwedaung by an attack from the north.

The Japanese in Shwedaung were the leading elements of *215th Regiment* which had crossed to the east bank of the river at Kyangin and moved north through Nyaungzaye. On reaching the village they had adopted their now familiar tactics and established a series of road blocks north and south of it. Throughout the night and the following day, 17th Division made repeated attempts from both north and south to clear them. The enemy, however, was steadily reinforced from across the river and during the afternoon was sup-

---

[1] All the infantry units were under strength and the striking force was thus equivalent to about one and a half battalions.

12. Sir Reginald Dorman-Smith and General the Hon. Sir Harold Alexander.

13. Lieut.-General Shojiro Iida.

14. Major-General J. Bruce Scott, Sir John Wise (Counsellor to the Governor), General the Hon. Sir Harold Alexander, General Sir Archibald Wavell, Lieut.-General W. J. Slim, Brigadier H. L. Davies.

15. Air Chief Marshal Sir Richard Peirse.

ported by aircraft which bombed the divisional transport with devastating effect. Although a passage through the blocks was eventually forced, enabling the guns, tanks and infantry to break out, most of the transport had to be abandoned. The British diversion to help the Chinese had resulted in considerable loss for, in addition to much transport, two guns and ten tanks, the already depleted infantry lost a further twenty-one officers and 290 other ranks.

Meanwhile the detachment on the west bank of the river had been ambushed in Padaung and lost half its strength, with the result that the enemy was able to move along the river bank unchecked and, by the evening of the 30th, had reached a point immediately opposite Prome. On the east of the river, hard hit in the fighting of the 29th and 30th, the enemy did not follow up, and during the 31st there were only patrol actions in the vicinity of Shwedaung and Sinmizwe.

On the 1st April Wavell and Alexander visited Slim at Burcorps' headquarters at Allanmyo. It was now becoming obvious that, after the action at Shwedaung and the loss of Toungoo by the Chinese, the continued occupation of Prome involved a considerable risk. Alexander therefore decided, with Wavell's approval, to withdraw from Prome and concentrate Burcorps in the Thayetmyo–Allanmyo area. Since it might be found advisable to continue the movement northward to an area where the country was more open and tanks could operate to greater advantage, Slim was ordered to speed up the backloading of stores.

The dispositions of 17th Division on this date were: 63rd Brigade (Brigadier A. E. Barlow) at Prome, which was now in ruins as a result of air attack; 16th Brigade (Brigadier J. K. Jones) immediately to the east of the town, roughly on the line of the road to Paukkaung; 48th Brigade (Brigadier R. T. Cameron) near Hmawza; and 7th Armoured Brigade at Tamagauk. Further north 1st Burma Division was disposed with 1st Burma Brigade at Dayindabo and 2nd Burma Brigade at Allanmyo.

Bringing up their troops in motor transport from Shwedaung, the Japanese launched a general attack against Prome at about midnight on the 1st/2nd, and in bright moonlight *215th Regiment* fought its way into the town threatening to overwhelm 63rd Brigade Headquarters and the gun positions, and forcing Barlow to withdraw to positions astride the road and railway on its eastern exits. Meanwhile *214th Regiment* had struck at Hmawza, but had been repulsed.

At about 3 a.m. on the 2nd Cowan, expecting that the enemy would attack eastwards from Prome, decided to pull back and take up a new position astride the road on the general line of the Nawin Chaung. He ordered 48th and 63rd Brigades to disengage before dawn and move back to the selected position through 16th Brigade, while 7th Armoured Brigade covered the left flank along the

Wettigan road. At about 10 a.m., however, he received a report from an officer of the Burma Military Police that an enemy column had passed north through Prome during the early hours and might be heading for Dayindabo.[1] If this report were true, 17th Division was likely to find itself in an awkward predicament since the main road, along which it must fall back to Allanmyo, passed through fifteen miles of forest reserve which provided ideal conditions for enemy road block tactics. Cowan consulted Slim by wireless and the latter agreed that the division must march at once for Dayindabo.

At 11.30 a.m. the retirement began. April in Burma is one of the hottest months of the year and the division was now entering the most arid region of the country. The heat was intense, the road dusty and the march a severe trial to the troops. Water was scarce and it was difficult to prevent the men crowding round the infrequent water holes. Japanese aircraft attacked at intervals, but the enemy made no attempt to close and that night the division reached Dayindabo. Next day it continued its withdrawal northward, again being attacked from the air on the line of march and, passing through 1st Burma Brigade and Dayindabo, reached the Allanmyo area.

On the 3rd April Major-General T. J. W. Winterton arrived from India and took over the appointment of Chief of Staff to General Alexander from Hutton, who had asked Wavell to replace him by an officer of appropriate rank as and when convenient. At Alexander's request Hutton remained attached to Army Headquarters till the 26th.

Slim issued an instruction on the 3rd outlining his future plans. His intention was to deny to the enemy the oilfields at Yenangyaung and Chauk[2], to cover upper Burma and to maintain touch with V Chinese Army operating in the Sittang River valley. Delaying positions were to be taken up in succession covering Allanmyo, Sinbaungwe and on the general line Minhla–Taungdwingyi. Burcorps would stand and fight on the general line of the Yin Chaung some twenty miles south of the Yenangyaung oilfields.

Before the withdrawal to the selected battle ground could be completed, a pause of two days was necessary to give time for the small oilfields north of Thayetmyo to be demolished and for the backloading of stores, the successful clearance of which was now of vital importance as the premature withdrawal from Prome had resulted in heavy losses of material. These tasks completed, Allanmyo and Thayetmyo were evacuated on the night of the 5th/6th, and by the 8th the whole force reached the Minhla–Taungdwingyi line, with

---

[1] There is no evidence that any column was directed on Dayindabo.
[2] See Map 9.

2nd Burma Brigade west of the Irrawaddy at Minhla.[1] After the withdrawal from Prome on the 2nd there had been no contact with the Japanese main forces, but the consequences of the disasters which had overtaken the Allied air forces at Magwe and Akyab were now beginning to be felt, and enemy aircraft were becoming more and more active over Burcorps' forward areas.

Requests for additional air support had already been made. On the 28th March the Governor had told the Secretary of State for Burma that more transport aircraft were urgently required to meet the critical military and civil situation, adding that his telegram was sent on the advice of Burma Army Headquarters. Wavell, after his meeting with Alexander and Stilwell on the 1st April, had told the Prime Minister that the Japanese complete command of the air was setting the commanders in Burma an extremely difficult task. On the 5th, Alexander cabled Wavell that the lack of any air support was already adversely affecting the morale of the troops. He asked that fighters should be made available and that the three or four transport aircraft serving the Burma theatre should be supplemented from American resources so that reinforcements could be flown in. Next day he followed this up with a personal letter in which he admitted that the state of the troops under his command was causing him anxiety. The 17th Division was, he said, tired and dispirited, and consequently did not fight well at Prome. Unit commanders were complaining that they had been fighting for over three months without relief, that as no reinforcements were arriving their units were getting weaker and weaker, and that they had had to suffer constant bombing and machine-gunning from low altitudes without any support from British aircraft. If the Imperial forces were to give of their best their morale must be raised. This could be done only by flying in fresh reinforcements to bring units to a reasonable strength and enable them to be relieved from time to time, by providing adequate air support and by propaganda. Wavell replied that he had sent six Blenheims and eight Hurricanes to 'Burwing' to operate for a limited period. Although, he said, he appreciated that morale was bound to suffer from the lack of air support, this was all he could spare in view of the necessity for conserving his resources for the air defence of north-east India. The Chiefs of Staff also recognized the effect upon morale of leaving the Army in Burma almost entirely without air support, but agreed that Wavell was right to conserve his resources.

The lack of air support had another aspect not specifically mentioned in this interchange of telegrams. Alexander and Slim had no means of carrying out air reconnaissance over enemy-held territory in Burma and had to rely entirely on ground patrols for information

---

[1] The 2nd Burma Brigade had crossed from Allanmyo to Thayetmyo on the 4th April.

of enemy movements. They were thus unable to obtain early indication of Japanese plans and, not knowing when and where the enemy was concentrating, were never able to take the initiative for the rest of the campaign.

The preliminary skirmishes were now over and the stage set for the main battle for central Burma, with everything in the enemy's favour. The Japanese army was homogeneous, with undisputed air superiority, and, with sea communications secure and control of the port of Rangoon, could easily be reinforced. The Allied armies on the other hand, although ostensibly under a single commander, served two masters, for the Chinese formations obeyed only orders countersigned by the Generalissimo. They were almost entirely without air support, and the British forces were bound to diminish in strength and efficiency as the campaign continued since they could be neither reinforced nor re-equipped.

Map 9

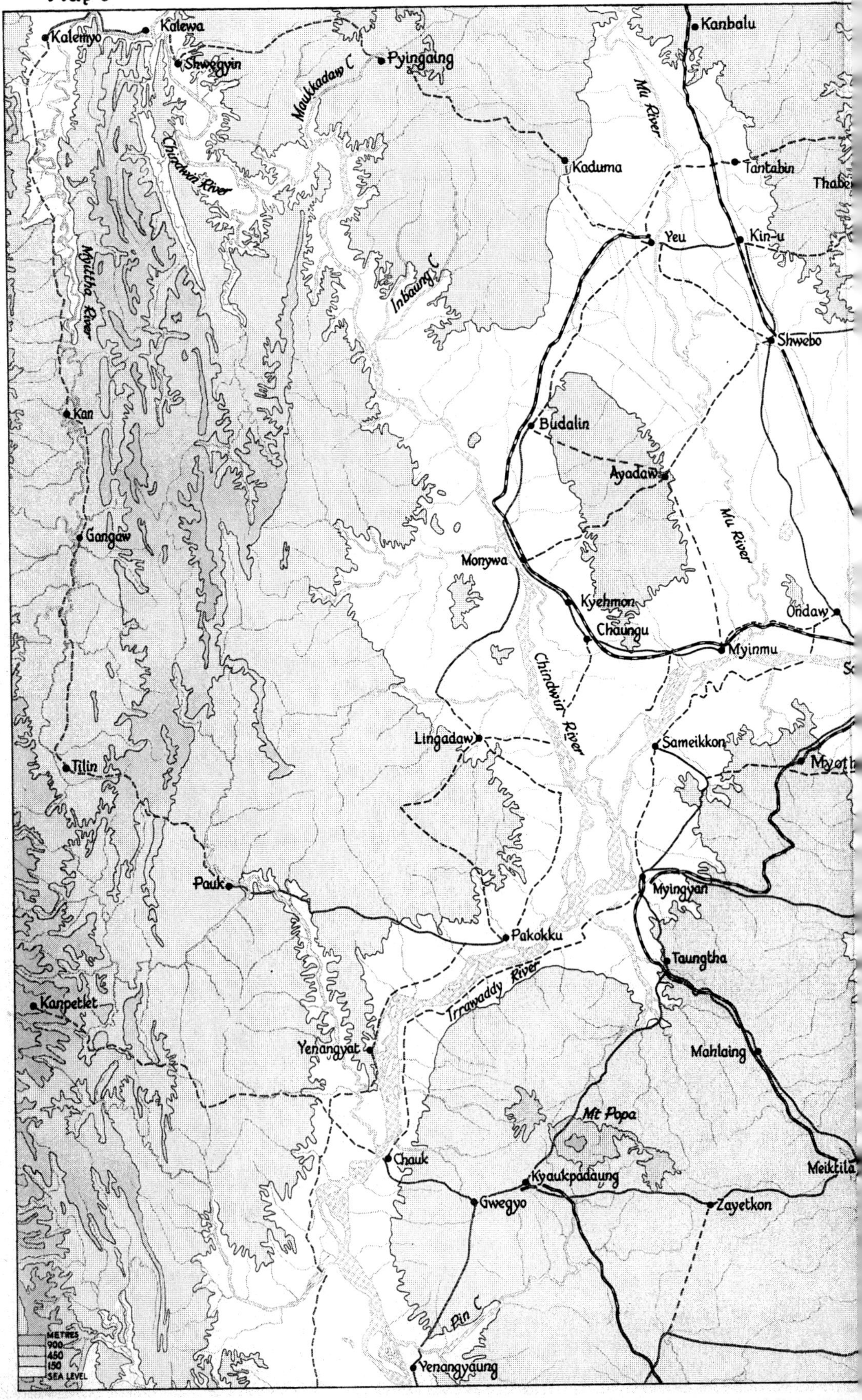
Kalemyo
Kalewa
Shwegyin
Pyingaing
Kanbalu
Maukkadaw C
Mu River
Chindwin River
Kaduma
Tantabin
Thabe
Yeu
Kin-u
Myittha River
Inbaung C
Shwebo
Kan
Budalin
Ayadaw
Gangaw
Mu River
Monywa
Kyehmon
Ondaw
Chaungu
Myinmu
Chindwin River
Lingadaw
Sameikkon
Tilin
Pauk
Myingyan
Pakokku
Taungtha
Irrawaddy River
Kanpetlet
Yenangyat
Mahlaing
Mt Popa
Chauk
Kyaukpadaung
Meiktila
Gwegyo
Zayetkon
Pin C
METRES
900
450
150
SEA LEVEL
Yenangyaung

Map 9
MANDALAY – KALEWA
April–May 1942

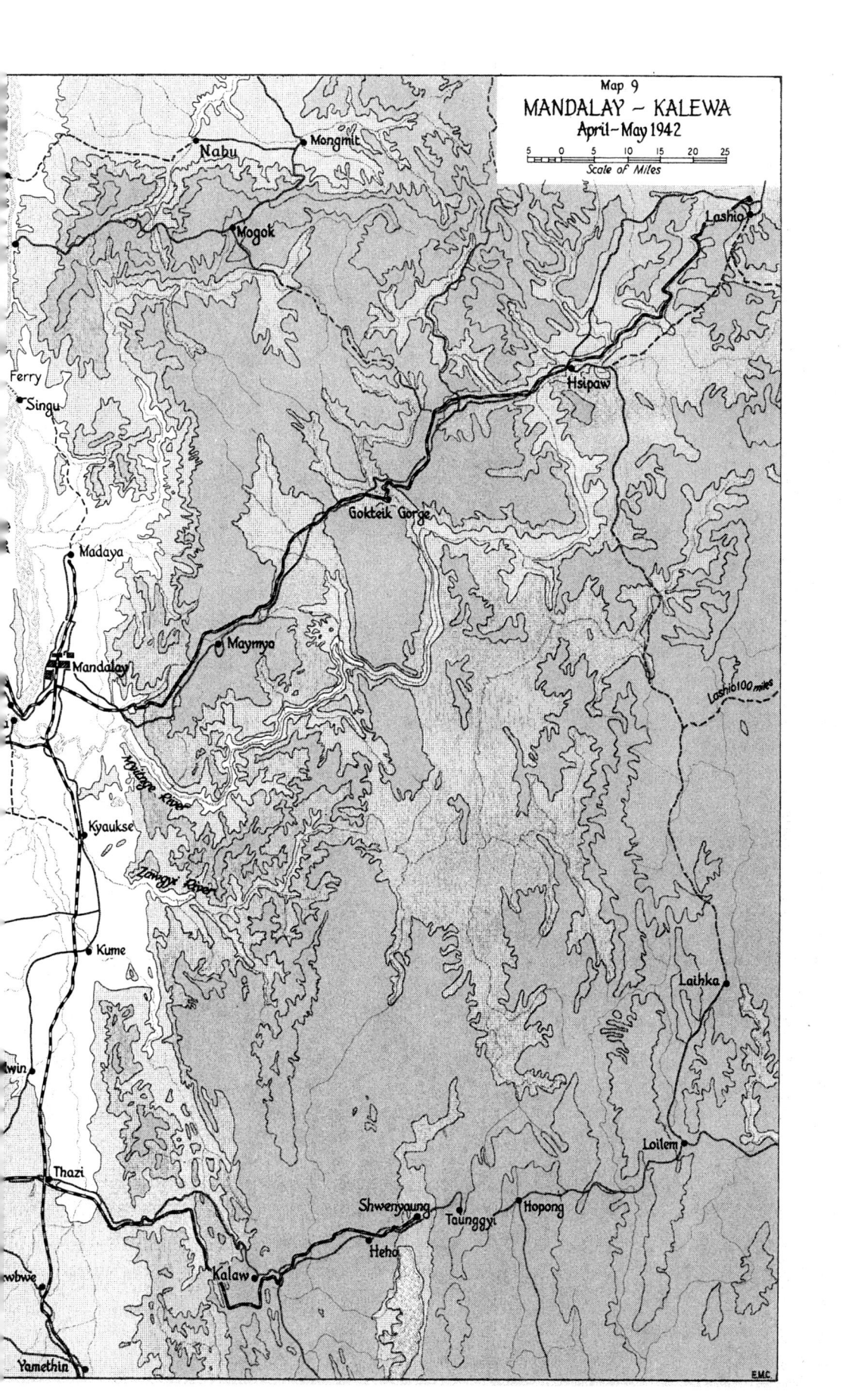

CHAPTER X

THE LOSS OF CENTRAL BURMA
(April 1942)

See Strategic Map, Maps 8 and 9 and Sketch 6

THE Japanese were quick to take advantage of the capture of Toungoo which gave them control of the road leading into the Karen Hills and Shan States. General Iida moved his headquarters there on the 2nd April and the following day issued a revised plan for the Mandalay battle. His plan of the 15th March had laid down the starting line for this battle as Taunggyi–Meiktila–Yenangyaung but, as a secret document captured at Toungoo had shown that the major portion of the Chinese expeditionary force was already south of Mandalay, he decided to adopt a new starting line further south, namely Loikaw–Yamethin–Yenangyaung. He planned to cut the Burma Road, and thus the Chinese line of communication, in the vicinity of Lashio and, by encircling the Allied forces in the Mandalay area, force them to fight with their backs to the Irrawaddy. On the right flank *56th Division*, supported by a tank regiment and two battalions of artillery and given extra mobility by the attachment of an independent motor transport battalion of 250 vehicles, was to advance rapidly on Lashio by way of Bawlake, Loikaw and Hsipaw. In the centre, *18th Division* and *55th Division* were directed to advance along the axis of the main road and railway to Mandalay; the former was then to cut the Burma Road immediately east of Mandalay while the latter drove the Allied forces up against the river. Simultaneously on the left flank *33rd Division* was to advance up the eastern bank of the Irrawaddy to Myingyan, outflanking the Allied right, and be prepared later to cross the river and move direct on Shwebo.

General Alexander on his part had decided to stand on the line Minhla–Taungdwingyi–Pyinmana–Loikaw. Burcorps was to be responsible for the forty-mile front as far east as Taungdwingyi, V Chinese Army for the Pyinmana area and VI Chinese Army for the Loikaw area. Alexander realized that the front allotted to Burcorps was far too long and could only be held by the sacrifice of all depth in the defence. Nevertheless the retention of Taungdwingyi was essential, for its loss would expose not only the right flank of V Chinese Army but the British left flank as well. On the 4th April therefore he asked V Army for assistance. General Tu Yu-ming agreed to send a Chinese regiment to Taungdwingyi. On the 6th, at Maymyo, Alexander met the Generalissimo, who insisted that there must be no further retirements and undertook to stand at Pyinmana, provided that the British also stood on the Minhla–Taungdwingyi line. Both agreed that the time had come to stand and fight. Alexander then pointed out that so wide was the front covered by Burcorps that in order to form a reserve he wanted a substantial Chinese force sent across the Pegu Yomas to Taungdwingyi. The Generalissimo agreed to send a complete Chinese division in place of the promised regiment, but three days later wrote to Stilwell telling him not to send one. Although constantly pressed to send a division, the Generalissimo vacillated for several days and in the end no Chinese formation was ever sent to help Burcorps hold the Minhla–Taungdwingyi line.[1] The long front had therefore to be held without any mobile reserve.

On the 6th April General Slim issued his orders for the eventual dispositions of Burcorps on the line Minhla–Taungdwingyi. The 2nd Burma Brigade, operating under corps control, was to hold Minhla on the west bank of the Irrawaddy; 1st Burma Division (1st Burma, 13th and 48th Brigades and 7th Armoured Brigade), referred to as the Corps' Striking Force, was to hold the line of the road from Migyaungye to Kokkogwa with 1st Burma Brigade at Migyaungye, 13th Brigade at Thityagauk, 48th Brigade at Kokkogwa and 7th Armoured Brigade just east of it;[2] and 17th Division (16th and 63rd Brigades) was to hold the Taungdwingyi–Satthwa area.[3] Slim's plan was that each part of the Corps' Striking Force was to reconnoitre tracks leading into the area from the south so that it could rapidly concentrate against any enemy columns moving north on its flanks or attack in flank any enemy advance on Taungdwingyi. He ordered an observation screen to be established along the whole corps front on a line some sixteen miles to the south of the general position.

Burcorps was now operating in the thinly populated dry zone where the country was generally undulating, though in places steep and rugged, with thin vegetation and scanty patches of forest. Water courses bit sharply into the hills but, save for the main tributaries of the Irrawaddy, were dry at this season of the year. As a result the dispositions of the Corps' Striking Force had to be governed to a large extent by considerations of water supply. As roads in the

---

[1] One Chinese battalion did appear at Taungdwingyi but was withdrawn before making contact with 17th Division.
[2] Both 13th and 48th Brigades had a small detachment of tanks from 2nd Royal Tank Regiment under command.
[3] For order of battle of Burcorps see Appendix 15.

area were even fewer than in lower Burma, Burcorps ordered the engineers to improve the existing communications, particularly the Magwe–Natmauk road and the railway line from Taungdwingyi through Natmauk to Kyaukpadaung, which was to be converted into a motorable road.[1] The Minhla–Taungdwingyi position was to be occupied during the 8th.

The Japanese plan for the capture of Yenangyaung was as follows: *215th Regiment* was directed on Yagyidaw and Kokkogwa to protect the right flank against interference from the British forces known to be in Taungdwingyi; *213th Regiment*, supported by *33rd Mountain Artillery Regiment* (less one battalion), was to advance up the east bank of the Irrawaddy through Sinbaungwe and capture Magwe, while *214th Regiment*, with one battalion of *33rd Mountain Regiment*, moved by way of Thityagauk, Nyaungbinywa and Tanbinzu to seize the ferry over the Pin Chaung north of Yenangyaung, thus cutting the British line of retreat. The *214th* and *215th Regiments* were to leave Allanmyo on the evening of the 9th and the morning of the 10th respectively. The *213th Regiment* was to occupy Sinbaungwe by the morning of the 12th.

Patrol clashes during the 10th indicated that the Japanese were advancing towards the centre of Burcorps' front between Alebo and Yagyidaw. In accordance with the general operational plan, Bruce Scott at 9 p.m. that night ordered 1st Burma Brigade to move from Migyaungye eastwards to attack in the flank the enemy forces approaching 13th Brigade's area. On the 11th the Japanese probed both flanks of the position held by 13th Brigade at Thityagauk, and during the day large enemy forces were observed some two miles north of Alebo. After dark that evening 1st Burma Brigade attacked Alebo and occupied it without opposition, and found evidence that the enemy had hurriedly evacuated it a little earlier. At dawn on the 12th, patrols from both 13th Brigade and 1st Burma Brigade failed to make contact with any enemy forces in the Alebo area. Meanwhile during the night of the 11th/12th a heavy attack had been launched on 48th Brigade at Kokkogwa and had penetrated deep into the perimeter west of the village. A counter-attack during the 12th drove the enemy out after fierce fighting and, although the enemy attacked again that night, the brigade held firm.

During the morning of the 12th, Bruce Scott heard that the Japanese had occupied Sinbaungwe and were moving north in strength. He immediately ordered 1st Burma Brigade to withdraw westwards from the Alebo area, sending a battalion as quickly as possible to reinforce the company which had been left to hold Migyaungye. Before the battalion reached the village, however, it had been occupied by the enemy. Efforts to recapture it at dawn on

---
[1] See Appendix 18 for details.

the 13th failed and at 11.30 a.m. 1st Burma Brigade, in order to escape envelopment, had to withdraw towards Sainggya.

At 12.30 p.m. Slim met Bruce Scott at Magwe. Slim had come to the conclusion that the Japanese were attempting to work round the flanks of 13th Brigade and might well move north across the main road by night. Although this might be dangerous, he felt that the loss of Migyaungye, which had completely exposed the right flank of the corps, and the subsequent enemy advance northwards along the eastern bank of the Irrawaddy constituted a threat which had to be countered at once. He therefore ordered 2nd Burma Brigade to send 5/1st Punjab and 7th Burma Rifles across the river to Magwe, and Bruce Scott to send the reserve battalion of 13th Brigade (2nd K.O.Y.L.I.) to Myingun and use 13th Brigade to help 1st Burma Brigade to disengage. He was then to withdraw both brigades to the line of the Yin Chaung. This line was not to be relinquished except under extreme pressure since, owing to the lack of water, the next defensive line would have to be forty miles further north on the Pin Chaung. At the same time he ordered 7th Armoured Brigade to send one regiment to the ford where the road crossed the Yin Chaung, to act as reserve to 1st Burma Division. The 2nd Royal Tank Regiment was detailed for this and on its way from Kokkogwa carried 2nd K.O.Y.L.I. to its destination.

Later in the day 48th Brigade and 7th Hussars were placed under the orders of 17th Division at Taungdwingyi, Headquarters 7th Armoured Brigade was sent to the Yin Chaung ford to resume command of 2nd Royal Tank Regiment and constitute a reserve north of the Yin Chaung, and 1st Burma Division was ordered to prepare Magwe airfield for final destruction. The 17th Division then withdrew 48th Brigade and 7th Hussars from Kokkogwa to Taungdwingyi and moved 16th Brigade to Natmauk to protect its line of communications. Thus, by the night of the 13th/14th April, Burcorps was disposed with 1st Burma Division in the Myingun–Sainggya–Yin Chaung area, 17th Division in depth along the Taungdwingyi–Natmauk road and 2nd Burma Brigade at Minhla.

Early on the 14th April, 2nd K.O.Y.L.I. was surrounded and forced back into a defensive perimeter in Myingun. During the day 1st Burma Division moved back and occupied the line of the Yin Chaung between the main road and the river, with 1st Burma Brigade on the right nearest the river, 13th Brigade on the left and 7th Armoured Brigade (less 7th Hussars) in reserve on the road behind the centre of the position. A reserve, named Magforce, was hurriedly formed in Magwe.[1] Meanwhile on the west bank of the

---

[1] Magforce consisted of 5th Mountain Battery, 1st Cameronians and 7th and 12th Burma Rifles.

Irrawaddy, 2nd Burma Brigade had withdrawn to Minbu. During the night of the 14th/15th 2nd K.O.Y.L.I., by this time only 150 strong, broke out from Myingun and, crossing the Yin Chaung at dawn, moved to Magwe.

Although it was essential that the destruction of the Yenangyaung oilfields should be completed before they fell into enemy hands, the requirements of the Allied forces demanded the continued production of petrol until the last possible moment. Hence it was not until 1 p.m. on the 15th that Slim gave the demolition signal. The task was completed by the afternoon of the 16th. The whole of the storage area containing millions of gallons of crude oil was by then a vast sheet of flame. Wells, plant and vital installations were also burning amid resounding explosions, and the sky was darkened by a huge pall of smoke. Both on the Yin Chaung and in 17th Division area the day passed quietly and the troops obtained some rest.

Meanwhile Japanese aircraft, carefully refraining from destroying anything in the vicinity which might later be of use, had on the 11th and 12th severely bombed Twingon where several roads converged on the one road giving access to the ford at the Pin Chaung.[1] The enemy clearly realized the importance of this crossing which formed the only northern outlet for wheeled traffic from Yenangyaung.

On the afternoon of the 15th April, Bruce Scott decided not to withdraw that night from the Yin Chaung. His men were very tired, 1st Burma Brigade was somewhat disorganized as a result of its hurried withdrawal from Migyaungye and Slim had told him to delay his withdrawal for as long as possible in order to give the Chinese time to attack the flank of the Japanese forces advancing northwards between Magwe and Taungdwingyi. His decision to halt a day longer on the Yin Chaung was to have serious consequences, for it enabled the Japanese *214th Regiment*, which had occupied Thityagauk on the 13th after the withdrawal of 13th Brigade, to move round his left flank through Nyaungbinywa, Tanbinzu and the Paunggwe Chaung and cut his line of retreat across the Pin Chaung. After he made his decision, Bruce Scott heard that 2,400 Japanese had been seen on the Yin Chaung north of Thityagauk on the 13th. He ordered a sweep by a squadron of tanks to be made next morning south-east of Magwe to locate this force.

The sweep did not take place, for at 1 a.m. on the 16th the Japanese attacked 1st Burma Division on the Yin Chaung, and by daylight both 1st and 13th Brigades had been driven back to the line of the main road and the armour was fully occupied in stemming the enemy advance. Bruce Scott thereupon instructed Magforce to take up a covering position at the road junction seven miles north-east of Magwe, and ordered the remainder of the division to begin to fall

---
[1] See Sketch 6.

back across country to the Kadaung Chaung at 9.30 a.m. These moves were harassed by low-flying aircraft but not followed up and, by the evening of the 16th, 1st Burma Division had harboured astride the Kadaung Chaung for the night, covered by Magforce. Rear divisional headquarters and all transport not required were then sent off escorted by elements of 7th Armoured Brigade, with orders to make for Gwegyo.[1] During the day Burcorps ordered 2nd Burma Brigade west of the Irrawaddy to withdraw from Minbu to Sagu and, in the evening, instructed 17th Division to operate in strength against the flank of the enemy following up 1st Burma Division.

While 1st Burma Division was halted for the night on the Kadaung Chaung all was not going well north of Yenangyaung. The divisional transport column and its armoured escort, having passed through the blazing town, had crossed the Pin Chaung. At 11 p.m., just as the head of the column had reached the point selected as a harbour for the night five miles north of the chaung, the enemy cut the road between the advanced guard and the main body of transport vehicles and established a road block. An attempt to clear the block failed and the column came to a halt. At the same time the enemy seized the Pin Chaung ford behind the rearguard and, having established a second road block at Twingon, attacked Yenangyaung from the north, driving the small garrison—1st Gloucestershire—to the south end of the town. The 1st Burma Division's line of retreat was now cut, and most of its transport and armour was separated from it by a strong enemy force in Yenangyaung.

While these events were taking place, LXVI Chinese Army had begun to enter Burma and its leading division (38th) had reached the Mandalay area.[2] At one period, when he was constantly changing his mind, Chiang Kai-shek had instructed Stilwell to send a division to support Burcorps, and on the 12th the latter had ordered the leading regiment of 38th Chinese Division to move to Kyaukpadaung and come under Slim's command. Although the Generalissimo had later cancelled his instruction, Alexander and Stilwell agreed that the whole of 38th Division (Lieut.-General Sun Li-jen) should be placed under Slim's command.[3] Thus it came about that Sun agreed with Slim to co-operate with any offensive action he might wish to take, and, on the 16th, 113th Chinese Regiment reached Kyaukpadaung.

---

[1] The 2nd Royal Tank Regiment (less two companies), 414th Battery, R.H.A. and 1st West Yorkshire (less two companies).

[2] See page 155.

[3] Lieut.-General Sun Li-jen received his military education at Virginia Military Institute and spoke English well. British commanders who fought in co-operation with him found him an able tactician, alert, aggressive and cool in battle. He was on occasion given British troops under his command and earned their respect. Straightforward and co-operative, he was perhaps the outstanding man among the Chinese leaders and certainly the most competent.

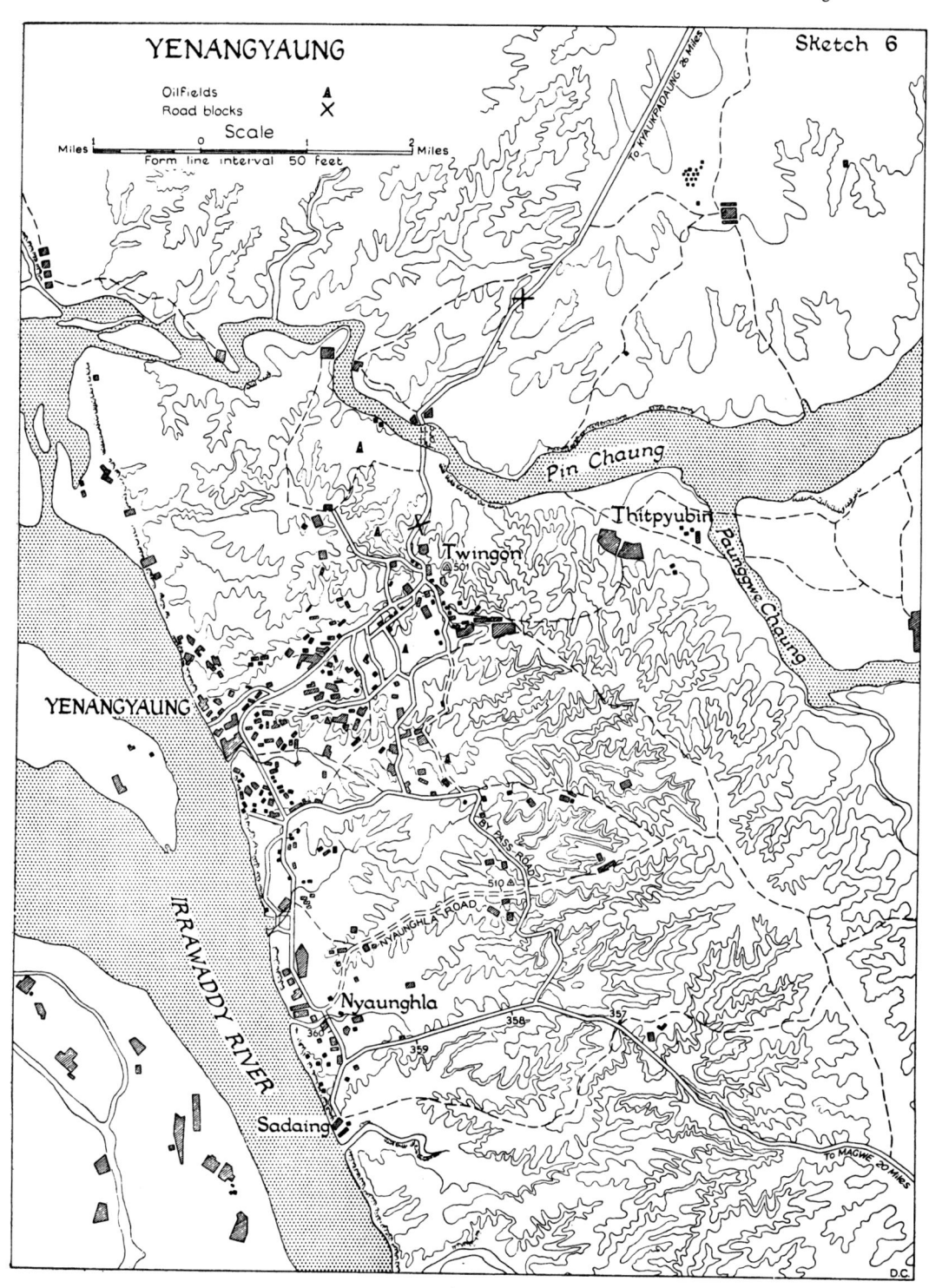

YENANGYAUNG

Sketch 6

Oilfields ▲
Road blocks ✕

Scale: Form line interval 50 feet

Bruce Scott had ordered the retreat of 1st Burma Division to continue on the 17th, with Magforce, from its covering position south of the Kadaung Chaung, becoming the advanced guard and 1st Burma Brigade with a squadron of tanks as rearguard. At 2 a.m. on the 17th, however, he received a report of the situation at Yenangyaung. He immediately arranged to use motor transport to speed up the move of Magforce, and moved with his tactical headquarters and the divisional engineers to Nyaunghla. There he met the Yenangyaung garrison commander and, having obtained first-hand news of the situation in the area, ordered the engineers to reinforce 1st Gloucestershire and establish a defensive line north of Nyaunghla.

The withdrawal of 1st Burma Division to the southern outskirts of Yenangyaung was unmolested, but the rearguard did not complete its march till midnight on the 17th/18th. The scarcity of water made it necessary to concentrate the division near the river, so Magforce harboured at Sadaing, 13th Brigade immediately south of Nyaunghla and 1st Burma Brigade at Milestone 358. Meanwhile early on the 17th the armoured escort with the transport column had cleared the road block north of the Pin Chaung, and the bulk of the transport had reached Gwegyo in the afternoon. But the Japanese still held the Pin Chaung ford, Twingon and Yenangyaung.

The leading troops of 38th Chinese Division were now beginning to arrive from the north and during the day Slim arranged that two Chinese regiments, supported by the elements of 7th Armoured Brigade north of the Pin Chaung, should attack at dawn on the 18th to clear the ford, and told Bruce Scott by wireless to break out through Yenangyaung under cover of this attack. Bruce Scott ordered Magforce to capture the ridge north-east of Nyaunghla, and then exploit northwards. Simultaneously 13th Brigade was to attack astride the Nyaunghla road, capture Point 510, and then move on Point 501 and Twingon. Having forced the road block north of the village, it was to exploit towards the Pin Chaung. Magforce was to be supported by 5th Mountain Battery, and 13th Brigade by 2nd and 23rd Mountain Batteries and a squadron of tanks. Once the by-pass road had been cleared, the division was to move up it towards Twingon covered by a rearguard formed by 1st Burma Brigade.

The country around Yenangyaung was barren, exceedingly broken and intersected by many deep, dry watercourses. In this shadeless, arid region the British force, short of water and rations, was now to fight for two days under the blazing sun. The burning ruins of the town and the oilfields provided a fitting background to the action.

The attack began at 6.30 a.m. on the 18th. Magforce (1st Cameronians) reached the first objective with little opposition. The 7th Burma Rifles then passed through and gained enough ground to prevent the Nyaunghla road coming under small-arms fire, but neither it nor 12th Burma Rifles, a territorial battalion which reinforced it, could make any further progress. These two battalions had little artillery support, since owing to ammunition shortage 5th Mountain Battery could keep only one gun in action. By the afternoon, only the Cameronians could be counted on for effective action. They succeeded in preventing the Japanese from working southward along the river bank, but lost heavily in the process.

The 13th Brigade meanwhile had gained Point 510 and continued the advance on Twingon, but its leading battalion (5/1st Punjab) found the enemy holding the high ground about Point 501, east of the village. The Punjabis gained a precarious foothold on the ridge and held it till mid-afternoon when a strong counter-attack forced them back with heavy casualties. The other two battalions of the brigade then attacked. The 1st Royal Inniskilling Fusiliers, on the left, failed to break into Twingon. Two companies, however, worked round the village and reached the Pin Chaung where, mistaking the Japanese for Chinese, they were taken prisoner. The 1/18th Royal Garhwal Rifles on the right was held up by wire and suffered severely, but by nightfall had entered the village, which was in flames and could not be held.

During the afternoon the transport remaining with the division had been moved forward up the by-pass road, the head of the column halting at the road junction a mile north of Point 510. At 3.30 p.m. Magforce was withdrawn from the river area by the Nyaunghla road to rejoin the main body of the division, and by the evening the whole division was concentrated south of Twingon. The enemy still held a road block north of the village and was firmly established on both sides of the Pin Chaung ford. Meanwhile 38th Chinese Division, supported by British guns and tanks, had attacked and reached the northern bank of the chaung, some distance east of the ford.

During the afternoon Bruce Scott had proposed to Slim that the division should abandon its transport and fight its way out across country, but Slim ordered him to hold on, since the Chinese would renew their attack at dawn next day. Bruce Scott had therefore no alternative but to form a defensive perimeter astride the by-pass road, in an area where there was no water, with troops who had been fighting all day in intense heat.

During the night the Japanese closed in from the north, west and south. Just before dawn on the 19th April, 13th Brigade, holding the northern face of the perimeter, repulsed an attack from the direction of Twingon and, as it became light, enemy machine-gun and mortar fire caused casualties and inflicted much damage on the massed transport. At 7 a.m. 13th Brigade delivered an unsuccessful attack on the road block south of the ford. The 2nd K.O.Y.L.I. and 2/7th Rajputs (1st Burma Brigade) then began to make a detour to the east to attack from that direction, but their move was cancelled by Burcorps, who feared it would clash with the advance of the Chinese, which had been delayed.

An erroneous report now affected the whole action. About noon on the 19th a company of 1st West Yorkshire Regiment, supported by tanks, had forced the Pin Chaung well east of the ford and had made contact with 2nd K.O.Y.L.I.; but in the meantine a report had reached Burcorps that the Japanese were in Kyaukpadaung. All available vehicles and infantry were immediately ordered to hasten north for the defence of the road junction at Gwegyo, and consequently the troops which had crossed the Pin Chaung, instead of being reinforced, were suddenly recalled. In actual fact it was the Chinese and not the Japanese who were in Kyaukpadaung. As a result of this mistake, the last chance of opening the road for 1st Burma Division was lost.

While these events were taking place the troops in the perimeter were under a galling fire. Moreover, owing to the heat and lack of water, men were beginning to die from exhaustion. Since the tanks had discovered a track which led away to the east, thus offering a chance of saving the transport, the vehicles were formed into a column with guns in front and lorries containing the wounded behind. By 2 p.m. there was still no sign of the Chinese attack and Bruce Scott, realizing that any further delay would endanger the whole force, began to move along the track towards the Pin Chaung. The column soon came under mortar and gun fire. A tank, two anti-aircraft guns and many vehicles were knocked out, but progress was steady till loose sand brought the transport to a halt. As there was now no hope of getting wheeled vehicles through, they were abandoned, and the guns were put out of action. Despite machine-gun fire from the nearby village of Thitpyubin, the division managed to get across the Pin Chaung about one and a half miles north-east of Twingon with the tanks carrying the wounded, and by nightfall had reached a point on the Yenangyaung-Kyaukpadaung road about five miles north-east of the ford.

Meanwhile at about 3 p.m. on the 19th, but too late to assist Bruce Scott, 38th Chinese Division had renewed its attack. Crossing the Pin Chaung it reached Twingon late in the evening and, in the course of its advance, released the men of the Inniskilling Fusiliers who had been captured on the previous day. On the 20th, General Sun Li-jen was given authority by Burcorps to use his discretion whether to continue his offensive in the Yenangyaung area or, in the event of the Japanese opposition proving too strong, to withdraw to the Gwegyo-Kyaukpadaung area. That day, still supported by part of 2nd Royal Tank Regiment, the Chinese division again attacked and penetrated into Yenangyaung, but finding that there were indications that the Japanese would counter-attack in strength at dawn, Sun Li-jen decided that night to withdraw. Accordingly on the 21st the Chinese fell back to Gwegyo, where they covered 1st Burma Division being reconstituted in the Mount Popa area, north-east of Kyaukpadaung.[1]

The whole of the Japanese *33rd Division* had been committed in the Yenangyaung action, for, when the divisional commander learnt on the 18th that *214th Regiment* was engaged, he had ordered both *213th* and *215th Regiments* to move north as quickly as possible. The *213th Regiment*, moving by road, reached Yenangyaung at noon on the 19th, and the *215th*, moving by water, arrived at 2 a.m. the following day. The enemy's object of securing the oilfields before they could be destroyed had not been achieved, but the unobserved and rapid advance of *214th Regiment* to the Pin Chaung deep in rear of the British line had succeeded, though at substantial cost, in inflicting heavy punishment on 1st Burma Division. The British casualties were about a fifth of their strength and much irreplaceable transport and equipment had been lost, including four 3·7-inch howitzers, four 25-pounders and most of the Bofors guns and mortars.

As a result of the orders received from Burcorps on the night of the 16th/17th, Cowan (17th Division) had early on the 17th sent out two columns, each consisting of a battalion and a squadron of 7th Hussars, from Taungdwingyi and Natmauk respectively with the object of drawing off part of the enemy forces engaging 1st Burma Division by demonstrating against their flank and rear. The Natmauk column moved out west along the Magwe road and during the next three days fought two successful minor engagements, first at a road block at Nyaungbinywa and then near the junction of the Magwe and Yenangyaung roads. The Taungdwingyi column established a road block some nine miles east of Migyaungye on the 19th without meeting any opposition. Both columns were attacked from the air during these operations. By that time it had become obvious that demonstrations in this area could not influence the action at Yenangyaung, and the columns were withdrawn. These demonstrations were made far too late to have any effect, for *214th Regiment* had passed through Nyaungbinywa several days before, and *215th Regiment* had gone north by river transport before the column from Taungdwingyi had started. Thus the only contact made was that by the Natmauk column which struck the rearguard of *213th Regiment* on its way north by road to Yenangyaung.

---

[1] See Map 9.

It will be recalled that the Chinese were responsible for the Sittang valley, the Karen Hills and the Shan States. At the beginning of April their armies were deployed as follows: V Chinese Army in the Sittang valley with 96th Division holding a defensive position covering Pyinmana, 200th Division in echelon behind the 96th to the northeast of Pyinmana and 22nd Division holding Yedashe; VI Chinese Army was widely dispersed in the Karen Hills and the Shan States with 93rd Division in the Kengtung area, 49th Division around Mongpan and 55th Division with its 1st Regiment and one battalion of 2nd Regiment, together with some Karen Levies, between Mawchi and Bawlake, 3rd Regiment at Thazi and 2nd Regiment (less one battalion) at Loilem in reserve.

General Stilwell's plan at this stage was for 22nd Division to fall back slowly to Pyinmana and then to move to the north-west of the town, allowing the Japanese to become involved with 96th Division, whereupon 22nd and 200th Divisions would launch a counter-offensive from both flanks. On the 7th April enemy pressure at Yedashe forced 22nd Division to begin its withdrawal. It fell back slowly, reaching Thagaya on the 13th, but it was not until the 16th that the Japanese came into contact with 96th Division at Pyinmana. The first part of Stilwell's plan (which for political reasons had become known as General Tu Yu-ming's plan) had been accomplished, but events in both the Irrawaddy valley and the Shan States were to lead to the rest of it being abandoned.

Meanwhile the Japanese *56th Division* had begun its advance towards Bawlake and Loikaw, sending an advanced guard towards Mawchi and a flank guard of one battalion across country from Toungoo directed on Hpruso. On the 9th, as a result of a number of clashes with enemy troops in the vicinity of Mawchi, Stilwell called a conference with General Tu Yu-ming and his staff. He had at that time little knowledge of the enemy's dispositions. Nevertheless he appreciated the menace which these contacts foreshadowed and gave what turned out to be a very accurate forecast of the Japanese plan, though he underestimated the strength of the Japanese force moving into the Shan States.[1] To counter this move he proposed that 49th Division and one regiment of 93rd Division should remain in the Mongpan and Kengtung areas respectively to watch the frontier with Siam; that 93rd Division (less one regiment) should move at once to Loikaw and that LXVI Chinese Army, then on its way into Burma, should concentrate as quickly as possible south of Mandalay. These proposals were accepted by the Chinese and the necessary orders to implement them issued.

Two days later Stilwell paid a visit to VI Chinese Army and to some of the formations under its command. He formed the opinion

---
[1] For the Japanese plan, see page 163.

16. Central Burma: dry zone crops (Toddy palms, millet and ground nuts).

17. Central Burma: rice fields in the Prome area.

18. The Ava Bridge—northbank.

19. The Chindwin north of Kalewa.

that its commander, General Kan Li-chu, and the commander of 55th Division, General Ch'en Mien-wu, were incapable of controlling the actions of their subordinates and that neither was obeying the orders received from his superiors. On his return to his headquarters, he asked General Lo Cho-ying to reprimand Kan Li-chu and to provide a new commander for 55th Division. Other Chinese commanders were little better. General Lu Kuo Ch'uan (93rd Division), with the support of Kan Li-chu, but unknown to Stilwell, had refused on the 13th to move as ordered to Loikaw unless motor transport were provided. Since none was available at the time the division remained where it was, and when the move eventually took place it was too late. The 1st Regiment (55th Division) had in the meanwhile abandoned the Mawchi–Kemapyu area contrary to orders and had retired to Bawlake, through 2nd Regiment which was in a position covering the bridge at Htuchaung.

Hearing on the 12th that the Chinese were holding a defensive position at Htuchaung, Lieut.-General Watanabe (*56th Division*) ordered an advanced guard to occupy the river bank opposite the village in order to prevent the suspension bridge from being destroyed. He sent a column consisting of one battalion and an engineer unit to cross the Htu River some three miles north of Htuchaung with orders to cut the enemy's lines of retreat to Bawlake, and a detachment to cross the river further north with instructions to seize and hold a section of the road halfway between Namhpe and Bawlake.

On the 16th, assaulted from the front and the flank, 2nd Regiment abandoned Htuchaung and fell back to a position covering Bawlake. With the arrival at Namhpe of 3rd Regiment from Thazi that day, 55th Division was concentrated for the first time. Its effective strength was however only some 4,000 rifles.

On the evening of the 17th the Japanese established a road block between Namhpe and Bawlake and attacked Bawlake from the south. The 3rd Regiment was ordered to counter-attack eastwards from Namhpe at dawn on the 18th, but the Japanese repelled all efforts to dislodge them from the road block. During the night, communication between Headquarters VI Chinese Army and 55th Division suddenly ceased. Early on the 19th Japanese armoured vehicles were encountered at Naungpale, only nine miles south of Loikaw. The 55th Division had been overrun. What actually happened in the Bawlake–Namhpe area during the 18th is not known, but Japanese accounts state that their forces inflicted a decisive blow, occupied both villages and sent forward armoured troops to join hands with the flank guard which, after its cross-country march from Toungoo, had reached Hpruso during the night of the 18th/19th. Remnants of VI Chinese Army in the area withdrew hurriedly to Hopong, having failed to destroy the bridge at Loikaw, and later to a position halfway between Hopong and Loilem. The Japanese occupied Loikaw on the 20th and both Hopong and Taunggyi on the 22nd. By this time they had run out of petrol and would have been completely immobilized but for the fact that the Chinese had left considerable supplies at Taunggyi.

On the 18th April, Alexander received a letter from Wavell giving the policy to be adopted if it became necessary to withdraw from Burma. Wavell told him that his objects were: to keep in close touch with the Chinese, with a portion of Burcorps fighting alongside them; to cover the Tamu–Kalewa route into Assam; and to keep a force in being and as many 'cards of re-entry' as possible so as to facilitate future offensive operations into Burma. This, Wavell said, might involve dividing the British forces into several parts in order to cover the Chindwin River and the road to Kalewa, the Mandalay–Myitkyina railway and the Irrawaddy River, and to enable touch to be kept with the Chinese retreating along the road and railway to Lashio. In view of the weakness of India, he would like as much of the Army in Burma as possible to cover the Assam road; nevertheless touch with the Chinese must remain the paramount consideration, and no grounds given them for accusing the British forces of running away to India.

At that time Alexander's plan, in the event of the loss of Mandalay, remained the same as that accepted by Wavell on the 4th April.[1] The 1st Burma Division was to cover the approaches to India by Kalewa; 17th Division (less one brigade) to withdraw on the axis Mandalay–Shwebo–Katha so as to cover the projected route from Ledo through the Hukawng Valley; 7th Armoured Brigade, together with one infantry brigade from 17th Division, to withdraw with V Chinese Army on the axis of the Burma Road through Lashio; and the troops of VI Chinese Army west of the Salween to withdraw by way of Lashio and those east of the Salween through Kengtung. All administrative arrangements had already been put in hand so that the plan could be adopted as and when the necessity arose.[2]

During the first half of April, however, it had become apparent that, owing to the loss of the rice-producing areas of Burma, the closing of the rice mills and the breakdown of the railways, it would not be possible to accumulate in the Lashio area sufficient stocks to feed the Chinese armies for more than a few weeks. Thus, as the plan stood, the withdrawal of the Chinese troops towards Lashio might well mean their starvation since, owing to a famine in Yunnan, it was very unlikely that sufficient stocks of rice could be sent from China.

---

[1] See page 153.
[2] This plan had been issued to all concerned on the 6th April.

ATTEMPTS TO SECURE THE LEFT FLANK

In these circumstances Alexander considered that he would have to invite the Chinese to withdraw some of their forces by way of Shwebo, where there was a better chance of securing supplies of rice. This factor, and the events in the Irrawaddy valley and the Shan States already described, were to cause the plan to be radically altered.

On the 17th Alexander had discussed with Stilwell his projected counter-attack south of Pyinmana, and had undertaken to place 7th Hussars at his disposal to give it additional punch. From that day, however, events moved so rapidly that both Generals had frequently to modify their plans. In view of events on the Irrawaddy front, Alexander decided on the 18th that the Pyinmana counter-attack was no longer feasible and arranged to meet Stilwell and Slim at Pyawbwe on the 19th to discuss the situation. Meanwhile Stilwell, becoming anxious as to the security of his right flank, had himself abandoned the idea of an offensive and ordered 200th Chinese Division to move to Meiktila. General Tu Yu-ming, to whom this order was given, accepted but failed to execute it.

At the conference on the 19th, Alexander stressed the importance of holding the centres of communication at Chauk, Kyaukpadaung, Meiktila and Thazi.[1] Slim then proposed that, as the deep penetration made by the Japanese *33rd Division* in the Irrawaddy valley offered a favourable opportunity for a counter-attack, Burcorps, reinforced by the Chinese, should attack westwards. If successful, the corps would then move east to help the Chinese. Alexander and Stilwell concurred and Slim was instructed that Burcorps, reinforced by 38th and 200th Chinese Divisions and one regiment of 22nd Chinese Division, was to launch an offensive on the 22nd against the exposed Japanese flank south of Yenangyaung.

On the 20th, however, it became known that the Japanese had occupied Loikaw and were moving towards Hopong. The danger to the left flank was such that the proposed counter-offensive towards Yenangyaung had perforce to be abandoned, and steps taken to guard against the increasing threat in the Shan States where both the Loilem–Hsipaw and the Taunggyi–Thazi roads looked as if they might be uncovered at any moment. Stilwell accordingly ordered 49th and 93rd Chinese Divisions to concentrate at Loilem; the mechanized 200th, together with one regiment of 22nd Chinese Division, in the Kalaw–Taunggyi area; and the remainder of the 22nd in the Thazi–Pyawbwe area. Meanwhile 96th Chinese Division, which was already heavily engaged, was to delay the Japanese between Pyinmana and Yamethin. Slim was not, however, informed of this change in plan and the first information he had of the move of 200th Division was the thunder of the motor vehicles as they moved

---
[1] See Map 9.

eastwards through Kyaukpadaung during the night of the 20th/21st. On the 22nd, in order to secure the more important centres of communication south of Mandalay, Slim ordered 1st Burma Division to move to Taungtha, 2nd Burma Brigade to Yenangyat, 38th Chinese Division to Kyaukpadaung, 17th Division to send one brigade to Zayetkon and the remainder to Meiktila, and 7th Armoured Brigade to Meiktila, where it was to come under command of V Chinese Army in support of the hard-pressed 96th Chinese Division.

General Alexander met General Lin Wei (the Generalissimo's chief liaison officer) at Maymyo on the 21st to discuss with him the plan to be adopted should a retreat from Burma become necessary. Bearing in mind the directions given in Wavell's letter, Alexander explained all the various factors which had to be taken into consideration and made the offer that 7th Armoured Brigade should accompany any Chinese forces moving along the Mandalay–Lashio axis. After a careful review of the whole situation, however, they agreed that it would be better that no British forces should withdraw towards Lashio and that 7th Armoured Brigade should be used in the more suitable ground in the Shwebo area where it could support V Chinese Army, which would retreat along the Mandalay–Shwebo axis. Burcorps would be disposed so as to cover the route to India by way of Kalewa.

Two days later Alexander issued an operation instruction embodying the decisions reached on the 21st. This stated that, in the event of a withdrawal north of Mandalay, all Chinese forces east of the Mandalay–Pyawbwe railway would move north and north-east for the defence of the Lashio road under Stilwell's orders; the reason being that any withdrawal from Meiktila would uncover the communications of the Chinese forces operating in the Taunggyi area. The instruction then indicated the probable grouping of the forces west of the railway. The 22nd and 96th Chinese Divisions supported by 7th Armoured Brigade were to defend the Meiktila–Thazi–Pyawbwe area under the command of General Lo Cho-ying; 1st Burma, 17th Indian and 38th Chinese Divisions the general line Chauk–Zayetkon–Meiktila under command of Burcorps; while 28th Chinese Division (the second division of LXVI Chinese Army to reach Burma), less one regiment, was to defend Mandalay. In the event of a withdrawal across the Irrawaddy, Burcorps would cover the approaches to Monywa and Yeu, with 1st Burma Division astride the Chindwin and a detachment guarding the track from Pakokku through Pauk and the Myittha valley to Kalemyo; 38th, and possibly another Chinese division, with 7th Armoured Brigade would move along the Sagaing–Shwebo road and the remaining Chinese divisions on the Mandalay–Lashio road.

Alexander had no intention of allowing his forces to be hemmed in in the loop of the Irrawaddy and forced to fight with their backs against the river. With this in view and bearing in mind the bottleneck of communications in the Mandalay area and the need to protect both the Chindwin and the Shwebo routes, he made it clear in this instruction that Burcorps was not to become involved in the close defence of Mandalay on the south bank of the Irrawaddy. The decision to cross the Irrawaddy would therefore be given as soon as the Meiktila–Thazi–Pyawbwe area became untenable. Burcorps was given the task of preparing and blowing all demolitions south of Mandalay, including the bridges over the Myitnge and the Ava bridge over the Irrawaddy.[1] Meanwhile to facilitate the crossing of the rivers, Burma Army Headquarters had arranged to have ferries prepared across the Myitnge and Irrawaddy Rivers west of the Ava bridge and at Sameikkon. The stage had thus been set for the withdrawal when the moment arrived, and it was not to be long delayed.

While the events described above were taking place the Japanese *56th Division*, meeting with very little opposition, had continued its advance and had occupied Loilem on the 23rd. It had thus obtained access to the road which led directly north to Hsipaw and Lashio on the Burma Road. The quick fall of Loilem was due to the lack of co-operation between formation commanders of VI Chinese Army. On the 20th Stilwell had ordered 49th and 93rd Divisions to concentrate there at once. The leading regiment of the former division, moving very fast, arrived just in time to offer some opposition to the Japanese west of Loilem, but was not strong enough to prevent them from entering the town. When next day the whole division was concentrated east of Loilem and poised for attack, General Kan Li-chu refused to allow the attack to take place and ordered the division to withdraw to Takaw. The same day, the leading troops of 93rd Chinese Division were approaching Loilem from the east, but hearing that the town had fallen the whole division promptly withdrew to Takaw. Here both divisions concentrated and were joined by the survivors (some 1,000 men) from 55th Division who had come across country from Bawlake. The VI Chinese Army then retreated through Puerh to China.

By the 22nd, 200th Chinese Division had reached the western outskirts of Taunggyi, where it was held up by the Japanese flank guard holding the village. The following day Stilwell visited the Chinese and, finding that little action had been taken, succeeded in persuading them to attack by offering 50,000 rupees if Taunggyi were secured that evening. The bribe proved effective and the village was recaptured before dark. Little further progress was, however, made

---

[1] These bridges had been prepared for demolition in February 1942.

and it was not until the 29th that the division reached Loilem. Finding the town burnt out and deserted, it then withdrew to China by way of Takaw and Kengtung.

The *56th Division*, having replenished its supplies of petrol and food from Chinese dumps in the Loilem area, had between the 24th and 29th moved north through Laihka to the road junction forty-five miles north of Loilem. The *113th Regiment* was then directed on Hsipaw and *148th Regiment* turned east and moved by way of Mongyai to Lashio.[1]

These events were not known to either Alexander or Stilwell, but they were both well aware that the enemy drive through Hopong was a serious threat to Lashio; so much so that Stilwell ordered 28th Chinese Division to move towards Lashio instead of undertaking the defence of Mandalay as ordered in Alexander's operation instruction of the 23rd. There it was to join 29th Division (the third division of LXVI Chinese Army), then on its way from China, and defend the town, since Stilwell knew that if Lashio were lost the road to Bhamo and Myitkyina was wide open. Unfortunately the move of 28th Division was greatly delayed by the complete disorganization of the railways and the lack of sufficient road transport. The same day, to guard against a surprise attack on Mandalay from the east, Alexander sent an improvised detachment drawn from training depots at Maymyo to hold the Gokteik Gorge, some eighty miles east of Mandalay on the Lashio road.

On the 25th Alexander met Slim and Stilwell at Kyaukse. He found that the Japanese were closing in on Pyawbwe, that 96th Chinese Division was beginning to break up under constant and heavy enemy pressure and that Stilwell was not sanguine about the outcome of the operations in the Shan States. In the belief that resistance on the Pyawbwe front was likely to collapse at any moment, and because Meiktila was devoid of infantry since the regiment of 22nd Chinese Division allotted to this area had been sent to Kalaw, Alexander decided that the time had come to retreat across the Irrawaddy. He therefore issued orders for the withdrawal plan to be put into operation on the night of the 25th/26th April, and for Burcorps to provide a rearguard in the Meiktila–Thazi area so as to cover the movement of the hard-pressed Chinese divisions.

Two days after this decision had been taken, Wavell reported to the Prime Minister that although events were moving fast in Burma he still hoped to retain sufficient of northern Burma to cover the roads from Assam and maintain touch with the Chinese. He added however that this was not going to be easy strategically, tactically, administratively or politically. After reviewing the general air and naval situation as it affected India, as well as the situation in China

---
[1] See Map 14 for Mongyai.

and Burma, he ended up with that characteristic flash of humour which he often displayed in the face of adversity: 'Our tails are well up, but not wagging very much as yet'.

The probable course of events could now be seen clearly enough for a decision to be made on the future rôle of the Army in Burma. The fall of Lashio appeared to be only a matter of time. There would then be nothing to prevent the loss of Bhamo, and the consequent rupture of communications with Myitkyina, for it was not possible to spare any troops for its defence. The condition and numerical weakness of the Chinese troops south of Mandalay also precluded the possibility of any lengthy stand on the Irrawaddy.

In these circumstances Alexander decided that his main object must be the defence of India. The withdrawal of as much as possible of the Burma Army to India for reorganization, the maintenance of touch with the Chinese and the retention of a position for re-entry into Burma were subsidiary objects. This decision was communicated to Slim on the 26th April and may be said to have initiated the last stage of the campaign. The plan to be adopted, after the withdrawal across the Irrawaddy, was for Burcorps to fall back towards Kalewa. Two brigades were to be disposed astride the Chindwin to delay the enemy as far south as possible; the Myittha valley was to be covered by a strong detachment and the remainder of the army was to move through Yeu to Kalewa leaving a detachment to protect this route. Some portion of the Chinese armies, in particular the hard-fighting 38th Division, was if possible to be taken back to India with the British troops. This plan was adjusted when information, judged to be reliable, was received on the 27th that a Japanese force moving up the west bank of the Irrawaddy had reached a village sixteen miles north-west of Yenangyaung, and had orders to move up the Myittha valley to cut the Kalewa–Tamu route. Alexander visited Burcorps on the 28th and confirmed an alteration to the plan, already made by Slim, whereby the whole of 2nd Burma Brigade, instead of only a detachment, would withdraw up the Myittha valley. He directed that a second brigade from 1st Burma Division (1st Burma Brigade) should be sent at once by river to Kalewa and thence to Kalemyo. The force left astride the Chindwin at Monywa would then be 1st Burma Division with its one remaining brigade (13th), which was to be reinforced by one brigade (63rd) sent from 17th Division. This would leave only 17th Division (less one brigade), 7th Armoured Brigade and the army and corps troops to withdraw along the Yeu–Kalewa track. These changes were incorporated in an operation instruction issued on the 29th.

The problem of maintenance was now far from easy. Preparations had been put in hand on the 26th for making the rough jungle track from Yeu to Shwegyin, on the Chindwin River, fit for motor transport—a track already being used by large numbers of refugees, who fouled the water points and blocked the Shwegyin ferry. Although the track was the link with the projected road to India from Kalewa to Tamu, little work had been done on it and it was still little more than a bullock cart track. A stretch of about thirty miles was waterless. The total length was some 107 miles, or six marches. Major-General A. V. T. Wakely (commanding the lines of communication), assisted by as many engineer units as could be made available, was placed in charge of the work of stocking the route with supplies and providing adequate water points. It was estimated that this would take seven days. As Alexander doubted if the line of the Irrawaddy could be held for this period, he urged the administrative staff to accelerate its arrangements. In order to provide sufficient transport for the purpose, all non-fighting vehicles which could be spared were withdrawn from Burcorps and handed over to Wakely. Dumps of rations, water and petrol were established at five staging points, and further supplies were accumulated at Shwegyin.

On the 30th April, Wavell told Alexander that he would deliver 800 tons of supplies at Kalewa between the 6th and 12th May, but warned him that the condition of the track between Kalewa and Tamu was so poor that, once the monsoon had set in about the 15th May, the movement of stores south of Tamu would have to be by the Chindwin and would suffice for only one brigade group. If, therefore, the Army in Burma were forced back to Kalewa, only a small force could be maintained there; the remainder would have to go back as far as Tamu or even further. Wavell added that he proposed sending IV Corps Headquarters (Lieut.-General N. M. S. Irwin) to the Imphal area to control the Imphal–Tamu–Kalewa line of communication and take command of 1st Indian Brigade, already in the area, and of 23rd Indian Division, which he was sending to Assam.

Burcorps began its withdrawal to the Irrawaddy on the night of the 25th/26th April. Slim ordered 2nd Burma Brigade to move to the Myittha valley by way of Pauk; 38th Chinese Division to the Ava bridge area, covered by 1st Burma Division (less 2nd Burma Brigade) which was then to move back to the ferry at Sameikkon; 17th Division (less 63rd Brigade) to the Ava bridge and 63rd Brigade to join 7th Armoured Brigade at Meiktila as a rearguard to the whole force.

Since the greater part of Burcorps had to cross at the Ava bridge, threatened by the advance of two enemy divisions astride the main railway to Mandalay, events on this axis are of importance. On both the 25th and 26th April, 7th Armoured Brigade, operating between

Meiktila and Pyawbwe, had clashes with Japanese armour and motorized columns, inflicting casualties on them and checking their advance. On the night of the 26th/27th both 63rd Brigade and 7th Armoured Brigade moved to Wundwin, 48th Brigade reached Kyaukse, where it prepared a strong defensive position, and 16th Brigade crossed the Irrawaddy to Ondaw. Throughout the 27th, 7th Armoured Brigade checked the enemy south of Wundwin. That night the remnants of 22nd and 96th Chinese Divisions withdrew through Kyaukse and 63rd Brigade was ferried by the tanks as far as Kume, where it was met by motor transport and moved to a position covering the road and railway bridge across the Myitnge River, south of Mandalay. The armoured brigade (less 7th Hussars) moved across the Ava bridge to Ondaw during the nights of the 27th/28th and 28th/29th.

The 48th Brigade supported by 7th Hussars was thus left to hold Kyaukse with orders to impose sufficient delay on the enemy to permit the safe passage of the Irrawaddy by the British forces, and also to give time for the Chinese to concentrate about Mandalay. At a point some ten miles south of the village, armoured patrols encountered each other on the 28th. By evening the enemy had reached the southern exits of Kyaukse. Here his tanks were stopped by a road block covered by anti-tank artillery. At about 9 p.m. the Japanese infantry appeared and during the next twelve hours made attack after attack on 1/7th Gurkhas astride the road and 2/5th Gurkhas east of it, but in the moonlight the British close-range fire proved deadly and all attacks were repelled.

The following morning a most successful counter-attack took heavy toll of the enemy. The Japanese, identified as *18th Division*, then began their usual encircling tactics. By the early afternoon they had considerable forces both east and west of Kyaukse, and at 3.30 p.m. they put in another but unsuccessful attack from the south. Thereupon Cowan ordered 48th Brigade to pull out. At 6 p.m. on the 29th the road and railway bridges over the Zawgyi River were blown and the brigade withdrew, covered by 7th Hussars.

The fortnight's rest enjoyed by 17th Division at Taungdwingyi had been of inestimable benefit to its morale. Admirably supported by tanks and artillery, 48th Brigade, reorganized after its successful defence of Kokkogwa, had fought a most successful rearguard action and temporarily brought the Japanese advance to a halt, inflicting such severe loss at little cost to itself that it was able to continue its retreat across the Irrawaddy unmolested. On the night of the 29th/30th the brigade, having destroyed the bridge over the Zawgyi River halfway between Kyaukse and the Myitnge River, crossed the Ava bridge and moved to Myinmu near the junction of the Mu River with the Irrawaddy.

Meanwhile on the 26th, 38th Chinese Division had withdrawn to Myingyan, and on the 27th was carried back to Ava in transport of 7th Armoured Brigade, emptied for the purpose at Slim's orders. On the 28th it had crossed the Irrawaddy by the ferry near the Ava bridge and occupied the Sagaing–Ondaw area. The 1st Burma Division (less 2nd Burma Brigade) sent its motor transport to cross by the Ava bridge, but the troops were ferried across the Irrawaddy at Sameikkon in a fleet of river transports, operated by the divisional engineers assisted by a detachment of Royal Marines. The operation was completed between dawn on the 27th and dusk on the 28th; the river fleet was then destroyed.[1] During the 29th the exhausted division remained resting on the north bank and for administrative reasons did not start its onward march to Monywa till the evening of the 30th. As 2nd Burma Brigade had left Pakokku for Pauk at 6.30 p.m. on the 28th, the Pakokku–Monywa road was left unprotected from the night of the 28th/29th and this, as will be seen, was to have serious results.

During the 29th April, Burcorps evacuated as much of its accumulated stores from the burnt-out city of Mandalay as could be removed by the transport available. Some supplies and equipment were handed over to the Chinese, but a considerable quantity had to be destroyed.

The same day Alexander met Stilwell at Shwebo. Stilwell proposed that the remnants of V Chinese Army holding the Myitnge river line south of Mandalay should, when the town was evacuated, move to Katha and possibly from there to Bhamo, but that the exhausted 96th Chinese Division should be moved by rail to Myitkyina, leaving only 22nd Chinese Division, which was short of a regiment, to hold the Myitnge line.[2] When this latter division was ordered to withdraw it should move through Mandalay to the Singu ferry and there cross to the west bank of the Irrawaddy. He indicated that the Japanese might be expected to capture Lashio at any moment and V Chinese Army might therefore be forced to withdraw to India. He requested that 38th Chinese Division, owing to the extreme weakness of V Chinese Army, should revert to his command so as to cover the army's withdrawal. Alexander felt obliged in the circumstances to agree to this request, although any retrograde movement by this division from the Sagaing area would uncover the flank of Burcorps when it was in position on the north bank of the Irrawaddy. In view of the unsatisfactory arrangements for the defence of the Myitnge River south of Mandalay disclosed by Stilwell, Alexander decided that, in order to protect the Ava bridge, 63rd Brigade would have to

---

[1] In addition to the men of the division, 450 mules and ponies, 260 bullock carts, 560 bullocks and 30 motor vehicles were put across the river.

[2] See Map 14.

occupy a bridgehead position on the south bank of the Irrawaddy without delay. Thus as soon as 48th Brigade had passed through on the night of the 29th/30th, 63rd Brigade destroyed the road and railway bridges over the Myitnge and moved back to the bridgehead position.

While Alexander and Stilwell were discussing the withdrawal of the Chinese forces in the Mandalay area, the disaster on the left flank feared by Stilwell occurred. As the leading regiment of 29th Chinese Division was entering Lashio from the north-east, it met the Japanese *148th Regiment* which had rapidly moved up from Loilem. In the ensuing action Lashio fell. The 28th Chinese Division, on the move from Mandalay to Lashio, was on the 28th still strung out along the road and was unable either to assist the 29th Division at Lashio or prevent *113th Regiment* from occupying Hsipaw. Thus the Burma Road was cut in two places and the way to Bhamo and Myitkyina lay open.

Throughout the 30th, 63rd Brigade remained on the eastern bank of the Irrawaddy, but it was evident that the destruction of the Ava bridge could not be long postponed, for the enemy was advancing rapidly on Mandalay from the south. The remnants of 96th Chinese Division and other units of V Chinese Army had already crossed the river on their way northwards to Shwebo and 22nd Chinese Division was withdrawing towards the crossing at Singu. The last troops of the Allied forces crossed the great bridge after darkness on the 30th and at midnight it was blown, two of its huge spans collapsing into the river. The final phase of the campaign was now about to begin.

CHAPTER XI

THE DEVELOPMENT OF INDIA AS A BASE
(April–May 1942)

See Maps 4 and 14

WHEN it was becoming evident that the Army in Burma would be forced to withdraw into Assam before the break of the monsoon in mid-May, General Wavell was faced with new and complex problems of administration. There was always the possibility that despite monsoon conditions the Japanese would attempt an invasion of Assam. He had now therefore to be prepared not only to defend eastern Bengal and the long Indian coastline from Chittagong to Palk Strait but the frontier of Assam as well. This meant a large movement of troops up to the border and a consequent added strain on the administrative services in India, which were still in the process of reorientation from west to east. The build-up of an efficient system of communications in eastern India was a prerequisite to a campaign for either the defence of the frontier, the recapture of Burma or the maintenance of an air ferry route to China. Communications were mainly dependent on the railways and so, in order to understand Wavell's difficulties, it is necessary to examine in some detail the many demands which had already been made on the Indian railway system by the exigencies of war.

When war broke out in Europe in 1939 the Indian Government had, at the request of the British Government, placed at its disposal a large tonnage of its coastal shipping. Indian coastal shipping in peacetime had been carrying, exclusive of cargoes to and from Burma, three and a half million dead weight tons a year, half of which represented coal shipments. Most of the Indian coal was mined in Bihar and was sent to Calcutta, whence it was distributed by sea. The reduction in coastal shipping threw most of this load on the railways which were already carrying ninety per cent. of all internal traffic. The railways had not only to carry this additional load but also to meet increased military demands for the transport of troops with their vehicles and equipment, the increased movement of raw materials required for the expanding industrial output, the movement of the vast amount of material required for the large airfield programme and the supply to eastern India of rice which was normally imported by sea from Burma.

In April 1942, after the Japanese raids on Ceylon, the four east coast Indian ports were closed leaving only Karachi, Bombay and the as yet undeveloped port of Cochin to handle the whole of the Indian seaborne trade. Cargoes normally imported through Madras, Vizagapatam and Calcutta now had to be routed through Bombay and carried by rail across India. This again increased the already heavy load on the railways.

Before 1939 the Indian railways had insufficient locomotives and wagon stock to meet the annual peak demands in full as they occurred, and a reasonable spread of peak traffic had always been enforced. The replacement of rolling stock, particularly locomotives, had been inadequate, and on the outbreak of war there were few reserves. During the years 1939 and 1940, when it appeared unlikely that India would be directly involved in the war, she generously released some ten per cent. of her railway equipment and many key operators to assist in meeting the military transportation requirements in the Middle East and Iraq. This used up all her reserves as well as some of the rolling stock required for her normal peacetime services. The railways were thus hard put to it to meet the additional strain thrown on them.

The most urgent requirement was more locomotives and wagons. These were normally obtained from the United Kingdom. Although many were on order when war broke out in Europe and additional orders had been placed during 1940, none had been delivered, since the concentration of British industry on the production of munitions and military equipment, added to the general shortage of raw materials, had virtually stopped the production of locomotives and railway equipment. An attempt to get locomotives and wagons from the United States was made in 1941, but was vetoed by the British Government on the grounds that the dollar expenditure was unjustified and that the placing of orders in the States would hinder America's all-important tank production programme. India was forced therefore to make do with what she had. She reduced her passenger traffic by about one-third in order to free locomotives and save coal, and set to work to keep the maximum number of existing locomotives in service by shortening the time required for their maintenance. But here another difficulty was encountered, for the railways were forced to give up some of their workshops for the manufacture of munitions and the maintenance of aircraft.[1]

---

[1] See page 112.

General Wavell found it necessary to send an official demand himself for 185 broad gauge locomotives as the minimum necessary to meet India's requirements. Knowing the difficulties which would be involved in meeting this demand, he followed it by a personal telegram to the Chief of the Imperial General Staff, a telegram which was interpreted by the railway authorities in India as meaning, 'In India it is guns before butter and railway locomotives before guns'. This telegram read:

> 'I cannot stress too strongly that Indian railways are already unable to meet full requirements owing to lack of sufficient locos and stock. These requirements will increase. I must depend on and accept the assurance of the Chief Commissioner of Railways in India that all resources are being utilized to the limits of safety. You will realise that the great distances in India force us to rely almost entirely on railways since road facilities, whether for through traffic or for local service, are inadequate. Moreover petrol limitations and shortage of road transport preclude full use of such roads as do exist. The railways will not be able to meet our requirements with their present equipment if simultaneous demands, such as those resulting from [the] destruction [of the] Digboi oil refinery[1], operations in north-east India, and movements in the west due to the Middle East situation combined with deterioration in internal situation, should occur.
>
> I fully realise that meeting this demand for locomotives involves interference with the production of other important war material but nevertheless in India the situation is such that the provision of locomotives is of more importance at this stage than of the other war material affected.'

In reply he was told that the world-wide demand for locomotives for military and other war purposes far exceeded the total productive capacity, and that every locomotive produced meant fewer tanks. The existing programme for India allowed for four locomotives to be completed in 1942 and forty in 1943.[2] With this India would have to make do. Meanwhile she should place orders for such spare parts and boilers as would enable her to repair and retain in service the existing fleet of locomotives, and by this means save new construction. The demands placed on the railways had therefore to be kept within their maximum capacity. Throughout 1942 this acted as a brake on the build-up of the administrative services and slowed down all India's military preparations.

Another administrative problem was that of providing India's increased requirements of petrol, oil and lubricants (P.O.L.). In 1941 India was able to meet fifteen per cent. of her requirements from her

---

[1] A plan existed to destroy this oil refinery in the event of a Japanese invasion of north-east Assam.

[2] The four were part of a pre-war order which it was agreed should be completed.

oilfields at Digboi in north-eastern Assam and at Attock in the Punjab. The remainder was imported from the Burma and Netherlands East Indies oilfields, and from the Persian Gulf. After the loss of the Netherlands East Indies and Rangoon all supplies from the east ceased. With the Digboi oilfields threatened and the east coast ports closed to tankers, the problem of meeting the demands of eastern and north-eastern India became acute.

The Government of India thereupon appointed a central authority to co-ordinate and allocate the output from Indian oilfields and all imported products. Faced with the rapidly rising demand for P.O.L. from the armed forces and the greatly increased difficulties of distribution caused by the closing of the east coast ports, immediate steps were taken to increase the severity of petrol rationing, control the use of oil for industrial purposes and conserve stocks of lubricants. India's requirements for 1942 were estimated at two and a half million tons, including 600,000 tons for shipping purposes. Of this, 280,000 tons could be produced in Assam and 85,000 tons in the Punjab. The remainder had to be imported from the Persian Gulf or the United States and, so long as tankers could not use the east coast ports, had to be distributed by the already overloaded railways from Bombay to eastern and southern India.

The problem was therefore threefold: firstly, to increase the Indian output by further drilling in the existing oilfields, secondly, to improve the communications to Digboi and, thirdly, to assist the railways to meet the additional load of moving petrol across the Indian continent. Additional drilling was put in hand at both oilfields. A long-term project was devised to relieve the railways of the 850 miles' haul from Bombay to Allahabad, where the broad gauge met the metre gauge to Assam. This took the form of a 6-inch pipeline complete with pumping stations and tankage. Finally, some 600 miles of 4-inch pipeline were ordered, to relieve in part the roads and railways in Assam of the carriage of P.O.L. to the newly-constructed airfields and the Manipur Road base.

Owing to the shortage of material and the time involved, the project to lay a pipeline from Bombay to Allahabad was reduced to one of constructing a pipeline as far as Bhusawal (276 miles east of Bombay) which by-passed the worst bottleneck—the section over the Western Ghats with its steep gradients—thus accelerating the tank wagon turn round. The pipelines were to prove their value in 1943 and the following years, and were the forerunners of a comprehensive system of British and American pipelines from Calcutta and Chittagong through eastern Bengal and Assam to the north-eastern frontier and later into Burma. Fortunately, the fact that the Japanese did not follow up their incursion into the Bay of Bengal allowed some tankers to reach Calcutta by the end of June, and enabled the vital

20. Near Taunggyi in the Shan States.

21. The Burma Road on the China border near Wanting.

flow of P.O.L. to eastern India to be maintained while the pipelines were being completed.[1]

Meanwhile the discussions between General Headquarters, Air Headquarters and the Government of India on the construction of some two hundred airfields resulted in a project being approved in May 1942, and in the airfield construction programme being given priority over everything except the requirements for concentrating troops and the needs of actual operations.[2]

Most of the airfields were to have two bitumen-treated or paved runways of metal or concrete 3,000 yards in length, and dispersal areas with paved surfaces connected to the runways by taxi tracks where aircraft could be parked, loaded, serviced and repaired. They also required operation control rooms, wireless stations and storage accommodation for bombs, ammunition and fuel, as well as living accommodation for large numbers of officers and men. In many areas electrical power stations and water supply systems had to be built. The project was therefore not only vast but complex, even though many airfields were at first built to the most temporary specifications.

The construction programme was controlled centrally from Delhi by the Engineer-in-Chief at General Headquarters, India (Major-General R. L. Bond), with arrangement for local liaison between the Chief Engineers of commands (or armies), officials of the Public Works Department and the R.A.F. groups. Many of the airfields were built by the Public Works Departments of the Central, Provincial and Indian States Governments. The acquisition of the necessary vehicles, plant, material and labour, and their movement to selected sites had begun in April, but it was not till June that the organization began to get into its stride. It soon found that the supply of steam-rollers, concrete mixers, materials and labour was inadequate, and that work could be undertaken only at some sixty sites simultaneously. The greatest difficulties were experienced in north-east India where, in addition to the almost complete lack of roads to the selected sites, there was a shortage of stone or gravel. As a result, coal had to be brought by rail from the Bihar coalfields and bricks burnt in order to provide the foundations for the roads and runways.

These great efforts soon began to produce results and by the end of 1942 five operational airfields were complete in all respects, eighty-eight had one all-weather runway of over 1,600 yards in length and sixty fair-weather airstrips had been completed. But these results were obtained to the detriment of work on the construction of many administrative and industrial installations, both military and civil,

---

[1] During July and August two tankers a month reached Calcutta. In September the number was increased to three.

[2] See pages 112–13.

and of the maintenance of India's internal communications. The concentration of effort on airfield construction was nevertheless of vital importance, for without these airfields air superiority over the Japanese, so necessary for the successful conduct of the war, could not be attained.

While Wavell was tackling these administrative problems, the danger of a Japanese invasion of Assam had increased. He therefore decided to organize a force from the hill people along the 600 miles of India's eastern frontier to undertake guerilla operations against the Japanese lines of communications, should they pass through the area. The initial strength envisaged was 2,000 men recruited from Tripura State, from the Chittagong district and the Chin, Lushai and Naga Hills, with a proportion of one British officer to approximately 200 tribesmen. If sufficient recruits were forthcoming, the strength would be increased to 10,000 men.

The organization, raising, arming and training of this force, which became known as 'V' Force, began in April 1942 with the help of the Assam Government. It was built up on the foundation of platoons loaned from the Assam Rifles (a force of five military police battalions maintained by the Assam Government and composed of Gurkhas under British officers seconded from the Indian Army). It was planned that 'V' Force should be organized into a headquarters and six groups, one to each of the six operational areas stretching along the frontier,[1] each group consisting of a small headquarters, four platoons of Assam Rifles and eventually up to 1,000 enrolled tribesmen. The force was to be self-supporting and live on the country.

When, as will be seen, the Japanese did not follow up their successes in Burma, the original rôle of 'V' Force was gradually changed to that of obtaining information. In addition, the force provided guides and porters and became a link between the army and the local inhabitants. But first and foremost they became the eyes of the troops in the dense jungle in which they were born and bred. If only on this account the experiment of raising 'V' Force was fully justified by results.

The force first went into action patrolling across the frontier to locate, guide and assist the hundreds of thousands of refugees who were making their way on foot from central Burma to the frontier near Tamu, from Myitkyina by way of the Hukawng Valley and from Fort Hertz over the Chaukan Pass to Ledo. Of those who followed the easier route to Tamu, about 190,000 eventually reached

---

[1] The six operational areas were: Tripura, Aijal, Chin Hills, Imphal, Kohima and Ledo. A seventh area was added in September in Arakan, and two more were formed during 1943.

Imphal. Their arrival, in varying stages of distress, created a very serious problem for the Assam Government, for not only had some system to be organized to prevent enemy agents among them infiltrating into India, but thousands had to be fed, given medical assistance and transported into India. That this was satisfactorily accomplished was due largely to the efforts of the Indian Tea Association, which put its organization in Assam at the disposal of the Government for this purpose. Many of those refugees who had attempted to escape by the longer and more difficult northern routes were overtaken by the monsoon, which turned the jungle tracks to mud and the unbridged streams and rivers into torrents. Rescue parties had to be organized and food and medical supplies dropped on groups of refugees marooned by the flooded rivers, as and when they were located by air reconnaissance. Some 100,000 refugees also crossed the Arakan Yomas and made their way along the coast to Akyab whence they were taken by ship to Calcutta. Including those evacuated by sea and air, a total of some 400,000 refugees from Burma succeeded in reaching India. But many thousands died on the way.

When considering the problem of the defence of India, Wavell found that the organization of the army in India into three commands (Northern, Eastern and Southern) and Western Independent District, which had been satisfactory in peacetime and in war so long as India was engaged only in raising and training new formations, was unsuitable at a time when the country was open to invasion. On the 21st April therefore, he reorganized India Command with the main object of freeing the senior officers, in threatened areas, of the mass of administrative detail which would prevent them from giving their full attention to the urgent task of preparing to repel a possible invasion. He formed Central Command with headquarters at Agra, covering, as far as geographical and political conditions permitted, the central areas of India in which most of the training establishments and depots were situated. He also formed three armies: North Western, responsible for the security of the North West Frontier with headquarters at Rawalpindi; Eastern, responsible for the defence of Assam, Bengal, Bihar and Orissa with headquarters at Ranchi; and Southern, responsible for the defence of southern India and the administration of the many training centres, hospitals and depots already in that area, with operational headquarters at Bangalore and administrative headquarters at Poona. At the same time he converted the original military districts in Eastern and Southern Armies into line of communication areas and sub-areas.[1] These areas were responsible for the training and administration of troops allotted to

---
[1] This conversion was not completed till August 1942.

the area, for the local administration of field force formations quartered there, for internal and railway security, for the defence of vulnerable points and for passive air defence.

On the 21st April, Eastern Army was disposed so as to meet any enemy forces attempting to land on the coast of eastern Bengal, in the Calcutta area or in Bihar and Orissa. The defence of Assam, at that time covered by the Army in Burma, was the responsibility of a temporary formation named the Assam Division, which had been formed out of the former Assam District Headquarters and 1st Indian Infantry Brigade. The newly-formed XV Indian Corps, consisting of 14th Indian Division in eastern Bengal and 26th Indian Division at Calcutta, was responsible for the defence of Bengal, Bihar and Orissa.[1] The IV Corps, consisting of 70th British and 23rd Indian Divisions (each of two brigades only), was retained as a mobile reserve at Ranchi. Akyab, controlled from General Headquarters, was garrisoned by one battalion and some anti-aircraft artillery. Southern Army was disposed so as to protect Vizagapatam, Madras and Trichinopoly. It consisted of 19th Indian Division, 20th Indian Division (which was in the process of being formed), 50th Army Tank Brigade and 251st Indian Armoured Brigade.[2]

General Wavell was well aware that whatever the final outcome of his exchanges with the Prime Minister (as described in Chapter VII) he would for the time being have to do the best he could with his attenuated forces. He decided to accept the risk of a seaborne invasion of eastern Bengal and Orissa before the arrival of the two British divisions which he had been promised[3], and to move formations into Assam at once to defend the frontier. Accordingly on the 1st May he ordered IV Corps to Imphal to assume responsibility for the protection of the frontier and for the reorganization of Burcorps on its withdrawal from Burma. At the same time he divided Eastern Army into three operational areas: Eastern, Central and Western. The Eastern Area was to be responsible for the defence of Assam and was allotted IV Corps, with headquarters at Imphal, consisting of 23rd Indian Division, brought up to the strength of four brigades by the addition of 1st Infantry Brigade from the Assam Division (which was abolished) and 49th Infantry Brigade from 14th Division. The Central Area was to be responsible for the defence of eastern Bengal and the Calcutta area and was allotted XV Corps, with headquarters at Barrackpore, consisting of 14th Division (now one

---

[1] The 26th Division was originally formed for the local defence of Calcutta, and until May 1942 was known as the Calcutta Division.

[2] See Appendix 16.

[3] See page 130.

brigade only) at Comilla, 26th Division at Calcutta, the Sundarbans Flotilla and 109th Brigade (one battalion only); this last brigade had already been moved to Silchar, with orders to proceed to Aijal as soon as possible, to secure the tracks radiating from it towards eastern Bengal. The Western Area was to be responsible for the Orissa coast and was to act as a general reserve. It was allotted 70th British Division at Ranchi. Owing to the state of communications in Assam, it was expected that the move of IV Corps would not be completed until the end of May, and that 109th Brigade would not be able to reach Aijal from Silchar till the monsoon abated.

Meanwhile at Akyab the situation had gradually worsened. With the virtual withdrawal of the civil administration at the end of March, and despite the gallant efforts of the Burmese Deputy Commissioner (Oo Kyaw Khine) who remained behind and attempted singlehanded to retain control, the administration of Arakan had disintegrated and lawlessness prevailed. Communal warfare broke out between the Arakanese Muslims and the Maughs (Arakanese Buddhists who were pro-Japanese) and both plundered the hapless refugees.

On the 6th April, as a result of an air attack on Akyab, the R.I.N. sloop *Indus* was sunk. On the 16th Japanese troops were reported to be at Taungup, and on the 18th and 19th Maughs attacked detachments of the Rajputs in the vicinity of Akyab. By this time the constant air attacks had practically destroyed the power station, disrupted the water supply and had made it almost impossible to keep the telegraph line to India functioning; consequently on the 22nd the greater part of the R.A.F. detachment with its supplies was withdrawn to India. On the 28th Oo Kyaw Khine was killed in a clash with the Japanese some twenty miles from Akyab, and on the 1st May a motor launch patrol found Japanese troops at Minbya. A heavy air raid on the 3rd, which did great material damage, and reports that Japanese in strength were closing in on the island made it clear that the defence of Akyab was no longer possible. Wavell therefore decided that the island was to be evacuated. On the 4th, after demolitions had been carried out in the town, the main jetty destroyed and all craft in the harbour sunk, the garrison was withdrawn by sea to Chittagong. The Japanese occupied the island the same day and shortly afterwards began using its airfield.

The defence of eastern Bengal now rested on 14th Indian Division at Comilla, which had only one brigade under command. Fear that the Japanese might attempt to seize Chittagong by a seaborne landing caused orders to be issued for the removal of port equipment and the preparation of the harbour works for destruction. With the exception of one garrison battalion left to cover the demolitions if ordered, all other troops were withdrawn. At the same time all forms of transport in eastern Bengal east of the Feni river, including country boats and bicycles, were collected by the civil authorities and moved to the west of the river.

On the 4th May Wavell warned Eastern Army to make arrangements for the reception of Burcorps. He estimated that the numbers to be maintained would be about 8,000 British, 25,000 Indian and 21,000 Chinese troops, and that these would arrive without guns, tanks and much of their equipment, owing to the difficulties of the route and the absence of means for crossing the Chindwin. The arrival of Chinese troops in India was quite unexpected and created a formidable administrative problem. It was eventually decided that all Chinese troops would be sent to Ramgarh near Ranchi, where suitable buildings existed, and arrangements made for their re-equipment and training under American control.

On the 8th Wavell held a conference at Palel, attended by the commanders of Eastern Army, IV Corps and 23rd Indian Division, to discuss the arrangements to cover the withdrawal of the Burma Army into Assam. On the 9th an Eastern Army operation instruction stated that IV Corps was to prevent the Japanese from entering Assam and either occupying the Imphal valley, cutting the Bengal–Assam railway or capturing the Digboi oilfields. The corps was to assume command of all troops in Assam, including 'V' Force and the Assam Rifles, and Burcorps on arrival at Tamu. It was to undertake the refitting of Burcorps, evacuating units not required in Assam to Ranchi.

To enable IV Corps and Burcorps to be maintained in Assam, Eastern Army took over the control of the Manipur Road advanced base depot at Dimapur from General Headquarters, India, and established further self-contained advanced bases at Gauhati (as a lay-back to the Manipur Road base), at Mymensingh (to serve eastern Bengal) and at Asansol and Chandil (to serve Bihar and Orissa). It was intended to hold some forty to sixty days' reserves of supplies east of the Brahmaputra. It was therefore planned that each of these was to hold thirty days' stocks, supplied from the reserve depots which General Headquarters, India, had already begun to build up,[1] and forward field depots, carrying from ten to thirty days' supplies of all kinds for the troops based on them, were to be established as tactical requirements demanded. Administrative units to put the whole scheme into effect were not available at the time since most of those raised by India earlier in the year had been sent to meet the requirements of the Middle East and Burma, and there was none in reserve. Thus, while new units were being hurriedly raised, reliance had to be placed on the few which could be spared

---
[1] See page 53.

from the North West Frontier. Matters were further complicated by the need to put this large scheme into force in so short a time. Stocks were often insufficient and the lack of experienced movement staff as well as the congestion on the railway held up deliveries, so that the depots could not be filled up quickly. There was also a shortage of military and civil road transport and of petrol containers, tankage and can-filling plant.

As IV Corps began to move forward, congestion on the railways and roads in both Bengal and Assam became rapidly worse. So great was it that, as Wavell told the Chief of the Imperial General Staff on the 12th, it took seven weeks, even before the arrival of the Burma Army at Tamu, to move a brigade from Ranchi to the Assam frontier and the maintenance of even this small force in that area was a strain on the line of communication. From the administrative point of view, with the monsoon about to break, the outlook was grave.

CHAPTER XII

THE ALLIED WITHDRAWAL FROM BURMA
(May 1942)

See Maps 9 and 14 and Sketches 7 and 8

IN Burma, the end of April saw the beginning of the final phase of the campaign. On the last day of the month, except for the rearguard of 63rd Brigade covering the Ava bridge and 22nd Chinese Division which was withdrawing northwards through Mandalay, both Burcorps and V Chinese Army were already across the Irrawaddy. General Alexander's object at this time was to hold the line of the Irrawaddy for as long as possible. When the withdrawal of the Allied armies became imperative, Burcorps was to move by the Myittha valley, the Chindwin River and the Yeu–Kalewa track towards Assam, the remnants of V Chinese Army to China or India as circumstances permitted and the remnants of LXVI Chinese Army to Yunnan.

Burcorps was disposed with 2nd Burma Brigade approaching Pauk and about to withdraw up the Myittha valley; 1st Gloucesters (some 150 strong) and a part of Force Viper at Monywa; 1st Burma Division (1st Burma and 13th Brigades) about to move to Monywa from the Sameikkon ferry; 17th Division with 48th Brigade at Myinmu, 16th Brigade at Ondaw (about to move to Myinmu) and 63rd Brigade in the Sagaing–Ava bridge area. The V Chinese Army was disposed with 38th Division covering the Irrawaddy crossings east of the Mu River, supported by 7th Armoured Brigade, 96th Division in the Shwebo area, about to move by rail to Myitkyina, and 22nd Division (less one regiment) withdrawing to Shwebo by way of the Singu ferry.

The Japanese had failed in their attempt to trap the Allied armies in the loop of the Irrawaddy. In consequence General Iida had on the 26th April ordered his four divisions to strike wide and deep in rear of the Allied forces, so as to cut their lines of retreat and thus destroy them in one blow. The *56th Division* was to capture Lashio and then advance towards the Salween; *18th Division* was to move to Lashio; *55th Division* was to clear the Mandalay area while *33rd Division* moved on Monywa and Shwebo, detaching a portion of the division to cut the Allies' line of retreat northwards at Bhamo and Katha. After learning that *56th Division* had captured Lashio, Iida adjusted his plan and on the 30th directed that division to swing north-westwards towards Bhamo and Myitkyina, while *18th Division* cleared the Shan States south of the Burma Road of all Chinese forces remaining in that area.

The *33rd Division* had begun its advance from Yenangyaung on the 26th, divisional headquarters and *213th Regiment* moving along the east bank of the Irrawaddy to Myingyan, and *215th Regiment* in motor transport, followed by *214th Regiment* (less one battalion), moving west of the Chindwin to the Monywa area. One battalion of *214th Regiment* and an engineer battalion were to move up the river in landing craft to Monywa to assist *215th Regiment* to cross the river at that point. By the evening of the 28th, both Myingyan and Pakokku had been occupied and by dusk on the 30th the advanced guard of *215th Regiment* had reached the west bank of the Chindwin opposite Monywa. The battalions moving up the river arrived there by dawn on the 1st May without meeting any opposition.

On the evening of the 30th April, Headquarters Burcorps was established near Budalin on the Monywa–Yeu road. Headquarters 1st Burma Division (Bruce Scott) and the divisional engineers were at Ma-U, four miles south-east of Monywa.[1] The 13th and 1st Burma Brigades, marching across country from Sameikkon, were approaching Chaungu. Some 2,400 clerks and servants sent off from Army Headquarters at Shwebo the previous evening, together with their wives and children, were concentrated at Alon awaiting transport up the Chindwin River to Kalewa. Everything appeared to be going according to plan when machine-gun, mortar and artillery fire was suddenly opened on Monywa from the western bank of the river; but the enemy made no attempt to cross it and seize the town.

From information which reached his headquarters, Slim received the impression that Monywa had been lost. This, if true, was serious, for not only did it completely disrupt his plans for the withdrawal, but exposed the undefended Yeu road and the vital Shwegyin–Kalewa crossing, thus providing the Japanese with the opportunity of cutting his one remaining line of withdrawal along the Yeu–Shwegyin track. He decided therefore that it was essential to recapture the town, and at 8.45 p.m. ordered 1st Burma Division to concentrate at Chaungu and move on Monywa as quickly as possible, and 48th and 63rd Brigades (then at Myinmu and Sagaing respectively) to move by rail to Chaungu where they were to come under command of the division. The 17th Division was to send

---

[1] See Sketch 7.

16th Brigade by the quickest route to Yeu with orders to cover the approaches to that town from the south. At the same time Alexander ordered 7th Armoured Brigade to send one squadron to reinforce 1st Burma Division and one squadron to operate along the Yeu–Monywa road.[1]

During the night Bruce Scott put his headquarters into a state of defence, sent 50th Field Park Company to reinforce Monywa and despatched all his engineer transport to Chaungu to ferry forward 63rd Brigade which expected to detrain there next morning. At about 5 a.m. on the 1st May, his headquarters was suddenly attacked but fought its way back to Chaungu, taking all essential documents with it. At dawn a Japanese battalion crossed the river and was soon in possession of Monywa, having forced the small garrison to withdraw towards Alon.

The 63rd Brigade from 17th Division was the first formation to arrive within striking distance of the town. Its two leading battalions detrained at Kyehmon on the morning of the 1st and advanced astride the main road. Assisted by a squadron of tanks they overcame strong opposition at Ma-U, but were unable to penetrate into Monywa. The remainder of the brigade arrived later in the day. A perimeter camp was then formed at Ma-U and held during the night, despite two enemy counter-attacks.

Alexander and Stilwell met at Yeu on the evening of the 1st. In view of the situation at Monywa, they decided that the withdrawal from the Irrawaddy line should begin without further delay. Stilwell agreed to the release of 7th Armoured Brigade which was in support of 38th Chinese Division east of the Mu River, and it was ordered to fall back through Yeu and operate down the Yeu–Monywa road. He told Alexander that he intended to withdraw V Chinese Army to the Katha area and, though uncertain as to his subsequent plans, was preparing for a possible withdrawal to India. This was the last occasion on which the two commanders met before the close of the campaign and, owing to the failure of Stilwell's wireless, there was no further communication between them.

Meanwhile Bruce Scott had planned to attack Monywa on the 2nd on a two-brigade front: 63rd Brigade, with a squadron of 7th Hussars under command, was to make a frontal assault astride the railway while 13th Brigade, which had arrived on the evening of the 1st, made a night march across country to Zalok and attacked from the east. Each attacking brigade was to have a field and a mountain battery under command. The 1st Burma Brigade, expected to arrive during the afternoon, was to be in divisional reserve.

The 13th Brigade's attack from Zalok made good progress and penetrated to the railway station, but by mid-afternoon was brought

---
[1] For order of battle see Appendix 17.

to a halt. The 63rd Brigade got as far as the outskirts of the town but was then held up. The 1st Burma Brigade, which had reached Ma-U during the morning, reinforced by a battalion from 48th Brigade passed through 63rd Brigade at 3.45 p.m. but succeeded only in making contact with 13th Brigade. Under cover of these attacks the divisional transport, escorted by two battalions of Burma Rifles, made its way through Zalok and Ettaw and despite frequent air attacks reached the Alon-Budalin road without serious loss.

At 5 p.m. 13th Brigade, acting on orders passed to it by an officer of 7th Armoured Brigade, disengaged and withdrew north to Alon. Bruce Scott, on hearing of this order, decided to ignore it and continue with the attack. No further progress was made, and at 8 p.m. he broke off the engagement and moved both 1st Burma and 63rd Brigades round Monywa to Alon without interference from the enemy.

The origin of the order to 13th Brigade remains a mystery. That it was delivered by an officer of 7th Armoured Brigade, who said he got it in clear on the wireless from the Army Commander, is certain. Both Army Headquarters and Burcorps later disclaimed all knowledge of it. It is now known that the Japanese, despite their desperate resistance in Monywa, had begun to recross the Chindwin to the west bank in the early afternoon. The most reasonable explanation seems to be that the message received at 7th Armoured Brigade Headquarters emanated from the Japanese, for there is evidence that the enemy had tried this ruse on a previous occasion, but fortunately without success.

By the night of the 2nd May, 1st Burma Division and 7th Armoured Brigade had concentrated at Alon and 16th Brigade of 17th Division at Yeu. The road from Monywa to Yeu and the Yeu–Shwegyin track were now secure, but the Japanese still had control of the direct route up the Chindwin to the vital Shwegyin–Kalewa crossing. To deal with this danger, 16th Brigade was ordered to move that night to Shwegyin to secure the crossing, and the withdrawal of the whole force was accelerated.

On the 3rd, 1st Burma Division (1st Burma, 13th and 63rd Brigades) covered by 7th Armoured Brigade began to withdraw towards Yeu, the starting point of the track to the Chindwin through which the whole of the British force would have to pass. During the withdrawal 7th Armoured Brigade had several encounters with enemy tanks supported by anti-tank guns near Budalin, but no infantry action developed and the withdrawal was completed by nightfall without further incident. On the same day Headquarters 17th Division and 48th Brigade (less one battalion), which had remained at Myinmu to reinforce the Monywa front should that become necessary, moved by way of Ondaw and Shwebo to Yeu. Burcorps was in a position to begin its final withdrawal from Burma.

Sketch 7
MONYWA

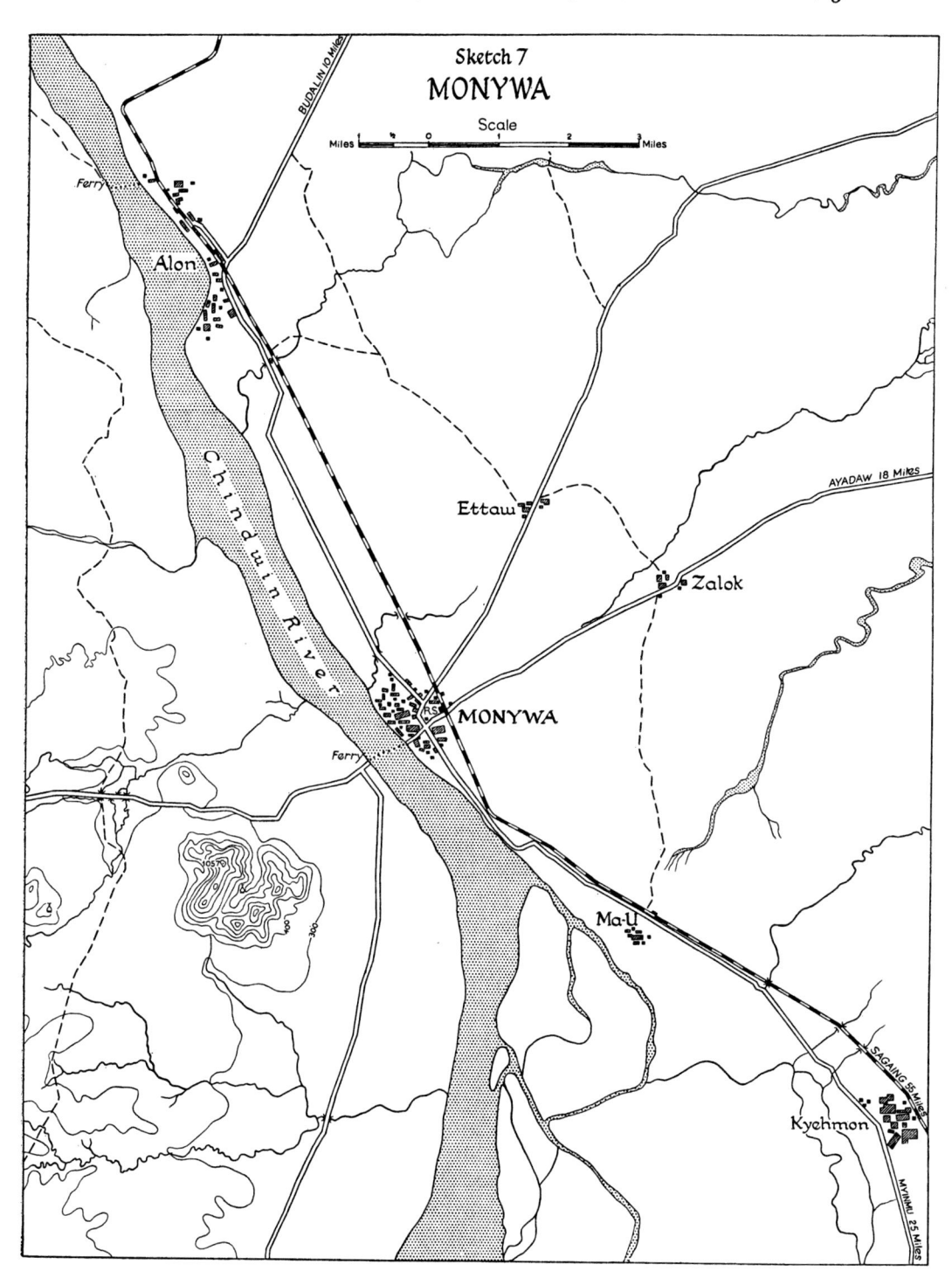

While these operations were in progress 2nd Burma Brigade, which had left Pakokku on the 28th April, was marching towards the Myittha valley. The brigade reached Pauk on the 1st May, which it found had been burnt and looted by Thakins. After leaving Pauk, the brigade saw no more of the enemy and, despite a difficult march, made contact on the 12th May with the Chin Hills Battalion of the Burma Frontier Force some fifteen miles south of Kalemyo. There it was met by motor transport supplied by IV Corps and taken back to Tamu. This brigade had, during the hottest time of the year, covered the 216 miles between Pakokku and Natchaung in 14 days along a poor track, and hampered by slow-moving bullock transport. All marches had been made by night, defensive positions being manned by day. Once the brigade had passed through the Pauk district, Brigadier Bourke received every assistance from the local inhabitants throughout the march. He was fortunately able to pay for everything that he requisitioned, for when the brigade had been about to leave Nyaunglebin in March the local magistrate had handed 150,000 rupees over to him.

While the Japanese *33rd Division* was thrusting up the Chindwin River valley, *56th Division* on the extreme right was advancing rapidly northwards from Lashio. The *56th Reconnaissance Regiment*, having forced 29th Chinese Division to evacuate Hsenwi, moved up the road to Bhamo which was now open and succeeded at dawn on the 3rd May in capturing intact the suspension bridge over the Shweli River, four miles west of Namhkan, held by a battalion of the Burma Frontier Force. The following day, *146th Regiment*, which had arrived at Rangoon from the Netherlands East Indies on the 19th April and had been sent up to join its division at Lashio, and *148th Regiment* inflicted a severe defeat on 29th Division which had withdrawn to Wanting.

About this time, General Iida, having heard that General Lo Cho-ying was at Katha on the 3rd and that General Tu Yu-ming had arrived at Myitkyina on the 4th, assumed that strong Chinese forces were still in the area north of Mandalay. Accordingly on the 6th he issued instructions to *15th Army* to destroy all Allied forces between Myitkyina and Tamanthi on the Chindwin. The *56th Division* was to continue its allotted task, advancing on Bhamo and Myitkyina, but in co-operation with *55th* and *33rd Divisions*. The *55th Division*, already advancing through Sagaing with Shwebo and Kin-u as its objectives, was to deal with the Allied forces in the Bhamo and Mongmit areas, while *33rd Division* destroyed any retiring up the railway towards Shwebo and Myitkyina. The *33rd Division*, in accordance with its previous orders, had on the 4th May already despatched *213th Regiment*, supported by a mountain artillery battalion and an engineer regiment, up the Chindwin River from Alon to seize Kalewa and Kalemyo so as to cut off the British forces retiring towards India. The main body of the division was now directed on Shwebo.

After the capture of the suspension bridge at Namhkan, *148th Regiment*, together with *56th Reconnaissance Regiment*, moved rapidly north and by the 8th had occupied Myitkyina and its airfield. The *146th Regiment*, continuing its advance north-east from Wanting, had occupied the heights on the west bank of the Salween on the 8th just after the Chinese had destroyed the vital bridge which carried the Burma Road over this mighty river. Simultaneously *18th Division* had begun mopping-up operations in the Shan States along the axes of the Mandalay–Lashio and Loilem–Takaw roads. Since VI Chinese Army had already withdrawn towards China, the only opposition met with came from stragglers and Takaw was occupied on the 11th May.

We must once again turn to the operations on the British front, which had developed into a race for the possession of Shwegyin. To Alexander, speed had by this time become more than ever vital, for not only was the Burma Army trying to reach Shwegyin before the Japanese, but the monsoon was about to break and the first heavy rains would make the chaungs impassable and turn the tracks into quagmires. Thanks to the efforts of the administrative staff in establishing and stocking a series of staging camps on the Yeu–Shwegyin track, there was no real shortage of supplies, but as a precautionary measure the troops were placed on half rations. Petrol was available in sufficient quantity to take all vehicles through to Shwegyin.[1]

The fact that all casualties as well as large numbers of refugees, whom he was determined not to abandon, had to accompany the force presented Alexander with a serious problem. Casualties had been evacuated by air from Shwebo until Japanese aircraft had bombed the airfield and rendered it useless. They were then sent by rail and river to Myitkyina but, when on the 6th May enemy bombers had destroyed three out of the five aircraft while loading, that line of evacuation was also closed. By the time the final withdrawal began, the number of casualties which had to be taken along the Yeu–Shwegyin track amounted to some 2,300 and in addition there were many thousands of refugees. These latter were not only fed by the army but given lifts whenever possible in military vehicles.

---

[1] See Appendix 18.

That the withdrawal was successfully accomplished reflects great credit on the engineer, transport and medical services, especially in view of the appalling road conditions and the shortage of serviceable motor vehicles. The narrow sandy track passed through innumerable chaungs and over a difficult hill section with many flimsy bridges. Alexander has stated that anyone seeing this track for the first time would find it difficult to imagine how a force with motor transport could possibly move over it. The engineers were, however, able to make such improvements that the whole force passed through without serious delays, though not without difficulty.

From Shwegyin all troops, motor vehicles and guns had to be ferried across the Chindwin up to Kalewa, for the path through the hills on the east bank of the river to Kaing,[1] though passable on foot and therefore usable by refugees, was not considered to be possible for fully-equipped infantry and pack animals. There were only six river steamers available, each with a carrying capacity of some 600 men, but these could carry only two lorries and two jeeps each. This made it necessary to abandon the guns and nearly all vehicles, leaving only sufficient motor transport to evacuate the wounded and carry essential equipment and ammunition. The fact that IV Corps had placed a transport company at Alexander's disposal and established staging camps stocked with supplies between Kalewa and Tamu made it unnecessary for units to carry rations.

To assist him in winning the race to Shwegyin, Alexander had ordered the Chindwin to be blocked by a boom near Gaundi (two miles south of Shwegyin), covered by a detachment of Royal Marines. He had also asked General Headquarters, India, to arrange for air attacks to be made on any enemy craft moving up river from Monywa. These were made on the 3rd, 4th and 5th and imposed considerable delay on the Japanese advance. On the 3rd Wavell told Alexander to withdraw Burcorps to the Tamu area as rapidly as the tactical situation allowed, since it would not be possible to maintain it in the Kalewa area. Two days later Alexander learnt that 1st Indian Brigade, which he had assumed was marching from Palel to Kalewa, would not move beyond Tamu.

General Sun Li-jen, whose division (38th) was acting as rearguard to V Chinese Army, visited Alexander at Kaduma on the 3rd May. The purpose of his visit was to ensure that his flank was not uncovered by too rapid a withdrawal of Burcorps, and indirectly to request that his division should retreat with the British forces to India. Alexander was unable to invite Sun Li-jen to move to India with Burcorps, for had he done so the rearguard of the Chinese armies would have been removed and political repercussions resulted; but he again impressed on Slim that his withdrawal from

---
[1] See Sketch 8.

the Yeu area was not to be completed until the Chinese rearguard had moved north to Shwebo.

Immediately after the despatch of 16th Brigade to the Kalewa area, the withdrawal of Burcorps from Yeu began. Slim ordered 17th Division (to which 63rd Brigade was to revert), with 7th Hussars under command, to occupy a series of lay-back positions at Kaduma and Pyingaing and establish a flank guard at the point where the Maukkadaw Chaung joined the Chindwin. As soon as the division was in position, 1st Burma Division (1st Burma and 13th Brigades) and 7th Armoured Brigade (less 7th Hussars) were to move to Shwegyin and cross the ferry to the Kalewa-Kalemyo area, followed by the remainder of Burcorps.

The 17th Division moved back on the 3rd and 4th. The 38th Chinese Division having moved north to Shwebo, 1st Burma Division began its withdrawal on the evening of the 5th. The 13th Brigade moved straight through to Shwegyin where it arrived on the 7th, and 1st Burma Brigade staged at Pyingaing on the 6th where the rearguard (48th Brigade) was already in position.

In order to protect the left flank of Burcorps and ease the load on the ferry at the Shwegyin–Kalewa crossing, Slim then ordered 1st Burma Brigade to move on the 8th northward by the track from Pyingaing through Indaw to Pantha, cross the river at Yuwa and march to Tamu.[1] That day 63rd Brigade reached Shwegyin and the rearguard and the flank guard at Maukkadaw Chaung began their withdrawal. On the night of the 8th/9th, 13th Brigade crossed the river to Kalewa. On the following night 63rd Brigade and 2nd Royal Tanks (having destroyed its armoured vehicles) crossed and thus by the morning of the 10th the only troops still east of the river were Headquarters 7th Armoured Brigade, 48th Brigade with its attached troops, and 1/9th Royal Jats (less two companies) of 16th Brigade which had been left to protect Shwegyin against any enemy advance up the east bank of the Chindwin.

So far all had gone according to plan. But the Japanese *213th Regiment* which had left Alon on the 4th May had been steadily moving up the Chindwin by river craft and route march. On the 5th, Japanese aircraft had bombed and broken the boom across the Chindwin at Gaundi and on the 7th had bombed Shwegyin, losing two aircraft from anti-aircraft fire. On the afternoon of the 9th, one Japanese battalion landed on the east bank of the river near Kywe some eight miles below Shwegyin, and that night the main body of the regiment landed at Ingongyi on the west bank of the Chindwin almost opposite. The battalion which had landed at Kywe moved without delay away from the river towards Thanbaya, from where a jungle track led to the lower reaches of the Shwegyin chaung. During

---
[1] See Map 12.

its withdrawal from the mouth of the Maukkadaw Chaung, the small British flank guard reached Kywe just after the Japanese battalion had moved north, and witnessed the arrival of the enemy at Ingongyi. Since its wireless batteries had run down it could not send a report of these landings to 1st Burma Division, which therefore remained unaware of the proximity of the Japanese to Shwegyin.

The embarkation point at Shwegyin was a small sandy bay where the engineers had constructed a jetty. The track approached this bay through a depression known as the Basin, about half a mile long and 400 yards broad, which was overlooked by steep jungle-clad hills. As the withdrawal proceeded the Basin inevitably became filled with tanks, guns, lorries, stores and equipment. So great was the congestion that many vehicles, guns and animals had to be kept back at Mutaik, two miles north-east of Shwegyin. The bombing on the 7th had seriously restricted the work of ferrying, for the Indian and Burmese crews would thereafter work only at night. Moreover, the river had suddenly risen some three feet and the newly-constructed jetties were partially submerged. Thus, despite the utmost endeavours of a detachment of Marines, officers of the Irrawaddy Flotilla Company, staff officers and others, the work of loading went on very slowly and on the 9th it was estimated that several days were still required for the clearance of the wounded, guns, animals and any transport and equipment not earmarked for destruction.

On the evening of the 9th, Headquarters 17th Division, 48th Brigade (less 1/7th Gurkhas) and 7th Hussars were at Mutaik. The 1/7th Gurkhas had arrived at Shwegyin during the day to reinforce the two companies of the Jats and take over some of the defensive positions round the Basin on the following morning. Further downstream 5/17th Dogras and a handful of Marines were deployed on both sides of the river near Gaundi, covering the broken boom and patrolling southwards.

At about 5.45 a.m. on the 10th, just as the Jats stood to, enemy parties appeared and began to advance towards the Basin, covered by light machine-gun fire. On being checked, they worked along the ridge dominating the eastern side of the Basin and, despite repeated local counter-attacks, succeeded in capturing a prominent knoll which commanded the jetty; one party managed to break into the Basin itself but was quickly driven out. Although the jetty could not be used, three river vessels, by drawing in under an almost sheer cliff some two hundred yards upstream, were able to embark all the wounded and transfer them safely to Kalewa.

As soon as the news of the Japanese attack on the Basin reached him, Cowan ordered 1/3rd Gurkhas (by this time only one company strong) and 1/4th Gurkhas to piquet the track between Mutaik and the Basin. The 1/4th arrived just in time to prevent the enemy seizing the southern end of the track which ran north from the Basin through Kongyi to Kaing. Cowan also moved 2/5th Gurkhas and a squadron of 7th Hussars direct to the Basin, where they were held in reserve.

In order that the jetty could be used and the remainder of the force ferried to Kalewa, it had now become essential to drive the Japanese from the commanding knoll on the eastern side of the Basin. A counter-attack, launched at 2 p.m. by 1/7th Gurkhas supported by a battery of 1st Indian Field Regiment from Mutaik and 3rd Indian Light Anti-Aircraft Battery from the Basin itself, failed to dislodge the enemy, although pressed with great resolution. During the late afternoon, enemy pressure on the positions held by 1/9th Royal Jats near the mouth of the chaung covering the jetty increased. Cowan had intended to launch another attack on the knoll at about 5 p.m. but, realizing that the Japanese were being steadily reinforced and that it was unlikely that the jetty could be used that night, he decided to fall back on Kalewa by the track to Kaing. He had indeed no alternative, for the flotilla on the Irrawaddy had by this time disintegrated. Though detailed information on this point is lacking, it seems probable that at least part of the main body of *213th Regiment* had crossed the river from Ingongyi during the day and taken part in the action.

The withdrawal began at once, but only the minimum of equipment could be carried as the track to Kaing crossed precipitous hills and was known to be exceedingly difficult. Tanks, guns, motor transport and the remaining stores and equipment had all therefore to be destroyed. At 5 p.m. the guns and mortars began wasting down their remaining ammunition; this held the enemy in check and the first stages of the withdrawal proceeded without interruption. Two layback positions were established by 2/5th Gurkhas to protect the final withdrawal of the covering troops through the northern exit from the Basin. At 7.55 p.m. the covering troops began to leave their positions and all guns increased their rate of fire, working up ten minutes later to an intense concentration. This last phase of the operation has been described in a unit war diary in the following words:

> 'The chief contribution came from the Bofors whose tracer shells lit up the descending darkness. It was a cheering sound the like of which we had not heard during our time in Burma. At 8.15 p.m. the guns ceased fire and five minutes later we received the order to go. As we left the Basin enormous fires were getting a good hold on the dumps of stores and ammunition, tanks and lorries. It was an eerie sight in the gathering gloom and distressing to think so much material had to be left behind. From the enemy there wasn't a sound. They had apparently had enough.'

It was fortunate that the Japanese did not follow up since the narrow steep path soon became blocked with troops and animals. By dawn on the 11th the tail of the column had only reached Kongyi, but there was no sign of the enemy. Although no one at the time realized it, the last action of the campaign had been fought.

On the night of the 11th/12th May, 48th Brigade and 2nd Duke of Wellington's (16th Brigade) left Kalewa by river steamer and reached Sittaung on the 14th. All the boats were then sunk and the troops marched to Tamu. The main body of 17th Division, marching up the Kabaw Valley, reached Tamu by the 17th and 63rd Brigade, which formed the rearguard, on the 19th. With the exception of some guns, very little in the way of armament, ammunition or equipment had been brought out of Burma; all the tanks and motor vehicles, except fifty lorries and thirty jeeps, had been destroyed or abandoned as unserviceable.[1]

During the campaign the Army in Burma, without once losing its cohesion, had retreated nearly one thousand miles in some three and a half months—the longest retreat ever carried out by a British army—and for the last seven hundred miles had virtually carried its base with it.[2] The British and Indian forces in Burma suffered some 10,036 casualties of which 3,670 were killed and wounded and the remaining 6,366 missing. To these figures must be added the losses of the Burma Rifles and other Burmese units amounting in all to 363 killed and wounded and 3,064 missing, making a grand total of 13,463 casualties. As against this, Japanese casualties, and the figures can be considered reliable, were 4,597 killed and wounded. The air losses sustained by the Allies and the Japanese were, on the other hand, almost equal. The Allies lost 116 aircraft, of which 65 were destroyed in aerial combat, whereas the Japanese records show a loss of 117 aircraft, of which 60 were destroyed in the air.

The first heavy rains of the monsoon fell on the 12th May. It was therefore by only a very narrow margin that Alexander had extricated his troops. Another week's campaign east of the Chindwin might well have led to complete disaster. As it was, dysentery and malaria were to take a heavy toll of the exhausted men, for the final stages of the withdrawal up the notoriously malarial Kabaw Valley were made in heavy rain and under conditions which would have tried even the fittest troops. On the 20th May, IV Corps assumed operational command of all the units from Burma, and Alexander's command came to an end. He had, as Wavell reported to the Prime Minister, performed a fine feat in bringing back the army.

---

[1] Twenty-eight out of forty-eight field, mountain and anti-tank guns reached Indian soil.
[2] See Appendix 18.

Sketch 8
SHWEGYIN

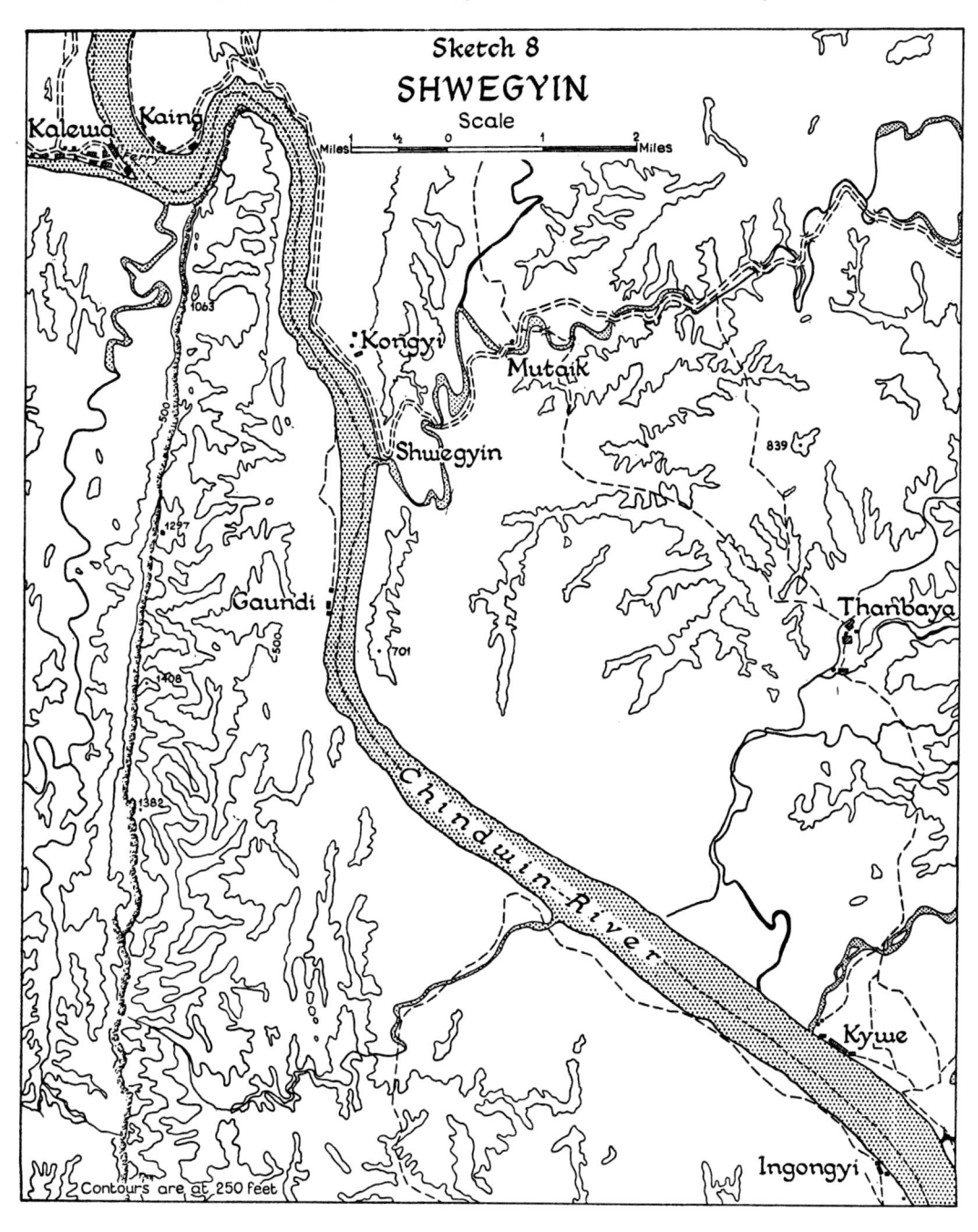

After Burcorps had left Yeu for the Chindwin, all contact was lost with the Chinese. The 22nd Chinese Division had crossed the Irrawaddy at Singu as planned and rejoined 96th Chinese Division at Shwebo. On the 4th May the Generalissimo ordered these two divisions, with 38th Chinese Division acting as rearguard, to withdraw to Myitkyina. On reaching Indaw, it was discovered that the Japanese were already in Myitkyina. The remnants of 22nd Chinese Division left the railway and retired north-west up the Hukawng Valley, eventually reaching Ledo by this very difficult route at the end of July. The 96th Chinese Division managed to by-pass the Japanese and reached Fort Hertz; then, turning east, made its way into China. General Sun Li-jen (38th Chinese Division) decided, however, to march westward to India. He moved south to Wuntho where he fought an engagement, and then crossed the hills to the Chindwin. There, at Paungbyin on the 11th,[1] the division encountered the Japanese. Two of his regiments got across and reached Imphal on the 24th covered by the 113th which, having fought a fine rearguard action, eventually crossed the Chindwin on the night of the 30th/31st May.

Meanwhile Stilwell, on his way to Myitkyina, had arrived near Indaw on the 5th; there he learnt that the Japanese were already in Bhamo and that the railway was blocked. He too decided to make for India. Abandoning his transport near Pinbon, he walked with a small party across the Zibyu Taungdan hills to Maingkaing and then travelled by raft down the Uyu River to Homalin. He crossed the Chindwin at this point on the 13th and reached Assam on the 15th. His remarks on arrival were characteristic: 'I claim we got a hell of a beating. We got run out of Burma and it is humiliating as hell. I think we ought to find out what caused it, go back and retake it.'[2] This was just what Wavell was planning to do as soon as circumstances permitted.

Mention has already been made of the use of aircraft for the evacuation of casualties from Burma during the campaign. Before the fall of Rangoon, 31 (Bomber-Transport) Squadron began to ply between Calcutta and Rangoon, carrying urgently required stores to Burma and evacuating civilians and troops on the return flights. When, after the fall of Rangoon, the air offered the only means by which reinforcements could be sent to Burma and casualties and refugees speedily brought out, every effort was made in India to increase the airlift. The squadron was temporarily joined by bomber aircraft of the 10th U.S.A.A.F. which were being assembled in India. These

---

[1] See Map 12.
[2] White, *The Stilwell Papers* (Macdonald, 1949) page 116.

were later replaced by a number of transport aircraft. Assistance was also given by British commercial houses in Calcutta, which, on their own initiative, chartered any available civil aircraft to help in the evacuation of civilians from upper Burma, and by American business men, some of whom obtained transport aircraft from the United States and presented them to the R.A.F. to be used for dropping supplies on the columns of refugees and the retreating Burma Army.

Between the 8th and 13th March American bombers, acting as transports, flew a fully-equipped battalion (1st Royal Inniskilling Fusiliers) to Magwe and on their return flights brought out over 400 civilian refugees and many casualties.[1] After the fall of Mandalay, British and American air crews defied every normal limit of pay-load in their endeavours to rescue as many as possible of the sick, wounded and refugees before the Japanese army could close in upon the few airfields still remaining in Allied hands. In all, by the close of the campaign, a total of some 8,600 people, including 2,600 wounded, had been flown out of Burma by the Allied air forces. Their efforts ceased only when all the airfields in Burma had been lost. They then turned their attention to dropping supplies, whenever and wherever possible, in an attempt to aid the pitiable columns of refugees making their way to Assam across difficult mountain tracks which, after the break of the monsoon, were to become almost impassable.

The use of aircraft for evacuation was not, however, allowed to interfere with their operational use. After the disasters at Magwe and Akyab,[2] in which the greater part of the air forces in Burma was destroyed on the ground, air operations over Burma had to be undertaken by two squadrons only—5 (Mohawk) Squadron at Dinjan and 113 (Blenheim) Squadron based in Bengal. From the middle of March the latter, using Magwe as an advanced landing ground until it had to be abandoned, began attacks on military objectives in the Irrawaddy valley, including vessels using the rivers, and on specific targets in support of Burcorps. In April the squadron was joined by long-range bombers of the 10th U.S.A.A.F. which began attacks on the docks at Rangoon. In May enemy shipping on the Chindwin was attacked and the enemy-occupied airfield at Myitkyina was heavily bombed, since it represented a threat to the airfield at Dinjan. In all, during the period from March to May, fifty-eight raids (thirteen by the 10th U.S.A.A.F. and forty-five by the R.A.F.) were carried out over Burma.

The First Burma Campaign illustrates once again the handicap under which an army fights when it is without adequate air support and what disasters can occur when the air defence is deprived of an

---

[1] See page 148.
[2] See pages 149-50.

effective warning system. Perhaps the greatest lesson learnt from the campaign was the possibility of air supply for an army cut off from all other means of support. The history of air supply in the Far East can be traced from the modest beginnings on the Burma front to the colossal army/air supply organization based in India, which was destined to revolutionize support for the land forces and have a profound influence on the future conduct of the war against Japan.

The five and a half months' campaign in Burma came to an end on the 20th May 1942, with the withdrawal of the Allied forces across the Chindwin. It can be divided into two distinct phases: the first, the struggle for Rangoon which lasted till the fall of the city on the 8th March 1942, and the second, the battle for central and upper Burma which continued from that date until the 20th May. The former has been reviewed in Chapter V. The latter must now be examined.

After the fall of Rangoon, the objects of the defence were to ensure the security of the Mandalay–Lashio road (the link with China), the new base area around Mandalay which held all the reserves of supplies and ammunition for the British forces, and the Yenangyaung oilfields on which the Allied forces depended for their supplies of oil and petrol. In addition, the defence had to hold as much of the rice-growing area of Burma as possible and secure the use of sufficient airfields to enable reinforcements and essential technical supplies to be flown in and casualties flown out. The Allies, if they were to achieve these objects, had to fight as far south of the general line Prome–Toungoo as possible in order to give depth in front of Toungoo. This town was the key to the defence, for it was from there that the Mawchi–Bawlake road left the Sittang valley and led straight into the heart of the Shan States and to Lashio. Once Toungoo was in enemy hands, the Burma Road could be cut and the whole Allied defence turned.

General Alexander wished to fight well in advance of Toungoo on the two comparatively narrow fronts in the Irrawaddy and Sittang valleys, which were separated by the Pegu Yomas. But, despite his promises on the outbreak of war, the Generalissimo was never prepared to commit Chinese forces wholeheartedly to the defence of Burma, and not only refused to allow V Chinese Army to move south of Toungoo but insisted on concentrating it back in the Mandalay area. This, and the concentration of Burcorps in the Irrawaddy valley, left 200th Chinese Division (approximately the strength of one British brigade) entirely unsupported to hold Toungoo. It put up a gallant fight and for eleven days held the town against a complete Japanese division. But the result was never in doubt. On the 29th March Toungoo fell and the Japanese, having found the bridge over the Sittang undamaged, were then in a position to develop quickly an encircling attack through the Shan States and thus threaten the Allies' left.

With 200th Chinese Division unsupported, it must have been clear to the Generalissimo that this danger existed and that it was essential to reinforce Toungoo and to concentrate VI Chinese Army in the Karen Hills to meet the Japanese drive which would inevitably follow if Toungoo were lost. Stilwell did his best to induce V Army to move to the aid of its isolated division and concentrate part of VI Army for the defence of the Karen Hills, but his wishes were disregarded and his orders disobeyed. When the Japanese had broken through the weak 55th Chinese Division, the remainder of VI Army was eventually concentrated further north much too late. Admittedly, the concentration of VI Chinese Army in the Karen Hills would have uncovered the routes from Indo-China into the Shan States, but the acceptance of this risk would in the circumstances have been well worth while. The Generalissimo was, however, of two minds as regards the defence of Burma and he mistrusted his allies. He was thus not prepared to instruct his army commanders to obey either Stilwell or Alexander. Once the Allied left flank was turned, the campaign in Burma was lost and it was only a question of time before the Allies would be forced to withdraw.

With the forces available and without a proper line of communication to India, it would have been very difficult to hold central Burma till the onset of the monsoon, especially as the enemy could be easily reinforced. Given full Chinese co-operation and a united command, it might have been done, but the Chinese neither co-operated wholeheartedly in the defence of Burma nor placed their forces completely under Allied command. Although certain Chinese formations and units fought magnificently, the poor training and equipment of most of their troops, the low standard of leadership and the lack of administrative services made their gallantry of no avail.

Certain aspects of the operations after the loss of Rangoon merit further examination. Alexander's decision to concentrate Burcorps in the Irrawaddy valley, leaving the defence of the main road and railway up the Sittang valley to Mandalay entirely in the hands of the Chinese, is one of these, especially as an advance up the Sittang valley offered the Japanese considerable strategic advantages. Alexander felt he required more strength in the Irrawaddy valley since 17th Indian Division, after its experiences at Sittang and Pegu, was scarcely fit to hold an enemy advance unaided. Moreover, the concentration of Burcorps balanced his army, and the removal of

1st Burma Division from the Sittang valley, as soon as the Chinese troops were established in Toungoo, had the advantage of enabling him to comply with the Chinese request for a front of their own with their own line of communications. When he made the decision he could not foresee that the Generalissimo would retain two Chinese divisions at Mandalay, and thus leave Toungoo to be defended by one Chinese division only.

It was planned to defend the Prome area to the last by brigades holding the two centres of communication at Prome itself and at Allanmyo while the rest of Burcorps remained mobile, prepared to counter-attack any Japanese formations operating against these towns. Both towns were therefore stocked with ammunition and supplies from those being backloaded to the Mandalay area on which the army had to subsist so long as it was in Burma.[1] But on the 28th March, Alexander, requested by both the Generalissimo and Stilwell to make an attempt to relieve pressure on V Chinese Army, ordered Burcorps to undertake offensive operations on the Irrawaddy front. It is difficult to see how an offensive in the Irrawaddy valley, separated as it was from the Sittang valley by the Pegu Yomas which were traversed only by rough tracks, could have quickly relieved pressure on the Chinese and saved Toungoo. One can only presume that the decision to launch Burcorps into a counter-offensive, at a time when 17th Division was still unfit for any offensive action and the corps was not fully concentrated, was taken for the sake of Allied unity. It resulted in an encounter battle south of Prome in which the exhausted 17th Division, not yet really recovered from its experiences during the retreat to Rangoon, was severely mauled and suffered further heavy casualties. This, and the loss of Toungoo, led to the decision of the 1st April to withdraw from Prome.[2] Thus it was that the defence plan for this area was never put into operation, most of the valuable stores placed in Prome were lost and Burcorps was forced back to the Minhla–Taungdwingyi line which was much more difficult to defend.

The withdrawal from the Prome area was accelerated by the decision on the 2nd April to fall back on Dayindabo, instead of standing astride the road on the general line of the Nawin Chaung immediately north of Prome.[3] Cowan's original decision, when he pulled back to the line of the Nawin Chaung, was taken to avoid envelopment, for he believed that the Japanese having broken into Prome would swing right against his positions east of the town. But he had not ruled out the possibility of a counter-attack to regain Prome, and the Nawin Chaung provided a good position from which

---

[1] See Appendix 18.
[2] See page 159.
[3] See page 160.

it could be launched. When, however, he received a report, which appeared to him at the time to be reliable, that an enemy column had passed through Prome during the night with the apparent object of cutting in behind 17th Division, it seemed as if the division were in grave danger. Both he and Slim knew of Alexander's plans to withdraw from the Prome area. They were therefore justified in their decision to play for safety. The area was in fact evacuated prematurely since the threat did not materialize.

Once the Prome area had been abandoned, the question arises whether the attempt to hold the long Minhla–Taungdwingyi line was justified. In point of fact there was no choice: obviously the Japanese line of advance up the Irrawaddy had to be blocked; obviously, too, Taungdwingyi had to be retained, for its loss would have exposed both the right flank of V Chinese Army and the British left.[1] This meant that Burcorps had to hold a front of forty miles, and no one realized better than Alexander the risk which this involved. He accordingly took the only course open to him: he obtained from Chiang Kai-shek a promise to send a complete Chinese division to Taungdwingyi. Had this reinforcement arrived in time, Slim would have been in a position to form a reserve and might have prevented the Japanese from passing a regiment unobserved through a gap in the defences and cutting Burcorps' communications at the Pin Chaung. Responsibility for the failure to hold the position must rest with the Chinese, who did not keep their promise to send a division to Taungdwingyi.

The only other phase of the operations on which comment seems called for is the period at the end of April when the road to Monywa was left unguarded and the town itself without adequate garrison. It will be recalled that, when Burcorps began its withdrawal to the Irrawaddy on the night of the 25th/26th April, Slim's orders were for 2nd Burma Brigade to move through Pakokku to Monywa, less a detachment which was to move by way of Pauk into the Myittha valley. But later, when information was received that a Japanese force located on the west bank of the Irrawaddy might be about to move up the Myittha valley with the object of cutting the Kalewa–Tamu road, the whole brigade, instead of only a detachment, was ordered to withdraw up the valley.[2] It left Pakokku on the evening of the 28th on its way to Pauk. That very night the Japanese entered Pakokku and so were able to move on to Monywa without opposition. By the evening of the 30th, the advanced guard of *215th Regiment* reached a point on the west bank of the river opposite the weakly-held town and had no difficulty in occupying it next day.[3]

---
[1] See page 163.
[2] See page 181.
[3] See page 200.

It would seem from the above that neither Burma Army nor Burcorps foresaw the speed with which the Japanese could reach Monywa once 2nd Burma Brigade had left Pakokku. The nearest troops to Monywa at that time were 1st Burma Division which, by the evening of the 28th April, had completed its crossing of the Irrawaddy at Sameikkon.[1] The troops were very tired after long marches over sandy tracks—part of 1st Burma Brigade had covered thirty-five miles in twenty-four hours—and the division was at that time dependent on bullock cart transport. For administrative reasons, General Bruce Scott did not start his march to Monywa till the evening of the 30th. He had no reason to move earlier, for he had received no orders indicating any necessity for speed in getting troops either to Monywa or to block the river and road approaches from the south. Had the danger to Monywa been realized when the whole of 2nd Burma Brigade was diverted to the Myittha valley, 16th Brigade could have been sent by rail from Ondaw and have reached Monywa in time to forestall the Japanese.

The loss of Monywa disrupted the whole plan of withdrawal: instead of there being, as planned, a force of two brigades astride the Chindwin with one brigade at Kalemyo, leaving only 17th Division (less one brigade) and 7th Armoured Brigade to withdraw by way of Yeu on Kalewa,[2] practically the whole British force had to retire up the Yeu–Shwegyin track. This in itself was serious enough in view of the state of the track, the shortage of motor transport, the necessity for evacuating a large number of sick and wounded and the difficulty of arranging supplies. But the situation was rendered critical by the fact that the river route to Kalewa was now open to the Japanese, and it thus became a race between the two forces. In view of the imminence of the monsoon, the need for speed in the withdrawal was fully appreciated, but the loss of Monywa turned what should have been a controlled time-table retirement into a hurried retreat which might easily have ended in disaster. It was carried through successfully, but a great deal of valuable equipment was lost, much of which would have been saved had the Shwegyin–Kalewa ferry been able to operate under more normal conditions.

We must conclude the story of the First Burma Campaign by examining it as a whole. The primary causes of the Allied failure to hold Burma will have become apparent to the reader in the course of the narrative. They were, firstly, the British unpreparedness in practically every respect to meet an invasion of the country. This was

---
[1] See page 184.
[2] See page 181.

reflected in the lack of troops and equipment, the lack of aircraft, which led to the defence being without proper intelligence of the enemy, and the lack of proper administrative services. British commanders had to meet a well-trained enemy with hurriedly collected formations and partly-trained troops. Moreover, such training as they had been given was designed to fit them for operations in the sandy deserts of the Middle East and, except for operations in the dry belt, was unsuitable for the type of country in which they had to fight. Secondly, the failure to bring Chinese troops quickly into Burma to assist in its defence; this resulted in British and Allied troops being defeated piecemeal. Lastly, the vacillation of the Chinese and, with one exception, the low standard of command in those Chinese armies which were allocated to the defence of central and upper Burma.

The British army in Burma was called upon to carry out a task beyond its powers. The troops were unsuitably equipped for the type of country in which they had to fight. They had not been trained for jungle warfare and, since in the early part of the campaign they had only motor transport, they were largely tied to the roads. The fact that the enemy soon established air supremacy over the battle area deprived the troops of close support from the air. That their morale, seriously affected by the Sittang disaster and the fall of Rangoon, which cut them off from outside help and left them without amenities and many of the essentials of life, recovered sufficiently to enable the army to deal the enemy severe blows, says much for the courage and resilience of both the British and the Indian troops.

There were two factors which played a part in reviving and sustaining morale. The first was the fine work of such administrative services as there were, which, by shifting the base from Rangoon during the fighting for the city and moving it in successive stages northward as the retreat continued, were able to keep the fighting troops provided with food, water and ammunition throughout the campaign.[1] The second was the presence of 7th Armoured Brigade. This formation with its mobility and fire power was able to give depth to the defence, provide support without delay in a crisis and break the ubiquitous road block; was able to transport infantry units quickly to threatened points and bring in casualties who would otherwise have had to be abandoned. There is no doubt that the armoured brigade played a leading part in the campaign after the fall of Rangoon, and that without it Burcorps might well have collapsed. It was sad that the brigade had to come out of Burma without its tanks. It deserved to have marched proudly with them into India at the head of Burcorps.

---

[1] See Appendix 18.

Strategically, the loss of Burma was a most serious reverse. The blockade of China had become complete for she was cut off from all Allied aid, except for the little that could be sent by air over some of the worst flying country in the world. It was doubtful whether the Chinese will to resist could survive this isolation. If it did not, large Japanese forces would be freed for use elsewhere. For the Allies, too, it was infinitely more difficult to establish and maintain on Chinese soil air forces with which to threaten the mainland of Japan and the enemy line of communications to the Southern Region. The loss of Burma dictated the future strategy of the war in South-East Asia. The efforts of the Allies in this theatre were thereafter directed to recapturing at least enough of Burma to secure the air route and, if possible, open a land route to China so as to keep her in the war—a most difficult military operation across the grain of a country of jungle-covered mountain ranges and broad rivers.

Map 10

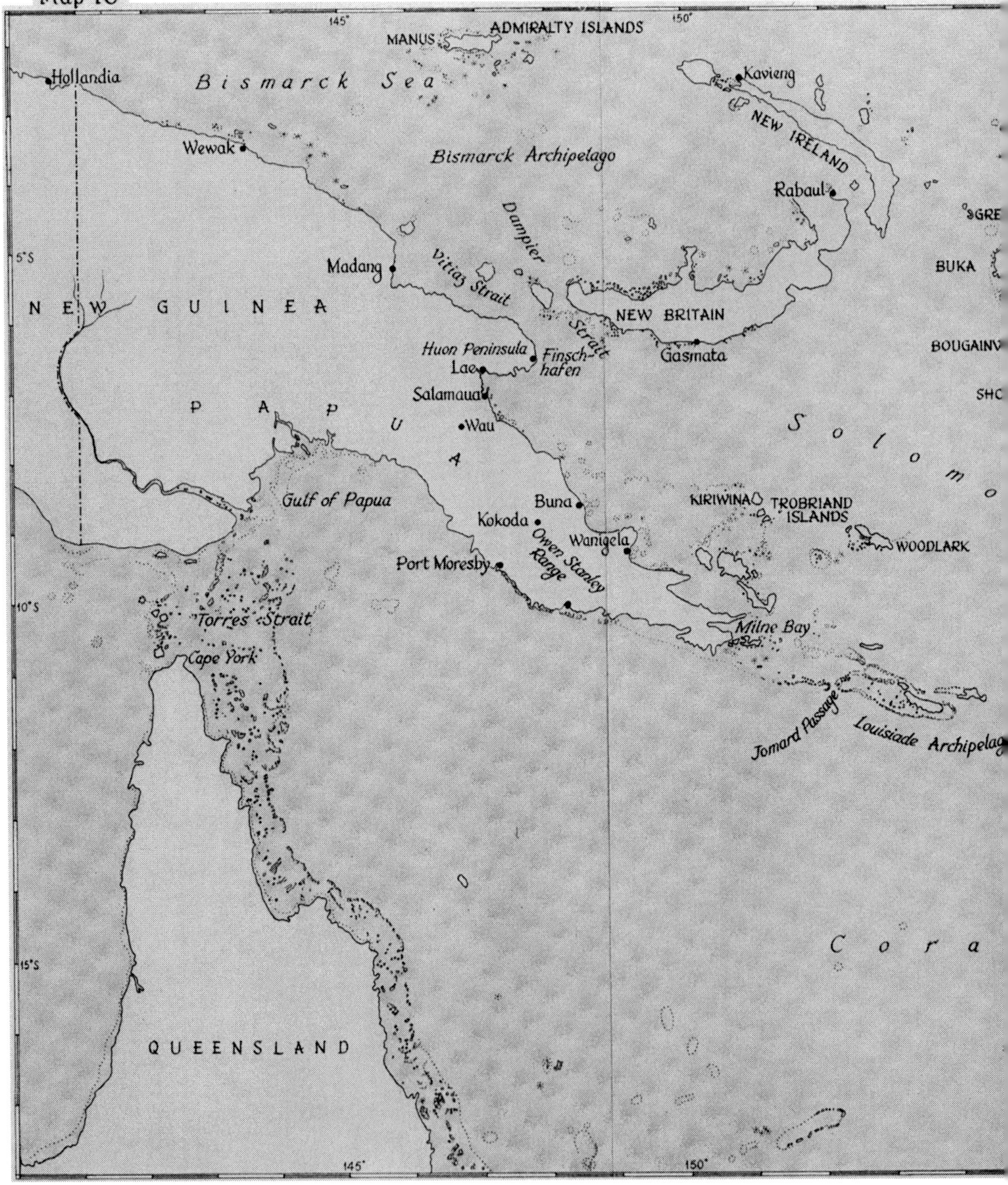
145°
150°
MANUS
ADMIRALTY ISLANDS
Hollandia
Bismarck Sea
Kavieng
NEW IRELAND
Wewak
Bismarck Archipelago
Rabaul
Dampier
Vitiaz Strait
Strait
5°S
Madang
BUKA
NEW GUINEA
NEW BRITAIN
Huon Peninsula
Finschhafen
Lae
Gasmata
BOUGAINV
Salamaua
SHC
PAPUA
Wau
Solomo
Gulf of Papua
Buna
KIRIWINA
TROBRIAND ISLANDS
Kokoda
Owen Stanley Range
Wanigela
WOODLARK
Port Moresby
10°S
Torres Strait
Milne Bay
Cape York
Jomard Passage
Louisiade Archipelag
Cora
15°S
QUEENSLAND

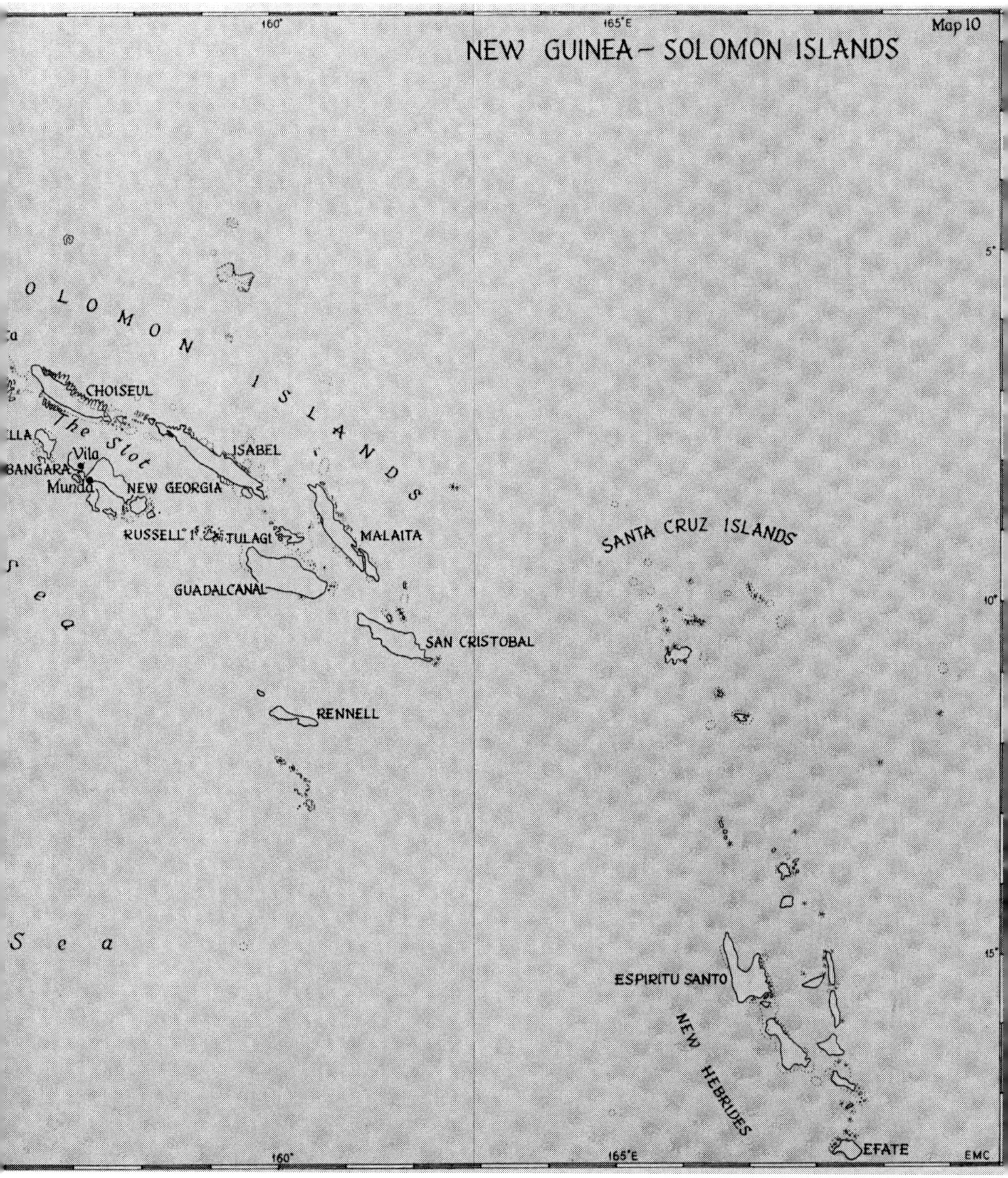
Map 10
NEW GUINEA – SOLOMON ISLANDS
160°
165°E
5°
10°
15°
SOLOMON ISLANDS
CHOISEUL
The Slot
Vila
BANGARA
Munda
NEW GEORGIA
ISABEL
RUSSELL Is.
TULAGI
MALAITA
GUADALCANAL
SAN CRISTOBAL
RENNELL
SANTA CRUZ ISLANDS
ESPIRITU SANTO
NEW HEBRIDES
EFATE
Sea
Sea
EMC

CHAPTER XIII

THE PACIFIC
(January–June 1942)

See Maps 10 and 15

WHILE the Japanese army was engaged in the conquest of Burma, their navy, over 4,000 miles away in the waters of the Solomon Sea, had been closing the ring round their newly-won empire in the Pacific.[1] Rabaul in New Britain, captured on the 23rd January 1942, had been quickly developed as the main advanced base. From there, units of the *South Sea Detachment*, escorted by Admiral Inoue's *4th Fleet* and covered by the *24th Air Flotilla*, began to advance towards Port Moresby and down through the Solomon Islands towards Guadalcanal. From Gasmata in the south of New Britain they crossed to New Guinea and on the 8th March took Lae and Salamaua. Two days later they occupied Finschhafen and thus gained control of the whole of the Huon Peninsula. By the end of the month a naval landing force had landed on Buka, the northernmost island of the Solomons, and on the adjoining islands of Bougainville and Shortland. On each of these they built airstrips. During April there was a pause while they assembled forces at the naval base at Truk in the Carolines for an attack on Port Moresby, which in January they had decided to include in their perimeter.

During the opening months of the war, the main purpose of American strategy in the Pacific was the creation of a secure line of communication to Australasia. The fortification of islands in the southern Pacific had been prevented by the *status quo* clause of the Washington Treaty, and little had been done by the United States towards their defence after that treaty expired in 1936.[2] After Pearl Harbour the American Joint Chiefs of Staff had reinforced Hawaii, Panama and the west coast of the United States and had begun to assemble forces to garrison the island bases on the line of communication to Australasia.

Early in January 1942 a marine regiment was sent to garrison American Samoa. A fortnight later a task force of about 17,000 men was sent by way of Australia to New Caledonia where the Free

---

[1] See Volume I, Chapter VI.
[2] See Volume I, Chapter I.

French authorities had taken control.[1] This island, with its fine natural harbour at Noumea, was one of the main links in the chain of island bases and an obvious target for Japanese attack. At the end of the month, two convoys were despatched by way of the Panama Canal with garrisons for Palmyra, Canton and Christmas Islands which were to be used as staging posts on the air route to Australasia, and also some 4,000 technicians and equipment to construct a naval fuelling base at Bora-Bora in the Society Islands. An American fighter squadron was sent to Fiji, where the garrison had been brought up to a strength of two brigades by New Zealand, and the strength of the Australian garrison at Port Moresby had been increased to a brigade. During the next few months the island bases were reinforced and developed in varying degrees to house, fuel and repair ships and aircraft coming from the United States. In March, Tongatabu in the Friendly Isles and Efate in the New Hebrides were added to the chain of bases, and in May work was started on the development of a forward naval and air base at Espiritu Santo (New Hebrides) which was to play an important part in the recapture of the Solomons.

The south Pacific route, which at the outset had been envisaged mainly as an air ferry route by way of Australia to the Philippines, had soon become the main channel for the supply of aircraft to the ABDA area. For this purpose, an American advanced base had been established at Darwin and United States units added to the Australian force which was protecting the naval station and airfields. But it was not till the 14th February, the day before Singapore fell, that it was decided to send United States army formations to Australia so as to build up a reserve from which the island bases could be reinforced, and to form the nucleus of a force with which a counter-offensive could eventually be launched. The 41st United States Division was the first to be sent, the leading contingent leaving San Francisco for Sydney in the middle of March. At about the same time 1st Australian Corps, except for 9th Australian Division in Syria and two brigades left temporarily as a garrison for Ceylon,[2] was on its way back from the Middle East.

To find shipping to carry these large bodies of troops over the vast distances involved created unprecedented difficulties. To land and equip American forces in Australia required more than twice the shipping tonnage needed to carry similar forces to Europe. Although at the Arcadia Conference in Washington in December 1941, Germany had been accepted as the prime enemy and the President was anxious to get American troops across the Atlantic as quickly as possible to fight Germany, the Combined Chiefs of Staff held the

---

[1] This force became known as the 'Americal Division'.
[2] See page 106.

opinion that the situation in the Far East had to be stabilized before a second front could be opened either in Africa or in Europe. Thus from January to March shipping for the Pacific was supplied at the expense of the Atlantic, and the number of American troops leaving the United States for the Pacific was nearly four times as great as the number making the much shorter voyage across the Atlantic to the United Kingdom.

The build-up of American strength in Australia and the dissolution of ABDA Command caused a reorganization of the chain of command in the Pacific. On the 22nd February 1942, the President ordered General Douglas MacArthur to take command of all American forces in Australia. At the same time he proposed that definite areas of strategic responsibility should be laid down. These were finally agreed upon at the beginning of April. In the Far East the defence of India and the Indian Ocean including Sumatra remained a British commitment, while the United States assumed responsibility for the whole of the Pacific including Australia and New Zealand. The Pacific was divided into two main areas—the South West Pacific Area which included the whole of the Netherlands East Indies except Sumatra, the Philippines, New Guinea, the Bismarcks, the Solomons and Australia; and the Pacific Ocean Area which comprised the whole of the rest of the Pacific, except the waters east of meridian 110° west guarding the approaches to the Panama Canal and the west coast of South America, which was known as the South East Pacific Area. The Pacific Ocean Area was in turn sub-divided into three areas: North, Central and South.[1]

On the 4th April, General MacArthur, who had arrived in Australia from the Philippines on the 17th March, was given command of the South West Pacific Area and Admiral Chester Nimitz was appointed Commander-in-Chief, Pacific Ocean Area. Their directives, which were virtually the same, required them to hold key military positions in their respective areas, to check the Japanese advance and to prepare major offensives against the enemy positions, the first of which was to be launched from the South Pacific and the South West Pacific Areas. The Combined Chiefs of Staff would dictate grand strategy and the American Joint Chiefs of Staff operational strategy. The two commanders would be directly responsible to the latter body, for whom General G. C. Marshall, Chief of Staff, United States Army, was executive agent for the South West Pacific and Admiral E. J. King, Commander-in-Chief, United States Fleet, for the Pacific Ocean area. Each area was to support its neighbour's operations. When task forces moved beyond their own boundaries, co-ordination of their activities with those of other forces would be exercised by the Combined or Joint Chiefs of Staff as appropriate.

[1] For details of these areas see Map 15.

General MacArthur was informed that the 41st and 32nd United States Divisions were being sent to Australia and that the air forces already assigned—two heavy, two medium and one light bomber and three fighter groups—would be brought up to full strength. Owing to shortage of shipping, which was at the time acute, and because of critical situations elsewhere, the strength of the United States forces in the South West Pacific would, for the time being, be limited to these.

While, during these first months of the war, the island route across the Pacific was being secured and Allied strength was gathering in Australia, the United States Pacific Fleet, though forced on the defensive, had not been idle. There was at the time no battle fleet, but the three fleet carriers, *Enterprise*, *Lexington* and *Saratoga*, and the bulk of the cruisers and destroyers of the Pacific Fleet had escaped the holocaust at Pearl Harbour. A fourth carrier, the *Yorktown*, was sent from the Atlantic, but the number was soon reduced to three again when on the 11th January the *Saratoga* was put out of action by a Japanese submarine while carrying out a sweep south of Pearl Harbour. Task forces formed round the carriers, when not engaged in covering the convoys crossing the Pacific, made harassing attacks on the enemy as opportunity occurred. Early in January the *Enterprise* and *Yorktown* task forces, under command of Vice-Admiral W. F. Halsey, bombed and bombarded enemy bases in the Marshall and Gilbert Islands. The damage inflicted was not great, but the fact of having for the first time struck back at the enemy acted as a tonic to the fleet and encouraged a repetition of raids on a similar pattern.

An attack on Rabaul by the *Lexington* task force under Vice-Admiral W. Brown was planned for February. During the approach the force was met by Japanese twin-engined bombers, most of which were shot down by the carrier's fighters. But, as surprise had been lost and fuel was running short, the Admiral decided to call off the attack. Wake and Marcus Islands were bombed and shelled by Admiral Halsey's *Enterprise* force a few days later. In order to cover the movement of American troops from Brisbane to New Caledonia early in March, Admiral Brown was ordered to make a second attack on Rabaul with the *Yorktown* and *Lexington* forces and an Australian cruiser squadron under Rear-Admiral J. G. Crace, R.N. While on the way he received news of the Japanese landings at Lae and Salamaua. Abandoning the attack on Rabaul, he set course for the Gulf of Papua from where he launched over 100 aircraft to fly over the Owen Stanley Mountains and bomb the two ports in the hope of catching the enemy unprepared. The attack, though well executed, achieved little.

THE AIR RAID ON TOKYO

Though they had met with some success and provided valuable experience, the raids up to the end of March had been no more than pin pricks. Another pin prick was soon to be given, but this time in a particularly tender part of the Japanese anatomy. On the 2nd April the newly-commissioned carrier *Hornet*, with sixteen army bombers (B.25s) loaded on deck, sailed with an escort of cruisers and destroyers to a rendezvous with Admiral Halsey's *Enterprise* force between Midway and the Aleutians. The combined force refuelled on the 17th and the carriers and cruisers, leaving the destroyers behind, went on alone. Early on the following morning the bombers were precariously but successfully launched in the teeth of a gale at a point some 650 miles east of the coast of Japan. Shortly after noon thirteen of the bombers, led by Lieut.-Colonel J. H. Doolittle, arrived over Tokyo and unloaded their bombs. The other three dropped incendiaries on Nagoya, Osaka and Kobe. The aircraft, not having the range for the return flight to the carrier, had orders to fly on to friendly airfields in China. All got away successfully. One landed near Vladivostock; the remainder reached China. Of these, four made crash landings and the crews of the other eleven baled out over country strange to them, in darkness and rain. Yet only eight of the eighty men lost their lives, including three who were captured and shot by the Japanese. Most of the survivors, cared for by Chinese peasants, eventually made their way to Chungking. Though pursued by a powerful force which included three fleet carriers, the American carrier force made good its retirement and entered Pearl Harbour on the 25th April.

The effects of the raid were out of all proportion to the damage inflicted. It was no more than a nuisance raid but it was spectacular and daring. It caught the public imagination and gave a tremendous fillip to American morale which had had little encouragement during the previous four months. In Japan, it created alarm for the safety of the homeland and, as will be seen, was to have a considerable influence on Japanese plans. Savage reprisals were taken against the Chinese. An expedition was sent to seize any airfields which might have been used by the aircraft, and men, women and children who were even remotely suspected of having aided American airmen were mercilessly butchered.

By the middle of April the Japanese had all but completed the first phase of their strategic plan. In four months Hong Kong, Malaya and the vast rich area of the Netherlands East Indies had been conquered. Guam, Wake and the Bismarck Archipelago had been captured. In the Philippines only a small pocket of resistance remained in Corregidor. In Burma the British army was being steadily forced back to the Indian border and the road to China was closed.

All this had been successfully accomplished without the loss of a single major warship; except for four destroyers, the Japanese Fleet remained intact. It was an astounding achievement.

The ease and speed with which it had been carried out surprised even the Japanese themselves and led them, instead of setting to work to consolidate their gains as they had planned, to expand their perimeter so as to give greater depth to their defence. Opinion in Tokyo was divided as to the method of execution, and even the wisdom, of this expansion. Whereas hitherto the Army had been the more venturesome, it was now the Navy which wished to press boldly forward and the Army which held back. Plans to strike westwards into the Indian Ocean and capture Ceylon, prepared by the staff of the *Combined Fleet*, were submitted to *Imperial General Headquarters*. Both the Army and Navy rejected them on the grounds that the time was not suitable and the necessary forces not available. The Navy could not then agree as to the best area in which to expand the perimeter. Admiral Nagano, the Chief of the Naval Staff, advocated an advance to the south-east to cut the line of communications from the United States to Australasia. Admiral Yamamoto, Commander-in-Chief, *Combined Fleet*, was insistent however, that priority should be given to bringing the United States Pacific Fleet to action before it had time to rebuild its strength.

The raid on Tokyo took place while the discussions were still in progress. It disclosed a gap in the ring of defences which lent force to Admiral Yamamoto's argument and convinced waverers of the need to close it. A compromise was finally reached. It was decided to advance in the south-east to Tulagi in the Solomons and Port Moresby in New Guinea as already planned so as to gain forward bases from which an advance could later be made to New Caledonia, Fiji and Samoa. The *Combined Fleet* would meanwhile escort an expedition to occupy Midway which would threaten Pearl Harbour and thus force a fleet action on the Americans. As a diversion to the attack on Midway and to block the shortest route from the United States to Japan, landings were to be made in the western Aleutians.

Forces had already begun to assemble at Truk for the attack on Port Moresby, and the *4th Fleet* had been reinforced by two fleet carriers from Admiral Nagumo's *1st Air Fleet* which had just returned from the attack on Ceylon.[1] An intelligence report that these movements had been ordered and that a heavily escorted group of transports would enter the Coral Sea about the 3rd May reached Admiral Nimitz in mid-April. That Port Moresby was its destination was not difficult to guess. He at once began to assemble every ship he could muster in the Coral Sea. Rear-Admiral F. J. Fletcher in the *Yorktown* with three heavy cruisers was already there; he was joined

---
[1] See Chapter VII.

on the 1st May by Rear-Admiral A. W. Fitch with the *Lexington* and two heavy cruisers from Pearl Harbour and three days later by Admiral Crace's Australian squadron. The only other two carriers in the Pacific were at the time still on their way back from the raid on Tokyo. They were sent south as soon as they had refuelled at Pearl Harbour, but arrived too late to take part in the battle.

On the 3rd May, when 400 miles south of Guadalcanal, Fletcher received news that the Japanese had landed at Tulagi, which is separated from Guadalcanal by a narrow strait. In view of the obvious threat, its small Australian garrison had been withdrawn two days earlier. Leaving Fitch's force refuelling at sea Fletcher set course at high speed towards the island. On the following day aircraft from the *Yorktown* made a series of strikes on shipping in the harbour but, as the Japanese covering force had already withdrawn, the results were disappointing. The following morning Fletcher made a rendezvous 300 miles to the southward with Admirals Fitch and Crace.

By this time the Japanese invasion force had left Rabaul for Port Moresby with an escort of destroyers. It was joined on the 5th by the light carrier *Shoho* and four heavy cruisers which had covered the Tulagi landing. A striking force of the two fleet carriers *Zuikaku* and *Shokaku* and two heavy cruisers under Rear-Admiral Takagi, which had come south to the east of the Solomons so as to be out of range of air reconnaissance, entered the Coral Sea on the night of the 5th in the hope of being able to take in the rear any American forces sent to intercept the transports.

Throughout the 5th and 6th May many reports of enemy forces reached Admiral Fletcher, but it was not until the evening of the 6th that the general direction of movement became evident and it could be deduced that the invasion force would probably pass on the 7th or 8th through the Jomard Passage in the Louisiades off the southern tip of New Guinea. He set course to intercept and on the early morning of the 7th sent Crace's cruisers on ahead to cover the southern exit from the Jomard Passage. They were sighted by a Japanese air patrol and that afternoon were heavily attacked by waves of land-based bombers and torpedo-bombers, but by good fortune and skilful manoeuvre not a ship was hit.

Meanwhile Fletcher's dawn air search had reported the Japanese carrier force. The report proved to be erroneous but the powerful air striking force sent out to attack it sighted the *Shoho*, and in a quarter of an hour sent her to the bottom. Not knowing Fletcher's position the Japanese sent out a dusk attack, but the American ships were covered by low cloud and, being without radar, the enemy aircraft failed to find them. They jettisoned their bombs, but on their way back were intercepted by the *Yorktown's* aircraft which shot down six for the loss of three. Eleven more Japanese aircraft failed to find their ships in the darkness and rain and were lost.

As a result of dawn reconnaissances on the 8th, both Admirals discovered each other's whereabouts and both launched strikes of about ninety aircraft. This time the Japanese had the advantage of cloud cover. Although their carriers were sighted shortly before 11 a.m., the *Zuikaku* was able to take cover in a rain storm, and as a result the American attack was concentrated on the *Shokaku* which was hit by three bombs. Although she appeared to the American pilots to be doomed, she was able to get back to Japan for repairs. Meanwhile in clear weather the Japanese bombers struck at the *Yorktown* and *Lexington*. By skilful handling the *Yorktown* evaded all but one bomb, but the *Lexington*, less fortunate, was hit by two torpedoes and three bombs which left her burning fiercely and listing to port. Within a few hours however the fires were extinguished, the list corrected, and she was making 25 knots. The battle was over, for both Admirals rejected the idea of renewing the attack next day. That evening both fleets withdrew from the Coral Sea.

In the five days of attack and counter-attack a Japanese light carrier, a destroyer and some small craft had been sunk and a large carrier disabled. The Japanese invasion fleet had been turned back and Port Moresby for the time was saved. American losses were an oiler and a destroyer which had been detached by Admiral Fletcher on the 6th and sunk by aircraft from the Japanese carriers; the two large carriers though damaged were still efficient fighting units. Honours so far were with the Americans, but the game was not yet played out. The *Lexington* had barely recovered her aircraft when a heavy internal explosion, caused by an accumulation of petrol vapour, shook the ship. This started fires which quickly got out of control and that evening the ship was abandoned and sunk.

If the result of a naval battle were determined by a comparison of the number and value of the ships sunk by each side then, with the loss of the *Lexington*, victory in the Coral Sea must go to the Japanese. But victories are not always measured by comparative losses. It is the effect on the enemy's plans and future strategy which is the ultimate criterion. The transports, deprived of their air cover by the sinking of the *Shoho*, were turned back and the invasion of Port Moresby was postponed until July. But by then the *1st Air Fleet*, short of two carriers, had been annihilated at the battle of Midway, and plans for a seaborne attack on Port Moresby had to be abandoned. The battle of the Coral Sea is memorable as the first sea battle in history the issue of which was decided in the air, and in which ships of the opposing fleets never exchanged a shot. It was the first check to the hitherto irresistible Japanese advance.

The advance into the Coral Sea was only the first move in the Japanese revised programme of expansion. The result of the battle was not the success for which they had hoped, but *Imperial General Headquarters* looked upon it as a minor setback and were not unduly worried. One light carrier had been lost, it is true, and the transports had been turned back, but Tulagi was in Japanese hands and they were confident that Port Moresby could be taken later, either by assault from the sea or by an overland advance. Meanwhile preparations for the capture of Midway, the second and more ambitious item on the programme, were already under way, but final arrangements had to wait until the 23rd April, by which time Admiral Nagumo's carriers would have returned from their attack on Ceylon. Admiral Yamamoto's broad plan was to use the main strength of the *Combined Fleet* to support the capture of Midway and to engage the American Fleet if it intervened; to the north a smaller force, containing two light carriers, would create a diversion by bombing Dutch Harbour at the eastern end of the Aleutians, followed by the capture of the islands of Adak, Kiska and Attu in the west. The widely separated points of attack, the approach from various directions and the preliminary air attacks were typical of Japanese naval practice at that time. Similar strategy had been used with easy success in the Philippines and the Netherlands East Indies, but there the Japanese had usually had the advantage of surprise. This time their enemy was forewarned.

Admiral Yamamoto issued his orders to the *Combined Fleet* on the 5th May. It was not long before Admiral Nimitz became aware, through his intelligence service, of the Japanese intentions, and began to gather forces to meet the impending attack. Three carriers were all he could muster and one of these was damaged. The *Enterprise* and *Hornet* were hurriedly recalled from the south Pacific and nineteen of the twenty-six submarines in the central Pacific, all that could reach the area in time, were brought in to patrol the approaches to Midway. The garrison in the island was reinforced and the airfields filled to capacity with aircraft from Hawaii.

The *Enterprise* and *Hornet* reached Pearl Harbour on the 26th May and sailed with six cruisers and nine destroyers under Rear-Admiral R. A. Spruance for a rendezvous about 350 miles north-east of Midway. The damaged *Yorktown* arrived on the following day. Repairs which normally would have taken ninety days were completed in two, and on the 30th she left with two cruisers and five destroyers under Admiral Fletcher to join the *Enterprise* and *Hornet*. The rendezvous was made on the afternoon of the 2nd June, and the combined force under Admiral Fletcher moved to an area north of Midway.

During the last week in May the Japanese invasion forces had been waiting in readiness at their appointed ports. The first to leave was the Aleutian diversionary force. On the 25th May two light carriers, the *Ryujo* and *Junyo*, with an escort of two cruisers and three destroyers left Japan for the air strike on Dutch Harbour. They were followed during the next three days by the Kiska and the combined Adak/Attu forces. Admiral Nagumo's striking force of four carriers, the *Akagi*, *Kaga*, *Soryu* and *Hiryu*, which were to soften up the defences of Midway before the landing, sailed on the morning of the 26th. Admiral Yamamoto with the battle fleet sailed some three hours later to support them. He was accompanied by the *2nd Fleet* under Admiral Kondo, which was later detached to the northward to give distant cover to the Aleutian invasion and to intercept any American forces which might come that way. The twelve transports of the Midway occupation force, carrying about 5,000 men with an escort of four heavy cruisers and two destroyers under Admiral Kurita, left Saipan and Guam in the Marianas on the evening of the 27th. As the great armada converged on Midway there can have been few misgivings in the minds of the officers and men. In the past six months the Japanese Navy had swept all before it. Hardly a ship had been lost and few even damaged. They must have been confident that Midway would prove as easy a conquest as the rest and that what was left of the American Fleet, if it could be brought to battle, would be outfought without difficulty. They underestimated the determination and vigilance of their enemy and the efficiency of his intelligence service.

The Japanese invasion force was first sighted on the morning of the 3rd June. A Catalina, at the extreme limit of its patrol 700 miles west of Midway, reported a group of eleven ships as the main body of the Japanese Fleet making to the eastward; that afternoon and during the night they were attacked by aircraft from the island, but without success. Admiral Fletcher however took the group of ships to be transports, which, in fact, they were. He had been led by his intelligence reports to expect that Admiral Nagumo's carrier striking force would approach from the north-west and launch an attack on Midway at first light on the 4th. He accordingly set course and speed so as to be 200 miles north of Midway at daylight next morning, from where he would be in a position to attack it on the flank. The accuracy of his intelligence was proved when, at 5.30 a.m. on the 4th, carriers were reported by a Midway patrol 200 miles west-south-west of him. A few minutes later a large formation of enemy aircraft was reported making for Midway. Admiral Fletcher at once ordered Admiral Spruance with the *Enterprise* and *Hornet* to close the enemy and launch a strike, telling him that he would follow in the *Yorktown* as soon as her aircraft had returned from their dawn search.

Admiral Nagumo's bombers struck the island at about 6.30 a.m. The defending fighters put up a gallant resistance and took their toll of the enemy but could not prevent heavy damage to the island installations. The airfield runways however remained serviceable. Radar had given warning of the impending attack and there had been time to launch a counter-attack on Admiral Nagumo's fleet. The American bombers from Midway were met by Japanese fighters in overwhelming numbers and withering anti-aircraft fire from the ships, and scored no hits. Their losses were severe.

The first round in the battle had gone to the Japanese. In the opening exchange of blows, most of the American island-based bombers had been destroyed or damaged and the buildings on the island had been reduced to ruins. Japanese losses were light in comparison and their fleet had withstood a number of attacks and remained intact. So far they were leading handsomely on points, but Admiral Nagumo was to make a decision which gave the Americans a chance which they seized with both hands. As his aircraft were returning from Midway he was told by their commanding officer that a second strike was necessary; he accordingly ordered the ninety-three aircraft which were ranged on deck in readiness for an attack on surface ships to be sent below to rearm for another attack on Midway. Hardly had he given the order when he received a report of enemy ships. After a short hesitation he cancelled his order for the attack on Midway but by that time it was too late: his striking force was already rearming and he had in any case to keep his decks clear for his returning aircraft. He held on his course towards Midway until these had landed on, and shortly after 9 a.m. altered course 90° to port towards the American ships which he now knew included at least one carrier.

Admiral Spruance had meanwhile launched a full strike of dive-bombers and torpedo-bombers from the *Hornet* and *Enterprise*. Admiral Fletcher, keeping half the *Yorktown's* aircraft on board in case of emergency, launched the other half some two hours later. The dive-bombers from the *Hornet*, unaware of the Japanese change of course, missed their target, turned south to search and took no part in the battle. The torpedo-bombers from all three carriers however turned north, found their target and made their attacks almost simultaneously. The Japanese fighters and intense anti-aircraft fire took terrible toll of the low-flying aircraft and of the forty-one sent only six returned. They scored no hits but the gallantry of their pilots did not go unrewarded. Before the Japanese fighters had time to regain height, the *Enterprise* and *Yorktown* dive-bombers arrived on the scene and attacked virtually unopposed. They concentrated on the *Akagi*, *Kaga* and *Soryu*. Their bombs, bursting among the aircraft crowded on deck, reduced the carriers in a few minutes to flaming wrecks which had to be abandoned by their crews. The *Kaga* and *Soryu* sank that evening; the *Akagi* drifted helplessly throughout the night and was sunk the following morning by torpedoes from a Japanese submarine.

As soon as the American aircraft had disappeared, bombers were sent out from the only undamaged Japanese carrier, the *Hiryu*, to attack the *Yorktown* which had been reported two hours earlier. A strike of torpedo-bombers followed them. The first wave attacked Admiral Fletcher's flagship shortly after his victorious bombers had returned and scored three hits, but the ship was still able to carry on although at reduced speed. The second wave put three torpedoes into her, causing damage which was to prove fatal. The ship was abandoned that evening but remained afloat for two days, until she was finally sunk by a Japanese submarine on the morning of the 7th while an American destroyer was trying to take her in tow.

The *Hiryu* did not survive her victim. She was set on fire by bombers from the *Enterprise* that evening, abandoned next morning and sunk by one of her own cruisers. By noon on the 5th June not one of Admiral Nagumo's carriers remained afloat: with them had gone some 250 valuable aircraft and the pick of the pilots of the Japanese naval air arm.

Despite the loss of his air power, Admiral Yamamoto for a time refused to abandon the assault on Midway. Ordering his fleet to concentrate on the evening of the 4th, he sent Admiral Kurita's four heavy cruisers on ahead to bombard the island. The bombardment did not take place: two of the cruisers rammed each other in trying to avoid an American submarine and Kurita withdrew his squadron. The news of the damage to the cruisers, coupled with fuller reports of the fate of his carrier force, at last decided Yamamoto to accept the inevitable and on the morning of the 5th June he ordered a general retirement to the northward.

Admiral Spruance, who had assumed command of the carrier force after the *Yorktown* had been disabled, had retired to the eastward during the night of the 4th/5th, unwilling to risk a night action with probably superior forces. On receiving a report of Kurita's cruisers he turned back to cover Midway. On the morning of the 6th his aircraft found the damaged cruisers; one was sunk but the other, though hard hit, eventually reached Japan.

When he received word of the attack on his cruisers and that the *Enterprise* and *Hornet* were to the eastward of them, Admiral Yamamoto saw a chance to lure Spruance into a trap. He sent a squadron of cruisers south to attack the American carriers while he followed with his concentrated battle fleet. But Spruance was not to be drawn. At nightfall on the 6th June, he turned his victorious carriers homeward. It was not until the following day that Yamamoto at last abandoned all hope of bringing the American Fleet to action and set course back to Japan. A few days later the Japanese naval forces, which on the 7th had assisted in the capture of Attu and Kiska Islands in the Aleutians, were also withdrawn.

If the reader wishes to know the full story of the battle of Midway he must turn to the American histories.[1] It has been given here in the barest detail, but even this short summary of the great American victory may be considered to have been given more space than is appropriate to a British history. It has been included deliberately because of its importance not only to the Americans but to the whole of the Allied cause. It was the turning point in the war against Japan. The battle of the Coral Sea checked for the first time the Japanese advance. Midway put a stop to it. Though his fleet was still greatly superior to Admiral Nimitz's in battleship strength, without his carriers Admiral Yamamoto no longer dared risk a fleet action in waters outside the range of his land-based aircraft. Japan's attempt to expand her already over-stretched perimeter proved an irretrievable mistake. In reaching for the shadow of further conquests she lost the bone of naval supremacy, without which she could not hold the vast area she had already won. She was never able to regain it. In the next few months American shipyards had replaced and repaired the ships of the Pacific Fleet, and were turning out new ships at a speed and in numbers which the Japanese industrial capacity could not hope to match.

---

[1] For list, see pages xiii–xiv.

CHAPTER XIV

FRUSTRATIONS DURING THE 1942 MONSOON

See Strategic Map and Map 14

AFTER the naval battles of Coral Sea and Midway, the possibility of a full scale seaborne invasion of Ceylon and the Madras or Orissa coasts, though it could not be entirely discounted, was greatly reduced. General Wavell could now expect that any Japanese attempts to advance towards India would be confined to the Assam frontier, Arakan and the eastern Bengal coast. Reinforced by 70th, 5th and 2nd British Divisions he had been able to rebuild his central reserve at Ranchi, and felt for the first time since the loss of Rangoon that the immediate danger to India had receded and that he could plan a counter-offensive.

But even before the battle of Midway had been fought, he had begun to consider plans for the recapture of Burma. The first essential was to establish air superiority over Burma from airfields in north-east India, but with the meagre resources, especially in long-range aircraft, which he expected to have by the end of 1942, he felt he could plan only for very limited operations to secure part of upper Burma north of Mandalay during the period of the dry weather from December 1942 to May 1943. By early June 1942 he had decided that at the end of October he could, subject to delays imposed by climatic and other conditions, operate a number of small columns on a wide front from Assam so as to gain the line of the Chindwin River from Kalewa to Homalin, and then advance if possible to the line Kalewa–Katha–Myitkyina. If these operations were successful, they would serve both to raise morale in India and re-establish a combined front with the Chinese.

On the 12th June, after the news of the battle of Midway became known, the Prime Minister cabled him that these minor operations were 'very nice and useful nibbling' but what he was really interested in was the capture of Rangoon and Moulmein, followed by an advance on Bangkok. He believed that the Japanese naval losses, particularly in aircraft carriers, would impose caution on their navy, and suggested that Wavell might plan to move down the coast from Chittagong to Akyab and, at the right time, launch an expedition of forty or fifty thousand troops with suitable armour across the northern part of the Bay of Bengal, thereby seizing the initiative and carrying the war back into southern Burma and towards Malaya. He added a rider to the effect that such an operation would only be possible if all went well on the Russian and Middle East fronts.

Wavell had already been reconsidering his tentative plans. He concluded that, as a result of Midway, the threat to India from the Japanese Navy had been reduced to one of raids on shipping in the Bay of Bengal which, although harmful from the point of view of material and morale, would not endanger the security of the country. He was now therefore in a position to begin to make definite plans for the recapture of the whole of Burma. He accordingly ordered Eastern Army to undertake detailed planning for the limited operations he had in view, and his planning staff at General Headquarters to consider the problems of launching a major operation with Rangoon as the objective, to which the code name of 'Anakim' was to be given. He informed the Prime Minister that his pressing need was an effective air striking force, including long-range fighters, and that until such a force had been built up he would be unable to support any offensive against Burma. He also urged that there should be some clear understanding with the Americans on the question of 'command'. He suggested that General Stilwell and the 10th U.S.A.A.F. should be placed under his command, Stilwell also acting as a link with the Chinese. Later he expressed the opinion that, if his air force were quickly and adequately reinforced and he were given enough shipping and landing craft (with trained crews) to lift two divisions in time to enable the troops to be trained, operation 'Anakim' was feasible, provided that the Eastern Fleet was built up to the necessary strength and American operations in the Pacific timed to keep the main Japanese Fleet occupied. It could not, however, be launched before January 1943.[1]

While the Chiefs of Staff were examining the possibility of providing the resources for 'Anakim', the war in the European theatres had taken a turn for the worse. In the Middle East the Germans had defeated the British 8th Army in the Libyan desert and forced it to retreat to Egypt, Tobruk had fallen, and the rapid German advance towards the Don at the southern end of the Russian front had created a threat to both Iraq and Persia. The flow of aircraft from the Middle East to India was stopped, and all the heavy bombers of the 10th U.S.A.A.F., the spearhead of Wavell's small air striking force, were temporarily diverted to the Middle East. The Chiefs of Staff warned Wavell that at least one of the British divisions which

---

[1] The air force requirements were assessed at 1,150 first line aircraft and, apart from naval forces, about 100 ships of not more than 500 feet in length or more than 24 feet in draught were required.

PLANS TO RECAPTURE BURMA

had just arrived in India might have to be sent to Iraq or Persia, but nevertheless proposed that all preparations and planning for 'Anakim' should go on. The Prime Minister, however, laid down that conditions for its launching would be favourable only if the Germans were defeated in the Middle East, if the Russian front held, if neither Iraq nor Persia was invaded, if American-Australian operations in the south-west Pacific area caused continuous wastage of the Japanese air forces and if the naval situation in both the Pacific and Indian Oceans remained propitious. He envisaged the operations in three stages: increased pressure on the enemy front in Assam, the seizure of Akyab and finally an attack on the Rangoon–Moulmein coast. The wish to launch an offensive early in 1943 to recapture Burma and carry the war into Siam existed therefore in both London and Delhi. But the shortage of aircraft and shipping imposed by the

A note sent by General Wavell in September 1942, to the Deputy Chief of the General Staff, India.

demands of other theatres of war, as well as climatic and political factors in India, created such insuperable obstacles that it was to be a long time before so large an offensive could be undertaken.

Meanwhile in Assam with the onset of the monsoon, which coincided with the arrival of Burcorps, the administrative position at Imphal had begun to give cause for anxiety and the maintenance of the flow of supplies along the Imphal Road had become IV Corps' primary task. As a result of the torrential rains conditions on the road rapidly worsened and the wear and tear on the vehicles of the transport companies became so heavy that, although mobile workshops were stationed at intervals along it, repairs could not keep pace with the wastage of vehicles. The position was further aggravated by the inefficiency of the drivers in the newly-raised transport companies, and by the high rate of sickness of both drivers and mechanics, due mainly to malaria. As a result the flow of traffic on the road was very much reduced, and there were occasions when rations for the troops in the Imphal area had to be reduced to half the authorized scale and only the barest minimum of equipment and engineering stores could be delivered.

These difficulties on the line of communication occurred at the very worst moment. There were still thousands of civilian refugees in the area who had arrived in an exhausted condition, and whose plight was such that military assistance, including the allocation of transport, had to be given at the expense of all other requirements. On the Imphal plain, in addition to IV Corps Headquarters, 23rd Indian Division and many administrative units, some 20,000 men of Burcorps had to be cared for. They were without blankets, ground sheets or cooking facilities and were in urgent need of tents and tarpaulins for shelter from the monsoon rain. The situation was eased by the fact that the civil population of Imphal had taken to the jungle after the town had been bombed by the Japanese on the 10th and 16th May. Empty houses and buildings were thus available and were used to give shelter to the troops. Nevertheless there were many for whom no cover could be found. It was among these, weakened by the trials they had endured during the long withdrawal, that malaria and dysentery took their greatest toll; the hospital services were strained to the utmost.

The limitations of both road and rail transport, as well as the congestion at the half-built Manipur road base at Dimapur, made it impossible to ease matters quickly by evacuating to India those troops of Burcorps not required at Imphal. Since there was at that time no certainty that the monsoon would stop any further Japanese advance, IV Corps needed all the troops who could be maintained

DEFENCE OF NORTH-EAST FRONTIER

forward of Imphal. But the administrative position in June was such that the ration strength on the Imphal plain could not be allowed to exceed 40,000. After ruthless pruning and the retention of essential units only, General Irwin found that he could keep in the forward area one of the Burcorps divisions in addition to 23rd Indian Division. He therefore decided to retain and re-equip 17th Indian Division at Imphal, to move 1st Burma Division (to be reconstituted and re-named 39th Indian Division) to Shillong and to send all surplus units to India, as and when these moves became possible.[1]

He disposed 23rd Indian Division so as to cover the south-eastern and eastern approaches to the Imphal plain, with orders to patrol actively as far forward as the Chindwin River, placed 17th Indian Division in reserve at Imphal with one battalion at Kohima, and covered the rest of the frontier with the Assam Rifles and 'V' Force. He also organized a North Assam Brigade to defend the Digboi oilfields against any enemy advance up the Hukawng Valley on to Ledo.

During June, July and August the administrative situation grew worse, since the exceptionally heavy monsoon rains caused frequent land-slides on the Imphal Road and breached the Assam trunk road and the railway between Parbatipur and Amingaon. Nevertheless by the end of July 1st Burma Division had been moved back to Shillong and all the surplus units had reached India. During the same period the Japanese, reorganizing after the capture of Burma and equally affected by the monsoon, made no attempt to advance and the only contacts between the opposing forces were occasional patrol clashes on the Chindwin. On the 29th July, General Irwin handed over command of IV Corps to Lieut.-General G. A. P. Scoones, and himself relieved General Sir Charles Broad as Commander of Eastern Army.

In eastern Bengal 14th Division, with only one brigade under command, was holding a defensive position behind the Feni river. Towards the end of June, reports were received that small enemy parties were moving northwards from Akyab and up the Kaladan valley towards Kyauktaw. To meet this threat Eastern Army ordered the division to move to the Chittagong area, and reinforced it with 123rd Indian Infantry Brigade (less one battalion) from Assam, where it had formed part of 23rd Indian Division. This brigade, seriously depleted by malaria while in Assam, arrived at Chittagong on the 11th July; here it was brought up to strength by the addition

---

[1] The 17th Indian Division consisted of 16th, 48th and 63rd Indian Infantry Brigades.
The 39th Indian Division as re-formed consisted of 106th and 113th (late 13th) Indian Infantry Brigades, each of one British and two Indian battalions.
The surplus fighting units returned to India consisted of two British and three Indian battalions and the remnants of the Burma Rifles.

of 10th Lancashire Fusiliers, a battalion which had recently arrived in India from England. At the same time the defence policy for eastern Bengal was modified to the extent that Chittagong was to be given up only if the defence were forced back by overwhelming enemy pressure.

During the monsoon Japanese air activity over Burma was very much restricted, for advantage was taken of the poor flying conditions to reorganize *5th Air Division*. The *10th Air Brigade, 27th Air Regiment* and *15th Independent Air Unit* were transferred to China and replaced by *14th* and *81st Air Regiments*. Most of the air units of the division were then withdrawn to Malaya and Siam for training and re-equipment, leaving only one fighter regiment and a few light bombers, totalling some forty aircraft, for the defence of Rangoon. In order to provide a suitable air component for *Southern Army*, the Japanese in July formed *3rd Air Army* with headquarters at Singapore, under the command of Lieut.-General H. Obata who was succeeded in command of *5th Air Division* by Lieut.-General N. Tazoe.[1]

Allied air operations were also on a small scale, but were notable for the skill and determination with which the aircraft were flown in bad weather. Targets on the Burma coast, in the Chindwin valley and at Akyab were attacked with success, and reconnaissance over the Bay of Bengal, enemy airfields in Burma and the port of Rangoon was regularly maintained. At one time it was thought that the Japanese intended to move from the Chindwin and Myittha valleys into the Chin Hills, which were held only by weak detachments and local levies. It was feared that the Chins would become alarmed and, depressed by a shortage of food, might make terms with the Japanese. The dropping of food in the area and vigorous bombing of the enemy troops wherever they could be found was consequently undertaken.

Throughout the monsoon, a small detachment of transport aircraft of 31 Squadron R.A.F., stationed at Dinjan in northern Assam, was constantly engaged in searching for parties of refugees who were still trying to make their way through the dense jungle to the safety of India. It was assisted occasionally by American Dakotas whenever they could be spared from their vital task of carrying supplies to China. Wherever groups were seen in jungle clearings or by the banks of swollen rivers, supplies were dropped to them. A small party of British men and women without food, money, arms or spare clothing, succeeded in reaching Fort Hertz. When it was reported that the Japanese were moving north from Sumprabum a determined attempt was made to rescue these unfortunate people

---

[1] See Appendix 19.

by air; but it was only after several sorties had been frustrated by the bad weather that on the 13th June an aircraft of 31 Squadron managed to reach Fort Hertz. After a landing and take-off from a very confined space, twenty-three people were successfully flown out.

Towards the end of June it was planned to reoccupy Fort Hertz, since it was thought to have possibilities as an emergency landing ground on the air supply route to China and as a base from which to raise and support Kachin Levies to operate against the Japanese between it and Myitkyina. As there was no road from India to Fort Hertz, a garrison had to be sent by air. On the 4th July, a reconnaissance party was dropped by parachute near Myitkyina to get information about the Japanese dispositions in that area, but its wireless broke down and no report was received. On the 22nd July, air reconnaissance reported that there was no activity at Fort Hertz and that the landing ground appeared to be water-logged and unfit for use. An attempt to fly in an army officer together with a wireless set and an operator failed owing to the weather, with the loss of one of the two aircraft used. Eventually two army officers and nine men were successfully dropped near Fort Hertz on the 13th August, to find that the reconnaissance party had reached the fort. By the 24th a landing ground 1,100 yards long had been prepared and, after a trial landing, a company of Indian infantry was flown in on the 10th September. Thereafter the garrison at Fort Hertz was entirely dependent upon air supply, which was successfully undertaken by the detachment of 31 Squadron operating from Dinjan.

During the spring and summer of 1942 development of the American Assam–Burma–China Ferry Command was retarded by the need to divert many of its aircraft to help in the evacuation of civil refugees and wounded from upper Burma, and to drop supplies to the retreating Burma Army.[1] The fact that the airfield at Myitkyina, which it had been hoped would provide a staging post between Assam and China, was in the hands of the Japanese by the end of May, greatly increased the difficulties of ferrying supplies to China, for all aircraft thereafter had to fly the 500 miles direct to Kunming over the mountains—a route which became known as the Hump. This route, much of which was unmapped, passed over snow-capped peaks which reached a height of over 15,000 feet and was considered at the time to be the most difficult in the world. During the monsoon much of the flying had to be done by instruments. There were no aids to navigation and there was a danger of meeting incredibly turbulent air currents over the mountains, capable of breaking up the stoutest aircraft. To add to their difficulties the pilots of the unarmed transport aircraft had to face the

---

[1] See pages 113–14. This command was renamed the India–China Ferry Command on the 15th July.

possibility of encountering Japanese fighters. Losses were thus heavy in the early days. Nevertheless the American pilots persevered and were later so successful that in 1943 the ferry command was greatly expanded, and eventually was delivering more supplies to China than ever passed along the old Burma Road.

Meanwhile the many administrative preparations and the airfield construction programme begun in India, as outlined in Chapters III and XI, were being pushed ahead as fast as the particularly severe monsoon conditions of 1942 and the supply of men and materials would permit. At the same time, Wavell was taking steps to improve the organization and training of the forces under his command.

Immediately after the withdrawal from Burma, commanders of formations and units, together with staff officers of all ranks, were summoned to Delhi in order to examine the lessons learnt from the recent campaigns and apply them to the organization and equipment of Indian Army formations. It soon became apparent that the Indian division was over-mechanized and road-bound and, owing to the lack of animal transport, at a disadvantage when forced to fight away from a main road in jungle country. It was therefore decided to introduce a new type of formation to be called an Indian light division. This formation was to be provided with only a light scale of mechanical transport vehicles (mainly jeeps and light four-wheel drive lorries), and was to depend largely on pack mule transport companies. It was to consist of a divisional headquarters and a support battalion, equipped with carriers and medium machine-guns, and two brigades only, each consisting of a headquarters defence platoon, one reconnaissance and three infantry battalions.[1] The artillery was to be two mountain regiments on a full pack basis, one mechanized field regiment and a mixed light anti-aircraft and anti-tank regiment. The engineers were reduced to one field park company and two field companies. The division was allotted six mule companies and four jeep companies as its first and second line transport. It was hoped that the light divisions would have much greater mobility and, as they would be able to operate if necessary well away from roads, would be able to defeat the normal Japanese encircling tactics. The 17th and 39th Indian Divisions were selected for conversion. At the same time the degree of mechanization of 7th, 20th and 23rd Divisions was reduced and some animal transport introduced; these became known as 'animal and motor transport' (A. and M.T.) divisions. The remaining Indian divisions (14th, 19th, 25th,

---

[1] The support battalion was described by General Wavell as 'mobile shock' troops. The reconnaissance battalion was to consist of two jeep companies and two mounted infantry companies.

26th and 34th) and the three British divisions (2nd, 5th and 70th) were unchanged.[1]

During the summer and autumn of 1942, a review of the Indian armoured formations was undertaken. In June of that year these consisted of 31st Indian Armoured Division (251st and 252nd Armoured Brigades) of which the headquarters and 252nd Armoured Brigade had been sent to Iraq; 32nd Indian Armoured Division (254th and 255th Armoured Brigades); and 43rd Indian Armoured Division which was about to be formed. There was in addition 50th Indian Tank Brigade (146th, 149th and 150th Regiments, R.A.C.).[2] It was decided that the composition of the Indian armoured divisions should be brought into line with that of the British armoured divisions, which consisted of one armoured brigade and one (lorried) infantry brigade per division instead of two armoured brigades. The 32nd Indian Armoured Division was reconstituted with 255th Indian Armoured Brigade and 73rd Indian (lorried) Infantry Brigade, while 43rd Indian Armoured Division was to be raised with one armoured (267th) and one lorried infantry (268th) brigade. At the same time the two surplus Indian armoured brigades (251st and 254th) were redesignated Indian tank brigades.[3]

This period also marked the beginning of the long-range penetration force. At the end of January the War Office had offered Wavell the services of Lieut.-Colonel O. C. Wingate, who had carried out guerilla operations in Palestine and Abyssinia with conspicuous success. Wavell, under whom Wingate had served, recognized 'his excellent if unorthodox qualities' and, seeing a rôle for him in Burma or China, accepted this offer. Wingate arrived in India shortly after the fall of Rangoon and Wavell immediately sent him to carry out a reconnaissance of upper Burma where it was thought that guerilla types of operation might be useful.[4]

On completion of his reconnaissance, Wingate returned to Delhi and submitted a scheme for long-range penetration into Burma. He propounded the theory that, given power to maintain forces by air and direct them by wireless, regular army formations could operate for indefinite periods in the heart of enemy-held territory. The only limit to the strength of such forces would be the air supply potential (i.e. the degree of air superiority and the number of suitable aircraft available). The value of such forces, he believed, was dis-

---

[1] The 26th Division was later converted to an A. and M.T. division.

[2] The 50th Indian Tank Brigade was formed from three British battalions sent from the United Kingdom for the purpose.

[3] The armoured formations were to be equipped as under: 50th Indian Tank Brigade—Valentine tanks, 251st and 254th Indian Tank Brigades—General Grant and General Stewart tanks, 32nd and 43rd Indian Armoured Divisions—General Grant tanks.

[4] Wingate was accompanied on this reconnaissance by Major J. M. Calvert, who had been in charge of the Bush Warfare School at Maymyo, training British guerillas for use in China. He later became one of Wingate's most successful column commanders.

proportionate to their cost, for one fighting man at the heart of the enemy's military machine was worth many hundreds in the forward battle zone. The governing principle of long-range penetration was that columns must be large enough to deliver blows of the necessary weight and small enough to evade the enemy in case of need.

He proposed, therefore, that a specially organized and trained brigade should be raised and used to penetrate deep into Burma and operate there by means of air supply and wireless, without depending on the normal military lines of communication. Such a force, properly used, would not only affect the enemy's ability to maintain his armies in the field by disrupting his lines of communication, but would be able to supply detailed air intelligence and so assist in the direction of the strategic air offensive. It would also be in a position to exploit any opportunities created by its presence within enemy territory.

After careful consideration of all the factors involved in the creation of such a specialized force, including that of the British manpower shortage in India, Wavell approved the formation of one long-range penetration brigade which was to be known, for deception purposes, as 77th Indian Infantry Brigade. The brigade was to be composed of a headquarters, one British and one Gurkha infantry battalion, a signals section, a specialized sabotage unit and a reconnaissance unit. It was to be organized to function on an all-pack basis in eight mixed columns, each column being accompanied by a platoon consisting of men enlisted from the country in which the operations were to take place. Since it would be entirely dependent on air supply, each column was to be provided with a small R.A.F. section equipped with wireless sets for liaison purposes.[1]

The 77th Indian Infantry Brigade, under Wingate's command, was formed during July 1942 and moved to a suitable area in the Central Provinces where it began intensive training in jungle warfare. Wingate selected as the emblem of the long-range penetration group a mythological beast—the Chinthe—statues of which, half lion and half eagle, were frequently found in Burmese pagodas. He considered that this emblem symbolized the close co-operation between the ground and air forces required in such operations. It was from this emblem that the name 'Chindits', by which the brigade became known, originated.

In preparation for an eventual offensive, Wavell also decided to press forward with the training of 50th Parachute Brigade (Brigadier G. H. Gough) for which volunteers from Indian Army units had been invited in 1941. Early in 1942 sufficient volunteers were forthcoming to start forming the brigade, and it began training with 215 (Wellington) Squadron, withdrawn for the purpose from its

---

[1] For composition of 77th Indian Infantry Brigade see Appendix 26.

operational rôle, from which at that time it could ill be spared. Arrangements were made in India for the manufacture of statichutes for the Chindits and parachutes and other equipment for the parachute brigade.[1] The provision of gliders was also investigated in order that an airborne brigade could be formed at a later date.

One other important reorganization was undertaken. After the withdrawal from Burma some 8,000 Chinese troops, from 22nd and 38th Chinese Divisions, had reached India and had been sent to Ramgarh for training.[2] Stilwell proposed later in the year that more Chinese troops should be flown from China to India to increase the numbers at Ramgarh to some 20–30,000. His object was to train and equip a Chinese corps of two divisions and corps troops, which would eventually be used to advance from Imphal to join hands with the Chinese from Yunnan. Wavell accepted this proposal in October 1942 but, considering that an advance from Imphal was impracticable, directed that one should be made from Ledo by the Hukawng Valley to Myitkyina. The necessary equipment, transport and training staff would be provided from American, and the accommodation and rations from British, sources. The transport of Chinese troops by air to bring the divisions up to strength began immediately. As a corollary to this decision, the plan to build the Ledo road over the Pangsau Pass and down the Hukawng Valley was revived, and it was agreed that the construction of the road and the stocking of an advanced base at Ledo would be undertaken by the Americans.[3]

After the rejection by Indian leaders of the British Government's proposals brought by the Cripps Mission, the political situation in India had progressively deteriorated during the summer of 1942. Since the resulting disturbances had a considerable effect on the ability of the Indian Army to take the offensive during the dry season of 1942–43, they must be described. By the end of April 1942 Mahatma Gandhi, the Congress leader, had begun to give public expression to the doctrine which was to develop into his 'Quit India' movement, and on the 1st May the All-India Congress Committee passed a resolution, the essence of which was:

> 'The present crisis, as well as the experience of the negotiations with Sir Stafford Cripps, makes it impossible for the Congress to consider any schemes or proposals which retain, even in partial measure, British control and authority in India. Not

---

[1] A statichute is a type of automatic parachute. It was adopted as standard equipment for dropping men and supplies.

[2] See page 196.

[3] See page 54.

only the interests of India but also Britain's safety, and world peace and freedom demand that Britain must abandon her hold on India. It is on the basis of independence alone that India can deal with Britain or with other nations.'

By the end of May it was clear that Congress was moving towards a civil disobedience campaign. By mid-July, although the stationing of Allied troops in India to ward off a Japanese attack was accepted, the Congress Working Committee passed a resolution to the effect that, should the appeal to Britain to withdraw fail, Congress would then 'be reluctantly compelled to utilize all the non-violent strength it might have gathered since 1920 when it adopted non-violence as a part of its policy . . .' Since the issues raised were so vital, the Working Committee decided to refer them to the All-India Congress Committee for final decision. After the passing of this resolution Mahatma Gandhi said, 'There is no room left in the proposal for withdrawal or negotiation. There is no question of one more chance. After all it is open rebellion'.

Instructions for the civil disobedience campaign then began to be circulated in Madras, the United Provinces and Bihar, and Congress leaders in speeches urged the masses to be prepared for the fight to the finish against the British which Congress would shortly launch. The All-India Congress Committee met at Bombay on the 8th August and resolved 'to sanction . . . the starting of a mass struggle on non-violent lines on the widest possible scale'. Since such a struggle had inevitably to be waged under the leadership of Mahatma Gandhi, the Committee requested him to take the lead and guide the nation in the steps to be taken.[1]

The following day the Government of India arrested Gandhi and other Congress leaders throughout the country. The initial reaction to these arrests was mild, but on the 11th August concerted and planned outbreaks of mob violence, arson, murder and sabotage began; in almost all cases these were directed against railway, postal and telegraphic communications or against the police. The areas most affected were Madras, Bihar and the United Provinces.[2] These were the areas of greatest strategic importance for they covered the Indian coalfields, lay on the lines of communication to the field armies and were close to those parts of India most obviously exposed to enemy attack. Within a very short time whole districts were isolated, the broad gauge railways connecting Calcutta with Delhi and Bombay were cut in many places and much of the metre gauge system in north-east India, on which the communications to the Assam frontier depended, was put out of action.

---

[1] Comd. 6430 (1943).
[2] See Map 4.

Wavell was forced to employ some fifty-seven infantry battalions to deal with these disturbances, as well as aircraft to demonstrate in the areas which the troops could not reach at first because of the dislocation of the railways.[1] The disturbances continued unabated for about a fortnight. During the third week there were indications of growing disapproval of mob violence amongst the general public, and by the fourth week the firm action taken by the authorities had largely restored law and order. It was, however, to be six weeks before normal conditions were restored throughout most of the country. The main effect of these disturbances on the military situation can be thus summarized: the training of certain field army formations and of reinforcements was retarded by some six to eight weeks; owing to the damage to the railways, Eastern Army's movement programme was delayed for at least three weeks; because of shortage of materials and labour difficulties, airfield construction in Assam and eastern India was held up for four to six weeks and there was a general loss of production in all factories turning out arms, clothing and equipment.

As the areas affected by the disturbances were either strategic centres or on important lines of communication, it was thought at the time that there was direct collusion between Congress and the Japanese. The Japanese Embassy in Afghanistan had been organized as a centre for the collection of intelligence from India, but there is no evidence of any association between it and Congress. Furthermore, although during the summer of 1942 the Japanese had been landing agents and Fifth Columnists from submarines on the east coast of India, they had not been ordered to make contact with Congress leaders. The available evidence shows that the Japanese, far from being in control of the Congress campaign, were constantly seeking information on its course and aims and the localities in which the disturbances were taking place.

These were not the only disturbances which Wavell had to tackle during the summer. In Sind a fanatical sect of Moslems, known as the Hurs, had long terrorized a considerable stretch of country through which ran the main railway line from Karachi to Lahore. In May a gang of Hurs derailed a mail train and then attacked it. It was impossible to tolerate further outrages of this kind on one of the principal lines of communication in India and, as the police and civil authorities were unable to control the situation, a military force was sent and martial law declared in the area. Thereafter the position soon improved, but so deep-rooted was the terrorism and so difficult the country, which consisted of large stretches of marsh and

---

[1] Of these battalions twenty-four were found from the Field Army, seven were specially formed from reinforcement camps and training centres and the balance was taken from those already allotted to internal security duties.

desert, that for the rest of the year the troops were engaged in restoring order.

In July there was a further distraction when tribesmen on the North West Frontier, inspired by the notorious Fakir of Ipi, cut the road between Miram Shah and Datta Khel, as a result of which the post at Datta Khel had to be supplied by air. To deal with the outbreak a mobile column was formed from 3rd, 33rd and 55th Indian Infantry Brigades and the Razmak Brigade. It was supported by 28 (AC) and 34(B) Squadrons, R.A.F., and, in the short but successful operations which followed, the road was reopened and Datta Khel relieved early in August. The lashkar, which had never exceeded more than some 700 tribesmen, was dispersed. The strength of the column employed, apart from restoring order, served as a salutary reminder to the tribesmen that adequate troops were available in India to take action against them should they make it necessary. From then onwards the situation on the North West Frontier in general remained satisfactory.

Another factor which complicated planning and delayed preparations for an offensive was the uncertainty regarding the arrival of 29th Independent Brigade. Wavell had been informed that it would reach him from Madagascar late in July or early in August. By mid-July it was clear that the brigade was to be retained in the island for further operations, and at the end of the month he was told to return all assault shipping and landing craft which had been sent him after the capture of Diego Suarez.[1]

Nevertheless, Wavell pressed on with his arrangements for training in amphibious operations. He established a small directorate of combined operations at General Headquarters, India, and a Force Headquarters at Bombay to direct training. The army portion of this headquarters was given the name of 36th Indian Division and placed under command of Major-General F. W. Festing.[2] He also formed a combined operations training school near Bombay, requisitioned two ships, converting one to a headquarters ship and the other to an assault ship, and started to train 6th Brigade of 2nd British Division. Since he was unable to obtain crews from either the Royal Navy or the Royal Indian Navy for the 477 landing craft which he estimated would be required for 'Anakim', he was forced to transfer the equivalent of some three battalions from the Indian Army to the Royal Indian Navy for training as landing craft crews.

The course of the war on the Russian front and in the Middle East also affected India. On the 11th July, Wavell was told that in view of the Russian situation he might have to send one or two

---

[1] See Chapter VIII.
[2] General Festing had commanded 29th Independent Brigade in the Madagascar campaign.

divisions to Iraq. He selected 5th and 2nd British Divisions in that order and made arrangements for their despatch if the necessity arose. On the 14th he called the attention of the Chiefs of Staff to the weakness of India's defences by sea and air, saying:

> 'India is . . . still practically defenceless against sea-borne invasion and will remain so until we have Air Force capable of making it as dangerous for enemy ships to approach shores of India as it was for them to approach Midway, and until our own Fleet can go into Bay of Bengal with their sterns well up [*sic*] looking for Japs. Surely we can afford to make available comparatively small (if modern) Air Force required to safeguard India. Until we do so India cannot be regarded as secure'.

After the unsuccessful campaign in Libya and 8th Army's retreat to Egypt, the Prime Minister held a conference in Cairo to which Wavell was summoned. At the conference it was decided among other things that India should send 5th British Division and 7th Armoured Brigade to Iraq, which with Persia was to form a new Persia and Iraq Command (PAIC) separate from Middle East Command. The 2nd British Division was to remain in India. The conference, prolonged by a visit to Moscow, lasted from the 4th to the 22nd August, and kept Wavell and several of his senior staff officers from attending to the many pressing problems awaiting them in India. Their absence and the loss to India of two trained formations caused further postponement of Wavell's preparations for 'Anakim'.

The delays caused by all these climatic, political and strategical factors, the time required to reorganize, equip and train British and Indian formations for their tasks, and the inability of Britain to provide the resources for a major campaign in the Far East owing to the demands of the war in the Middle East and Russian theatres, made it clear by the end of August 1942, that operation 'Anakim' could not be mounted in the dry weather 1942–43 and would have to be postponed for a year. The limited operations planned for IV Corps had also to be postponed owing to delays imposed by the Congress riots on the preparations in Assam, the effects of the heavy monsoon and the ravages of malaria. In these circumstances Wavell began to consider an operation to reoccupy Akyab, which could be staged independently of both operations from Assam against upper Burma and of a seaborne expedition directed on Rangoon. Such an operation would inevitably force the enemy air force into a struggle for air superiority over Burma which would increase its rate of wastage, thus assisting the Allied cause, particularly in the south-west Pacific. The capture of Akyab would reduce the air threat to Calcutta, and provide an advanced base from which air attacks could penetrate more deeply into enemy-occupied territory further east. An early offensive would moreover have a considerable moral effect both on the Indian Army and on India as a whole.

This did not mean that Wavell had abandoned his ideas for a limited offensive into upper Burma at the first opportunity to establish IV Corps in a favourable position for reconquering Burma and reopening the Burma Road. On the 17th September he issued an operation instruction ordering Eastern Army to capture Akyab and reoccupy north Arakan, to strengthen the position in the Chin Hills, to occupy Kalewa and Sittaung and thence raid the Japanese lines of communication and finally to make administrative preparations to permit the rapid advance of a force towards upper or lower Burma, should opportunity offer during the campaigning season of 1942–43.[1]

In preparation for the advance on Akyab, 14th Indian Division (Major-General W. L. Lloyd) was brought up to strength during September by the addition of 55th Indian Infantry Brigade from the North West Frontier, and three unallotted battalions on garrison and internal security duties in eastern Bengal were formed into 88th Infantry Brigade for duties on the line of communication. Lloyd was ordered to establish advanced forces as near Akyab as possible commensurate with security. He was warned, however, that there was a possibility that the Japanese might attempt an advance on Chittagong and that he was to hold this port against all enemy attacks by land, sea and air.

Although he was aware that Akyab once captured might become an exposed outpost difficult to maintain, and that the Japanese when attacked might increase their garrison in Burma, Wavell told the Chiefs of Staff towards the end of September that he proposed to attempt the occupation of the island early in December 1942. This would be dependent on there being no further delay in the build-up of the R.A.F. in India and on the arrival of 29th Independent Brigade with the necessary specialist personnel and landing craft from Madagascar not later than the 20th October, a prospect which at that time appeared to be reasonable. At the same time, he ordered Eastern Army to hasten the movement of 14th Division southwards without waiting for the arrival of its reinforcing brigade, since it was now essential to forestall any Japanese movement northwards from Akyab.

By this time the original small air force in India Command had expanded to thirty-one squadrons, and it was forecast that its strength would reach fifty-two squadrons by February 1943.[2] The

---

[1] See Appendix 20.

[2] For the order of battle of air forces in India and Ceylon, September 1942, see Appendix 21.

bomber squadrons withdrawn from Burma and re-equipped with Blenheim IVs, and a squadron formed from the few Wellingtons which had reached India, provided the main striking force. The fighter defence which had at one time depended on a single Mohawk squadron had been augmented by six Hurricane squadrons, three of which had come from the United Kingdom. A photographic reconnaissance unit had been formed from Hurricanes and some Mitchell aircraft taken over from the Dutch, the former for short-range and the latter for long-range reconnaissance. But although these thirty-one squadrons appeared on paper to be a reasonably strong force, six were unfit for operations, nine had to be retained for the defence of Ceylon and five for reconnaissance and transport duties. This left only seven fighter and four short-range bomber squadrons for the defence of north-east India. The proposed expansion of the air forces was also being hampered by the fact that the Vengeance dive-bombers being sent to India were meeting with serious technical difficulties, and it was unlikely that any Vengeance squadrons would be fit for operations before the end of 1942. The 10th U.S.A.A.F. had some long-range Liberator bombers but these, not being directly under the command of Air Headquarters, could not be counted on.

By early October, air reconnaissance showed that the Japanese were constructing airfields and aircraft shelters in Burma sufficient for several hundred aircraft, and there were indications that they had already begun to increase their air strength. In these circumstances, Air Marshal Peirse urged the Air Ministry to expedite the despatch of long-range bombers and fighters so as to enable him to organize an effective striking force. At the same time he advised Wavell that, until these arrived, the operation to reoccupy Akyab would be feasible only if the Japanese refrained from materially reinforcing their own air forces, and so make it possible for the island to be captured by surprise. The Air Ministry did their best to meet the Air Marshal's request and told him that they were increasing the monthly flow of Hurricanes from fifty to seventy-five and of Blenheims from twenty to twenty-four, and sending six Liberators and enough Wellingtons to allow a second squadron to be formed, as well as sufficient Beaufighters to enable one long-range fighter squadron to be formed in each of the months from October to December.

In view of these promises, Wavell decided in mid-October to go ahead with the Akyab operation. His plan, to be carried out by Eastern Army, was that 14th Division was to occupy the Maungdaw–Buthidaung area and Kyauktaw in the Kaladan valley by the 1st December as a diversionary operation, and that a direct assault on Akyab from the sea was to be made by 29th Independent Brigade and 6th Brigade of 2nd British Division.[1] No date however was fixed

---
[1] See Map 13.

for the seaborne assault on Akyab, since it was still not known when 29th Brigade and the assault shipping would arrive.

In November, Eastern Army instructed IV Corps to use 23rd Division to patrol the northern end of the Kabaw Valley and establish a brigade in the Sittaung area by the middle of February,[1] and 17th Division to cover the construction of the road to Tiddim and continue intensive training. The stage was thus set for the first deliberate British offensive for the reconquest of Burma.

---

[1] This necessitated the completion of the Imphal Road to Tamu and the construction of a road from Tamu to Sittaung.

Map 11
MAUNGDAW – BUTHIDAUNG – RATHEDAUNG

Scale of Miles
Contours at intervals of 250 ft.

Pi Chaung
Kyauktaw
Kaladan River
Pi Chaung
To Myohaung
Apaukwa
Ngasanbaw Chaung
Kanzauk
Prindaw
Mrawchaung
Awrama
Banyo
Htizwe
Thaungdara
Mayu River
Batarai
Kamai
Rathedaung
Gwedauk
Myinbu
Kaladan River
Tawbya R
Thayetpyin
Kalachaung
Ponnagyun
Magyichaung
Ferry
Padali
Point
Akyab Is

CHAPTER XV

THE FIRST ARAKAN OFFENSIVE

(September 1942 – February 1943)

See Maps 11 and 13 and Sketches 9 and 13

ARAKAN is a country of densely forested parallel hill ranges running from north to south, separated by narrow cultivated valleys filled with ricefields and intersected by tidal creeks known as chaungs. Most of the forest is dense evergreen jungle, impassable except where tracks exist. The ricefields during the monsoon are anything up to three feet deep in water. In the dry weather the fields themselves offer no impediment to movement, but the banks between them are high enough to hinder the free movement of tanks.

The coastal strip from Maungdaw to the tip of the Mayu peninsula is forty-five miles long and some two miles wide in the northern part, narrowing to a few hundred yards in the south between Donbaik and Foul Point. It is much intersected by tidal chaungs, and here and there by areas of jungle or mangrove swamp. It is flanked throughout its length on the east by the narrow and precipitous Mayu Range which rises to over 2,000 feet above sea level. In 1942 it was crossed by one metalled road running from Maungdaw to Buthidaung which passed through two short tunnels at the summit of the pass, and by a few jungle tracks.

To the east of this range lies the Mayu River which is known as the Kalapanzin in its upper reaches. The Mayu valley is some eight to ten miles wide near Buthidaung, broadening to the south and narrowing to the north. In it there are a series of parallel and heavily forested narrow ridges from fifty to one hundred and fifty feet high running from north to south, which in places are little more than knife edges and in others widen out to a tangle of low knolls covered in elephant grass, scrub or bamboo. To the east of the valley lies the great mass of the Arakan Hill Tracts, which separate it from the Kaladan River valley. This broad belt of hills, rising to close on 3,000 feet, is a network of knife-edge ridges and deep precipitous gorges covered by thick jungle and pierced by mountain torrents, of which all but the largest dry up in the spring. These hills are crossed by a few tracks which wind along the narrow valleys and climb steeply to the passes over the ridges.

The Mayu–Kalapanzin River and its tributary chaungs are tidal as far north as Goppe Bazar. Even the smaller chaungs were often tank obstacles since their banks were precipitous, crumbly and frequently undercut by tidal action. They became obstacles to infantry at high tide, for most of them were unfordable for a considerable distance from their junction with the main river; consequently great attention had to be paid to tide tables when operations were being planned. Villages are invariably built on the banks of these chaungs, which are often the only means of communication during the monsoon.

Such tracks as existed usually followed the banks of the chaungs or the edge of the jungle along the foothills. Wheeled traffic was brought to a standstill during the monsoon, and even patrols could move away from the few tracks for short distances only. In the dry season, tracks for wheeled vehicles could be easily made in the valleys by cutting gaps through the banks between the ricefields.

From mid-May to October rain is almost unceasing, malaria is rife and the jungle is full of the small black leech, while the even more repulsive yellow and green elephant leech lurks in pools in the jungle fringe, but neither form of leech is found in the ricefields. Apart from malaria and leech bites, the main scourges are prickly heat and jungle ringworm. Men manning defences had to live in bamboo bivouacs raised some two feet off the ground sited close to their alarm posts, carefully camouflaged and defiladed from view. Alarm posts had to be of the bunker type with overhead cover to keep out the rain. Stores and medical aid posts had to be housed in specially constructed bamboo huts known as bashas.

In the dry season from November to May, there are four months when the climate is delightful. Leeches disappear, though they are replaced by the less obvious but much more dangerous jungle tick which is the bearer of scrub typhus. Snakes are seldom seen and there are no scorpions, but there are large numbers of 'armour-plated' reddish-brown poisonous centipedes. The chief characteristic of the dry season climate is the heavy dew, accompanied by a mist which blankets the valleys from two or three hours before dawn until any time up to ten o'clock.

On the 21st September 1942, General Lloyd (14th Division) had been ordered to move towards Akyab without waiting for the arrival of 55th Infantry Brigade, in order to forestall the enemy on the line Maungdaw–Buthidaung.[1] He thereupon relieved 123rd Brigade of

---
[1] For order of battle of 14th Division see Appendix 22.

THE ADVANCE TOWARDS AKYAB BEGINS

its responsibility for the security of Chittagong and ordered it to move to Cox's Bazar. This movement was not to prove easy.

The railway line ended at Dohazari some twenty miles to the south of Chittagong. A metalled road ran for a further ten miles, but beyond this point there was only a four-foot earth track which the monsoon had made almost unusable. Lloyd decided to move the brigade by sea to Cox's Bazar,[1] and to set his divisional engineers to build an all-weather road to Ramu and Cox's Bazar to serve as a permanent line of communication, a formidable task for at that time of the year the country was waterlogged and there was no stone in the area. It was not until mid-October that the road was fit for animal transport and light motor vehicles in fair weather.[2]

Meanwhile 123rd Brigade had been concentrated in the Cox's Bazar–Ramu area and, assisted by local labour, had begun to improve the track from Cox's Bazar through Ukhia to Tumbru at the head of the navigable portion of the Naf River. Heavy rainstorms often flooded the new track and made it unusable; the advancing troops had therefore to be supplied by porter and, often cut off from their base, had to go on half rations. Nevertheless, by the third week in October the brigade was disposed with its leading battalion (1/15th Punjab) at Tumbru and Bawli Bazar, a second battalion at Ramu and the remainder at Cox's Bazar. The Punjabis were ordered to send forward a company to Maungdaw, and on the 23rd October a fighting patrol reached Buthidaung.

On the 17th October Eastern Army issued an operation instruction giving details of the plan for reoccupying Akyab. By the 1st December 14th Division was to establish one brigade in the Maungdaw–Buthidaung–Rathedaung area, a second in support in the Cox's Bazar–Tumbru area and a third at Chittagong. Since a Japanese force reported by 'V' Force to be at Kyauktaw in the Kaladan valley presented a threat to 14th Division's eastern flank,[3] Eastern Army ordered a detachment of a hundred men from the Independent Western Tribal Legion to move to Paletwa.[4]

The Japanese had gradually reinforced their garrison at Akyab during the summer and by September it consisted of *213th Infantry Regiment* (less *I/213th Battalion*). Learning towards the middle of October of the British southward advance, *II/213th Battalion* was sent forward to occupy Buthidaung and Maungdaw. Its advanced parties, moving up the Mayu River in launches, arrived at Buthidaung on the 23rd October almost simultaneously with the Punjabi patrol and a sharp action ensued. The patrol did what it could to delay the

---

[1] He had only two small coastal steamers.
[2] See Appendix 31.
[3] This was a platoon of *III/213th Battalion*.
[4] A semi-regular unit composed of Mahsuds from the North West Frontier.

Japanese disembarkation and then withdrew to Maungdaw. The isolated Punjabi company thereupon withdrew to Bawli Bazar, where it rejoined its battalion. The Japanese then occupied an outpost position astride the Mayu Range on the general line Buthidaung–the Tunnels–Maungdaw.

Despite interference by Muslim refugees moving north, appalling weather (thirteen inches of rain fell on the 5th November) which closed all roads, and typhoon conditions in the Bay of Bengal which brought shipping to a standstill, 14th Division's advance continued. By the end of November, 123rd Brigade was in the Zeganbyin–Goppe Bazar–Bawli Bazar area with 47th Brigade along the line of communication through Ukhia and Cox's Bazar to Dohazari and 55th Brigade in reserve at Chittagong. The Tripura 'V' Force had just been put under Lloyd's command in place of the Western Tribal Legion which, having proved unreliable, had been disbanded.

The line of communication to 14th Division was still precarious. From Chittagong to Cox's Bazar the sea route was the main artery, with the track from Dohazari to Ramu as a subsidiary. South of Cox's Bazar, motor transport was used as far as Tumbru and thence sampans to Bawli Bazar and Teknaf. Forward of these places pack transport, assisted by porters over the passes, had to be used. The divisional engineers were working to extend the Dohazari–Tumbru–Bawli Bazar track to Zeganbyin and make it fit for light lorries. To relieve the strain on this long road, Eastern Army reorganized the Sundarbans Flotilla for use on the Chittagong–Maungdaw sea route as soon as Maungdaw had been occupied, renaming it 2000 Flotilla.[1]

While 14th Division was making its slow and arduous progress southwards, constructing its line of communication as it went, the prospect of launching the proposed seaborne operation to reoccupy Akyab had been gradually diminishing. Wavell had always held that the reduction of enemy air strength was an essential preliminary to a seaborne assault. Partly because the growth of the Allied air forces had been slower than expected when the operation was mooted, and partly because the Japanese had kept their aircraft well back and used forward airfields for refuelling only, air operations so far had clearly failed to reduce their strength appreciably. During October, Wavell had come to the conclusion that a direct seaborne assault on Akyab, in which transports and warships would be exposed to a heavy scale of air attack for some three days, was no longer practicable.

---

[1] See Appendix 31 and page 55.

Quite apart from the question of air superiority, it was clear to him by the end of the month that, even if the landing craft and their crews arrived in India during November, they could not be ready for the operation until the end of December. The 29th Brigade, delayed at Durban, could not reach India in time for an assault in mid-January. The necessary assault shipping and naval escorts were unlikely to be forthcoming in January or February, and by March the weather on the Arakan coast would be unsuitable for a landing. Wavell therefore began to examine an alternative plan for reoccupying Akyab by an overland advance, combined with a short-range seaborne assault on the island from the Mayu peninsula, using small craft. Having discussed it with General Irwin (Eastern Army) early in November and later in the month with Admiral Somerville, he told the Chiefs of Staff on the 17th that he had abandoned his original plan and substituted an alternative which would make a much smaller demand on shipping and on naval and air cover. On the 19th he ordered Eastern Army to undertake the alternative operation, and placed 6th Infantry Brigade Group, five motor launches, seventy-two landing craft and three paddle steamers at Irwin's disposal.

Under the new plan the speed of the overland advance became of importance. Accordingly, despite his administrative difficulties, Lloyd planned to attack the Japanese defensive positions on the general line Maungdaw–Buthidaung on the 2nd December with 123rd Brigade reinforced by one battalion of 47th Brigade. This was the maximum strength he could at that time maintain in the forward area, but he considered that with these four battalions he would be able to overwhelm the small Japanese force before it could be reinforced. Determined however that there should be no risk of failure in the first action in Arakan, Irwin decided that it would be unwise to commit 14th Division piecemeal against a position which the Japanese had had time to prepare. He therefore ordered Lloyd to delay his attack until the line of communication south of Cox's Bazar as far as Zeganbyin had been improved, the tracks over the hills to Goppe Bazar and Taung Bazar made fit for mule traffic and 47th Brigade concentrated in the forward area. Twenty-four hours of heavy rain on the 7th closed all roads and tracks in Arakan for two days and stopped work on the line of communications, with the result that the concentration of 123rd and 47th Brigades was delayed and the offensive had to be postponed until the middle of the month.

On the 13th December, 'V' Force reported that the enemy had reinforced his forward troops with part of a second battalion. The Japanese however, deeming it too risky to attempt to hold an outpost position so far forward as Maungdaw–Buthidaung with only two battalions available, withdrew *II/213th Battalion* on the 16th to the general line Gwedauk–Kondan on the western bank of the Mayu

River opposite Rathedaung. Thus when the leading British patrols moved forward at dawn on the 17th December, they found both Maungdaw and Buthidaung abandoned.

The great efforts made during 1942 to build up the air forces in north-east India had begun to show results by the autumn. Bomber and fighter operations had been the responsibility of 221 and 224 Groups respectively, but the area over which their units were dispersed was too large for the effective control of squadrons.[1] Moreover, the possibility of reoccupying Akyab later in the year had made it desirable for a group headquarters to be in the forward area close to the army formation which was to undertake the operation. The two groups were therefore made into composite formations. 221 Group, with headquarters at Calcutta, was placed in control of the bomber, coastal and fighter squadrons in western Bengal, and 224 Group, with headquarters at Chittagong, of the fighter and light bomber squadrons operating over the whole of the Burma front from Assam to the Bay of Bengal. Within these groups mobile wings were organized, each wing having its own air stores park and salvage unit. When this reorganization was completed, the 10th U.S.A.A.F. took over the air defence of the north-eastern corner of Assam and of the air route to China.

As the monsoon abated, bomber squadrons began a systematic offensive against Japanese airfields and communications in Burma. Owing to the great distances involved, these raids were both exhausting and uneconomical and some bomber and fighter squadrons were therefore moved to fair-weather airstrips hurriedly prepared at Feni, Agartala and Jessore.[2] Since the range of day bombing attacks was limited to a distance of about the 140 miles from the advanced airstrips within which the fighters could provide escorts, it was decided during October to form a night bomber force. A few heavy bombers from 159 (Liberator) Squadron and medium bombers from 34 (Blenheim) Squadron and 99 (Wellington) Squadron were accordingly withdrawn from day operations for training.[3] On the 17th November they bombed the airfields at Magwe and Meiktila, the first night attack on military objectives deep in Burma. The day bombers with fighter escort were meanwhile used to attack Japanese communications in the forward areas. The fighter squadrons stationed at Calcutta and Chittagong were used to defend those ports, and to give cover to shipping in the northern part of the Bay of Bengal and along the Arakan coast.

---

[1] See pages 111–12.
[2] See Map 14.
[3] 99 and 159 Squadrons had just been formed.

By the end of October, the 10th U.S.A.A.F. had also been sufficiently reinforced with heavy bombers to undertake raids on Rangoon, Mandalay and other targets. On the 26th November, eight Liberators flew a round trip of some 2,760 miles in a surprise attack on an oil refinery and power plant at Bangkok. Rangoon however remained the principal target for the American long-range bombers, regular attacks being made on the docks and shipping there. In November agents were dropped by parachute into Burma to report on the arrival and departure of ships, the movement of troops up country and activity at the Rangoon and Meiktila airfields.

Meanwhile the fighter units of *5th Air Division* which had been re-equipping and training in Malaya and Siam during the monsoon had moved back to Burma. The bomber units remained based in Malaya and Siam and, to avoid loss from persistent Allied bombing, used the Burma airfields as advanced refuelling bases only. The *4th* and *7th Air Brigades* were ordered to attack the Imphal and Chittagong areas so as to interfere with any Allied preparations for a counter-offensive, while *12th Air Brigade* was left to cover the Hukawng Valley and Yunnan fronts. Attacks were first made on the airfields in northern Assam used as supply bases for American transport aircraft operating the air lift to China. The raids caused little damage, except at Dinjan where the defending fighters could get only three minutes warning. As a result, some transport aircraft and fighters were destroyed on the ground.

On the 26th October Chittagong was attacked by some thirty fighters. No warning was received and the enemy aircraft were not intercepted. Although this raid caused little damage to the port, it showed up the inadequacy of the warning system. During the following weeks a few light raids were made on the port, but on the 5th December shipping and the jetties were attacked by twenty-four bombers and twelve fighters. Most of the bombs fell in the river and there was little damage. On the 10th a slightly larger force succeeded in destroying some rolling stock and damaging the railway. Five more raids on the 15th and 16th were intercepted by the defending Hurricane and Mohawk aircraft, but very few enemy aircraft were destroyed because the warning was too short to enable the fighters to gain the requisite height.

The Japanese next turned their attention to Calcutta and made five night attacks on the city between the 20th and 28th December, using not more than nine bombers at a time. Though the bombing was widespread and indiscriminate, on each occasion the docks received some hits. Casualties were light, but about 350,000 people left the city. The docks were denuded of labour and public services were seriously affected, with the result that refuse was left in the streets to rot, thereby increasing the ever-present risk of an epidemic.

The inability of the Hurricanes defending Calcutta to intercept the enemy bombers at night led Wavell to appeal for a squadron of specially equipped night fighter aircraft. A flight of Beaufighters of 176 Squadron, equipped for night interception, arrived from the Middle East on the 14th January 1943, and the very next night three enemy bombers attacking the city were shot down by one Beaufighter. Five nights later two out of four enemy bombers were destroyed for the loss of one Beaufighter. The Japanese made no further attempts to bomb Calcutta for the time being.

Enemy air activity, so marked during the autumn of 1942, unexpectedly decreased since the desperate situation in the south-west Pacific forced the Japanese to transfer *12th Air Brigade* and *14th Air Regiment* of *4th Air Brigade* to that theatre in December 1942.[1] The *5th Air Division* was thus left with only some hundred and fifty aircraft to meet the growing Allied air strength.

Although by this time the air forces in India had been greatly expanded and outnumbered the enemy over the battle area, they were unable to gain air superiority and the enemy air force still held the initiative. Except at high altitude the Hurricane fighter was no match for the Japanese Zero. Moreover, there was a complete lack of long-range fighters without which an offensive against the enemy air bases could not be sustained.[2] Thus, from bases largely out of reach of the Allies, the Japanese could attack objectives anywhere they chose from northern Assam to southern Bengal including Calcutta. The Allies could do no more than distribute their fighter squadrons to cover those sectors where enemy aircraft were most likely to be intercepted. On such a vast front, it was not surprising that formations of enemy aircraft were frequently able to make attacks without being intercepted.

On the 10th December, a week before the occupation of Maungdaw and Buthidaung, General Irwin gave 14th Division detailed instructions for the overland advance on Akyab. The division, supported by 224 Group R.A.F., was to occupy the Mayu peninsula and Rathedaung, and build a fair-weather track to Foul Point at the southern end of the peninsula by the 15th January 1943. The 6th British Brigade was to concentrate at Chittagong by the 25th December, and then move to Foul Point and launch a short-range seaborne assault on Akyab Island at a date to be fixed near the end of January. The plans for the assault would be prepared by Eastern Army. A naval force of armed motor launches, landing craft and river steamers (Force 'Z') was to be formed at Chittagong during Decem-

---

[1] See Chapter XVI for events in the Pacific.
[2] See Appendix 23 for performance of British and Japanese aircraft.

ber to patrol the Naf and Mayu Rivers, attack enemy seaborne communications south of Akyab and provide the assault craft for 6th Brigade's landing on the island.

Although the sea route from Chittagong to Maungdaw could now be used, the maintenance of 14th Division in the Maungdaw and Buthidaung area was still not easy. Six vessels had been removed from 2000 Flotilla for the training of 6th Brigade, throwing a heavy load on the already inadequate road communications. The advance to Foul Point and Rathedaung greatly increased the difficulties. West of the Mayu Range, a partially bridged unmetalled track went as far as Alethangyaw. Beyond that point, a road to Foul Point had to be made at the base of the foothills clear of the beach—a slow process as it necessitated the bridging of the numerous tidal chaungs. During the dry season the beach could be used at low tide for periods varying from two to four hours according to the direction and strength of the wind, but any vehicle caught by the tide was inevitably lost.[1] East of the range the Mayu River provided the only line of communication. Its capacity was strictly limited owing to the shortage of river craft and the fact that the enemy held the estuary and lower reaches.[2]

On the 21st December, Lloyd received information from 'V' Force of the presence of some 800 Japanese at Kondan which suggested a possible defensive position, but air reconnaissance was unable to corroborate this.[3] On the 22nd he ordered 47th Brigade to advance down both sides of the Mayu Range and clear it of the enemy, and at the same time protect the line of communication south of Bawli Bazar and build the fair-weather track along the coastal strip to Foul Point. The 123rd Brigade (less one battalion) was to advance down the eastern side of the Mayu River to capture Rathedaung. Its third battalion, 8/10th Baluch (Lieut.-Colonel J. H. Souter), known as Soutcol, was to move across the hills from Taung Bazar to Kyauktaw on the Kaladan River, where a column known as Tripforce was already operating to protect the left flank of the division.[4] The plan had inherent tactical and administrative defects as it left 123rd Brigade with only two battalions for its attack on Rathedaung, while 47th Brigade had to advance with its two wings separated by the Mayu Range.

Brigadier E. H. Blaker (47th Brigade) ordered 5/8th Punjab to move down the coast and, constructing the track with engineer assistance, reach Indin by the 27th December. The 1/7th Rajput was to move east of the range and reach the line Atet Nanra–Prinshe by

---

[1] During the advance, 47th Brigade lost some vehicles in this way.

[2] See Appendix 31.

[3] Air reconnaissance over jungle-covered country could not locate defences which were well camouflaged and hidden in the undergrowth.

[4] See Appendix 31 for the arrangements to maintain Soutcol. Tripforce consisted of 1st Tripura Rifles (I.S.F.) and Tripura 'V' Force.

the 31st December. The 1st Inniskillings was to remain in the Maungdaw area for the time being to protect the rear communications of the brigade. The 1/7th Rajput was to be maintained by 123rd Brigade until it reached Atet Nanra; its maintenance was then to revert to 47th Brigade by the track which crossed the range from Kyaukpandu. By the 31st December the forward elements of 47th Brigade had reached Shinkhali and Thitkado, and the Inniskillings Alethangyaw. The 5/8th Punjab had met with no opposition but 1/7th Rajput had made contact with an enemy defensive position near Kondan, thus confirming 'V' Force's reports.

Brigadier A. V. Hammond (123rd Brigade) ordered 10th Lancashire Fusiliers to move without its carriers and animal transport by boat down the Mayu River to Zedidaung and thence by the Ngasanbaw Chaung to Htizwe, from where there was a track to Rathedaung. He estimated that the battalion could reach Htizwe by the evening of the 4th January and Rathedaung by the 7th. The 1/15th Punjab in brigade reserve was to follow the Lancashire Fusiliers as transport permitted. On the 25th December a patrol of the Fusiliers, working well in advance of the battalion, entered Rathedaung and returned to report that the enemy had left the village on the 22nd. On the night of the 27th/28th, a company of the same battalion moved down the river by boat to occupy the village, but on attempting to enter it met with machine-gun and mortar fire and was driven back. The following day the battalion unsuccessfully attacked Rathedaung with two fresh companies—all the strength that it could at that time bring into action. By the 31st December the whole battalion was concentrated forward in contact with the enemy holding the hills on the northern side of Rathedaung.

On the coastal strip, a carrier patrol of 47th Brigade reached both Foul Point and Magyichaung on the 1st January 1943, without meeting any opposition, and 1/7th Rajput dispersed enemy patrols near Thitkado and Atet Nanra. When Lloyd visited Blaker that day it appeared that, although the coastal strip to Foul Point was undefended, the Kondan area east of the range was held by the enemy. Since possession of this area would enable the Japanese to interfere with 6th Brigade's attack on Akyab, Lloyd decided, despite his administrative difficulties,[1] to dislodge them without delay, and told Blaker to do this before occupying Foul Point. Blaker ordered 1/7th Rajput to attack southwards from Thitkado while 1st Inniskillings (less one company) and 5/8th Punjab crossed the range, the former directed on Laungchaung and Thayetpyin, and the latter on Kondan and the line of the Gwedauk Chaung from Myinbu.[2] The coastal

---

[1] All units of 47th Brigade were on half rations. See Appendix 31 for the maintenance position on this date.
[2] See Sketch 14.

strip was to be protected by one company of the Inniskillings and the carriers of all three battalions. The lack of wireless sets within the brigade made co-ordination of the attack difficult, and the crossing of the range proved to be extremely arduous as the troops had in places to cut their way through virgin jungle. Nevertheless, the attack was launched on the 4th as planned. It met with no opposition for the enemy had disappeared from the area.

The Japanese had expected no more than patrol action east of the Mayu River and had occupied the Kondan area so that they could threaten the communications of any troops advancing along the coast to Foul Point. The 123rd Brigade's advance took them by surprise but, by sending a company of *II/213th Battalion* across the river, they were able to forestall the Lancashire Fusiliers at Rathedaung on the night of the 27th/28th December. Having checked 1/7th Rajput north of Thitkado, they moved the rest of the battalion from Kondan to Rathedaung, and hurriedly sent forward *III/213th Battalion* from Akyab with orders to hold Laungchaung and Donbaik, at the tip of the Mayu peninsula, at all costs.

As soon as Lloyd heard that Kondan was clear of the enemy he told 47th Brigade to continue its advance to Foul Point, leaving 1/7th Rajput in the Thitkado area to guard against an enemy counter-attack across the river, and to be ready to cross the river to assist 123rd Brigade if the proposed attack on Rathedaung on the 9th January failed.[1] Blaker immediately ordered 1st Inniskillings (then occupying Laungchaung) to return to the west of the range and 5/8th Punjab (then in the Kondan–Myinbu area) to move to the southern tip of the peninsula and occupy Kalachaung, Magyichaung and Foul Point. The Inniskillings crossed the range early on the 5th but, owing to a report of enemy landings at the mouth of the Gwedauk Chaung, the advance of 5/8th Punjab did not begin till 5 p.m. on the 5th. The Inniskillings had hardly left Laungchaung when enemy patrols moved in, and when the Punjabis reached the outskirts of the village on the 6th they found the Japanese holding a defensive position supported by mortars and machine-guns. The Punjabis, who had been unable to get their mortars across the range, failed to drive them out and on the evening of the 8th took up a defensive position at Thayetpyin.[2]

Meanwhile on the coast, carrier patrols ranged freely to Foul Point. On the 4th and 5th January they met small bodies of the enemy and drove them into the foothills without difficulty, but on the 6th they ran into organized opposition on the chaung, one mile to the north

---

[1] In preparation for this eventuality, Lloyd began to collect a fleet of folding boats and rafts at Buthidaung.

[2] Havildar Parkash Singh of 5/8th Punjab gained the Victoria Cross during these operations.

of Donbaik, and lost two carriers. On the 7th a company of the Inniskillings tried unsuccessfully to occupy Donbaik and attempts on the 8th and 9th by the whole battalion, supported by a field and mountain battery, to break through to Foul Point failed at the cost of about a hundred casualties.

On the other side of the Mayu River Hammond, still entirely dependent on river transport, spent the first week of January in concentrating his two battalions and in bringing forward stores and ammunition. On the 9th, under cover of bombing and machine-gunning by the air force and supported by all the available artillery (two mountain batteries), the Lancashire Fusiliers again attacked Rathedaung but, although they at first gained ground, by evening were back in their original position. The following day the reserve battalion (1/15th Punjab) was brought up and succeeded in occupying Temple Hill, but could make no further progress.[1] Thus by the 10th, on both sides of the Mayu River and when almost within sight of their goal, the two leading brigades of 14th Division had been brought to a standstill by determined enemy resistance.

The following day Irwin, accompanied by Wavell, visited Arakan and held a conference at Shinkhali with Lloyd and Blaker. Irwin blamed Lloyd for not having used all his resources at Donbaik on the 8th and 9th, and ordered him to break through at once along the coastal strip to Foul Point with all the strength he could muster. Lloyd accordingly released 1/7th Rajput, which he had been holding east of the range in readiness to help 123rd Brigade capture Rathedaung, and ordered 47th Brigade to make a two-battalion attack on Donbaik.

Blaker, who estimated that Donbaik was held by one company,[2] ordered it to be attacked on the 18th. The Inniskillings were to move along the coastal strip, and the Rajputs along the foothills, supported by 130th Field Regiment (less one battery), 8th Mountain Battery and one company of the Jat (machine-gun) battalion, which had just joined the brigade. By the evening of the 18th the Inniskillings had reached the mouth of F.D.L. Chaung, but could get no further.[3] The Rajputs had occupied Shepherd's Crook and the area between North and South Promontories, but were forced back to South Knob during the night. Repeated attacks by both battalions during the 19th failed with heavy loss, particularly in officers, and that evening Blaker ordered both battalions to withdraw to a defensive position between the sea and the foothills some 400 yards north of F.D.L. Chaung.

On the other side of the Mayu River, Hammond had decided to

---

[1] See Sketch 9.

[2] This was correct. On the 16th the Japanese garrison of Donbaik was one company of *III/213th Battalion*.

[3] See Sketch 13.

attack from the east supported by fire from Temple Hill. During the night of the 11th/12th an enemy attempt to drive 1/15th Punjab off this hill failed, but when next morning the Lancashire Fusiliers launched an attack from the east they were unable to reach their objectives. They attacked again on the 18th, but once more without success, and by the evening of the 19th, despite repeated attempts to capture Shaving Brush Hill, the position remained much as it had been on the evening of the 12th. On both sides of the Mayu River the second attempt to break through had failed.

Meanwhile on the 13th two motor launches from Force 'Z' had moved up the Mayu River to Buthidaung to secure for 123rd Brigade the uninterrupted use of the river, and interfere with the Japanese communications to Rathedaung, Laungchaung and Donbaik. The launches made no contact with the enemy until the 27th, when one of them rammed and sank a launch filled with troops and drove another ashore. In the Kaladan valley, Soutcol (8/10th Baluch), reduced by sickness to 375 all ranks, had occupied Kyauktaw on the 17th, having driven off a small Japanese patrol. On the following day Tripforce, which had moved south from Paletwa along the east bank of the Kaladan River, found the Japanese in occupation of the villages opposite Kyauktaw.[1]

Realizing the importance of retaining the use of the airfields at Akyab, General Iida (*15th Army*) had decided early in January 1943 to reinforce Arakan and had ordered *55th Division* (Lieut.-General T. Koga), at that time in the area Toungoo–Prome,[2] to move to Taungup and thence along the cost to Akyab. He placed under its command the two battalions of *213th Regiment*, which were holding Akyab, and instructed *33rd Division* to send its third battalion (*I/213th*), then at Pakokku, with a mountain battery by the jungle track across the Arakan Yomas to Paletwa in the Kaladan valley. He ordered Koga to hold Rathedaung, Laungchaung and Donbaik at all costs until reinforcements arrived, orders which, as will be seen later, were carried out to the letter. He also arranged for *5th Air Division* to allot one air brigade (*4th*) to support *55th Division* and to use the other (*7th*) to attack Allied lines of communication in the Chittagong area.

General Koga with a few staff officers flew to Akyab on the 24th January. Owing to the shortage of coastal vessels and the delays caused by the constant British air attacks on coastal shipping and on the line of communications across the Arakan Yomas, he did not

---

[1] Tripforce was placed under command of Soutcol on the 14th January.

[2] See Strategic Map. The infantry of *55th Division* consisted at this time of *112th* and *143rd Infantry Regiments*.

expect the leading regiment, even if it left behind its animal transport and artillery, to reach Akyab until the first half of February or the division to be concentrated there till the end of that month.[1]

To Koga the situation appeared to be desperate. At first he thought that he might have to withdraw *213th Regiment* to the main defensive positions at Akyab, but in accordance with his instructions he decided to attempt to hold the existing front, particularly the southern end of the Mayu peninsula. He therefore ordered *213th Regiment* to maintain its position at all costs, and sent forward to Donbaik all the troops he could as they arrived. The issue now depended on whether the Japanese could prevent 14th Division breaking through at Donbaik and Rathedaung and launching a seaborne assault on Akyab before their reinforcements arrived.

Time was slipping away, and impatience at the delay in clearing the Mayu peninsula and occupying Rathedaung was giving way to anxiety lest the opportunity should be lost. The reserve brigade and the remainder of the artillery were brought forward as quickly as possible, and 14th Division regrouped for a deliberate assault on Donbaik and Rathedaung. Lloyd ordered 55th Brigade (less one battalion) to relieve 47th Brigade in the Mayu peninsula by the 24th January, taking under command 5/8th Punjab at Laungchaung and the depleted 1/7th Rajput at Indin: the brigade was thus increased to four battalions. The 123rd Brigade was brought up to strength with 8/6th Rajputana Rifles from 55th Brigade. The artillery at Donbaik was reinforced by one and a half field batteries and a light anti-aircraft battery. He also asked Eastern Army for some of the Valentine tanks which were at Chittagong ready to take part in 6th Brigade's amphibious operation.

In the Kaladan valley, Tripforce had reached Kyauktaw and Soutcol had moved forward to Apaukwa and Kanzauk to open up the direct line of communication to Htizwe. Both forces had been ordered to stand on the defensive and not to operate east of the Kaladan River. The 6th Brigade had arrived at Chittagong and had begun training for its attack on Akyab, and Irwin had ordered 71st Brigade (Brigadier G. G. C. Bull) from 26th Indian Division to move forward to Chittagong as a reserve for 14th Division.

On the 22nd January the R.A.F. repeatedly attacked a Japanese column, some fifteen miles long, moving from Prome towards Taungup. It was now quite clear that there was no time to waste and

---

[1] There were only seven motor boats, each with a capacity of five tons, available at Taungup. It thus became a bottle-neck on the line of communication to Akyab. Additional craft were built and others requisitioned and repaired, but only the barest minimum of supplies could be carried. The Japanese had thus to live on the country as they moved up the coast.

that, unless the Japanese defence could be overcome early in February, an amphibious attack on Akyab would be out of the question. Irwin therefore ordered Lloyd to attack as soon as possible and, to give the attack additional punch, ordered XV Corps to send forward eight Valentine tanks.[1] Lloyd then ordered 55th Brigade (Brigadier J. M. Hunt) supported by the tanks and the bulk of the artillery to attack Donbaik on the 1st February, and 123rd Brigade (Brigadier Hammond) to attack Rathedaung on the 3rd.

As a preliminary to the main attack on Donbaik, 2/1st Punjab was to occupy North and South Knobs on the 30th January and 1/7th Rajput from brigade reserve was to relieve 1/17th Dogra in the coastal area. The main attack on the 1st February was to be made in two phases. In the first the Dogras assisted by tanks would advance from North Knob westwards along F.D.L. Chaung to Wooded Village, the tanks making two sorties: one, under cover of an artillery bombardment but unaccompanied by infantry, from Shepherd's Crook along F.D.L. Chaung to Wooded Village and back again, and the other in support of 1/17th Dogra's attack. In the second phase the Dogras would advance from F.D.L. Chaung to the general line Wadi Junction–South Knob. The plan went awry. As the tanks did not arrive till the night before the attack there was no time for reconnaissance, and their first sortie was made on the north instead of the south of F.D.L. Chaung. Three of the eight tanks were ditched; the Dogras became involved with enemy patrols on the western slopes of North Knob and failed to reach their start line during the morning, so the second phase of attack did not even begin.

The 2/1st Punjab, moving along the foothills, succeeded in spite of considerable losses in occupying Wadi Junction by the evening of the 1st, and on the morning of the 2nd attacked and took Wooded Village from the rear. Although attacked from front and rear, the Japanese in F.D.L. Chaung stood firm and reinforcements arriving at Donbaik launched several counter-attacks on Wooded Village, Shepherd's Crook and South Knob. All these were beaten off and stalemate resulted. On the 4th Brigadier Hunt had to admit failure, and during the night of the 4th/5th withdrew the Punjabis from Wooded Village back to South Knob.

On the 3rd Hammond again attacked the Japanese positions on the hills north of Rathedaung, employing all his three battalions supported by one light and two mountain batteries and by R.A.F. bombers. The attack was to be in three phases: 1/15th Punjab was first to capture Taunghlamaw village and Taunghlamaw Spur, then 10th Lancashire Fusiliers West Hill and finally the Punjabis, assisted

---

[1] General Slim pointed out at the time that the number of tanks was insufficient for the purpose and that they did not even form a properly constituted sub-unit. His view was not accepted on the ground that it was too difficult to transport or deploy a larger force.

by 8/6th Rajputana Rifles, were to occupy Hill 75 and Shaving Brush Hill. The Punjabis captured the village, but could make no progress up the slopes of the spur. Although they attacked prematurely, the Rajputana Rifles succeeded in gaining a footing on Shaving Brush Hill but were later driven off it, incurring many casualties. Despite repeated attempts, 10th Lancashire Fusiliers succeeded in occupying only the northern half of West Hill. Once again the tenacious Japanese defence had won the day, and that night Brigadier Hammond withdrew to a defensive position on the general line from the northern half of West Hill to Temple Hill.

For a month all attempts by 14th Division to break through the enemy defences had failed. The Japanese had thus been given time to bring up reinforcements, and the capture of Akyab which at the beginning of the year had seemed comparatively simple had now become a most formidable task.

Sketch 9
RATHEDAUNG

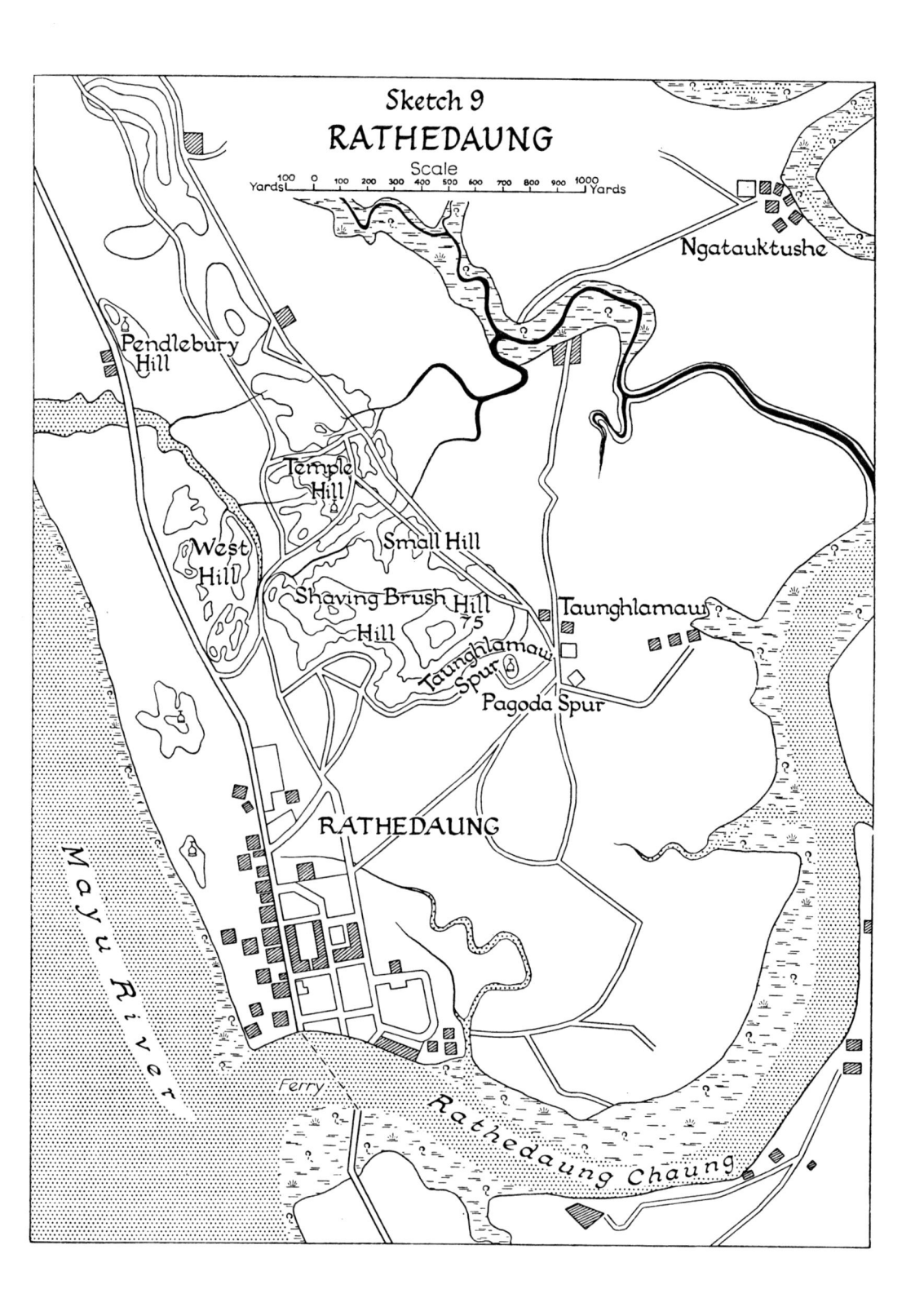

CHAPTER XVI

THE PACIFIC

(June 1942–February 1943)

See Maps 10 and 15 and Sketches 10 and 11

WE must now turn back some six months in time and review events in the Pacific after the battle of Midway at the beginning of June 1942, but before doing so it might be well to recall the momentous events which were taking place in the West. The month of June was one of the most critical of the war. The battle of the Atlantic was at its height; with the entry of the United States into the war the German U-boats had found new and profitable hunting grounds in the western Atlantic, and by the end of June Allied shipping losses had reached a peak. In the first half of 1942 nearly four million tons of shipping had been sunk. In Europe, the Russian Army had been steadily forced back across the Don under the fury of the German assault and there were grave doubts if it could withstand the summer offensive which was about to start. In the Middle East, Tobruk had surrendered to Rommel's army on the 21st June and the British 8th Army had been driven back to El Alamein where it was re-forming to meet the expected advance on Cairo. The British Fleet had been withdrawn from Alexandria to Haifa and Port Said. Malta for the past few months had been under constant air attack by the Luftwaffe; only two ships of the last two convoys carrying supplies had been able to get through and the island was facing starvation. It looked as if the defence of the Middle East might collapse and the two gigantic German pincer movements through the Caucasus and Cairo meet. The British and Chinese armies had been driven out of Burma and there were fears that China, cut off from Allied help, might drop out of the war.

The Allies had not as yet decided on their future strategy. The Russians were clamouring for a second front; the Americans were pressing for a landing in north-west Europe, and the British for an invasion of north-west Africa. Mr Churchill was in Washington trying to reach agreement: while he was there Tobruk fell, and at the end of the month he returned to face a vote of censure in the House of Commons on the conduct of the war. He was given an overwhelming vote of confidence, but it must have needed all his fortitude and vision to see the way through the dark clouds which for the past six months had enveloped the Allied cause. But there was a ray of light in the Pacific, where at the great sea battle of Midway the Japanese had received their first decisive defeat.

Although the Japanese Fleet remained numerically superior to the United States Fleet in the Pacific, the loss of the greater part of its carrier force restricted its power and mobility and enabled the Americans to embark on a limited offensive. By this time the life line to Australia had been made reasonably secure. By May the Americal Division was in New Caledonia,[1] and 37th U.S. Division, which had been awaiting shipment in New Zealand, had reached the Fiji Islands. The 7th Marine Regiment was in eastern Samoa. In the New Hebrides, Efate and Espiritu Santo were in the process of development as forward air bases. A seaplane base and airstrip were already in operation at the former and a Marine defence battalion had been sent there as garrison. In Australia, 7th Australian Division had recently arrived from the Middle East and two American divisions, 32nd and 41st, had disembarked in May.[2]

The Japanese occupation of Tulagi on the 3rd May had created a new threat to the vital line of communications.[3] At the end of May Admiral Nimitz had suggested a raid on the island, but the idea was discarded on the ground that there was insufficient strength to hold it if captured. Immediately after the battle of Midway, General MacArthur put forward a new and more ambitious proposal—the capture of Rabaul by a division trained in amphibious warfare, escorted by a task force which included two carriers. But Admiral King would not expose his valuable carriers to the danger of air attack in the Solomon Sea, nor was he willing to transfer them to MacArthur's command. He had in mind a step-by-step advance through the Solomon Islands to Rabaul and made a counter proposal that 1st U.S. Marine Division, then on its way to New Zealand, should start an offensive with the capture of Tulagi on about the 1st August, covered by the *Enterprise* and *Hornet* carrier task forces then at Pearl Harbour.

Admiral King's proposal found favour with General Marshall and, after some difficulty over the question of command, the American Joint Chiefs of Staff issued a directive on the 2nd July for two parallel advances up through the Solomons and along the coast of New Guinea with the occupation of the New Britain–New Ireland–New Guinea area as the ultimate objective. Three phases were envisaged: the first—to occupy the Santa Cruz Islands, Tulagi and adjacent islands; the second—to seize the rest of the Solomons, Papua and the coast of north-east New Guinea as far north as the

---

[1] See pages 221-22 and footnote.
[2] See page 222.
[3] See page 227.

Huon Peninsula; and the third—to capture Rabaul and the New Britain–New Ireland area. Admiral Nimitz was to control the first phase and General MacArthur the second and third phases.[1]

The target date for the first phase (operation 'Watchtower') was originally fixed for the 1st August, but it was found impossible to assemble the forces in time and it was therefore postponed until the 7th August. Both General MacArthur and Admiral R. L. Ghormley, who had recently been appointed Commander-in-Chief, South Pacific Area, wished to postpone the date still further until means were available to follow up immediately with the remaining phases. The American War Department, however, could make no promise of further reinforcements for the Pacific, since the troops already there exceeded the total it had planned to allocate to the theatre up to the end of the year, and the forthcoming Allied invasion of North Africa would make heavy demands on American resources. Rapid action became necessary when it was learned early in July that the Japanese had moved across to Guadalcanal and were building an air base near Lunga Point, the completion of which would prejudice the success of 'Watchtower'.[2] The capture of the airfield thus became the immediate Allied objective.

Meanwhile, the Japanese too had been preparing for a new offensive. The conclusion of the Netherlands East Indies campaign and the surrender of Bataan had enabled them to strengthen their south-eastern front. Early in May *Imperial General Headquarters* had issued orders for the formation of a new *17th Army* to be concentrated by the end of June at Truk, Rabaul and Palau, composed of units drawn from the Philippines, Java and the original *South Sea Detachment*. Lieut.-General Hyakutake had been appointed army commander and instructed to prepare plans for the capture of New Caledonia, Fiji, Samoa and Port Moresby but, after the battle of Midway, the attack on the islands was cancelled for the time being and it was decided to capture Port Moresby by an overland advance.

On the 14th July the *8th Fleet* was created to take over from Admiral Inoue's *4th Fleet* the responsibility for the south-east area.[3] The new Commander-in-Chief, Vice-Admiral Mikawa, arrived at Rabaul on the 30th July. His fleet at first comprised five heavy and three light cruisers, five submarines and a number of destroyers. The land-based air force in the south-east area (the *25th Air Flotilla*) based on Rabaul was reinforced and the construction of airfields on Buka and Bougainville speeded up.

---

[1] The boundary between the South Pacific and South West Pacific Areas was moved on 1st August so as to include Guadalcanal in Admiral Nimitz's command. See Map 15.
[2] See Sketch 10.
[3] The Japanese south-east front covered the south-west Pacific.

Guadalcanal lies in the southern half of the Solomons group, which comprises a great many islands running for about 600 miles in a south-easterly direction from Rabaul. Buka and Bougainville (its largest island) lie at its northern, and San Cristobal at its southern end. The remaining islands form a double chain separated by a deep water channel which was given by the Americans the name of 'The Slot'. The area is one of the wettest in the world and the climate throughout the year is humid, enervating and malarial. The islands are mountainous and thickly covered with jungle and tall knife-like kunai grass; in 1942 they were sparsely inhabited and the only cultivation was on the coastal plains where there were scattered coconut plantations. There are few good harbours but the narrow channels between the islands are usually calm. The group was divided politically, Buka and Bougainville being part of the Australian Mandated Territory of New Guinea and the remainder forming the British Solomon Islands Protectorate. Soon after the First World War, the Australian Government had created a coast-watching organization composed mainly of planters and civil servants. These gallant men remained hidden in the jungle behind the Japanese lines after the occupation, and at the risk of their lives gave invaluable information of enemy movements.

By the end of July Admiral Ghormley's expedition was ready. It consisted of an amphibious force under Rear-Admiral R. K. Turner, U.S.N., and an air support force under Rear-Admiral L. Noyes, U.S.N. Vice-Admiral F. J. Fletcher, U.S.N., who had commanded the carrier task force at Coral Sea and Midway, was in tactical command of the whole operation. The air support force consisted of the carriers *Saratoga*, *Enterprise* and *Wasp* supported by the new battleship *North Carolina*, six cruisers and a large number of destroyers.[1] The convoy carrying 1st U.S. Marine Division (less 7th Marine Regiment) and 2nd Marine Regiment from 2nd U.S. Marine Division,[2] commanded by Major-General A. A. Vandegrift, was supported by four cruisers and eleven destroyers and screened by a squadron of three Australian cruisers and one American under the command of Rear-Admiral V. A. C. Crutchley, V.C.[3] Naval aircraft of the South Pacific Command, reinforced by five marine air squadrons and some heavy bombers, and army aircraft of Mac-Arthur's South West Pacific Command were to reconnoitre the area and act in general support of the operation.

The amphibious force left Wellington on the 22nd July and met

---

[1] The *Wasp* had recently arrived from the Mediterranean where she had been aiding the Royal Navy to get convoys through to Malta.

[2] The 1st U.S. Marine Division comprised 1st, 5th, 7th and 11th Regiments.

[3] Rear-Admiral Crutchley had relieved Rear-Admiral Crace in command of the Anzac Squadron. The cruisers were H.M.A.S. *Australia*, *Canberra* and *Hobart* and U.S.S. *Chicago*.

the air support force south of Fiji; after four days of rehearsals on one of the remoter islands of that group, both forces sailed for their destination on the last day of the month. Heavy haze and intermittent rain squalls helped to conceal the ships and their approach was undetected. On the morning of the 7th August, landings were made on Guadalcanal near Lunga Point and at Tulagi. Both were completely successful. There was no opposition at Guadalcanal and before dark some 11,000 Marines had been landed. On the following day the almost completed airstrip, which was later to become famous as Henderson Field, was in their hands. At Tulagi and on two adjacent islets twenty miles across the strait to the northward of Guadalcanal the Japanese were better prepared, and the three battalions landed met fierce opposition. By the 8th the Marines had captured the islands, but 108 of their number were dead and 140 wounded. The Japanese garrisons of about 1,500 were wiped out almost to a man. It had taken only forty-eight hours to get a footing on Guadalcanal. It was to take six months and cost the lives of thousands of American soldiers, sailors and airmen and the loss of many fine ships before the island was finally secured.

The Japanese reactions were swift: within a few hours of the American landings, a striking force from the *25th Air Flotilla* had left Rabaul. In the early afternoon of the 7th and on the following day bombers attacked the transports off Lunga Point but, owing to timely warning from an Australian coast-watcher in Bougainville, the attacks on each occasion were broken up by fighters from American carriers. Two destroyers were hit and a transport was set on fire and became a total loss. These attacks, as might be expected, were but the precursors of stronger measures.

As soon as the news of the landings reached Rabaul, Admiral Mikawa, who was in the midst of preparations for the attack on Port Moresby, decided to send what ships he could lay hands on to attack and destroy the American naval forces. By the evening of the 7th he had assembled five heavy and two light cruisers south of Rabaul and had set course for Guadalcanal. Meanwhile *Imperial General Headquarters* had issued orders that the garrison of the island was to be reinforced and a convoy carrying some 500 troops, escorted by destroyers, had left Rabaul. Shortly after sailing, one of the transports was torpedoed by an American submarine and the remainder were recalled. At daylight on the 8th, Mikawa flew off aircraft to reconnoitre and that afternoon entered 'The Slot' south of Choiseul Island.

The Japanese squadron was sighted by American aircraft on the evening of the 7th and again on the following morning but, owing to a combination of an erroneous and belated report, thick weather and bad luck, the enemy was not again located that day. Thus

Mikawa was able to make his approach down 'The Slot' undetected, having learnt from his own aircraft the strength and disposition of his enemy.

The small volcanic island of Savo lies at the entrance to Iron Bottom Sound which divides Guadalcanal from Florida Island.[1] On the evening of the 8th August the Allied screening force took up its dispositions for the night; the cruisers *Australia* (R.A.N.), *Canberra* (R.A.N.) and *Chicago* (U.S.N.) and two American destroyers patrolled the seven-mile wide channel south of Savo, and the American cruisers *Vincennes*, *Astoria* and *Quincy* and two destroyers the northern channel; two destroyers formed an extended radar patrol north-west of the island. On the evening of the 8th Turner to his dismay learnt from Fletcher that, owing to shortage of fuel and the risk of further torpedo-bomber attacks, the air support force was being withdrawn. Crutchley was at once called to a conference on board Turner's flagship in Lunga Roads to discuss with General Vandegrift the implications of the withdrawal of the carriers. Turning over command of the southern patrol to the Captain of the *Chicago*, he sailed soon after dark in the *Australia* for the transport anchorage, unaware of the imminence of attack.

As Mikawa approached Savo island, he flew off his aircraft for another reconnaissance of the sound. At about midnight on the 8th unidentified aircraft were reported overhead by the American transports, and at about 1.45 a.m. an aircraft from the *Chokai* dropped flares over the transports. By this time the Japanese cruisers had sighted one of the two destroyers on extended patrol but were themselves unseen and had entered the channel south of Savo island undetected. As they passed the island, heavy rain clouds blacked out their silhouettes and it was not until 1.43 a.m. that the alarm was given by an American destroyer. By then the Japanese already had their sights on the unwitting *Canberra* and *Chicago* and opened fire with guns and torpedoes at point blank range. The *Canberra*, hit by two torpedoes and riddled with shell, burst into flames and had to be abandoned. The *Chicago* next astern was more fortunate: although hit by one torpedo she received no serious damage, but before she had time to reply the enemy cruisers were out of range and making at high speed to the northward in two columns to round Savo island. Unhappily, no enemy reports were made by the southern forces. The northern force, assuming the gunfire to have been directed against aircraft, was thus also taken by surprise when at 1.49 a.m. it came under heavy fire from two directions. Within a few minutes the cruisers *Vincennes*, *Astoria* and *Quincy*, hit by torpedo salvoes, were burning fiercely. The *Quincy* and the *Vincennes* capsized and sank, the *Astoria* survived until the afternoon when she too sank after an

---

[1] See Sketch 10.

explosion in one of her magazines. After a brush with one of the extended patrol destroyers, the Japanese ships withdrew at high speed up 'The Slot' at 2.15 a.m., leaving behind them four Allied heavy cruisers sunk or sinking and another damaged. The damage to the Japanese ships was almost negligible.[1]

It was a crushing defeat, although it might have been worse. Had Mikawa but stuck to his main object and followed up his victory with the destruction of the transports, he could have brought to a halt the American offensive at its inception, for all the transport and supply ships of the South West Pacific Command were lying almost defenceless in Lunga Roads. It must be remembered however that the Admiral was unaware of the withdrawal of the American carriers. His squadron was scattered and, by the time he had re-formed it, it would be nearly daybreak. If he had turned back into the sound he must have expected an attack on his ships by Admiral Fletcher's bombers.

Turner had intended to withdraw the amphibious force at daylight on the 9th, but the Japanese night attack had seriously delayed unloading. Despite the risk of renewed air attack, he decided to continue to land supplies until well into the afternoon. But even so, when the ships sailed that evening, not all the troops of 2nd Marine Regiment had been landed, and the Marines on Guadalcanal and Tulagi were left with only about a month's supply of food and half their supplies of ammunition. Admiral Ghormley was forced to keep his carriers well south of Guadalcanal to patrol the line of communication between Noumea and Espiritu Santo and the island. Thus for the next two weeks the Marines were virtually isolated: they were without naval support and, until Henderson Field was in use, without air cover. Since the completion and supply of the airfield was of the first importance, three converted destroyers, with their high speed and manoeuvrability, were used to make two runs to deliver petrol, bombs and ammunition to the island. Even so by the 20th, when the first flight of Marine Corps aircraft was flown in, supplies on the airfield were still very inadequate.

The American landings had come as a complete surprise to the Japanese. The newly-formed *17th Army* was not yet concentrated; an infantry group headquarters and two brigades were at Davao in the Philippines and a brigade (the *Kawaguchi Detachment*) at Palau. An infantry regimental group (the *Ichiki Detachment*) however, which had been attached to the navy for the landings on Midway and was on its way back to Japan from Guam, had on the 7th August been recalled to Truk and was expected to arrive there on the 12th. The only striking force at Rabaul was the *South Sea Detachment* (an infantry

---

[1] One of Admiral Mikawa's heavy cruisers was, however, sunk on the 9th by an American submarine on patrol off the approaches to Kavieng in New Ireland.

group headquarters and an infantry regiment) but it was already earmarked for the attack on New Guinea, and an advanced force had been landed at Buna on the 21st July.

On the 13th August, *Imperial General Headquarters* issued new orders to *17th Army*. Port Moresby was to be taken as soon as possible and, in order to seize the advantage of naval control gained by the victory at Savo island, an expeditionary force was to be sent to Guadalcanal. General Hyakutake, the army commander, assessed American strength in Guadalcanal as 2,000 men and estimated that a force of 6,000 men would be sufficient to recapture the island. He decided to use the *Kawaguchi* and *Ichiki Detachments* and a special naval landing force of 1,000 men. An advanced force from the *Ichiki Detachment* (also 1,000 men) sailed for Guadalcanal via Rabaul in destroyers and landed on the 18th August twenty miles east of Lunga Point. At the same time 500 men of the special naval landing force landed at Kokumbona, seven miles west of the American positions. Without waiting for the follow-up convoy the advanced force attacked and in a sharp encounter was practically annihilated. Colonel Ichiki committed suicide. The convoy carrying the second contingent of the *Ichiki Detachment* (1,500 men) and the rest of the naval landing force left Rabaul on the 19th, escorted by a light cruiser and four destroyers.

The transports were covered by a powerful force consisting of two of Admiral Nagumo's few remaining fleet carriers, the *Zuikaku* and the *Shokaku* and the light carrier *Ryujo*, two battleships, five cruisers and seventeen destroyers under Admiral Kondo. Timely warning of the movement was received from coast-watchers, and by the 21st Admiral Ghormley had concentrated three task forces south-east of Guadalcanal built round his carriers, the *Saratoga*, *Enterprise* and *Wasp* and the battleship *North Carolina*. On the morning of the 23rd the Japanese transports were reported by reconnaissance aircraft about 250 miles north of the island, by which time the *Wasp's* group had been detached to refuel further south. The *Saratoga* sent out a strike but the aircraft were unable to find their target since, on being sighted, Admiral Kondo had turned his force to the northward—a course which he maintained during the night. At daybreak he resumed his southerly course, having sent the *Ryujo* on ahead in the hope that, as in the Coral Sea battle, the Americans would concentrate their attacks on the smaller carrier, thus giving Admiral Nagumo's fleet carriers a chance to strike back at them while most of their aircraft were away.

The plan worked, but not quite as Kondo had intended. The *Ryujo* was sighted on the morning of the 24th, and the *Saratoga* and *Enterprise* both sent out strikes which sank her shortly before 4 p.m. Meanwhile the *Shokaku* and *Zuikaku* had been sighted and, when the expected Japanese air attacks came in, the American carriers had their full strength of fighters in the air to meet them. American fighters assisted by anti-aircraft fire from the *North Carolina* took heavy toll of the attackers. Three bombs which hit the *Enterprise* failed to do fatal damage. The battle of the Eastern Solomons, as it was called, was indecisive; both fleets withdrew during the night. The enemy transports which held on towards Guadalcanal with their escorts were attacked with such good effect by bombers from Henderson Field and Espiritu Santo that they were recalled, the surviving troops being transferred to destroyers, which landed them near Cape Esperance a few nights later.

After this battle there was a comparative lull, although on Guadalcanal the weak Japanese forces made a number of unsuccessful attempts to break through to Henderson Field. Both the Americans and the Japanese took advantage of this lull to improve their position on the island. The Japanese with their superior naval strength were able to do so more easily than the Americans, but American aircraft operating from Henderson Field forced them to confine their activities to the hours of darkness. Light cruisers and destroyers came down 'The Slot' with such regularity to bombard the American positions and to land troops and supplies that they were named by the Marines the 'Tokyo Express'. By the middle of September the whole of the *Kawaguchi Detachment* had been landed.

The Americans too were able to bring in a few reinforcements and supplies. On the 1st September the first of the naval construction units, known as the 'Seabees', and some Marine Corps engineers were landed for the maintenance of the airfield, and on the 14th September 7th Marine Regiment (about 4,000 men) arrived from Samoa.

During these weeks no fleet action took place, but Japanese submarines and aircraft were active round Guadalcanal and there were numerous scattered actions in which American losses were severe. On the last day of August the *Saratoga* was torpedoed by a submarine; the ship had to return to Pearl Harbour for repairs but her aircraft were flown off to reinforce Henderson Field. Fifteen days later a group of submarines sank the *Wasp* and damaged the *North Carolina* and a destroyer, while they were engaged in covering the passage of 7th Marine Regiment. As the *Enterprise* was still repairing battle damage the *Hornet*, for the time being, was the only carrier left in the south Pacific.

It will be recalled that the second phase as laid down by the American Chiefs of Staff in their directive of the 2nd July was the occupation of the rest of the Solomons and the capture of Lae and Salamaua and the north-eastern area of New Guinea. At that time the

Australian forces in New Guinea were few and widely separated. An independent Australian company and a handful of New Guinea riflemen, known as 'Kangaforce', were at Wau, a mountain village in the heart of the New Guinea goldfields inland from Salamaua. Two Australian militia brigades were at Port Moresby, a third was being assembled at Milne Bay where airstrips were being prepared and a Papuan battalion and an incomplete Australian battalion were between Kokoda and Buna. While preparing his plans and collecting his forces, General MacArthur, who was in strategic control of the second phase, decided as a preliminary step to send a small Australian force overland to Buna, where there was a fighter strip, to establish an air base from which to support his eventual amphibious advance. He timed the movement to begin early in August to coincide with the landings on Guadalcanal. But he was to be forestalled.

Having been prevented by the battle of the Coral Sea from making a frontal assault on Port Moresby from the sea, the Japanese had planned to take it by an overland advance across the Owen Stanley Mountains and, in order to protect their flank, capture the airstrip at Milne Bay. On the 21st July an advanced force of some 2,000 men was landed unopposed west of Buna, from where a jungle track over the mountains crossed the peninsula to Port Moresby.[1] The track led by fairly easy stages to Kokoda, which stood on a plateau 1,200 feet above sea level flanked by high mountains. From there it climbed to 7,000 feet over steep ridges and through deep valleys where the narrow trail was walled by thick bush before it descended to the southern coastal plain. By the 29th July the Japanese had occupied Kokoda.

General MacArthur had meanwhile been assembling his forces, and early in August 7th Australian Division was on the way to New Guinea.[2] The 18th Australian Brigade was sent to reinforce the garrison at Milne Bay and 21st Australian Brigade, to be followed by 25th Brigade, to Port Moresby. On the 12th August, Lieut.-General F. F. Rowell, commanding 1st Australian Corps, took command at Port Moresby and at once ordered 21st Brigade forward into the mountains.

Between the 18th and 21st August the main body of the Japanese invasion force, under the command of Major-General Horii, was landed at Buna, bringing the strength of the force up to some 13,500 men. During the next month the Japanese steadily drove the Australians southwards, but their administration was poor and their line of communication along the difficult mountainous track broke down under constant attack by Allied aircraft, with the result that their troops were half-starved and many died from dysentery and

---
[1] See Sketch 11.
[2] The leading battalion embarked at Brisbane on the 6th August.

food poisoning. Thus their advance gradually lost its impetus and, after 25th Australian Brigade arrived in mid-September to reinforce 21st Brigade, was brought to a halt when only thirty-two miles from Port Moresby.

Meanwhile two Japanese transports, escorted by two light cruisers and three destroyers, had entered Milne Bay on the night of the 25th August and landed a naval force of about 1,200 men a few miles to the east of the airstrip. After five days of fierce fighting the Japanese, reinforced by another 775 men, had reached the edge of the airstrip. On the 31st, 18th Australian Brigade counter-attacked and drove the Japanese back to their base, which it occupied on the 6th September to find that the greater part of the landing force had by then been withdrawn.

By the second half of September, General MacArthur had concentrated the equivalent of two divisions in New Guinea[1] and, with his flank secure and the Japanese firmly held on the Kokoda trail, was ready to take the offensive and recapture Buna. He would then be in a position to begin the second phase of the main offensive as soon as Guadalcanal had been secured and the advance along the Solomon Islands resumed. On the 23rd General Sir Thomas Blamey, the Australian Commander-in-Chief, Allied Land Forces in the South West Pacific, arrived at Port Moresby to take control of operations.

After the failure of their attempts in August to break American resistance in Guadalcanal, *Imperial General Headquarters* issued a new directive on the 18th September in which the recapture of that island was given precedence over operations in New Guinea. General Hyakutake (*17th Army*) had by this time realized that he had underestimated American strength in Guadalcanal, but he still miscalculated. He believed that there were 7,500 troops in the island instead of the 19,000 who were actually there. On the basis of this erroneous estimate, he decided to throw in another division and at the end of August issued a new plan which he had later to revise several times. Henderson Field was to be retaken and its capture followed by the seizure of the islands of Tulagi, Rennell and San Cristobal; attacks were to be intensified against General MacArthur's forces in New Guinea, and Port Moresby captured by the end of November. The offensive against Guadalcanal was to be a joint operation in which the *Combined Fleet* would co-operate fully until two weeks after the fresh division had landed. A tentative date for the opening attacks was set for the 21st October.

---

[1] The 7th Australian Division, 6th Australian Division (less one brigade) and 128th Regiment of 32nd U.S. Division.

By drawing troops from China, the Netherlands East Indies, the Philippines and Truk, *Imperial General Headquarters* had by October assembled a strong force in the Rabaul area under *17th Army's* command. The infantry consisted of two divisions (*2nd* and *38th*), one regimental group and one reinforced battalion, with supporting troops. Of this, the group and the reinforced battalion (the *Kawaguchi* and *Ichiki Detachments*) had already met defeat in Guadalcanal. The movement of this force from Rabaul to Guadalcanal, which had begun in August, was speeded up during September by means of the 'Tokyo Express', landing craft and transports.

The implications of this steady flow of reinforcements were not lost on the Americans. It was obvious that their own garrison in the island faced a serious threat, for its strength was gradually diminishing as the enervating and humid heat, inadequate diet and disease began to take their toll. It was not, however, till the beginning of October that it was decided to reinforce the garrison. On the 9th, transports carrying a regiment of the Americal Division left New Caledonia for Guadalcanal[1], escorted by three destroyers and covered by a squadron of four cruisers and four destroyers under command of Rear-Admiral N. Scott, U.S.N., whose orders were to protect the convoy by offensive action. He faithfully carried these out, for on the night of the 11th/12th he surprised a Japanese force of three cruisers and two destroyers between Cape Esperance and Savo island about to bombard Henderson Field in order to cover the landing of reforcements. He was fortunate enough to be able to bring off the time-honoured manoeuvre of crossing the enemy's T, and succeeded in sinking one cruiser and two destroyers and damaging another cruiser. Aircraft followed up this success next morning and sank a third destroyer. His own losses were one destroyer sunk and two cruisers and a destroyer damaged. The regiment with its supplies was safely landed during daylight on the 13th and the transports sailed before nightfall.

Meanwhile on the 12th Japanese bombers had made heavy and accurate attacks on Henderson Field. On the night of the 13th/14th a naval squadron which included two battleships completed the work of the aircraft in the heaviest bombardment of the campaign, making it unusable by heavy bombers for nearly a month and putting half of the ninety aircraft in Guadalcanal out of action. On the 15th, American aircraft from Henderson Field and the New Hebrides bombed enemy transports unloading at Tassafaronga, sinking three, but not before some three to four thousand Japanese troops and most of their supplies had been landed.

---

[1] See pages 221-22 and footnote.

The second half of October saw the first major attempt by the Japanese to regain control of the island. By the 15th a large proportion of the *Combined Fleet* had been brought south of the Marianas and its commander, Admiral Yamamoto, could deploy against the Americans no less than five carriers, five battleships, fourteen cruisers and twenty-four destroyers. By the same date General Hyakutake had succeeded in concentrating some 20,000 troops on the island and felt he could take the offensive. He planned that the main body of *2nd Division*, under command of Lieut.-General Maruyama, should make its way from Kokumbona through the jungle to a starting line due south of the American perimeter and attack north, while a diversionary force under Major-General Sumiyoshi, composed mainly of artillery, covered its rear, shelled the airfield and, moving parallel with the coast, attacked the perimeter from the west. 'X' day was originally set for the 18th October, but torrential rain and thick jungle held up *2nd Division's* advance and the attack did not begin until the 24th. Not only were the attacks badly co-ordinated but the Americans, warned by the landings on the 15th, were prepared; by the 26th the offensive had failed and the Japanese had been forced to withdraw.

Meanwhile a supporting Japanese fleet, which included four carriers, was at sea awaiting word of the capture of Henderson Field before carrying out its part of the combined plan; this, to use Japanese phraseology, was 'to apprehend and annihilate any powerful forces in the Solomons area as well as any reinforcements'. The American Fleet was also at sea with very much the same purpose. At General Vandegrift's urgent request for naval support, Vice-Admiral W. F. Halsey, who on the 18th October had relieved Admiral Ghormley as Commander-in-Chief, South Pacific, had sent a battleship, three cruisers and ten destroyers to the westward of Guadalcanal ready to attack any supporting enemy naval force. The carrier *Hornet* and the remaining four cruisers were sent east of the New Hebrides with orders to round the Santa Cruz Islands to the northward and be in a position to intercept any enemy forces approaching the Guadalcanal–Tulagi area. The *Hornet's* force was joined on the 25th by a task force from Pearl Harbour under Rear-Admiral T. C. Kinkaid, U.S.N., composed of the battleship *South Dakota*, the carrier *Enterprise*, newly fit for service again, two cruisers and eight destroyers.

The enemy fleet was sighted by a Catalina north-west of the Santa Cruz Islands on the 25th, and early on the morning of the 26th Kinkaid was ordered to attack it. Shortly after daylight both sides sighted the other's carriers and both sent out strikes. In the ensuing air battle the Americans, although outnumbered, lost seventy aircraft against Japanese losses of about one hundred. The *Hornet* and a destroyer were sunk and the *Enterprise*, the *South Dakota* and a cruiser damaged. All the Japanese ships remained afloat but two carriers, a heavy cruiser and two destroyers were damaged; the carrier *Shokaku* was so hard hit that, although able to get home, she was out of action for nine months.

The battle of Santa Cruz left the Americans once again with only one carrier in the south Pacific, the veteran *Enterprise*, and she was considerably damaged. The Americans had already appealed to their British allies for the loan of a carrier, but the demands of operation 'Torch' (the landing in North Africa), due to start in a matter of days, had already reduced the Eastern Fleet to a carrier and two battleships and it was not until December, when the success of 'Torch' was assured, that the Admiralty was able to see its way clear to release the carrier *Victorious* from the Home Fleet for the Pacific.

The Americans were determined not to lose their hold on Guadalcanal. As the struggle for the island reached its climax, the President instructed his Chiefs of Staff to send everything they could to the two active theatres—the Pacific and North Africa—even if it meant reducing commitments elsewhere. Admiral King could send no carriers, but diverted to the south Pacific a considerable force which included a battleship, six cruisers, twenty-four submarines and about 130 naval aircraft. General Marshall sent seventy-five army aircraft from Hawaii to reinforce the south-west Pacific but would not increase the existing allocation of troops to the Pacific. This did not, however, prevent the reinforcement of Guadalcanal by troops drawn from the island bases. On the 4th November, two regiments from 2nd Marine Division were landed without opposition and four days later two convoys left Noumea and Espiritu Santo carrying another 6,000 officers and men of the Americal Division. The two convoys, commanded by Rear-Admiral Turner, were escorted by two squadrons, one commanded by Rear-Admiral Scott and the other by Rear-Admiral D. J. Callaghan, and were covered by a task force re-formed round the damaged *Enterprise* and the battleships *Washington* and *South Dakota*.

The Japanese were no less determined than the Americans to gain control of Guadalcanal, and in November made another major attempt to reinforce the island and drive the Americans out. Their plan followed the same now familiar pattern as the previous ones. Two naval squadrons were to bombard and neutralize Henderson Field, a third was to convoy the transports carrying the rest of *38th Division* from Rabaul, while a fourth gave general support.

The leading American convoy, escorted by Scott's squadron, arrived off Lunga Point on the morning of the 11th November and was joined the next day by the second convoy escorted by Callaghan's squadron. Within a few hours of their arrival, a strong Japanese force including two battleships (*Hiei* and *Kirishima*) was reported coming down 'The Slot'. Turner calmly continued unloading the transports until all troops and supplies had been landed, and then sailed them in convoy for Espiritu Santo at dusk, escorted by three destroyers. He left the remainder of the combined escort forces under command of Callaghan to fight a delaying night action with the greatly superior Japanese, so as to give the covering task force, which was on its way up from Noumea, time to intercept the Japanese invasion convoys believed to be en route for Guadalcanal.

After escorting the transports clear of the anchorage, Callaghan turned west to meet the enemy. It was a dark night with no moon and in the early hours of the morning of the 13th the two forces met almost head on before a gun was fired. The ensuing battle which lasted only twenty-four minutes was one of the most furious sea battles ever fought: two American light cruisers and four destroyers were sunk or left sinking and all the remainder were damaged. Both Scott and Callaghan were killed and casualties were very heavy. The Japanese lost two destroyers. The battleship *Hiei* was crippled, left dead in the water and sunk next day by American aircraft. Callaghan's night action saved Henderson Field from bombardment by battleships but did not prevent it from being shelled by cruisers and destroyers the following night; nor did it prevent the arrival of the Japanese transports. It achieved its main object however of giving the task force time to intervene.

The following afternoon, aircraft from the *Enterprise* sank a cruiser and damaged other ships of the Japanese cruiser bombardment force, while aircraft from Henderson Field wrought havoc among the transports unloading on the north of the island and sunk seven out of eleven. Meanwhile, the Japanese heavy bombardment force which had been mauled in the night action returned reorganized and reinforced, to cover the transports. It consisted of the surviving battleship *Kirishima*, four cruisers and nine destroyers. Admiral Halsey sent Rear-Admiral W. A. Lee with the *Washington*, *South Dakota* and four destroyers to attack it. Lee led his battleships round the southeast tip of Guadalcanal and shortly after midnight met the enemy in the narrow channel south of Savo island. The encounter was fought at longer range than that of the 13th but was almost as savage. The *Kirishima* was so badly damaged that she had to be scuttled by her crew. One Japanese and three American destroyers were sunk. The *South Dakota* was heavily hit but remained afloat.

When day broke on the 15th the remaining four Japanese transports were seen by the Americans beached and helpless; they were bombarded by shore batteries and aircraft from Henderson Field and in a few hours were blazing hulks. Only 4,000 of the 10,000 troops which sailed in the ill-fated Japanese convoy reached Guadalcanal and they were left with insufficient supplies and rations.

The three-day naval battle of Guadalcanal was the American Navy's first decisive victory of the campaign in spite of its heavy losses. It put a quick end to the November offensive on which the Japanese had set high hopes. The enemy did not however give up his struggle to reinforce the island; the 'Tokyo Express' still ran, though at less frequent intervals, but brought only small shipments of troops and supplies. Heavy ships were never again to be used in support, but the Americans of course could not know this.

At the end of November another Japanese attempt to bring in large reinforcements was suspected, and Halsey sent out a striking force of five cruisers and four destroyers to prevent it. On the night of the 30th, it intercepted eight enemy destroyers carrying supplies to Tassafaronga. Although the Americans had the advantage of surprise the Japanese fired their torpedoes with such deadly effect that four of the American cruisers were hit. Three survived but one had to be abandoned before she capsized. Only one Japanese destroyer was sunk. The battle of Tassafaronga was the last of the fierce night encounters in the narrow waters of the South Solomons.

In spite of its success on this occasion the Japanese Navy realized that, in the face of growing American naval and air strength, reinforcement of the garrison would become more and more difficult. Its own losses at sea and in the air during the past four months had been severe, and shipping, as always, was scarce. The Navy therefore wished to abandon the operation. The Army however was determined to continue the struggle until a decision had been reached. The Army's view prevailed and *Imperial General Headquarters* formed a new area army headquarters to control *17th Army*, responsible for the Solomons area, and a newly-formed *18th Army*, responsible for New Guinea. Lieut.-General Imamura, commanding *16th Army* in Java, was appointed Commander-in-Chief, *8th Area Army*. On the 27th November, *6th Air Division* was formed to support the new area army. But although by the end of the year Imamura had 50,000 troops at his disposal, he was unable to deploy them, as he had no means of transporting them to battle or of supplying them.

On the last day of 1942 *Imperial General Headquarters* decided to abandon Guadalcanal and hold a line further back in New Georgia. From then on only small consignments of essential supplies were sent to the Japanese garrison. They came chiefly by submarine, for Allied air power had grown to such an extent and air attacks were so persistent that even the 'Tokyo Express' dared venture only on rare occasions to run the gauntlet of 'The Slot'. The Americans on the contrary were able to reinforce with comparative ease. On the 9th December, General A. M. Patch relieved General Vandegrift and during the next six weeks 1st Marine Division, which had endured four months fighting in the steamy malaria-ridden jungles of Guadalcanal, was withdrawn for much needed rest and reorganization in Australia. It was relieved by 25th U.S. Division, some 7,500 officers and men of which were landed unopposed on the 31st December. On the 4th January, 2nd U.S. Marine Division Headquarters and 6th Marine Regiment arrived from New Zealand, thereby bringing the strength of the garrison to about 50,000 men.

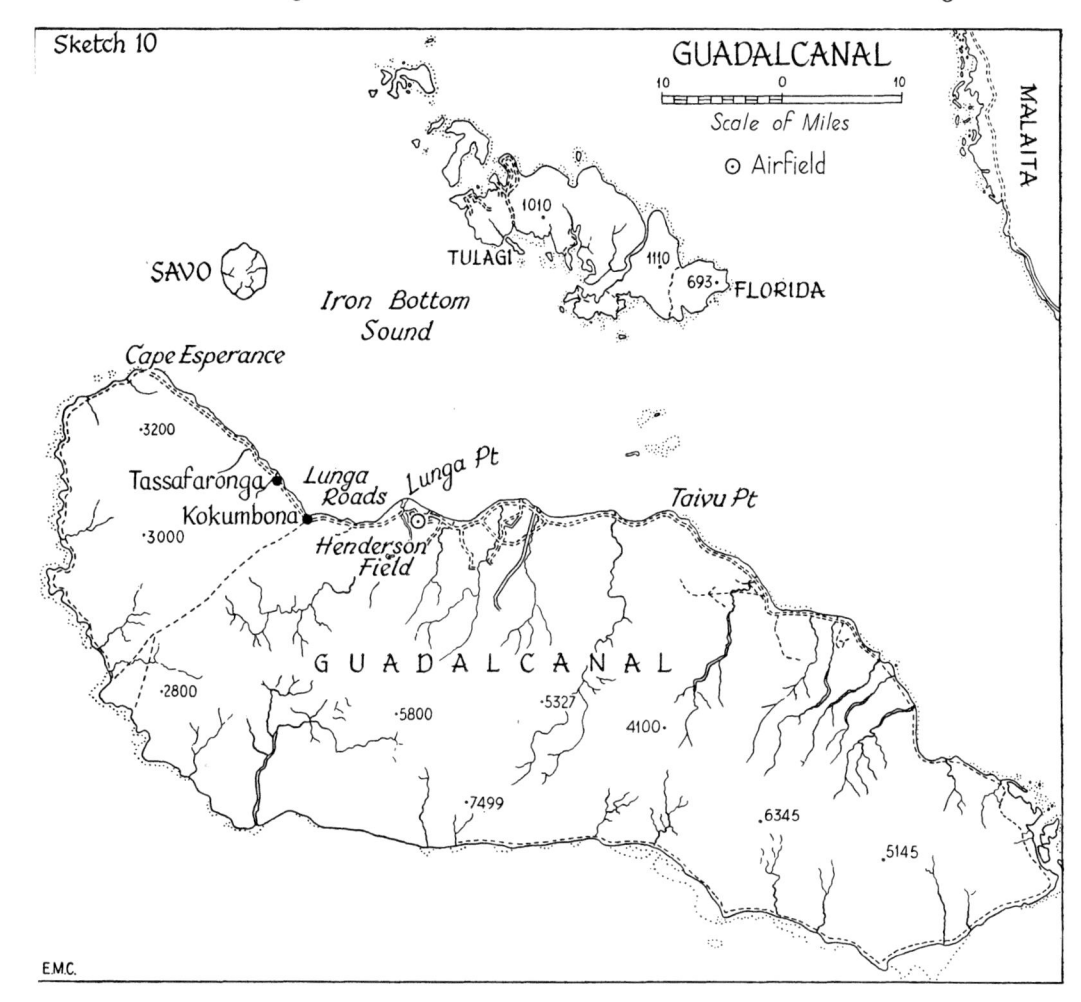

The Japanese strength on Guadalcanal had by that time declined from the peak of 30,000 men, reached in November, to about 25,000. The garrison had received practically no reinforcements since the survivors of the ill-fated convoy had struggled ashore during the naval battle of Guadalcanal. The troops, underfed and riddled with disease but fighting desperately to the last, were gradually driven back. At the end of January 1943 they withdrew by order of General Imamura to Cape Esperance, from where, during the first week in February, they were ferried in barges under cover of darkness to destroyers. By the 7th, exactly six months after the Marines had first landed in the Solomons, the Japanese evacuation of the island was completed. Some 13,000 men, all that was left of the garrison, had made their escape without the Americans having the least idea of what was happening. General Patch was thus left in undisputed control of the island. The first phase of the operations planned on the 2nd July 1942 was over.

While the battle for Guadalcanal was in progress, an equally fierce struggle was taking place in New Guinea for control of the Papuan peninsula. When General Blamey arrived at Port Moresby on the 23rd September to assume control of operations, the whole of the 7th and the best part of 6th Australian Division had reached New Guinea, and the leading units of 32nd U.S. Division were beginning to arrive by air. An Australian squadron of Hudsons and some Catalinas were at Port Moresby, and two squadrons of Kittyhawks and a Beaufighter squadron were at Milne Bay. In Australia, Major-General C. C. Kenney, U.S.A.A.F. (Commander Allied Air Forces, South West Pacific) had three fighter and five bomber groups, but the squadrons were widely scattered. There was practically no naval support. The Allied naval forces in the South West Pacific (known as 'MacArthur's Navy') consisted of only five cruisers, eight destroyers (fully occupied on escort duties), twenty submarines and seven small craft.

General Blamey decided that his first task was to secure his base at Port Moresby by driving the enemy back over the Kokoda trail and, having done this, to evict him from his bridgehead on the north coast. The interior of Papua was in 1942 practically roadless: there were only two tracks overland from Port Moresby to the Buna area, the Kokoda trail which the Japanese had followed and another further to the south-east, known as the Kapa Kapa trail, which was more direct but even steeper and more mountainous.[1] His difficulty therefore was to concentrate and maintain sufficient forces north of the Owen Stanley Range. The sea route from Milne Bay to the Buna area was hazardous and badly charted. The only naval vessels which could be profitably employed for the transport of troops and supplies on this route were landing craft, and there was none of these in the South West Pacific Command. He therefore decided to fly part of 32nd U.S. Division to Wanigela, a mission station on the coast one hundred miles north-east of Milne Bay, where there was an

---
[1] See Sketch 11.

airstrip. From there, it was thought, it could make its way up the coast to join hands with 7th Australian Division and with an American column advancing across the mountains by the Kokoda and Kapa Kapa trails respectively.

On the 23rd September, 25th Australian Brigade began to advance towards Kokoda and on the 28th found the Japanese positions on the ridge above Port Moresby abandoned. At the same time a battalion of 126th Regiment from 32nd U.S. Division left Port Moresby by way of the Kapa Kapa trail. Papuan porters followed the advance bringing up supplies and carrying back the wounded. As the line of communications lengthened, Hudsons from Port Moresby ('biscuit bombers' as the troops called them) flew in food and ammunition which they dropped on open patches in the jungle. Supplies often fell in the jungle and could not be recovered, but enough reached the troops to enable them to go on. The Japanese, forced owing to their lack of air support to exist on what they could carry, had withdrawn to a series of three prepared defensive positions in depth, one behind the other, at Templeton's Crossing at the top of the range. A frontal attack combined with wide outflanking moves by 25th Australian Brigade drove them from the first of these positions on the 16th October, but the brigade could make little further progress. It was then relieved by 16th Australian Brigade, which, after very severe fighting under appalling conditions of mud and rain in the thick jungle, succeeded by the 28th October in driving the Japanese from the remainder of their prepared positions. The division then began to descend towards the northern plain and by the 2nd November had occupied Kokoda without opposition. Two days later the existing airstrip near this village had been repaired and was in use, thus enabling a further advance to begin.

The Japanese meanwhile had fallen back to fresh positions west of the Kumusi River. Between the 4th and 12th November, 7th Australian Division, assisted by close support from the air, broke the Japanese resistance after fierce fighting and reached the river which at that time was in flood and over a hundred yards in width. The remnants of the Japanese then hastily withdrew to their perimeter on the coast covering Buna. This consisted of a series of cleverly prepared and well-constructed defences running from Cape Endaiadere to Gona covering both Buna and Sanananda.

Bridging material was dropped by air at the Kumusi crossing, and by the 16th the Australians were able to resume their advance, with 25th Brigade directed on Gona and 16th Brigade on Sanananda. By the 19th, both brigades had made contact with the Japanese defences and were brought to a halt. As soon as the Dobodura plain had been occupied, airfields were constructed at Popondetta and at Dobodura itself, thus enabling the Allied forces north of the Owen

Stanley Range to be easily supplied and reinforced and artillery to be brought forward.

Meanwhile an Australian battalion had been flown on the 5th October to Wanigela to secure the airstrip, and on the 14th had been followed up by 128th U.S. Regiment. The whole of this force was then moved by native craft to Pongani, where a new airfield was prepared. By the middle of November, Headquarters 32nd U.S. Division and 126th Regiment (less one battalion) had been flown into Pongani, and on the 15th the division began its advance along the coast with one column directed on Cape Endaiadere and another on Buna. The American battalion which had crossed the range by the Kapa Kapa trail reached Bofu on the 16th November and then, having sent a detachment to join 7th Australian Division at the Kumusi River, rejoined its division. By the 20th the Americans had also made contact with the south-eastern face of the Japanese ring round Buna and their advance had been brought to a halt.

General Blamey had hoped that the speed of the advance would enable the Japanese position covering Buna to be quickly overcome. It soon became evident, however, that it was going to be an extremely difficult matter to eject the enemy, always tenacious in defence, from well sited, prepared positions, which could be attacked only frontally and to which the approaches were limited. He realized that a change in policy would be necessary and that fresh troops would have to be brought forward. Accordingly, 21st and 30th Brigades of 6th Australian Division were flown in to relieve the weary 16th and 25th Brigades, and 127th Regiment was flown in to bring 32nd U.S. Division to full strength. At the same time the command organization was adjusted. Lieut.-General E. F. Herring (General Officer Commanding, 1st Australian Corps) was placed in command of all troops on the northern plain so that the operations of 7th Australian and 32nd U.S. Divisions could be co-ordinated[1], and General MacArthur sent forward Lieut.-General R. L. Eichelberger (Commander 1st U.S. Corps) with most of his staff to take command of all American troops in the area, with orders 'to take Buna or not come back alive'.[2]

About the same time General Adachi, who had assumed command of *18th Army* on the 25th November, attempted to reinforce the beleaguered garrison at Buna by running destroyers down the coast from Lae and Salamaua, but these attempts were largely frustrated by Allied aircraft which so harried the enemy vessels that only a trickle of troops reached the garrison.

---

[1] Lieut.-General Herring had relieved Lieut.-General Rowell as G.O.C. 1st Australian Corps on the 1st October 1942.

[2] Eichelberger, *Jungle Road to Tokyo* (Odhams Press, 1951), page 42.

THE JAPANESE DRIVEN FROM PAPUA

The arrival of fresh troops soon produced results, for after ten days fighting 21st Australian Brigade captured Gona on the northern flank of the perimeter on the 9th December. But elsewhere on the front repeated attacks made only local progress and broke down in the face of fierce enemy resistance. It was therefore decided to concentrate the available forces on the capture of the Cape Endaiadere–Buna area, leaving Sanananda to be dealt with later. At the same time the Allied forces were further strengthened by bringing in 18th Australian Brigade and some tanks from Milne Bay. All through December the battle to drive the Japanese from their last footholds in Papua raged. Conditions were appalling and both sides suffered terribly from the ravages of the climate and disease, and the casualties were heavy. One by one the Japanese defences were reduced, but it was not till the 3rd January 1943 that the whole of the coastline from Cape Endaiadere to Buna was occupied and the last of the Japanese liquidated. Meanwhile on the 1st January, 163rd U.S. Regiment (part of 41st U.S. Division) had been flown in. This regiment, with 18th Australian Brigade and 127th U.S. Regiment, attacked enemy positions in the Sanananda area on the 12th January. By the 16th these were overrun and their garrisons annihilated. By the 21st the last of the Japanese pockets along the coastal strip had been mopped up and, all resistance having ceased, the campaign was brought to its close.

The Papuan campaign had lasted six months and cost nearly 5,700 Australian and 2,800 American casualties.[1] It might have ended sooner if more naval support had been available or if the channels leading to Buna had been less treacherous. As it was, General MacArthur had had to depend almost entirely on his small air force for the supply and reinforcement of his troops. Air transport for the support of an army gained a new significance in the Papuan campaign as it was later to do in Burma. In the South West Pacific Area, and indeed in every theatre of war, it was to open the way to operations hitherto deemed impossible.

The two campaigns for the capture of Papua and Guadalcanal ended within a fortnight of each other. Both were similar in many respects. In both, the armies fought under appalling conditions in the tropical damp heat of the jungle, often up to their knees in mud, short of food and plagued by malaria and jungle sores. In both campaigns the air played a vital part. There was one difference however. In Papua sea power played little part while in the Solomons it had a dominant rôle. During the six months of the campaign no less than six great sea battles were fought in the narrow waters round Guadalcanal. American losses in warship tonnage were little less than the Japanese, but the Americans could replace them at far

---
[1] American documents give the Japanese losses as about 12,000.

greater speed than could the enemy.[1] The cost of victory in each campaign had been high, but not too high for the result achieved. In both, victory was complete. The Japanese advance had at last been halted; the threat of invasion to Australia had passed and the vital line of communication between her and the United States was secure. A new phase had opened in the Pacific. After over a year of fighting on the defensive, the Allies could now turn to the offensive. The initiative had been taken from the hitherto victorious Japanese.

---

[1] The comparative losses were:

	Allies Number	Allies Tonnage	Japanese Number	Japanese Tonnage
Battleships	–	—	2	62,000
Fleet carriers	2	34,500	–	—
Light carriers	–	—	1	8,500
Heavy cruisers	6	56,925	3	26,400
Light cruisers	2	12,000	1	5,700
Destroyers	14	22,815	11	20,930
Submarines	–	—	6	11,309
	24	126,240	24	134,839

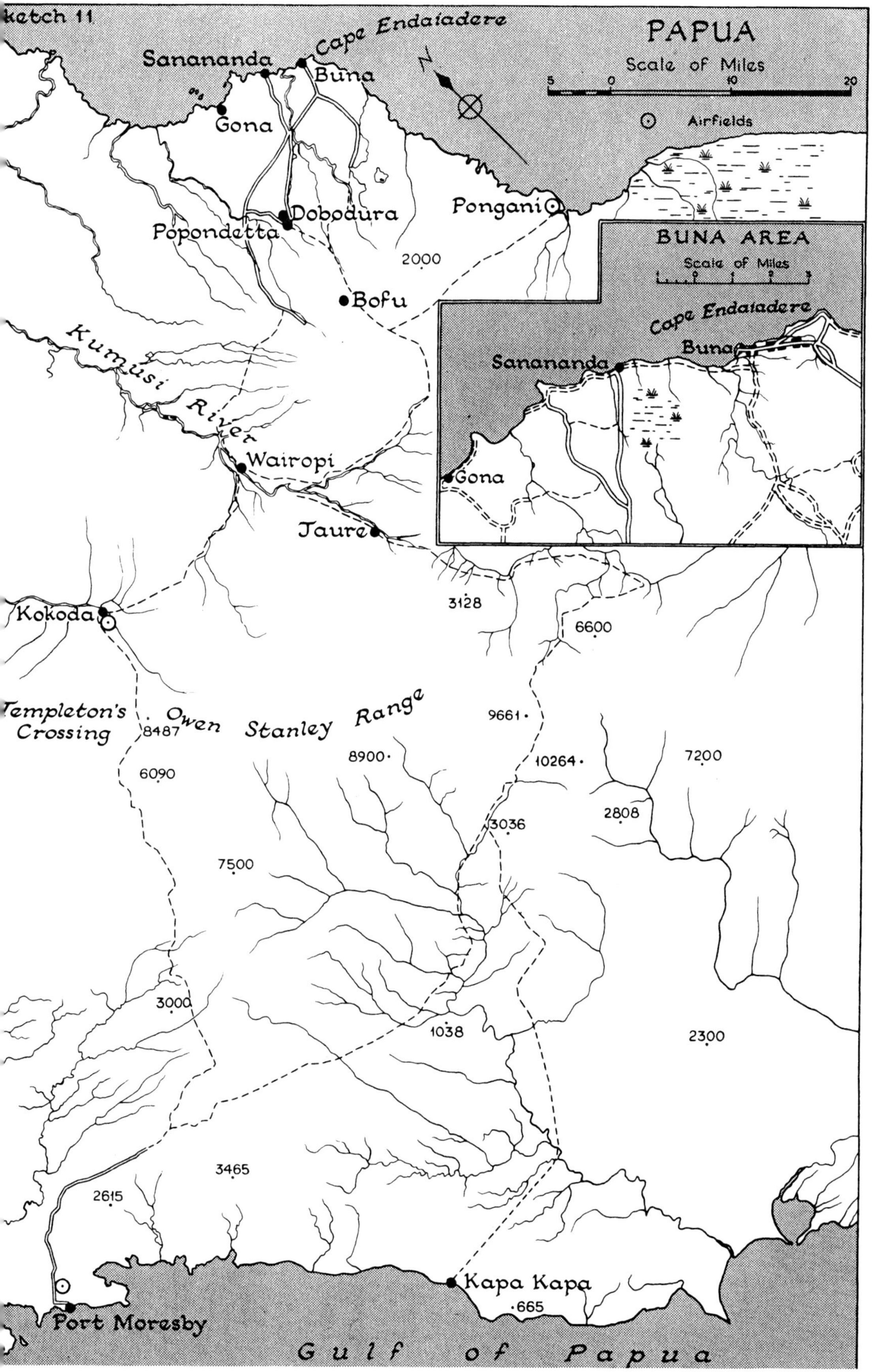

ketch 11
PAPUA
Scale of Miles
5
0
10
20
Airfields
Cape Endaiadere
Sananada
Buna
Gona
Dobodura
Popondetta
Pongani
2000
Bofu
Kumusi River
Wairopi
Jaure
Kokoda
3128
6600
Templeton's Crossing
8487
Owen Stanley Range
9661
8900
10264
7200
6090
2808
3036
7500
3000
1038
2300
3465
2615
Kapa Kapa
665
Port Moresby
Gulf of Papua
BUNA AREA
Scale of Miles
Cape Endaiadere
Buna
Sananada
Gona

CHAPTER XVII

PLANS FOR THE REOCCUPATION OF BURMA IN 1944

See Strategic Map and Map 14

GENERAL WAVELL had been prevented by administrative difficulties, lack of resources and the ravages of malaria among the troops from attempting to launch 'Anakim' during the dry season of 1942–43. Thus, in his operation instruction of the 17th September 1942, he had been able to give Eastern Army limited objectives only.[1] He had not, however, abandoned hope of taking some action before May 1943 towards the reoccupation of upper Burma, and particularly for the capture of the airfield at Myitkyina. To be successful, any operation in this area called for simultaneous action from Assam by the British-Indian and the American-trained Chinese armies on the one hand, and from Yunnan by the Chinese armies on the other. Wavell therefore opened discussions with Stilwell and through him with Chiang Kai-shek, with a view to formulating a combined plan of action with the Chinese.

On the 18th and 19th October 1942, a conference between Wavell and Stilwell took place in Delhi. After Wavell had outlined his operational plans and explained the difficulties which beset him, Stilwell produced a Chinese plan approved by the Generalissimo for 'the retaking of Burma under the joint effort of the Chinese, British and American forces'. It proposed that the Chinese should attack west and south from Yunnan with fifteen to twenty divisions (each of 7,000 men) while five to seven divisions and parachute troops, provided by Britain and America, would, together with the Chinese forces in India, attack from Assam and make landings at Rangoon. The combined British and American air forces would attack enemy air bases, gain control of the air and cover the naval and land operations. A strong combined British and American fleet (consisting of at least three to four battleships, six to eight aircraft carriers and a large number of submarines) would enter the China and Java Seas to cut the enemy's line of communications, then attack the Andaman Islands, gain control of the Bay of Bengal and cover the landings at

[1] See Appendix 20.

Rangoon. To prepare the way for the land operations, the United States would increase the air transport of supplies to China to equip the Chinese divisions, and Britain would develop road communications from India into Burma.

Wavell pointed out that the number of aircraft carriers and submarines asked for by the Generalissimo was nowhere in sight. The control of the Bay of Bengal must depend on air superiority over Japanese land-based aircraft and by March 1943, the date proposed for the offensive, the combined British and American air forces would not be strong enough to gain it. Moreover, there was no possibility of a fleet, except perhaps submarines, operating in the China and Java Seas until the air bases to cover it had been secured. The Generalissimo's plan, however, appeared sufficiently in accord with his own ideas to form a basis for future planning for the recapture of the whole of Burma. The immediate problem was the date on which a limited offensive into northern Burma could be launched and how far it could go, since to be caught by the monsoon in a position where troops could not be maintained and might even have to be withdrawn would be most inadvisable.

The Chiefs of Staff instructed Wavell to establish, at his next meeting with Stilwell, the principle that any Chinese forces operating from India into Burma must come under control of the Commander-in-Chief in India, and to endeavour to get agreement that the 10th U.S.A.A.F. should be placed under control of the Air Officer Commanding, India, for the duration of the operations. At a second conference on the 27th October, Stilwell and Wavell agreed firstly, that the Chinese force at Ramgarh should advance from Ledo down the Hukawng Valley to capture the airfield at Myitkyina before the next monsoon and then move towards Bhamo to join hands, if possible, with the Chinese from Yunnan; and secondly, that the Americans should establish and stock a base at Ledo. Since transportation to Assam was limited, the decision on how and when the Ledo base could be stocked would be made by Wavell. They confirmed that the construction of the Ledo–Hukawng Valley route should be an American responsibility.[1]

Wavell made it quite clear that the Ramgarh force must come under his command; Stilwell agreed to the necessity for this and undertook to obtain the Generalissimo's concurrence. On the question of the control of the 10th U.S.A.A.F., Stilwell said that the Generalissimo would never agree to its coming under the control of the Air Officer Commanding, India, for operations in Burma since he regarded it as being definitely allotted to China. He thought however that in practice there would be no difficulty in the British and American air commanders making plans for joint operations by

---
[1] See page 245.

their respective forces, both for the defence of India and the offensive against Burma.

When reporting on this conference to the Chiefs of Staff, Wavell said, 'I think we must accept with good grace and willingness this American–Chinese co-operation in recapture of Burma. It will introduce some complications and inevitable difficulties of inter-Allied co-operation, but am sure we can manage to work with Americans as combined staff'.

Early in November, Stilwell reported that the Generalissimo accepted in principle the plans made in Delhi and would be ready to move by the 1st March with fifteen divisions, five of which would form the initial attacking force. They would have little artillery support. The Generalissimo agreed to the Chinese force in India coming under British command at first, but expressed the desire for a unified command when the attacking forces converged on Mandalay. He insisted, however, on being given a reasonable assurance that naval domination of the Bay of Bengal and air superiority over Burma would be secured; otherwise he would not participate in the plan. On learning this, Wavell again warned Stilwell that it was impossible to say how strong the Eastern Fleet or the air forces would be by March 1943; Admiral Somerville was however shortly leaving for London to discuss the question of reinforcements for the Eastern Fleet.

Early the following month, Wavell heard from Field Marshal Sir John Dill, the head of the British Joint Staff Mission in Washington, that Stilwell expected the Ledo base to be stocked and ready and the Chinese corps concentrated there by the 1st March 1943. Some 6,000 American specialist engineers and 63,000 shipping tons of road building and maintenance equipment were being sent from the United States for the purpose of constructing the all-weather two-way road down the Hukawng Valley; the engineers and the equipment would arrive at Calcutta between mid-March and early April.

Just before Christmas 1942 two further conferences between Wavell and Stilwell took place at Delhi. At the first, Stilwell represented that, in view of the economic situation in China, it was imperative that a road from Ledo to Myitkyina, and thence by Tengchung to Paoshan in Yunnan, should be constructed at the earliest possible moment. Pending its completion Stilwell hoped that, with the use of the airfield at Myitkyina and the control of the Bhamo area, it would be possible to operate the air ferry service as far as Myitkyina instead of to Kunming; goods would then be taken down the Irrawaddy as far as Bhamo and finally by motor transport by way of existing roads into China. With the shorter air lift, he hoped that the tonnage carried could be increased two and a half times.

Wavell pointed out that, since troops would have to advance at least as far as the Bhamo–Katha area, and possibly even to Lashio, in order to cover the construction of such a road and make Stilwell's interim plan feasible, the problem was not so much one of getting the troops to these areas as of maintaining them there during the 1943 monsoon. He had, he said, had the experience of trying during the 1942 monsoon to build roads, and of maintaining troops at the end of the Imphal Road which had been made and metalled for years. He did not think that an all-weather road could be put through to Myitkyina before, or troops maintained beyond it during, the monsoon. He suggested as an alternative that the advance of troops, both from Ledo and from Yunnan, should be so controlled that they kept pace with the progress of road construction and that, to ease the maintenance problem, only the minimum number of covering troops should be employed.

Despite these arguments, Stilwell continued to hold the view that a large Chinese force from Ledo should be pushed beyond Myitkyina and that a full-scale advance should be undertaken by the Chinese from Yunnan by the 1st March 1943. He brushed aside all the maintenance difficulties which Wavell had enumerated by saying that they would have to be overcome by air supply, and insisted that the danger to troops from malaria during the monsoon could be overcome by preventive measures.

When reporting the gist of this to the Chiefs of Staff, Wavell said that the crux of the problem was how far to go before the monsoon and where to effect a junction between the British and Chinese forces—a problem which he thought time alone would solve. He went on, 'I may have to resist pressure to push on during dry weather to support Chinese further than maintenance during the wet season will allow, but I am determined not to get troops into position of last May when we had to withdraw through inability to maintain ourselves':

The Chiefs of Staff reminded Wavell that Burma was a British theatre of war and that he must retain responsibility for all operations based on India. He must therefore reserve for himself the ultimate responsibility for the conduct and scope of the Chinese offensive from Ledo. They realized the political and psychological advantages to be derived from a successful offensive during the dry weather on the lines that Stilwell had proposed; nevertheless they considered 'Anakim' the more important operation and held that its chances of success should not be prejudiced by operations in upper Burma.

At the second conference, Wavell explained that operation 'Anakim' would have to wait till the autumn and winter of 1943. He fully recognized, however, the considerable advantages which would accrue from the early occupation of upper Burma and he was most anxious to undertake operations for this purpose. How far he could go was governed by administrative factors. He estimated that IV Corps could be assembled by the 15th February 1943, Ledo could be stocked with forty-five days' supplies by the 1st March and the Chinese corps assembled there by the 22nd March. American specialist engineers would arrive at Ledo about the same time, but only one-third of the road-making machinery required would be available by the 15th April and the remainder would not be on the site till the end of May, too late to begin work before the monsoon. He again warned Stilwell that he did not consider it possible to put an all-weather road through to Shingbwiyang before the rains, and emphasized that once they began he could not operate east of the Chindwin. He could raid across the Chindwin, but could not advance to the Katha–Shwebo area and thus give direct assistance to the Chinese in Yunnan before the monsoon broke. He hoped however to be able to send his long-range penetration formation (77th Infantry Brigade) to the Katha area and possibly across the Irrawaddy.[1]

Admiral Somerville, who had returned from his discussions in London and was present at the conference, told Stilwell that, as a result of the diversion of ships to cover the landings in North Africa,[2] the Eastern Fleet was too weak to do more than protect shipping routes to the Middle East, India and Australia. He could not maintain a squadron for a spring offensive in the Bay of Bengal where it would be within reach of enemy shore-based aircraft. For action against enemy ships in that area, reliance would have to be placed on the air forces. He asked Stilwell to make it quite clear to the Generalissimo that, if they were to fight on equal terms, ships operating within reach of enemy shore-based aircraft must themselves be supported by similar forces.

In summing up the conference, Wavell said he was most anxious for the Generalissimo to understand that, if the Chinese troops from Yunnan were to meet a concentration of Japanese forces in upper Burma, the British would not be able to help them by operating large forces east of the Chindwin. It was therefore the Generalissimo's responsibility to say whether he would advance in these circumstances. Stilwell then returned to Chungking, having agreed to convey the substance of the discussions to the Generalissimo.

The Generalissimo's reactions were immediate. On the 28th December, he cabled the President that the Prime Minister had assured the members of the Pacific War Council early in 1942 that before the end of that year's monsoon eight battleships, three aircraft carriers and auxiliary craft would be in the Indian Ocean to assist in the recapture of Burma.[3] Stilwell had now told him that

---

[1] See pages 243-44.

[2] The Allies invaded French North Africa on the night of the 7th/8th November 1942.

[3] For the composition of the Pacific War Council see page 56 footnote.

Somerville had at his disposal only a few destroyers and submarines for operations in the Bay of Bengal. Wavell had promised to make seven divisions available to assist in the recapture of Burma, but now only three divisions were to be employed in limited operations towards Akyab and the Chindwin River. He asked the President to urge the British to provide the naval, air and land forces to carry out their part of the bargain, adding that he could rely on the Chinese forces being concentrated and ready for action in time and in accordance with the plans made. The President in reply told the Generalissimo that the opening of the Burma Road was more important than the reoccupation of the whole of Burma and that this problem would be considered without delay.[1]

Mr. Churchill assured the President that at no time had he given any promise or assurance to the Pacific War Council about the fleet, but had merely stated what was then intended. It had been proposed to form an Eastern Fleet by July 1942, but since then all Admiral Somerville's essential aircraft carriers had been taken away from him and his destroyers had been drawn on for the North African landing and the convoys to Russia. Therefore, although the battleships for the Eastern Fleet were, or soon would be, ready, they would be without their screen and could not enter the Bay of Bengal until they had been reinforced by carriers. In any case a fleet was unnecessary for the operations. As for the seven divisions, at no time had Wavell given an undertaking to use them to recapture Burma before the next monsoon.

On the 1st January 1943, Wavell, who that day had been promoted to the rank of Field Marshal, was told by Sir John Dill that the Generalissimo, while making the necessary arrangements to concentrate the Chinese divisions in Yunnan (though Stilwell was worried that the concentration would not be carried out in time), was insisting that the British kept their promise to have sufficient naval forces in the Bay of Bengal to ensure its control. He was saying that he would make all preparations to start on the date set and then see what the British would do about their promise; if the fleet appeared he would start, if not he would not move a finger. On the 11th Wavell received copies of the Generalissimo's cable of the 28th December and the subsequent exchange of views between the Prime Minister and the President. On hearing of these two telegrams from Chungking he remarked, 'Stilwell has not been able to make the naval position clear to the Generalissimo, who is perhaps taking the opportunity to put on us the blame for not carrying out an operation the difficulties of which he is now only beginning to appreciate, and into which he has possibly been unwillingly pushed by the Americans'. On the 16th Chiang Kai-shek

---
[1] Romanus and Sunderland, page 258.

THE CASABLANCA CONFERENCE

informed the President that, because of the lack of naval forces in the Bay of Bengal, he would not take part in the coming offensive.

About the middle of January 1943 Major-General G. E. Grimsdale, who had on the 6th November 1942 assumed command of 204 Mission in Chungking, arrived in Delhi.[1] He brought information of a growing difference of opinion between Brigadier-General C. L. Chennault, who was in command of the China Air Task Force (C.A.T.F.), and General Stilwell. Chennault claimed that his air force, which had been remarkably successful in China, might accomplish great results with a small expenditure of force, since the Japanese line of communication was very vulnerable to air attack. But he complained that Stilwell was starving and misusing the C.A.T.F. in order to build up a land offensive into China which could accomplish little. Wavell passed this information on to the Chiefs of Staff with the comment that he considered it probable that Chennault's proposals would show a better dividend than a Yunnan offensive since Japanese industrial capacity was insufficient to maintain their air forces and shipping, and that attacks on these would, at this stage, pay better than land operations; nevertheless this was an American issue into which it would be inadvisable for the British to enter.

A conference, attended by the Prime Minister, the President of the United States and their Chiefs of Staff, was held at Casablanca from the 14th to 23rd January 1943. It was called for the purpose of reaching definite conclusions on the general strategic policy for the year. The basic assumption underlying all decisions taken at the meeting was that the Allies' primary aim was to procure the defeat of Germany before undertaking a full-scale offensive against Japan. But, although the Far East took a secondary place in their deliberations, the situation there was discussed in some detail and important recommendations as to the future conduct of operations were made by the Combined Chiefs of Staff and accepted by the Prime Minister and the President. These recommendations covered operations against Japanese forces in Burma, the island-by-island advance on Japan in the Pacific and plans for the general disruption of Japanese communications.

The main aim in Burma was to be the mounting of operation 'Anakim' with the object of recapturing Rangoon, for which a

---

[1] Major-General Dennys, who commanded the mission at the outbreak of war had been killed in an air crash on the 14th March 1942. His place was taken by Major-General J. G. Bruce. The latter recommended the withdrawal of the small British contingents in China (see Chapter I) since they were not being properly used by the Chinese. They were withdrawn by October 1942 and in November General Bruce handed over the command of the mission to Major-General Grimsdale, who was at that time British Military Attaché in Chungking.

provisional date, the 15th November 1943, was fixed. This date was to be reconsidered in July 1943, because the essential naval forces, assault shipping and landing craft could not be made available until the late summer at the earliest. To facilitate the accomplishment of 'Anakim', the operations to secure bases in the Akyab area were to continue; they would be followed by a limited advance from Assam and across the Chindwin into upper Burma to gain bridgeheads from which further operations could be mounted and the air transport route to China improved. In the Pacific, without prejudice to 'Anakim', an advance towards the Truk–Guam line was thought practicable, particularly in conjunction with the operations in hand for the recapture of Rabaul, if time and resources allowed.[1] Of great importance to the general scheme were the plans for a concentrated attack on Japanese shipping on routes from Korea to Siam by submarines and by aircraft based in China. It was decided to provide additional transport aircraft for the ferrying of supplies to China and to build up the C.A.T.F. there to the maximum extent. This last decision was expected to show results in the spring.

Immediately the Casablanca conference ended, it was arranged that Lieut.-General H. H. Arnold (Commanding General, United States Army Air Force), Lieut.-General B. B. Somervell (Commanding General, United States Services of Supply) and Brigadier-General A. C. Wedemeyer (American Joint Planning Staff), accompanied by Sir John Dill, should visit Delhi and Chungking, returning by way of Delhi, with the object of forging a closer link with the Generalissimo and co-ordinating plans for the recapture of the whole of Burma. The party was due to arrive at Delhi on the 31st January.

On the 25th, Colonel F. D. Merrill (Stilwell's Chief of Staff) arrived in Delhi and told Wavell that the concentration of Chinese troops in Yunnan was behind schedule, but that Stilwell hoped the offensive might still be launched on the 1st March. If it did not take place, he proposed to cancel the operation from Ledo but keep forward one Chinese regiment to cover the construction of the Ledo–Myitkyina road, which would be pushed ahead as rapidly as possible.

On the 30th, Wavell received from the British Military Attaché in Chungking a report that there were no signs of any reorganization of the Chinese forces in Yunnan, or of the arrival of the promised new army for the offensive of the 1st March. Most of the air transport operating across the Hump was engaged in bringing in supplies for this mythical Yunnan army to the exclusion of petrol supplies for Chennault's air force. Chennault was saying that his aircraft were practically grounded, and that he would be unable to protect the air route for longer than another week unless petrol supplies were

[1] See Map 15.

immediately resumed. The report ended with the Military Attaché's personal opinion that the proposed offensive was most unlikely to start and even if started would be a fiasco. It was with this background that a conference at Delhi opened on the 1st February 1943.

The conference began with a report on the build-up of India as a base and on the existing state and proposed development of the communications from India to the north-eastern frontier, since all plans had of necessity to hinge on these.

The build-up of India as the base for the war in the Far East had been carried out as resources permitted during 1942. By December, agreement had been reached that the base should eventually be capable of maintaining a force equivalent to thirty-four divisions, thirty-one in India and three in Ceylon (this total to include 240,000 British troops), and an air force of eighty-five R.A.F. squadrons as well as fifteen squadrons of the 10th U.S.A.A.F. The base was to be laid out so that India could maintain the forces required for the defence of her North West Frontier, for internal security and the troops under training within her boundaries, as well as the forces operating on her north-east frontier and any expeditionary force which might be despatched from Indian ports against Japanese-held territories. In January 1943, agreement was reached that the size of the force required for 'Anakim' would be one armoured and ten infantry divisions, one tank brigade and an air force of seventy-six squadrons.

Early in 1943, arrangements were made to start work on improving the ports in India to enable them to receive increased quantities of goods from overseas and to fit them for mounting expeditionary forces. Work was also begun on the construction of four reserve bases to hold thirty days' requirements of all kinds for the forces allotted to 'Anakim', and also for the internal needs of India. These bases were: No. 1 Reserve Base at Lahore to maintain all troops in north-west India; No. 2 at Benares, for the maintenance of forces in Assam, eastern Bengal and Arakan[1]; No. 3 at Panagarh (between the towns of Asansol and Burdwan), for the maintenance of forces supplied through the port of Calcutta; and No. 4 at Avadi (twenty miles west of Madras) for the maintenance overseas of forces supplied through the port of Madras.[2] These reserve bases were to be stocked with goods brought in from overseas at west coast ports, and from the many central depots holding commodities produced within India Command and by the Indian munition factories.[3] In addition a

---
[1] See page 53.
[2] See Map 4.
[3] See Appendix 24.

transit area (a miniature of the Avadi base) was to be constructed at the port of Vizagapatam and the existing transit area at Calcutta expanded.

On the lines of communication to the north-east frontier much had been done during 1942 to improve the roads. Although work had been proceeding on it for some time, an Assam access road, running from the broad gauge railway system at Siliguri to the vehicle ferry at Jogighopa in Assam, could not be ready for use in time for the projected operations and thus all vehicles had to be carried by rail to Bongaigaon or Amingaon. The roads from Bongaigaon to the Jogighopa–Goalpara vehicle ferry, and the Assam trunk road south of the Brahmaputra from Goalpara and Pandu (Gauhati) to Ledo, as well as the new spur from Golaghat (near Jorhat) to Dimapur, had all been brought up to a single-way all-weather standard. The Imphal Road, which had been made a two-way all-weather road as far as Imphal and was being extended to Tamu, had already reached Palel as a single-way road and it was estimated that it would be completed by the end of the monsoon. It was then to be extended to Sittaung. A new road was under construction from Imphal to Tiddim and, as a one-way fair-weather road, had reached Milestone 82 beyond Imphal, about half way to Tiddim.[1] The Ledo road had been constructed to a point some three miles east of the Pangsau Pass and was progressing at the rate of half a mile a day. The roads from Tamu to Sittaung, from Imphal to Tiddim and the Ledo road through Shingbwiyang to Mogaung and Myitkyina were eventually to be brought to an all-weather two-way standard. In eastern Bengal, a one-way fair-weather road had been constructed from Comilla through Chittagong and Cox's Bazar to Maungdaw, and was to be converted into a one-way all-weather road when possible.

The capacity of the railways to and in Assam and eastern Bengal in February 1943 was as shown on Sketch 17. Owing to damage by the 1942 floods, the capacity of the railway between Bongaigaon and the important ferry at Amingaon (which could carry 250 wagons a day and an additional 700 tons a day transhipped on flats) had been reduced from fourteen to eleven trains each way daily, and the inland water transport system on the Brahmaputra was still working much below capacity owing to the shortage of power units and barges; nevertheless much more could be delivered at railheads and river ports than could at that time be taken forward by the existing roads. On the basis of the three ton lorry, the only type of load-carrying vehicle then available, the Imphal and Ledo roads could not maintain more than two and a half to three divisions each. It was planned to increase the capacity of the Imphal Road by introducing a system

---

[1] See Sketch 16.

of road traffic organization under which a loaded lorry went from end to end of the road, a fresh driver taking over at each stage. There would be continuous day and night running, no waste of time on the turn-round, and driver operating only on stages they knew. This would speed up delivery and enable better arrangements to be made for the maintenance of the vehicles.[1] If, however, the three ton lorry with its two and a half ton pay load could be replaced by a lorry with a five to six ton pay load, the roads would be able to carry forward all that the railways and rivers could deliver, and this would be sufficient to maintain a maximum of about five divisions on each of the two roads. Larger lorries were thus badly needed.

Steps had been taken to improve the capacity of the transportation system as a whole. Arrangements had been made for some of the river craft and barges which had been sent to Iraq to be returned to India, but it was doubtful whether these could be released in time to undertake the sea passage before the 1943 monsoon; they could not therefore be counted on for use in Assam till late in the dry weather of 1943–44. Work was in hand to improve the operational efficiency of the Assam and eastern Bengal railways, which was expected eventually to increase their carrying capacity by about twenty per cent. Orders had been placed in the United Kingdom for locomotives, port equipment and river craft, but very little had been received during the past twelve months. The greatest difficulty was still the shortage of locomotives.[2]

By February 1943 great progress had been made in the construction of airfields. The immensity of the task can be gauged by the fact that at one time in 1942 over a million men were engaged on this work. Despite the considerable delays caused by the Congress disturbances in August 1942, out of the total of 220 new airfields under construction approximately 100 had been completed to an all-weather standard, though some were without all their buildings, and 60 were ready for use in dry weather[3]. Owing however to the nature of the ground, the construction of the airfields in Bengal had lagged behind the rest of the programme, and it was estimated that these would not be fully ready until the middle of April.

There was one other administrative matter which affected all future planning. India (including Ceylon) relied on outside sources for aircraft, for the greater part of her engineering and transportation requirements, for military equipment and vehicles and for many of the raw materials required by her industry. She therefore needed a regular supply of goods from overseas. This meant the allocation

---

[1] See Appendix 24.
[2] See pages 188–89.
[3] The cost of the airfield programme when completed came to £92 million.

from the Allied shipping pool of a monthly quota of tonnage. When 'Anakim' was first mooted, it became clear that a considerable shipping tonnage over and above normal requirements would be necessary during each month of 1942 and 1943 in order to provide India with the wherewithal to undertake the proposed operation.

Experience had shown that there was approximately a four-month interval between the time that stores were shipped from the United Kingdom or the United States and the time they were in the hands of the users in India. Assuming therefore that 'Anakim' would be launched in November 1943, and that time would be allowed for troops to be trained in the use of new weapons and equipment before that date, everything required for 'Anakim' had to be shipped from Britain or America by June 1943 at the latest. When the conference at Delhi opened in February, it was estimated on this basis that some 183,000 tons of shipping would be necessary (60,000 tons from the United Kingdom and 123,000 from the United States) each month from February to June inclusive, and after that 160,000 tons each month. This tonnage would be over and above that needed for the normal monthly troop convoys[1], and the conveyance between March and August 1943 of 45,000 airmen (needed to complete the expansion of the R.A.F. in India) and the reinforcing formations and units required for 'Anakim'.

The tonnage allotted to India up to November 1942 had not been far short of the figure of 183,000 tons a month, but during December 1942 and January 1943 it had fallen to about a third of this amount. It was clear to the conference that unless the tonnage allotted could be raised at once to the figures indicated, which were considered to be the minimum, it would not be possible to mount 'Anakim' during the dry season 1943–44. In making these calculations, it was assumed that the equipment and stores would be provided by due date and shipped in an order of priority laid down by India Command, and further that all losses during the sea voyage would be made good as quickly as possible.

Bearing in mind these administrative factors, the conference set out to consider what could be attempted towards the recapture of Burma both before the 1943 monsoon and during the dry weather of November 1943–May 1944. Stilwell told the conference that he had planned to have twenty-six Chinese divisions ready in Yunnan by the end of March, some of which he proposed to use for an offensive into Burma. The progress of the concentration had been very slow

---

[1] A troop convoy (known as W.S. convoy) left the United Kingdom each month for the Middle East and India. The monthly convoy usually carried 7,000 reinforcements to India to replace normal wastage.

and the state of readiness was less than he had hoped. He therefore felt that, if the offensive were launched in March, it would not be strong enough to achieve its object. Consequently he proposed to confine activity from China to patrols, thus giving the Chinese troops time to train, and to wait until the monsoon was over before launching the proposed offensive into upper Burma. But he would continue the construction of the Ledo road with a view to extending it as far as possible by the end of the monsoon; the Japanese, he said, had begun to build a road from Myitkyina to Tengchung.

Wavell explained that he hoped it might be possible for IV Corps to attack the Kalewa–Kalemyo area by the end of March or early April, but it would not be possible to carry out a further advance before the monsoon broke. It had been his intention to send 77th (L.R.P.) Brigade across the Chindwin to the Katha area, and perhaps across the Irrawaddy, in support of the Yunnan offensive, and had concentrated it at Imphal for this purpose. If, however, this brigade were used at a time when no major offensive was in progress, there was the risk that it might be lost, and in any case its special training and tactics would be revealed to no purpose. With the postponement of the Yunnan offensive he had now to decide whether it would be better to use this specially trained force immediately, or save it for more effective use in conjunction with a main offensive at the end of the year.

The question of British naval action in the Bay of Bengal, which the Generalissimo continued to raise, was also discussed and it became evident that no large scale naval operations would be possible before the monsoon. Stilwell explained that the Generalissimo's insistence on this was due to his fear that the Japanese would considerably reinforce Burma by sea during the offensive. The conference agreed that, until the Eastern Fleet could be brought up to a state which would enable the Allies to regain command of the sea, it would not be possible to prevent the Japanese from bringing reinforcements into Burma by sea. Their difficulties could, however, be increased by the use of submarines in the Bay of Bengal and by stepping up air attacks on the docks and shipping in Rangoon and on communications in Burma.

The conference came to the conclusion that it was essential that the whole of Burma should be reoccupied in one season, namely the dry period from the 1st November 1943 to the 15th May 1944. It was agreed that, until the beginning of the 1943 monsoon, the activities of the Allied forces should be confined to attacks by submarines on the Japanese sea line of communication to Rangoon; limited offensive operations from Yunnan so as to gain positions for an offensive after the monsoon; limited operations from Ledo to cover the construction of the road which was to be pushed forward as far as

w

possible towards Mogaung; an advance from the Imphal area to the Chindwin between Sittaung and Kalewa, followed by raids east of the river with a view to establishing bridgeheads; operations to gain control of the Chin Hills; the capture of Akyab and if possible Ramree Island; air attacks on river shipping and internal lines of communication, airfields, and port installations and shipping at Rangoon; operations to maintain local air superiority and to destroy enemy aircraft; the completion of airfields and administrative preparations in India as rapidly as possible; and operations by American aircraft from bases in China against Japanese shipping.

The outline plan for the capture of Burma in the dry weather of 1943–44 was to include an offensive from Yunnan towards the Mandalay area by about eleven Chinese divisions each 10,000 strong; an advance from Ledo towards the same area by the Chinese corps which was being trained at Ramgarh; an advance by three British divisions from the Tamu–Kalewa area towards Mandalay; a series of assaults by British forces along the Arakan coast on Ramree Island (if not already taken), on Sandoway and Gwa with the object of capturing airfields, on Taungup to open the way for an overland offensive to Prome, and on the coast opposite Bassein to open the way for the capture of that town and the airfields in that area, and finally a direct sea and airborne assault on Rangoon. The advance into upper Burma was timed for November 1943, the operations on the Arakan coast, including the capture of Bassein, for December 1943 and the attack on Rangoon for January 1944.

The conference finally agreed that the plan for the recapture of Burma could be carried out only if the Eastern Fleet were reinforced, particularly by aircraft carriers, and could meet the potential threat from the enemy naval forces based on Singapore; if the promised air reinforcements were sent as planned; if shipping tonnage, estimated at 183,000 tons a month for six months in addition to the monthly troop convoys, was provided from March onwards; if equipment and stores required for 'Anakim' were despatched by due date; and if certain reinforcements in men, aircraft and assault shipping were made available to India. These included one parachute brigade group, five assault brigade groups, two reserve divisions (one British), two hundred transport aircraft, two hundred and forty fighters, one hundred and twenty-five heavy bombers, ninety light and medium bombers and enough assault shipping, landing craft and crews to carry the five assault brigade groups.

Field Marshal Dill, General Arnold, General Stilwell and Brigadier-General C. L. Bissell (10th U.S.A.A.F.) then flew to Chungking to discuss future strategy with the Generalissimo. On the 6th and 7th February, accompanied by General Chennault (C.A.T.F.), they met the Generalissimo, his Minister for War (General Ho Ying Chin) and other Chinese senior staff officers. At the first meeting, General Arnold outlined the existing and contemplated measures for increasing the air lift from India to Chungking before the monsoon from the figure of 1,700 to 4,000 tons a month[1], provided that the facilities in China were promptly increased to match the increases being made in India; no firm commitment beyond these figures was possible at the moment. He said that a heavy bombardment group of thirty-five aircraft had already left the United States and was due to arrive in China during March; it would undertake four to six missions a month and attack vital Japanese targets and shipping. In addition, the United States was prepared to begin forming Chinese fighter and bomber squadrons to serve with the C.A.T.F. Sir John Dill then outlined the plans on which the British and American commanders had agreed in Delhi, and asked the Generalissimo for an assurance that the Chinese would carry out their part in the co-ordinated operations to pin down large Japanese forces in north Burma. The Generalissimo agreed to send letters to both the Prime Minister and the President giving the required assurance. During the course of the discussion, the Generalissimo was given to understand that adequate naval forces would be available to cover the proposed operations in the Bay of Bengal at the end of 1943.

On the 7th the Generalissimo, having promised that he would provide the additional terminal facilities for the proposed increase in the air lift, stated that China could not fully prosecute the war unless he were given by November 1943 an independent air force under Chennault, a monthly air lift tonnage from India of 10,000 tons and a minimum of 500 aircraft operating from Chinese territory. The administrative difficulties inherent in increasing the air lift from 4,000 to 10,000 tons per month, and in maintaining and operating a large air force in China, were explained to him, as also was the fact that the build-up of the air lift to a higher figure could be accomplished only over a considerable period of time: in fact that administration and supply were the determining factors. Despite these explanations, the Generalissimo reiterated that, although China was ready to play her part in the plan, the increased air lift tonnage demanded was essential and must be provided. Unless it and 500 aircraft were forthcoming by November, he could give no assurance of the success of the proposed campaign.

As soon as the Delhi conference was over, Field Marshal Wavell flew to Assam to see for himself the state of affairs in IV Corps area. He had to decide, now that there was to be no major offensive before the

---
[1] 2,250 tons for the Chinese Yunnan armies and 1,750 tons for the C.A.T.F.

1943 monsoon, how best to employ the corps during the remaining months of the dry season. What it could accomplish during the dry weather of 1942–43 on the Chindwin front depended largely on the progress in road construction. In the autumn of 1942, when an offensive by the corps into upper Burma was under consideration, it had been decided to construct two roads leading to the Kabaw Valley and the Chindwin: the Imphal–Tamu road (64 miles long) which could be extended by way of the Kabaw Valley to Sittaung and Kalemyo; and the Imphal–Tiddim road (162 miles long) giving access through Fort White and the Chin Hills to Kalemyo. Both roads would join the existing all-weather Kalemyo–Kalewa road at Kalemyo. The Tiddim road had certain obvious advantages in its approach to Kalemyo since it was screened by a mountain range throughout its length, whereas the road down the Kabaw Valley from Tamu was exposed to enemy interference from across the Chindwin. For this reason, priority had been given to the construction of the longer Tiddim road, which was to be covered by 17th Division, while 23rd Division patrolled the northern end of the Kabaw Valley and made arrangements to establish a brigade in the Sittaung area by mid-February 1943.[1]

At the time of Wavell's visit to the Assam front, the Tiddim road had been completed to an all-weather standard as far as Milestone 32, though the roadhead had reached Milestone 82; and the Palel–Tamu road needed considerable improvement it if were to remain usable during the monsoon, while its extension from Tamu had only just begun. After discussion with the Chief Engineer, IV Corps, Wavell recognized that with the engineering resources available the long Tiddim road could not be completed before the rains, and that there might be no reliable access road to the Chindwin in existence by the time the 1943 monsoon broke. Consequently he told Scoones that both 17th and 23rd Divisions were to be employed on road making, that engineering resources were to be diverted from other projects and that the activities of IV Corps for the remainder of the dry weather were to be restricted to offensive patrolling on a scale unlikely to precipitate a Japanese offensive. He directed Scoones to undertake an examination of the whole road construction problem, so that a decision on priorities could be reached in time to ensure the existence of at least one road to the Chindwin by the middle of May. As a result of this examination, all engineering resources were concentrated in March on the Palel–Tamu road, which was to be made a two-way all-weather road capable of taking three ton lorries by the break of the monsoon.

Wavell then flew back to Calcutta, where on the 9th February he met the Allied representatives, including General Ho Ying Chin, on

---
[1] See page 252.

their return from Chungking, and held a conference in order to ensure that the decisions reached at Casablanca, Delhi and Chungking were perfectly clear to all concerned. Ho Ying Chin explained that the Chinese planned to employ ten divisions (each 10,000 strong) from western Yunnan towards Myitkyina, Bhamo, Lashio and Kengtung, starting as soon as the roads had dried out sufficiently to allow of offensive operations, which he estimated would be about the end of October. Three Chinese armies, each of two divisions, would be held in reserve in the Kunming area to deal with any possible Japanese counter-thrust from Indo-China. Wavell said that the Chinese corps from Ramgarh and three British-Indian divisions, with one in reserve, would advance into upper Burma; one division was already operating in Arakan and five would be available for the contemplated seaborne operations against Rangoon, the details of which had still to be worked out. In all, ten British-Indian divisions would be available to operate against the Japanese in Burma during the dry season 1943–44.

Once again the Chinese representative emphasized that the provision of naval forces was essential and that without them success would be impossible, a view to which all present agreed. It was also recognized that the air lift tonnage should be increased as rapidly as possible by the provision of the necessary facilities at both termini, for these, not aircraft, would be the limiting factor. Wavell summed up this final conference by saying that the Allies were all in agreement, and that it only remained for them to press on, with the greatest possible energy, the preparations necessary to enable the battle to start immediately after the monsoon.

These conferences produced one quick result. On the 8th March President Roosevelt told the Generalissimo that the 14th U.S.A.A.F., separate from the 10th U.S.A.A.F., was to be formed in China under the command of General Chennault and built up to 500 aircraft as soon as they could be maintained; and that the air lift was to be expanded until 10,000 tons a month were being flown into China.[1] The 14th U.S.A.A.F. came into being on the 11th March 1943, but the supply of aircraft to bring it up to strength and the increased tonnage to be carried by the India China Ferry Command were to present the Combined Chiefs of Staff and Field Marshal Wavell with problems which exercised their ingenuity for many months to come.

While the Allies were considering their plans for a counter-offensive, the Japanese were reviewing their strategic policy. Their original plan was that, after the occupation of Burma, *15th Army* should stand on the defensive, since the western limit of the Greater

---
[1] Romanus and Sunderland, page 278.

East Asia Co-Prosperity Sphere had been fixed as the frontier between Burma and India.[1] The ease with which the early objectives had been gained led *Southern Army* to consider the possibility of an advance into north-east Assam, and on the 22nd August 1942 *15th Army* was ordered to draw up a plan for an invasion of Assam, which was to be called Plan 21. The intention was to exploit the successful campaign in Burma by continuing the advance at the end of the 1942 monsoon and striking the British-Indian army before it had had time to recover from the effect of its defeats, thus maintaining the initiative both politically and strategically *vis-à-vis* India.

The *15th Army* proposed that *33rd Division*, with certain units from *55th Division* attached, should advance on the axis Kalewa–Imphal–Kohima and occupy Dimapur and Silchar. The main body of *18th Division*, reorganized as a mechanized force, would then pass through *33rd Division*, advance to Golaghat and deal with expected British counter-attacks. At the same time, a detachment from *18th Division* would move up the Hukawng Valley on Ledo. On completion of these operations, *15th Army* would occupy defensive positions on the general line Golaghat–Silchar.

During the autumn, the plan was examined by the divisional commanders concerned. They one and all held the view that an advance by one bound into the heart of Assam would be extremely difficult, for the lack of transport and communications would impose insuperable administrative obstacles. Towards the end of 1942, however, the critical situation which had developed in the south and south-west Pacific led *Imperial General Headquarters* to direct *Southern Army* on the 23rd December to suspend all work on Plan 21. Nevertheless, in order to be prepared in case the operation were ordered at a later date, *15th Army* as the responsible formation in Burma continued to plan, collect information, improve communications and build up reserves. The official Japanese policy for Burma for the dry weather 1942–43, however, remained defensive.

---

[1] See Volume I, Chapter V.

Map 12

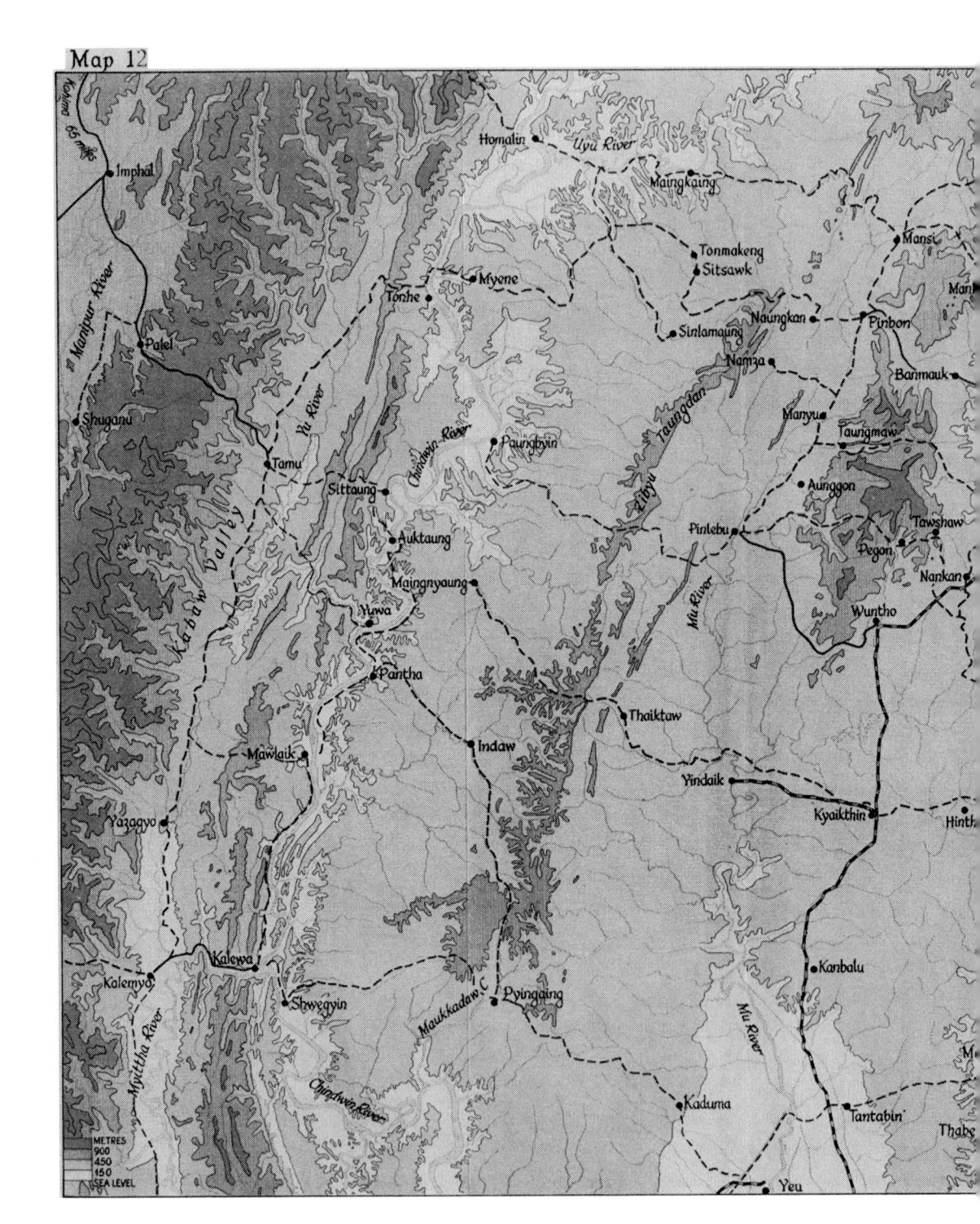

Map 12
BHAMO-TAMU
February-May 1943

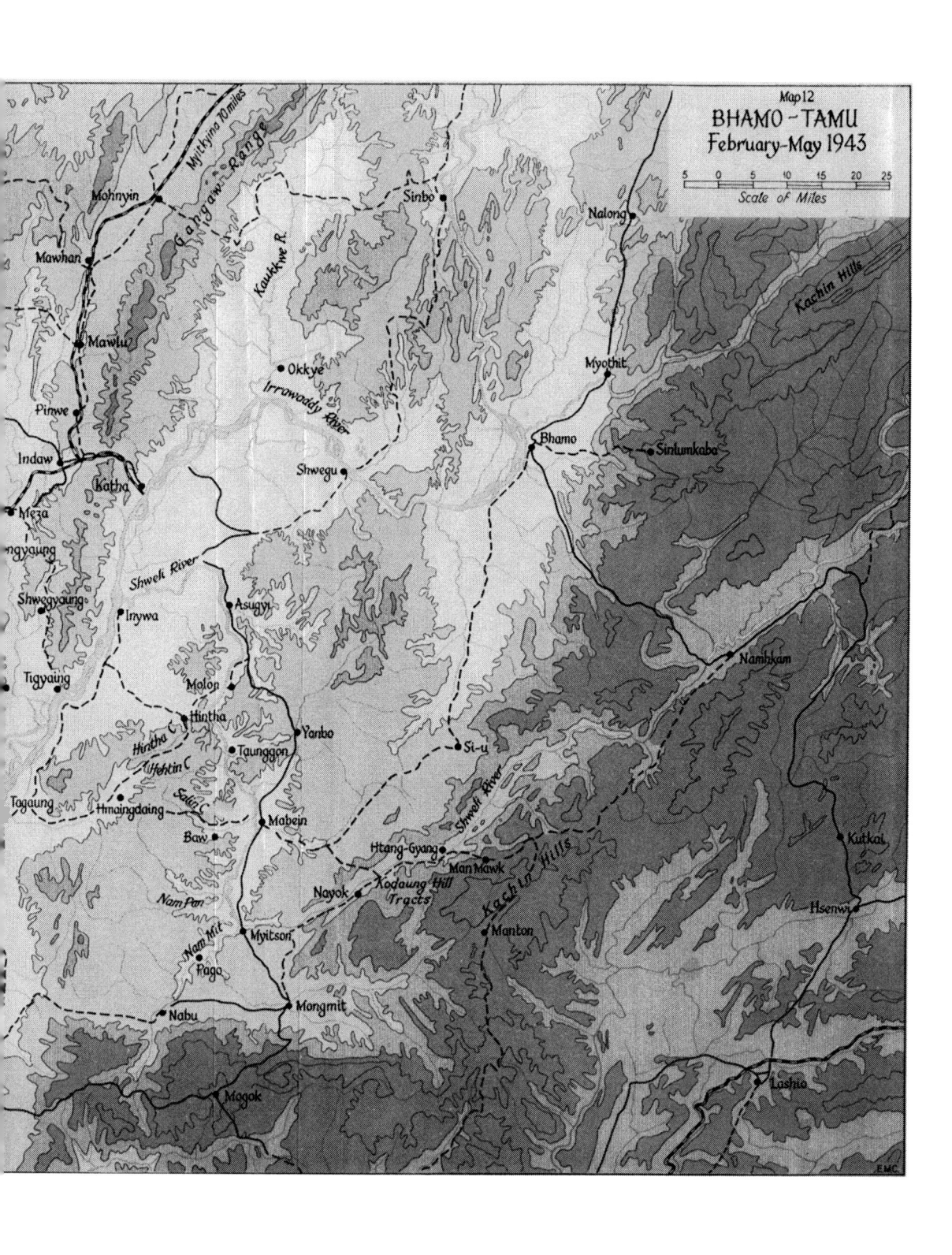

CHAPTER XVIII

THE FIRST CHINDIT OPERATION

(February–April 1943)

See Maps 12 and 14

WHEN after the Delhi conference Field Marshal Wavell visited Assam, he had to consider how best to employ 77th (L.R.P.) Brigade. He had originally intended that, co-ordinated with the advances by the Chinese armies from Yunnan, the Chinese-American forces from Ledo and IV Corps across the Chindwin, it was to enter Burma about the middle of February through IV Corps front. It was to cut the railway between Shwebo and Myitkyina, harass the enemy in the Shwebo area and, if circumstances were favourable, cross the Irrawaddy and cut the enemy communications with the Salween front. The final stage of the proposed operation was left to be decided in the light of events, but the brigade was to be withdrawn to India before the onset of the monsoon, unless the general situation indicated the possibility of its remaining in, living on, and operating from the dry belt of Burma throughout the rains. The abandonment of the main offensive meant that the operation would lose its strategic value, and Wavell had now to decide whether or not to continue with it.

At the end of January 1943 the Japanese were thought to have four or five divisions in Burma disposed as under: *18th Division* in the Shan States astride the Taunggyi–Kengtung road; *56th Division* on the Salween front, astride the Burma Road; *55th Division* in the area Myitkyina–Bhamo–Shwebo–Katha; *33rd Division* (less one regiment in Arakan) on the Chindwin, responsible for the Kabaw and Myittha valleys; and a fifth, and unidentified, division in the vicinity of Rangoon. It was considered that the Japanese intention at that time would be to stand on the defensive, that they would concentrate on the defence of the Chindwin and Salween fronts and that the division in the Myitkyina–Katha area would be very sensitive to any threat to its lines of communication.

Brigadier Wingate put forward six reasons for going on with the operation: firstly, the whole theory of employment of long-range penetration groups had to be tested and proved; secondly, the brigade had been raised and specially trained for an operation to take place in early 1943 and any delay might cause deterioration both physical and psychological; thirdly, the proposed operation would provide an opportunity for finding out the chances of getting Burmese co-operation in the liberation of their country—a subject on which opinion was diverse; fourthly, it would prevent the Japanese starting an offensive towards the Fort Hertz area[1]; fifthly, it would stop enemy infiltration across the Chindwin; and finally, the incursion of the brigade would confuse and interrupt any Japanese plan for an offensive towards Assam.

There was much to be said for these arguments. Wavell, however, had to consider whether the risk of losing all or part of the brigade on a mission of no strategic value, in order to prove whether this type of operation could succeed against the Japanese, would be balanced by the experience gained, and whether it was wise to use this new technique by itself and thus lose the value of surprise when it was used later as a part of the main offensive. After weighing up all the arguments Wavell came to the conclusion that, although it was theoretically wrong to employ the brigade before a follow-up by the main forces could take place, the valuable information and experience which would be gained was well worth the risk. Accordingly, he instructed the brigade to leave Imphal on the 8th February with its objectives unchanged. At the same time he gave instructions that a second similar formation (111th Brigade) should be raised and trained in India.

During January the brigade had been moved forward from central India to Imphal, where it had come under command of IV Corps, and an air supply detachment of transport aircraft from 31 Squadron, R.A.F., had been moved to the airfield at Agartala in eastern Bengal. Three months' reserve had been accumulated at this airfield; an army staff with a section of expert packers had been installed and a rear base for the expedition established under the direct control of Eastern Army.[2] While the brigade was on its way to Imphal, supply dropping exercises had been held and had proved to be very satisfactory. They all took place at night since it was thought that, to avoid detection and almost certain interception, drops could be carried out only under cover of darkness.

Wingate realized that before he could reach the railway, which was his objective, he first had to overcome the obstacles of the Chindwin River and the Zibyu Taungdan, a range of steep hills lying between it and the Mu River valley; in this valley, moreover, lay Pinlebu and Pinbon where he could expect resistance. He then

---

[1] The detachment at Fort Hertz was organizing Kachin Levies and attempting to gain control of the country as far south as Sumprabum.

[2] See Appendix 25.

had to cross a further range of hills through which there was only a limited number of routes to choose from, all of which passed through defiles. He had, therefore, to plan his operation in such a way that the Japanese would be given the least possible warning of the movement of his force across the Chindwin and the Zibyu Taungdan, and be misled as to his real intentions.

He decided to divide his force into two groups.[1] The Northern (main) Group, consisting of his own headquarters, the Group and Burma Rifles Headquarters and five columns (Nos. 3, 4, 5, 7 and 8), numbering some 2,200 all ranks and 850 mules, was to cross the Chindwin at Tonhe, traverse the range to the Pinbon–Naungkan area and, moving south-east, strike the railway between Bongyaung and Nankan. After carrying out demolitions, the group would make for Tigyaing to cross the Irrawaddy. The Southern (subsidiary) Group, consisting of Group Headquarters and two columns (Nos. 1 and 2), numbering some 1,000 all ranks and 250 mules, was to cross the Chindwin thirty-five miles further south at Auktaung, move south-east across the hills to Thaiktaw, blow up the railway at Kyaikthin and then cross the Irrawaddy near Tagaung and make for Mongmit.

The Southern Group was to cross the Chindwin one day in advance of the Northern Group. Since the crossing was close to enemy posts known to be in the Mawlaik area, it was hoped that the Japanese would be led to believe that this column was part of an orthodox flank attack on Kalewa. To strengthen this deception, IV Corps was to send a company of Patiala infantry, supported by some mountain guns, in advance of the Southern Group to simulate an attack on Pantha, and a battalion (4/5th Mahrattas) down the Kabaw Valley to Yazagyo. At the same time Major J. B. Jeffries, commanding 142nd Commando Company but wearing the badges of rank of a Brigadier, was to show himself conspicuously in the area south of Auktaung with a view to making the Japanese think that the Southern Group was moving south instead of east. To mislead the enemy still further, Headquarters 2nd Burma Rifles (part of the Northern Group) was to cross the Chindwin at Tonhe on the 13th February. Under cover of these diversions, the Southern Group was quietly to disappear into the hills on its way to Kyaikthin. The Southern Group was to receive daylight supply drops on both the 14th and 15th near Auktaung (in sight of the enemy posts) and cross the river on the nights of the 14th/15th and 15th/16th. It was hoped in this way to induce the Japanese to think that the crossing at Tonhe, if they discovered it, was intended to distract attention from the crossing further south.

---

[1] See Appendix 26 for composition of 77th Brigade.

The march to Palel was made openly by day and from there to Tamu by night. Wingate issued his final instructions and his stirring Order of the Day at Tamu.[1] The brigade then divided into its two groups and, moving by night, each advanced to its respective crossing point over the Chindwin. On saying farewell to the Southern Group, Wingate made a slight but important change in his original plan. His parting words to Lieut.-Colonel L. A. Alexander were, 'I shall meet you at Tagaung Taung' (a group of hills east of the Irrawaddy between Tagaung and Hmaingdaing). The daylight supply drops on the 14th and 15th took place, and the Patiala infantry crossed the river as planned on the afternoon of the 14th without meeting with opposition. The Southern Group crossed on the following two nights and on the 16th the Mahrattas made contact with the enemy in the Kabaw Valley. The Chindits had their first skirmish on the 18th near Maingnyaung and inflicted some casualties. Some of the mule loads were lost and the group was delayed by having to make a detour to the south over difficult country; as a result it did not reach Kyaikthin till the 2nd March, well behind its schedule. On approaching the railway it split up, Group Headquarters and No. 2 Column moving down the branch line from Yindaik and No. 1 Column moving parallel with it some miles further north. No. 1 Column succeeded in destroying a railway bridge some four miles north of Kyaikthin. But Group Headquarters and No. 2 Column were ambushed that evening some three miles west of the railway and, owing to a misunderstanding about the rendezvous, No. 2 Column lost cohesion and dispersed. Most of the men eventually recrossed the Chindwin. Some however joined up with Group Headquarters and No. 1 Column on the 7th at the original rendezvous near Hinthaw; the whole party then moved towards the Irrawaddy. They reached Tagaung on the 9th March and completed their crossing unopposed on the 10th.

The Northern Group began to cross the Chindwin at Tonhe on the 14th February, and Headquarters 2nd Burma Rifles moved to Myene, where the first supply drop took place. In the course of sixteen sorties during the three nights from the 15th to the 18th, some 70,000 pounds of supplies were dropped. The drops were made in open country, for neither Wingate nor the R.A.F. thought that supply dropping was possible in jungle; chance later on proved them wrong. The main body crossed the river unopposed and by the 18th reached Myene where it picked up its supplies. By the 22nd the whole group was concentrated at Tonmakeng. While waiting there for a supply drop on the night of the 24th/25th, Wingate sent three columns (Nos. 3, 7 and 8) to attack Japanese troops reported to be

---

[1] See Appendix 27.

in Sinlamaung.[1] The enemy had just left and the columns, after breakfasting on Japanese supplies, returned to Tonmakeng, taking with them a horse and an elephant with its mahout, which later proved to be most useful.

On the 26th, Wingate decided to move on towards the Mu River valley avoiding the known tracks. One column (No. 3) again moved south towards Sinlamaung and, crossing the hills to Namza, reached Manyu on the 1st March. The main body followed a little-used track which reached the river about half-way between Naungkan and Pinbon. Its march had to be made in single file and took three days, but by evening on the 1st March it was bivouacked some five miles west of Pinbon which, as it knew by that time, was held by the enemy. Wingate then decided that the main attack on the railway should take place as soon as possible, and ordered No. 3 Column (Major J. M. Calvert) and No. 5 Column (Major B. E. Fergusson) to move by separate routes to the railway at Nankan and Bongyaung respectively to carry out the planned demolitions. The remaining columns of the group were to create diversions which would draw the Japanese away from the railway. No. 4 Column (Major R. B. G. Bromhead) was to ambush the road running north from Pinbon and then, bypassing the town, link up with Wingate at Indaw. At the same time No. 7 Column (Major K. D. Gilkes) and No. 8 (Major W. P. Scott) were to demonstrate towards Pinlebu, which was known to contain an enemy garrison. In addition to drawing the Japanese away from the railway, these moves were designed to convince them that the brigade's object was to invest Pinlebu as a prelude to an advance by 23rd Division.

On the 4th, No. 4 Column was about to move towards Indaw when Wingate, having abandoned his proposed attack on the town, ordered it to link up with the main force in the Pinlebu area.[2] The column on its southward move clashed with the enemy. In the ensuing action mules and equipment were lost and Bromhead, finding himself without wireless, extremely short of ammunition and unable to contact the rest of the group, decided to make his way back to the Chindwin. Meanwhile No. 8 Column had made a series of demonstrations near Pinblebu supported by No. 7; these, together with the bombing of Wuntho and Pinlebu by the R.A.F. on the 4th, at Wingate's request, had the desired effect and induced the Japanese to reinforce Pinbon from Banmauk and Pinlebu from Wuntho, thus drawing troops away from the railway.

---

[1] Reports had reached Wingate on the 18th that there were enemy garrisons in both Homalin and Sinlamaung.

[2] This change of plan was due to information that the track to the railway at Nankan by way of Aunggon and Pegon was not guarded by the Japanese.

While the main body of the group was carrying out these diversions, No. 5 Column, moving by way of the Taungmaw valley, reached Tatlwin on the 5th. The following day, after a brush with an enemy patrol to the west of the railway, the column destroyed a bridge at the station and blocked the track by dynamiting the gorge south of the village. No. 3 Column, moving through Pegon, had reached the vicinity of Nankan on the 4th and, after waiting till the 6th to synchronize with No. 5 Column, blew up two large railway bridges and cut the railway track in more than seventy places, in spite of minor enemy interference. Both columns then moved to their respective rendezvous east of the railway in readiness to make their dash to the Irrawaddy.

On the 6th, the day of the attacks on the railway, Wingate, with his headquarters and Nos. 7 and 8 Columns, was still in the Aunggon area. On the 7th he moved eastwards through Pegon to Tawshaw, which he reached on the 9th. There he remained for a few days awaiting news of the rest of his force, for he had not heard from Southern Group since its successful attack on the railway on the 3rd. He realized that by now the Japanese would probably have discovered his intentions and the strength of his force, and would have set forces on the move to isolate and destroy it. In the month since the start of the operation, his columns had successfully attacked the railway and, although he had had for the time being to abandon his plan to seize the landing ground at Indaw, he had dealt the Japanese communications several shrewd blows with comparatively little loss, and all ranks had gained much experience. Notwithstanding his successes, he considered that what he had achieved so far was not a full and convincing demonstration of the value of long-range penetration groups and that his task would not be completed unless he contained considerable Japanese forces for the remaining two months of the dry weather.

With these considerations in mind he concluded that, if he could remain in the area, carry out sustained attacks on the railway and seize the Indaw landing ground, he would not only provide convincing proof of the efficacy of his methods, but would at the same time contain the Japanese. He therefore contemplated forming a permanent rendezvous in the mountains north of Wuntho, where he could collect all his columns and whence battle groups could raid the enemy's communications. On the evening of the 9th, however, he heard that the Southern Group was in the process of crossing the Irrawaddy at Tagaung. He also received signals from Nos. 3 and 5 Columns, which were approaching the river, saying that crossings in the vicinity of Tigyaing would be unopposed if made at once, and asking for permission to proceed. With part of his force already across the river, and knowing that it might be difficult for those columns east of the railway to retrace their steps, Wingate gave permission for Nos. 3 and 5 Columns to cross the Irrawaddy and decided to follow with the remainder of the force.

After his success on the railway, Fergusson (No. 5) began to move as quickly as possible to the Irrawaddy, for he was short of supplies and could not, he thought, arrange for a supply drop with any safety until he reached the vicinity of Hmaingdaing, some twenty miles beyond the river. The column reached Tigyaing on the 10th. On that day Japanese aircraft dropped leaflets on the village saying that the bulk of the British forces had been surrounded and destroyed on the 3rd March and calling upon the column to surrender.[1] Knowing that the Japanese would be closing in on him, Fergusson hurriedly bought as much food as he could get and, having commandeered local craft, began his crossing. Late in the afternoon he heard that a force of some two hundred Japanese was approaching the town from the south. The crossing was however completed under cover of darkness without loss, and the column began its move to the vicinity of Hmaingdaing where the next supply drop was to take place.

No. 3 Column was not so fortunate. Calvert, very short of supplies, arranged for a drop on the 11th on the banks of the Meza River, twelve miles south of Nankan. Hearing during the day of the presence of Japanese troops in both Tawma and Tigyaing, he decided to slip between them by night. At 2 a.m. on the 13th he reached the western side of the Irrawaddy, some six miles south of Tigyaing. His move however had been discovered and at 7.30 a.m., just as the column was moving off to the point selected for the crossing, the Japanese made a surprise attack. While the column waited for the local craft which the Burma Rifles platoon was collecting, a hastily organized rearguard put up a fierce resistance. The crossing began at noon but, as the Japanese were obviously bringing up reinforcements, it soon became clear that most of the mules and supplies would have to be left behind. The column succeeded in crossing by evening with all its weapons, wireless sets and demolition explosives, but some of the mules, ammunition and medical equipment had to be left. Having arranged for its wounded to be left with some Burman villagers, the column moved eastwards on the 15th and joined up with No. 5 Column some four miles southeast of Hmaingdaing.

Meanwhile, Wingate with Nos. 7 and 8 Columns had arranged for a supply drop on the 13th in an open area some three miles south of Tawshaw. A party of Japanese however was found to be holding a

---

[1] The Brigadier's badges lost by Major Jeffries during the ambush at Kyaikthin on the 2nd/3rd March may have been picked up by the Japanese, and led them to the conclusion that they had destroyed the force headquarters.

defensive position near the southern end of the selected area. The supply aircraft arrived just as an attempt to drive the enemy away had failed. The signal to drop was not therefore given and they returned to their base. This was the first intimation the Japanese had that the Chindits were being supplied by air. Wingate then crossed the railway between Bongyaung and Nankan and on the 16th reached Shwegyaung, where supplies were safely dropped. The following day, the group moved down to the Irrawaddy and on the 18th it crossed unopposed two miles south of Inywa.

What effect had Wingate's operations had on the Japanese? In the middle of February the dispositions of *15th Army* were: *56th Division* astride the Burma Road on the Salween front, *18th Division* in the Sumprabum–Myitkyina–Katha–Maymyo area, *33rd Division*, less one regiment, covering the Kabaw and Myittha valleys, and *55th Division*, plus one regiment from the *33rd*, in Arakan.[1] It was thus the *18th* and *33rd Divisions* which were affected by the British incursion into upper Burma. The *18th Division* was disposed with *114th Regiment* at Myitkyina, *56th Regiment* at Maymyo and *55th Regiment* at Katha, with one battalion split up into small garrisons in Naungkan, Sinlamaung, Pinbon, Pinlebu, Wuntho and Indaw, with standing patrols at a number of points along the railway line. In order to get information on the nature of the ground along the Chindwin River valley, the divisional commander had given orders early in February for the garrisons at Naungkan and Sinlamaung to be moved to Homalin and Tonhe respectively. The moves began about the time that 77th Brigade was crossing the Chindwin. The *33rd Division* was disposed with *215th Regiment* at Aungban near Kalaw and *214th Regiment* at Pakokku.[2] The *215th Regiment* was responsible for the Chindwin between Mawlaik and Kalewa, and had one battalion forward at Kalemyo with small detached garrisons at various places along the river. The *214th* was responsible for the Myittha valley.

The first reports of the British crossing of the Chindwin were received from Pantha; columns of unknown strength were said to have crossed the Chindwin near Sittaung about the 11th February. The commanders of *15th Army* and both *18th* and *33rd Divisions* assumed that these columns were small groups, possibly of intelligence personnel, and consequently took no action, leaving the subordinate commanders on the spot to deal with the situation. Although he heard nothing from his forward posts at Sinlamaung and Naungkan,

---

[1] The *55th Division* was at the time short of one regiment which was in the south-west Pacific.

[2] See Map 9.

the commander of *55th Regiment* at Katha gradually became aware, from the engagements at Pinbon and Pinblebu, that British forces of about brigade strength were operating in the Mu River valley, and ordered his two battalions at Katha to locate and engage them in the area west of Indaw. Both battalions moved off in this direction but failed to find them.

It was not until they received reports of the demolition of the railway bridge at Kyaikthin on the 3rd March that the commanders of *15th Army* and *33rd Division* began to revise their original estimate of the strength and intentions of the British forces across the river. The *33rd Division* then ordered *215th Regiment*, less its battalion in the Kalemyo area, to move to Kyaikthin. At the same time, *18th Division* ordered *III/56th Battalion* to move from Maymyo to Tagaung along the eastern bank of the Irrawaddy. The two battalions of *215th Regiment* concentrated at Kyaikthin, and sent patrols up the railway line to make contact with the troops of *55th Regiment* at Wuntho. Unable to discover the whereabouts of the British forces, and unaware that they were being supplied by air, the regimental commander concluded they had moved westwards, and turned in that direction. After a few days of fruitless search, the regiment was ordered to return to its base at Kalaw. At that time *15th Army Headquarters* believed that the main part of the British force had been destroyed in the Mu River valley and along the railway line, and that the remnants had withdrawn westwards.

About the 10th March, however, information reached *55th Regiment* that some British forces had been seen crossing the Irrawaddy, and shortly afterwards the Japanese realized that they were being supplied by air. The *15th Army*, concluding that Bhamo was their objective, ordered *18th* and *56th Divisions* to hem in and destroy those who had crossed the Irrawaddy. The commander of *55th Regiment* had already sent, on his own initiative, two battalions from the Indaw area to move to the Irrawaddy, south of its junction with the Shweli at Inywa, with orders to destroy any other British forces attempting to cross the river. It was portions of these two units which arrived just too late to prevent the crossing of Nos. 3 and 5 Columns in the Tigyaing area. On receipt of its instructions from *15th Army*, *18th Division* ordered *III/56th Battalion* to accelerate its move to Tagaung and *II/56th Battalion* to guard the crossings over the Shweli River north of Myitson. Simultaneously, *56th Division* ordered *II/146th Battalion* to move to Yanbo and the lower regions of the Shweli River in order to co-operate with units of *18th Division*.

It will be seen that, as Wingate had planned, the first information received by senior Japanese commanders came from the action of the deception parties and had provoked little reaction. This, and the fact that the Southern Group was moving along the boundary between two Japanese divisions resulted in the group meeting little opposition till it reached the railway. The Northern Group would have met the Japanese before reaching the Mu River, but for the lucky chance that the garrisons at Naungkan and Sinlamaung happened to be on the march to the Chindwin at the same time as the group was moving in the opposite direction. Thus it was that both groups reached the Mu River valley and the vicinity of the railway without being discovered and were completely free to strike when and where they would.

The actions at Pinbon, Pinlebu and Kyaikthin made the Japanese search to the west in the hope of cutting the columns' supply routes. It was not till the abortive supply drop south of Tawshaw on the 13th disclosed the fact that the British forces were being supplied by air, and the columns were actually seen crossing the Irrawaddy, that the enemy fully realized the scope and nature of the British operation. Assuming that if some parties were making the crossing of the Irrawaddy, others had already crossed or would cross, the Japanese then planned to confine and destroy the British within the triangle formed by the Irrawaddy on the west, the Shweli River on the east and the roads from the Irrawaddy to Mongmit and Myitson in the south.

In anticipation of operations east of the Irrawaddy, Wingate had agreed to a request by Captain D. C. Herring (who commanded a platoon of the Burma Rifles composed of Kachin tribesmen attached to No. 7 Column) that he might move into the Kachin Hills in order to find out whether the tribesmen were prepared to support the British, and whether the time was ripe to raise a revolt against the Japanese occupation.[1] Herring with his party left the Northern Group on the 1st March to make his way into Kachin territory. Wingate had arranged that, on completion of the reconnaissance, Herring was to meet a representative of the Southern Group on the 25th, at a rendezvous on the upper Shweli River, some eight miles north-east of Htang-Gyang. He hoped that Herring's report would help him to decide whether or not to move into Kachin territory after crossing the Irrawaddy.

Herring reached the Kachin Hills to the north-east of Bhamo on the 15th without encountering any Japanese. He decided that a Kachin rising on a much larger scale than expected could be organized and a guerilla campaign launched against the Japanese, provided that arms and equipment could be supplied by air. He had

---

[1] No. 7 Column had been earmarked to penetrate the Kachin Hills, if circumstances permitted, and join with the Chinese forces across the Salween. Herring and his Kachins had been attached to this column for that reason. Herring, however, considered his men unsuitable for guerilla operations amongst Shans and Burmans; hence his request.

22. General Sir Claude Auchinleck.

23. Major-General O. C. Wingate.

24. Deciduous forest north of Shweli R. looking west towards Katha.

25. Supply drop by a Dakota (C.47).

not however been given a powerful enough wireless set, and was thus unable to pass on this information.[1] On the 19th he set off for the rendezvous, which he reached on the appointed date, having been helped by the Kachin tribesmen who everywhere received him with the greatest enthusiasm. He remained there till the 29th but saw no signs of any representative of the Southern Group, and it was not till the 18th April, when he made contact with Headquarters 2nd Burma Rifles far to the north, that he was able to report. By that time 77th Brigade had dispersed.

On crossing the Irrawaddy, Wingate was full of confidence. Although two out of his seven columns had dispersed, he had succeeded in damaging the railway and crossing both major river obstacles. Air supply, despite a few failures, had proved generally successful, and Herring with his Kachins would probably have prepared a good reception for the brigade in the Kodaung Hill Tracts. He felt that he was now entering the second and more fruitful phase of his operations. In an Order of the Day issued after he had crossed the river he held out to his men the prospect of rest among friendly tribesmen (presumably in the Kachin Hills). His optimism was to be short-lived, for he was soon to find that the country immediately east of the Irrawaddy and between it and the Shweli River was very different from his assessment of it. It proved at that time of the year to be a dry, hot belt of waterless and trackless forest, surrounded by country well served by motorable roads and tracks. By crossing the Irrawaddy he had disclosed his position and the Japanese, by patrolling the roads and rivers, were soon able to limit his activities. Wingate thus found himself trapped in a triangle formed by the Irrawaddy and Shweli Rivers and the east-west roads from Mongmit and Mogok to the Irrawaddy and, turn which way he would, could not extricate his columns as a cohesive fighting force.

Before crossing the river on the 17th, he had ordered Nos. 3 and 5 Columns to join forces, under the command of Calvert, and destroy the Gokteik Gorge viaduct on the Lashio road some fifty miles southeast of Mogok.[2] At that time he apparently thought that the Southern Group, in conformity with his original instructions, would be moving towards the Mongmit area and the rendezvous with Herring. With the eventual intention of moving to Mongmit himself, he moved his headquarters and Nos. 7 and 8 Columns southwards towards Baw where he had arranged for a supply drop for the 24th March. He

---

[1] There were no light-weight sets available in India with the requisite range. The only suitable sets were so heavy that the large artillery mules had to be used for their carriage. Had the reconnaissance party taken such a set, its mobility, and thus its chances of reaching its destination sufficiently far ahead of the main body in time to carry out its mission, would have been greatly reduced. Wingate decided to send it without a long-range wireless set and gamble on being able to receive its report at the selected rendezvous.

[2] See Map 9.

was soon to realize that matters were not developing as he had expected, since his columns reported that they had begun to encounter difficulties owing to the rapidly increasing activity of Japanese patrols and the growing exhaustion of their men and animals, both from the lack of water and from the need to be constantly on the move.

Meanwhile Alexander (Southern Group) and Dunlop (No. 1 Column), unable to gain touch with brigade headquarters by wireless[1], had been waiting in the vicinity of Hmaingdaing in accordance with Wingate's parting instructions at Tamu, expecting either to meet him or to receive orders. On the 15th March, Calvert bivouacked near them. Hearing from him that brigade headquarters was making for Baw, they moved there on the 16th in order to contact Wingate personally. But, unable to find his headquarters, they set out for Mongmit on the 18th and by the 22nd had reached the Nam Pan at a point some ten miles north-west of Myitson. The following day they received what proved to be their final supply drop and, at last, had a wireless message from Wingate which read, somewhat cryptically, 'Jesus remembers his little children'. At a loss as to its meaning, they decided to continue their move to the Mongmit area and make an attempt to reach the rendezvous with Herring.

On the 22nd, No. 5 Column also reached the Nam Pan and there met the Southern Group. Fergusson had reached the Nam Mit on the 19th, some four miles south-west of Myitson, to find the country alive with Japanese patrols and the town itself strongly held. He passed this news to Wingate, who arranged for the town to be heavily bombed that day and ordered the column to go to a selected point on the Nam Pan, where it was to receive a supply drop on the 23rd, and then move north to cover the southward advance of Nos. 7 and 8 Columns. This was to Fergusson a complete change of plan. No. 3 Column had also moved south and by the 23rd was near Pago on the Nam Mit where Calvert, learning that a Japanese battalion was patrolling the river between Myitson and Nabu, organized an ambush. During the day an enemy company walked into it and suffered heavy casualties without loss to the column. Having broken off the action, Calvert moved into the hills some eight miles to the south-west to rest his men and carry out reconnaissances before attempting to cross the Nabu and Mogok roads on his way to the Gokteik Gorge.

Meanwhile, IV Corps had questioned Wingate on the possibility of further operations. He had replied that he proposed to move eastwards into the Kachin Hills and operate towards Lashio—

---

[1] The Southern Group could communicate with brigade headquarters only when headquarters chose to communicate with it.

Bhamo. Scoones thereupon had warned him that this was not feasible because of the difficulty of air supply at such a distance, and suggested instead an attack on Shwebo. When Wingate said this was not possible as the Japanese had moved all boats from the Irrawaddy, he was ordered on the 24th to begin his withdrawal to India.

The same day an action developed from which a valuable lesson was learnt. Wingate had arranged for a supply drop to take place near Baw but, knowing that the Japanese were in strength at Mabein and suspecting that they might also be in the village, he blocked all access to it and gave orders that it was to be entered only in overwhelming force at first light. A party however blundered into it during the night and found it occupied. The enemy reacted sharply and Wingate had to lay an emergency flare path in the jungle some distance to the north-west. The aircraft duly arrived and began their drop. The pilots however became suspicious and, after parachuting two wireless operators and dropping only two days' rations, discontinued the operation. The group (headquarters and Nos. 7 and 8 Columns) then withdrew north-west along the Salin Chaung. Since the enforced change in the dropping zone at Baw had shown that supplies could be dropped successfully at short notice in jungle-covered country, an emergency drop was arranged for the 25th, and four days' rations, the balance of the abortive attempt at Baw, were safely received. The group then moved north to the Hehtin Chaung, where No. 5 Column rejoined it after an absence of nearly four weeks.

When on the 24th Wingate had been told to withdraw, he ordered No. 3 Column to return to the Chindwin independently, unless it were already very close to the Gokteik Gorge. He now decided to allow the Southern Group, which had begun to make for the rendezvous with Herring, to continue its movement eastwards, since it would tend to widen the area of operations and mystify the Japanese. On the 26th he sent the group a second message, also couched in biblical language, indicating that it was to make for the Kachin Hills. He then held a conference with his remaining column commanders to plan the retreat to India. As it was thought that there might be boats at Inywa, at the junction of the Irrawaddy and Shweli Rivers, he decided that the Northern Group (less No. 3 Column) should move there as quickly as possible in one body. He considered that the Japanese would not be likely to expect him to return to the point of his original crossing, and that with a fighting strength of some 1,200 men he would be able to overcome any opposition. In order to deceive the Japanese, he arranged for bogus supply drops to be made in the area between the Mongmit–Shwebo and Lashio–Mandalay roads. Since the withdrawal could not be carried out with the full complement of animals and equipment, owing to the time it would take to ferry them across the Irrawaddy, all non-essential equipment was dumped and all mules, except those required to carry wireless sets and other essentials, were turned loose. On the 27th the group moved off to the north, covered by a rearguard formed by No. 5 Column.

During the march the group became dispersed: Lieut.-Colonel L. G. Wheeler, with Headquarters 2nd Burma Rifles, reached a village some four miles from Inywa by the Shweli River, and Fergusson (No. 5) became involved on the 28th in a clash at Hintha in which he was forced to scatter his column and order it to rendezvous south of Inywa. The remainder of the group reached Inywa at 3 a.m. on the 29th to find that the Japanese were in force on the west bank of the Irrawaddy and that there were few boats. Although a few men succeeded in getting across, it soon became clear that the group as a whole would be unable to manage the crossing. Wingate thereupon decided that the moment had come to break it down to dispersal groups, which could fan out and cross the Irrawaddy more or less simultaneously on as extended a front as possible—a method for the withdrawal which had been fully discussed before the operation had been launched and was understood by all concerned. A final supply drop took place on the 30th in the jungle to the east of Inywa. Nos. 5, 7 and 8 Columns, Headquarters Burma Rifles and the dispersal groups from Wingate's and Northern Group's headquarters then began their individual efforts to get back to the Chindwin.

No. 3 Column and the Southern Group did not begin their return journey till some time later. Calvert was some five miles north of Nabu when on the 24th he received the order to withdraw. He decided to replenish his supplies from a dump which he had made near Baw on his way south, attempt to cross the Shweli and then either move into China or cross the Irrawaddy between Bhamo and Katha. On the night of the 27th/28th, having made an unsuccessful attempt to cross the Shweli at a point some five miles south of Taunggon, he arranged for a final supply drop and then, with great reluctance, divided his column into ten dispersal groups and started them on their homeward trek.

The Southern Group meanwhile had crossed the Mongmit–Nabu road without meeting with opposition and, having abandoned most of its mules, moved south-east into the hills. There on the 26th it received the biblical message from Wingate which read, 'Remember Lot's wife. Return not whence ye came. Seek thy salvation in the mountains. Genesis XIX'. This message was interpreted to mean that the group was to carry on to the rendezvous with Captain Herring and then make for the Kachin Hills. By the 31st March, it was on the escarpment overlooking the Mongmit–Mogok road, about half-way between the two villages. It was soon located by the Japanese and a spirited engagement ensued, in which British fighter aircraft called up by wireless from Agartala took part. The group, after giving its probable route and asking for a supply drop at Manton on the 6th April, then abandoned its remaining mules, destroyed its wireless sets and slipped across the road. On the 6th April, however, it found itself at least one day's march from Manton and had the mortification of seeing the supply aircraft circling over the village and being unable to attract their attention. This unfortunate event naturally had a most depressing effect on morale, and Alexander and Dunlop decided that the only course was to withdraw to India. They came to the conclusion that the best plan was to cross the Shweli and attempt to reach Fort Hertz, but on the 10th the crossing over the Shweli at Htang-Gyang was found to be held by the Japanese, and the idea of reaching Fort Hertz had to be abandoned. The group, as a formed body, then turned back and began to retrace its steps to the Chindwin.

It is not within the scope of this volume to follow the fortunes of the dispersal groups and the various columns on their return journey. It suffices to say that Headquarters Burma Rifles and Nos. 5 and 8 Columns managed to cross the lower reaches of the Shweli in the vicinity of Asugyi. The Burma Rifles eventually reached Fort Hertz having collected Captain Herring's party on the way; Nos. 5 and 8 Columns, turning north, crossed the Irrawaddy between Bhamo and Katha and reached the Chindwin at Tonhe and Tamanthi respectively.[1] No. 7 Column, moving south, crossed the Mongmit–Myitson road and then moved north-east to Nayok on the Shweli. Having crossed the river, the column moved into the Kachin Hills and eventually reached Paoshan in China, from where it was flown back to India in American aircraft. The majority of the Southern Group and Wingate's and Calvert's parties reached the Chindwin at various points between Tonhe and Auktaung, crossing ground already familiar.

Some of the columns which had lost their wireless equipment were unable to call for air supply, but, despite this, several parties received supplies after having been located by reconnaissance aircraft. The help received in this way included in one instance the dropping of rubber dinghies, lifebelts, medical supplies and rations to a column attempting to cross the Shweli River. After crossing the Irrawaddy, one column was unable to make progress, encumbered as it was with its wounded and sick. Most of these had no chance of reaching India unless they could be rescued by air. The column commander therefore arranged for a small jungle clearing to be prepared and for

---
[1] For Tamanthi see Map 14.

smoke signals and strips of parachute silk to be displayed on the ground. These were seen from the air and, after supplies had been dropped and an improvised runway marked out, a transport aircraft with fighter escort arrived, and landed safely on the uneven ground. Seventeen sick and wounded men were taken on board, and after a hazardous take-off the aircraft returned safely to base. The risk was too great for more aircraft to attempt landings, but further supplies including a complete outfit of clothes and boots were dropped with a note explaining the position and giving advice about routes, gained from columns which had already reached safety. The remainder of the column, then in good condition, continued its westward march. Columns which received no supplies by air had to rely on local purchase; the troops passing through the Kachin Hills fared best, the friendly tribesmen giving them food, shelter and guides as well as much information of enemy movements.

Of the 3,000 men who had marched into Burma at the beginning of February, about 2,182 had returned to India some four months later. They had marched at least 1,000 miles and some had covered as many as 1,500. They had penetrated far into enemy territory. They had endured intense physical trials and, although they had had to abandon most of their mules and equipment, they had returned with their personal arms and equipment. So ended a remarkable exploit.

Before we consider whether the decision to employ 77th Brigade in an unsupported operation proved, in the light of events, to be sound and what effect the operation had on the course of the war, its planning and conduct must be examined. Wingate, with a wealth of experience of guerilla and partisan warfare behind him, had the vision to see what might be accomplished in Burma by properly trained and organized mobile columns supplied by air and thus free to move at will. He had also the determination to get his ideas accepted and brought to fruition against all opposition. To him must go the credit for the concept, organization and training of a long-range penetration force and the careful planning which enabled him to get his brigade behind the enemy lines without opposition.

His initial plan, however, lacked flexibility, for it is clear that he intended to take the whole or part of his force across the Irrawaddy and even contemplated moving into the Kachin Hills and possibly into China. Thus, at a time when conditions in Burma under Japanese occupation were largely unknown and the reaction of the enemy could only be surmised, he issued definite orders before the operation began which committed at any rate part of his force to crossing the

Irrawaddy. Further, although there was a wealth of first-hand knowledge of the climate and topography of Burma then available in India, both he and the Joint Planning Staff in Delhi appear to have formed a completely false picture of the nature of the country which would be encountered between the Irrawaddy and the Shweli Rivers.

The crossing of the Chindwin, the measures to deceive the enemy and the move to the Mu River valley were well planned and co-ordinated. By the time the railway had been reached and damaged, the Japanese, as Wingate had anticipated, had very little idea of the scope, size and intention of the operation. When he halted on the 9th March to await news of the progress of the Southern Group and of Nos. 3 and 5 Columns, Wingate still retained the initiative and was in a position to take full advantage of the enemy's ignorance of his position and intentions. It is clear from the records that he was fully aware of the strength of his position, but it was at this point that the inflexibility resulting from the issue of orders too far in advance affected his actions.

The Southern Group, by crossing the Irrawaddy as ordered, had focussed Japanese attention on the river line and given them not only a clue as to his intentions but a definite, instead of indefinite, line on which to concentrate their forces. This, and the fact that Nos. 3 and 5 Columns were also close to the river and were about to cross it, compromised his freedom of action. He realized that the Japanese, having been alerted by the attacks on the railway and the crossing of the Irrawaddy by the Southern Group, might make it difficult for Nos. 3 and 5 Columns to get safely back into the shelter of the more secure hill country west of the railway, if ordered to do so. For this reason and because both column commanders were anxious to carry out the original plan and thought they could get across the river unopposed if they crossed at once, he allowed them to proceed and followed them with the remainder of his force nine days later.

Determined to prove his theories to the utmost and urged on by what might be accomplished in the Kachin Hills, if Herring's report on conditions were favourable, Wingate, despite the fact that his motto was 'Don't be predictable', played into the hands of the Japanese by committing his entire force to the triangle between the Irrawaddy and Shweli Rivers. What would have happened had he decided to divide his force, allowing the Southern Group and Nos. 3 and 5 Columns to operate east of the river while, with the rest of the brigade, he moved to a rendezvous north of Wuntho, as he had earlier contemplated, can only be a matter for conjecture. Such a decision would at least have kept the Japanese guessing, and would have prevented them from concentrating on the destruction of the columns which had crossed the Irrawaddy. By following his advanced columns across the river, he committed his entire force to an area unsuited to its characteristics and to operations which had very little value.

Once he had taken the decision to concentrate the whole brigade across the Irrawaddy, it appears from his subsequent actions that he had no clear picture of his object. He afterwards complained that the slowness with which Nos. 3 and 5 Columns and the Southern Group carried out his orders after they had crossed the Irrawaddy resulted in the whole brigade being bunched in the restricted area between the Irrawaddy and Shweli Rivers. That the columns which had crossed the Irrawaddy early in March moved slowly was not their fault. Nos. 3 and 5 Columns did not receive their specific orders to move to the Gokteik Gorge till the 17th, some time after they had crossed the river. Wingate had told the Southern Group to meet him in the Tagaung Taung area. Although he later ordered it to meet Herring on the 25th at the rendezvous on the upper Shweli, he did not cancel his earlier instruction, unless the first obscure biblical message was meant to do so. In the circumstances Alexander and Dunlop were perfectly justified in waiting there for orders, provided that they left themselves sufficient time to get to the rendezvous. When they did get some idea of Wingate's whereabouts, they moved on the 16th towards Baw to get orders and it was not till the 18th, the day on which Wingate himself crossed the Irrawaddy, that they began their move to Mongmit and the rendezvous. It was thus that eight precious days were lost.

Both the Southern Group and Nos. 3 and 5 Columns soon found themselves further delayed by the nature of the country and the fact that the Japanese, by this time fully alerted, had had time to surround the Irrawaddy–Shweli triangle. Had Wingate realized what the country east of the Irrawaddy was like, divided his force on the 9th March, as he had then contemplated, and given orders to those columns already across or crossing the river to push on to the area east of Mongmit at once, the bunching of the brigade in the trap would have been avoided.

But he failed to appreciate the position correctly and neither Calvert nor Fergusson received orders till eight days later. As for the Southern Group, he appears to have looked upon it purely as a detachment for deception purposes and consequently largely ignored it. After it had crossed the Irrawaddy he sent it only the two cryptic messages and finally, in order to cover his own retirement, despatched it on a mission which might well have resulted in its destruction. All he accomplished after he took the decision to move his whole force across the Irrawaddy was to gain experience in crossing a major obstacle.

It is fortunate that Wingate did not receive Herring's report, for he subsequently made it clear that, had he received it, he would have marched into the Kachin Hills in spite of the warning he had received from IV Corps that supply dropping would become more difficult the further east he moved. Although the Kachins would undoubtedly have come to his aid, he would in the circumstances have been unable to hold the area and would have been forced to withdraw to China. The loyal Kachins would then have had to suffer the retaliatory measures which the Japanese would have taken to ensure that they would never again assist the British. Spared this fate, they were able greatly to assist the L.R.P. groups when they returned in 1944, and other organizations both then and later.

We must now consider what effect the operation had on the conduct of the war as a whole. In the circumstances in which it was launched, the operation had no strategic value from the British point of view, and the military damage and casualties inflicted on the Japanese were small compared with the effort involved. Nevertheless the fact that the Chindits had entered upper Burma, damaged the railway, inflicted casualties and been able to return, albeit without their equipment and animals, acted as a welcome tonic and to a large extent offset the failure in Arakan.[1] Moreover it showed that properly trained and well led troops could infiltrate through difficult jungle country and operate in the heart of enemy-held territory. The experience gained was later to prove of great value.

By far the most valuable lesson learnt was that forces could be maintained in jungle country by air supply, demanded by wireless as and when required. Provided air superiority could be retained and sufficient transport aircraft made available, an offensive into Burma across the grain of the country was no longer of necessity tied to roads which could only be built slowly and with great difficulty. Given these two conditions, commanders were to find themselves once again with strategical and tactical freedom. Thus, even though the enterprise had little or no strategical value, it was well worth the effort expended.

There was at the time, however, a possibility that much of the value of the lessons learnt would be lost if they were not kept in their proper perspective. The danger was not lessened by the fact that Wingate, as the originator and leader of the first successful land operation against the Japanese in Burma, found himself almost overnight a national hero. In the circumstances there was a risk that his unorthodox views might be over-exploited in the belief that in his methods, and his alone, the road to victory lay and that, not for the first time, a form of private army would result. Indeed, shortly after

---
[1] See Chapter XX.

his return to India, Wingate, a most determined and uncompromising man, began advocating the raising of six L.R.P. brigades of specially selected men and the building-up of a separate organization under his personal command for their administration, supply and training.

In the early stages of the operation, the Japanese thought that the British force which had crossed the Chindwin consisted either of intelligence groups or perhaps small guerilla units sent into Burma to reconnoitre their defensive lay-out and to create confusion within the country. After the crossing of the Irrawaddy, the Japanese thought that the Chindits might attempt to join up with the Chinese in Yunnan. But when the columns began to withdraw towards Assam, they came to the conclusion that the object had been a reconnaissance to gain practical experience in the jungle and tactical and topographical information in preparation for a major offensive at a later date, and to build up in Burma a network of intelligence agents.

The Japanese have since admitted that the Chindits were difficult to deal with effectively, particularly as they moved only by night and avoided places where the inhabitants might possibly be unfriendly. Hampered by the lack of up-to-date information, by the fact that their troops were facing a type of operation which had never been envisaged (and for which they had not been trained) the Japanese believed nevertheless that on balance the counter-measures they had adopted were successful, in that all the British columns suffered loss and were compelled to disperse and withdraw under very difficult circumstances. On the credit side, they claimed that they were able to find out a great deal about the preparations in the Imphal area for a British offensive by interrogating their Chindit prisoners. They also realized that the hitherto pro-Japanese attitude of many of the local inhabitants in Burma had to some extent changed. On the debit side, the Chindits had frustrated their plans for the period February–May 1943, which they had proposed to use to rest their troops and to give them battle training in preparation for the next phase of the war.

It is now known that at the end of 1942 Japanese policy in Burma was entirely defensive.[1] They had no intention of infiltrating across the Chindwin, capturing Fort Hertz or launching an offensive into Assam. Thus of the six reasons put forward by Wingate in February, three were invalid.[2] Nevertheless the operation had one unexpected effect on the Japanese. Their adoption of a defensive policy had been based on the assumption that the movement of large bodies of troops

---
[1] Plan 21 was abandoned on the 23rd December. See page 308.
[2] See pages 309–10.

across the grain of the country anywhere along the Assam–Burma frontier would be extremely difficult. In consequence, by the end of 1942, they had concentrated their formations on the general axis of the Myitkyina–Mandalay railway and in the highlands of the Shan States, with detachments at Akyab and watching the Chindwin crossings in the vicinity of Kalewa.

As a result of the Chindit operation, the Japanese commanders and staffs in Burma, and in particular General Mutaguchi (commander of *18th Division*), who was shortly to succeed to the command of *15th Army*, saw that movement across the grain of the country was not after all impossible and that they had an insecure flank on the Chindwin. They also began to realize that their assessment of the capabilities and battle efficiency of the British-Indian troops, based on their comparatively easy victories in 1941–42, was incorrect. They could therefore no longer uphold the view that, provided the main tracks across the frontier were held, infiltration into Burma could be prevented and that any offensive on a large scale across the Assam–Burma frontier by either contestant would be impossible unless the main roads were repaired and improved. *Headquarters 15th Army* immediately set to work to review the problem of the defence of upper Burma and came to the conclusion that the British, having evolved new tactics, might repeat the operation on a larger scale in conjunction with a major offensive. They thereupon decided that, in the circumstances, an offensive-defensive policy was sounder and more economical than a purely defensive one; a decision which was eventually to lead them to disaster.

The incursion into Burma by the Chindits was thus instrumental in bringing about a change in Japanese military thinking and led them to adopt a new policy in Burma. This was the outstanding outcome of the operation.

CHAPTER XIX

THE JAPANESE OFFENSIVE IN ARAKAN
(February–March 1943)

See Maps 11 and 13 and Sketches 9, 12, 13 and 14

IN Arakan 14th Indian Division, having tried unsuccessfully for a month to break through the Japanese defences at Donbaik and Rathedaung, was disposed at the end of the first week in February with 55th Brigade on the Mayu peninsula, 123rd Brigade east of the Mayu River facing Rathedaung and 47th Brigade in reserve. Soutcol (8/10th Baluch), with Tripforce under command, was in occupation of Kanzauk and Apaukwa in the Kaladan valley. In Calcutta on the 9th February, after his visit to IV Corps in Assam, Field Marshal Wavell discussed the situation in Arakan with General Irwin.[1] By this time it was known that the Japanese were being reinforced; units of a new regiment had been identified in the Rathedaung area and there were indications that another was moving along the Prome–Taungup track, which would bring their strength in Arakan to about a division. The increase in the enemy's strength as well as the time factor inclined Wavell to the view that there was little chance of capturing Akyab before the break of the monsoon. Nevertheless, he was determined to make another effort to clear the Mayu peninsula and told Irwin that he might use 6th British Brigade for that purpose. Irwin thereupon placed 71st Brigade of 26th Indian Division, then on the move to Maungdaw, at the disposal of 14th Division, gave instructions that 6th Brigade should be moved forward from Chittagong and ordered Lloyd to launch another attack on Donbaik as soon as possible after the 25th February, using 6th Brigade to co-operate with 71st Brigade in a 'coastwise operation'.

After the failure on both sides of the Mayu River early in February, Lloyd had realized that he had to make a supreme effort to break through at Donbaik as quickly as he could so that the coastal track, already completed to a point some two miles north of Donbaik, could reach Foul Point in time to enable 6th Brigade to assault Akyab before the bad weather set in. Assuming that superiority in

---
[1] See page 305.

numbers and fire power would enable him to overcome Japanese resistance on a narrow front, he ordered 55th Brigade to renew the attack on the 18th February, using four battalions (1/7th Rajput, 1/17th Dogra, 2/1st Punjab and 1st Inniskillings) supported by all the available artillery.

The attack was launched frontally by two battalions at 4.30 a.m. on the 18th, under cover of a timed artillery barrage. The 1st Inniskillings on the right occupied F.D.L. Chaung from the coast to M.17 and infiltrated into the Wooded Village area, but 2/1st Punjab on the left was held up by Japanese posts in M.18, M.16, S.4 and S.5, and suffered about one hundred and thirty casualties.[1] During the day, the enemy infiltrated westward down F.D.L.Chaung and reoccupied M.17. A second attack at 1 p.m. by the reserve battalion (1/7th Rajput), under cover of heavy artillery concentrations on S.4 and S.5, also failed. By evening all the attacking troops were back in their former positions and the day ended without any territorial gain. The 1/17th Dogra holding the left flank in the foothills had not been involved.

After this failure, Lloyd had no alternative but to undertake a general reorganization of his forces before making a further attempt to break through to Foul Point, and on the 20th he ordered 71st Brigade, which had by then reached Maungdaw, to relieve 55th Brigade. The latter was ordered to leave one battalion (1/17th Dogra) at Donbaik and move to Buthidaung in divisional reserve for a short rest before in turn relieving 123rd Brigade. In order to allow the commander of 71st Brigade to give his undivided attention to the problem of breaking through at Donbaik, 47th Brigade was ordered to take over responsibility for the area between the Mayu Range and the river.

On the Kaladan front, Soutcol, under command of 123rd Brigade since the 14th, was disposed with Headquarters 8/10th Baluch and two companies at Apaukwa, one company at Kyauktaw and one at Kanzauk.[2] Tripforce was at Paletwa with detachments at Daletme and Kaladan. On the 15th, 'V' Force reported an enemy column, 700 strong, at Ngamyinthaung, five miles east of Kaladan.[3] Lloyd thereupon ordered Tripforce to withdraw its detachment at Kaladan and concentrate at Paletwa. The withdrawal took place on the 21st and the Japanese immediately occupied Kaladan, thus interposing between Tripforce and Soutcol. The same day 'V' Force reported that Japanese reinforcements had been seen landing at Ponnagyun on the Kaladan River, and air reconnaissance provided evidence that work was in progress on a coastal road from Taungup towards

---

[1] See Sketch 13.
[2] See page 266.
[3] This was *I/213th Battalion* from Pakokku. See page 265.

Akyab. Force 'Z' was at once ordered to raid selected points along the coast.[1] On the 21st February, four motor launches carrying a platoon of infantry and a detachment of a field company made a surprise assault on Myebon.[2] They arrived at their objective without incident and some Japanese obligingly made fast the launches' lines before finding out their mistake. The jetties and a cargo ship were destroyed and the force got away unharmed. A similar raid on Kyaukpyu was planned for the 26th, but was called off after the force had met and sunk some enemy launches during its approach.

It had meanwhile become evident that the Japanese were taking an increasing interest in the area to the east of Rathedaung. Both on the 16th and 18th there were patrol clashes in the Kamai–Batarai area and two days later in the hills south of Awrama, uncomfortably close to the line of communication to Soutcol. Hammond appreciated, as it turned out correctly, that the Japanese were contemplating a counter-offensive to turn his left flank and isolate Soutcol, but Lloyd thought that his intended attack on Donbaik would fully occupy the enemy's attention and make such action unlikely.

Within a few days, however, Lloyd realized that 71st Brigade could not relieve 55th Brigade and be ready to attack Donbaik before the 26th February. Since at least a fortnight would be required after the capture of Foul Point to mount the amphibious attack on Akyab (the latest possible date for which was, owing to weather, the 15th March), Lloyd realized that there was no possibility of its capture before the monsoon and that the Japanese would be free to mount the counter-offensive that Hammond feared. He therefore told Irwin that, as the danger to his left flank was increasing, he considered he should adopt a defensive rôle and that no further attempt should be made to secure the tip of the Mayu peninsula.

Irwin discussed the situation with Lloyd on the 22nd. The following day he told Wavell that the enemy strength was increasing, that there was a growing threat to Lloyd's left flank and that any further attempt to occupy the whole of the Mayu peninsula would be unjustified. It could lead to no important result, would be costly in men and material and, if successful, would add to his difficulties should the enemy threat to the left flank develop. He had therefore ordered Lloyd to consolidate the positions gained, hold them until the monsoon made a withdrawal inevitable and prepare defensive lay-back positions in depth in the Indin area, at Buthidaung and Kyauktaw. He proposed to relieve 14th Division by 26th Division at the end of March or early April.

---

[1] See pages 260–61.
[2] See Strategic Map.

Wavell however disagreed with both Irwin and Lloyd, since he felt that a marked success was essential to restore the confidence of the troops in their ability to beat the Japanese. At a conference on the 26th February at Delhi, he directed Irwin to order Lloyd to use 6th Brigade to attack in conjunction with 71st Brigade and overwhelm the Donbaik position by sheer weight of numbers.

Lloyd ordered 6th Brigade to take over part of the Donbaik front from 71st Brigade by the 8th March. He planned that 6th Brigade would attack down the coastal plain, 71st Brigade along the foothills and 47th Brigade along the summit of the range. When Donbaik had been captured, 47th Brigade, assisted by 71st Brigade, was to take Laungchaung. On being told of this plan, Irwin overruled it. In a letter to Wavell on the 9th he explained that he considered it amounted to two independent operations, that 6th Brigade's attack would vary very little from the unsuccessful attacks which had preceded it and 71st Brigade, if it were to do its task properly, would be utterly exhausted. He himself had gone forward and, after studying the ground for an hour, had told Lloyd that the first phase of the attack was to be highly concentrated, made on very limited objectives after detailed planning, and that the rôle of nearly every man was to be taken into account. Since the preliminary planning would require at least a week, he had given the 15th March as the earliest date for the attack.

In the same letter, however, Irwin struck note of warning, saying,

> 'As regards the operations on the Donbaik front, however successful the first phase attack should be (if we carry it out) I cannot forecast a rapid ending to operations to clear the Mayu peninsula and therefore I reach the conclusion that from the point of view of training and experience, the attack should go on whatever the result and whatever the cost, but from the general point of view I doubt whether it will materially affect the general situation on the 14th Divisional front and may, in fact, tie up forces which we would be glad to have east of the Mayu'.

The operation was not however to take place for, as will be seen, the Japanese gained the initiative by a counter-offensive east of the Mayu River and forced a redisposal of 14th Division.

While 14th Division had been trying in vain to break the enemy resistance at Donbaik and Rathedaung, the Japanese *55th Division* had been gradually assembling at Akyab.[1] By the end of February all but one battalion had arrived, but animals, baggage and those unfit to march had been left behind in south Burma. General Koga, whose instructions were to occupy the general line Htizwe–Indin in

---
[1] See page 265.

26. Lieut.-General N. M. S. Irwin, Major-General W. L. Lloyd.

27. Lieut.-General Takishi Koga.

28. Animal Barge on the Naf River near Tumbru.

29. Kalapanzin valley near Buthidaung looking south-west, Mayu Range in the background.

THE JAPANESE PLAN

order to protect Akyab, had decided to launch a counter-offensive as soon as his division was concentrated. He saw that he had an opportunity of defeating the British piecemeal for, holding as he did a central position at the confluence of the Arakan rivers, he could concentrate rapidly in any area he chose, while geographical conditions divided his opponents into three separate groups. He therefore planned a three phase advance. In the first the Kaladan valley was to be secured. In the second the British forces on the east bank of the Mayu River were to be defeated by an encircling attack based on Rathedaung, aided by a flank attack across the hills from the Kaladan valley. In the third the Mayu River and the range were to be crossed and Indin occupied so as to cut off the British forces in the Donbaik area.

He organized his division into four columns[1]: the *Kawashima Column* (one battalion less one company) to defend Akyab Island; the *Uno Column* (three battalions less one company) to hold Laungchaung and Donbaik on the Mayu peninsula; the *Tanahashi Column* (two battalions and a mountain artillery regiment) to attack British forces north of Rathedaung on the 7th March, and the *Miyawaki Column* (one battalion plus one company and a mountain artillery battalion) to concentrate at Banyo on the 6th March and on the following day advance to secure the Kaladan valley, where it was to join hands with *I/213th Battalion* which had crossed the Chin Hills and occupied Kaladan on the 21st February.[2] Leaving a company to garrison Kaladan, the *Miyawaki Column* was then to cross the hills by the Awrama track to Mrawchaung, where it would make contact with the *Tanahashi Column*. When the eastern bank of the Mayu River had been secured, the *Tanahashi Column*, taking under command a battalion from the *Uno Column* and one from the *Miyawaki Column*, was to cross the river and move on Indin, while the *Miyawaki Column*, now reduced to one battalion, operated east of the river and protected the right flank. The *Uno Column* (reduced in strength to two battalions) would meanwhile advance north from Donbaik.

Reports that the Japanese intended to launch an offensive on the 25th February began to reach 123rd Brigade from 'V' Force and local inhabitants. Brigadier Hammond consequently withdrew 1/15th Punjab from its position facing Rathedaung to the general line Sabahta Chaung–Kyauktan to protect his exposed left flank.[3] On the 26th and 27th, patrols found strong Japanese forces in the

---

[1] For the detailed composition of these columns see Appendix 28.
[2] See page 265.
[3] See Sketch 12.

Thayetchaung and Nwatingok areas, and on the night of the 3rd/4th March Hammond withdrew the rest of his brigade from the hills north of Rathedaung to a position covering the crossings of the Ngasanbaw Chaung in the Htizwe–Kyauktan area and the western end of the track to the Kaladan valley.

On the 7th March Wavell wrote to Irwin saying:

> '. . . It looks as if the Japanese were going to make some sort of long-range penetration against our L. of C. from the direction of the Kaladan, but you should be able to deal with this; and a strong blow on the Mayu Peninsula and a real success here will do more than anything to help the situation. I should like to finish up this campaigning season with a real success which will show both our own troops and the Jap that we can and mean to be top dog.'

The same day, the *Miyawaki Column* attacked the Baluch company at Kanzauk and occupied the high ground between Kanzauk and Apaukwa. Colonel Souter (Soutcol) immediately recalled the detached company of 8/10th Baluch at Kyauktaw to Apaukwa, and asked for an air strike on the following day to support an attack on the high ground with the object of regaining touch with Kanzauk and re-establishing the line of communication to Htizwe. In spite of support by the whole fighter and bomber strength of 224 Group R.A.F. on the afternoon of the 8th, the Baluchis were unable to force their way through to Kanzauk. That evening Lloyd decided to evacuate the southern part of the Kaladan valley, and ordered the garrison of Apaukwa to fall back up the Yo Chaung and thence west to Buthidaung, and the garrison of Kanzauk through Awrama to Htizwe. The 1/17th Dogra of 55th Brigade, then in reserve at Buthidaung, was ordered to patrol the land and water routes from the east between Buthidaung and Taung Bazar, while 2/1st Punjab (also from 55th Brigade) reinforced 123rd Brigade in the Htizwe bridgehead.

Simultaneously with the offensive in the Kaladan valley, the *Tanahashi Column* attacked 123rd Brigade north of Rathedaung. Before dawn on the 7th, enemy forces landed west of Hkanaunggyi, occupied two small hills in the rear of the main position held by 10th Lancashire Fusiliers at Kanbyin, and began to push eastwards. Counter-attacks during the day, in which the Fusiliers suffered some sixty casualties, halted the eastward move but failed to dislodge the enemy from the two hills. On the 8th, the enemy drove 8/6th Rajputana Rifles across the Sabahta Chaung, and wrested the southern half of the sausage-shaped hill south of Nawlagyaw from 1/15th Punjab. Brigadier Hammond thereupon withdrew the right flank of 10th Lancashire Fusiliers to Ywathit, near the mouth of the Thaungdara Chaung.

The Japanese advance at Nawlagyaw was not pressed, and the track from the Kaladan valley remained open until the 10th March, by which time the garrison of Kanzauk had been safely withdrawn. The same day 2/1st Punjab arrived at Htizwe and during the night relieved the battle-weary 1/15th Punjab which had been continuously in action for five months. On the 12th, it was discovered that the Japanese had occupied Mrawchaung and were in the hills on either side of the Awrama track, thus threatening the northern flank of the bridgehead at Kyauktan. On the following night, they renewed their attacks in the Nawlagyaw area. During fierce fighting on the 13th, successful infiltration by small enemy parties forced 2/1st Punjab to withdraw to a new line facing southeast through the Point 199 feature. The same day the Japanese again attacked at the southern end of the bridgehead, but without success. That evening Brigadier Hunt with 55th Brigade Headquarters took over operational control from Brigadier Hammond but, as all the infantry of his brigade were already in the battle area, the strength of the force remained the same. His first act was to pull back the right flank of the bridgehead from Ywathit to the northern bank of the Thaungdara Chaung.

Realizing that the position of 55th Brigade in the Htizwe bridgehead was rapidly becoming precarious, and to free Lloyd's hands for the contemplated attack on Donbaik, Irwin decided on the 13th March to form a special headquarters (Mayforce) to take control, under Lloyd's general direction, of all operations east of the Mayu–Kalapanzin River. Mayforce, under command of Brigadier Curtis, came into being at midnight on the 14th/15th, but did not take over command of 55th and 123rd Brigades and operational control east of the Mayu River till the 19th.[1]

Lloyd had intended that 71st Brigade, after its attack on Donbaik, and 4th Brigade, then on its way by sea from Calcutta to Chittagong, should relieve 55th and 123rd Brigades during the second half of the month, but the position east of the Mayu River had become so dangerous by the 14th that he sent 71st Brigade to Buthidaung to reinforce Mayforce, leaving 1st Lincolnshire behind with 6th Brigade for the attack on Donbaik.

At dawn on the 14th, the enemy launched an attack on Kyauktan from the north-east which penetrated to the animal transport lines on the outskirts of the village. An immediate counter-attack by 2/1st Punjab drove the Japanese into the open at the point of the bayonet, where they were caught by accurate artillery fire. A wounded prisoner was found to belong to *II/112th Battalion* which had previously been identified in the Kaladan valley. Next morning, the Japanese managed to secure a bridgehead across the Thaungdara

---
[1] Brigadier Curtis had commanded 13th Brigade throughout the retreat from Burma.

Chaung near its mouth from which they could command the road from Htizwe to Thaungdara. At the same time they increased their pressure south-west of Nawlagyaw, forcing Hunt to evacuate Kyauktan on the night of the 15th/16th. After withdrawing across the Ngasanbaw Chaung at Kyauktan, 2/1st Punjab recrossed that night at Htizwe to form a two-battalion bridgehead with 10th Lancashire Fusiliers. This smaller bridgehead, supported by artillery fire from across the chaung, was held throughout the 16th while arrangements were being made to withdraw 55th Brigade that night to the Taungmaw–Zedidaung area, twelve miles to the north.

Next day, 71st Brigade moved forward from Buthidaung to Taungmaw to cover the withdrawal of 55th Brigade to the Buthidaung area where it was to be in divisional reserve; two motor launches and two landing craft patrolled the Mayu River to prevent the enemy crossing from Htizwe. On the 19th Brigadier Curtis (Mayforce), having taken control of operations east of the river, ordered 71st Brigade to take up a defensive position along the general line of the Aungtha Chaung east of Zedidaung and carry out offensive patrolling to the south. The same day 4th Brigade (Brigadier S. A. H. Hungerford) began to arrive at Maungdaw, and Lloyd ordered Tripforce to evacuate the upper reaches of the Kaladan valley and withdraw to the railhead at Dohazari.

Meanwhile, the removal of 71st Brigade from the Mayu peninsula had made it necessary to change the plan for the proposed attack on Donbaik. Brigadier R. V. C. Cavendish (6th Brigade) now had six battalions: his own four[1], 1st Lincolnshire (left behind by 71st Brigade) and 5/8th Punjab (loaned from 47th Brigade), supported by two field regiments. Information had been received that there were by this time three enemy battalions holding the Donbaik–Laungchaung area. In view of this considerable increase, and in accordance with Irwin's wishes, Cavendish ordered a deliberate attack to be made on the 18th March west from Shepherd's Crook down the F.D.L. Chaung[2], and southwards from the Knobs to Wadi Junction and North and South Promontories, starting at 5.40 a.m. in a series of timed phases, each with covering artillery support. The attack fared no better than those which had preceded it. The troops attacking westwards from Shepherd's Crook were unable to reduce the Japanese strong points along the F.D.L. Chaung, while those attacking southwards towards the Promontories, though making progress at first, had by-passed enemy posts which, in the very close country, they could not afterwards subdue. A night attack in the early hours of the 19th was no more successful. By

---

[1] The 1st Royal Scots, 2nd Durham Light Infantry, 1st Royal Berkshire and 1st Royal Welch Fusiliers.

[2] See Sketch 13.

HTIZWE BRIDGEHEAD

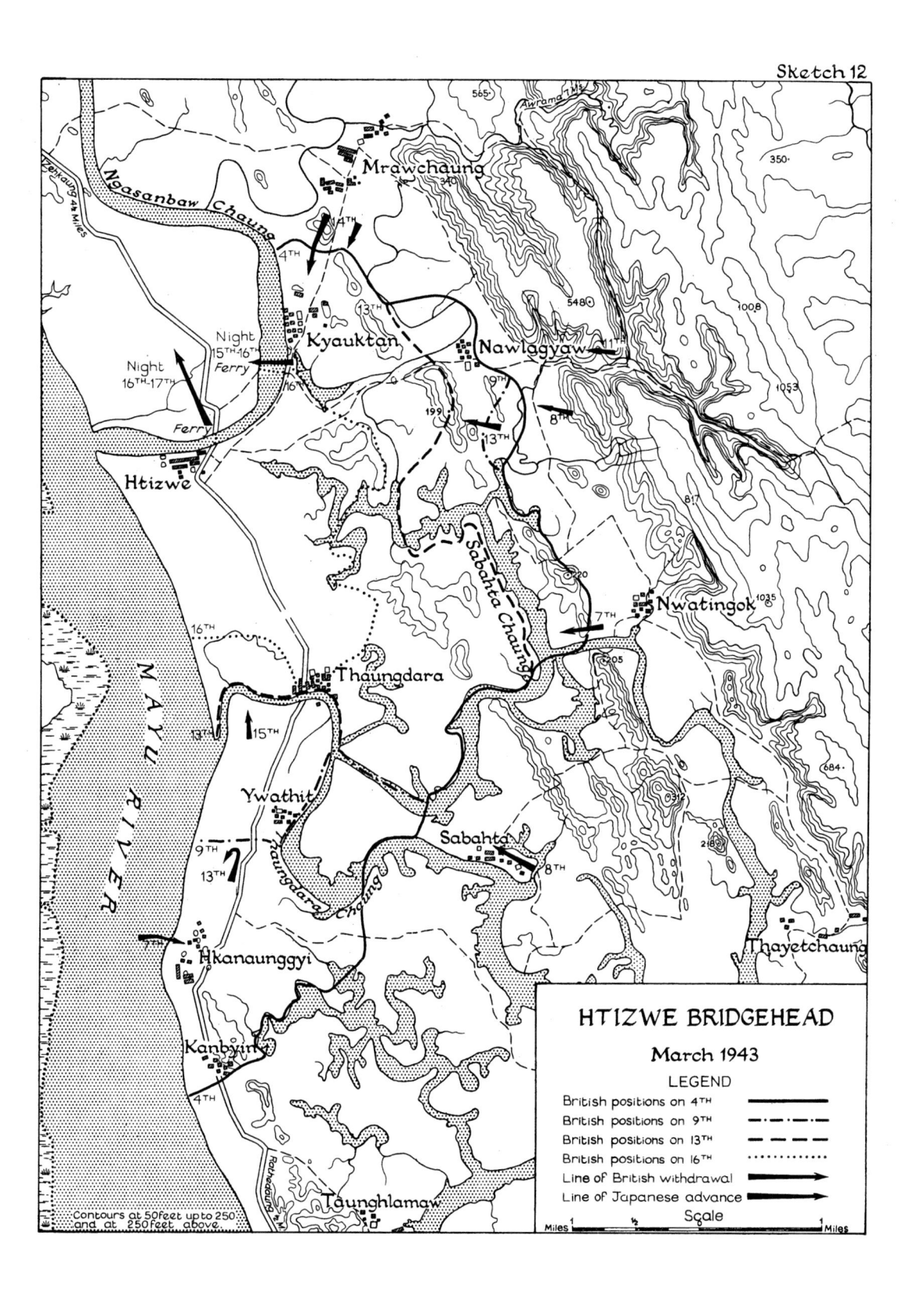

March 1943

LEGEND

British positions on 4TH	———
British positions on 9TH	—·—·—
British positions on 13TH	- - - -
British positions on 16TH	··········
Line of British withdrawal	⟶
Line of Japanese advance	⟶

Sketch 12

Contours at 50 feet up to 250 and at 250 feet above.

morning, the brigade had suffered more than 300 casualties and had made no appreciable gain. Thereupon Lloyd decided to make no further attempt to capture Donbaik. He ordered 6th Brigade to stand on the defensive, and released Headquarters 99th Field Regiment with one battery and 1st Lincolnshire to join 71st Brigade in the Zedidaung area.

On the 20th, Wavell and Irwin discussed the situation with Lloyd at his headquarters and later that evening Irwin formulated his policy for the short period before the break of the monsoon. He considered that no further offensive action was desirable on the Mayu peninsula and that defensive positions in depth should be taken up as early as possible; this was in effect the policy he had recommended on the 23rd February which had been overruled by Wavell. Buthidaung was to be secured as a base and 71st Brigade used to carry out offensive operations to harass the enemy rather than to gain ground. No ground was to be given up in any circumstances until it was obviously too late for any further Japanese offensive. Wavell however still hoped for a success at Donbaik and on the 25th wrote to Irwin, 'I feel it is no use ordering it while Lloyd is in command, since he obviously does not believe in it. But, if Lomax takes over and after examination thinks it can be done, I am quite prepared to support another attempt'.[1]

During the period from the 7th to 19th March, the Japanese had been uniformly successful. They had cleared the Kaladan valley, forced the British-Indian troops east of the Mayu River to withdraw some twelve miles to Zedidaung, thereby uncovering the left flank of the formations in the Mayu peninsula, and repulsed with heavy loss a strong attack on Donbaik by well-trained British troops. The first and second phases of their counter-offensive had been completed. When, by the end of March, General Koga saw no indication of any British counter-attack east of the Mayu River, he decided the time had come to proceed with the third phase of his plan, which was to destroy the British forces in the toe of the Mayu peninsula after cutting their communications at Indin. He ordered the *Miyawaki Column* to contain the British forces known to be in position near Zedidaung, the *Tanahashi Column* to cross the river and move on Indin, and the *Uno Column* to hold the Donbaik–Laungchaung area.[2] On the night of the 24th/25th March, the *Tanahashi Column* crossed the Mayu River between Prindaw and Thamihlaywa and moved westwards, covered by aircraft of *5th Air Division*. Leaving a battalion to guard his right flank in the vicinity of Praingdaung and

---
[1] Major-General C. E. N. Lomax, commanding 26th Indian Division.
[2] For detailed composition of Japanese columns for the third phase see Appendix 28.

sending a special detachment (*Kakihara*) to cross the range from Adwinbyin and cut the British communications north of Gyindaw, Tanahashi with the rest of his column planned to occupy the high ground north and west of Atet Nanra and then move across the range and reach Indin by the 3rd April.[1] Having contained the British forces at Laungchaung and Donbaik, the *Uno Column* was to advance and assist in the destruction of the British forces south of Indin.

The fact that the Japanese had crossed the Mayu River became known to Lloyd on the 25th March when enemy troops were seen to be entering the foothills north of Atet Nanra. Estimating their strength as two battalions, he ordered 47th Brigade (Brigadier R. A. A. Wimberley) to attack them from the south, while maintaining its positions at Thayetpyin, and 4th Brigade, supported by 31st Mountain Battery, to concentrate at Hparabyin by 7 a.m. on the 27th and attack from the north. The 47th Brigade was strung out over some eleven miles of country; it was thus unable to concentrate sufficient strength to undertake an immediate offensive.

Fighting began on the 26th, and the next day the Japanese occupied the crest of the range about one and a half miles west of Atet Nanra and so cut 47th Brigade's line of communication to Kyaukpandu. Lloyd then ordered the track from Indin to Sinoh to be improved so that the brigade could be supplied and its mules moved to the west of the range[2], and formed a special force called Hopforce (Colonel B. H. Hopkins) to attack from the west and clear the Kyaukpandu–Atet Nanra track.[3] The 47th Brigade and Hopforce failed on the 28th to dislodge the enemy either from the Atet Nanra area or from the crest of the range astride the Kyaukpandu track. Further to the north 4th Brigade, whose concentration at Hparabyin had been delayed by lack of transport, was held up at Praingdaung. Since its position was rapidly becoming untenable, Lloyd on the afternoon of the 29th ordered 47th Brigade to withdraw to the west of the range and join hands with 6th Brigade, which was to withdraw to Kodingauk.

Irwin had for some time considered that Lloyd's handling of

---

[1] See Sketch 14.

[2] This track was made passable for animals in some forty-eight hours and all the mules of 47th Brigade withdrawn.

[3] To begin with Hopforce consisted of: two companies 1st Royal Berkshire, three carrier platoons from 6th Brigade, one troop from 130th Field Regiment and one company from 10th Indian Engineer Regiment. It was later reinforced by the remainder of 1st Royal Berkshire.

Sketch 13

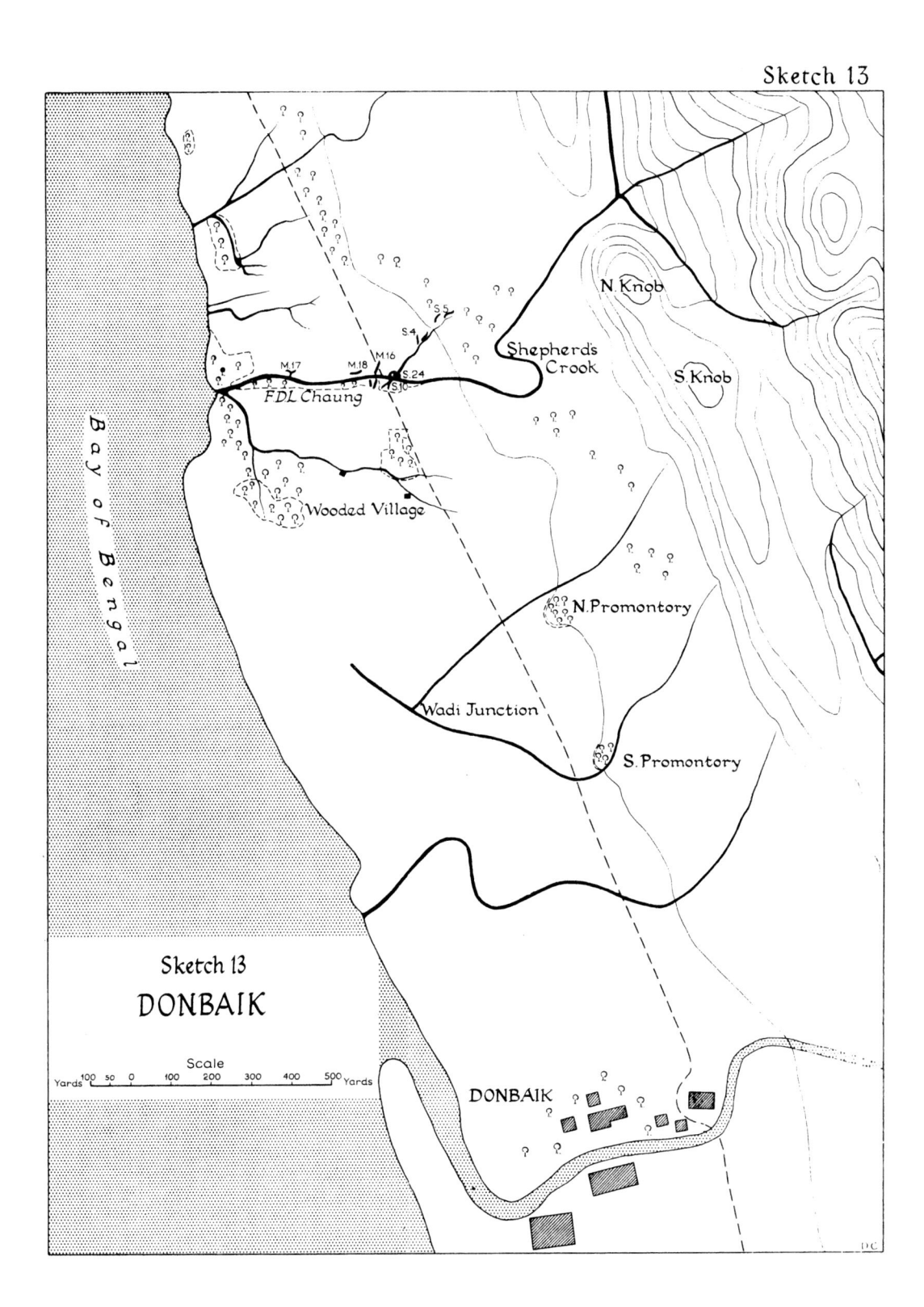

Sketch 13
DONBAIK

operations was faulty and, as already stated, had overruled his plan for the renewed attack on Donbaik. Having lost confidence in Lloyd's ability to handle the operations and realizing that a nine-month's campaign had placed a great strain on the whole of the divisional headquarters staff, Irwin had already arranged to relieve Headquarters 14th Division by Headquarters 26th Division (two brigades of 26th Division were already under command of 14th Division) and planned that Major-General C. E. N. Lomax (26th Division) should go to Maungdaw in advance of his staff and take over from Lloyd early in April.

Lloyd's withdrawal order of the 29th was in direct conflict with Irwin's specific instructions that the ground gained was to be held until the monsoon, and still more so with Wavell's wish, to which he had deferred, that the effort to clear the Mayu peninsula should continue. Irwin therefore decided to take command of 14th Division himself, pending Lomax's arrival. He reached Maungdaw that evening and sent Lloyd on leave. On the 30th he visited 4th Brigade and, during the afternoon, sent a message to 47th Brigade saying, '4th Brigade is on the move, stick it out'. That night he told both 6th and 47th Brigades that no withdrawals were to take place until further orders. On the 31st he visited 6th Brigade.

The position of 47th Brigade had meanwhile worsened, for Wimberley had been forced to withdraw southwards from the Atet Nanra area to Sinoh, the pressure on Hopforce on the Atet Nanra–Kyaukpandu track east of Ywathit had increased and the enemy was clearly making preparations for an attack on Thayetpyin. On the 1st April this attack was made in strength and forced 1/7th Rajput to withdraw to Thitkado. The same day 4th Brigade, in an attempt to drive south and make contact with 47th Brigade, failed to force the crossing of the Ngwedaung Chaung at Praingdaung.

On the morning of the 1st, Irwin sent 47th Brigade a message confirming his previous order that there should be no immediate withdrawal. Shortly after noon, he sent Wimberley new and detailed orders based on the fact that the approach of the monsoon would necessitate the brigade's eventual withdrawal from its existing position. The move was to be carried out deliberately and without loss of equipment along the pack track from Sinoh to Indin and the footpath from Kondan to the Sangan Chaung. The 1/7th Rajput was to move by stages, the first to Myinbu and the second to Thitkado. The first stage was to begin as soon as it could be methodically planned and the insignificant danger to the left flank of 6th Brigade, exposed as a result of the withdrawal, would have to be accepted. The date for the second stage would be given later but it would probably not begin before the 10th April. The brigade would eventually be withdrawn to the west of the range in co-operation with

6th Brigade, on the lines of Lloyd's order of the 29th March, since cancelled; this would probably not take place until the 15th April. It was, the order continued, of the utmost importance that the brigade should gradually close northwards and operate aggressively north from Sinoh to keep the enemy at a distance.

On receiving these orders on the telephone during the afternoon, Wimberley told Headquarters 14th Division of the morning's events at Thayetpyin.[1] He was promptly ordered to reoccupy Myinbu to cover the Sangan track, and Irwin's orders for an eventual withdrawal were reaffirmed, despite the changed situation. Myinbu was reoccupied that night by two companies 1st Inniskillings. On the 2nd April, however, pressure from the south increased and they were driven back to the Thitkado area, with the result that the Sangan track could no longer be used for a withdrawal west of the range. Wimberley thereupon moved 1/7th Rajput to strengthen the defences of Sinoh and thus secure the only track across the range still available to him. The same day, in the face of increasing enemy pressure, Hopforce withdrew 1st Royal Berkshire (less one company) from its positions east of Ywathit to an area about one mile south of the village, from where the tracks to both Kyaukpandu and Indin could be kept under daylight observation, but not under small arms fire. The Japanese were thus given access to the coast north of Indin of which they were not slow to take advantage. The 1/15th Punjab, which was at Maungdaw preparing to return to India, was hurriedly brought back to Gyindaw that evening to secure the line of communication to Indin against Japanese infiltration.

On the 3rd April, Irwin received an instruction from Wavell (dated 1st April) that the object of future operations was to regain the initiative and inflict a severe defeat on the enemy. To this end, offensive operations were to be carried out on both sides of the Mayu River. Such action, Wavell said, should be not only possible but successful if the advantages over the enemy in numbers, equipment and air support were skilfully used, and particularly if the enemy's over-confidence led him to expose himself to an effective counter-stroke east of the Mayu River. Without prejudice to offensive action, monsoon positions, with as much depth as possible in front of them, were to be selected and prepared to cover the Maungdaw–Buthidaung road, the airfield at Maungdaw and the mouth of the Naf River. If possible, the landing ground at Indin and the Mrawchaung–Apaukwa track to the Kaladan valley were also to be covered during the monsoon. At the same time, Force 'Z' was

---
[1] It is not known whether written confirmatory orders were received by the brigade. Brigadier Wimberley has since said that when given their gist on the telephone he took no heed since they bore little relation to the situation of his brigade, which was hard pressed. His immediate object was to hold his ground until permitted to withdraw, a most difficult task in the circumstances.

directed to assist 14th Division by operating against the enemy's line of communication across the Mayu River, and the Air Officer Commanding, Bengal, was told to keep the Japanese air forces on the defensive and maintain air superiority over the area of land operations.

At 4 p.m. on the 3rd, Irwin handed over command of 14th Division to Lomax and explained how he wished the operations in Arakan to develop. For the immediate operations, 6th and 47th Brigades, having driven the enemy from the Atet Nanra–Kyaukpandu area, were to hold their ground and if possible take the offensive southwards. During the monsoon, two brigades were to hold the Cox's Bazar–Maungdaw–Buthidaung area while a third brigade held Chittagong. The withdrawal to the monsoon positions, with the forward troops on the general line Gyindaw–Taungmaw, was to begin on about the 15th April. On his return to Calcutta, he issued a directive confirming these instructions with slight adjustments.[1]

Before this directive reached Lomax, it was already invalid. Early on the morning of the 3rd, the Japanese had occupied the Point 251 feature and established a road block at the bridge over the chaung north of Indin, thus cutting the line of communication to 6th and 47th Brigades and 1st Royal Berkshire. The blocking of the road came as a shock to 6th Brigade. On orders from Cavendish, 1st Royal Scots and a troop of field artillery moved quickly north and attacked the Indin road block at 6 p.m. at the same time as Hopforce attacked it from the north, but the block held firm.

Events were now rapidly reaching a crisis. The 4th Brigade made an attempt to drive south along the foothills with two battalions on the 4th, but again made no progress, while further south 1st Inniskillings in the Thitkado area was driven back to Sinoh. The Japanese occupation of Point 251 did not however prevent the use of the beach road at low tide, and during the day a supply convoy was able to reach 6th Brigade and return with surplus stores. Obliged by the circumstances to ignore Irwin's directives for a gradual withdrawal, Lomax ordered 6th Brigade to concentrate at Indin during the night of the 4th/5th, clear it of the enemy on the 5th and regain touch with 47th Brigade by way of the Sinoh track.

The 6th Brigade reached the Indin–Kwason area early on the 5th. Lomax told Cavendish during the morning that he had ordered 4th Brigade to move to Gyindaw, leaving one battalion and a mountain battery to hold a defensive position at Hparabyin, that 47th Brigade was being concentrated at Sinoh in preparation for a withdrawal to the west of the range as soon as the western exits of the Sinoh track were secure and that his task was to secure the Indin–Kyaukpandu area.

---
[1] See Appendix 29.

That afternoon 6th Brigade launched an attack across the chaung north of Indin. By 5 p.m. the southern half of Point 251 had been captured but, owing to approaching darkness, a further attack to clear the remainder of the high ground had to be postponed until the next day. By nightfall 2nd Durham Light Infantry and 1st Royal Welch Fusiliers held part of the Point 251 feature, 1st Royal Scots the northern and eastern outskirts of Indin, 130th Field Regiment was in Kwason and brigade headquarters in Indin.

During the night of the 5th/6th disaster befell 6th Brigade. An enemy force, which had passed between 1st Royal Berkshire and 47th Brigade, attacked Indin from the east, and another infiltrated into the village from the north with the result that 6th Brigade Headquarters was surrounded. At 3.30 a.m. Cavendish, unable to communicate with his battalions, told the Officer Commanding 130th Field Regiment at Kwason of the position by field telephone. He instructed him to give orders on his behalf to 1st Royal Welch Fusiliers and 2nd Durham Light Infantry to attack southwards at first light to relieve pressure on brigade headquarters, and asked him to make an attempt to gain contact with 47th Brigade and direct it to withdraw at once to Kwason. Shortly afterwards, brigade headquarters was overrun and Brigadier Cavendish and most of his staff were captured or killed.[1] The dawn attack which he had ordered succeeded, however, in driving the enemy out of Indin.

When at about 10 a.m. on the 6th General Lomax heard of these events, he ordered Colonel Hopkins to take command of 6th Brigade and withdraw it by the beach route to Kyaukpandu, secure the area and remain there till 4th Brigade was firmly established at Gyindaw. To suit the tide, the withdrawal began in the afternoon and the brigade reached Kyaukpandu without difficulty. At the same time a message was dropped on the isolated 1st Royal Berkshire, still south of Ywathit, ordering it to withdraw to Kyaukpandu[2], which it did during the night of the 6th/7th without much difficulty.

The withdrawal of 6th Brigade left the enemy in control of the western exits of the Sinoh–Indin track, and isolated 47th Brigade east of the range. As the brigade's liaison officer, despite repeated attempts, had failed to get through to 6th Brigade during the night of the 5th/6th, Brigadier Wimberley ordered the withdrawal to Indin to begin at dawn. It soon became evident that the track to Indin could no longer be used. Wimberley therefore decided to break out across country in the direction of Kwason, where he thought he would find 6th Brigade. All equipment which could not be carried, including the 3-inch mortars, was abandoned. The un-

---

[1] Brigadier Cavendish was captured. According to Japanese reports he was killed shortly afterwards by British artillery fire.

[2] The Berkshires had been supplied by air during the previous afternoon.

reconnoitred route soon led the column (which was in single file) into almost impassable country and it had to return to the summit of the range and attempt to find an easier route. When in the early hours of the 7th April a reconnaissance showed that the enemy was already in Kwason, Wimberley split the brigade into small parties to find their way out as best they could. Most of them managed to reach the beach at various points and, without their equipment, rejoined 6th Brigade between the 8th and 14th April. As a fighting formation, 47th Brigade had temporarily ceased to exist. The survivors were sent back to India where the brigade was re-formed and re-equipped.

Meanwhile 71st Brigade, guarding the left flank east of the Mayu River, had attacked Point 201 south-east of Zedidaung on the 28th March and made good progress. In view of the situation on the Mayu peninsula, the operation was called off on the 29th and the brigade withdrawn into its defensive position. Thereafter, action on this front was confined to patrolling. Meanwhile in pursuance of its instructions to interfere with enemy traffic across the Mayu River, Force 'Z', based on Buthidaung, had destroyed three, and damaged one, enemy craft on the night of the 30th/31st March. The enemy then sited guns and mortars on the river banks which made its task more hazardous, but on the night of the 6th April another enemy vessel was sunk. Further attempts to interrupt traffic up the chaung to Kyaungdaung, which the enemy was using as a line of communication to his formations west of the river, were however unsuccessful.

The third phase of the Japanese offensive had been completed in just under a fortnight. General Koga, in exactly one calendar month, including a pause of five days between the second and third phases, had not only reached the objectives allotted to him, but had inflicted a severe defeat on a considerably superior British force.

ATET NANRA–INDIN

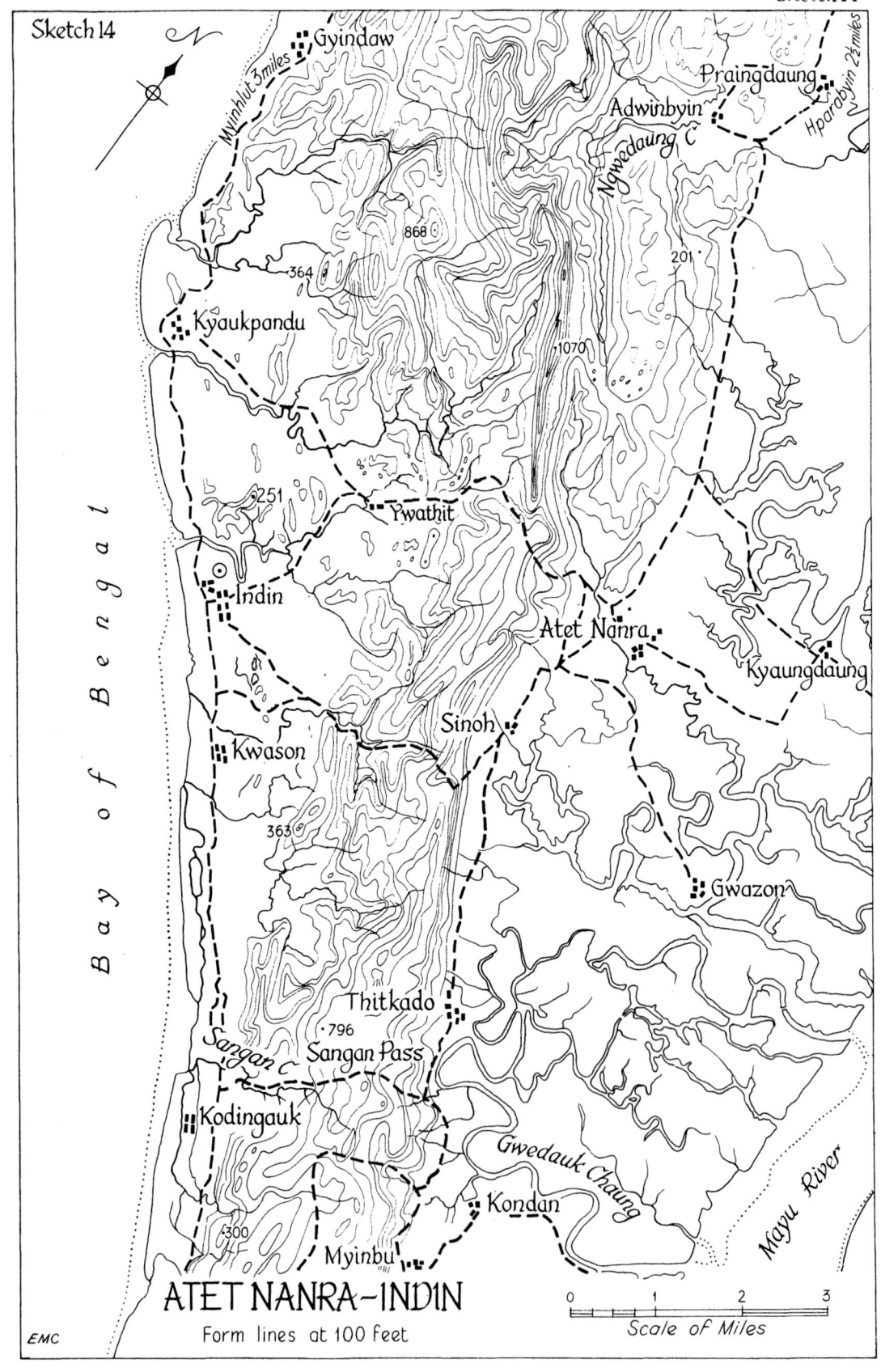

Sketch 14

Form lines at 100 feet

Scale of Miles

CHAPTER XX

THE END OF THE ARAKAN CAMPAIGN

See Maps 11 and 13 and Sketch 15

THE Arakan campaign now entered its final phase. Having gained all the objectives given him, General Koga, whose force had been increased by the arrival of *II/214th Battalion*, asked and received *15th Army's* sanction to continue his offensive with a view to gaining, and holding during the monsoon, the general line Buthidaung–Maungdaw[1], since it gave better protection to Akyab and its occupation would make it much more difficult for the British to re-open an offensive in Arakan at the end of 1943.

He decided to leave *I/112th Battalion* to follow up and contain the retreating British forces on the coastal strip, and to concentrate both the *Uno* and *Tanahashi Columns* (now each of three battalions) between the range and the Mayu River, while the *Miyawaki Column*, as before, contained the British forces east of the river.[2] The *Uno* and *Tanahashi Columns* were to advance north on the 25th April, capture Buthidaung and the Tunnels and then wheel left and seize Maungdaw. Simultaneously the *Miyawaki Column*, east of the Mayu River, was to make for Taung Bazar. The offensive was to be completed early in May.

It was not long before Lomax received information through 'V' Force and from escaped Indian prisoners of war indicating that the Japanese might attempt to capture the Maungdaw–Buthidaung line before the monsoon broke. He accordingly redisposed his forces for the defence of this line, which Irwin had already decided to make his monsoon position. He withdrew 6th Brigade to the Dilpara–Kingyaung area on the night of the 10th/11th April, and two nights later 4th Brigade to the Lambaguna–Godusara area.[3] The move of the latter led to a clash with an enemy detachment which had established itself during the night across the route at Myinhlut.[4] On the 13th he

---

[1] This line was the one abandoned on the 16th December 1942, see pages 257–58.
[2] For composition of columns in this phase see Appendix 28.
[3] See Sketch 15.
[4] This was the *Kakihara Column* which had belatedly reached its allotted objective, see page 340.

ordered Mayforce to assume responsibility for the area west of the Mayu River up to the crest of the range, to withdraw 71st Brigade to the line of the Saingdin Chaung and to arrange for 55th Brigade to take command of 6/11th Sikhs and 31st Mountain Battery, left behind by 4th Brigade to hold a defensive position at Hparabyin.

On the 14th April command of all troops in Arakan, from and including Chittagong southwards, was made over to XV Indian Corps (Lieut.-General W. J. Slim), and Lomax's 26th Divisional Headquarters replaced 14th Divisional Headquarters. Slim found a most unsatisfactory state of affairs. Many of the units under command of 26th Division had had their morale lowered by the series of abortive attempts to capture Rathedaung and Donbaik, and those which had not been involved in the attacks on these villages had frequently been manoeuvred out of their positions and had taken part in minor unsuccessful attacks. The losses from battle casualties and latterly malaria had been heavy and had been replaced by young, partly-trained men.[1] As a result, the morale of the troops was generally poor and in some units very low.

Slim appreciated that the Japanese would launch their main attack east of the range before the monsoon, using the Mayu River as their line of communication, and make the Tunnels area their objective. Having gained control of this area, they might then attack Maungdaw. There was also the possibility that they might make a wider turning movement east of the Mayu River directed on Taung Bazar. In his first operation instruction, Slim made it clear that his object was to hold the Maungdaw–Tunnels area. Buthidaung, though not vital, was to be held unless its retention endangered the main object.[2] He instructed 26th Division to prepare to fight a battle with the greatest force that could be concentrated, and to inflict so many casualties on the Japanese that they would be incapable of further large-scale operations before the break of the monsoon. In addition to the four brigades (4th, 6th, 55th and 71st) already under command of 26th Division, he met Lomax's request to be given 36th Indian Brigade (Brigadier L. C. Thomas), then at Cox's Bazar as a reserve, and gave orders that it was to move to Maungdaw by the end of the month.[3]

The following week was one of little activity. Although Japanese patrols were encountered in the hills east of Lambaguna and west and

---

[1] Five hundred cases of malaria were reported in the nine days from the 6th to 14th April.

[2] The Buthidaung area was the headquarters of the Military Administrator, Arakan (Lieut.-Colonel D. C. P. Phelips). Phelips was provided with a security force consisting of 'C' Company, 4th Burma Regiment. This company was later placed under command of Mayforce. See Donnison, *British Military Administration in the Far East, 1943-46* (H.M.S.O. 1956).

[3] For the composition of the brigades under command of 26th Division see Appendix 30. The 36th Brigade reached Maungdaw on the 23rd April.

south-west of Hparabyin, information from 'V' Force confirmed the belief that the main Japanese thrust would be made east of the range. Accordingly, Lomax instructed Mayforce on the 21st April to withdraw 55th Brigade from its exposed position at Hparabyin to the general line Kanthe–Seinnyinbya, with its left flank on the river and its right flank on the Point 302–Point 297 ridge; 'C' Company, 4th Burma Regiment, under orders of the brigade, was to act as a link with 4th Brigade across the crest of the range.

During the next few days the Japanese advanced. On the 23rd, a column of about battalion strength was seen moving north along the foothills near Point 318 east of Lambaguna. Since the movement threatened to turn the left flank of 4th Brigade in the coastal plain, Lomax told it to occupy the foothills east of Godusara up to and including Point 1102, and 6th Brigade to send a battalion to the Kingyaung area. On both the 24th and 25th, Japanese attacks on 55th Brigade in the Kanthe area were repulsed. On the 25th an enemy column was reported advancing northwards along the crest of the range towards Point 1102. To counter this, 7/15th Punjab of 4th Brigade made an attempt on the 26th to occupy Point 1213 but found it already held by the enemy. On the 28th, despite bombardment by a combined force of fighters and bombers, the Japanese were still in strength on the hill and the battalion was unable to gain any ground. Nevertheless, the counter-attack appeared to have brought the enemy to a standstill.

On the 29th fighting broke out in 4th Brigade's area around Point 318 which, after changing hands several times, was eventually occupied by the enemy. On the same day Lomax received a report from 'V' Force that the Japanese were thinning out west of the Mayu River with the possible intention of carrying out an encircling movement towards Taung Bazar. This information, subsequently found to be erroneous, led him to the conclusion that the Japanese advance along the foothills and the crest of the range as well as at Kanthe had been checked, and that an opportunity might occur to make an effective counterstroke against their communications while they were moving their reserves across the river in preparation for their move on Taung Bazar. He therefore ordered 36th Brigade from Maungdaw to move up behind 55th Brigade in readiness to launch an attack from the Kanthe position on the 1st May to occupy the high ground north-west of Hparabyin astride the enemy's communications.

Meanwhile, both opponents had been reconsidering their plans. Slim believed that the Japanese would exploit their successes and attempt to gain the Tunnels by outflanking 26th Division. The enemy had already used outflanking tactics successfully against the troops under his command, whose will to resist was now so low that they were unlikely to be able to hold even the strong Maungdaw–Tunnels position if it were turned, as it undoubtedly could be. He therefore made an appreciation on the 24th April to evolve a plan in case the Japanese succeeded in taking Buthidaung and that part of the Maungdaw–Buthidaung road lying east of the range and possibly the Tunnels.

Since taking over command in Arakan, his object had been to cover the general line Maungdaw–Buthidaung but, owing to the immensity of the country and their control of the two rivers which formed the main lines of communications, the Japanese were always in a position to lever the corps out of one position after another unless drastic counter measures were taken. To bring this state of affairs to an end, he had either to launch an immediate counter-offensive or to make a total change in the previously accepted strategic ideas.

If the Japanese were to move north up the Kalapanzin valley with a view to cutting the communications to Maungdaw, they would cover their exposed flank with a strong force in a prepared position. Any counterstroke would therefore meet similar conditions to those at Donbaik, and to commit his one fresh (but not yet battle tried) brigade to such an attack in country where it was not possible to deploy adequate supporting arms was courting failure. The rest of his force was in no condition to launch an offensive. It was evident that an immediate counterstroke was not possible.

A change of strategy was therefore essential. In any theatre where troops were few and the country vast, lines of defence could always be turned. What were needed were large, strong, well stocked and easily maintained pivots of manoeuvre from which striking forces could operate, not to hold or gain ground but to destroy the enemy forces. Such pivots would have to be so placed that the Japanese would have to attack them in order to open a line of communication for their advance.

For the defence of Arakan, the airfields at Chittagong, Cox's Bazar and Ramu were vital.[1] Forward of these, there were four possible areas for the kind of pivot he envisaged. The first, Maungdaw, had certain advantages, but Slim discarded it because it could be so easily hemmed in, there was no time to stock it for a lengthy siege and the Japanese could close the Naf River on which it would have to rely for maintenance in the monsoon. The second position was Bawli Bazar with its good stopping line—the Pruma Khal—but during the monsoon that river formed its only suitable line of communication, and the country behind it was ideal for Japanese infiltration and envelopment tactics. The same applied to the third—the Tumbru area. This left the Cox's Bazar–Ramu–Ukhia area, which the Japanese could not by-pass and where the

---
[1] See Map 13.

30. Maungdaw from the north.

31. Donbaik (F.D.L. Chaung. Shepherds Crook in the foreground).

ground was comparatively open and suitable for the deployment of artillery and tanks, weapons in which he held the superiority. Of this area Slim wrote:

> 'If we hold the Cox's Bazar Area firmly the Japanese will find it extremely difficult to maintain large forces over so long an L. of C. through hill country. Let him. Pursuing this policy we give the Japanese all the dirty work. If he comes on he must do so in small bodies—we then kill them. If he goes back we send mobile columns after him to harry him. If he turns round and snarls we withdraw . . . once more . . .
>
> The surest way of quick success in Burma is, not to hammer our way with small forces through jungle where the Japanese has every advantage, but to make him occupy as much area as possible, string himself out until he is weak, and then, when we have got him stretched, come in at him from the sea and air. By luring him northwards into the Chittagong and Cox's Bazar districts we get a better chance to get in behind his forward troops. His L. of C. runs along the coast and is vulnerable throughout its length. It gives us an opportunity of striking anywhere from Teknaf to Moulmein, a long coastline whereon we are almost bound to find an undefended beach. A block by a division landed astride this L. of C., and kept there, would finally ensure the putting of all troops northwards into the bag or at least force them to adopt a difficult getaway across the hills.'

He therefore prepared a plan for a phased withdrawal to that area. That his plan was not carried out in full was due to the fact that, after occupying Maungdaw and Buthidaung in May, the Japanese did not move northwards.

Having failed to break through the Kanthe position on the 24th and 25th April, the Japanese decided to abandon their original plan and attempt to advance along an elephant track which ran along the crest of the range, and form a corridor between the British troops to the west of the range and those east of Kanthe. They planned to occupy Point 1102 and Point 1440 on the their left and Point 302 and Point 297 on their right flank. Having secured the flanks of the corridor, they would then send a force straight through to seize Point 551, which commanded the Maungdaw–Buthidaung road immediately to the east of the Tunnels. They expected that once this important tactical feature was in their hands the British troops east of the range would be forced to withdraw from Buthidaung. The *Uno Column* was therefore ordered to contain the British east of Kanthe and occupy the Point 302–Point 297 feature, while the *Tanahashi Column*, having secured Points 1102 and 1440, advanced to Point 551.

The 36th Brigade's reconnaissance, in preparation for the proposed attack towards Hparabyin, showed clearly that the enemy was in considerable strength on the high ground south-west of Seinnyinbya and that any advance would commit it to a frontal assault on a strong position. Feeling that it would be unjustifiable to commit his only reserve to an operation which could have no immediate effect on the Japanese line of communication to their forces east of the river, Lomax cancelled the operation on the 1st May, and withdrew 36th Brigade into divisional reserve in the Letwedet area.

On the 2nd, XV Corps judged that the enemy strength in the Kanthe–Seinnyinbya area indicated that the Japanese would thrust towards the Tunnels and Point 551, between the crest of the range and the area held by 55th Brigade. If they adopted such a plan, Lomax saw that there was a possibility of trapping them in a box with 7/15th Punjab of 4th Brigade in the Point 1213–Point 1102 area and 1st Royal Scots of 6th Brigade in the Kingyaung–Point 1440–Point 1443 area forming the western side, 55th Brigade the eastern side and 71st Brigade, which he reinforced with 2/8th Punjab from Maungdaw, in the north forming the lid. Accordingly, 71st Brigade was disposed with 10th Lancashire Fusiliers holding the Tunnels area with a detachment on Point 551, 2/8th Punjab between Sinoh East and Sinoh West covering the Kin Chaung and Ale Chaung valleys, 1st Lincolns in Buthidaung with a detachment forward on the Saingdin Chaung and 9/15th Punjab in reserve.

The Japanese launched their northward drive on the 2nd, attacking both sides of the box simultaneously. By evening they had captured the whole of the Point 302–Point 297 ridge and the crest of the range between Point 1102 and Point 1213. They then quickly moved further north, capturing Point 1440 and Point 375 and infiltrating round and through the newly-arrived 2/8th Punjab, and by the morning of the 3rd were seen to be digging in on the east side of the Point 551 ridge within a mile of the Buthidaung road. That afternoon, 10th Lancashire Fusiliers detachment was driven off Point 551.

On the night of the 3rd/4th, Lomax ordered Mayforce to use 36th Brigade, reinforced by 9/5th Punjab from 71st Brigade, to recapture the vital Point 551 ridge which overlooked four miles of the Buthidaung road. The 8/13th F.F. Rifles succeeded on the 4th in mopping up several small enemy positions on the northern end of the ridge while 9/15th Punjab established a line behind it; but the other two battalions of the brigade, attacking the ridge from the east, were unable to make headway. During the day the enemy crossed the Buthidaung road at Milestone 4, burning the wooden bridge across the Letwedet chaung.

Slim visited Lomax on the afternoon of the 5th and authorized him to give up Buthidaung, if it were necessary to do so in order to ensure that 55th Brigade and the troops east of the Tunnels were extricated intact, but emphasised that Maungdaw and all the ground necessary for its prolonged defence must be made secure. In order to deal with any threat to the division's line of communication from the direction of the Taung Bazar area, he placed 23rd Brigade and 160th Field Regiment of 70th British Division, then at Chittagong, under Lomax's command from midnight on the 6th/7th.

By the evening, however, it was clear that 55th Brigade's situation was becoming critical and Lomax was forced to order Mayforce to cancel the counter-attack and use 36th Brigade to extricate the 55th. During the 6th it became evident that Buthidaung would have to be abandoned, and at noon Lomax decided that the withdrawal should take place that night. He told Mayforce that 71st Brigade was to defend the Tunnels area[1], and that 36th Brigade was to cover the withdrawal of 55th Brigade and 1st Lincolnshire to the Ngakyedauk Pass. The 1/17th Dogra, then concentrating at Taung Bazar, was to watch the tracks running north up the Kalapanzin valley and come under orders of 23rd Brigade on its arrival in the Bawli Bazar–Goppe Bazar area.

In a message to Irwin that day, Slim ascribed the failure of Lomax's plan to trap the Japanese on the 2nd and 3rd May to the fact that the sides of the box had crumbled, and the lid had opened without adequate reason. This, he said, was mainly due to the very low morale of some units which had been in Arakan without relief since the beginning of operations the previous year. Late that afternoon, Irwin (at that time in IV Corps area in Assam) sent Slim a message stressing the vital necessity of holding Maungdaw and, still hoping that the enemy might be cleared from the Buthidaung–Maungdaw road, suggested that 55th Brigade should continue to cover Buthidaung and 36th Brigade control the Tunnels area. The message arrived too late to be acted on since 55th Brigade was already on the move.

Force 'Z' helped to destroy the Buthidaung ferry and all surplus craft, and then withdrew upstream to Taung Bazar.[2] The 55th Brigade and 1st Lincolnshire destroyed their wheeled transport, which could not by-pass the destroyed bridge at Milestone 4, and withdrew across country during the night of the 6th/7th. Having fought a rearguard action in the Letwedet area throughout the 7th, 36th Brigade broke contact after dark and, without interference from

---

[1] The 8/13th F.F. Rifles from 36th Brigade and 7/15th Punjab from 4th Brigade were placed under command of 71st Brigade.

[2] Force 'Z' left its remaining craft with the battalion at Taung Bazar and withdrew overland to Chittagong.

the enemy, withdrew to the pass, and took over its defence from 55th Brigade. On the 8th, Lomax redisposed his division for the defence of Maungdaw with 4th and 6th Brigades supported by 99th Field Regiment in the coastal area, 71st Brigade supported by 8th Mountain Battery in the Tunnels area, 36th Brigade supported by 31st Mountain Battery holding the Ngakyedauk Pass, 55th Brigade supported by 130th Field Regiment in reserve in the Razabil area and 23rd Brigade supported by 160th Field Regiment in the Bawli Bazar–Goppe Bazar area, with 1/17th Dogra forward in Taung Bazar.

There was no contact with enemy troops on the 8th, but enemy aircraft attacked Maungdaw, Bawli Bazar and other points on the line of communications. The fact that the enemy made no attempt to cross the range and cut the road north of Maungdaw, as had been expected, tended to corroborate 'V' Force reports of wide and deep outflanking movements to the east. Thus, when during the day Irwin arrived at XV Corps Headquarters to urge that Maungdaw be held[1], Slim was insistent that the time had come to put into force his plan for a withdrawal right back to the Cox's Bazar area. A compromise was eventually reached. Irwin agreed to the evacuation of Maungdaw, which he now realized could be easily isolated and had little tactical value except as a base for troops holding the Tunnels area, but insisted that the general line Nhila–Bawli Bazar–Goppe Bazar–Taung Bazar should be held. This plan was later approved by General Headquarters, India.

That evening Slim ordered Lomax to prepare to withdraw, but left it to him to decide when the withdrawal should begin. The new positions were to be held until the beginning of the monsoon and, if possible, all stores were to be evacuated from Maungdaw, any left behind being destroyed. The following day passed comparatively quietly, but bombing of Maungdaw caused all civilian labour to disappear. Mayforce was abolished (71st, 55th and 36th Brigades reverting to direct control by 26th Division), and that evening Lomax issued detailed orders for a phased withdrawal on a four-day programme. No move except for backloading of surplus stores was to be made, however, without his orders. On the 10th further information, indicating an imminent attack in strength on Maungdaw from the north-east and south, began to come in. Lomax was not prepared to risk a fight for Maungdaw with his battle-weary troops, and in the evening carried out the preliminary moves for his phased withdrawal. At 11.15 a.m. on the 11th he issued the code word for the general withdrawal to the new line of defence.

---

[1] Irwin took his Major-General in charge of Administration (General Goddard) with him to Maungdaw to make the administrative arrangements to supply the area, if held during the monsoon.

WITHDRAWAL FROM MAUNGDAW

The withdrawal began little more than twenty-four hours after the receipt, by those who had to carry it out, of the detailed plan and much earlier than had been envisaged by Lomax when he issued it. This, together with the disappearance of civilian labour, resulted in demolitions being incomplete and more stores left to be backloaded than the available river craft and motor vehicles could deal with in the time available. Much of value to the enemy was therefore left behind. An attempt was made by the R.A.F. to destroy what was left by bombing, and on the night of the 16th/17th a raiding party made a gallant but unsuccessful effort to recover some badly needed folding boats.

The reports from 'V' Force which had led to the hasty withdrawal from Maungdaw proved in fact to be incorrect. The Japanese occupied Buthidaung on the 9th and Maungdaw (*I/112th Battalion* moving in from the south) on the 14th. In view of the depth of the British retreat and the approach of the monsoon, General Koga decided to take up a defensive position on the general line Buthidaung–Maungdaw. He disposed *143rd Regiment* (less *III/143rd Battalion*) in the Buthidaung area, *112th Regiment* in the Maungdaw area and withdrew the rest of his division to Akyab in reserve.

The 26th Division was now disposed with 71st Brigade on the right at Nhila covering the Teknaf peninsula and the Naf River, 36th Brigade in the centre on the Maungdaw–Bawli Bazar road, 4th Brigade on the left covering the Taung Bazar–Goppe Bazar area and 6th Brigade in reserve at Tumbru. The 23rd and 55th Brigades were in the Faqira Bazar and Panzai Bazar areas respectively to prevent any attempt at a wide and deep outflanking movement on Cox's Bazar. The 14th Brigade of 70th British Division, moved forward from Calcutta, was at Cox's Bazar as an additional reserve.

Irwin was anxious to retake Maungdaw by surprise, but Slim, who had accurate knowledge of the Japanese dispositions in Buthidaung and Maungdaw, maintained that such an operation would be comparable with the attack on Donbaik and advised against it. The idea was abandoned, and, in view of the onset of the monsoon, it was decided to thin out 26th Division and leave it with its own three brigades (4th, 36th and 71st). By the end of May all formations had taken up their new (monsoon) positions, and those surplus to requirements had been moved back to India.

Throughout the campaign, the R.A.F. (Bengal Command) had been active in support of the land forces, and both Hurricanes and Blenheims were constantly engaged in attacks against ground targets. Between January and May 1943 some 5,000 sorties were flown in direct and indirect support of the land operations, while a further 700 were flown in the defence of airfields and installations in the

Chittagong area and the Mayu peninsula. Close support for the army however proved exceptionally difficult. The nature of the country imposed conditions quite unlike those in Europe and the Middle East: air attacks had more often than not to be made on unseen objectives in thick jungle, the position of which the ground forces indicated by firing smoke shells or by giving map references. Moreover, the number of aircraft available was so small that an attack by even eight Blenheims was considered to be heavy and, as at this stage more suitable types of aircraft for attacking ground targets were not available, it is hardly surprising that air strikes in support of infantry were usually ineffective.[1] Nevertheless, during this period the R.A.F. succeeded in gaining temporary local air superiority over Arakan and in inflicting considerable losses on the Japanese.

The attempt to recapture Akyab in the early part of 1943 thus ended in complete failure. With overwhelming numerical superiority in the early stages, preponderance in artillery and a monopoly in armour, a British success must at the outset have appeared to be certain. The failure was to have wide repercussions, and its causes therefore merit examination.

The task given 14th Division in October 1942 was to reach the Maungdaw–Buthidaung area in order to draw enemy troops away from Akyab, while a seaborne attack was launched on the island by a fully-trained amphibious force.[2] There was no need for haste, and administrative considerations were therefore allowed to dictate the pace of the division's advance. In November 1942, the delay in the arrival of 29th Independent Brigade and its landing craft forced Wavell to substitute a short-range assault on Akyab from Foul Point for his original plan. The division was then ordered to occupy the Mayu peninsula and build a road to Foul Point so that the assault could be mounted. Speed therefore became of paramount importance. Even with additional engineering resources, the capacity of the long line of communication from Dohazari and Cox's Bazar southwards could not be quickly improved, and the only hope of increasing the rate of the division's advance lay in the speedy capture of Maungdaw and the development of the direct line of communication by sea from Chittagong.

At the end of November, Lloyd was able to maintain four battalions in the Zeganbyin–Taung Bazar area and proposed to attack the weak and extended Japanese outpost position on the 2nd December.

---

[1] Hurricane fighter bombers and Vengeance light bombers, which later proved more efficient for close support, were not operational in India until October 1943.

[2] See page 255.

Irwin, knowing the poor state of training of his troops and unwilling to risk an initial failure, decided to wait till two brigades were concentrated and the line of communications had been improved.[1] His caution at this moment not only resulted in a fortnight's delay in reaching Maungdaw, but enabled the Japanese to withdraw unmolested to ground of their own choosing and thereby regain the initiative.

In order to exploit fully the possession of Maungdaw and the motorable road to Buthidaung, additional coastal steamers were required. Both Lloyd and Irwin made repeated requests to General Headquarters, India, for more of these, but owing to the general shortage in India they could not be supplied. To make matters worse, Irwin had to use six steamers from his existing fleet for training 6th Brigade for its assault. Thus during the critical weeks at the end of December the lack of supplies hampered the division's progress down the Mayu peninsula.

With caution forced on him early in December, it is understandable that Lloyd, when faced with a threat to his left flank from Kondan, used all his available strength to cross the range and deal with it, instead of masking it and driving boldly for Foul Point, the occupation of which, together with the threat to Rathedaung, might have compelled the Japanese to strengthen their Akyab garrison quickly. As their only troops in the vicinity available to reinforce Akyab were those at Kondan and Rathedaung, the occupation of Foul Point might have forced the Japanese to conform to the moves of 14th Division and lose the initiative.

The failure of partially trained troops at Donbaik and Rathedaung, despite their numerical superiority, is not surprising. Throughout the war in Burma, frontal attacks against well dug-in and skilfully sited positions held by determined troops never succeeded unless there was overwhelming artillery strength or close support by tanks and aircraft. During the first Arakan campaign, air and artillery support was always weak. On the one occasion when tanks were employed, the advice of the tank brigade commander on their tactical use was not taken, with the result that their attack was not co-ordinated with the infantry.[2] Furthermore the troops were so dependent on their communications that, when they had surrounded the enemy defences, they were recalled before their presence in rear of the defenders could have any effect.

The failures at Donbaik and Rathedaung gave the enemy time to bring up reinforcements and take the offensive with a well-trained division which had fought throughout the First Burma Campaign. General Koga carefully avoided any frontal attack and, enjoying the

---

[1] See page 257.
[2] The technique of tank attacks on bunker defences had not then been developed.

advantages of a central position and control of the rivers, manoeuvred 14th and later 26th Divisions out of their positions by deep and wide outflanking attacks aimed at their communications. In this he was greatly assisted by the fact that the British commanders, believing that weight of numbers could achieve success, persisted in trying to break through at Donbaik and to hold on to the southern end of the Mayu peninsula, even after their left flank had been exposed by the withdrawal east of the Mayu River.[1]

When, at the end of February, Irwin accepted Lloyd's view that any further attempt to break through at Donbaik was unjustified, he made up his mind that there should be no withdrawal until it became necessary to take up monsoon positions further north. Despite the failure of the further attempt on the 18th March to clear the peninsula and the growing threat to Lloyd's flank on the peninsula, he held to his decision. When on the 29th March, after the Japanese had secured the crest of the range near Atet Nanra, Lloyd ordered his two brigades to withdraw from what has aptly been described as the 'toe of the sock' where they were in danger of being trapped, Irwin, presumably to meet Wavell's desire to try once again to break through at Donbaik, decided to countermand the order. As he had already overruled Lloyd's plans on more than one occasion, to countermand an order already given left Irwin with no option but to relieve Lloyd of his command and, as Lomax had not yet arrived, take over command himself.

His instructions on handing over to Lomax, confirmed in writing on the 4th April, show how far his views were from the realities of the situation. Wavell's operation instruction of the 1st April for offensive operations on both sides of the Mayu River was impracticable. Had a withdrawal of the forces from the Donbaik-Laungchaung area taken place in the third week of March when the enemy was poised to cross the Mayu River and strike the exposed flank of the troops holding the peninsula, a mobile reserve could have been collected, and the effective blow envisaged by Wavell in his instruction might have been delivered. But a success at Donbaik and the retention of ground had become the paramount considerations, with the result that two brigades became exposed to encirclement. Complete disaster was averted only by the fact that Lomax, on assuming command, realized the imminent danger and was able to extricate 6th Brigade by the beach road. He could not save 47th Brigade intact, but Wimberley's decision to split it into small groups to make their way through the jungle enabled most of the troops to reach safety, albeit with the loss of all their equipment.

The failures and withdrawals on both sides of the Mayu River had by this time begun seriously to affect the morale of many units,

---
[1] See page 339.

LETWEDET – MAUNGDAW
Form lines at 100 feet

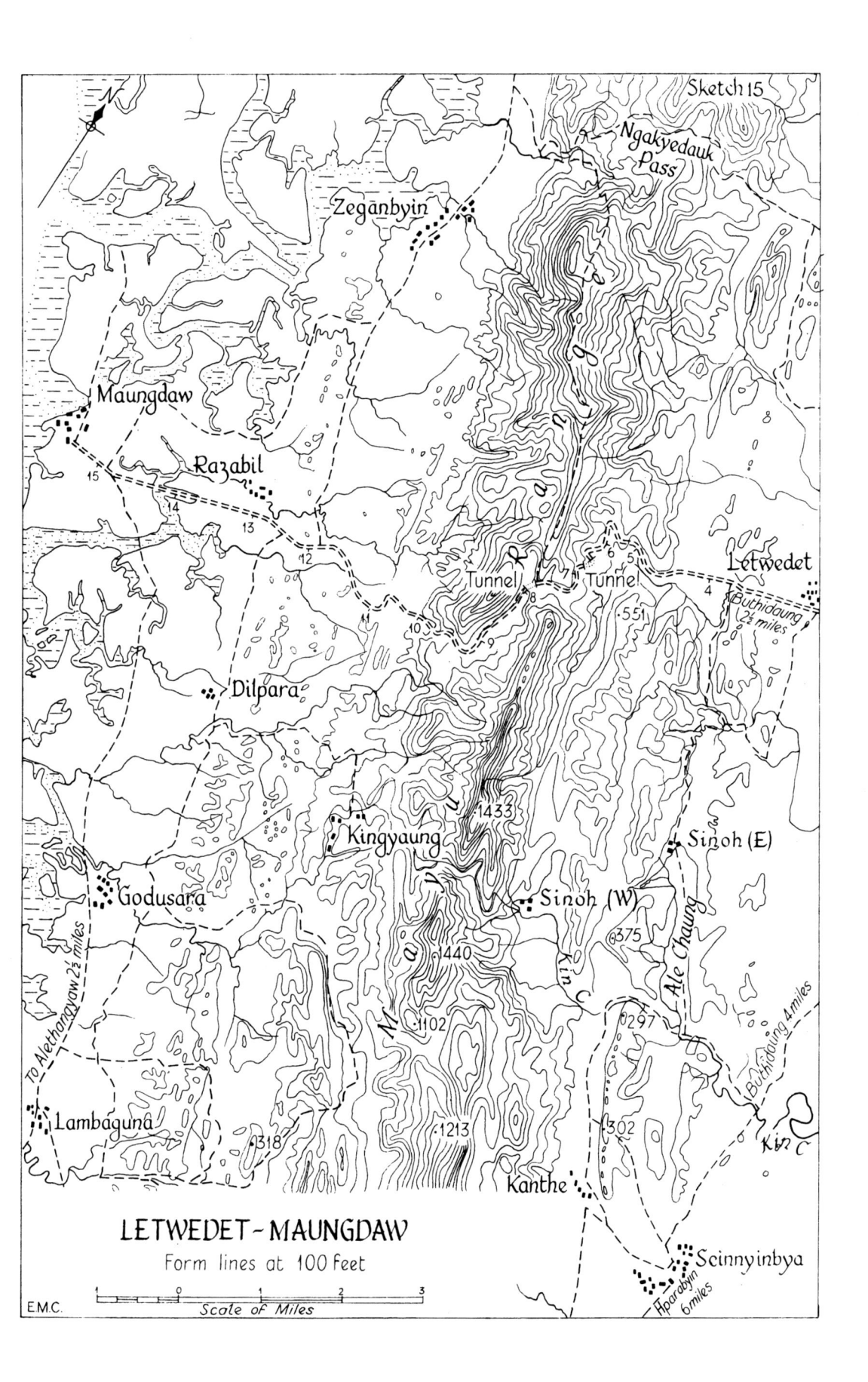

especially those which had been in Arakan for a long period without relief. Morale could have been restored only by withdrawing them from Arakan, since the reinforcements sent from India were almost entirely untrained and no unit can absorb large numbers of untrained men in the face of the enemy. Thus it was that the well conceived plans prepared by Slim and Lomax, which might have succeeded with determined troops, failed, and a withdrawal to monsoon positions far further north than Irwin had ever envisaged became necessary.

As first planned, the advance into Arakan and the attempt to capture Akyab was undoubtedly justified. But when almost at the beginning of the campaign the initiative passed into enemy hands, and the coastal craft required to build up the capacity of the line of communication quickly could not be provided, Wavell might have been well advised to cancel the attempt to capture Akyab in 1943, and content himself instead with a limited operation well within the administrative capabilities at the time, such as the capture and consolidation of the Maungdaw–Buthidaung area in order to seize a good jumping-off place for future operations and give his troops battle experience. As it was, he paid the penalty for committing inexperienced troops to a difficult operation at the end of a tenuous line of communication.

When morale was beginning to ebb as a result of the repeated failures in the six weeks ending 18th/19th February to break through at Donbaik and Rathedaung, Wavell was courting disaster in ordering that a further attempt to overwhelm the Donbaik position should be made in March, in the hope that victory might restore morale and prestige. The Japanese had been reinforced, the capture of Akyab was no longer possible and there was no strategic value to be gained from such an operation. After the inevitable failure of the attack on the 18th March, the decision to try to hold the ground gained on the peninsula, even though outflanked, played straight into the enemy's hands, and so the British forces found themselves in May 1943 back where they had started in October 1942.

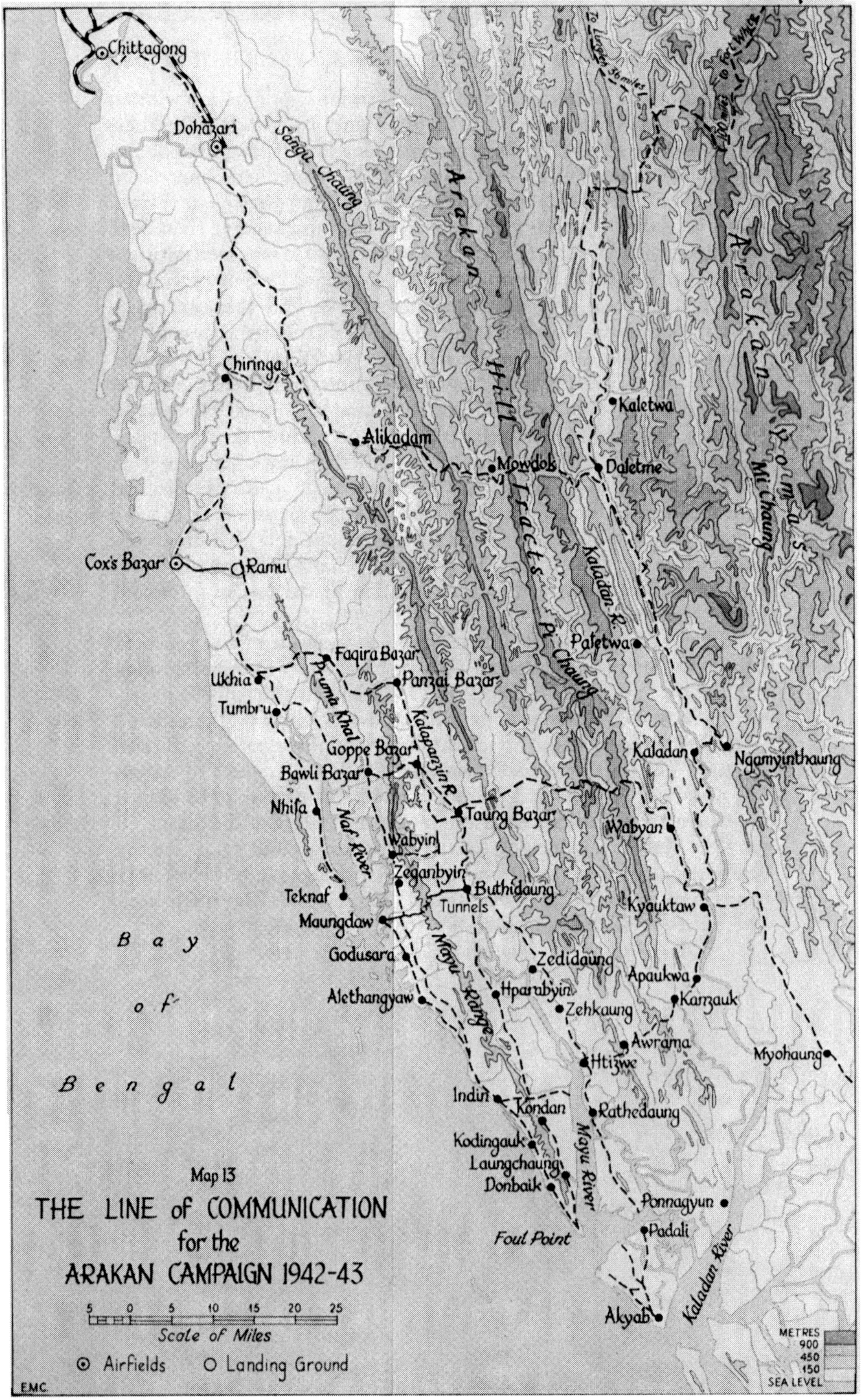

Map 13

Map 13
THE LINE of COMMUNICATION
for the
ARAKAN CAMPAIGN 1942-43

⊙ Airfields   ○ Landing Ground

CHAPTER XXI

PLANS FOR AN OFFENSIVE IN 1944 FRUSTRATED

See Strategic Map and Map 14

WHILE the Chindit columns were penetrating deep into Burma and the Arakan offensive was drawing dismally to its close, Field Marshal Wavell, in accordance with the agreements reached at the Calcutta conference on the 9th February, began to accelerate the preparations to launch the 'Anakim' offensive at the end of the 1943 monsoon.

At the end of 1942 he had suggested the use of African troops in operations in Burma and elsewhere in the Far East, for it seemed to him that West African formations, used to tropical jungles and to moving with porter transport, would be invaluable in parts of Burma and Malaya, while the mechanized East African formations could be sent to Ceylon to release British and Indian troops for 'Anakim'. In February 1943, with War Office approval, plans had been made to send 81st West African Division to India if shipping could be found during the summer and autumn, and to bring the East African force (21st Brigade) already in Ceylon up to the strength of a division (11th East African) by the despatch of the additional brigades from East Africa when they were ready, thus releasing 20th Indian Division for 'Anakim'.

To provide the two reserve divisions needed for 'Anakim'[1], Wavell, in February, asked for another British infantry division to be sent to India by December 1943, and for the return of 4th Indian Division which had been in the Middle East for three years. On the suggestion of the War Office, he agreed to accept 5th Indian Division from the Persia–Iraq command, then being reduced in size, since it could be moved to India as soon as shipping became available. The Chiefs of Staff decided that a British division, if sent, would come from the Middle East, but deferred its nomination till a later date.

When considering the command structure for the planning and execution of 'Anakim', Wavell came to the conclusion that it would be necessary to have two commands directly under his control. He

---
[1] See page 304.

therefore proposed that Eastern Army should command all formations operating in Arakan and from Assam, including the Chinese corps. A new command would have to be set up to control the seaborne forces assaulting the coasts of Burma. Accordingly, he began to raise an Indian Expeditionary Force Headquarters and asked the Chiefs of Staff to provide a suitable commander. General Sir George Giffard, who had been General Officer Commanding-in-Chief, West Africa, was appointed on the 18th March, and ordered to India immediately so that the detailed planning for the operation could begin.

Meanwhile at the end of February Wavell, together with Admiral Somerville and Air Marshal Peirse, had made a more detailed study of the 'Anakim' plan agreed on at the conference earlier in the month. They devoted their attention mainly to the problem, which had not been fully investigated, of launching seaborne assaults along the Arakan coast, on Bassein and in the Rangoon area. They decided that a large naval force would be required in case the Japanese sent a strong fleet into the Indian Ocean, and to provide convoy escorts and the necessary inshore squadrons. As the Japanese were in possession of conveniently placed airfields, and it was unlikely that their air strength could be so reduced before November 1943 as to give a sufficient margin of superiority, air cover would have to be given by carrier-borne aircraft for some weeks, and a large number of auxiliary aircraft carriers would therefore be required. Even if the requisite number of carriers were provided, convoys would still be very vulnerable to attack. The success of the operation therefore depended almost entirely on the Japanese land-based air force being prevented from intervening. But, as they were unable to envisage the circumstances which would bring this about, they recognized that the risks involved in the operation were substantial.

In reporting these views to the Chiefs of Staff, Wavell said that he fully appreciated the necessity for recapturing Burma at the earliest possible moment, but that the 'Anakim' plan was a gamble involving great difficulties and risks. It was, however, the only way in his opinion by which Burma could be regained in one campaigning season and, so far as operations from India were concerned, nothing but the reoccupation of Burma and the reopening of the Burma Road could do much to hasten the defeat of Japan. He therefore proposed that planning on the basis of 'Anakim' should continue, since it offered the best and only chance of shortening the war with Japan. It might however be that Japanese strength and counter-preparations in Burma would render the plan too hazardous. In that case, alternative plans for the use of the expeditionary forces being organised in India would be required and he was taking steps to prepare them.

In a note to his planning staff written on the 16th February, Wavell had said:

'... It is obvious that the natural difficulties [inherent in 'Anakim'] are such that, even if the Japanese forces in Burma are not increased, we may have to look elsewhere for a speedy and effective blow against the Japanese line. It is also clear that we can expect little military aid from China; and that we shall get far more effective co-operation from the U.S.A. and Australian forces in [the] south-west Pacific. I have in fact had a telegram from General MacArthur suggesting we might plan a combined operation together.

So far we have been operating separately from India and the Pacific against the extreme flanks of the Japanese line—the Solomons and New Guinea and Northern Burma. We can only progress very slowly and at considerable cost in these areas. If we could make a sudden combined assault against the centre of the Japanese line we might catch our enemy off his guard and achieve great results.

The objective I have in mind for such a blow is the control of the Sunda Straits between Sumatra and Java. This would threaten Singapore and the whole Japanese position in the Netherlands East Indies. If we could at the same time seize a base in northern Sumatra from which to control the Malacca Straits, we should have gone far towards the defeat of Japan.

I do not underrate the formidable nature of this undertaking, but I believe that it is no more formidable than the capture of Burma would be.

We cannot hope to secure surprise in an attack on Burma, since this is an obvious move and must be expected by the enemy; but we could hope for surprise in the Sumatra–Java attack, since this would be unexpected and could be concealed by continuing preparations against Burma (and in Australia against south-west Pacific islands).

Our operation in southern Sumatra would be aimed at the port of Oosthaven and the Palembang airfields. Incidentally we should, if successful, prevent the Japanese from using oilfields and refinery at Palembang. The operation in Java might include Batavia. The attacks would in the first instance have to be supported by carrier-borne aircraft. We should therefore have to ensure surprise by every possible means so as to prevent heavy attack on our convoys by shore-based aircraft.

For political reasons it will be necessary to conceal our intentions from the Chinese who are naturally anxious to see the reconquest of Burma. This very fact can be made to help our plans; we can continue preparations and discussions with the Chinese on an offensive into Burma, and this will quite likely come to the knowledge of the Japanese. We shall in fact make a limited offensive into Upper Burma, with the object of confirming the Japanese of our intentions to attack in Burma...'

It is clear from this that Wavell was beginning to turn away from the hard nut of Burma and favour an attack on other areas where, he thought, the strategical gain would be more commensurate with the cost. The alternatives would however make heavy demands on shipping, landing craft and naval forces, and Allied resources in these were limited.

It had been made clear at the time of the Delhi conference early in February 1943 that the launching of 'Anakim' on the 15th November depended on the monthly receipt in India of some 183,000 shipping tons of stores and equipment during the six months from March to August, and the inclusion in the shipping programme of specific items which had to arrive in India by definite dates so that the troops could be trained.[1] It was therefore somewhat of a shock to Wavell when he received a cable on the 10th March from the Chiefs of Staff telling him that the general shortage of cargo shipping was causing them increased anxiety, and asking him to scrutinize his shipping programmes carefully in order to eliminate all items not absolutely necessary for the mounting of 'Anakim'. To this Wavell replied that careful scrutiny had shown that no significant reduction could be made in the estimates given in February, and pointed out that the March allotment of shipping to India had been some 100,000 tons short of the amount required. If, he said, 'Anakim' were to be mounted in 1943, no cuts could be made in the basic allotments for April and the succeeding months, and the existing shortfall would have to be made good in the period from April to June.

The actual allotment of shipping for February had been 73,000 tons and for March 65,000 tons. During March, Wavell was told that the April allotment would be approximately 65,000 tons. He therefore had the whole situation reviewed again. He found that 18,000 load-carrying vehicles and 238 units of earth-moving machinery, which were urgently required for the construction of airfields and roads, as well as 800 tanks and 1,770 guns, amounting in all to some 101,000 tons, awaited shipment at British and United States ports. But on the limited space allotted there was room for only 15,000 tons a month for these essential items.

As a result, he reported to the Chiefs of Staff on the 1st April, that, far from receiving the weapons, equipment and material to build up for 'Anakim', India was not even being sent sufficient to complete her 1943 expansion programme and to maintain operations on the existing and very limited scale.[2] Moreover, the proportion of the total tonnage which could be allotted to civil requirements had already been

---
[1] See page 302.
[2] The Arakan and Chindit operations.

limited almost entirely to items required for essential production for the defence services, causing the small reserves of raw materials still in hand to be reduced to a dangerous level. Depending on the amount of shipping available, there appeared to be three possible alternatives for India: firstly, full preparations for 'Anakim' as planned, for which 174,000 tons a month (a reduction of 9,000 tons on the original estimate) from March were required; secondly, maintenance of land and air forces at their existing strength plus development to the 1943 expansion target, for which 127,000 tons a month (64,000 military and 63,000 civil) were required; and thirdly, a policy of stringent retrenchment, a course which India was already being forced to adopt by the actual allocation of shipping during February, March and April. If forced to adopt the last of these, India would soon become unable to arm and equip the new units being raised or to replace wastage in vehicles, weapons and equipment; the armed forces would in consequence be forced to accept a rôle of passive defence. But even if military requirements were reduced by the acceptance of this rôle, the minimum civil needs could not possibly be met; prices would rise, labour would give trouble and civil and political discontent might make India unsuitable as a base. Once recruiting, factory production and morale had been allowed to drop, it would be difficult to restore them to their original level. He asked what allocation of shipping tonnage he could expect and, if it were to continue at the present level of 65,000 tons, how long it would continue. He ended, 'My primary weapon for the defence of India is the air force and, assuming that this force must continue operations for the defence of India at the present standard, I shall be forced to cut down the remaining Services and the requirements of industry still further and thus accentuate the dangers enumerated [above]'.

Two days later he was told by the War Office that there was a possibility of the Mediterranean being opened to shipping in August, which would enable ships sailing in July by this shorter route to arrive at Indian ports in August at the same time as ships sailing in May by way of the Cape. Owing to the general shipping shortage, it would be impossible to meet fully the requirements for 'Anakim' at least till the Mediterranean was opened and, even then, provided only that no other circumstances impinged on the shipping position. It was therefore necessary to aim at extracting the greatest benefit from the opening of the Mediterranean route, despite the risk that at the last moment this would not become possible and the ships might still have to go by the Cape route with its consequent six weeks' delay. Some ships would therefore be loaded in May to sail by the Cape, and the balance of the August arrivals in India made up by loading the rest of the ships in July to sail by way of the

Mediterranean. Wavell was asked to submit a list of the items which were so important that delay in their arrival could not be risked. These would be sent by the normal May allotments.

Wavell replied that the shipping allotments for both March and April had been over 100,000 tons short. There was now apparently a qualified hope that the first increase in the monthly allotments (some 65,000 tons) would reach India in August, but the total tonnage received by August would still be over 100,000 tons short of the minimum requirements for 'Anakim'. Even if it were intended to send increased allotments by the shorter route in June and July to make up for these deficiencies, he would still be faced with a number of other difficulties. Among these were: the Indian ports could not handle more than 250,000 tons of shipping a month; communications in India were, owing to the effects of the monsoon, at their worst from September to October; ordnance depots and other channels for distribution to the troops would be blocked by the rush of material at a time when the transportation services would be suffering from the lack of equipment which should have already been received; the capacity of the assembly and erection plants would be insufficient to deal with the accumulation of vehicles and craft; the 4-inch pipe-lines, which would have to be laid in Assam to ensure that the supply of petrol was adequate, would not be available in time; and the essential specialized assault equipment would not be in the hands of the troops in time to give them adequate training in its use.

The original target date of the 15th November for 'Anakim' was already impossible to achieve, and these factors would now retard it still further. Wavell reminded the Chiefs of Staff that the campaigning season was short. Any delay in launching the operation would make it more difficult to reach a position where the troops could be maintained before the beginning of the 1944 monsoon; and most of the landings in the later stages of the operation, designed to seize airfields and deep water ports, had to be made on open beaches which would be affected by the weather before the monsoon actually broke. In other words, Wavell hinted strongly that, unless the Chiefs of Staff could overcome their difficulties and find the necessary shipping tonnage, the launching of 'Anakim' in the dry weather 1943–44 would become extremely hazardous, if not impossible.

But yet another administrative factor was to delay preparations for that part of 'Anakim' which involved an advance into upper Burma from Assam. At the conference in Chungking, General Arnold had offered to increase the air lift from India to 4,000 tons a month, but Chiang Kai-shek had insisted that this figure should be raised to 10,000 tons a month by November if China were to play her part in the dry weather offensive.[1] As a direct result of the Generalissimo's insistence, General Bissell (10th U.S.A.A.F.) told Wavell that four or five more airfields would be required in northern Assam. At this time there were seven airfields available, of which five were allotted to the Americans and two to the R.A.F.[2] Bissell asked that, as a first step, the two airfields used by the R.A.F. should be handed over to him or that they should be shared. A further three airfields would have to be constructed at high priority and he suggested that, to save time, steel planking from the U.S.A. should be used for the runways. Additional hardstandings and other improvements would be needed at all the existing airfields to enable them to take heavier transport aircraft, large numbers of which were expected shortly.

Owing to the location of the airfields and the shortages of material, labour and vehicles in Assam, these demands created further engineering and administrative problems. By this time the organization for the construction of airfields and roads, introduced early in 1942[3], had proved unsuitable for Assam, where the normal difficulties were greatly increased by local conditions. Wavell had therefore agreed early in March 1943 to the creation of a self-contained and independent organization known as the General Reserve Engineering Force (G.R.E.F.) which would work directly under the orders of General Headquarters, India. It would have its own headquarters and be organized into three echelons: the first of military units, the second of quasi-military units and the third of supervisory staff only, who would employ local labour. It would be responsible for all airfield and road construction in Assam and any other engineering projects in that area that might be necessary from time to time. Four airfield construction groups had also been formed: two for the construction of forward landing strips in pace with an advance, and two to follow up later to convert these strips to airfields of an all-weather standard, as required.

In April, the G.R.E.F. was made responsible for the completion to the required standards of all roads in Assam east of Bongaigaon and the airfields already allotted to the 10th U.S.A.A.F. in north-east Assam; for the construction of the new airfields now required in that area; and for the laying of a 4-inch pipe-line, some 150 miles in length, from Chandranathpur to Dimapur to save the carriage of petrol over the difficult Badarpur–Lumding hill section of the railway.[4]

---

[1] See page 305.

[2] The U.S.A.A.F. airfields were Sookerating, Dinjan, Chabua, Mohanbari and Misamari, and the R.A.F. airfields Jorhat and Tezpur. The three new airfields were Moran, Nazira and Golaghat. See Sketch 17.

[3] See page 191.

[4] See Sketch 17.

From the administrative point of view, the increase in the air lift and the construction of additional airfields involved the delivery to Assam not only of the 10,000 tons a month of stores for air transport to China, but all the steel planking (some 20,000 tons) required for the new airfields and some 10,000 tons a month of 100 octane petrol, as well as the stores required to accommodate and maintain the additional aircraft crews and American ground staffs. On the 9th March, Wavell told the Prime Minister that, as a result of the increased load on both his engineering resources and the transportation system in and into Assam, he could not provide the three additional airfields without destroying all chance of being ready for an advance into northern Burma by November 1943.

Since the shortage of shipping would probably result in 'Anakim' being postponed till the dry weather of 1944-45, Wavell thought it more than ever desirable to do everything possible to deliver the 10,000 tons per month to China. Accordingly he told the Chiefs of Staff on the 10th April that he had decided to give airfield construction priority over all other engineering projects in Assam, and had ordered that the three new airfields were to be ready for use by the 1st October.

In London, the Prime Minister and the Chiefs of Staff were becoming increasingly uneasy about 'Anakim' from both its administrative and its operational aspects. Thus when on the 1st April Wavell suggested that he should visit the United Kingdom in June to discuss it and the Far Eastern situation as a whole, they decided that he should come as soon as possible so that decisions on 'Anakim', or any of its alternatives, could be taken at once. On the 18th April Wavell, with Peirse, Somerville and two staff officers left for London, where they arrived on the 22nd.

After some days of discussion with the three commanders, the Chiefs of Staff reached the conclusion that 'Anakim'—an operation which the Prime Minister had likened to attacking a hedgehog by pulling its bristles out one by one—could not be attempted during the dry weather of 1943-44. Their reasons were firstly, that the provision of naval forces, assault ships, landing craft and special equipment for the Far East would rule out any major combined operations in the Mediterranean after the invasion of Sicily in July, and thus lessen pressure on Germany at what might be a critical time in the fighting on the Russian front; secondly, that the success of 'Anakim' depended ultimately on a direct assault on Rangoon which, if the Japanese fortified its seaward approaches, would almost certainly fail; thirdly, that the launching of 'Anakim' would commit British forces to a major operation not essential towards the ultimate defeat of Japan, in some of the worst campaigning country in the world; and lastly, that, even if 'Anakim' were successful, the Burma Road could probably not be opened to its full capacity (some 20,000 tons a month) until the middle of 1945: the immediate effect on China of the operation would thus be little more than psychological.

After studying a number of alternative proposals, the Chiefs of Staff recommended the following programme for the dry weather 1943–44. The available resources were to be concentrated on developing the air facilities in Assam and increasing the capacity of the air route to China with three objects in view: an increase in the flow of airborne supplies to China, the maintenance of a larger American air force in China to strike at Japanese shipping in the Formosa Strait, and the intensification of air operations against the Japanese in Burma. Land operations from Assam were to cover as far as possible the development of the air facilities, but were not to be on a scale which would prejudice this development by causing excessive demands on the already overloaded Assam transportation system. Finally, Akyab and Ramree Islands were to be captured in order to provide air and naval bases further south from which the control of the Bay of Bengal could be increased, Japanese communications in central Burma more easily attacked and later coastal operations towards Gwa and Sandoway covered.

On the 26th April, the United States Chiefs of Staff suggested that the three commanders should return to India by way of Washington where they would have the opportunity of discussing operations in the China–Burma–India theatre with the Combined Chiefs of Staff and with Stilwell and Chennault, who were to be there till early May. They therefore travelled with the Prime Minister and the Chiefs of Staff on the 4th May to Washington to attend 'Trident', the Anglo-American conference to be held to consider plans for the defeat of Germany, Italy and Japan.

During the voyage across the Atlantic, the Prime Minister studied the Chiefs of Staff's recommendations. He commented that 'going into swampy jungles to fight the Japanese is like going into the water to fight a shark. It is better to entice him into a trap or catch him on a hook and then demolish him with axes after hauling him out on to dry land'. Although he thought the proposed operations were a 'bleak and skinny programme', he accepted the recommendations of the Chiefs of Staff, but he asked them to consider 'how then to deceive and entrap the shark', indicating that a landing might be made at one or more unexpected points in the crescent from Moulmein to Timor.[1] The Prime Minister was expressing a view which coincided closely with that already expressed by Wavell when, in

---
[1] Churchill, *The Second World War*, Volume IV (Cassell, 1951) pages 702-705.

February, he had begun to realize the difficulties in the way of launching 'Anakim' in the campaigning season of 1943–44.

Another important matter came up for discussion in London and during the voyage across the Atlantic. Similar reasons to those which had led Wavell to form an Indian Expeditionary Force and appoint a separate commander to control the seaborne portion of 'Anakim' had led him and the Viceroy (the Marquess of Linlithgow) in February to review the whole problem of command in South-East Asia. It was not however till the 21st April that the Viceroy cabled Mr. L. S. Amery, the Secretary of State for India, giving his views on the subject.

He realized, he said, that the business of defeating the Japanese was one of first class magnitude and that a Commander-in-Chief, Asia, would be required to organize and carry through the necessary campaign; this would become even more necessary if, after the defeat of Germany, British, American and other Allied troops were based on India. There was also, he said, a strong case for relieving the Commander-in-Chief in India of some of the burden he was at the time carrying in connection with active operations, in order to give him more time to discharge his normal duties as adviser to the Governor General in Council; these included not only his general military responsibilities for the security of India and for the supervision and inspection of training and administrative establishments, but political duties as well.

He proposed therefore that consideration should be given to creating the post of Commander-in-Chief, Asia (or Far East) which would include India within its control for operational purposes. This post might well be offered to Field Marshal Wavell. The post of Commander-in-Chief in India, which would thus fall vacant, should, he suggested, be offered to General Auchinleck, who was for the moment unemployed, since he was greatly respected by the Indian Army and would be able to raise its morale to the pitch necessary to enable the Japanese to be met and defeated in battle.

As a consequence of this cable, Mr. Amery submitted a concrete proposal to the Prime Minister on the 27th April. He suggested that the Commander-in-Chief in India should be entirely relieved of all operational responsibility for the South-East Asia campaigns and should concentrate upon the administration of India as a base and on the organization, training and sending forward of the forces under his command in conformity with the operational orders of the Supreme Chief, who would be in undistracted charge of the campaigns. The Commander-in-Chief in India would be responsible only for local operational matters such as internal security, the defence of the North West Frontier and India's coastline outside the area controlled by the Supreme Chief. He proposed various forms which the Supreme Command might take should the basic idea be accepted.

The Prime Minister showed Wavell these proposals during the voyage and asked him for his views. On the 17th May Wavell replied that he too had been considering the problem of command in the Indian theatre of war. He felt that there were obvious advantages in having a command in South-East Asia separate from that of the Commander-in-Chief in India, who was overloaded with duties as a member of the Government of India, head of the Indian Army and the man in charge of the planning and conduct of operations against Japan. A separate commander who could give his whole time to operations was undoubtedly required. He pointed out that the United States forces in India were tending to set up entirely independent intelligence and administration organizations, thus leading to overlapping and confusion. He therefore advocated a combined British and American command and staff, if possible on the lines of the command set up in North Africa under General D. D. Eisenhower. In addition to overcoming the difficulties he had specified, such a combined command would ensure better co-ordination of the resources available for operations to defeat the Japanese.

He said that he assumed that the Supreme Commander, if it were agreed to appoint one, would be British, since the forces operating from India would be mainly British, and, if the North African model were followed, he would have an American deputy. In any case a combined British-American intelligence organization was essential to co-ordinate the existing overlapping systems. The extent of a South-East Asia Command would require definition. No difficulty would arise in fixing a boundary between the new command and General MacArthur's South West Pacific Command, but the division between the new command and the Generalissimo's in China might be a matter of delicate negotiation. He considered that all operations in Burma, including the control of any Chinese forces operating in the country, should be under the new command. He outlined his views on the internal organization of the command and proposed that its headquarters should at first be in Delhi, since it would take over the existing General Headquarters, India, Planning Staff. Since Delhi was overcrowded, it should move elsewhere later: Ceylon might be the best place, for there the Supreme Commander could maintain close touch with the Commander-in-Chief, Eastern Fleet.

Those concerned were all in agreement that a new South-East Asia Command was needed, but there was to be much discussion before a decision on its final form was reached a few months later.

CHAPTER XXII

THE PACIFIC

(February–April 1943)

See Maps 10 and 15 and Sketch 19

TO give the reader the background to the strategic decisions taken at the Trident Conference, it is necessary here to review the progress of the war in the Pacific since February 1943. But, before doing so, some of the great events which took place in the West, while the struggles for Guadalcanal and Papua were going on in the East, should be recalled. The last months of 1942 and the beginning of 1943 had seen a dramatic change in the fortunes of the Allies. The battle of El Alamein had sounded the knell of Axis hopes in the Middle East; by February the British 8th Army had driven Rommel's forces nearly 1,000 miles from the Egyptian border, and further west General Eisenhower's Anglo-American armies, which had landed in North Africa in November, had gained control of Morocco and Algeria and had crossed the Tunisian border. In Europe, a German army had been almost annihilated at Stalingrad and the Russian counter-offensive, having pushed the enemy back over the Don, was beginning to gain momentum. Everywhere the Allies' star was in the ascendant. Only in the Atlantic, where German U-boats and aircraft were still taking terrible toll of merchant shipping, was the issue still in doubt.

In the Pacific, the hitherto victorious Japanese advance had been brought to a halt.[1] In occupying Tulagi and Guadalcanal, 700 miles away from their nearest air base at Rabaul, the Japanese Navy had, contrary to its usual practice, moved outside the effective range of its land-based fighter aircraft. Before it could move its air squadrons forward, the Americans had taken possession of the partly-completed Henderson Field on Guadalcanal. Possession of this airfield gave to the Americans, and denied to the Japanese, a forward base for air striking forces and a valuable advanced position for reconnaissance covering the reinforcement routes to the island. Throughout the campaign, the Americans again and again received timely warning of the approach of the enemy from their reconnaissance aircraft, as well as from the gallant band of coast-watchers hiding in the jungle on the islands to the north. This

---
[1] See Chapter XVI.

enabled them to dispose their forces so as to intercept Japanese attempts to reinforce their garrison on the island. The result, as we have seen, was a series of naval and air battles none of which was decisive until the three-day battle of Guadalcanal. The Japanese had then found that their losses in ships and aircraft were more than they could afford for the recapture of the island. The unexpected strength of American resistance had a twofold effect. Firstly, it forced the Japanese to embark on a contest of attrition in which the greater recuperative power of the United States finally told, and secondly, it led them to reinforce Guadalcanal at the expense of New Guinea, with the result that their campaign for the control of Papua failed through lack of adequate support. By February 1943 *Imperial General Headquarters* had realized that with the almost simultaneous defeat of their forces in Guadalcanal and Papua a major turning point in the war had been reached, and they now had to turn from the offensive to the defensive.

Rabaul, lying at the northern end of New Britain, one of the ring of islands in the Bismarck Archipelago—aptly called by the Americans the Bismarck Barrier—was the key point of the Japanese south-eastern front, for it covered the approaches to the Phillippines from the south-east and guarded the main Japanese naval base at Truk from the south. *Imperial General Headquarters* was in no doubt that this would be the next main Allied objective and it was determined to hold Rabaul at all costs. It assumed that MacArthur's South West Pacific and Halsey's South Pacific forces would approach it through New Guinea on the one hand and by the chain of the Solomons to Bougainville on the other. Even before the fall of Guadalcanal, it had decided that the next line of defence was to run from Isabel and the New Georgia islands in the central Solomons to Lae in New Guinea, and had begun to strengthen both the central Solomons and the north-east coast of New Guinea. The Navy was to be primarily responsible for the defence of the central Solomons and the Army for the northern Solomons and New Guinea.

Admiral Yamamoto (Commander-in-Chief, *Combined Fleet*) believed that Japan's only hope of winning the war lay in the decisive defeat of the American Fleet while the odds were still in his favour. Having lost two battleships and six carriers in less than a year, he wished to husband his remaining strength. He intended therefore to keep his heavy ships in the background until a favourable opportunity for a fleet action occurred. On Christmas Eve 1942, Vice-Admiral Kusaka had been appointed Commander, *South-Eastern Area Fleet*, and given command of the *8th Fleet* and all naval forces in the Bismarck, Solomons and New Guinea area in addition to his own *11th Air Fleet*. Knowing that he could expect little help from the *Combined*

ALLIED PLANS FOR THE PACIFIC

Fleet, he took steps to speed up the development of the new airfields at Munda and Vila, intending to rely largely on air power for the defence of the central Solomons. Lieut.-General Imamura (*8th Area Army*) at the same time began to strengthen the defences of Rabaul and to reinforce the garrisons in the northern and central Solomons. Early in the new year he sent two divisions to Wewak[1], bringing the total strength of New Guinea up to about three divisions.

The Allies meanwhile, with the initiative at last in their hands, were discussing plans for the next move. The general direction of the advance had been laid down in the directive of July 1942[2], and confirmed at the Casablanca Conference in January 1943.[3] In the south and south-west Pacific, the advance through New Guinea and the Solomons was to be continued until Rabaul was taken and the Bismarck Barrier broken. Munda airfield was selected as the next main objective in the approach to the Bismarck Barrier. In New Guinea, the capture of Lae and Salamaua was the obvious prerequisite to the clearance of the Huon Peninsula and entry to New Britain. After the desperate fighting of the past six months, time was needed to recuperate and reorganize before the next phase, and it was thought that the offensive could not be resumed till April. Admiral Halsey, however, obtained Admiral Nimitz's approval to take the Russell Islands as a stepping stone towards Munda and to develop them as an advanced naval and air base. During the evacuation of Guadalcanal, the Japanese had landed several thousand men on the islands and, in the belief that they were still there, Admiral Halsey greatly overweighted the assault. On the 21st February a force of 9,000 men was landed to find no trace of the enemy. The operation is chiefly noteworthy for the repulse by gun fire of a night torpedo-bomber attack on the transports during their passage north.

During February, the only fighting which took place in New Guinea was centred round the mining village of Wau, thirty miles south-west of Salamaua, where the small Australian Kangaforce had driven off repeated Japanese attacks on the airfield during January.[4] In the second part of the month 17th Australian Brigade was flown to Wau, and Kangaforce thus reinforced drove the enemy back to the coast. Regarding the airfield at Wau as a threat to his hold on the Huon Peninsula, General Imamura then decided, in consultation with Admiral Kusaka, to augment the garrison at Lae. Eight transports escorted by a similar number of destroyers left Rabaul on the last day of February carrying *Headquarters 18th Army* and the main body of *51st Division*, nearly seven thousand troops in all. The convoy was sighted by reconnaissance aircraft on the 1st March

---
[1] The *20th* and *41st Divisions*.
[2] See pages 270–71.
[3] See pages 297–98.
[4] See page 278.

and shadowed until well after dark, when contact was lost. It was picked up again the next morning as it was about to enter Dampier Strait, and for the next forty-eight hours was subjected to repeated attacks by American and Australian bombers from the Papuan airfields. A new technique of very low attack using delayed action fuses, called by the Americans 'skip bombing', was employed with devastating effect. The convoy was completely destroyed and only four of the escorting destroyers escaped and returned to Rabaul. These and some submarines rescued about half of the men from the convoy, but over three thousand were missing. Twenty to thirty of the Japanese aircraft giving cover to the convoy were shot down for the loss of only five of the three hundred and thirty-five Allied aircraft engaged. As a result of the air battle of the Bismarck Sea, the Japanese had to resort to sending in supplies and reinforcements to Lae and Salamaua by barge and submarine, as they had been forced to do during the Guadalcanal campaign.

As in New Guinea, so in the central Solomons the Japanese were feverishly trying to build up their defences to meet the expected Allied offensive. Admiral Halsey, while planning and preparing, was doing his best to stop them. Aircraft of the South West Pacific Command made day and night raids on the airfields at Munda and Vila. On the night of the 6th/7th March, a destroyer task force under Rear-Admiral A. S. Merrill, U.S.N., entered Kula Gulf between the islands of New Georgia and Kolombangara, sank two destroyers bringing supplies to Vila and carried out a bombardment of Vila airfield.[1] The bombardment was heavy, but the coral airstrip was easily repaired and the airfield was soon in action again.

Admiral Halsey had by now a powerful fleet. Although the *Saratoga* and *Enterprise* were his only surviving fleet carriers, he had been reinforced by three escort carriers. In addition he had four battleships, two of which had been salvaged after the Pearl Harbour débâcle, and a considerable number of cruisers and destroyers. The South Pacific air force also had been greatly strengthened: there were now over 300 aircraft of all types in Guadalcanal alone, and another 200 in the New Hebrides and New Caledonia. General MacArthur's naval forces in the south-west Pacific were however still very slender. Admiral Crutchley's squadron of three cruisers formed the only battle force[2], and there was a serious shortage of flotilla vessels, but a growing force of American submarines was working from Brisbane. Landing craft, which had been so badly needed in the Papuan campaign, were beginning to arrive, and an amphibious force was being built up and trained at Brisbane. General Kenney's air force had grown in strength, as the Japanese

---
[1] See Sketch 19.
[2] H.M.A.S. *Australia* and *Hobart* and U.S.S. *Phoenix*.

had learnt to their cost at the battle of the Bismarck Sea, when over 300 aircraft were operating from airfields in New Guinea alone. On the 15th March the South and South West Pacific naval forces were renamed the 3rd and 7th Fleet respectively; each was divided into task groups and task forces and each contained an amphibious force bearing the same number as the fleet to which it belonged.

By the beginning of March, Admiral Halsey felt ready to begin the offensive and proposed that the South Pacific Area forces should attack Munda early in April. General MacArthur, who had been given responsibility for the conduct of the second phase of operations in the Joint Chiefs of Staff directive of the 2nd July, wished to establish air bases in the Trobriand Islands off the east coast of Papua as a preliminary to the clearance of the Huon Peninsula, and to synchronize the opening attacks in New Guinea and the Solomons. His amphibious forces which were building up at Brisbane would not be ready by April, and he therefore asked that Halsey's offensive should be timed for mid-May.

A conference, attended by the American Chiefs of Staff and leading representatives of the South and South West Pacific Commands, was held in Washington in March to decide on the strategy to be adopted in the Pacific. It resulted on the 28th March in the issue of a new directive. In the South West Pacific Area, the Trobriand Islands (Kiriwina and Woodlark) were to be taken and airfields established there. Lae, Salamaua, Finschhafen, the Madaung area and western New Britain were then to be seized. In the South Pacific Area, the Solomons were to be occupied as far north as Bougainville. General MacArthur was to have strategic control of all operations and Admiral Halsey tactical command of operations in the Solomons area, subject to the general direction of MacArthur. The 15th May was provisionally set for the opening attack but, as we shall see, it had to be postponed for another six weeks.

The Japanese, while preparing to meet the expected offensive, had no intention of letting MacArthur and Halsey perfect their plans unhindered. During March the *11th Air Fleet* had, so far as its resources permitted, made sporadic attacks on Allied bases in New Guinea and the Solomons. At the end of the month Admiral Yamamoto arrived at Rabaul to conduct an all-out air campaign on the Allied forward bases, designated the 'I Operation', with the object of reducing the growing Allied air power and delaying their impending offensive. Over a hundred aircraft from Admiral Nagumo's four fleet carriers and their pilots, the pick of the naval air arm, were disembarked and based on the airfields in New Britain and the northern Solomons to augment the *11th Air Fleet*. In all, Yamamoto assembled over three hundred torpedo-bombers, dive-bombers and fighters. The 'I Operation' opened on the 1st April with a preparatory sweep down 'The Slot' by fifty-eight fighters, eighteen of which were shot down for the loss of six American aircraft. A week later about seventy bombers escorted by over a hundred fighters, the heaviest concentration of aircraft since Pearl Harbour, attacked shipping at Guadalcanal and Tulagi. American fighters, warned by coast-watchers, were airborne to meet them and in the ensuing air battle nineteen Japanese aircraft were shot down at a cost of seven American, from which all but one of the pilots were saved. Despite the number of aircraft employed, damage done to the ships crowded in the roads was slight: only a destroyer and two auxiliary craft were sunk. The offensive switched to New Guinea on the 11th April when Oro Bay (near Buna), now the main supply base for the airfields north of the Owen Stanleys, was heavily attacked. Although only five minutes warning was received, once again the damage to shipping was slight. On the following day Port Moresby received the heaviest raid yet in the south-west Pacific. Forty-three bombers, escorted by over a hundred and thirty fighters, struck at the airfield and at shipping in the harbour. Not a ship was hit. Two days later it was the turn of Milne Bay. Timely warning had enabled most of the ships to leave their anchorages and only two ships, one British and one Dutch, were sunk.

The raid on Milne Bay ended the 'I Operation', and the Japanese carrier aircraft were recalled to their ships. The pilots made extravagant claims, which bore no relation to the truth, of the number of ships sunk and aircraft shot down. Allied losses in the series of raids were in fact no more than a destroyer, a corvette, a tanker and two merchant ships sunk and approximately twenty-five aircraft shot down. From the point of view of the Japanese, the operation proved to be a dismal failure. It failed to restore the balance of air power in their favour as they had hoped—if anything it swung it the other way. The *1st Carrier Squadron* was so disorganized by the losses of aircraft and pilots that it had to be sent back to Japan to reorganize and refit. Admiral Yamamoto himself, accepting his airmen's claims, believed he had achieved his purpose. He did not live to learn the truth. Four days after the final attack on Milne Bay, he and some of his staff officers flew in two bombers, escorted by nine fighters, from Rabaul to visit air bases in the south of Bougainville. American intelligence gave warning of the visit, and a strong force of fighters sent from Guadalcanal intercepted them on the 18th April as they were about to land. Both bombers were destroyed with all their passengers. The death of Admiral Yamamoto, one of the outstanding figures in Japanese naval history, was a severe blow to the morale of the Imperial Navy. His body was recovered from the jungle and his ashes taken to Tokyo where on the 5th May he was given a state funeral. He was succeeded by Admiral Mineichi Koga.

CHAPTER XXIII

THE TRIDENT CONFERENCE
(May–June 1943)

See Strategic Map and Maps 14 and 15

BEFORE turning to the Trident Conference in Washington, it may be well to give the opposing views held by Stilwell and Chennault on the programme for the China theatre, since these had a considerable effect on United States policy and thus on the decisions reached at the conference.[1] The divergence arose from the fundamentally different approach on the part of these two officers towards the problem of keeping China in the war, and of making the greatest use of her territory and her armed forces for the defeat of Japan. The question was one for consideration by the American Chiefs of Staff, since it affected the whole strategical concept of war in South-East Asia.

In April the two Generals arrived in Washington to present their views. Chennault proposed that the 14th U.S.A.A.F. should be built up to a strength of about 150 fighters and 80 bombers and used to protect the terminal air bases in Yunnan, to wrest air superiority from the Japanese *3rd Air Division*, to attack shipping in the coastal ports, the Formosa Strait and on the Yangtze, to disrupt the enemy's lines of communication within China and later to bomb the Japanese mainland. He claimed that he could sink some half a million tons of enemy shipping in six months and force the Japanese to withdraw from the interior of China. He realized that the immediate Japanese reaction to such an air offensive would be to advance into central China to capture the airfields from which he was operating. But, since they had failed in similar efforts before, he discounted their ability to carry such an operation to a successful conclusion. In order to build up the air force to the required strength, he would need some 4,700 tons of supplies flown into China monthly for four months, increasing later to 7,000 tons.

Stilwell on the other hand considered that, though the building up of the 14th U.S.A.A.F. would result in considerable disruption of Japanese shipping lanes, it would not lead to decisive results. As soon

---

[1] Rumours of differences of opinion between the two Generals had reached Wavell's ears in January. See page 297.

as the proposed attack began to affect the Japanese seriously, they would launch an offensive from Indo-China to capture the Kunming area and the eastern terminal of the air route to China which, if successful, would put China out of the war. It was therefore necessary to re-equip and organize sufficient Chinese divisions to defend Yunnan. For this he would require a second group of thirty Chinese divisions over and above the first thirty which he was in the process of reorganizing. He estimated that for this purpose he required some 2,000 tons of supplies to be flown into China monthly. He expressed the opinion that, though the air supply route might eventually be able to carry 10,000 tons per month[1], the only way of getting large quantities of material into China was by road, and thus a land route would ultimately be essential.

From the wording of a telegram the Generalissimo sent to the President early in January 1943, it was clear that he inclined towards the view expressed by Chennault, and was tending to rely on American air power rather than on his own armies, reorganized by Stilwell and re-equipped with American arms, for the defeat of Japan. In it he said:

> 'The remarkable potentialities of an air offensive in China have already been demonstrated by a small and ill-supported force. I believe that an early air offensive is feasible, since, owing to the peculiar tactical conditions which prevail here, neither the supply, material and personnel requirements are such as to embarrass the United Nations' air effort elsewhere. The return, I predict, will be out of all proportion to the investment, and by further weakening the Japanese air arm and striking at the seaborne communications with their new conquests, an air offensive in China will directly prepare for the ultimate general offensive to which we both look forward.'[2]

It was no doubt with this thought in mind that the Generalissimo had insisted at the Chungking conference in February on the organization of a separate air force in China and the increase of the air lift to 10,000 tons a month.

As can be imagined, the opposing views held by Chennault and Stilwell each had their separate supporters in Washington. It therefore fell to the President, as Commander-in-Chief, to decide which to accept as the policy of the United States. He believed that the most effective way of defeating the Japanese was by striking at their shipping as it left Japan. This could best be done from China or Russia. Much depended therefore on keeping China going, and there was a danger of her collapsing. He felt that politically he had to support the Generalissimo, who considered the fulfilment of the

---
[1] See pages 366-68.
[2] Romanus and Sunderland, page 260.

proposed air programme of prime importance. He decided therefore that there should be no delay in carrying out the Chennault programme, though the necessary supplies for the Yunnan force should also be sent in.[1]

When the conference opened on the 12th May, both the British and American views on strategy for the Far East were discussed at length. While accepting that the build-up of the air lift and 14th U.S.A.A.F. should be given priority, the American Chiefs of Staff thought that a great increase in the tonnage carried, without effective ground operations, would produce a strong Japanese reaction and that the lack of aggressive action in Burma would be fatal for China. They therefore advocated more vigorous and far-reaching operations from Assam than were envisaged by the British Chiefs of Staff.

The Combined Chiefs of Staff finally put forward five recommendations:

(1) The concentration of available resources, as first priority within the Assam–Burma Theatre, on the building up and increasing of the air route to China to a capacity of 10,000 tons a month by early autumn, and the development of air facilities in Assam with a view to:
  (a) intensifying air operations against the Japanese in Burma;
  (b) maintaining increased American air forces in China; and
  (c) maintaining the flow of airborne supplies to China.
(2) Vigorous and aggressive land and air operations at the end of the 1943 monsoon from Assam into Burma via Ledo and Imphal, in step with an advance by Chinese forces from Yunnan, with the object of containing as many Japanese forces as possible, covering the air route to China, and as an essential step towards the opening of the Burma Road.
(3) The capture of Akyab and of Ramree Island by amphibious operations, with possible exploitation.
(4) The interruption of Japanese sea communications into Burma.
(5) The continuance of administrative preparations in India for the eventual launching of an overseas operation of about the size of Anakim.

These were approved by the Prime Minister and the President and became the policy to be followed in the South-East Asia theatre of operations. The conference also examined the various courses of action to be adopted in the Pacific and agreed that operations should be undertaken to eject the Japanese from the Aleutians; to seize the Marshall and Caroline Islands as well as the Solomons, the Bismarck Archipelago and Japanese-held New Guinea and to intensify attacks on enemy lines of communication.[2]

---
[1] Romanus and Sunderland, pages 320-27.
[2] See Map 15.

It will be seen that, except in one respect, the decisions on policy for South-East Asia reached at the Trident Conference followed closely the British Chiefs of Staff's recommendations made in London at the end of April. The difference lay in the scope of the land operations across the Assam frontier into Burma. In order to avoid overloading the already extended Assam transportation system, the British view had been to limit operations from Assam to those necessary to cover the development of the air facilities. The Trident conclusions however spoke of vigorous land and air operations from Assam into Burma in conjunction with an advance from Yunnan by the Chinese forces as an essential step towards the opening of the Burma Road. This in fact was 'Anakim' without the seaborne portion of the operation. The conclusions demanded the allocation of considerable resources of men and material to operations for the recapture of upper Burma, which could be provided only at the expense of the immediate expansion of the air supply to China and the build-up of the line of communication from India to the Assam border. They were therefore to increase India's administrative difficulties.

During the course of the Trident Conference, news of the final reverses in Arakan resulting in the loss of Buthidaung and Maungdaw reached Washington.[1] Wavell, the Indian Army and the commanders in Arakan all came under very severe criticism from the Prime Minister, who described the campaign as one of the most disappointing and indeed discreditable which had occurred during the course of the war. He demanded that new commanders should be found, that troops whose morale had been lowered should be severely disciplined and that, if regular Indian Army troops were incapable of fighting the Japanese in the jungle, commando formations should be developed.

Wavell's reaction to these criticisms was to point out that the operations in Arakan had to be viewed in their proper perspective. They had been undertaken on his instructions at a time when there was every prospect of landing craft and other equipment being available for a seaborne assault on Akyab. When it had become clear that these would not be forthcoming, he had decided to risk trying to reach Akyab by an overland advance rather than keep his troops idle, though they were neither fully trained nor of the best quality. At the time he took this decision, he had reason to suppose that the Japanese would be fully occupied in upper Burma and unlikely to be able to send reinforcements to Arakan, since IV Corps and the Chinese, both from India and Yunnan, were to carry out a com-

[1] See Chapter XX.

bined attack on upper Burma. The Chinese had not moved and plans for the attack had had to be abandoned; as a result, the Japanese were able to reinforce Akyab and Arakan with the equivalent of a complete division, which had altered the whole situation in that area. Although it was clear that Akyab could not be reached, he had decided to carry on with the operations in order to keep the Japanese extended and to inflict losses, and on balance he thought they had suffered the more heavily. From the standpoint of morale, however, the balance was of course entirely on the Japanese side, which was serious, but the operations had not been without some advantage to the Allies. They had shown that the known weaknesses in the expanded Indian Army were more pronounced than had been realized. It was better, he said, that these should have been disclosed then rather than later, as would have happened had the operations not been undertaken.

On being told of the Prime Minister's criticism of the Arakan operations, General Sir Alan Hartley (Deputy Commander-in-Chief in India) observed that it should be remembered that the Indian Army had been grossly over-expanded to meet Imperial needs and as a result had for the time being become a second-class army. It had been used against a first-class enemy in terrain which had in pre-war days been considered impossible for active operations, but which, as the Japanese had realized, could be fought over provided the troops were adequately trained. In such terrain the infantry had to be the '*corps d'élite*', yet it was this arm which had been most affected by over-expansion and had become the weakest branch of the Indian Army. The problem was to raise the standard of the British and Indian infantry to that of the enemy's, and to ensure that the scale of operations planned for the next dry weather was such that, with the resources then available, success would be certain. If this aspect of the matter were forgotten, and the impossible asked, the effect on the morale of the whole of the Indian Army might be disastrous.

Meanwhile Mr Amery (the Secretary of State for India) had been considering the morale of the Indian Army from an entirely different point of view. For some months it had been becoming plain that great efforts were being made by the Japanese to undermine its loyalty. They had set up a school at Penang for training Indian nationals as agents who, on completing their training, were to be sent to India to create internal unrest and promote sabotage. They had formed an 'Indian National Army' (I.N.A.) from Indian prisoners of war and Indian civilians resident in Malaya and Burma. They were giving assistance to an organization styled the 'Indian Independence League' (I.I.L.), which had been formed round a nucleus of certain notorious political absconders who for many years had found refuge and support in Japan and elsewhere. Both these organizations were being given opportunities to broadcast subversive propaganda to India. This was the background to a memorandum sent by Mr Amery to the Prime Minister in Washington.

He explained that the enormous expansion of the Indian Army had resulted in the exhaustion of the manpower of the pre-war military classes with their long tradition of military service and loyalty, and the recruitment into the Services of many classes with no such traditional background. This position was not improved by the fact that a large number of British and Indian officers, lacking in experience of the Indian soldier, his language and traditions, had to be given temporary commissions: these officers were unable to engender confidence and faith in their men as had the regular Indian Army regimental officer or his counterpart in the Indian Navy and Air Force. Another factor which, he felt, rendered the Indian armed forces particularly susceptible to Japanese subversive activities was the deterioration of the economic situation in India. The great increase in the cost of living had been a potent recruiting agent; many men had been driven to joining the colours solely for the pay and material benefits of the army, and in the desire to receive training which might be of value in civil life after the war. The Indian Army, he pointed out, had always been mercenary in that the men were volunteers, but the pre-war army had been composed of a body of men who chose the profession of arms as good in itself and, as part of their professional instinct, were imbued with devotion to their regiment and to the Government.

Despite all these difficulties, Mr Amery continued, there were no signs as yet that the attacks, both internal and external, on the loyalty of the Services in India had met with much success. The danger existed, however, and would have to be met. It was clear to him that any further expansion of the Indian Army would be dangerous, and he recommended that every effort should be made to improve its quality rather than quantity by keeping the standard high and weeding out unsuitable men.

Wavell agreed that up to that time there had been little evidence that subversive elements had affected the loyalty of the Indian Army. The situation was being carefully watched by General Headquarters, India, but the army appeared to be indifferent to politics, though showing considerable concern at the deteriorating economic position. Its morale remained good, as was shown by its behaviour during the Congress-sponsored riots in August and September 1942. Had there been any widespread disaffection, it would have come to light at that time. He thought however that a potential source of danger lay in the Indian Air Force, where the men enlisted were almost entirely from the politically conscious and non-martial classes.

The Prime Minister was greatly concerned at Mr Amery's report, and expressed the view that not only should all expansion of the army cease, but that its size should be substantially reduced to improve its quality. The Chiefs of Staff agreed that no new formations should be raised, but preferred to postpone any decision on the desirability of reducing the size of the army till the matter had been fully investigated. To this the Prime Minister agreed, and on the 20th May the Cabinet decided that the target for the expansion of the Indian Army, already reduced to fifteen divisions and two armoured divisions (a reduction of three divisions), should be retained but not exceeded.[1] A watch should be kept on the economic situation so that, if necessary, the pay of Indian ranks could be increased.

Wavell was well aware that the failure in Arakan, following as it did the disastrous campaigns in Malaya and Burma, had dealt the army in India a severe shock. He knew that it had fostered among all ranks a false idea of Japanese skill and a belief in Japanese invincibility, and as a result they had come to place the need to protect themselves against the enemy before the need to take the offensive and defeat him. Their morale was basically sound, but the myth of Japanese invincibility had clearly to be destroyed before an offensive spirit could be re-established throughout the army. The reasons for the Japanese successes were that in physical fitness and morale and, above all, in organization for and training in jungle warfare they were greatly superior to the hastily formed, partially equipped Indian Army formations whose training was not only inadequate, but had been based on the requirements of warfare in the open desert country of the Middle East and Iraq. The army in India had therefore to be reorganized, re-equipped and given intensive training in tactical methods suitable for the terrain in South-East Asia before any further operations against the Japanese could safely be launched.

On the 16th May, Wavell told his deputy in Delhi that steps should be taken to profit by the lessons learnt from the Arakan and Chindit operations, so as to ensure that the Indian Army could meet the Japanese on equal terms when operations began again in the dry weather 1943–44. Since the failure in Arakan was clearly due to the inability of the British and Indian infantry to deal with Japanese infiltrating and enveloping tactics in the jungle and to overcome their tenacious defensive methods, Wavell gave instructions that a strong representative committee was to be set up 'to examine and report on the present standard of readiness for war of British and

---

[1] The 4th, 6th, 8th and 10th Infantry Divisions and 31st Armoured Division in the Middle East; 5th, 7th, 14th, 17th, 19th, 20th, 23rd, 25th, 26th, 36th and 39th Infantry Divisions and 44th Armoured Division (formed out of 32nd and 43rd) in India. The 34th Infantry Division in Ceylon was broken up in May/June 1943, and 9th and 11th Infantry Divisions had been lost in Malaya.

Indian Infantry Battalions in India, and to make recommendations for their improvement'.

Accordingly the Infantry Committee, India, was formed and sat from the 1st to the 14th June 1943. It found that the repeated failures in Arakan arose from a number of factors which could not be attributed to any fault of the infantry soldier himself. These were: the lack of adequate basic training and of experienced leadership in the infantry units employed in the operations; the absence before the operations began of any collective training of the formations employed; prolonged periods in contact with the enemy, which included much hard fighting without relief or replacement of casualties, leading to exhaustion of the troops; the high incidence of malaria and the delay in the return of malaria casualties to units; and the inability of exhausted, under-strength and battle-weary units to absorb inadequately trained recruits in large numbers. The accumulative effect of all these factors led inevitably to a drop in both efficiency and morale.

The committee expressed the opinion that fundamentally the morale, fighting spirit and physique of the infantry in India were sound. But, although it had been recognised that in any operations against the Japanese in jungle and hill country the infantry was predominant, this arm of the Service, which had become highly technical, had not been given the necessary priority in the selection of recruits, in training and in many other ways. It had not been fully realized that the adage 'any man can be an infantry man' had been out of date for many years. The committee concluded by saying that a stage had been reached in the war with Japan when nothing except success would stimulate morale to the highest pitch. They stressed therefore that inadequate support of isolated units or formations, fighting interminably without relief and without trained reserves and reinforcements, would have an immediate and disastrous effect on morale.

The committee made five major recommendations: firstly, that the status of the infantry arm should be improved by giving the Indian infantry first claim in the selection of cadet officers and educated recruits, by increasing the rate of pay of both British and Indian infantry[1], and by stopping the practice of 'milking' the infantry of trained men or specialists for the benefit of other arms of the Services; secondly, that the period of basic training for the Indian infantry recruit should be increased to eleven months, training to be progressive and to include two months in a training division where jungle warfare would be taught, while all British

---

[1] Increased rates of pay for Indian troops were announced by General Auchinleck in the Council of State on the 13th March 1944. The rate of pay of British troops was a matter for decision by His Majesty's Government.

infantry drafts should on arrival in India undergo a period of acclimatization and toughening, combined with training in jungle warfare; thirdly, that arrangements should be made to improve collective training of infantrymen with other arms before they went on active operations; fourthly, that steps should be taken to improve the quality of officers and non-commissioned officers in the infantry; and lastly, that the reinforcement system for active battalions should be improved. The system whereby recruits who had not finished their basic training at infantry training centres were drafted as reinforcements must cease, and drafts should include an adequate proportion of good and experienced non-commissioned officers. The committee proposed that two training divisions should be formed without delay so that the reinforcement machinery could function efficiently by the time operations began in the dry weather of 1943-44.

These recommendations were accepted. Arrangements were made for 14th and 39th Indian Divisions to be converted into training divisions for Indian troops, for a new brigade (52nd) to be formed out of three British battalions for training British troops and for the necessary measures to be taken to improve the training given at the infantry training centres.[1] All brigades incorporated within active divisions were to be reorganized so that they should consist, as far as resources permitted, of one British, one Indian and one Gurkha battalion.

At the close of the Trident Conference, Air Marshal Peirse returned to India to speed up the development of air facilities in Assam so that the air lift to China could be increased to the agreed figure of 10,000 tons a month by the autumn. The Prime Minister asked Field Marshal Wavell and Admiral Somerville to meet him in London for further discussions, and arranged with the President that General Stilwell and General Chennault should return to China by way of London in order to exchange information with the India Office and the Service departments. He himself went on to North Africa, but with his return to London early in June the framework of the proposed new command in South-East Asia began to take shape.[2]

On the 15th June, the Prime Minister set out his views on the reorganization of command in South-East Asia in a memorandum to the Chiefs of Staff, and these became the basis for all further discussion. He advocated an organization in which there would be a

---

[1] One British battalion was also converted into a Basic Training Unit, for men not basically trained on arrival in India and all ranks joining the infantry from disbanded anti-aircraft artillery regiments.

[2] See pages 370-71.

British Supreme Commander, with an American deputy and an Allied staff, who would be responsible for the conduct of all operations against Japan in South-East Asia. There would continue to be a statutory Commander-in-Chief in India, co-equal in status to the Supreme Commander and responsible for the internal security of India, for the maintenance, administration and training of the Indian Army in conformity with the operational requirements of the Supreme Commander, and for the organization and administration of India as a base. The selection of a Supreme Commander was left open until the proposed organization had been agreed on in London, and discussed with the President and the American Chiefs of Staff.

During this time the Prime Minister had been considering the problem of finding a successor to the Marquess of Linlithgow, whose term as Viceroy of India would expire in October 1943. There is little doubt that the failure of the Arakan campaign had lowered the military prestige of Field Marshal Wavell in the eyes of both the Prime Minister and the American Chiefs of Staff. On the 18th June it was announced that he was to succeed to the Viceroyalty of India, and that General Auchinleck would assume the appointment of Commander-in-Chief in India at once.[1] 'It is proposed', went on the announcement 'to relieve the Commander-in-Chief, India, of the responsibility for the conduct of the operations against Japan, and to set up a separate [South] East Asia command for that purpose'.[2]

---

[1] Field Marshal Sir Archibald Wavell was created a Viscount on the 1st July 1943 and installed as Viceroy on the 20th October 1943. General Sir Claude Auchinleck became Commander-in-Chief in India on the 20th June 1943.

[2] *The Times*, 19th June 1943.

CHAPTER XXIV

THE AFTERMATH OF TRIDENT

(May–August 1943)

See Maps 13 and 14 and Sketch 16

DURING the period between Field Marshal Wavell's departure for London at the end of April 1943 and General Auchinleck's appointment as Commander-in-Chief in India in June, many changes had taken place in India and the Far East. The Eastern Fleet had been temporarily reduced to the strength of one battleship, nine cruisers, two destroyers and four armed merchant cruisers owing to the need to support current operations in the Mediterranean. It was based on Kilindini in East Africa and its activities were for the time being confined to the Indian Ocean since, in the absence of aircraft carriers, it could not operate in the Bay of Bengal.

A number of changes had been made in the organization and dispositions of the army in India to fit it better for future campaigns in Burma and Arakan and for amphibious operations. In the light of the strategical situation, the growing shortage of suitable manpower and the lack of skilled technicians, it had been decided once again to reorganize the Indian armoured formations.[1] The 32nd and 43rd Armoured Divisions had been amalgamated into 44th Armoured Division, which consisted of 255th Indian Armoured Brigade (from 32nd Armoured Division) and 268th Indian (lorried) Infantry Brigade (from 43rd Armoured Division). The surplus infantry brigade (73rd) had been disbanded; the three units forming 267th Indian Armoured Brigade reverted to infantry and became 72nd Indian Infantry Brigade. This formation, and 29th Independent Infantry Brigade, had been placed under command of a new formation, 36th Indian Division, for training in amphibious operations. The Indian Army was thus left with 31st Armoured Division in Iraq and 44th Armoured Division and three tank brigades (50th, 251st and 254th) in India.

At the close of the Arakan campaign and after the return of the Chindits in June, Eastern Army had been redisposed. The 14th and

---

[1] For details of the first reorganization see page 243.

39th Indian Divisions had been withdrawn from Arakan and Assam respectively to Ranchi for conversion into training divisions, so that reinforcements reaching field formations could be fully trained in jungle warfare. In Assam, IV Corps was disposed with 23rd Indian Division in the Kabaw Valley patrolling the upper Chindwin, and 17th Indian Division along the Tiddim road with one brigade forward in Tiddim itself. In Arakan, 26th Indian Division was holding the general line Nhila–Bawli Bazar–Goppe Bazar–Taung Bazar covering Cox's Bazar, in contact with the Japanese who were holding Buthidaung and Maungdaw.[1] The XV Corps Headquarters had been withdrawn from eastern Bengal and was in Ranchi, with 70th British Division under command. The 254th Indian Tank Brigade was in reserve at Ranchi.

On the 26th May, General Sir George Giffard had taken over command of Eastern Army from General Irwin. The modification of 'Anakim' by the deferment of the seaborne operations meant that the Indian Expeditionary Force would not be required for some time and, though at the Trident Conference the Chiefs of Staff had recommended that amphibious operations on the scale of 'Anakim' should be carried out later, it was not deemed necessary at this stage to appoint a new commander for the force. Giffard, however, continued to control its training and planning through its Chief of Staff. In June, the force controlled the Combined Training Centre in India[2], and consisted of 2nd British and 36th Indian Divisions, 50th Tank Brigade and some dock and transportation units.

Southern Army remained responsible for the defence of southern India and had under command XXXIII Corps (Lieut.-General A. F. P. Christison), consisting of 19th and 25th Indian Divisions, 44th Indian Armoured Division and 251st Tank Brigade. The garrison in Ceylon consisted of 20th Indian Division (32nd, 80th and 100th Brigades) and 34th Indian Division, composed of 99th Indian and one East African brigade. General Headquarters, India, had as a general reserve 5th Indian Division and two long-range penetration (L.R.P.) groups (77th Brigade re-forming after the Chindit operations and 111th being raised) and 50th Indian Parachute Brigade.

After their retreat from Burma, 22nd and 38th Chinese Divisions had been reconstituted, re-equipped and trained by the Americans at Ramgarh. The 38th Division was east of Ledo covering the construction of the Ledo–Myitkyina road, 22nd Division was in

---

[1] See Map 13.

[2] In August the Combined Operations Directorate at General Headquarters, India, was reorganized and strengthened, and was once again made responsible for the control of all basic training for assault at combined training centres. At the same time, a second combined training centre was established at Cocanada.

the process of moving to Ledo and at Ramgarh 30th Chinese Division was being formed from men flown in from China.

The expansion and re-equipment of the British and Indian air forces was proceeding apace.[1] By June 1943 there were fifty-two squadrons, of which thirty-four were operational and the remainder in various stages of re-equipment and training.[2] This compared favourably with thirty-one (twenty-five operational) squadrons in September 1942.[3] Some of the Blenheim squadrons had been re-equipped with Hurricanes for use as fighter-bombers, and light bomber squadrons had been formed with Vengeance aircraft for the close support of the army. Concurrently with the increase in squadrons, a number of training establishments had been formed throughout India. The expansion, re-equipment and training of the R.I.A.F. had continued but, owing to the difficulty of recruiting men suitable for training as aircrews and technicians, had made slow progress. By June there were seven R.I.A.F. squadrons, but owing to over-rapid expansion none of them was yet fit for active operations.

The 10th U.S.A.A.F. had also expanded and comprised twelve squadrons—three fighter, eight bomber and one photographic—mostly based in Assam. The American Air Transport Command had absorbed the Ferry Command and become entirely responsible for air supply to China. The 14th U.S.A.A.F. had replaced the C.A.T.F. and was quite independent of the 10th U.S.A.A.F.

The extensive airfield construction programme throughout India had progressed much more slowly than expected, owing to the general shortage of earth-moving and other machinery, to the vast amount of material required, much of which could not be moved quickly on the congested railways, and to the serious shortage of skilled engineers for supervision of the local contractors. The full programme was not expected to be completed before the end of 1943. Work on the airfields in Assam required by the American air force for the air supply to China, although given first priority, had also gone on slowly, mainly owing to the limitations of the Assam line of communications. The construction of additional hard standings and taxi-tracks on the existing airfields, although well behind schedule, was expected to be completed by the beginning of August and thus enable the agreed monthly air lift to China to be reached by the target date. Owing to constructional difficulties on the selected sites, it was not possible, in June, to forecast when the three new airfields required would be ready for use.[4]

---

[1] The Indian Air Force was honoured with the prefix 'Royal' on the 1st April 1943, the tenth anniversary of its formation.

[2] See Appendix 32.

[3] See Appendix 21.

[4] See page 367. Major-General H. Roome succeeded General Bond as Engineer-in-Chief, India Command, in May 1943.

The political situation in India had remained more or less satisfactory after the disturbances in the autumn of 1942, mainly owing to the internment of the leaders of the Congress Party. Economic factors had, however, begun to cause increasing anxiety. India's war economy had been fairly sound for the first few months of 1942 but, with the increasing number of troops in the country, Government expenditure began to assume colossal proportions. India's imports for civil consumption were much reduced by the loss of her Far Eastern sources of supply and the increasing world shortage of shipping. In consequence, a scramble for consumer goods set in and prices began to rise. The poor distribution of foodstuffs and other essential commodities, brought about by the congestion of the transportation system, coupled with the general shortages and the adverse course of the war against Japan had a demoralizing effect on the civil population. Hoarding, which could not be checked, became rife, and by the end of 1942 the spiral of inflation was already mounting. Poor grain harvests in the new year aggravated the situation and, since the complex Indian administrative system made a comprehensive and satisfactory scheme of rationing and price control almost impossible, India was by June 1943 in the grip of a serious economic crisis.

When General Auchinleck took over command in India, he found himself in the position of caretaker for the Supreme Commander and, until the new headquarters was set up, responsible not only for training and preparing the army and air force in India for their task, but also for planning the operations decided upon at the Trident Conference. Priority had been given at Trident to an increase in the air lift to China up to a monthly capacity of 10,000 tons by the early autumn. But, in addition, an offensive campaign had to be launched from Assam deep into northern Burma, and amphibious operations had to be undertaken to capture Akyab and other strategic points along the Arakan coast. Auchinleck had two problems to solve: the first was whether the Assam line of communication, with its strictly limited capacity, could be made to support the air lift as well as a land offensive; the second was whether, with the resources available in India and what could be supplied in time from the United Kingdom or elsewhere, he could carry out the amphibious operations planned for the dry weather with a reasonable chance of success.

Although the Assam line of communication had been considerably improved since the outbreak of war with Japan, the endeavours to increase its capacity had been based on a load factor which, though adequate in 1942, was proving in 1943 to be far too small. Not only had it to provide for the jute and tea industries—both indispensable to the Allied war effort—and the normal economic life of Assam, but it had also to meet the needs of the land and air forces likely to take part in an offensive into Burma, as well as the urgent and growing requirements of the air lift to China. It was estimated that the Services alone would require a lift of about 4,300 tons a day if the Trident plans were to be implemented, whereas the combined rail and river capacity of the line of communications for petrol and military stores was, in June 1943, only some 1,720 tons a day.

On the 2nd July, Auchinleck reported to the Chiefs of Staff that the feasibility of all operations (except those in Arakan) depended on whether the capacity of the Assam line of communication could be sufficiently increased in the time available. Furthermore, the depth of any advance into Burma must be governed by the speed at which all-weather roads could be built.

The theoretical capacity of the line of communication could, he considered, be raised to 3,400 tons a day, provided that one daily train path allotted to civil requirements in Assam was made available to the Services, that during the monsoon the greatest possible increase was made in the overall capacity of the Assam railway and that, at the expense of the jute and tea industries, the Services were allotted all the river shipping on the Brahmaputra, thus increasing the shipping tonnage available to them from 27,000 to some 81,000 tons. But his maximum of 3,400 tons a day fell far short of the requirements of the Trident plan, and he was therefore investigating possible further improvements in the operation of the Assam railway and increases in the capacity for military goods on the Brahmaputra. Meanwhile, he had no alternative but to reduce the overall demands on the line of communication by about one-fifth and would have to plan operations with this in mind.[1]

He pointed out that if IV Corps were to maintain throughout the 1944 monsoon the positions gained during the contemplated offensive, the gap between the all-weather Assam road system and the river and road systems of Burma would have to be considerably reduced. This would mean extending the Imphal Road as far as the Chindwin at Sittaung and to Kalemyo, but he had insufficient engineering resources at his disposal to do this at the same time as improving the line of communication. He therefore advocated that, during the dry weather 1943–44, the American-Chinese forces from Ledo should advance only as far towards Myitkyina as subsequent maintenance would allow, and that the British-Indian forces should confine their operations to reaching positions from which they could cover the construction of the essential roads.

---

[1] See Appendix 24.

Turning to the proposed operations along the Arakan coast, Auchinleck said that Akyab Island had by now been strongly fortified and its capture had become a formidable venture. He would require at least two assault brigades in the first flight, a third brigade, assault-loaded in its own craft, in the second flight, and a follow-up division ready to be put ashore as soon as the beaches had been secured. To provide the necessary air cover over Akyab, he would have to operate three to four fighter squadrons continuously during the hours of daylight and, in addition, would need sufficient carrier-borne aircraft to protect the convoys. In order to ensure the success of the assault, and it was most important from the point of view of prestige and morale that it should succeed, two divisions and a long-range penetration group would have to operate towards Akyab on the Arakan coast and down the Kaladan valley. The line of communication forward of Chittagong could, by the dry weather, be made capable of maintaining such a force, but at the expense of improving the airfields in eastern Bengal to heavy bomber standard. Considerable improvement would have to be made in the meantime to the port of Chittagong. There would have in any case to be an interval of three to four months from the time that Akyab was captured before the assault against Ramree could be launched, unless separate shipping were provided. This would give the Japanese time to strengthen their defences at Ramree, and it might therefore be preferable to attempt a *coup de main* with a small force from Akyab immediately after its capture, rather than stage a full-scale operation after such a long interval.

Auchinleck concluded by saying that, in view of all the administrative, training and climatic factors involved, the offensive from both Imphal and Ledo, although it might begin in November 1943, could not reach its greatest strength till February 1944, and the assault on Akyab could not take place before January 1944.

During July preparations went on, but towards the end of the month the monsoon unexpectedly but effectively upset all calculations. The Damodar River burst its banks some fifty miles northwest of Calcutta, sweeping away large sections of the main East India Railway broad gauge lines and the Grand Trunk Road connecting Calcutta and the Asansol industrial area with western India. To make matters worse, at the beginning of August floods in Bengal and Orissa breached the railway line from Calcutta to Vizagapatam and southern India. Little could be done to repair the breaches till the floods subsided, and it was soon found that one of them on the railway near Burdwan could not be repaired till the end of October and another till the end of November. Normal running would not be restored till early December, and until then the tonnage of supplies which could reach Calcutta, by way of unaffected lines, would be more than halved, since almost the whole capacity of the trains which could be run would be required for the carriage of coal, on which all the rail, river and seaborne transportation services further east depended. The reduction in rail traffic to Calcutta immediately affected delivery of goods to both Assam and eastern Bengal and seriously retarded all the preparations being made to carry out the Trident plans.

On the 10th August Auchinleck was told by the Chiefs of Staff that, in order to be in a position to exploit a possible Italian collapse in the eastern Mediterranean, they had authorized the Commanders-in-Chief, Middle East, to keep in the Mediterranean until further notice all the assault shipping allotted to India for the proposed assault on Akyab. This shipping had been due to sail for India that very day and the indefinite delay in its departure would clearly not only seriously hinder the training of the troops allotted to the operation, but would postpone *sine die* the date on which the assault on Akyab could be launched.

Three days later, Auchinleck reported to the Chiefs of Staff the position as he then saw it, and gave his views on the policy which might be adopted for the dry weather 1943–44. Further planning on the basis of the Trident decisions had shown that the load on the Assam line of communications had been underestimated. This was owing firstly, to the unexpectedly heavy demands of the airfield programme which had to be met in full; secondly, to an American demand for the whole of the oil output from Digboi, which made it necessary to bring more P.O.L. supplies into Assam from Calcutta than had been expected; and lastly, to the fact that the original figure of 3,400 tons a day had included no margin for contingencies, and these at an absolute minimum had to be reckoned at fifteen per cent.

But as demands on the line of communications had increased, so had its estimated capacity diminished, for the shortage of locomotives could not be made good till October at the earliest and the planned stepping-up of the railway and river lift from some 1,700 to 3,400 tons a day could not take effect till mid-September. Thus arrears of essential stores would steadily accumulate. These factors, together with the effect of the breaches in the railways west of Calcutta, would produce a deficiency in the lift to Assam by 1st March 1944 of some 128,000 tons. Even if reductions to the utmost limit in American and British requirements were accepted, a saving of only some 20,000 tons could be made and a deficit of some 600 tons a day for six months would still remain. The problem was whether the capacity of the line of communications could be stepped up still further in the time available and, if this were impossible, what changes would have to be made in the operational planning to bring requirements into line with possibilities.

An investigation by experts had shown that the majority of the effective improvements—such as doubling the railway track, increasing the river fleet and enlarging the capacity of the river ports—could not ease the position before October 1944. The only way to overcome present difficulties would be to increase the number of train paths and improve the operation of the railway by taking risks which would not normally be acceptable; to bring in rolling stock and locomotives from other metre gauge lines in India and accept the dislocation caused thereby; to instal navigational lights on the Brahmaputra River to enable it to be used by night, and to establish an air lift from Calcutta to the American Air Transport Command airfields in Assam. These measures were expected to provide some small increase in the capacity of the line of communications, but an overall deficiency would still remain.

This being the position, the possibility of having to call off the proposed advance in northern Burma from both Ledo and Imphal would have to be faced. 'If', said Auchinleck,

> 'we remain on the defensive on both fronts [the] saving effected would be six or seven hundred tons a day against anticipated deficit of about six hundred tons a day. We should then be able to meet fully demands of air ferry route and late in the season, when construction of airfields is reduced while capacity of L. of C. is increased by fresh stock from U.S.A. and completion of pipelines, we should have a growing capacity to spare for increased lift to China'.

He suggested that the advance down the Arakan coast and the assault on Akyab should be carried out as planned; but if the requisite assault craft, assault shipping and naval cover could not be supplied, he wondered whether it was worth while undertaking a land advance towards Akyab which would interfere with the completion of the airfields in eastern Bengal to an all-weather standard for heavy bombers. Since Air Marshal Peirse considered that the raising of the standard of these airfields would be preferable to acquiring new airfields in Akyab, Auchinleck suggested that the maintenance of a continuous air offensive against Burma, and particularly Akyab, would be the correct policy.

He was aware, he said, of the pressure which was being brought to bear on the Chiefs of Staff by the Americans in favour of large-scale offensive operations against Burma during the dry season 1943–44, and went on:

> 'The course of planning for even the limited operations included in Champion [the Trident decisions] has brought me to the conclusion that best military course would be to avoid wasting effort on this unprofitable objective and to concentrate on supply to China by air at the same time increasing and conserving

strength of India and preparing resources for Culverin [an attack on northern Sumatra] next winter. Preparation for Culverin would enable us to bring training of troops to high standard. If Culverin were definitely decided on for 1944–45 it would be desirable to divert resources for Bullfrog [the assault on Akyab] to Buccaneer [an assault on the Andaman Islands] in the late spring of 1944'.

The Chiefs of Staff felt loath to accept the abandonment of the entire campaign, which they felt might prolong the war for years, because of an estimated deficiency in the capacity of the Assam line of communication of only 600 tons a day for six months, especially as they knew that both rail and river transportation systems in Assam were operated on a lower standard of efficiency than would be acceptable elsewhere. Accordingly they asked Auchinleck on the 17th whether the capacity could be increased sufficiently to enable the planned objectives to be reached, if substantial American assistance in the form of technical military personnel and material (locomotives, trucks, motor vehicles and barges) were provided[1], if priority over all other activities in India were given to the Assam communications and if all transportation facilities east of the Brahmaputra were brought under military control.

Auchinleck agreed that the railways in Assam were being operated less efficiently than would be acceptable by British and American standards, and that military control on certain sections should result in improvement in the overall capacity. The same, he said, did not apply to river transport on the Brahmaputra with its narrow and continuously shifting channels, unsuitable banks and river ports liable to erosion and shoaling. The existing ports were already working to full capacity and the construction of new ports and their road or rail connections must be considered as a long-term project only; it would not help to solve the immediate problem. The next three months, during which the water level of the river would fall, would be the most critical.

Even with the American assistance offered and the adoption of the measures suggested by the Chiefs of Staff, he thought it unlikely that there would be a gain of more than 26,000 tons in the lift by March 1944, which would still leave a deficiency of some 102,000 tons. Thus, if land operations were to go on as planned during the coming dry season, they could only be at the expense of the air lift to China or at the expense of operations from Ledo. The shortfall in tonnage would also make it impossible to devote any additional lift to stores required for improving the lines of communication to enable them

---

[1] This assistance included the shipment between September and December of 114 metre gauge locomotives and in September and October of 4,000 metre gauge wagons, 2,400 motor vehicles over and above the normal quota and a considerable number of tow-boats and wooden barges.

to meet the requirements of the more extended operations clearly necessary for 1944–45.

He found it difficult to accept the view that the abandonment of the campaign for the dry weather would result in prolonging the war for years. The monsoon had caused so much damage to the communications that the concentration of resources to make the proposed operations feasible would inevitably delay until the spring of 1944 the allotment of any tonnage for the improvement of the lines of communication themselves. To enable a full-scale offensive to be undertaken in 1944–45, the capacity of the Assam line of communication would have to be doubled, and the allotment of tonnage for this purpose should begin at once and take priority over short-term operations.

While this interchange of views between Auchinleck and the Chiefs of Staff was taking place, the Prime Minister was becoming increasingly exasperated by the difficulties mounting up in South-East Asia and the vast expenditure of force required for what appeared to be trumpery gains. He advocated that the proper course for the campaign in 1944 should be: maximum aid by air to China, maximum pressure by operations similar to those conducted by Brigadier Wingate and the use of the flexibility of sea power to strike where the Japanese were not prepared and where fighting was not interrupted by the monsoon season. He said that operations on the Indian front had been characterized by a welter of inefficiency and lassitude, and suggested that Wingate, whom he described as a man of genius and audacity who had been discerned by all eyes as a figure quite above the ordinary level, should command the army to fight in Burma. No mere question of seniority, he said, must obstruct the advance of real personalities to their proper stations in war, and gave orders that Wingate should be brought to England for discussions at an early date. The Chief of the Imperial General Staff thereupon instructed Auchinleck to send Wingate to the United Kingdom without delay, and asked him to give his views on Wingate as a possible candidate for higher command.

Wingate left India by air on the 30th July. The following day Auchinleck told the Chief of the Imperial General Staff that, in his opinion, Wingate's chief value lay in his exceptional power to organize and inspire personally officers and men engaged on long-range penetration operations, but that the further he was removed from the troops employed the less valuable was he likely to be, particularly as he had no experience of large-scale operations or of the handling of considerable forces. He had already arranged that Wingate, during the forthcoming operations, should command both

32. Landslide on the Imphal Road.

33. Jogighopa–Goalpara vehicle ferry (north side).

34. Loading by hand, Dhubri.

35. Amingaon–Pandu rail ferry (Pandu on the far bank).

77th and 111th (L.R.P.) Brigades on IV Corps front. Wingate would be under the general direction of the corps commander, but this would in no way restrict his activities.

He was considering the conversion of another division into two more long-range penetration brigades. This was a long process which entailed weeding out unsuitable men (probably some forty per cent.), providing much special equipment, and the training of specialists. He felt, however, that for 1944–45 large numbers of both assault and follow-up airborne troops would be required, and that the provision of these was more important than an increase in the number of long-range penetration troops, valuable as they were under certain circumstances. He asked therefore that no drastic changes should be made in the existing plans for which preparations were actively proceeding.

Wingate arrived in London the day before the Prime Minister and the Chiefs of Staff were about to leave in s.s. *Queen Mary* for Quebec, where another Anglo-American conference—which became known as Quadrant—was about to be held to discuss 'the prospects of victory in Sicily, the Italian situation and the progress of the war'. The Prime Minister interviewed Wingate at once and, impressed by his personality and his views on 'how the Japanese could be mastered in jungle warfare by long-range penetration groups landed by air behind the enemy lines', arranged that he should accompany the British delegation to Quebec so that there would be an opportunity for him to put his views before the Chiefs of Staff.[1]

During the voyage across the Atlantic, Wingate on the 10th August submitted to the Chiefs of Staff a memorandum giving his views on how Burma north of a line from Lashio to Kalewa could be reoccupied during the dry weather of 1943–44 by using L.R.P. forces. He said that, as the possibilities of using L.R.P. groups against the Japanese had been demonstrated, it remained only to ensure that in the future they were used on a sufficient scale and on the right principles. The purpose of long-range penetration operations was to create a state of confusion within enemy-held territory by disrupting his communications and rear installations, which would lead to progressive weakening and misdirection of his main forces, and to indicate suitable targets for the tactical air forces which would enable the strategic air offensive to be driven home. Such operations would inevitably produce favourable opportunities for an offensive by the main Allied forces, but these would be of a fleeting nature and would have to be exploited to the full as they occurred. L.R.P. groups should therefore be used as an essential part of any plan for the reconquest of Burma, to create a situation favourable for the advance of the main forces.

---
[1] Churchill, *The Second World War*, Volume V (Cassell, 1952) pages 61–62.

He proposed that, for the forthcoming operations, three long-range penetration groups should be used to begin with. The first should operate from China against the Mandalay–Lashio–Bhamo line of communications, the second from the area north of Tamu against the Shwebo–Myitkyina railway and the third from the Chin Hills against the Kalewa–Kalemyo communications.[1] All three would have to be launched simultaneously and, if possible, coincidentally with an offensive in Arakan. They would be but the prelude to an advance by the main forces which, he suggested, might aim at reaching certain objectives as the Japanese interior economy became disrupted. These were Bhamo and Lashio, which should be occupied by Chinese forces from Yunnan and held throughout the monsoon; the Pinlebu area (with the airfield at Indaw) and the Kalemyo–Kalewa area, to be occupied by IV Corps; and Myitkyina, to be occupied by the American-Chinese forces from Ledo. The real threat to Myitkyina should not be developed till well after the entry of all three L.R.P. groups, since a premature threat would produce a strong Japanese reaction.

It was important, he said, that, since L.R.P. groups should not operate for more than twelve weeks without replacements and, since the enemy could be expected to strike back only when he had gauged the full scope and intention of the advance, the operations should be timed to end after the break of the 1944 monsoon. That being the case a suitable date for the three L.R.P. groups to cross their Rubicons—the Salween, Chindwin and Myittha Rivers—would be the 15th February 1944. It would be necessary to resume a full-scale offensive the moment the monsoon was over (i.e. by the end of October 1944) so as to forestall a Japanese attack on the positions gained and held throughout the monsoon. This offensive, too, should be planned on the new lines and three fresh L.R.P. groups, with others in reserve, would be required. Seeing that the objective of a 1944–45 offensive would be the reoccupation of the whole of Burma, with perhaps penetrations into Siam and Indo-China, it might entail large-scale amphibious operations which would demand further L.R.P. groups.

Since the only effective answer to penetration was counter-penetration, such action by the Japanese must be expected. This might be aimed at IV Corps line of communication area. To prevent its being successful, two L.R.P. groups should be ready to strike back deeply at the enemy's communications, should he attempt to interfere with the British communications. If not required for this purpose, these two groups would be available for an offensive in 1944–45. Maintenance of all L.R.P. groups would be by air, as also

---

[1] See Map 14.

that of the divisions used in the follow-up to occupy the Katha–Pinlebu area.

The total commitment in long-range penetration troops would be a force headquarters on the basis of a modified corps headquarters, two wing headquarters, each corresponding to the headquarters of a light division, two wings each of four L.R.P. groups, each of eight columns, and between twelve and twenty D.C.3 aircraft for supply purposes. The L.R.P. force Wingate envisaged would total some 19,000 British officers and men, 7,500 Gurkhas or Africans, 6,000 mules and ponies and 100 jeeps.[1] Against this total, he said, there were now only two L.R.P. groups in India, each of which had six instead of eight columns. The quality of most of the officers and men was below that needed, and there was as yet no force headquarters, no training machinery and a shortage of the indispensable experts (airmen, sappers and signalmen). All these deficiencies could be overcome without delay if the necessary priority were given. In the two existing groups, however, were to be found the nuclei of officers and men who had served in the first Chindit operation; it was on these that the edifice of the L.R.P. force could be built.

Wingate proposed that 77th and 111th (L.R.P.) Brigades should be reorganized and concentrated in IV Corps area by January 1944 to continue their training for instant counter-penetration, should the enemy attempt to move into IV Corps line of communication area; that four more groups should be added progressively before the monsoon in May 1944 and that further groups should be raised and trained for use in the 1944–45 dry weather offensive. The great need however, whatever the final plan, was the construction of a machine for turning out L.R.P. groups at a steady and increasing rate. The commander of the L.R.P. force should, he thought, be responsible for organization and training to General Headquarters, India, and for operational employment to Eastern Army.

The Chiefs of Staff were so impressed by this memorandum and plan that on the 14th August they told Auchinleck that they had decided to use L.R.P. groups extensively, since they felt that their value in the Japanese war had been proved. They sent him an outline plan for the organization and employment of an expanded L.R.P. force, which was virtually a copy of Wingate's memorandum, and asked him what effect it would have on his resources and on operations already being prepared. They said that the two groups of six columns already available should be expanded to the full size, and that a force headquarters, one wing headquarters and one complete group should be formed immediately, as the first stage of the expan-

---

[1] The British figures included 90 R.A.F. and some 1,000 army officers. The total involved was equivalent in manpower to at least two full divisions.

sion programme. The second stage, to be completed by the 1st October 1943, would include the formation of a second wing headquarters and three groups. The third stage, to be completed by the 1st January 1944, would include the last two groups, thus making a total of eight. All these groups were to be drawn predominantly from British formations, the ratio being three British to one Gurkha. To help meet the demand for specialists, they were prepared to send some from the United Kingdom.[1]

Auchinleck replied that L.R.P. groups on the lines proposed by Wingate were not capable of achieving results against organized forces of all arms, for their rôle was not to fight but to evade the enemy and harass him by using guerilla tactics. He emphasized therefore that, unless the main forces could take advantage of the situation created by the L.R.P. groups, their efforts would be largely wasted. Subsequent retaliation, too, against Burmese who had helped the columns would make them unwilling to offer aid in the future. Exploitation by the main forces was thus the important factor, and its possibilities must govern both areas of employment and timings of all L.R.P. activities.

Administrative factors prevented him, as he had already told them, from radically improving the capacity of the Assam line of communication before March 1944. Thus the proposed advance of the main forces in support of the suggested L.R.P. operations was impracticable, unless the advance by the American-Chinese forces from Ledo were abandoned and the air lift to China seriously reduced. Furthermore, neither the maintenance of the forward divisions during the monsoon nor the air transport of an L.R.P. group to China would be possible without four or five additional air squadrons, and the presence of these would add to the burden on the already overloaded line of communication. He queried the wisdom of relying on the Chinese to advance from Yunnan, even if led by an L.R.P. group from Paoshan.

In the circumstances he considered that it would be a waste of effort and material to cut up existing units into L.R.P. groups to the extent proposed, unless they were required to counter penetration by the enemy. If the suggested number of groups were formed, it would involve breaking up 70th British Division and one Indian (A. & M.T.) division as well as providing three British battalions, thereby disorganizing a third division. It would also mean finding some 3,000 British troops from other arms, some 600 signallers, over and above those offered by the Chiefs of Staff, and the extensive 'milking' of other units to provide suitable officers; these figures were

---

[1] These included the following: for demolition platoons, 64 officers and 960 men; for signals, 8 officers and 140 men; for headquarters, up to 30 staff officers; and for R.A.F. sections, 50 R.A.F. officers.

based on the assumption that one hundred per cent. of the men in any given unit would be acceptable for L.R.P. purposes, and that was most unlikely. He was opposed to the creation of a force headquarters, since he considered that there could be only one commander in each area of operations or corps front.

The effect of the proposals on projected operations would be considerable. The capture of Ramree would be impossible, for 70th British Division would not be available; the withdrawal of an A. & M.T. division would leave Eastern Army without a reserve and the assault brigades needed for the prosecution of the campaign in 1944–45 would not be available. Further, the army in India would have to start another reorganization scheme only two months after it had begun to train with new equipment and on a new organization based on experience gained in battle.

Nevertheless, Auchinleck agreed that L.R.P. operations would be of considerable value in Burma, and put forward suggestions whereby the existing L.R.P. force could be expanded without disorganizing the army in India. He proposed that part of 81st West African Division, which was due to arrive in India shortly, should be converted into an L.R.P. group. He had discussed the proposal with Major-General C. G. Woolner, the divisional commander, and they had both agreed that the division should be suitable, since its organization was flexible, it had been trained exclusively for war in dense jungle and it had porter transport. Although two of its brigades had already been earmarked for use in Arakan, one could be spared for an L.R.P. rôle. Auchinleck maintained that this brigade, together with 77th and 111th Brigades, each made up, if necessary, to eight columns, would be sufficient to meet the L.R.P. requirements for the campaigning season 1943–44. If further brigades were required, he suggested that, as soon as it was trained, 82nd West African Division should be brought to India and converted to L.R.P. groups.

The Chiefs of Staff asked Wingate for his comments on Auchinleck's views. Wingate stated quite categorically that, if it were seriously intended to proceed with the expansion of L.R.P. forces, they were quite unacceptable. If the groups were to be effective, they should consist mainly of British officers and men. The West Africans, and particularly their officers, had not been tried in battle and it would be a mistake to let the whole plan depend on their being a success in an L.R.P. rôle. Nevertheless he was prepared to accept one West African brigade as an experiment, on the understanding that he was given a free hand in its organization and training, that any further expansion based on West African troops would be subject to results and that he would not be asked to use West Africans in the 1943–44 operations. He considered that the retention of a battalion and brigade organization cut across his whole conception of the L.R.P. forces, which must be organized in columns; in this respect he demanded that he should be given a free hand. Unlike Auchinleck, he considered a force headquarters essential, not only during the earlier period when the force was being organized, but also during operations.

To recapitulate briefly: General Auchinleck, like his predecessor, found that administrative factors made it impracticable to carry out fully the plans decided upon by the Combined Chiefs of Staff for the dry weather 1943–44. He advocated instead that priority should be given to the building-up of the air lift to China and that any surplus administrative and engineering resources should be concentrated on improving lines of communication from Calcutta eastwards. If this were done, it would then be possible to launch a full-scale offensive with fully-trained troops, backed by adequate lines of communication, in the dry weather 1944–45.

Like the Prime Minister and Field Marshal Wavell before him, he came to the conclusion that strategically it would be better to launch an amphibious offensive against northern Sumatra than become involved in a difficult campaign for the recapture of Burma from Assam.

The Chiefs of Staff on the other hand, under pressure from the Americans, whose policy was at one and the same time to build up the air lift to China and recapture northern Burma so that road communications with China could be re-established, were looking round for any way which would enable the plans approved at Trident to be carried out.

They offered Auchinleck substantial aid from America in the hope that this would enable him to overcome his administrative difficulties in time for an offensive into northern Burma during 1943–44. Auchinleck pointed out, however, that it would arrive too late to have any appreciable effect on the administrative situation. They then accepted, as a means of breaking the deadlock, Wingate's proposals for expanding and using the L.R.P. force, without previous reference to the Commander-in-Chief in India. They made these their policy and asked Auchinleck, the responsible commander on the spot, for his views. Auchinleck admitted the value of L.R.P. groups in reasonable numbers as ancillary to his main forces but, believing that Wingate's proposals went too far, put forward an alternative which took into account the difficulties of administration and organization with which he was faced. When this alternative was put before Wingate, by then in the position of having power without responsibility, he dubbed it quite unacceptable.

During the monsoon of 1943, there was only one serious clash between the opposing armies along the length of the north-eastern frontier. Japanese forces had moved into the Kachin and Chin Hills as the monsoon approached. In the former, they occupied Sumprabum and thus threatened Fort Hertz; this threat did not develop, but plans were prepared for its evacuation.[1] Their advance into the Chin Hills however led to fighting between Fort White and Kalemyo.[2] General Scoones (IV Corps) had intended to withdraw the whole of 17th Indian Division from the Tiddim area at the beginning of the monsoon, since the newly constructed road was liable to landslides and flooding, and the mountain peaks, enshrouded in mist during the monsoon period, made air supply difficult, dangerous and unreliable. But when the Chin Levies were driven from both No. 2 and 3 Stockades and Japanese forces threatened Fort White, Scoones decided to take the offensive in the Chin Hills. He ordered 48th Brigade (Brigadier R. T. Cameron), which was working on the road north of Tiddim covered by 2/5th Royal Gurkhas in the Kennedy Peak area, to concentrate near Tiddim and then reoccupy the Stockades.

The brigade, maintained along the Tiddim road by jeep convoys supplemented by air supply, was without any artillery support, but it could call for tactical air support by means of an air tentacle attached to brigade headquarters. After considerable preliminary skirmishing during which several small posts changed hands, Cameron ordered a deliberate attack, covered by an air bombardment, to be made on the 26th May by a composite battalion found from 2/5th and 1/4th Gurkhas in order to clear the hill overlooking No. 3 Stockade as a preliminary to its capture. He kept 1/7th Gurkhas in reserve holding the Kennedy Peak area. Although rain and cloud prevented the air bombardment from being carried out, the attack succeeded in taking the hill at a cost of some 150 casualties after fierce hand-to-hand fighting.[3] It soon became evident that the Japanese strength and superiority in artillery precluded any possibility of retaking No. 3 Stockade. The 48th Brigade was therefore ordered to withdraw to Fort White and Kennedy Peak where it could be supplied with less difficulty. At the end of June, it was relieved by 63rd Brigade and withdrawn to Shillong for a rest.

Further north, the withdrawal of the forward troops of 23rd Division from the Kabaw Valley into the better climate in the hills to the west was marked by several sharp patrol fights. The Japanese did not follow up, and the notoriously malarious valley was left unoccupied throughout the monsoon, though visited at intervals by

---

[1] See Map 14.
[2] See Sketch 16.
[3] During this action, Havildar Gaje Ghale of 2/5th Gurkhas earned the Victoria Cross.

patrols. In Arakan, where there was a wide and extensively flooded 'no man's land' between the opposing forces, there were only minor clashes between patrols. To keep alive the offensive spirit and get identifications, General Lomax (26th Division) ordered two raids on company scale to be carried out: one on Maungdaw across the Naf estuary was highly successful and identified *143rd Infantry Regiment;* the other on the Maungdaw–Buthidaung road suffered casualties and achieved only moderate success.[1]

In the air, however, the weight of the offensive against targets in Burma was steadily increasing and advantage was taken of every break in the monsoon. No serious attempt had been made to fly over Burma during the 1942 monsoon, since it was more important at that time to concentrate on building up the air force in India. The growth of the Allied air force and its re-equipment with more modern aircraft and the greatly improved efficiency of the maintenance services made air operations on a large scale possible throughout the 1943 monsoon. It was at first planned to give priority to attacking the enemy air forces in Burma but, when the Japanese withdrew the bulk of their aircraft to Siam and Malaya shortly after the break of the monsoon, the whole of the air effort was switched on to their military formations and installations and nodal points on their lines of communication.

Strategic bombing was undertaken mainly by the 10th U.S.A.A.F. by day with about forty heavy and fifty medium bombers, while the R.A.F., with an average of only some twelve Liberators and Wellingtons, operated by night. Enemy communications in Burma and Siam and particularly the railways were the chief targets. The damage to the railways compelled the Japanese to rely more and more on road and river transport, thus increasing the targets for the tactical air forces. Although naturally reduced during the height of the monsoon, when conditions at times precluded all flying, the scale of these attacks increased rapidly as the weather improved and by October was approximately doubled.[2]

The tactical air force was mainly engaged in support of the army. On the central front, 221 Group gave direct support to IV Corps, with 170 Wing R.A.F. operating from Imphal so long as its airfield stood up to monsoon conditions, and then from other airfields in Assam and eastern Bengal. This group also carried out reconnaissance and attacked targets in the Kabaw Valley, on the Kalemyo–Fort White

---

[1] See Map 13.

[2]
	June	July	August	September	October
Fighter sorties	737	573	518	763	1,030
Bomber sorties	324	314	164	145	610
Weight of bombs dropped (tons)	108	131	66	56	404
Reconnaissance sorties	177	128	132	204	315
Photographic reconnaissance sorties	40	30	61	66	110

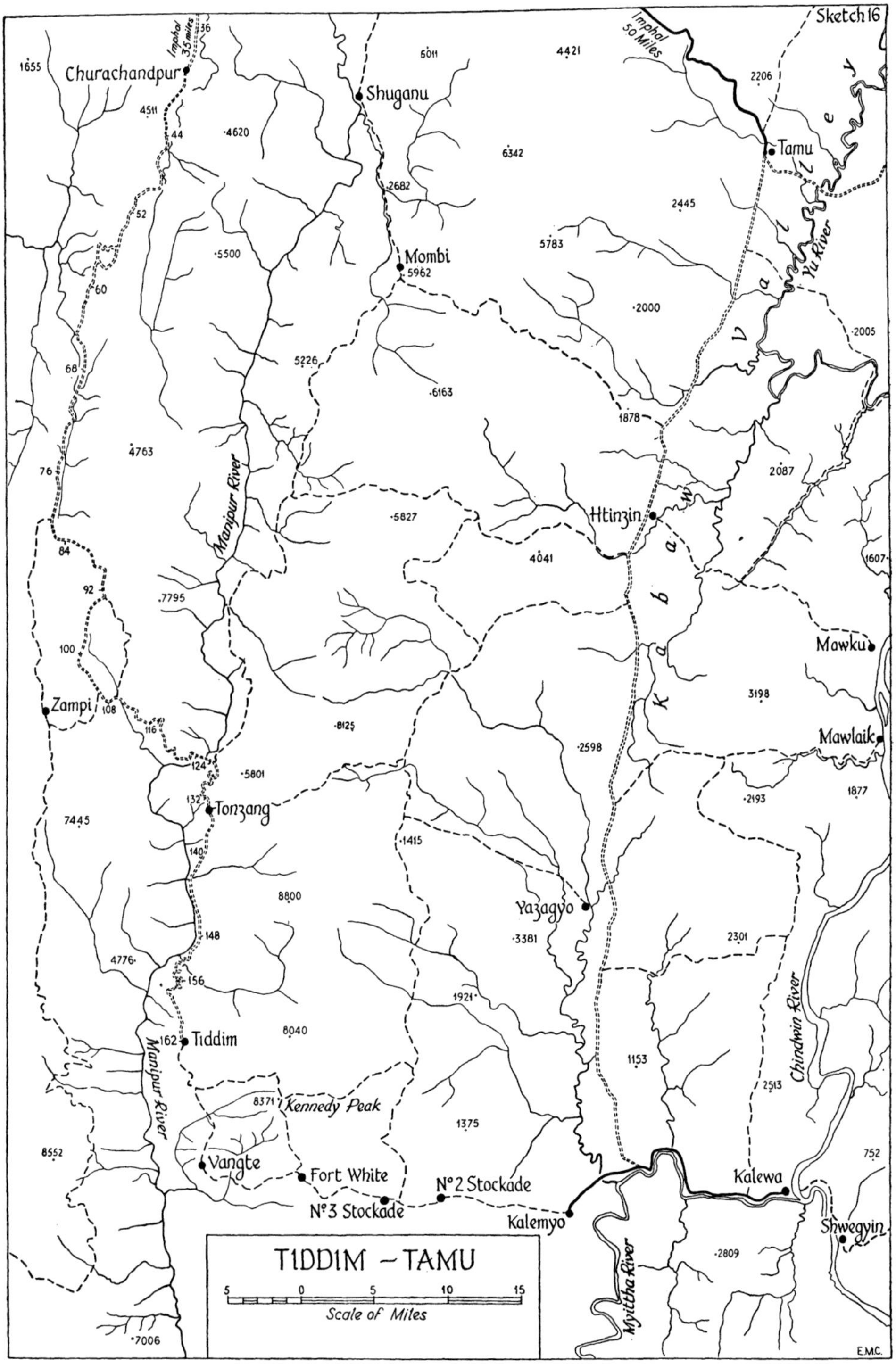
Sketch 16
TIDDIM – TAMU
Scale of Miles
5 0 5 10 15
Imphal 35 miles
Imphal 50 Miles
Churachandpur
Shuganu
Tamu
Mombi
Htinzin
Zampi
Tonzang
Tiddim
Vangte
Kennedy Peak
Fort White
No. 3 Stockade
No. 2 Stockade
Kalemyo
Kalewa
Shwegyin
Mawku
Mawlaik
Yazagyo
Manipur River
Yu River
Chindwin River
Myittha River
Kabaw Valley
E.M.C.

ASSAM LINE O

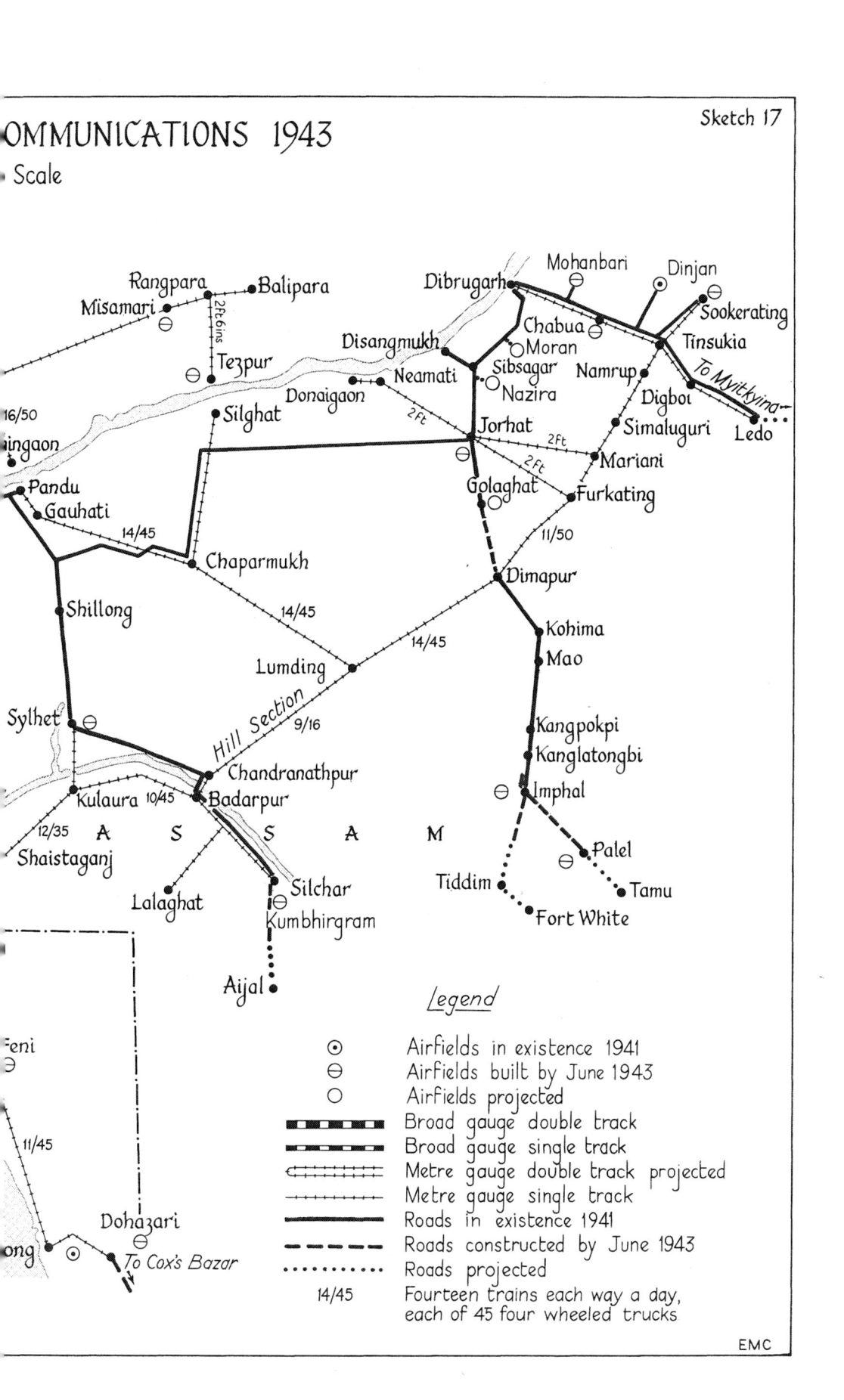

COMMUNICATIONS 1943

Sketch 17

Scale

Legend

- ⊙ Airfields in existence 1941
- ⊖ Airfields built by June 1943
- ○ Airfields projected
- ▬▬▬ Broad gauge double track
- ▬▬▬ Broad gauge single track
- ⟵⟶ Metre gauge double track projected
- ┼┼┼┼ Metre gauge single track
- ▬▬▬ Roads in existence 1941
- ─ ─ ─ Roads constructed by June 1943
- .... Roads projected
- 14/45 Fourteen trains each way a day, each of 45 four wheeled trucks

EMC

road and along the Chindwin. On the Arakan front, 224 Group at Chittagong with six fighter and two light bomber squadrons and a reconnaissance flight gave direct support to 26th Indian Division. Raids were often made against the enemy line of communications along the coast and on river craft, railways and roads in lower and central Burma.

The return of the Chindits did not lead to any reduction in the calls on 31 Squadron for air supply. On the contrary, the onset of the monsoon, which resulted in army units being isolated by floods or by breaks in the roads and railway, increased their commitments which included the Chinese-American troops in north Burma and the British-Indian forces in the Chin Hills, Arakan and Fort Hertz. The R.A.F. also carried out reconnaissance over the Indian Ocean in all weathers and provided shipping escorts, anti-submarine patrols and air-sea rescue sorties, flying in all during the monsoon some 70,000 hours. The cost of all these operations was forty-two British and twenty-seven American aircraft, mostly lost owing to bad weather.

It is not possible to assess the effect of this air activity on the Japanese, since it was essentially part of a war of attrition which did not reach its climax until much later. It can however be said that by the end of the monsoon in 1943, the Allied air forces, increased in strength and efficiency, were in a far better position to gain and hold air superiority over Burma during the forthcoming operations in the dry weather than they had been in the autumn of 1942.

CHAPTER XXV

THE PACIFIC
(May–September 1943)

See Maps 10 and 15 and Sketches 18 and 19

ALLIED plans for operations in the Pacific were largely unaffected by the Trident Conference, which did little more than confirm the decisions taken at Casablanca four months earlier. The general outline of strategy remained the same: the enemy was to be ejected from the Aleutians; the Marshall and the Gilbert Islands were to be seized; the advance along the coast of New Guinea and up through the Solomons was to be continued and, by the capture of the Admiralty Islands, a wedge driven between the Japanese positions in New Guinea and New Britain which would isolate and neutralize Rabaul. The plan to capture this strongly held naval and air base was discarded as too costly.

The decision to clear the Aleutians was dictated by the pressure of public opinion in the United States rather than by military necessity. The occupation by the Japanese of the islands of Kiska and Attu in June 1942 had raised the old bogey of invasion of Alaska by way of the Aleutian chain, and a demand for the expulsion of the enemy from American soil had followed.[1] The requirements of the south Pacific had prevented much being done in the first half of 1942, but in September American forces occupied Adak island and in January 1943 Amchitka, and airfields within fighter range of the Japanese-held islands were constructed on each. The fear that the loss of Attu and Kiska might open the way to attack on the Kurile Islands and even on Japan itself led the Japanese to reinforce their garrisons. On the 26th March 1943, a small American task group of cruisers and destroyers intercepted a number of transports, escorted by a Japanese force twice its size and fire power, off the Komandorskie islands. A long-range daylight gun action, of a type fast becoming obsolete, followed, in which neither aircraft nor submarines took part. Neither side lost any ships, but the enemy transports turned back. From then on the Japanese no longer dared risk their transports to run the blockade and, as they had been forced to do in the Solomons, employed only destroyers and submarines to reinforce their garrison.

---

[1] See Map 15.

It was not until May 1943 that preparations were completed for the first major attempt to regain the Aleutians. On the 4th, transports carrying an American division, escorted by a powerful task force which included three of the older battleships, left Alaska in cold and stormy weather, and on the 11th landed their troops on the beaches of Attu. The small Japanese garrison, though greatly outnumbered, fought to the death and it was not till the 29th that organized resistance ceased. Although American warships remained until the 17th to give fire support to the troops ashore, the Japanese Fleet made no attempt to seek action. This was due partly to the weakness of the Japanese *5th Fleet* and partly to the persistent fog which covered the whole of the Aleutians.

The Americans then turned their attention to Kiska, which they bombed and bombarded whenever weather permitted. In July the Japanese decided to evacuate the island. Under cover of thick fog, a force of cruisers and destroyers made a bold dash for Kiska and, having in little less than an hour embarked the garrison and civilians in the island—over 5,000 men, withdrew as secretly as it had come. The Americans had no inkling that the island had been evacuated, and early in August assembled an expeditionary force of over 35,000 men, of whom some 5,000 were Canadians, on Attu. On Friday the 13th, always a day of ill omen to sailors, the force with a strong escort including battleships sailed for Kiska. On the night of the 15th/16th the troops were landed to grope their way through fog and rain in search of a non-existent enemy.

The bloodless occupation of Kiska brought to an end the campaign in the Aleutians. For many months, American forces which might have been more usefully employed elsewhere had been engaged in the recapture of two remote islands of comparative insignificance. The Japanese had never had any intention of invading Alaska; their object was merely to prevent the Americans making use of the shortest route from the New World to Japan. In retrospect, it seems that the Japanese garrisons might well have been left to 'wither on the vine'.

While in the storms and fogs of the north Pacific the Aleutians were being reoccupied, the forces of the South and South West Pacific Commands, nearly 4,000 miles to the southward, had begun the second phase of their advances in New Guinea and the central Solomons.[1] General MacArthur had hoped to resume his offensive on the 15th May but, owing to unavoidable delays in the build-up of the 7th Amphibious Force, had to postpone it until the 30th June. For the proposed operations in New Guinea he had divided

---
[1] See pages 270-71.

the military forces of the South West Pacific Command into their national components: the Alamo Force, consisting of 32nd and 41st U.S. Divisions and part of a third division under command of Lieut.-General W. Krueger, and the New Guinea Force, under command of Lieut.-General E. F. Herring. The 3rd, 5th, 7th, 9th and 11th Australian Divisions and some American regiments served in the New Guinea Force at various times between May and August.

MacArthur's plan was that the Alamo Force would take Kiriwina and Woodlark Islands in the Trobriand group, and the New Guinea Force Lae, Salamaua, Finschhafen and Madang, while Admiral Halsey's South Pacific forces captured the New Georgia group in the central Solomons. The Alamo Force would then move across to western New Britain, supported by aircraft based on Lae and Salamaua, while the South Pacific forces seized Kieta on the east coast of Bougainville and neutralized the island of Buka.[1] The offensive was to begin on the 30th June with three simultaneous attacks: Woodlark and Kiriwina were to be occupied; a landing was to be made at Nassau Bay (sixty miles south of Lae) to provide a base for the supply of the New Guinea Force during its advance on Salamaua and for the landing craft required later for the attack on Lae[2]; and the invasion of the New Georgia group was to begin under cover of air attacks on Japanese bases in Bougainville and Buka. During the last weeks of June, Amboina, Timor and other bases in the Netherlands East Indies were to be kept under air attack in order to deceive the Japanese as to the main direction of the forthcoming offensive.

The equivalent of a brigade group from the Alamo Force was landed on Kiriwina and another on Woodlark as planned. It was known that there was no enemy garrison on the islands but, in order that they might gain the greatest possible experience from what was, except for the possibility of air attack, no more than a practice landing, the troops were purposely kept in ignorance of the fact. The Japanese were unaware of the landings and their air force did not interfere with the operation. The construction of airfields on both islands was immediately begun, and within a few months American and Australian fighter squadrons based on them were providing escorts for bombers raiding Rabaul, Bougainville and Munda.

After their failure in February 1943 to capture Wau, the Japanese in New Guinea had fallen back on defended positions on the main trails leading to Salamaua from the west and south. During March and April Kangaforce, which it will be remembered had been reinforced by 17th Australian Brigade[3], could do little more than

---

[1] See Map 10.
[2] See Sketch 18.
[3] See page 375.

make harassing attacks on their lines of communication. Towards the end of April, Headquarters 3rd Australian Division and one battalion of 15th Australian Brigade had been sent to Wau. Kangaforce was then disbanded and Major-General S. G. Savige, the divisional commander, took over control of all operations in the area. Headquarters 15th Brigade and its remaining battalions arrived at Wau in May and early June. At the end of May, Savige was informed of the impending occupation of Kiriwina and Woodlark Islands and ordered to secure Nassau Bay as a base for future operations.

On the 30th June, one battalion of 162nd U.S. Regiment landed at Nassau Bay. The same day General Savige began a concentric attack on Salamaua. On the left, 15th Australian Brigade soon gained a foothold on a ridge near Bobdubi which dominated a stretch of the enemy's line of communications to Mubo and gave observation over the airfield and harbour. In the centre, 17th Australian Brigade occupied the Mubo area after hard fighting on the 13th. On the right, 162nd Regiment, brought up to full strength and supported by artillery, advanced along the coast and by the end of July captured Tambu Bay, six miles south of Salamaua; this was immediately developed as an advanced base for the supply of forward troops, and additional artillery was landed.

The country round Salamaua was no less forbidding than that which lay between Port Moresby and Buna. Steep, sharp-ridged mountains covered with dense bush and occasional patches of kunai grass surrounded the town. Progress was painfully slow and difficult. General Eichelberger, who had commanded the 32nd U.S. Division in Papua, has given a vivid description of the difficulties experienced by the troops:

> '. . . it was about one part fighting to three parts sheer misery of physical environment. It was climbing up one hill and down another, and then, when breath was short, fording streams with weapons held aloft or wading through swamps. It was sweat and then chill; it was a weariness of body and spirit; and once again tropical illness was a greater foe than enemy bullets'.[1]

Nevertheless, by the 19th August the Japanese had been forced to withdraw to an inner ring of defences on the last remaining high ground covering the approaches to Salamaua. Since the main purpose of the attack on the town, which in itself was of little strategical importance, was to delude the Japanese into believing that it was the primary object of the Allied advance and to draw off enemy strength from Lae, General Savige was instructed to delay his final assault on the town until the assault on Lae had begun.

---

[1] Eichelberger, page 109.

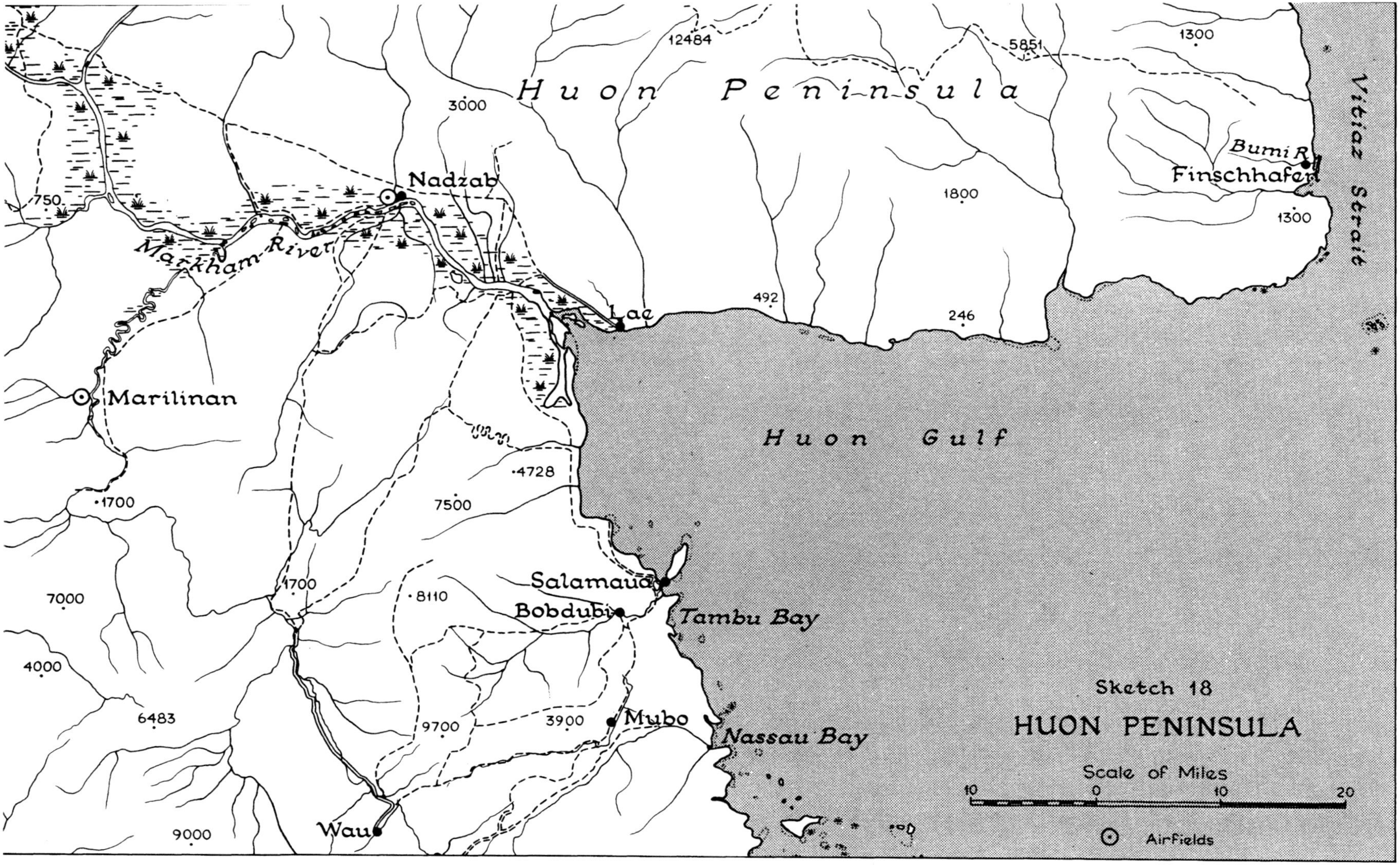
Sketch 18
HUON PENINSULA
Scale of Miles
10
0
10
20
Airfields
Vitiaz Strait
Huon Peninsula
Huon Gulf
Finschhafen
Bumi R.
Lae
Nadzab
Markham River
Marilinan
Salamaua
Bobdubi
Tambu Bay
Mubo
Nassau Bay
Wau
12484
5851
1300
3000
1800
1300
750
492
246
4728
7500
1700
1700
8110
7000
4000
6483
9700
3900
9000

While the Allied forces were closing in on the Japanese strongholds on the southern coast of the Huon Peninsula, Admiral Halsey's South Pacific forces in the central Solomons were engaged in gaining a footing on New Georgia, the largest of the group of islands of that name.[1] To the north-west of New Georgia lie Kolombangara and Vella Lavella, the three islands being separated by Kula Gulf and Vella Gulf. At the foot of Kula Gulf lies Arundel island, and seven miles south of Munda Point (the south-west tip of New Georgia) Rendova. Vangunu and Gatukai lie at the south-eastern end of the group which in all comprises hundreds of islands.

Admiral Halsey's plan was to make the main landing on Rendova with simultaneous subsidiary landings at Wickham Anchorage on Vangunu, and at Segi Point and Viru Harbour at the eastern end of New Georgia. As soon as Rendova was secured, troops were to be ferried across the seven-mile channel to a beach on New Georgia, five miles east of Munda Point, from where they were to advance across country to seize the airfield. A further landing, to take place simultaneously with that east of Munda Point, was to be made at Rice Anchorage in order to cut the Japanese reinforcement route to New Georgia which terminated at Bairoko Harbour.

Rear-Admiral Turner, commander of the 3rd Amphibious Force, was placed in command of the landing operations. He divided his force into two: a western under his own immediate command for the main landing and an eastern under Rear-Admiral G. H. Fort for the subsidiary landings. Admiral Halsey with a powerful carrier and battleship force provided cover for the whole operation, and Vice-Admiral Fitch's South Pacific Air Force gave air support. The bulk of the troops was found from 43rd U.S. Division.

Owing to a report from an Australian coast-watcher that the Japanese were moving into the area, the landings at Segi Point were made on the 21st instead of the 30th June and met with no opposition. As invasion day approached, Japanese airfields were kept under heavy attack. The Munda and Vila airfields were bombed by naval aircraft and Shortland island was bombarded on the night of the 29th/30th by cruisers and destroyers.

The landing on Rendova on the 30th came as a complete surprise to the Japanese, and met with only minor opposition from the small garrison of some 200 naval ratings. During the day, Japanese aircraft made two attacks on the transports and escorting craft but were held off until 3 p.m. by fighters based on Guadalcanal, by which time unloading had been completed. As the transports were withdrawing, a third attack broke through the fighter screen and, although all the enemy aircraft were eventually destroyed, they succeeded in disabling a destroyer and sinking a transport. The landing at Viru

---
[1] See Sketch 19.

Harbour was successfully accomplished on the 1st July and on the following day the ferrying of the troops from Rendova to the beach east of Munda Point began. By the 5th, two infantry regiments had been landed and the overland advance began. The same day two infantry battalions of 37th U.S. Division and a Marine raider regiment, escorted by three light cruisers and nine destroyers under the command of Rear-Admiral W. L. Ainsworth, were landed at Rice Anchorage on the north-west of New Georgia with orders to occupy the Bairoko Harbour area. The landings were effected without incident but, as the escorting force began its return journey to Espiritu Santo, a destroyer—the *Strong*—was torpedoed and sunk.

The Japanese commanders had meanwhile held a conference at Rabaul on the 4th to decide what steps to take to repel the American invasion. Their garrisons in the New Georgia group comprised a mixed force of soldiers and sailors numbering only some 11,000 all ranks. Bearing in mind *Imperial General Headquarters'* order that the central Solomons were to be held, General Imamura arranged with Admiral Kusaka to send four battalions to Kolombangara. The first detachment left at high speed in four destroyers that very afternoon and safely reached its destination.[1]

Admiral Ainsworth had passed Guadalcanal on his way back to Espiritu Santo when, in the early afternoon of the 5th, he received orders from Admiral Halsey to intercept a Japanese reinforcing convoy reported leaving Shortland island. This order led to the naval action of Kula Gulf. The Admiral at once turned back up 'The Slot'. As the American ships rounded the northern tip of New Georgia, ten Japanese destroyers entered Kula Gulf. Shortly before 2 a.m., the American cruisers' radar picked up two groups of enemy vessels. Forming line ahead, Ainsworth closed to within 7,000 yards before opening fire and concentrated on one of the destroyers of the leading group, which was quickly sunk. But the Japanese destroyers had already fired a salvo of torpedoes, and as the Admiral turned to attack the second group the cruiser *Helena* was struck by three torpedoes which blew her bows off. The Japanese destroyers then turned away and contact was lost. Ainsworth made a sweep to the north-west but was unable to find them, and at 3.30 a.m., leaving two destroyers to pick up survivors from the *Helena*, he headed back to Tulagi. Three Japanese destroyer transports, which had been detached before the action, landed 1,200 troops and supplies at Vila. One of them however ran aground and, reported by a coast-watcher, was destroyed by American aircraft during the morning of the 6th.

A week later, a second naval action which became known as the Battle of Kolombangara took place in Kula Gulf when Admiral Ainsworth again intercepted Japanese destroyers attempting to land

---
[1] The torpedo which sank the *Strong* came from one of these destroyers.

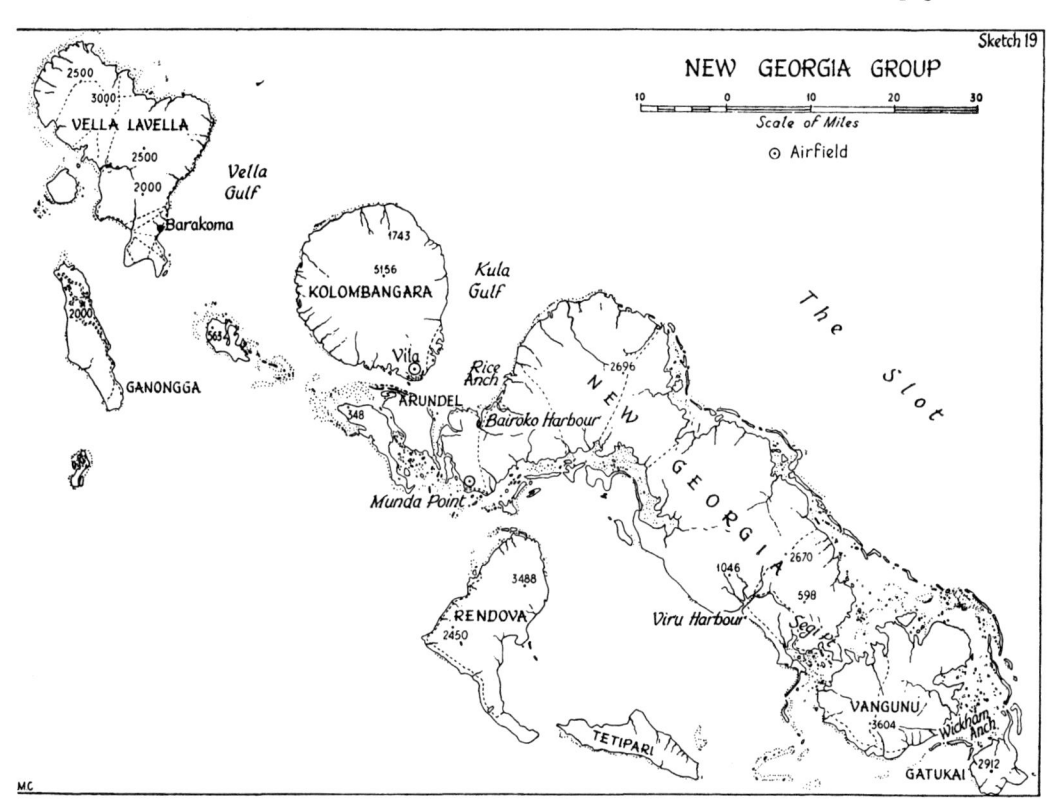

reinforcements at Vila. By this time, six destroyers had been added to his force and the *Helena* replaced by a light cruiser—the *Leander* (Captain C. A. L. Mansergh, R.N.) of the Royal New Zealand Navy. The Japanese force, which consisted of five destroyers led by the light cruiser *Jintsu* escorting five destroyer transports, was reported by a Catalina on patrol shortly after 12.30 a.m. on the 13th, and about half an hour later the enemy vessels showed on the cruisers' radar screens. The ensuing action followed very much the same pattern as the previous one. In the opening engagement the cruisers, on an opposite course to the enemy, concentrated their fire on the largest ship and in a few minutes the *Jintsu*, which had survived a score of fights in the Netherlands East Indies and the Solomons, broke in two and sank. But once again the Japanese beat their opponents to the draw: as the cruisers turned to the same course as the enemy, a torpedo struck the *Leander* and put her out of action. Meanwhile, the Japanese destroyer transports had moved unseen along the coast to Kolombangara and had landed another 1,700 troops as well as supplies at Vila. Having retired at high speed and reloaded their torpedoes, the Japanese covering destroyers again made contact with the American cruisers at about 2 a.m. Uncertain whether they were his own destroyers sent in pursuit or the enemy's, Ainsworth held his fire. The Japanese made full use of the delay. Before they could fire a shot, two American cruisers and a destroyer were torpedoed in quick succession. Nevertheless, all the three cruisers damaged in the action were able to make port under their own steam. The battles of Kula Gulf and Kolombangara cost the Americans dear; but they had the effect of deterring the Japanese from making any further attempts to run the gauntlet of Kula Gulf.

Ashore in New Georgia the American troops, though heavily reinforced, had been held up by rain, mud and tangled jungle, and had made little progress towards Munda airfield. On the 16th July, Lieut.-General O. W. Griswold, Commander 14th U.S. Corps, took charge of all operations in the south; fresh troops, tanks and guns were brought in and on the 25th the final assault on the airfield began. As the troops moved forward, destroyers gave fire support and aircraft carried out the heaviest bombardment yet made on an airfield in the south Pacific. Nevertheless the Japanese held out for a further ten days, and it was not until the 5th August that American tanks and infantry occupied it. Another nineteen days passed before American troops entered Bairoko. By the 24th August, the occupation of New Georgia was complete.

While the Americans were closing in on Munda, the Japanese had continued to reinforce Vila by way of Vella Gulf. The day Munda airfield was captured, Admiral Halsey received a report that Japanese destroyers, and possibly a cruiser, were about to land a fresh contingent. Six destroyers, sent from Tulagi to intercept, surprised a force of enemy destroyers in Vella Gulf shortly before midnight on the 6th August. In a brilliantly fought night action lasting only forty-five minutes, three of the four Japanese destroyers were torpedoed and sunk. For the first time American destroyers had fought a battle unaccompanied by cruisers, and for the first time they had achieved real success.

After the occupation of New Georgia, the Japanese still held three of the main islands in the group (Kolombangara, Vella Lavella and Arundel). Meeting with considerably stronger resistance than they had expected, American troops occupied Arundel between the 27th August and the 20th September. Vila airfield, the centre of Japanese strength on Kolombangara, was then neutralized, for it was within artillery range of the northern shores of Arundel.

Meanwhile Admiral Halsey had made a change in his original plan, which was to attack and occupy Kolombangara as soon as the New Georgia operations had been completed. Kolombangara had by this time a garrison of some 10,000 troops firmly entrenched in positions as strong as those at Munda. The garrison of Vella Lavella, on the other hand, had been reported by coast-watchers to consist only of some 250 lightly armed troops. Furthermore, there was a suitable site on the island for an airstrip which was all that Halsey wanted for the next phase—the capture of Bougainville. Thus, having no wish to embark on another long drawn out and costly struggle in Kolombangara similar to the one then going on in New Georgia, the Admiral had decided to by-pass it. This was the first instance of the deliberate use of the leap-frogging or by-passing strategy which had long been contemplated, and which from now on was to be generally used in the Pacific. It had already been practised inadvertently in the Aleutians, where the capture of Attu had led the Japanese to abandon Kiska as being too expensive to hold.

Admiral Halsey did not wait till the whole of New Georgia had been secured before putting his new plan into action. Towards the end of July, reconnaissance parties were sent to Vella Lavella and a beach and potential airstrip selected at Barakoma on the east coast of the island. In the early morning of the 15th August, a regimental combat team, a Marine defence battalion and supporting troops were landed under cover of aircraft. By sunset 4,600 men had been put ashore. The small enemy garrison was mainly concentrated in the north of the island and the only opposition came from the air, and that was ineffective. An enemy counter-landing was expected but did not materialize, for on the 13th August *Imperial General Headquarters* had decided to withdraw from the central Solomons and concentrate on strengthening the outer defences of Rabaul, especially Bougainville.

CHAPTER XXVI

ALLIED AND JAPANESE PLANS FOR THE DRY WEATHER 1943-44

See Strategic Map and Maps 10, 12, 14 and 15

THE Chiefs of Staff surmised that at the forthcoming Quadrant Conference in Quebec the Americans would be likely, for political reasons, to place considerable stress on the importance of helping China and, basing their plans on optimistic estimates of the date by which a new 'north Burma road' could be completed, would press for an early and powerful offensive into north Burma.

Three new factors affecting the possible course of operations from India had arisen since the Trident Conference in May. Firstly, Auchinleck had reported that the lines of communication to Assam could not be sufficiently improved in the time available to support both the proposed increase in the air lift to China and the offensive from Ledo and Tamu into northern Burma. Secondly, examination had shown that the demand for shipping for the attacks on Akyab and Ramree would place such a heavy drain on Allied resources for combined operations that it would interfere with the prosecution of the war in the Mediterranean, and that the strategic advantage would scarcely warrant the cost. Finally, Wingate's long-range penetration groups had emerged as a valuable means of carrying the war into enemy-held territory. The decisions made at the Trident Conference for operations from India in 1943-44 had therefore to be reviewed in the light of these factors.

The Chiefs of Staff and the Prime Minister were agreed that a 'strong new feature' should be made of the L.R.P. groups, but felt too much in the dark about the logistical problems in India to agree with Auchinleck that the north Burma operations should be cancelled. On the question of operations against Akyab and Ramree, the Chiefs of Staff and the Prime Minister were divided. Although the Chiefs of Staff were prepared to abandon them, they were willing, if the Americans pressed for it, to consider mounting them on the 1st March 1944. The Prime Minister, on the other hand, wanted them to be replaced by an operation against northern Sumatra ('Culverin').

The Chiefs of Staff's contentions were that, provided the Akyab and Ramree operations were cancelled and the strategic air offensive planned for Burma was diverted to Sumatra, the land and air forces needed for 'Culverin' could be found; but there would still be the problem of finding the naval forces, assault shipping and landing craft required for either operation. From a short-term view 'Culverin' would pay handsome dividends, since it would provide a strategic base for the Allied air forces, but from a long-term view it was open to serious disadvantages. Whatever the long-term plan for the defeat of Japan, both southern Burma and Singapore would have to be recaptured, and it was therefore important that plans should be kept flexible so that either objective could be attacked as circumstances permitted. The capture of northern Sumatra would, by indicating the next objective, commit the Allies to an immediate attack on Singapore before the Japanese could reinforce it. If, after northern Sumatra was captured, there were insufficient forces available to launch an attack on Malaya at once, operations for the capture of Singapore would be prejudiced and all flexibility in planning would be lost. It seemed, too, that southern Burma could be recaptured only by means of an amphibious attack on Rangoon, and for this Akyab and Ramree would have to be in Allied hands. They therefore thought that for the dry weather of 1943–44 it would be best to carry on with the plans agreed to at the Trident Conference, so that this essential strategic flexibility could be retained and either southern Burma or Singapore attacked later as events dictated.

The Prime Minister disagreed, and declared himself utterly opposed to the operations against Akyab. He was not prepared, he said, to get into a position where the dead hand of a long-term plan paralyzed action in the near future, and he reserved the right to raise the question of 'Culverin' with the Americans.

After taking into account all the developments in the Indian theatre, the Chiefs of Staff came to the conclusion that, as far as northern Burma was concerned, there were only three possible courses, though there were not enough resources to carry out more than one of them in full. These were firstly, to put the main effort during the dry weather of 1943–44 into the land and air operations necessary to establish land communications with China while improving and securing the air route, though such operations, until completed, would probably be at the expense of the air lift; secondly, to give priority to increasing the air lift to China, though, if this course were adopted, the remaining capacity of the Assam line of communications would be insufficient to sustain the offensive operations into northern Burma necessary for the protection of the air route; and thirdly, to adopt the long-term policy (advocated by Auchinleck) of putting the main effort during the dry weather into developing the line of communication into Assam and eastern Bengal, so that in the dry weather of 1944–45 a powerful offensive could be launched for the capture of northern Burma, and a far greater tonnage of supplies be delivered by air to China.

Further investigation of the administrative problems in India would be needed before definite decisions could be taken on which course to adopt, but it was clear to the Chiefs of Staff that a decision on general policy would be needed from the Combined Chiefs of Staff. After weighing up as far as possible the pros and cons of the three courses, they decided to suggest the adoption of the first at the Quadrant Conference. They considered that this would meet the wishes of their American allies and that if, by the capture of northern Burma, a junction could be made with the Chinese forces, it would go far towards compensating the Generalissimo for the temporary reduction in the tonnages delivered by the air route. It would appear that in deciding to adopt this course they were influenced by Wingate's contention that with the help of L.R.P. groups an offensive by the main forces could be successfully carried out, despite the warning from Auchinleck that the Assam line of communication could not support it.

The Quadrant Conference opened at Quebec on the 14th August.[1] At an early meeting of the Combined Chiefs of Staff attended by Wingate, the British Chiefs of Staff said that they had been examining the possibility of using L.R.P. groups, maintained by air well ahead of the main advances, to cut the enemy supply lines and had as a result decided to form six groups. To this end, they were proposing to undertake a comb-out of suitable men from the army in India. They considered that the operations proposed by Wingate would enable enough of upper Burma to be seized to open a road to China. Wingate then gave an account of the Chindit operation, and outlined his views on the future employment of L.R.P. groups in conjunction with the advance of the main forces for the recapture of northern Burma. The American Chiefs of Staff were so impressed by what he said that they decided to provide American jungle-trained troops to form part of his organization. Before the end of the conference, they had called for volunteers for this purpose.[2]

As expected, the American Chiefs of Staff were insistent on the need for re-opening road communication with China and maintained that, without doubt, the whole of Burma would eventually have

---

[1] See Ehrman, *Grand Strategy*, Volume V (H.M.S.O., 1956).
[2] Some 3,000 men were formed into 5307th Composite Unit (Provisional), which later became known as Merrill's Marauders.

to be recaptured. They advocated the launching of an offensive into northern Burma and the capture of both Akyab and Ramree during the dry weather of 1943–44, a programme almost identical with the Trident decisions. They held that any operations further south, such as 'Culverin', would be a diversion from the main effort which ought to be concentrated on securing Burma.

When the Prime Minister suggested that 'Culverin' should be substituted for operations on the Arakan coast, the President was unimpressed and outlined the American views on the strategy for the final defeat of Japan. He likened the area held by the Japanese to a slice of pie with Japan at the apex and the island barrier formed by the Netherlands East Indies as the crust. He considered that the strategy of the Allies should be to advance as far along the two edges of the slice towards the apex as was necessary to enable them to bomb the Japanese mainland and shipping on the routes to the various points on the crust. This meant an advance across the Pacific towards Formosa and the Chinese coast, and an advance from Burma into China proper.[1] He preferred this type of strategy to nibbling at the crust which, he said, would be the effect of adopting an operation such as 'Culverin'.

It was finally agreed that the capture of northern Burma should be given priority for the forthcoming dry weather, with the object of establishing land communications with China and improving and securing the air route, although it was realized that administrative difficulties might reduce the scale or delay the start of the operation. The Combined Chiefs of Staff, however, found it impracticable to arrive at all the necessary decisions for the conduct of operations against Japan in the forthcoming dry weather, and left open the selection of an objective for the proposed amphibious operation in 1944. The decisions of the Quadrant Conference affecting South-East Asia, though somewhat similar, were thus not so clear cut as those of the Trident Conference.

The plan for the dry weather of 1943–44 was to be firstly, to carry out operations for the capture of northern Burma in order to improve the air route and establish overland communication with China, with a target date mid-February 1944, the extent of these operations being dependent upon how much communications had been affected by the recent floods. Secondly, to continue preparations for an amphibious operation in the spring of 1944, but, pending a decision on the particular objective, the scale of these preparations should be of the order of those contemplated at the Trident Conference for the capture of Akyab and Ramree. Thirdly, to continue the preparation of India as a base for the operations eventually contemplated in the South-East Asia theatre. Finally, to continue to build up and

---
[1] See Map 15.

increase the air lift to China and air facilities in general with a view to keeping her in the war, while intensifying operations against Japan, maintaining and increasing United States and Chinese air forces in China and equipping Chinese ground forces.

Although it had been decided that the main effort was to be directed towards establishing land communications with China and improving and securing the air route, priorities to be accorded to the various operations could not be rigidly laid down. The responsible commanders would therefore have to regard the decision as a guide, and bear in mind the importance of long-term development of the line of communication. Subject to the requirements of military operations in Burma, approval was given for the intensified development of the supply routes into and in Assam so that a target of 220,000 tons capacity a month could be reached by the 31st December 1945, and for the construction of two 6-inch oil pipe-lines from Calcutta to Ledo, a 4-inch pipe-line from Ledo to Kunming and a 6-inch pipe-line following the road into China to facilitate air operations and ease congestion on the existing lines of supply.

The Combined Chiefs of Staff directed that a study should be made of the potentialities and limitations of developing the air route to China to a scale sufficient to make it possible to use all the heavy bomber and transport aircraft likely to be available for the South-East Asia theatre and China in 1944–45, on the assumption that Germany would be defeated in the autumn of 1944. The action required to implement the most comprehensive plan possible, without prejudicing operations being carried out in the interim, was to be specified. They further directed that the possibilities of the following operations and their relation one to another should be examined:

(a) an operation against northern Sumatra with target date of spring 1944;

(b) operations southwards from northern Burma with target date November 1944;

(c) operations south from Moulmein area or the Kra Isthmus in the direction of Bangkok, target date to be as early as practicable;

(d) operations through the Strait of Malacca and Malaya for the direct capture of Singapore, target date to be as early as possible;

(e) the capture of Akyab and Ramree, to determine whether this was necessary to the success of operations in (a) to (d) above or the operations planned for the capture of upper Burma.

As regards the Pacific, it was decided that operations were to be carried out in 1943–44 to capture the Gilbert and Marshall Islands, Ponape and the eastern Carolines, Palau (including Yap), Guam and the Japanese Marianas.[1] The current operation in New Guinea was to be extended with a view to the seizure or neutralization of eastern New Guinea as far west as Wewak, and of the Admiralty Islands and the Bismarck Archipelago; Rabaul in New Britain was to be neutralized if possible. An advance step-by-step along the north coast of New Guinea would then be undertaken.[2]

The setting up of the proposed new Allied command in South-East Asia was also discussed at the conference. The Prime Minister and the President had been in correspondence on the subject for the previous two months and, by the time the conference opened, the Chiefs of Staff were able to present a memorandum on it. The document listed the parts of the Prime Minister's original paper of the 15th June which had been approved by both the President and the Chiefs of Staff, and the points on which agreement had yet to be reached.[3] The two most important of these were the responsibilities of the Deputy Supreme Allied Commander, and the relationship to be established between the Supreme Command and the Combined Chiefs of Staff.

President Roosevelt had on the 30th June proposed that General Stilwell should be made the Deputy Supreme Commander, and double his duties as such with his present duties as United States Commander in the China–Burma–India theatre. He would thus be Commander-in-Chief of the United States air and ground forces in South-East Asia Command, Commander-in-Chief of Chinese forces in Burma and Chief of Staff to Chiang Kai-shek as well as Deputy Supreme Commander. Both the Prime Minister and the British Chiefs of Staff were very doubtful of the wisdom of this multiple command, but realized there would be advantages in accepting the President's proposal, and trusting to the Supreme Commander to make the necessary adjustments if difficulties arose.

While recognizing the faults inherent in such a command, the United States Chiefs of Staff emphasized the great importance of the appointment. It would have to be Stilwell's task, not an easy one, to ensure not only that the Chinese would play their part in operations, but that the 14th U.S.A.A.F. would co-operate as much as possible in Burma. It would have to be remembered, General Marshall said, that politically all United States forces in China or in the proposed South-East Asia Command were regarded as being there for the sole purpose of supporting China. A system had therefore to be evolved whereby, without sacrifice of this political principle, the maximum

---
[1] See Map 15.
[2] See Map 10.
[3] See pages 387-88.

S.E. ASIA COMMAND TO BE SET UP

support could be provided for operations in Burma. In the circumstances, the British Chiefs of Staff deferred to the United States views on Stilwell's responsibilities. They remained quite firm, however, about the pattern of command. They maintained that it should be similar to that in the south-west Pacific, where General MacArthur was under the Combined Chiefs of Staff for matters of strategic policy and under his own Chiefs of Staff for matters of operational policy. The American Chiefs of Staff favoured the system in General Eisenhower's North African command in which he was directly responsible to the Combined Chiefs of Staff. The Americans, in their turn, yielded to British wishes on this matter.

The conference finally agreed to set up a Supreme Allied Command in South-East Asia, the Supreme Commander to be British with an American deputy, and the command and staff to be Anglo-American. The Supreme Commander's Headquarters would be established at Delhi until a permanent location was decided on. The Deputy Supreme Allied Commander (General Stilwell) together with the Naval, Army and Air Commanders-in-Chief would, under the orders of the Supreme Commander, control all operations and command all forces assigned to the South-East Asia theatre. General Stilwell would, in addition, have direct command of all United States ground and air forces in South-East Asia and, in conformity with the overall plan of the British Army Commander, exercise control over all Chinese forces operating in Burma. He would continue to bear the same direct responsibilities to Chiang Kai-shek as before. The Combined Chiefs of Staff would exercise a general jurisdiction over strategy in the theatre and over the allocation of all resources between it and the China theatre. The British Chiefs of Staff would exercise operational control and be the channel through which all instructions to the Supreme Commander passed.

The India and South-East Asia Commands would be separate; the administration of India as a base for the forces in South-East Asia would remain the responsibility of the Commander-in-Chief in India. Since the co-ordination of the movement and maintenance of the operational forces assigned to S.E.A.C., but based in India, and of the internal garrison could best be carried out by one staff responsible in the last resort to one authority with power to decide priorities, this would be the task of the Government of India and General Headquarters, India. Conflicts of opinion over priorities in connection with the division of responsibilities between India and S.E.A.C. could be expected: the Viceroy, not in his statutory capacity but acting on behalf of the War Cabinet, would resolve these as they occurred. If not satisfied with the Viceroy's rulings on administrative matters, the Supreme Commander would be able to exercise his right of direct access to the British Chiefs of Staff.

On the 25th August 1943, the day after the conclusion of the conference, this announcement was made from the Citadel at Quebec:

> 'It has been decided to set up a separate South-East Asia Command for conducting operations based on India and Ceylon against Japan. It will be an allied command similar to that set up in North Africa.
> The King has been pleased to approve the appointment of Acting Vice-Admiral the Lord Louis Mountbatten, G.C.V.O., D.S.O., A.D.C., to be Supreme Allied Commander, South-East Asia.'[1]

Admiral Mountbatten was at that time Chief of Combined Operations and a member of the Chiefs of Staff Committee. During his voyage across the Atlantic, the Prime Minister had written that he might well be the man for the post of Supreme Commander: he knew the whole story from the top, was young, enthusiastic and 'triphibious'.

While the Allies were formulating plans to set up a new command in South-East Asia and launch an offensive against northern Burma, the Japanese were reconsidering their strategy in Burma. Their pre-war plan for the formation of a Greater East Asia Co-Prosperity Sphere had envisaged the India-Burma frontier as the north-western limit of their conquest.[2] Thus when *15th Army* had completed the capture of Burma in May 1942, it was ordered to consolidate its position and adopt a defensive rôle. Plans for an offensive into north-east Assam had been considered that autumn, but had been abandoned, and until the break of the 1943 monsoon the original policy of standing on the defensive remained.[3]

The Japanese came to the conclusion that any Allied counter-offensive for the recapture of northern and central Burma would be launched simultaneously from Yunnan, along the Hukawng Valley and across the Assam border near Tamu. They thought an offensive might also be launched along the Arakan coast at the same time, but this, for geographical reasons, would be a separate operation and not necessarily closely co-ordinated with operations further north. In view of the huge size of Burma and the fact that there were three distinct and widely separated areas in which fighting might take place, they considered that the task of defending it was too great for one army commander. The ideal defensive organization demanded one army for the Assam border, a second for the Chinese border and a third for the Arakan and coastal areas, all controlled by a *Burma Area Army Headquarters*. Further, since Burma was a con-

---

[1] *The Times*, 26th August 1943.
[2] See Volume I, Chapter V.
[3] See pages 307-308.

JAPANESE REORGANIZATION IN BURMA

venient base from which political attacks on British rule in India could be controlled, an organization higher than an army headquarters was needed so that the Commander-in-Chief could, through the Japanese Ambassador in Burma and representatives of the newly-formed puppet Government of Burma, keep in close touch with all internal matters affecting the country and direct political attacks on British rule in India.

On the 27th March 1943, *Burma Area Army Headquarters* was set up, under command of Lieut.-General M. Kawabe, to control *15th Army* and *55th Division*, which were allotted to the defence of central and northern Burma, and of Arakan respectively. Kawabe's primary task was to defend Burma, and draw up plans and complete preparations as far as possible for offensive operations beyond the frontier. At the same time, *15th Army* was reorganized to consist of *18th, 33rd* and *56th Divisions* and placed under command of Lieut.-General R. Mutaguchi (promoted from the command of *18th Division*).[1] This fell short of the ideal three-army organization but was apparently all that *Imperial General Headquarters* in Tokyo was prepared to sanction at the time. The reorganization was completed early in April, *Burma Area Army Headquarters* being located at Rangoon and *15th Army Headquarters* at Maymyo. In view of the possibility of a British counter-offensive and the size of the area to be defended, plans were made to reinforce *15th Army* by *31st Division* (Lieut.-General K. Sato). This division, which had some of its units in China and some in the Pacific area, began to reach Burma during June but was not complete till September 1943.

Since the sea route to Rangoon by way of Singapore and the Strait of Malacca was long and exposed to attack by Allied submarines and aircraft, the Japanese had to find an alternative and more secure line of communication to Burma. The only road from Siam to southern Burma, which ran from Raheng to Moulmein, had been hurriedly improved at the time of *15th Army's* advance into Burma early in 1942, and was not fit for prolonged heavy traffic. In June 1942, therefore, *Imperial General Headquarters* had directed *Southern Army* to build a single-line metre gauge railway, some 250 miles in length, to carry three thousand tons a day from Non Pladuk, two miles from Ban Pong in Siam, by way of Three Pagodas Pass to join the existing railway in Burma half way between Moulmein and Ye.[2] This was to be completed by November 1943. Work began in November 1942; and labour was found from Allied prisoners of war and from conscripted Malays and Burmese. In February 1943 it became evident

---

[1] Lieut.-General Kawabe had held the appointment of Chief of Staff, Japanese Expeditionary Force in China, for some time previously. At the time of the outbreak of the China Incident in 1937, both Kawabe and Mutaguchi were serving in north China the former as a brigade commander and the latter as a regimental commander

[2] See Strategic Map.

that, to meet the threat of an Allied counter-offensive, the troops in Burma would have to be reinforced. This, and the scale of Allied air attacks on shipping and on Rangoon, caused *Imperial General Headquarters* to direct *Southern Army* to speed up the construction of the railway and complete it by August. Although Japanese documents state that '*Southern Army* in accordance with this directive ordered units to increase their efforts to complete the work and to pay particular attention to the systematic mobilization of labourers', they attempted to achieve their object by slave-driving prisoners of war. Some sixty-one thousand were sent to work on what has since come to be known as the 'Death Railway'.[1] The British prisoners of war were mainly taken from the camp at Changi on Singapore Island and worked on the Siamese end of the railway. Conditions were appalling and the men, weakened by brutal treatment and malnutrition, and suffering from malaria, dysentery and jungle sores, were mercilessly driven. As a result, some twenty per cent. died before the railway was completed and scores of others had their health ruined for life. The same treatment was meted out to the impressed coolies, among whom the mortality was even higher. Despite the methods employed, the railway was not opened to traffic till the 25th October 1943.

When General Mutaguchi, a man of strong personality who had been uniformly successful as a commander from the time of the outbreak of the China Incident, assumed command of *15th Army* it was holding a general line from the Salween River in Yunnan through Myitkyina, Mogaung, Wuntho, Kalewa to Pakokku. Having been involved, as Commander, *18th Division*, in the operations to defend northern Burma against the incursion of the Chindits, Mutaguchi had closely studied Wingate's tactics and his use of ground and had realized that movement by units with pack transport was possible in many parts of northern and western Burma during the dry season.[2] He considered therefore that the defensive plan hitherto adopted by *15th Army* was inadequate, and that the general line of defence should be pushed forward at least to the Chindwin River or, since in dry weather the river would not present a serious obstacle to penetrations by British columns, to a line still further forward in the hills on the Assam–Burma border. The possession of this latter line would enable an offensive to be launched against the British bases in Assam.

Shortly after assuming command of *15th Army*, Mutaguchi ordered a detailed reconnaissance of the Chindwin River valley to be carried

---

[1] Approximately 30,000 British, 13,000 Australian, 18,000 Dutch and 700 American. From October 1943 to the end of the war, some 32,000 prisoners of war were kept on maintenance work on the railway.
[2] See page 329.

out in order to get information on British movements and intentions, and to ascertain whether he could maintain troops in that area. The reconnaissance party reported that the area was suitable for operations by troops equipped with pack transport; tracks from Pinlebu to Paungbyin and Pinbon to Homalin could be improved sufficiently for the purpose without great difficulty[1]; the local inhabitants were favourably disposed towards the Japanese, which meant that supplies could be obtained; and British reconnaissance activities in the valley were steadily increasing. Mutaguchi therefore decided to advance to the Chindwin River, cross it south of Homalin and occupy the line of hills between the Chindwin and Yu Rivers (operation 'BU'). He proposed to begin the operation at the end of May just before the beginning of the monsoon. The necessary improvements to the two tracks across the Zibyu Taungdan could not however be completed in time and, faced with the danger of the troops in the forward positions being cut off from supplies during the monsoon, Mutaguchi postponed the operation.

He was not however satisfied that operation 'BU' entirely met the situation. To stand on the defensive in the type of country to be found in upper Burma was, he believed, to court defeat, and the correct policy for the Japanese armies in Burma would be to take the offensive and forestall any British attempt to invade Burma. From the wider point of view of the general war situation, and especially of the unfavourable turn of events in the Pacific, Mutaguchi considered that an offensive against the productive province of Assam in the dry weather of 1943-44 would be a sound move and well timed. For these reasons he came to the conclusion that the capture of the British bases in Assam, followed by a further advance towards India as envisaged in Plan 21,[2] would be the best course of action, since it would result in a British set-back which would have world wide repercussions and encourage the Indian independence movement.

Major-General Obata, Mutaguchi's Chief of Staff, was opposed to an offensive on these lines on the grounds that *15th Army* had insufficient strength and that the administrative position was too weak to give adequate support to such an ambitious operation.[3] Obata infringed the rules of procedure and military etiquette by attempting to persuade the commander of *18th Division* to oppose the views of the army commander, and was replaced at the end of May by Major-General M. Kunomura.[4] The new Chief of Staff agreed with

---

[1] See Map 12.

[2] See page 308.

[3] Major-General Obata's early service had been with the Army Service Transportation Corps and he had therefore considerable administrative experience.

[4] Major-General Kunomura had previously been employed in the Inspectorate of Military Training in Tokyo and had no recent experience of active operations.

Mutaguchi that an offensive on the lines of Plan 21 was the right approach to the problem of the defence of Burma. A conference, attended by observers from *Burma Area Army*, was held at *15th Army Headquarters* about the middle of June to formulate a plan for the invasion of north-east India, the decisive battle to be fought west of Golaghat.

Meanwhile, General Kawabe (*Burma Area Army*) had also been studying the problem of how best to defend Burma in the light of the Chindit operations. He, like Obata, thought that Mutaguchi's plan was far too ambitious and did not take into account the improved fighting value of the British forces in Assam. He came to the conclusion that to forestall a British offensive, of which there were ample indications, he would have to capture the bases at Imphal and Kohima from which it could be launched, and then hold a defensive position in the hills to the west and north-west of the Imphal plain. With the forces at his disposal and any reinforcements he might get, he believed such an operation was feasible.

After the conference at *15th Army Headquarters* in mid-June, Kawabe asked *Southern Army* to obtain the sanction of *Imperial General Headquarters* for an offensive across the frontier to gain the general line Kohima–Imphal. *Imperial General Headquarters* replied that, before any decision could be reached, the problem should once again be carefully studied by *Burma Area Army*. Accordingly, another conference was held between the 24th and 27th June which was attended by all commanders and senior officers of army formations in Burma, representatives from *3rd Air Army* and *5th Air Division* and General Inada, Vice-Chief of Staff, *Southern Army*. The conference was instructed to carry out a war game to determine whether a British counter-offensive from India could best be defeated by advancing the main line of defence beyond the Chindwin to the high ground on the western side of the Kabaw Valley or, alternatively, to the hills on the west of the Imphal plain, after the British bases at Kohima and Imphal had been captured. The war game was based on the assumption that *15th Army* would use three divisions on the Chindwin front, while remaining on the defensive on the Hukawng Valley and Salween fronts.

The conference was far from unanimous in its views on what Allied action would constitute the greatest danger to Burma. *Burma Area Army* and *5th Air Division* were of the opinion that it lay in an attack from the sea, while *15th Army* took the view that it lay in an offensive from Assam into northern Burma. The latter view was accepted since there was insufficient information to enable any accurate estimate to be made of the Allied intentions regarding a seaborne attack. As a result of the war game, the conference reached the conclusion that, if the defensive line were pushed forward as far as the Kabaw Valley only and no attempt were made to deal with the main British forces at Imphal, it would be difficult to hold the expected British offensive. Such being the case, it was accepted that the best course would be to attack the British before they had time to complete their preparations for an offensive, capture their base at Imphal and prevent them launching any offensive into Burma. The administrative implications were then examined. It was considered that for the first phase one supply route would be required for each division, and after the capture of Imphal the main supply route should be Kalewa–Tamu–Imphal. To operate these, considerably more administrative units than were available in Burma would be required.[1]

An accident regarded by all ranks as an ill omen for the success of the contemplated operations followed the conference. The transport aircraft carrying the Chiefs of Staff of *18th* and *56th Divisions* and other staff officers crashed east of Pegu, and all the occupants were killed.

As a result of the conference, *Burma Area Army* reported to *Southern Army* that an advance into central Assam was beyond the capabilities of the army as it then was. An advance to Imphal was in their opinion strategically necessary for the proper defence of Burma, and would in the long run result in a saving of manpower. A successful operation would, in addition, offset the failures in the Pacific and raise the morale of the Japanese people. If such an advance were to be carried out, however, Burma would have to be reinforced by three divisions and provided with at least a thousand motor vehicles, a number of miscellaneous administrative units and sufficient ammunition for four divisions in an encounter battle. Although *Southern Army* could supply some of these requirements, many would have to come from outside sources. *Burma Area Army* therefore asked *Southern Army* to approach *Imperial General Headquarters* for the balance without delay. In the middle of July, Count Terauchi (Commander-in-Chief, *Southern Army*) sent his Vice-Chief of the General Staff to Tokyo to report in detail on the general situation in the Southern Region, and at the same time to stress strongly the necessity for an offensive policy on the Burma–India front.

Imperial General Headquarters viewed the problem from both the political and the military angles. During the Malayan campaign

---

	Required	Available
[1] M.T. companies	150	90
Supply companies	60	40
Transportation headquarters	3–4	2
L. of C. sector units	4	2
L. of C. hospitals	8–10	6
L. of C. medical units	4	3
Field road construction units	4–5	3
Independent engineer units	5	3

(December 1941 to February 1942), the Japanese had formed an Indian National League and an Indian National Army. An aggressive policy towards India based on these two organizations had been adopted as early as August 1942 in the hope of so strengthening the anti-British independence movement in India that the British would find it impossible to use it as a base for operations. At the same time Subhas Chandra Bose, who had at one time been President of the Congress Party in India and was now conducting the movement from Berlin, was invited to return to Asia. He travelled to Penang by submarine and from there by air to Tokyo where he arrived in May 1943. The Japanese Government agreed to give him every possible support in his efforts to build up a strong movement directed against India. On the 1st July Bose went to Singapore, where he established a Provisional Government of Free India, with himself as its head, and appointed himself Commander-in-Chief of the Indian National Army. Encouraged by his presence, the Indian independence movement throughout the Far East at once gathered strength, and Bose urged that the Japanese army in Burma should launch an invasion of India supported by units of the Indian National Army. Pressed by *Southern Army* and committed to supporting Bose and the Indian independence movement, *Imperial General Headquarters* gave its consent in July 1943 for preparations for an offensive to begin. It agreed to reinforce *Burma Area Army* with *15th Division*, *54th Division* and *24th Independent Mixed Brigade* and a number of engineer, transport and other administrative units and undertook to make the required motor vehicles and ammunition available.

Orders had in fact already been issued by *Imperial General Headquarters* on the 17th June for *15th Division*, at that time in Shanghai, to move to Burma for posting to *15th Army*. The division began to move by sea to Saigon in July, from where it was sent by orders of *Southern Army* to Siam. It was not until about the end of September that it was concentrated and began training in the Bangkok area. *Imperial General Headquarters* then arranged for *54th Division* to begin to move to Burma in October 1943 and be ready for operations by January 1944, for *24th Independent Mixed Brigade* to be brought up to a strength of four battalions and used to garrison Tenasserim and *2nd Division* to move to Malaya in December 1943 to act as a general reserve for *Southern Army*.

So that the offensive could be undertaken during the dry weather of 1943–44, vehicles and equipment required by *Burma Area Army* had to reach Burma before the end of the monsoon. Since the new Siam–Burma railway would not be ready for use till the end of October, they had to be sent by sea to Rangoon. To ensure the safe passage of the ships, the minesweeping organization and the air defences of Rangoon were strengthened; the port facilities at Mergui and Moulmein were improved and escort vessels were stationed at strategic points.

The *5th Air Division* had been reduced in December 1942 to a strength of six air regiments (two fighter, two reconnaissance and light bomber and two heavy bomber—a total of fifty fighters and ninety bombers) by the withdrawal of two fighter and one heavy bomber air regiments to the south-east Pacific.[1] During the 1943 monsoon, all the air regiments had been removed from Burma to Siam and Malaya to rest and refit, leaving only a nucleus air contingent behind, but both heavy bomber air regiments were temporarily used to cover the passage of the ships carrying stores to Rangoon. As a result, there was little loss and most of the essential stores reached Rangoon on time.

Owing to the increased Allied air strength and their own weakness (the air regiments sent to the Pacific front had not been replaced), the Japanese found that by the summer of 1943 they had lost air superiority over Burma, and military movement by day either by land or water had become extremely hazardous. In these circumstances *Headquarters Southern Army*, considering the adverse air situation in Burma to be one of their most pressing problems, ordered an investigation to be carried out to ascertain how best such air strength as remained could be used. *Headquarters 3rd Air Army* accordingly held a conference of all air unit commanders to study the tactical problems facing an air force fighting a numerically superior enemy.[2] It was evident that the number of fighter aircraft available for protection and escort duties was quite inadequate, and that the proportion of heavy bombers (and the defensive power of those available was weak) to other types was far too high. The conference therefore recommended that the majority of the heavy bomber units of *5th Air Division* should be reorganized into fighter units, and pilots and airmen in reconnaissance and light bomber units be transferred to bring fighter units up to strength. The recommendation was sent to *Imperial General Headquarters* in Tokyo, who did not accept it, but undertook as far as was practicable to increase the number of fighter units in southern Burma.

The shortage of fighter aircraft and the inability of the Japanese to replace losses in all types of aircraft in *Southern Army* illustrate their serious overall position at this stage of the war. Neither the Japanese air force nor the supporting aircraft industry had been organized for a long war. Japan had begun the war with an aircraft industry which could scarcely maintain her air force and

---

[1] See Appendix 33.

[2] The strength of *5th Air Division* at that time was only 150 aircraft (90 bombers and 60 fighters) since all units were much under strength.

Map 14

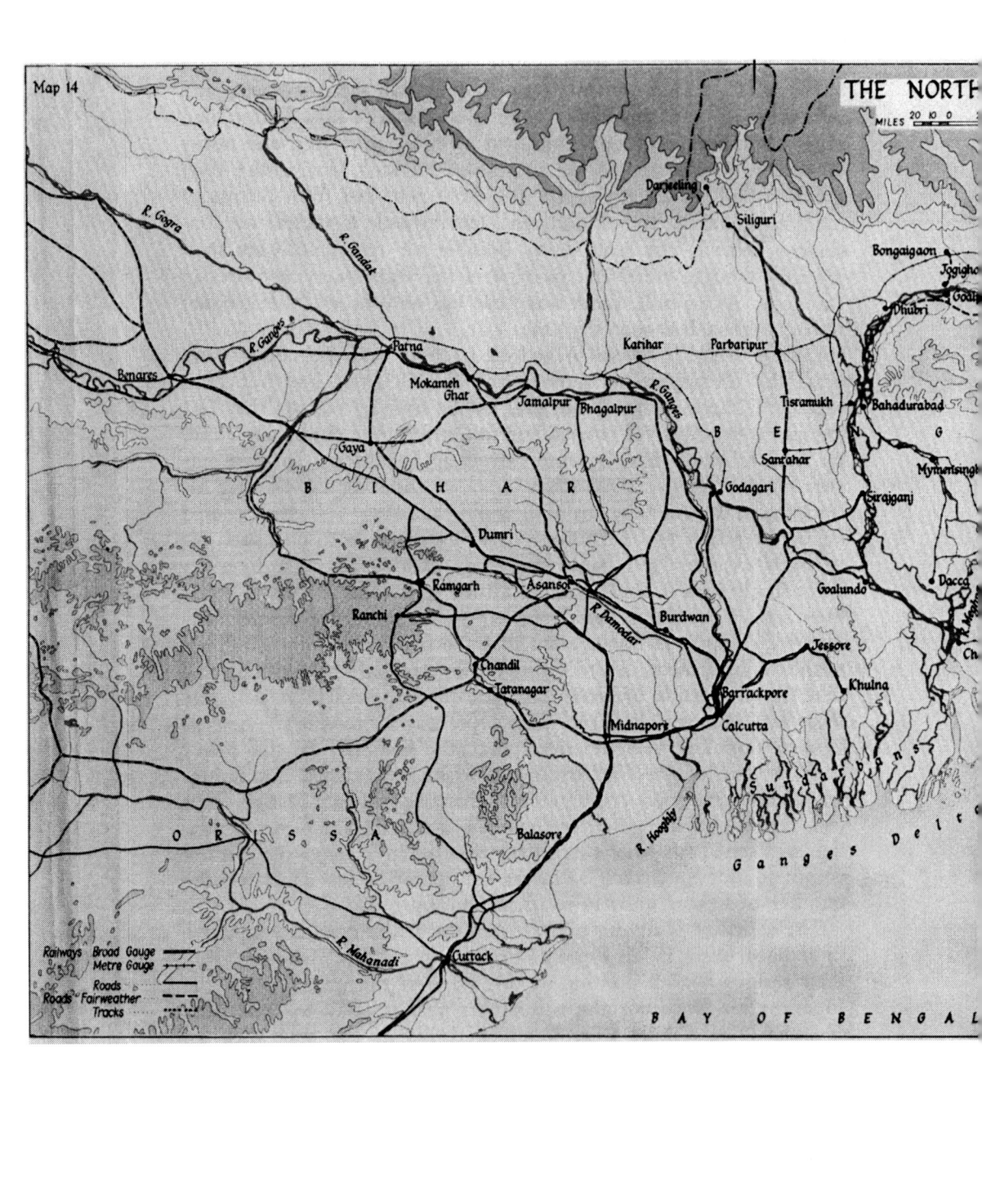

THE NORTH

MILES 20 10 0

Map 14

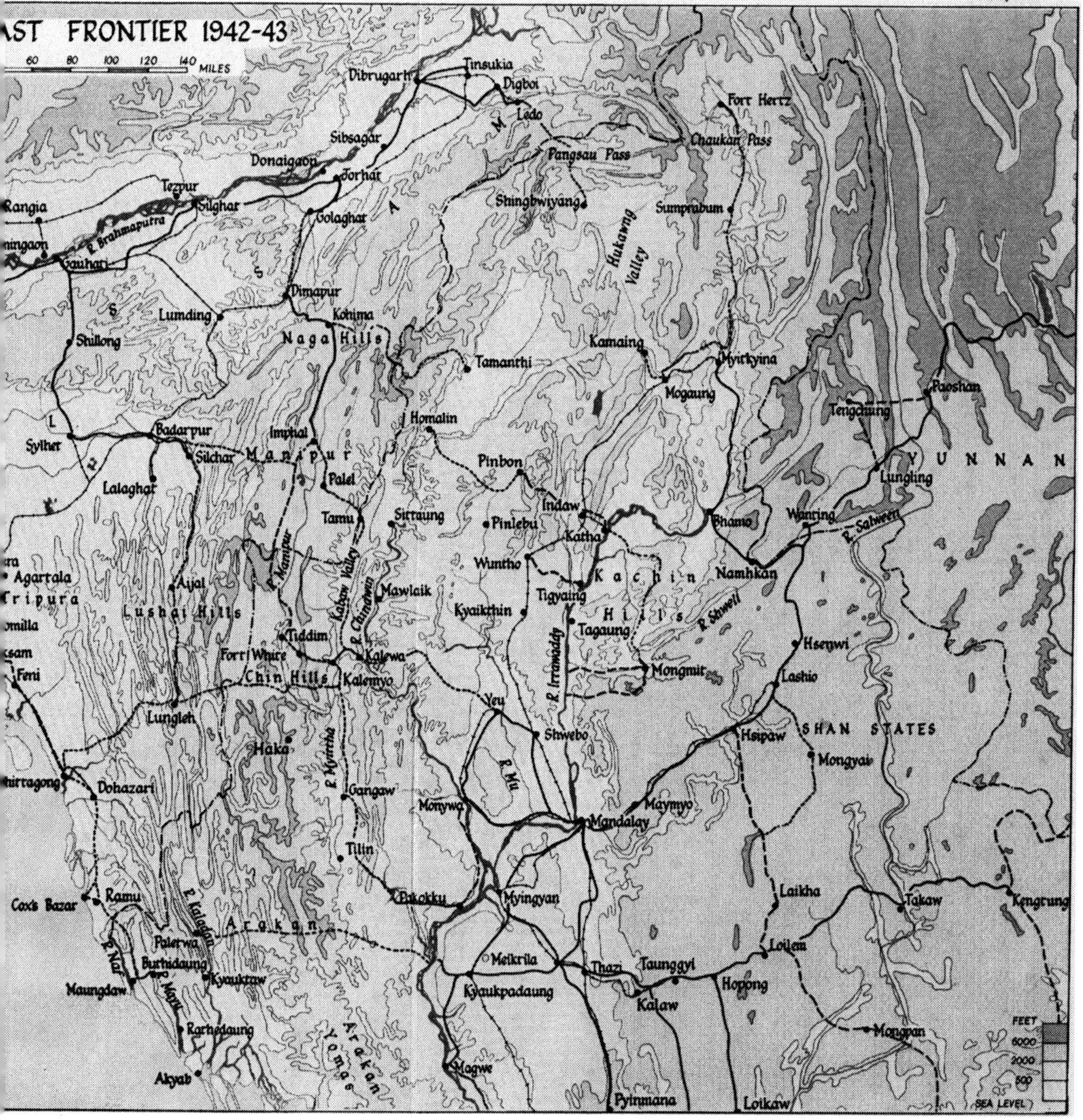
AST FRONTIER 1942-43
60 80 100 120 140 MILES
Dibrugarh
Tinsukia
Digboi
Ledo
Fort Hertz
Chaukan Pass
Pangsau Pass
Sibsagar
Donaigaon
Jorhat
Tezpur
Silghar
Rangia
R. Brahmaputra
Gauhati
Golaghat
Shingbwiyang
Sumprabum
Hukawng Valley
Dimapur
Lumding
Kohima
Shillong
Naga Hills
Kamaing
Myitkyina
Tamanthi
Mogaung
Paoshan
Tengchung
Homalin
Sylhet
Badarpur
Imphal
Silchar
Manipur
Lalaghat
Palel
Pinbon
Lungling
YUNNAN
Indaw
Tamu
Sittaung
Pinlebu
Bhamo
Wanting
R. Salween
Katha
R. Manipur
Kabaw Valley
Wuntho
Kachin
Namhkan
Agartala
Tripura
Aijal
Mawlaik
Tigyaing
Lushai Hills
R. Chindwin
Kyaikthin
Hills
R. Shweli
Tagaung
R. Irrawaddy
Tiddim
Hsenwi
Fort White
Kalewa
Mongmit
Feni
Chin Hills
Kalemyo
Lashio
Lungleh
Yeu
Shwebo
Hsipaw
SHAN STATES
Haka
Mongyai
R. Myittha
R. Mu
Dohazari
Gangaw
Monywa
Maymyo
Mandalay
Tilin
Cox's Bazar
Ramu
Pakokku
Myingyan
Laikha
Takaw
Kengtung
R. Kaladan
Arakan
Paletwa
R. Naf
Buthidaung
R. Mayu
Maungdaw
Kyauktaw
Meiktila
Thazi
Taunggyi
Loilem
Kyaukpadaung
Hopong
Kalaw
Rathedaung
Arakan Yomas
Mongpan
Akyab
Magwe
Pyinmana
Loikaw
FEET
6000
2000
500
SEA LEVEL

SOUTH WEST PACIFIC AREA

August 1942

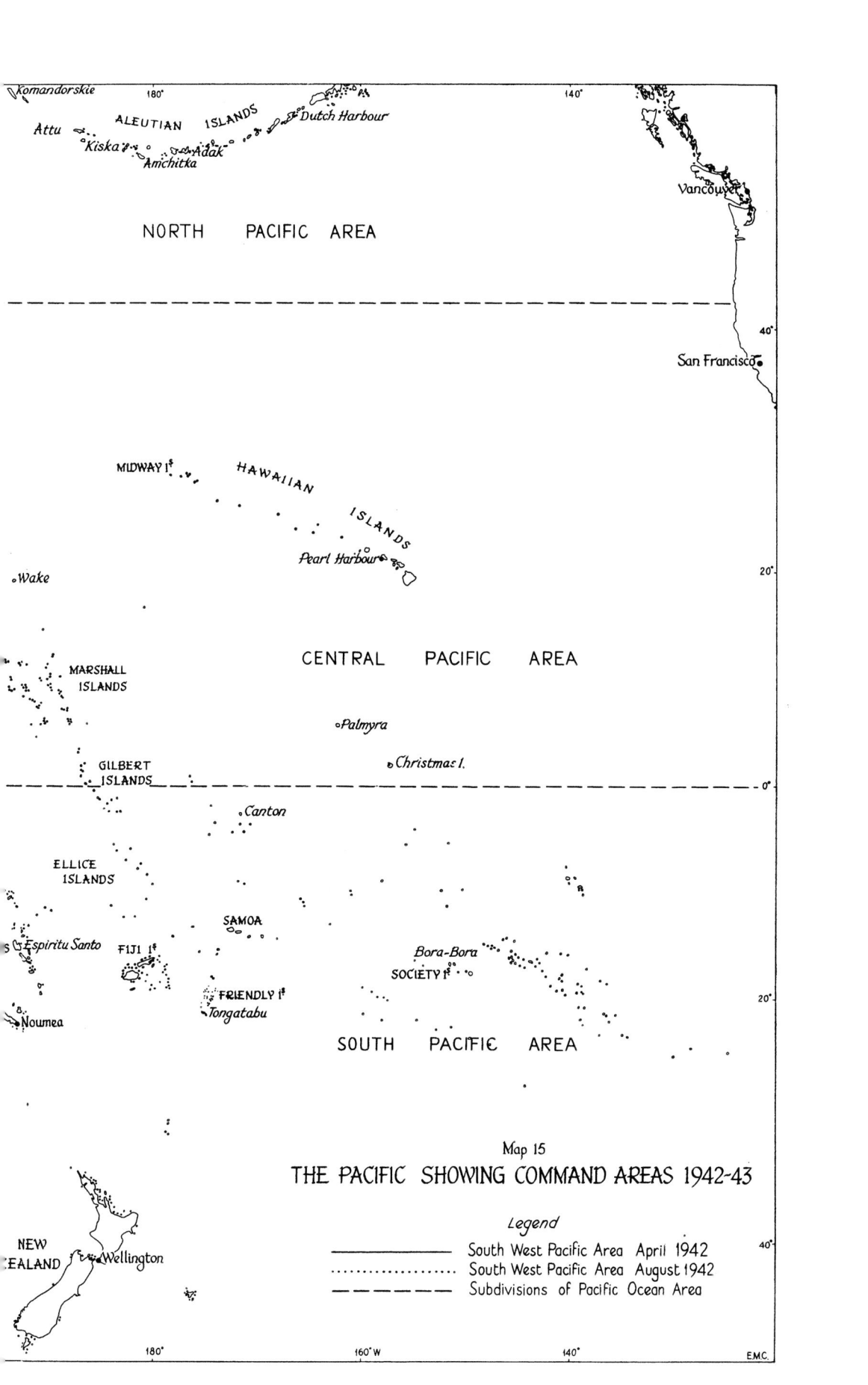

Map 15
THE PACIFIC SHOWING COMMAND AREAS 1942-43

Legend
———————— South West Pacific Area   April 1942
·················· South West Pacific Area   August 1942
— — — — — Subdivisions of Pacific Ocean Area

could not expand it. As the war progressed and the shortage of essential materials began to affect industry in Japan, so the strength of the Navy and Army Air Forces began slowly to decline. This, coupled with the heavy losses in the battle for Guadalcanal in the Solomons, forced the Japanese to adopt a purely defensive air policy in Burma during 1943.

Having obtained the necessary support from Tokyo for an offensive, *Southern Army* issued preparatory instructions on the 7th August. *Burma Area Army* was told to complete preparations for a counter-offensive (operation 'U-Go') towards Imphal to forestall a British offensive. The general idea was that the British should be defeated near the frontier, their bases in the Imphal area captured and a strong permanent defensive position established covering Kohima and Imphal from the west. In the event of the British opening their offensive first, they were to be met, defeated and the advance to the Imphal line carried out as planned. Operation 'U-Go' would probably be launched at the beginning of 1944 at the earliest, but the actual date would be subject to *Southern Army's* approval. Some seven divisions would be available in Burma early in 1944. On the 12th August, *Burma Area Army* ordered *15th Army* to begin planning on the lines of this instruction.

The fifteen months period following the end of the First Burma Campaign had been one of consolidation and planning by the Allies and Japanese alike, and consequently fighting on land and in the air had been on a small scale. The Allies had been doing their utmost to launch an offensive for the recapture of Burma, but had been prevented by their lack of resources and by the many administrative difficulties which had to be overcome before forces of the necessary size could be concentrated and maintained. By the end of the period, however, it seemed that, with American technical assistance and the use of air transport, most of the administrative problems could be solved, that trained army formations and air squadrons in sufficient numbers would at last be available and that, with the help of L.R.P. groups, on which great hopes were placed, an offensive might be launched with some prospect of success before the onset of the 1944 monsoon. But it was apparently assumed by those responsible for drawing up plans for offensive action that the Japanese would remain on the defensive, and the possibility of their invading Assam with the forces then at their disposal was not taken into account. The planners also seem to have consistently overestimated the strength of the enemy air force in Burma.

The Japanese on their part, mainly owing to the influence of the Chindit operation of 1943 on some of their senior officers in Burma, had come to the conclusion that they would be unable to defeat the threatened Allied offensive by standing on the defensive, and that an invasion of Assam in order to capture the Allied base at Imphal was their best course of action. Thus the end of the summer of 1943 found both sides planning an offensive during the forthcoming dry weather.

Appendices

APPENDIX 1

Order of Battle of the Army in Burma, 27th December 1941

Army Headquarters (Rangoon)

1st Burma Division (Southern Shan States)
Major-General J. Bruce Scott
    27th Indian Mountain Regiment
    2nd Indian Mountain Battery
    23rd Indian Mountain Battery
    5th Field Battery, R.A., B.A.F.
    56th Field Company, S. and M.
    50th Field Park Company, S. and M.
    1st Burma Field Company, S. and M.
    13th Burma Rifles
    14th Burma Rifles
    F.F.1, F.F.3, F.F.4, F.F.5.[1]

1st Burma Brigade
Brigadier G. A. L. Farwell
    2nd K.O.Y.L.I.
    1st Burma Rifles
    5th Burma Rifles

2nd Burma Brigade (Moulmein)
Brigadier A. J. H. Bourke
    12th Indian Mountain Battery (Moulmein)
    1/7th Gurkha Rifles (Moulmein)
    Tenasserim Battalion, B.A.F. (Moulmein) (less one company)
    2nd Burma Rifles (Mergui)
    4th Burma Rifles (Kawkareik)
    6th Burma Rifles (Tavoy)
    Two companies 3rd Burma Rifles (Mergui)
    One company Tenasserim Battalion, B.A.F. (Tavoy)
    8th Burma Rifles (Moulmein)
    F.F.2 (Mergui)[2]

13th Indian Brigade
Brigadier A. C. Curtis
    5/1st Punjab Regiment
    2/7th Rajput Regiment
    1/18th Royal Garhwal Rifles

16th Indian Brigade[2] (Mandalay)
Brigadier J. K. Jones
    1/9th Royal Jat Regiment
    4/12th Frontier Force Regiment
    7th Burma Rifles

Rangoon Garrison
    1st Gloucestershire Regiment
    3rd Burma Rifles (less two companies)

---

[1] F.F. units consisted of headquarters, two troops of mounted infantry and three infantry columns each of about one hundred men. In addition to pack transport they had a few lorries, and F.F.2 had some motor-driven native craft.

[2] In general reserve.

APPENDIX 2

The State of Training of Brigades forming 17th Indian Infantry Division in December 1941

1. Brigadier G. C. Ballentine, who commanded 44th Indian Infantry Brigade, originally part of 17th Indian Division, gave the following account of the state of training of his brigade in December 1941, just before it embarked for service in Malaya. The state of affairs disclosed applied equally to 46th and 48th Indian Infantry Brigades:

> 'The battalions were raised in the autumn of 1940, and the brigade was formed in Poona in July 1941. All battalions arrived in Poona under strength, consisting of equal proportions of trained regular soldiers, reservists and drafts straight from the Regimental Training Centres. 6/1st Punjab was minus one company which did not rejoin until November. The various ancillary units of the brigade group were raised from scratch in the autumn of 1941, except the signal section which was not complete until immediately before the brigade sailed for Malaya. The bulk of transport, equipment and weapons came in steadily, and the only serious shortages on departure were in Bren guns and anti-tank weapons.
>
> Excellent progress in all branches of training, designed solely for Middle East conditions, was made in Poona, but this was largely negatived by the appalling milking inherent in the large-scale Indian Army expansion. During the six months July to December 1941, each battalion threw off some 250 men, culminating in their sending, on the point of departure for Malaya, 45 V.C.O.s, N.C.O.s and potential N.C.O.s to form their respective training companies at the training centres. During the last month in India, each battalion took in some 250 recruits to replace wastage, many of whom had only 4 or 5 months service and were under 18 years of age. Thus the battalions were very largely composed of recruits who had been less than three months with them, some of whom joined during the journey to the port of embarkation; and the numbers of experienced V.C.O.s and N.C.O.s, few to begin with, had been gravely reduced. In common with all Indian Army units, British officers averaged rather less than three regulars per battalion, the remainder being E.C.O.s [Emergency Commissioned Officers] drawn from outside India with, at the most, twelve months' experience of Indian troops, their ways and their language'.

2. Brigadier J. K. Jones, who commanded 16th Indian Infantry Brigade which reached Burma in December 1941, wrote:

> 'Of the three battalions in the brigade none had been longer in it than 6 weeks. None of the battalions had carried out higher

training of any sort during that year. One battalion had come from Waziristan and had taken part in the usual 'frontier column'. Another battalion had been digging defences in the Kurram for some months and had done practically no training other than individual. There was no brigade signal section. This was picked up en route to port of embarkation, and the brigade as such had carried out no training whatsoever.

The three battalions, although regular battalions, had been milked to the last drop and drafts of recruits of approximately 300 reached two of the battalions, three hours and three days respectively before they entrained.

I took over command of the brigade six days prior to departure overseas . . . Before leaving for Burma it was discovered that very few had any practice in A.A. firing with L.M.G.s and some practice ammunition was taken and A.A. practice carried out during the short sea voyage. Further investigation showed that most of the young soldiers had not reached even a reasonable standard of efficiency in the L.M.G., C.M.T., and that the No. 36 Grenade was a strange thing to all others than the N.C.O.s and a few of the old soldiers. Nearly 40 per cent of the young officers had not fired a pistol course.

No one had any experience of jungle, except a few senior officers whose experience was confined to 'Shikar'. Every effort was made to try and put these matters right as far as it was possible, during the short time spent in Mandalay, but as it happened, the brigade, whose rôle was reserve for the Army in Burma, was one of the first formations to make contact with the enemy.

The disadvantages of no one knowing the Burmese language was realised but all efforts to obtain interpreters were abortive'.

APPENDIX 3

Order of Battle of the Japanese 15th Army, December 1941

15th Army Headquarters
(*Lieut.-General S. Iida*)

33rd Division
(*Lieut.-General S. Sakurai*)
    33rd Infantry Group (Major-General M. Araki)
        213th Infantry Regiment (Colonel K. Miyawaki)
        214th Infantry Regiment (Colonel T. Sakuma)
        215th Infantry Regiment (Colonel M. Harada)
    33rd Mountain Artillery Regiment
    33rd Engineer Regiment
    33rd Transport Regiment
    Divisional medical unit
    Two field hospitals
    Veterinary and ordnance sections

55th Division
(*Lieut.-General Y. Takeuchi*)
    112th Infantry Regiment (Colonel K. Obarazawa, later Colonel S. Tanahashi)
    143rd Infantry Regiment (Colonel M. Uno)
    55th Cavalry Regiment (less one squadron)
    55th Mountain Artillery Regiment (less one battalion)
    55th Engineer Regiment (less one company)
    55th Transport Regiment (less two companies)
    Divisional medical unit
    One field hospital
    Veterinary and ordnance sections

Army troops
    Two wire communication companies
    Two fixed radio units
    One line of communication sector unit
    Two independent transport companies (motor transport)
    Two independent transport companies (horsed)
    One line of communication hospital

Total strength
    Men   35,440
    Horses   701
    Troop-carrying vehicles   53
    Trucks   570

APPENDIX 4

Dispositions of Brigades of 17th Indian Infantry Division, 8th February 1942

2nd Burma Brigade

    12th Mountain Battery
    4/12th Frontier Force Regiment
    3rd Burma Rifles   } Kyaikto–Sittang area
    7th Burma Rifles

48th Indian Brigade

    1/3rd Gurkha Rifles
    1/4th Gurkha Rifles   } Kyaikto area
    2/5th Royal Gurkha Rifles

16th Indian Brigade

    1/7th Gurkha Rifles
    1/9th Royal Jat Regiment   } Bilin area
    8th Burma Rifles (less one company)
    One company 4th Burma Rifles   Shwegun
    One company 8th Burma Rifles   Kamamaung
    2nd Burma Rifles   Papun

46th Indian Brigade

    3/7th Gurkha Rifles   } Martaban
    One company 2nd K.O.Y.L.I.
    7/10th Baluch Regiment   } Kuzeik
    One section 5th Mountain Battery
    5/17th Dogra Regiment   Duyinzeik
    2nd K.O.Y.L.I. (less one company)
    4th Burma Rifles (less one company)   } Thaton (in reserve)
    5th Mountain Battery (less one section)

APPENDIX 5

Order of Battle of 17th Indian Infantry Division at the Bilin River Action

Headquarters 17th Indian Division
H.Q. 28th Mountain Regiment
24th Field Company, S. and M.
Malerkotla Field Company, S. and M.
60th Field Company, S. and M.
6th Indian Pioneer Battalion
One section 18th Indian Artisan Works Company
1st Burma Artisan Works Company
7/10th Baluch Regiment (250 strong re-forming at Kyaikto)
2nd Burma Rifles (Papun)
One company 4th Burma Rifles (Shwegun)
One company 8th Burma Rifles (Kamamaung)
F.F.2 (a column on each flank)

16th Brigade
- 2nd K.O.Y.L.I.
- 1/9th Royal Jat Regiment
- 1/7th Gurkha Rifles
- 5/17th Dogra Regiment
- 8th Burma Rifles (less one company)
- 5th Mountain Battery
- 15th Mountain Battery
- 28th Mountain Battery
- Section 5th Field Battery, B.A.F.
- Section armoured cars B.A.F.

48th Brigade
- 12th Mountain Battery
- 1/3rd Gurkha Rifles
- 1/4th Gurkha Rifles
- 2/5th Royal Gurkha Rifles

46th Brigade
- 4/12th Frontier Force Regiment
- 3/7th Gurkha Rifles
- 4th Burma Rifles (less one company)

APPENDIX 6

Parade State of the Infantry of 17th Indian Division, 24th February 1942

Total Strength
all ranks

16th Brigade
- 2nd K.O.Y.L.I. — 206 ⎫
- 1/9th Royal Jat Regiment — 568 ⎬ Rifles 210
- 1/7th Gurkha Rifles — 300 ⎬ L.M.G.s 6
- 8th Burma Rifles — 96 ⎭

46th Brigade
- 2nd Duke of Wellington's — 316 ⎫
  (one company crossed before bridge blown)
- 7/10th Baluch Regiment — 208 ⎬ Rifles 340
  (crossed before bridge blown)   L.M.G.s 4
- 5/17th Dogra Regiment — 104
- 3/7th Gurkha Rifles — 170 ⎭

48th Brigade
- 1/3rd Gurkha Rifles — 107 ⎫
- 1/4th Gurkha Rifles — 680 ⎬
  (crossed before bridge blown)   Rifles 870
- 2/5th Royal Gurkha Rifles — 227 ⎬ L.M.G.s 46
- 4/12th Frontier Force Regiment — 502 ⎭
  (crossed before bridge blown)

The total of 3,484 represents about 41 per cent. of the total authorized establishment, but it must be realised that most battalions were already below strength before the Sittang action. On the 27th, when stragglers had come in and available reinforcements had been brought up, the strength increased to 4,277 all ranks.

APPENDIX 7

Directive to Vice-Admiral Layton on Appointment as Commander-in-Chief, Ceylon, on the 5th March 1942

You are appointed Commander-in-Chief, Ceylon.[1] All naval, military, air and civil authorities in the area including the Governor and the civil administration will be subject to your direction.

2. Your immediate task is to ensure that all measures necessary for the defence of Ceylon are taken forthwith and that the military and civil measures are properly co-ordinated. The Governor has emergency powers under the constitution and the power to issue defence regulations which he can use to the extent you may require for any such measures.

3. You will convene and preside over any council or conference from time to time which you consider necessary for the effective co-operation of all services in Ceylon.

4. You will report as soon as possible whether in order to carry out the tasks specified in paragraphs 2 and 3 above it is necessary for you to assume supreme command of all the fighting services allotted to the defence of Ceylon and what staff and other arrangements this would entail.

5. On all military matters your immediate superior will be C.-in-C. India. As to civil matters the Governor of Ceylon will remain at his post and will exercise the civil functions of Governor subject to your over-riding authority and direction.

6. You will communicate with higher authority as follows:
   (a) on military matters you will address C.-in-C. India and repeat to Admiralty for communication to Chiefs of Staff.
   (b) on civil matters you will address Secretary of State for Colonies and will ensure that the Governor is consulted and informed to the necessary extent. You will consult with Governor as to the desirability of his continuing to communicate direct with Secretary of State for Colonies on civil affairs not touching upon defence issues.

7. In the exercise of your authority in civil affairs you will have regard to the importance and value of the maintenance of the services of the civil government as long as they can operate effectively in the prevailing conditions.

---

[1] 'which for this purpose includes the Maldive Islands' was added on the 18th March.

APPENDIX 8

Order of Battle of Air Forces, Ceylon, 31st March 1942

ROYAL AIR FORCE

30 (F) Squadron	Hurricane	Ratmalana, Colombo
258 (F) Squadron	Hurricane	Ratmalana, Colombo
261 (F) Squadron	Hurricane	China Bay, Trincomalee
273 (F) Squadron	Fulmar	China Bay, Trincomalee
11 (B) Squadron	Blenheim	Racecourse, Colombo
Det. 205 (FB) Squadron	Catalina	Koggala } at southern end
Det. 413 (FB) Squadron R.C.A.F.[1]	Catalina	Koggala } of Ceylon

FLEET AIR ARM (on shore)

803 (F) Squadron	Fulmar	China Bay, Trincomalee
806 (F) Squadron	Fulmar	China Bay, Trincomalee
788 (TSR) Squadron[2]	Swordfish and Albacore	China Bay, Trincomalee

---

[1] Royal Canadian Air Force.
[2] A torpedo spotter reconnaissance squadron.

APPENDIX 9

Naval Forces Taking Part in Operations off Ceylon, 29th March–10th April, 1942

British
Commander-in-Chief, Admiral Sir James Somerville

FORCE 'A'

Battleship	*Warspite* (Fleet Flagship)	Capt. F. E. P. Hutton
Aircraft Carriers (Rear-Admiral D. W. Boyd)	*Indomitable* (12 Fulmars) (9 Hurricanes) (24 Albacores)	Capt. T. Troubridge
	Formidable (12 Martlets) (21 Albacores)	Capt. A. W. La T. Bisset
Cruisers	*Dorsetshire*	Capt. A. W. S. Agar, V.C.
	Cornwall	Capt. P. C. W. Manwaring
	Enterprise	Capt. J. C. Annesley
	Emerald	Capt. F. C. Flynn
Destroyers	*Napier*	
	Nestor	
	Paladin	
	Panther	
	Hotspur	
	Foxhound	

FORCE 'B'
Acting Vice-Admiral A. V. Willis

Battleships	*Resolution*	3rd Battle Squadron	Capt. A. R. Halfhide
	Ramillies		Capt. D. N. C. Tufnell
	Royal Sovereign		Capt. R. H. Portal
	Revenge		Capt. L. V. Morgan
Aircraft Carrier	*Hermes* (12 Swordfish)		Capt. R. F. J. Onslow
Light Cruisers	*Caledon*		Capt. R. J. Shaw
	Dragon		Act. Capt. H. J. Haynes
A/A Cruiser	*Heemskerk* (Royal Netherlands Navy)		

448

APPENDIX 9

Destroyers	*Griffin*
	Norman
	Arrow
	Vampire (Royal Australian Navy)
	Decoy
	Fortune
	Scout
	Isaac Sweers (Royal Netherlands Navy)

Japanese

Commander-in-Chief, Vice-Admiral Kondo

STRIKING FORCE

Vice-Admiral Nagumo

Aircraft Carriers	*Akagi* (Flagship)
	Soryu
	Hiryu — Each ship carrying about 60 aircraft
	Shokaku
	Zuikaku
Battleships	*Kongo* (Flag of Vice-Admiral Mikawa)
	Hiei
	Kirishima
	Haruna
Cruisers	*Tone*
	Chikuma
Destroyers	Light cruiser *Abukuma* (Flag of Rear-Admiral Omori) and eleven destroyers
Submarines	Seven

MALAYA FORCE

Vice-Admiral Ozawa

Aircraft Carrier	*Ryujo*
Cruisers	*Chokai* (Flagship)
	Kumano
	Suzuya
	Mikuma
	Mogami
Light Cruiser	*Yura*
3rd Destroyer Flotilla	Light cruiser *Sendai* and eleven destroyers
Minesweepers	Five

APPENDIX 10
Naval Forces and Other Shipping Taking Part in The Operation to Capture Diego Suarez

Commander-in-Chief, Rear-Admiral E. N. Syfret

A: NAVAL FORCES

Battleship	*Ramillies* (Flagship)	Capt. D. N. C. Tufnell
Aircraft Carriers (Rear-Admiral D. W. Boyd)	*Indomitable*	Capt T. Troubridge
	Illustrious	Capt. A. G. Talbot
Cruisers	*Devonshire*	Capt. R. D. Oliver
	Hermione	Capt. G. N. Oliver
Destroyers	*Pakenham*	*Anthony*
	Lookout	*Panther*
	Active	*Lightning*
	Paladin	*Inconstant*
	Laforey	*Duncan*
	Javelin	
Corvettes	Six	
Minesweepers	Six	
Oiler	One	

B: OTHER SHIPPING

Assault Ships	*Winchester Castle*	⎱ No. 5 Commando and
	Royal Ulsterman	⎰ 2nd East Lancashire Regiment
	Keren	1st Royal Scots Fusiliers
	Karanja	2nd Royal Welch Fusiliers
	Sobieski	2nd South Lancashire Regiment (floating reserve)
Special Ships	*Derwentdale*	Motor landing craft and tanks
	Bachaquero	Tank landing ship
Troop Ships	*Oronsay*	⎱ 17th Infantry Brigade
	Duchess of Atholl	⎰
	Franconia	13th Infantry Brigade
Stores and M.T. Ships	*Empire Kingsley*	⎱
	Thalatta	⎬ 17th Brigade stores and M.T.
	Mahout	⎰
	City of Hong Kong	
	Mairnbank	⎱ 13th Brigade stores and M.T.
	Martand	⎰
Hospital Ship	*Atlantis*	

APPENDIX 11

Order of Battle of the Japanese 5th Air Division, March 1942[1]

Headquarters, 5th Air Division, Rangoon

4th Air Brigade, Toungoo		
50th Air Regiment	Fighters	Toungoo
8th Air Regiment	Reconnaissance and light bombers	Toungoo
7th Air Brigade, Bangkok		
64th Air Regiment	Fighters	Rangoon
12th Air Regiment	Heavy bombers	Bangkok
98th Air Regiment	Heavy bombers	Nakawn
10th Air Brigade, Lampang		
77th Air Regiment	Fighters	Lampang
31st Air Regiment	Light bombers	Phitsanulok
12th Air Brigade, Hlegu		
1st Air Regiment	Fighters	Hlegu
11th Air Regiment	Fighters	Hlegu
15th Independent Air Unit (two headquarters reconnaissance squadrons)		Rangoon
27th Air Regiment	Fighters	Toungoo

Note

The above gives a total strength of approximately 288 fighters, 126 bombers and reconnaissance aircraft.

---

[1] Includes reinforcements from 3rd Air Division on completion of operations in the Netherlands East Indies.

APPENDIX 12

Order of Battle of the Chinese Expeditionary Force in Burma

Lieut.-General Lin Wei — Chief of the Chinese General Staff Mission to Burma
Lieut.-General Lo Cho-ying — Executive Officer to General Stilwell

V ARMY

(Lieut.-General Tu Yu-ming)

22nd Division
(Major-General Liao Yao-shiang)
    64th Regiment
    65th Regiment
    66th Regiment

96th Division
(Major-General Yu Shao)
    286th Regiment
    287th Regiment
    288th Regiment

200th Division
(Major-General Tai An lan)
    598th Regiment
    599th Regiment
    600th Regiment

Training Depot
    1st Reserve Regiment
    2nd Reserve Regiment

Army Troops attached
    Cavalry regiment
    Artillery regiment
    Engineer regiment
    Armoured regiment
    Motor regiment
    Signal battalion

VI ARMY

(Lieut.-General Kan Li-chu)

49th Division
(Major-General Peng Pi-shen)
    145th Regiment
    146th Regiment
    147th Regiment

55th Division
(Lieut.-General Ch'en Mien-wu)
    1st Regiment
    2nd Regiment
    3rd Regiment

93rd Division
(Lieut.-General Lu Kuo Ch'uan)
    277th Regiment
    278th Regiment
    279th Regiment

Army Troops attached
    Engineer battalion
    Transport battalion
    Signal Battalion
    1st Battalion, 13th Artillery Regiment

APPENDIX 12

LXVI ARMY

(Lieut.-General Chang Chen)

28th Division

(Major-General Liu Po-lung)
    82nd Regiment
    83rd Regiment
    84th Regiment

38th Division

(Lieut.-General Sun Li-jen)
    112th Regiment
    113th Regiment
    114th Regiment

29th Division

(Major-General Ma Wei-chi)
    85th Regiment
    86th Regiment
    87th Regiment

Army Troops attached
    1st Battalion, 18th Artillery Regiment

Notes

(1) The strength of a Chinese regiment was equivalent to the strength of a British battalion, that of a division to a British brigade and that of an army to a British division.

(2) The Chinese formations had in general no supporting or ancillary units.

(3) The infantry were not all equipped with rifles.

APPENDIX 13

Order of Battle of Burcorps on Formation, 19th March 1942

Corps Troops
7th Armoured Brigade Group
    7th Hussars
    2nd Royal Tank Regiment
    414th Battery, R.H.A.
    'A' Battery, 95th Anti-Tank Regiment, R.A.
    1st West Yorkshire Regiment
8th Heavy Anti-Aircraft Battery, R.A.
3rd Indian Light Anti-Aircraft Battery (less one troop)
1st Field Company, Burma Sappers and Miners
17th and 18th Artisan Works Companies
6th Pioneer Battalion, Indian Engineers

1st Burma Division
H.Q. 27th Indian Mountain Regiment
2nd Indian Mountain Battery
23rd Indian Mountain Battery
8th Indian Anti-Tank Battery
50th Field Park Company, S. and M.
56th Field Company, S. and M. (less two sections)
Malerkotla Field Company, S. and M.
F.F.1, F.F.3, F.F.4 and F.F.5.

17th Indian Division
H.Q. 1st Indian Field Regiment
1st Indian Field Battery
2nd Indian Field Battery
12th Indian Mountain Battery
5th Indian Anti-Tank Battery
24th Field Company, S. and M.
60th Field Company, S. and M.
70th Field Company, S. and M.
1st Gloucestershire Regiment
5/17th Dogra Regiment
8th Burma Rifles
1st, 2nd and 3rd Detachments, B.F.F.
Royal Marine river patrol (Force Viper)
Rangoon Battalion, Burma Military Police
F.F.2 and F.F.6.

1st Burma Brigade
    2/7th Rajput Regiment
    1st Burma Rifles
    2nd Burma Rifles
    5th Burma Rifles

16th Indian Brigade
    2nd Duke of Wellington's Regiment
    1/9th Royal Jat Regiment
    7/10th Baluch Regiment
    4/12th Frontier Force Regiment

APPENDIX 13

1st Burma Division *(cont.)*
2nd Burma Brigade
    5/1st Punjab Regiment
    7th Burma Rifles
    F.F.8.

13th Indian Brigade
    1/18th Royal Garhwal Rifles

17th Indian Division *(cont.)*
48th Indian Brigade
    1st Cameronians
    1/3rd Gurkha Rifles ⎱ Composite
    2/5th Royal Gurkha Rifles ⎰ battalion
    1/4th Gurkha Rifles
    1/7th Gurkha Rifles ⎱ Composite
    3/7th Gurkha Rifles ⎰ battalion

63rd Indian Brigade
    1st Royal Inniskilling Fusiliers
    1/11th Sikh Regiment
    2/13th Frontier Force Rifles
    1/10th Gurkha Rifles

Army Troops

H.Q. 28th Indian Mountain Regiment
1st Heavy Anti-Aircraft Regiment, R.A., B.A.F.
Detachment Rangoon Field Brigade, R.A., B.A.F.
Depot, British Infantry
10th Burma Rifles
Bhamo Battalion, B.F.F.
Chin Hills Battalion, B.F.F. (less detachment)
Myitkyina Battalion, B.F.F.
Northern Shan States Battalion, B.F.F.
Southern Shan States Battalion, B.F.F.
Reserve Battalion, B.F.F.
Kokine Battalion, B.F.F. (less detachments)
Karen Levies

Line of Communication Troops

2nd Indian Anti-Tank Regiment
    (less two batteries—no guns)
8th Indian Heavy Anti-Aircraft Battery
One troop 3rd Indian Light Anti-Aircraft Battery
Rangoon Field Brigade, R.A., B.A.F.
Two sections 56th Field Company
2nd K.O.Y.L.I.
3rd Burma Rifles
4th Burma Rifles
6th Burma Rifles
11th, 12th, 13th and 14th Burma Rifles, B.T.F.
Tenasserim Battalion, B.A.F.
Burma Railways Battalion, B.A.F.
Upper Burma Battalion, B.A.F.

Mandalay Battalion, B.A.F.
Detachments Kokine Battalion, B.F.F.
Detachment Chin Hills Battalion, B.F.F.
M.I. Detachment, B.F.F.
1st, 2nd, 3rd, 4th, 5th, 6th, 7th, 8th, and
9th Garrison Companies

Notes

(1) The strength of the three brigades in 17th Division was 2,500, 2,500 and 1,700 respectively.

(2) The four battalions of the Burma Rifles in 1st Burma Division were well under strength since by that time they were without Karens and Burmans.

(3) 5th, 15th and 28th Indian Mountain Batteries of 28th Mountain Regiment were re-equipping at Mandalay.

APPENDIX 14

Directive to General J. W. Stilwell, February 1942 (as cabled by the War Office to Supreme Commander, A.B.D.A. Area)

1. General J. W. Stilwell has been appointed United States representative in China with concurrence of Chiang Kai-shek and with following functions:

   (a) Supervision and control of all United States defence air affairs for China.

   (b) Under the Generalissimo to command all the United States forces in China and such Chinese forces as may be assigned. Should it be necessary for any of these forces to engage in joint operations in Burma they will come under the command of the Supreme Commander of the A.B.D.A. area, who will issue necessary directions for co-operation of United States representative's forces with forces under British commanders in Burma.

   (c) Represent United States Government on any international War Council in China.

   (d) Control and maintain the Burma road in China.

2. General Stilwell will leave by air for China shortly.

3. To make this project reasonably effective the following points were agreed in Washington during the recent discussion between the Combined Chiefs of Staff:

   (a) In co-operation with commanders of adjacent areas United States representative is to be permitted to establish and/or use bases, routes and staging areas in India and Burma to support his operations in and north of Burma.

   (b) United States representative to be authorized to make every effort to increase the capacity of the Burma route throughout its length from Rangoon to Chungking. To do this, he will probably be given complete executive control of China section of route. On British section control will still be exercised by British authorities, both military and civil. To achieve general aim these British authorities will be instructed to carry out every possible improvement to route in accordance with requirements of United States representative, and will accept such American technicians and equipment as may be necessary for improvement of facilities in port of Rangoon and along the route itself.

(c) United States representative by arrangements with British commander in Burma to be permitted to construct and/or use necessary airfields in Burma.

(d) United States representative to be accepted as the principal liaison agency between Supreme Commander of A.B.D.A. area and Generalissimo Chiang Kai-shek.

4. United States Chiefs of Staff have subsequently agreed that there is no objection to General Wavell communicating direct with Chiang Kai-shek, using existing communications through British Military Attaché, Chungking, and keeping Senior United States Liaison Officer with Generalissimo informed.

APPENDIX 15

Order of Battle of Fighting Formations in Burcorps, 6th April 1942

7th Armoured Brigade
7th Hussars
2nd Royal Tank Regiment
414th Battery, R.H.A.
'A' Battery, 95th Anti-Tank Regiment, R.A.
1st West Yorkshire Regiment

Corps Troops
2nd Burma Brigade
    5/1st Punjab Regiment
      (transferred to 13th Brigade, 14th April)
    2nd Burma Rifles
    7th Burma Rifles
      (transferred to Magforce, 14th April)
    8th Burma Rifles
    F.F.8.

1st Burma Division
(Striking Force)
2nd Indian Field Battery
H.Q. 27th Mountain Regiment
    2nd and 23rd Indian
    Mountain Batteries
8th Indian Anti-Tank Battery
56th Field Company, S. and M.
Malerkotla Field Company,
    S. and M.
50th Field Park Company,
    S. and M.
1st Cameronians
    (transferred to Magforce)
12th Burma Rifles (Territorials)
    (transferred to Magforce)
F.F.1, F.F.3, F.F.4 and F.F.5.

17th Indian Division
H.Q. 1st Indian Field Regiment
1st Indian Field Battery
12th Indian Mountain Battery
15th Indian Mountain Battery
5th Indian Anti-Tank Battery
24th Field Company, S. and M.
60th Field Company, S. and M.
70th Field Company, S. and M.
5/17th Dogra Regiment
F.F.2 and F.F.6.

16th Indian Brigade
    2nd Duke of Wellington's
    Regiment
    1/9th Royal Jat Regiment
    7/10th Baluch Regiment
    4/12th Frontier Force Regiment

48th Indian Brigade
    1/3rd Gurkha Rifles ⎫ Composite battalion
    2/5th Royal Gurkha Rifles ⎬
    1/4th Gurkha Rifles
    1/7th Gurkha Rifles ⎫ Composite battalion
    3/7th Gurkha Rifles ⎭

63rd Indian Brigade
    1/11th Sikh Regiment
    2/13th Frontier Force Rifles
    1/10th Gurkha Rifles

13th Indian Brigade
    1st Royal Inniskilling Fusiliers
    2nd K.O.Y.L.I.
    1/18th Royal Garhwal Rifles

1st Burma Brigade
    2/7th Rajput Regiment
    1st Burma Rifles
    5th Burma Rifles

            Line of Communication Troops
              1st Gloucestershire Regiment
                (garrison of Yenangyaung)

Total strength, approximately:
British	13,700
Indian	37,000
Burmese	12,300
	63,000

Note

5th Mountain Battery was in army reserve, and was transferred to Magforce on the 12th April.

APPENDIX 16

Order of Battle of Eastern and Southern Armies, 21st April 1942

EASTERN ARMY (RANCHI)

Lieut.-General Sir Charles Broad

Assam Division (Jorhat)
1st Infantry Brigade
9th Anti-Aircraft Brigade

XV Indian Corps (Barrackpore)
Lieut.-General Sir Noel Beresford-Peirse

  14th Indian Division (Comilla)
  Major-General W. L. Lloyd
    47th Infantry Brigade
    49th Infantry Brigade
    Garrison battalions at
      Dacca and Chittagong

  26th Indian Division (Calcutta)
  Major-General T. G. G. Heywood
    4th Infantry Brigade
    71st Infantry Brigade
    109th Infantry Brigade
    1st Anti-Aircraft Brigade
    36th Indian Infantry Brigade
      (Kharagpur)
    Sundarbans Flotilla

IV Corps (Ranchi)
Lieut.-General N. M. S. Irwin

  70th British Division (Ranchi)
  Major-General G. W. Symes
    14th Infantry Brigade
    23rd Infantry Brigade

  23rd Indian Division (Ranchi)
  Major-General R. A. Savory
    37th Infantry Brigade
    123rd Infantry Brigade

SOUTHERN ARMY (BANGALORE)

General Sir Brodie Haig.

19th Indian Division (Madras)
Major-General G. A. P. Scoones
  62nd Infantry Brigade
  64th Infantry Brigade
  98th Infantry Brigade

20th Indian Division (Bangalore)[1]
Major-General D. D. Gracey
  32nd Infantry Brigade[2]
  51st Infantry Brigade[3]
  53rd Infantry Brigade

50th Army Tank Brigade (Poona)

251st Indian Armoured Brigade
  (moving to Secunderabad)

---

[1] Being formed.
[2] At Trichinopoly.
[3] At Secunderabad.

APPENDIX 17

Order of Battle of Fighting Formations in Burcorps, 30th April 1942

Corps Troops
    7th Armoured Brigade
        7th Hussars
        2nd Royal Tank Regiment
        1st West Yorkshire Regiment
        414th Battery, R.H.A.
        'A' Battery, 95th Anti-Tank Regiment, R.A.
    Artillery
        H.Q. 28th Mountain Regiment
        5th Indian Mountain Battery
        28th Indian Mountain Battery

1st Burma Division
H.Q. 27th Indian Mountain Regiment
2nd Indian Mountain Battery
23rd Indian Mountain Battery
56th Field Company, S. and M.
Malerkotla Field Company, S. and M.
50th Field Park Company, S. and M.
1st, 5th, 7th and 12th Burma Rifles
1st Gloucestershire Regiment

13th Indian Brigade
    1st Royal Inniskilling Fusiliers
    5/1st Punjab Regiment
    1/18th Royal Garhwal Rifles

1st Burma Brigade
    1st Cameronians
    2nd K.O.Y.L.I.
    2/7th Rajput Regiment

17th Indian Division
H.Q. 1st Indian Field Regiment
1st Indian Field Battery
12th Indian Mountain Battery
15th Indian Mountain Battery
5th Indian Anti-Tank Battery
8th Indian Heavy Anti-Aircraft Battery
3rd Indian Light Anti-Aircraft Battery
24th Field Company, S. and M.
60th Field Company, S. and M.
70th Field Company, S. and M.
5/17th Dogra Regiment

16th Indian Brigade
    2nd Duke of Wellington's Regiment
    1/9th Royal Jat Regiment
    7/10th Baluch Regiment
    4/12th Frontier Force Regiment

63rd Indian Brigade
    1/11th Sikh Regiment
    2/13th Frontier Force Rifles
    1/10th Gurkha Rifles

APPENDIX 17

1st Burma Division (*cont.*)
  2nd Burma Brigade
    2nd Burma Rifles
    8th Burma Rifles
    F.F.8.

17th Indian Division (*cont.*)
  48th Indian Brigade
    1/3rd Gurkha Rifles ⎫ Composite
    2/5th Royal Gurkha Rifles ⎬ battalion
    1/4th Gurkha Rifles
    1/7th Gurkha Rifles ⎫ Composite
    3/7th Gurkha Rifles ⎬ battalion

Note

By this date, the average strength of the battalions constituting these divisions was about 400.

APPENDIX 18

The Administrative Background to the First Burma Campaign, December 1941–May 1942

See Strategic Map, Maps 1, 8, 9 and 12.

PART I: GENERAL ADMINISTRATIVE PROBLEMS

Although until the 12th December 1941 Burma formed part of Far East Command and the War Office was responsible for its administration[1], the Commander-in-Chief in India had been told in November 1940 to co-operate with the Commander-in-Chief, Far East, in measures for its land and air defence and furnish as far as possible men and material which Burma could not provide herself, subject to the general approval of the Chiefs of Staff. In October 1941 the Adjutant-General, India, visited Rangoon and reported that the administrative situation in Burma gave cause for concern: the staff was inadequate, the medical organization was weak and, should the forces in Burma be engaged in mobile warfare and be dependent on long and difficult lines of communication, there were far too few administrative units. A former Director of Ordnance Services, acting as a liaison officer at General Headquarters, India, reported in even stronger terms on the ordnance situation. He expected a complete breakdown in war. No representative of the Quartermaster General's branch was, however, sent from General Headquarters, India, to investigate the position in Burma as regards the use by the Services of the ports, railways and inland water transport facilities.

These reports were by no means exaggerated but, although something was done, the administrative situation was still very serious when war broke out, especially as regards mechanical transport. By the 20th September 1941, Burma's outstanding demand for motor vehicles totalled 2,604. On the 24th October, the War Office told India to supply 1,030 vehicles of various types and arranged to supply the rest. India herself was very short of motor transport and her assembly plants could not meet the demand in full. Thus by the time war broke out, Burma had the equivalent of only seven mechanical transport companies. General Hutton said in his despatch: 'Transport has been very short and but for 620 lorries presented by the Generalissimo from lease-lend the force would have been immobilized'.

When responsibility for the defence of Burma was transferred to India on the 12th December 1941, General Wavell did what he could to improve the unsatisfactory situation. He could supply few of the administrative units required, since demands from the Middle East and Malaya had taken all those which India had ready for service by that date, but he sent sixty-one, mostly administrative, officers to Burma. These included

---

[1] See pages 6-7.

a Major-General i/c Administration (Major-General E. N. Goddard), a Deputy Chief Engineer, a Director of Transportation, an Embarkation Commandant, and a Director of Movements, as well as a number of other senior administrative officers.[1]

In an appreciation of the situation in Burma on the 22nd December, submitted to the Chief of the Imperial General Staff, Wavell explained that the staff was inadequate in quantity and quality, there were serious deficiencies in the medical services, and a repair organization for transport was non-existent; the great weakness of Burma, he said, lay in her dependence on a single port of entry in a most exposed position. The next day, Wavell was ordered by the War Office to organize the resources in Burma so that a maximum of four divisions, supported by fifteen squadrons R.A.F., could be maintained. The administrative services for such a force did not exist.

Of the many problems which confronted General Goddard on his arrival in Burma on the 31st December, the two most pressing were movement control and transportation. Movements were still being carried out on a peacetime system. Such movement control officers as there were worked under the local formation headquarters, and there was no centralized control. Local commanders made their demands direct to the civil agencies, who were often called upon to meet conflicting and sometimes impossible requests. When early in January Colonel J. N. Soden arrived from Iraq to become Director of Movements, Army in Burma, his first task was to frame an organization and his second to educate commanders and staffs in the duties and functions of movement control.

The civil rail and river transportation agencies in Burma were highly organized for peacetime requirements and adequately equipped to meet any expected military needs. When war broke out, it was generally believed that it would be fought on the frontiers remote from the main rail and river communications of Burma proper. Thus, though powers existed under which the Government of Burma could take over the railways, no immediate action was taken to militarize the transportation agencies or bring them under centralized control of the army. The port of Rangoon, the railways, river transport, roads and postal and telegraph communications, on which the army depended, all remained under civil control.

Later, after the air raids on Rangoon in December 1941, it was realized that the army might be almost completely immobilized at short notice, should further air raids cause staff and labour to take flight. On the 11th January 1942, the Chief Railway Commissioner suggested that the officers and men of the Burma Railways Battalion (B.A.F.) should be embodied, but should carry on their normal railway work. This he felt would raise the morale of the unit and all civilian staff and assist the authorities in maintaining disciplinary control among railway workers. He also suggested that the railways should be placed under the Defence of Burma Rules, which would give him power equivalent to martial law over all railway staff. It was thought at that time that the Japanese would launch their offensive before the end of the month. Neither Army Headquarters nor the Government therefore accepted the suggestions since,

---

[1] See page 14.

with invasion imminent, they considered it inadvisable to make any changes in organization. Moreover, in the absence of a Director of Transportation and an adequate staff, it would not have been possible to militarize the civil agencies in the time left. Instead an urgent demand was placed on India for the minimum requirements in military transportation, line of communication, and labour units to cope with the possibility of the complete disintegration of the civil organizations. Although most of the transportation units she had originally raised had been sent to Iraq, India sent a docks group headquarters and a dock operating company, a headquarters railways construction and maintenance group, followed by a detachment of a railway construction company, all of which had arrived by the middle of February. These proved invaluable, and without them there would have been a complete breakdown in the docks and on the railways.

Although at the end of January Wavell was able to report that the Rangoon docks had been cleared, that the railways were working well and that sufficient labour was available for immediate requirements, the general administrative situation was still precarious. Not only were large numbers of transport, supply and medical units still required, but there were grave defects in the minor administrative services. There was no provost service worthy of the name, and Brigadier Davies (Brigadier General Staff to General Hutton) has since said that half the losses of brigade and divisional transport, and the essential equipment it carried, were due to the lack of trained provost units. The postal service was unsatisfactory; brigades had field post offices, but these were dependent on the civil Post and Telegraph Department in their rear; mail, both official and private, remained undelivered and failure to hear from relatives for long periods affected morale. There was no canteen organization.

The fact that there were many cogs missing in the administrative machine must not, however, be taken to mean that Hutton and Goddard did not do all that was possible in the few weeks that elapsed before the Japanese opened their main offensive on the 20th January.[1] During this period, preliminary plans were drawn up to implement Hutton's decision, made early in January, to prepare a new base in the Mandalay–Meiktila–Myingyan area in upper Burma,[2] on an extension of the proposed new road being built by India from Imphal to Tamu on the Burmese border. Work was also begun on dispersing the Rangoon base area as far north as the line Pegu–Tharrawaddy.

Goddard at once ordered a reconnaissance of the new base area to be made, and began to clear the port of Rangoon of some of the reserves of army equipment, stores and supplies and, as far as transportation and labour difficulties allowed, of the large accumulation of lease-lend material for China. To provide a relief for the port of Rangoon, a survey of Bassein was undertaken. It showed that a year would be needed to develop it sufficiently to accommodate nine ocean-going steamers, and that even to

---

[1] See page 29.
[2] See page 26. An ordnance depot for the maintenance of 1st Burma Division had been established at Meiktila before the outbreak of war.

construct a wharf for three ships would take six months. Work on this and all other transportation problems was hampered by the fact that there was no Director of Transportation until the 27th January.

A Headquarters, Line of Communication Area, was formed in Rangoon to administer the Rangoon, Central Burma and Upper Burma Sub-Areas, and Major-General Wakely was appointed General Officer Commanding the Line of Communications. With the arrival of 17th Indian Division early in January, the administrative layout and chain of command was as follows:

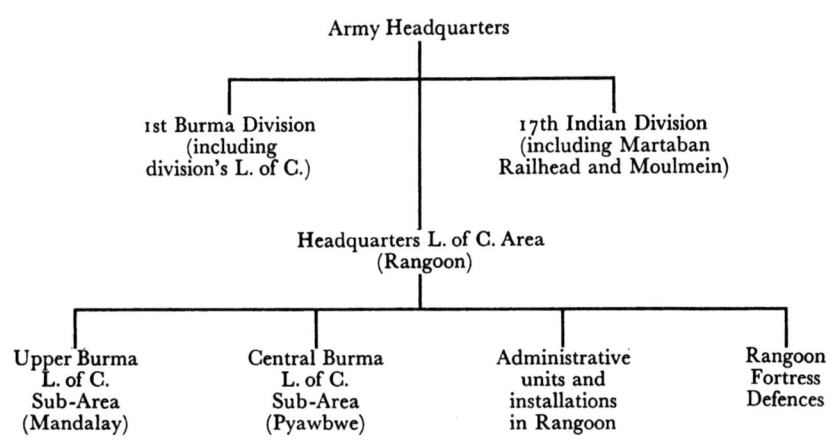

```
                        Army Headquarters
                               │
        ┌──────────────────────┼──────────────────────┐
  1st Burma Division                          17th Indian Division
     (including                                 (including Martaban
  division's L. of C.)                         Railhead and Moulmein)
                               │
                    Headquarters L. of C. Area
                            (Rangoon)
                               │
    ┌──────────────┬───────────┴──────────┬──────────────┐
Upper Burma      Central Burma       Administrative     Rangoon
  L. of C.          L. of C.           units and        Fortress
  Sub-Area          Sub-Area         installations      Defences
 (Mandalay)        (Pyawbwe)          in Rangoon
```

The transfer of three-quarters of all the reserves in Rangoon to the Mandalay area, ordered by Hutton on the 22nd January, involved many difficulties.[1] The major problem was how to keep the railways working, since the number of desertions rose rapidly as the threat to Rangoon increased. The Director of Transportation (Colonel F. J. Biddulph) reached Rangoon on the 27th January. At the end of the month he said that militarization of the transportation agencies was essential, and urged the heads of the agencies and Army Headquarters to take immediate action to this end.[2] But by this time the Japanese had reached Moulmein, and the military situation had deteriorated so much that they considered it too late to put his recommendation into effect, however advisable it might be. Early in February Biddulph proposed, among other things, that the Burma Railways Battalion (B.A.F.) should be embodied. The Chief Railway Commissioner, who by this time had been empowered under the Defence of Burma Rules to require railway staff to stay at their posts and to inform them that any infraction of the order rendered the employee liable to imprisonment, had now changed his mind on this issue. The threat of imprisonment was, however, no substitute for training and discipline, and provided no deterrent to would-be deserters; in consequence the position on the railways grew steadily worse.

---

[1] See page 33.

[2] Since they were not organized in any form of military units, it was impossible for the army to feed and pay the personnel of the railways and the Irrawaddy Flotilla Company. They thus remained dependent on local shops, many of which closed down due to bombing or the proximity of enemy forces. In such circumstances desertions were inevitable.

By the 24th February, the day after the Sittang disaster, the railway staff was so depleted, and those who remained at work under such immense strain, that the Chief Railway Commissioner declared that not another train could be run. Since it was vital to supply the troops at the front and evacuate stores and other material from Rangoon, the Director of Transportation insisted that a minimum of one train a day must be run to Pegu and Prome respectively, with the help of army engineers and the railway staff still on duty. Faced by the refusal of the Chief Railway Commissioner to consider this proposal, the Governor promptly acceded to the army's request and on the 25th ordered that the railways in lower Burma from Toungoo and Prome southwards should be placed under military control. The Chief Railway Commissioner and the three senior officials were sent to control the railways in upper Burma. Those who remained in lower Burma were commissioned, and one of them was appointed Deputy Director of Railways.

Directly this change took place, new life was infused into the railways and morale greatly increased. A number of railwaymen returned to duty, and the continuous shortening of the lines of communication enabled the shortages of staff, due to desertions, to be made up from those who stayed on duty, particularly Anglo-Burmese and Anglo-Indians who remained staunch throughout.

Railway working in and around Rangoon and between Rangoon and Prome was resumed and, with the assistance of 1st Burma Division, the railway between Nyaunglebin and Pyuntaza was put into working order and cleared of deserted trains. Further north, difficulties were greater since the bombing of Toungoo and other towns between it and Mandalay had produced chaos; the marshalling yards were full, and loaded trains were standing at stations all down the lines. At the urgent request of Army Headquarters, an officer of the Indian Engineers with a detachment of engine drivers and signalmen were flown in from India, and were placed at the disposal of the Deputy Director to help him in the task. Before Rangoon fell, the Director of Transportation sent the Deputy Director to organize railway services on the Rangoon–Prome line along which the army was to withdraw. On the 14th March, after the fall of Rangoon, the railways in upper Burma were placed under control of the Deputy Director.

Early in April, however, the morale of the railway staffs began to fall rapidly owing to the continued withdrawal of the army and the terror instilled by the behaviour of the Chinese troops towards them.[1] On the 15th, Sir John Rowland, a former Chief Railway Commissioner, who was then in charge of the construction of the Burma–China railway, was asked to use his influence to help in raising their morale. He laid down certain conditions, one of which was that the army would look after the railway staff and undertake to evacuate them to India before the withdrawal of all military forces. These conditions were accepted but, owing to the rapid advance of the Japanese, both parties to the agreement found themselves unable to carry it out.

---

[1] See page 474.

On the evacuation of Rangoon, the Army in Burma became dependent on stocks already in the country and on locally obtained supplies. The main base installations in upper Burma at this time were:

Mandalay area:	No. 2 Base Supply Depot
	No. 1 Ordnance Field Depot
	Ammunition Depot
	Engineer stores depot, with a sub-depot at Monywa
	Railway workshops at Myitnge
	Base medical units
Meiktila:	Advance base ordnance depot
Taunggyi:	No. 2 Ordnance Field Depot (in process of being moved to the Mandalay area)
Prome:	Ordnance field depot (being moved to the Mandalay area by river)
Pyinmana area:	Ammunition depot
Yenangyaung area:	Production of motor spirit, 800,000 gallons a month, with target of 2 million. (Distribution difficulties arose when production exceeded 1 million gallons). Refining arrangements were improved to produce 87 octane spirit for the armoured brigade and 90 octane spirit for the R.A.F.

On the 21st March, Headquarters L. of C. Area was told that, in addition to installations already existing, a hospital and medical stores depot should be established forthwith at Myingyan and at Shwebo, a supply depot in the Myinmu–Shwebo area, a P.O.L. depot in the Mandalay area, an ammunition depot near Shwebo, an ordnance stores depot at Myinmu, and an engineer stores depot (for transit only) at Monywa. Headquarters 2nd Echelon would be either at Sagaing or Shwebo.

A review of the state of the stocks in Burma made after the fall of Rangoon showed that the supplies of petrol and oil were satisfactory, provided the oilfields could be held. This was largely due to the initiative of The Burmah Oil Company officers, under the leadership of Mr. J. Drysdale, who arranged to refine crude oil at Yenangyaung. Medical stores were sufficient for six months; there was ammunition of the more common types to last till the rains, when expenditure was likely to be on a reduced scale; there was a shortage of clothing and equipment, but a reasonable stock of small arms; and supplies would be adequate for six months, provided there was no loss through enemy action. Considerable quantities of supplies were however lost when the Japanese captured Prome, and there were further losses when they bombed Mandalay.

India was pressing forward with the construction of the Imphal–Kalewa road on her side of the frontier, and by May had constructed a fair-weather road up to Tamu, but the section onwards to Kalewa (for which Burma was responsible) was still only a rough cart track.[1] It is

---

[1] See pages 53–54.

therefore relevant to investigate why comparatively little progress was made on the Burma section between Tamu and Kalewa. The Deputy Commissioner, Upper Chindwin District, had been relieved of routine duties and placed in charge of the Tamu–Kalewa section, and in February the resources of the local Public Works Department were increased as they became available, but the work was hampered by the influx of refugees, which upset the labour, the distance from Rangoon and the lack of equipment. On the 28th April a fair-weather road from Imphal reached Tamu. The same day Headquarters 'Z' L. of C. Area from India took over. Four days later a motorable track was bulldozed through to Kalewa, which enabled all staging posts between Kalewa and Imphal to be stocked with two days' rations for 36,000 men by the 6th May.[1]

PART II: THE SUPPLY OF THE ARMY IN BURMA DURING THE CAMPAIGN

The retreat of the Army in Burma from Kawkareik to Imphal covered a distance of approximately 1,000 miles and took three and a half months. As it progressed and reserves became scarcer, a proper handover by Army Headquarters to subordinate formations of depots and dumps, and the details of any road and water reconnaissances carried out was very necessary. When, as sometimes happened, handovers were not carried out properly, dumps were missed, found looted or even prematurely destroyed. Subordinate formations had at times during the retreat to carry out administrative reconnaissances of areas already reconnoitred, as no Service representative had stayed behind to hand over details.

The first stage of the withdrawal from Rangoon followed the road and railway to Prome along the Irrawaddy valley. By the 27th February, the stocking of this route was nearly complete and all formations, including Rangoon Fortress and Headquarters L. of C. Area, were told of the arrangements to maintain them along this route should a general withdrawal become necessary. Arrangements were also made to keep some locomotives and rolling stock on the Prome line to evacuate casualties and stores of the withdrawing formations, and to maintain them by supply train from Prome until the town itself was reached. As many river transport craft as possible sailed from Rangoon to the Mandalay area, so that a river link between the new base being established in upper Burma and the Prome area could be organized. At the same time, reserve supply dumps of rations and petrol were formed at Dayindabo and Allanmyo for use later in the defence of Prome and the Irrawaddy valley.

Rangoon and Pegu were evacuated at the end of the first week of March. In the early stage of the withdrawal, the troops were maintained from depots formed at Taukkyan and Tharrawaddy. From the 13th to 26th March, a daily train from Prome (carrying supplies, ammunition and P.O.L.) maintained the force and evacuated surplus stores. During this period, the motor transport of 17th Indian Division was reduced to pro-

---

[1] See page 206.

APPENDIX 18

vide vehicles for a divisional reconnaissance regiment and the two motorised battalions required as a support group for 7th Armoured Brigade. For its second line maintenance, the division was thus left with only one composite transport company of seventy-two vehicles, mostly 3 tonners, with a carrying capacity of approximately half a general purpose transport company, compared with the normal establishment of three general purpose transport companies for an infantry division on the lower scale of transport. Deliveries had therefore to be made on a bulk basis to supply and petrol points within brigade groups, instead of to unit lines. The second line maintenance of 7th Armoured Brigade remained based on 65th Company, R.A.S.C., which had accompanied it from the Middle East.

By the 10th March almost all the available river transport craft had arrived at Prome. The wounded and sick and military stores of all kinds, including locally purchased rice, were sent up river to the new base depots. Despite the most strenuous efforts, shortage of labour prevented the clearance of large quantities of reserves. The inadequacy of the road transport was accentuated by enemy air action and, in face of unopposed low-flying attacks, it became more and more difficult to make civilian crews go downstream. At the end of March, movement by day of river craft and road transport south of Allanmyo was stopped. The loss of the civil heavy repair installations in the Rangoon area made even normal maintenance of road transport a matter of great difficulty.

During the first half of March, 1st Burma Division (except for 13th Brigade still in the Karen Hills) was maintained from Toungoo by supply train. The withdrawal to the Irrawaddy valley began on the 15th March, and on the 21st the division (less 13th Brigade) assembled at Yedashe and entrained for Taungdwingyi, from where it finished the journey to Prome by motor transport and march route. The 13th Brigade reached Meiktila on the 2nd April *en route* to Allanmyo. It was intended that the active defence of the Irrawaddy valley by Burcorps should now pivot on defended localities at Prome and Allanmyo, holding twenty-two days' requirements and reserves for the whole force. Maintenance of Burcorps from upper Burma was to be by river, supplies and stores being shipped from the Mandalay area and petrol by barge from Yenangyaung. Should the river route for any reason be unusable, an alternative line of supply was to be by rail from Mandalay to Taungtha and Meiktila, thence by road to Kyaukpadaung, and finally by rail to Satthwa where supplies could be taken over by Burcorps. In early April, the Japanese unexpectedly cut the railway south of Pyinmana at a time when there were no locomotives on the branch line Kyaukpadaung–Pyinmana, making this branch of the railway unusable.

When circumstances compelled Burcorps to withdraw from the Prome area, orders were given to backload stores: the order of priority being 87/90 octane spirit, lubricants, ammunition and supplies; but many reserves had to be abandoned. Between the evacuation of Prome on the night of the 1st/2nd April and the evacuation of Allanmyo in the night of the 5th/6th, Burcorps was supplied from reserve dumps at Allanmyo and thereafter from Yenangyaung. Returning second line vehicles, when not engaged on troop-carrying, were used to backload stores to Taungdwingyi, and later to Yenangyaung.

From the 2nd to the 9th April, the remaining second line motor transport of 17th Division was made available for troop-carrying, and from the 5th to the 9th rations and stores for 17th Division and 7th Armoured Brigade were delivered daily by the R.A.S.C. company of the latter formation. On the 10th, second line transport of 17th Division resumed maintenance of its division in the Taungdwingyi area from Yenangyaung. The maintenance of 2nd Burma Brigade on the west bank of the river was by daily supply launch from a field supply depot at Magwe.

During the first three weeks of April, much was done to improve road communications in the Burcorps area and to link them to the road system running south and south-west from Mandalay. The conversion of the railway track from Taungdwingyi to Natmauk to a road suitable for motor transport had priority. It was cleared of rails by the 10th April, and three days later was fit for use by 3 ton lorries. Other roads made fit for use by 3 ton lorries were the Magwe–Natmauk–Yamethin–Pyawbwe road (ready by the 11th April), a new road to connect Natmauk to the Meiktila–Kyaukpadaung road at Zayetkon (ready by the 19th April) and the Myingyan–Myotha road (ready by the 19th April). A bridge over the Pin Chaung north of Yenangyaung was begun at the end of March, but work on it was discontinued on the 13th April and orders issued to concentrate on keeping the ford open for traffic.

After the destruction of the oilfields at Yenangyaung, the remaining stocks of petrol were estimated to be sufficient for two months, but these were widely distributed. Since the collection and distribution of rice for the Chinese forces depended almost entirely on motor transport, the destruction of the oilfields at once severely limited the length of time the Chinese troops could remain in the field.

The supply routes allotted to divisions by Burcorps on the 15th April were:

1st Burma Division: main road Myingyan–Taungtha–Kyaukpadaung–Gwegyo–Yenangyaung–Magwe.

17th Indian Division: Mandalay–Meiktila–Zayetkon–Natmauk–Taungdwingyi.

In preparation for the maintenance of the force after it had crossed the Irrawaddy and regrouped in areas north and west of that river and astride the Chindwin, Headquarters Burma Army had meanwhile placed one month's requirements in the area Yeu–Shwebo–Monywa–Okma (fifty-two miles north of Monywa on the east bank of the Chindwin), and arranged that 1st Burma Division and 17th Indian Division would be supplied from Monywa and both 7th Armoured Brigade and 38th Chinese Division from Shwebo.

The tentative plan that 7th Armoured Brigade and one infantry brigade should withdraw towards China entailed the stocking of the line Mandalay–Lashio. Work on this was progressing well when the plan was cancelled on the 21st April. Hospitals had to be hurriedly brought back and depots cleared, and the reorganization was completed only just before the blowing of the Ava bridge at midnight on the 30th April/1st May.

APPENDIX 18

Burcorps began its withdrawal across the Irrawaddy on the night of the 25th/26th April by the Ava bridge and the ferry at Sameikkon, and was shortly afterwards to begin its withdrawal towards India along the Yeu–Kalewa track and up the Chindwin, using river craft from Monywa. Monywa, however, fell to the Japanese on the 1st May and the whole force had to withdraw by the Yeu–Kalewa road. The river craft managed to get through to Kalewa. To maintain Burcorps during this withdrawal, there were in the area Yeu–Shwebo thirty days' supplies for 6,500 British, 22,000 Indian, 4,000 Burmese troops and 1,600 animals. There were in addition about one month's supplies dispersed over the railway north of Mandalay, but these could not be collected quickly. Stocks of ammunition, except A.A. ammunition, were considered adequate for the task ahead. The petrol situation was now serious: the sole remaining stocks were 25,000 gallons of M.T. and 10,000 gallons of 87/90 octane petrol at Shwebo and 20,000 gallons of 87/90 octane petrol with 65th Company R.A.S.C. and 'B' Echelon 7th Armoured Brigade. In case motor transport had to be discarded owing to lack of petrol, bullock carts, mules and ponies were purchased locally.

These reserves had to suffice until maintenance could be switched to India, with railhead at Dimapur (Manipur Road) and roadhead at Tamu—425 miles and 225 miles respectively distant from Yeu. Although India Command had sent some supplies to Kalewa and arrangements had been made to drop small quantities there by air in emergency, the state of the road forward of Dimapur and the approaching monsoon made the maintenance of the Burma Army at Kalewa impossible.[1] It had therefore to move back from Kalewa to M.T. roadhead north of Tamu, as the tactical situation permitted, and by the 6th May India Command had stocked staging posts to make this possible.

The withdrawal now became a race with the weather and the Japanese. Before Headquarters Burma Army could stock the Yeu–Kalewa track, it had to be made fit for motor transport and a ferry organized across the Chindwin from Shwegyin to Kalewa. As many 15 cwt. trucks as could be spared from formations were sent ahead to stock the road, as its improvement up to 3 ton standard progressed. Between Yeu and Shwegyin (107 miles) five staging posts, roughly twenty miles apart, were stocked and local water resources developed. When the passage of troops along the road began, stocking was incomplete, but by almost superhuman efforts the administrative staff completed the distribution of stocks as the withdrawal proceeded. Although the force was placed on half rations on the 4th May, there was never any real shortage of supplies and the stocks of petrol were sufficient for all the remaining vehicles to get to Shwegyin. The move of L. of C. troops from Yeu began on the 30th April, the leading elements reaching Kalewa on the 2nd May. The withdrawal of Burcorps to Kalewa began the next day.

The administrative story of the First Burma Campaign is one of masterly improvisation by the slender and overworked administrative staffs. The tools for the task were hopelessly inadequate, and thus, at

---

[1] Early rains began on the 12th May and became heavy on the 20th May.

times, confusion was inevitable. The problems which were successfully solved included the formation of a new base in upper Burma; the disembarkation of units and stores at Rangoon, despite labour and other difficulties; the final evacuation of Rangoon; the backloading of stocks from the Mandalay–Lashio line, concurrently with maintenance of Burcorps engaged in active operations south of the Irrawaddy; the evacuation of the upper Burma base, including Mandalay, and the stocking of the area north of the Irrawaddy. Perhaps the most formidable of all the problems was the last hundred miles of the retreat to the Chindwin, when enemy intervention resulted in the loss of the river route and the whole army had to use the Yeu–Shwegyin road and be ferried across the Chindwin under pressure from the enemy. Tribute must be paid to the excellent work carried out by the civil transportation agencies under appallingly difficult circumstances. The campaign shows, however, that some form of militarization of these agencies at the outbreak of war would have been invaluable.

The administration of the Chinese forces in Burma was also a problem of the first magnitude. They had no administrative services as understood in a modern army. There were no engineer, medical, ordnance, supply and transport corps, or pay organization. In the absence of a Chinese 'Q' staff, rail transportation proved peculiarly difficult. Chinese commanders had no conception of timed or balanced railway running. Chinese soldiers ordered engine drivers at the point of the bayonet to start or stop trains without any regard to safe railway working. Complete dislocation of train operation inevitably ensued and collisions resulted.

The Chinese policy was to transfer as much as possible of the slender stocks of petrol to China, while the British were, of course, husbanding their reserves. Again, although the shortage of motor transport was most acute, the Chinese failed to make available for general use the large number of lease-lend lorries which had been concentrated at Lashio. A generous allotment of this transport to VI Chinese Army might, by facilitating concentration, have made a great difference to the campaign in the southern Shan States in April 1942.[1]

The lack of any Chinese administrative staff meant that British liaison officers had to concentrate on making administrative arrangements to the detriment of their liaison duties.[2] This had the serious effect of lowering their prestige, for most of the Chinese commanders regarded administration as unworthy of the consideration of a fighting soldier. No satisfactory engineer liaison was established since there was only one engineer officer on General Stilwell's staff, and it was difficult to maintain contact with him. Thus it was impossible to ensure that important bridges were demolished in areas for which the Chinese were responsible.

---

[1] See pages 174–76. The lorries released (see para. 2, page 464) to the British, referred to by General Hutton, were from stocks in Rangoon.

[2] Many of these were from the Burma Civil Service. Their devotion to duty in circumstances of considerable strain was of a high order.

APPENDIX 18

The Chinese had a Liasion Mission with British headquarters. This, in addition to its operational function, acted as the channel through which payment was made to Chinese troops, including funds for the purchase of items which the British had guaranteed to supply but which could not be furnished in kind. British field cashiers attached to Chinese formations drew money from certain specified civil treasuries, and transferred it to representatives of the Chinese mission and to supply agents. The system was the best that could be devised in the circumstances.

The biggest administrative problem was, of course, the provision of supplies. The British were responsible for distribution down to Chinese divisions, and this entailed the collection of rice. Transport was obtained by requisitioning civilian lorries employed on the Burma Road. Eventually a civilian firm, complete with its staff, workshops and vehicles, was taken over and formed into army units; it proved invaluable.[1] This system worked satisfactorily up till the fall of Mandalay. After that, operations became too fluid and the Chinese armies lived on the country by purchase or looting.

One unexpected difficulty affecting supplies was the impossibility of ascertaining correct ration strengths. The official figures given to the Liaison Mission were: V Chinese Army 60,000, VI Chinese Army 40,000 and LXVI Chinese Army 30,000—a total of 130,000. The Chief Liaison Officer estimated that the correct figure was 70,000, but worked on a basis of 86,000 in order to allow a safety margin.

In addition to supplies, the British had agreed, if they could spare the stocks, to meet other Chinese requirements, including medical stores and mosquito nets. A casualty clearing station and a staging section, together with medical stores, were provided from the Burma Army's small resources and these, together with Dr Seagrave's unit, were the only medical units the Chinese had. This proved entirely inadequate even though, whenever possible, Chinese wounded were treated in British hospitals and in river steamers provided by the Irrawaddy Flotilla Company.

The ordnance situation was also unsatisfactory in that the Chinese had very few reserves of ammunition, clothing and equipment. As the types of stores required were not common to both armies, the British could do little to help except with engineer stores and explosives.

The Chinese forces in Burma presented a tremendous administrative problem. The fact that the British were able to move, feed and maintain them without the help of any regular administrative units at all, either British or Chinese, is another remarkable example of successful improvisation.

---

[1] See page 36.

APPENDIX 19

Order of Battle of the Japanese 3rd Air Army, July 1942

Headquarters 3rd Air Army, Singapore

Burma	Netherlands East Indies
5th Air Division	3rd Air Brigade
	59th Air Regiment
4th Air Brigade	75th Air Regiment
50th (F) Air Regiment	
8th (LB) Air Regiment	21st Independent Air Unit
14th (HB) Air Regiment	
	83rd Independent Air Unit
7th Air Brigade	
64th (F) Air Regiment	
12th (HB) Air Regiment	
98th (HB) Air Regiment	
12th Air Brigade	
1st (F) Air Regiment	
11th (F) Air Regiment	
81st (Recce) Air Regiment	

APPENDIX 20

G.H.Q. Operation Instruction No. 11

To: G.O.C.-in-C., Eastern Army

OBJECT

1. The object of operations in Upper Burma during the dry season of 1942/43 will be:
    (a) to develop communications and establish ourselves in a favourable position for reconquering Burma and reopening the Burma Road at the first opportunity;
    (b) to bring the Japanese to battle with the purpose of using up their strength, particularly in the air.

INTENTION

2. My immediate intention is:
    (a) to capture Akyab and to re-occupy Upper Arakan;
    (b) to strengthen our position in the Chin Hills;
    (c) to occupy Kalewa and Sittaung and thence to raid the Japanese L. of C.;
    (d) to make such administrative preparations as will allow of the rapid advance of a force towards Upper or Lower Burma should opportunity offer during the campaigning season of 1942/43.

METHOD

Capture of Akyab

3. This operation will form the subject of a separate instruction. You will make preparations for carrying it out as soon as possible. In particular, you will commence the construction of a road south from Chittagong and you will complete the landing ground at Cox's Bazar. The infiltration southwards of your forces in this area will commence as soon as their maintenance becomes possible.

OPERATIONS FROM ASSAM

4. You will establish regular forces at:
    (a) Tiddim, and
    (b) Tamu

as soon as the administrative situation and the condition of your troops will allow. You will then capture:
    (c) Kalewa and
    (d) Sittaung

and by the occupation of these places you will deny the use of the R. Chindwin to the enemy.

5. You will then be prepared to send raiding columns deep into enemy territory in order to interfere with his L. of C. and to take advantage of any weakening in his position. In this connection you will consider the employment of 77 Infantry Brigade and the use of small detachments of parachute troops. You will keep in mind the possibility of deep penetration by flying columns, and will consider how far they can support themselves on the country.

6. You will take the necessary steps to protect your L. of C. and advanced bases in Assam against enemy air attack. You will give priority in the allotment of resources to the construction of aerodromes from which fighters can operate to protect your advanced base at Manipur Road and the important railway junction at Lumding. You will also give the R.A.F. every possible assistance in the establishment of an efficient warning system.

7. You will construct the road Manipur Base–Palel to a two way all-weather standard, and the roads Imphal–Tiddim and Palel–Tamu to a one way all-weather standard before the rainy season of 1943.

8. Detailed air planning will be carried out by A.O.C. Bengal to whom A.O.C.-in-C., India will allot the necessary Air Forces.

9. G.H.Q. will be responsible for planning any diversionary operation or cover plan.

10. G.H.Q. Operation Instruction No. 4 dated 14th June 1942 is cancelled.

Acknowledge

A. P. WAVELL
General
Commander-in-Chief in India

New Delhi
17/9/42

APPENDIX 21

Order of Battle of Air Forces, India and Ceylon, September 1942

	Air Headquarters, India	
31 (BT) Squadron	D.C.2/D.C.3	Dinjan
3 (PR) Squadron	Hurricane/Mitchell	Calcutta
	221 Group, Calcutta	
34 (B) Squadron	Blenheim IV	Asansol
60 (B) Squadron	Blenheim IV	Asansol
113 (B) Squadron	Blenheim IV	Asansol
215 (B) Squadron	Wellington	Pandaveswar
62 (GR) Squadron	Hudson	Dum Dum
353 (GR) Squadron	Hudson	Dum Dum
20 (AC) Squadron[1]	Lysander	Jamshedpur
28 (AC) Squadron[1]	Lysander	Ranchi
	224 Group, Calcutta	
5 (F) Squadron	Mohawk	Dinjan
67 (F) Squadron	Hurricane	Alipore
135 (F) Squadron	Hurricane	Dum Dum
136 (F) Squadron	Hurricane	Alipore
607 (F) Squadron	Hurricane	Alipore
615 (F) Squadron	Hurricane	Jessore
146 (F) Squadron	Hurricane	Jessore
	225 Group, Bangalore	
240 (FB) Squadron	Catalina	Madras
	222 Group, Colombo	
30 (F) Squadron	Hurricane	Ratmalana
258 (F) Squadron	Hurricane	Ratmalana
261 (F) Squadron	Hurricane	China Bay
273 (F) Squadron	Fulmar	China Bay
11 (B) Squadron	Blenheim IV	Colombo
22 (TB) Squadron	Beaufort	Ratmalana
205 (FB) Squadron	Catalina	Koggala
321 (FB) Squadron, Dutch	Catalina	China Bay
413 (FB) Squadron, R.C.A.F.	Catalina	Koggala
	223 Group, Peshawar	
1 (AC) Squadron, I.A.F.[1]	Lysander	Peshawar
2 (AC) Squadron, I.A.F.[1]	Lysander	Peshawar
3 (AC) Squadron, I.A.F.[1]	Audax	Kohat
4 (AC) Squadron, I.A.F.[1]	Lysander	Kohat

[1] Non-operational.

APPENDIX 22

Order of Battle of 14th Indian Infantry Division

Headquarters 14th Infantry Division
(*Major-General W. L. Lloyd*)

    130th Field Regiment, R.A.
        314th Field Battery, R.A.
        315th Field Battery, R.A.
        494th Field Battery, R.A.
    23rd Indian Mountain Regiment
        3rd Mountain Battery
        8th Mountain Battery
        17th Mountain Battery
    26th Field Company
    73rd Field Company
    74th Field Company
    306th Field Park Company
    17th Auxiliary Pioneer Battalion
    9th Bridging Section

47th Indian Infantry Brigade
(*Brigadier E. H. Blaker*)
  1st Royal Inniskilling
    Fusiliers
  1/7th Rajput Regiment
  5/8th Punjab Regiment
	55th Indian Infantry Brigade
	(*Brigadier J. M. Hunt*)
	  2/1st Punjab Regiment
	  1/17th Dogra Regiment
	  8/6th Rajputana Rifles

123rd Indian Infantry Brigade
(*Brigadier A. V. Hammond*)
  10th Lancashire Fusiliers
  8/10th Baluch Regiment
  1/15th Punjab Regiment
	88th Indian Infantry Brigade
	(*Brigadier L. C. Thomas*)
	  5/9th Jat Regiment
	  14/12th Frontier Force
	    Regiment
	  1/16th Punjab Regiment

'V' Force
2000 Flotilla

APPENDIX 23

Particulars of British and Enemy Aircraft in use in South East Asia during the Period covered by this Volume

The figures in these tables are no more than a general guide to the characteristics and capabilities of each type of aircraft. The performance was affected by the climate, the skill of the pilot, the accuracy of navigation and by the uncertainties of flying in the presence of the enemy. For these reasons the operational range—not to be confused with the radius of action—was always much less than the still air range. Broadly speaking, after allowing for the running of the engines on the ground and for the climb to the height quoted, the still air range was the distance that could be flown in still air until the tanks were empty.

Notes: (i) The most economical cruising speed was the speed at which the greatest range was achieved.
(ii) The height given in Column IV was the optimum height for the maximum speed.

FIGHTER AIRCRAFT
BRITISH

Aircraft	Fuel and Still Air Range at Most Economical Cruising Speed (Gals.)	Fuel and Still Air Range at Most Economical Cruising Speed (Miles)	Most Economical Cruising Speed in Miles Per Hour	Maximum Speed in Miles Per Hour	Gun Armament	Remarks
Buffalo Single engine monoplane Crew 1	133	759	180 at 15,000 ft.	295 at 18,500 ft.	4 × ·50 in.	American design and manufacture. Was less manoeuvreable and much inferior to the Japanese Zero at heights of 10,000 feet and above. Also it had a relatively poor rate of climb: 6·1 minutes to 13,000 feet compared with 4·3 minutes for the Zero.
Beaufighter Twin engine monoplane Crew 2	550	1,515	226 at 15,000 ft.	324 at 11,750 ft.	6 × ·303 in. 4 × 20 mm	A long-range fighter which with special equipment was used for night fighter interception.

FIGHTER AIRCRAFT
BRITISH

Aircraft	Fuel and Still Air Range at Most Economical Cruising Speed (Gals.)	Fuel and Still Air Range at Most Economical Cruising Speed (Miles)	Most Economical Cruising Speed in Miles Per Hour	Maximum Speed in Miles Per Hour	Gun Armament	Remarks
Fulmar Single engine monoplane Crew 2	155	820	170 at 10,000 ft.	253 at 10,000 ft.	8 × ·303 in.	Fleet Air Arm.
Hurricane Mk. II Single engine monoplane Crew 1	97 183 (2 × 43)	480 970	200 at 15,000 ft.	342 at 22,000 ft.	12 × ·303 in. or 4 × 20 mm	Below 10,000 ft. the Hurricane was less manoeuvreable than the Japanese Zero but at medium heights and above 20,000 ft. the Hurricane proved to be superior.
Mohawk Single engine monoplane Crew 1	132	900	160–170 at 15,000 ft.	300 at 14,000 ft.	6 × ·303 in.	American design and manufacture. This aircraft was an earlier version of the Tomahawk. It was obsolete in 1941 but was retained in service by the R.A.F. in India.
Tomahawk Single engine monoplane Crew 1	132	695	185 at 15,000 ft.	340 at 16,000 ft.	2 × ·50 in. 4 × ·303 in.	American design and manufacture. Not used by the British in Far East but as it was standard equipment of the A.V.G. is included for ease of reference. This aircraft was very manoeuvreable and somewhat similar in performance to the Hurricane Mk. II at heights above 15,000 ft.

APPENDIX 23

FIGHTER AIRCRAFT
BRITISH

Aircraft	Fuel and Still Air Range at Most Economical Cruising Speed — Gals.	Fuel and Still Air Range at Most Economical Cruising Speed — Miles	Most Economical Cruising Speed in Miles Per Hour	Maximum Speed in Miles Per Hour	Gun Armament	Remarks
Spitfire Mk. V Single engine monoplane Crew 1	85	480	208 at 20,000 ft.	375 at 20,250 ft.	4 × ·303 in. 2 × 20 mm	First introduced as a fighter in India November 1943. Spitfires for photographic reconnaissance were in use in India from January 1943.

BOMBER AIRCRAFT
(including torpedo-bomber and reconnaissance)
BRITISH

Aircraft	Still Air Range with Associated Bomb-load — Miles	Still Air Range with Associated Bomb-load — Bomb-load	Most Economical Cruising Speed in Miles Per Hour	Maximum Speed in Miles Per Hour	Gun Armament	Remarks
Albacore Single engine biplane Crew 2 or 3	521	1 torpedo or 1,500 lb	105 at 6,000 ft.	163 at 4,800 ft.	2 × ·303 in.	Fleet Air Arm. Figures relate to use as torpedo-bomber.

BOMBER AIRCRAFT
(including torpedo-bomber and reconnaissance)

BRITISH

Aircraft	Still Air Range with Associated Bomb-load (Miles)	Bomb-load	Most Economical Cruising Speed in Miles Per Hour	Maximum Speed in Miles Per Hour	Gun Armament	Remarks
Blenheim Mk. I Twin engine monoplane Crew 3	920	1,000 lb	165 at 15,000 ft.	265 at 15,000 ft.	2 × ·303 in.	
Blenheim Mk. IV Twin engine monoplane Crew 3	1,457	1,000 lb	170 at 15,000 ft.	266 at 11,800 ft.	5 × ·303 in.	
Bisley Twin engine monoplane Crew 3	1,230	1,000 lb	170 at 15,000 ft.	244 at 6,000 ft.	5 × ·303 in.	
Beaufort Mk. I Twin engine monoplane Crew 4	1,390	1 torpedo or 1,650 lb	160 at 5,000 ft.	236 at 5,000 ft.	4 × ·303 in.	Figures relate to use as torpedo-bomber.
Lysander Single engine monoplane Crew 2	1,410	500 lb	123 at 10,000 ft.	212 at 4,500 ft.	4 × ·303 in.	Primary rôle was tactical reconnaissance and army co-operation but was also used as a light bomber. Was obsolete in 1941 but was retained by the R.A.F. in India until September 1942.

APPENDIX 23

BOMBER AIRCRAFT
(including torpedo-bomber and reconnaissance)

BRITISH

Aircraft	Still Air Range with Associated Bomb-load (Miles)	Bomb-load	Most Economical Cruising Speed in Miles Per Hour	Maximum Speed in Miles Per Hour	Gun Armament	Remarks
Liberator Mk. II Four engine monoplane Crew 8	1,940 / 2,730	8,000 lb / 4,500 lb	156 at 15,000 ft.	228 at 14,000 ft.	5 × ·50 in. 4 × ·303 in.	Heavy bomber. American design and manufacture.
Swordfish Single engine biplane Crew 2	528	1 torpedo or 1,500 lb	103 at 5,000 ft.	139 at 5,000 ft.	2 × ·303 in.	Fleet Air Arm. Figures relate to use as torpedo-bomber.
Vengeance Single engine monoplane Crew 2	915	1,500 lb	187 at 15,000 ft.	258 at 11,500 ft.	6 × ·303 in.	American design and manufacture. Light bomber in practice proved most useful as a dive-bomber.
Wellington Mk. I Twin engine monoplane Crew 6	2,550 / 1,200	1,000 lb / 4,500 lb	165 at 10,000 ft.	235 at 15,500 ft.	6 × ·303 in.	Medium bomber.

GENERAL RECONNAISSANCE AND TRANSPORT AIRCRAFT
BRITISH

Aircraft	Still Air Range with Associated Bomb-load (Miles)	Bomb-load	Most Economical Cruising Speed in Miles Per Hour	Maximum Speed in Miles Per Hour	Gun Armament	Remarks
Catalina Twin engine flying-boat Crew 9	1,395 2,950	2,000 lb Nil	123 at 5,000 ft.	177 at 5,000 ft.	2 × ·303 in. 2 × ·500 in.	American design and manufacture.
Hudson Mk. II Twin engine monoplane Crew 4	1,540	950 lb	195 at 10,000 ft.	225 at 7,900 ft.	4 Browning 3 × ·303 in.	American design and manufacture. Primary rôle was reconnaissance but was frequently used as a medium bomber.
Dakota Twin engine monoplane Crew 3 or 4	1,910	26 troops with full equipment or equivalent	160 at 10,000 ft.	220 at 10,000 ft.	None	Transport aircraft of American design and manufacture. The Dakota (C47) was the military version of DC2 and DC3 civil air line transports in use in 1941.

APPENDIX 23

FIGHTER AIRCRAFT
JAPANESE

Aircraft	Fuel and Still Air Range at Most Economical Cruising Speed — Gals.	Fuel and Still Air Range at Most Economical Cruising Speed — Miles	Most Economical Cruising Speed in Miles Per Hour	Maximum Speed in Miles Per Hour	Gun Armament	Remarks (Allied Code Name)
Navy Zero Mk. II Single engine monoplane Crew 1	112	885	160 at 18,000 ft.	335 at 18,500 ft.	2 × 7·7 mm plus 2 × 20 mm	'ZEKE 2'
Army 1 Mk. II Single engine monoplane Crew 1	126	950	155 at 18,000 ft.	325 at 18,500 ft.	2 × 12·7 mm	'OSCAR 2'

BOMBER AIRCRAFT
(including torpedo-bomber and reconnaissance)
JAPANESE

Aircraft	Still Air Range with Associated Bomb-load — Miles	Still Air Range with Associated Bomb-load — Bomb-load	Most Economical Cruising Speed in Miles Per Hour	Maximum Speed in Miles Per Hour	Gun Armament	Remarks (Allied Code Name)
Navy 1 Twin engine monoplane Crew 7	3,075	2,200 lb or 1 torpedo	145 at 15,000 ft.	283 at 13,800 ft.	3 × 7·7 mm 2 × 20 mm	Standard Navy bomber (land-based). 'BETTY'
Navy 97 Mk. II Single engine monoplane Crew 2	1,220	1,100 lb or 1 torpedo	130 at 13,000 ft.	222 at 15,000 ft.	4 × 7·7 mm	Standard torpedo-bomber, carrier-borne. 'KATE'

BOMBER AIRCRAFT
(including torpedo-bomber and reconnaissance)

JAPANESE

Aircraft	Still Air Range with Associated Bomb-load (Miles)	Bomb-load	Most Economical Cruising Speed in Miles Per Hour	Maximum Speed in Miles Per Hour	Gun Armament	Remarks (Allied Code Name)
Army 97 Mk. III Twin engine monoplane Crew 7	1,635	2,200 lb	150 at 13,000 ft.	294 at 15,500 ft.	6 × 7·7 mm or 5 × 7·7 mm plus 1 × 12·7 mm 1 × 20 mm	'SALLY'
Army 1 Mk. II Twin engine monoplane Crew 2	1,405	None	219 at 15,000 ft.	365 at 21,000 ft.	1 × 7·7 mm	Specially developed for photographic reconnaissance. 'DINAH'
Army 99 Twin engine monoplane Crew 2	1,030	660 lb	180 at 12,000 ft.	250 at 12,000 ft.	3 × 7·7 mm	'SONIA'

Notes: (i) The Japanese system of numbering each type of aircraft was related to the year of issue. Type numbers correspond to the last one or two digits of the year of issue according to the Japanese calendar, by which the year 1940 was the Japanese year 2600. Thus aircraft brought into service in 1939 were designated 'Type 99' and those issued in 1940 were 'Type O'.
To simplify reference to particular types, the Allies allotted a code name to each type.

(ii) The Japanese did not introduce basically new types of aircraft during the course of the war. Modified versions of types in production in 1941 or earlier were made, resulting in improved performance in some types. Variations in armament were also made. In general, however, the types of aircraft with which squadrons were equipped remained unchanged.

(iii) Japanese aircraft were not normally fitted with self-sealing petrol tanks or protective armour, nor were the aircrews equipped with parachutes. For these reasons their losses, particularly of aircraft damaged in action, may have been greater than they otherwise would have been.

APPENDIX 24

Administrative Problems in India Command, 1942–43

See Maps 4 and 14 and Sketches 17 and 20

On the outbreak of war in Europe in September 1939, the Indian Army was responsible for the defence of the North West Frontier and for internal security. It had also to provide three infantry brigade groups for service overseas. India's administrative lay-out was designed to maintain her peacetime forces and faced north-west. All her administrative installations had been placed near the ports of Bombay and Karachi, and along the main railway and road communications which led from the interior to the North West Frontier.

Between 1939 and 1941 the Indian Army was greatly expanded to meet the needs of the Commonwealth, and Indian formations were sent to Egypt, Iraq and Malaya. With the expansion of the armed forces from 200,000 to some 900,000 men, there had to be a corresponding increase in the administrative installations (ordnance depots, army service corps supply and transport bases, workshops, hospitals, barracks and hutted camps) within India. A large number of new installations, sited to maintain troops on the North West Frontier or forces overseas through the ports of Bombay and Karachi, were therefore built. This expansion and the increased production of munitions and equipment threw a considerable strain on India's engineering resources and railways, but their capacity was able to meet the additional load.

The situation changed abruptly with the outbreak of war with Japan in December 1941 and the loss, early in 1942, of Malaya, the Netherlands East Indies and southern Burma. India then faced the possibility of invasion across her north-eastern frontier or at any point along her coast-line on the Bay of Bengal. Formations had to be deployed in Assam and eastern Bengal, in the Calcutta area and in southern India in the vicinity of Madras and Vizagapatam; a new administrative lay-out facing east had to be organized, new airfields built and the capacity of the existing communications to Assam and eastern Bengal greatly expanded.[1]

PART I: THE BUILD-UP OF INDIA AS A BASE FOR SOUTH-EAST ASIA

In January 1942, work was begun on a reserve supply depot and an engineer depot at Benares and a reserve ordnance and ammunition depot at Jamalpur. These depots had access to the Assam and eastern Bengal rail systems at the Amingaon and Tistamukh ferries respectively by two routes: the metre gauge line north of the Ganges, or the broad gauge to the

---
[1] See Chapter III.

junctions with the metre gauge at Parbatipur and Santahar. At the same time advanced depots were established in Assam and eastern Bengal.[1]

This was but a beginning. During the spring of 1942, India Command began to consider the lay-out of the country as a base for the larger forces which would eventually be required for the recapture of Burma, Malaya and the Netherlands East Indies. On the 23rd June 1942, the War Office gave sanction for administrative planning to be based on 28 divisions (or their equivalent) of which $6\frac{1}{2}$ divisions could be assumed to be British and the remainder Indian. On the 29th December 1942 the Commander-in-Chief was told to plan the Indian base on revised figures: 31 divisions (or their equivalent) for India, 3 for Ceylon and 85 R.A.F. and 15 U.S.A.A.F. squadrons. The total number included some 240,000 British troops. The figures were arrived at in the following way: two British divisions (2nd and 70th); twelve Indian divisions (32nd and 43rd Armoured and 7th, 14th, 17th, 19th, 23rd, 25th, 26th and 39th Infantry Divisions in India, and 20th and 34th Infantry Divisions in Ceylon); one West African and one East African division; and the equivalent of fifteen more divisions including a parachute brigade, three tank brigades, four unattached brigades, a L.R.P. brigade, brigades for the defence of the North West Frontier, internal security troops, the remnants of the Burma Army, the Chinese forces in India and levies and local forces in Assam and Ceylon.

Early in 1943 plans were made to lay out the base so that, in addition to maintaining the forces in India for internal security, the defence of the North West Frontier and the training establishments, it could support the forces required for 'Anakim' through east coast ports or across the eastern frontier. These were assessed at eleven divisions, one tank brigade and seventy-six air force squadrons. On the 4th March 1943, sanction was given to increase the potential capacity of the base to allow for a 50 per cent. increase in the forces for 'Anakim'.

Actual planning for the lay-out of the base began in January 1943. Four 'Reserve Bases', each to hold thirty days' supplies for the forces it was to maintain, were to be established. No. 1 Reserve Base at Lahore and No. 2 Reserve Base at Benares were to maintain the forces retained in India (including Assam and eastern Bengal) and be developed out of the existing installations and depots. Two entirely new bases—No. 3 Reserve Base at Panagarh (98 miles west of Calcutta) and No. 4 Reserve Base at Avadi (20 miles west of Madras)—were to be built to maintain through the ports of Calcutta and Madras the forces earmarked for 'Anakim'. Both these had to be planned so that they could be greatly expanded if necessary. Since Panagarh was some distance from the port of Calcutta, the existing transit depot had to be extended, and a transit area had to be constructed at Vizagapatam which would have to be used as a subsidiary port for the maintenance of overseas forces.

In April 1943, Eastern Army began work on No. 3 Reserve Base at Panagarh. The whole area, some thirty square miles of flat rice-growing

---

[1] See page 53.

APPENDIX 24

country, was drained, the inhabitants of fourteen villages housed elsewhere, and railways, roads, bridges, power stations and accommodation for stores and men built. In May 1943, Southern Army began No. 4 Reserve Base at Avadi on an area of twenty-seven square miles of flat land adjoining the main Madras–Bombay railway line and the Madras–Bangalore road. This, as originally planned, was to hold 300,000 tons of engineer stores, 72,000 tons of supplies, 50,000 tons of petrol, 30,000 tons of ammunition, 90,000 tons of ordnance stores and 100,000 tons of R.A.F. stores, as well as medical, veterinary and N.A.A.F.I. stores. Both were colossal engineering projects and were (with expansions) still in hand when the war came to an end in 1945.

PART II: THE IMPROVEMENT OF THE RAIL AND RIVER COMMUNICATIONS FROM INDIA BASE TO THE NORTH-EAST FRONTIER IN ASSAM AND EASTERN BENGAL

The rail and river communications to Assam and eastern Bengal were long, difficult and liable to interruption. In 1941 they had a very poor carrying capacity. The distances from the nearest bases in eastern India (Calcutta and Benares) to the railheads in Assam (Dimapur and Ledo) and to Chittagong in eastern Bengal were immense. From Calcutta by way of Parbatipur to Dimapur and Ledo by rail the distances were 340 and 530 miles respectively; from Benares to these railheads were 730 and 920 miles respectively: from Calcutta to Chittagong by the shortest all-rail route by the Tistamukh ferry was over 500 miles; by rail and river through Goalundo 340 miles including a five-hour river journey to Chandpur, and by sea 330 miles. The river route to Dibrugarh from Goalundo or Sirajganj served by broad gauge railway from Calcutta was about 650 miles, and the turn-round of steamers took some 33 days. Most of the stores and equipment reaching India from overseas had to be disembarked at Bombay and carried a further 1,130 miles across India to the Calcutta area. The same applied to ammunition manufactured or filled at the Kirkee (near Poona) group of factories. In terms of European distances most of the imported requirements of the troops on the Assam frontier had to be transported by rail some 1,600 miles, a distance equivalent to that from London to the vicinity of Moscow, and all supplies had to be taken forward from the nearest bases in India for a distance equivalent to a journey from London to Madrid.

Distance was not the only difficulty. India's main railway lines were broad gauge, whereas those in eastern Bengal and Assam were metre gauge; this meant that goods had to be transferred from one set of trucks to others of a smaller carrying capacity at Benares, Mokameh Ghat, Santahar or Parbatipur. Since the unbridged Brahmaputra River separated the railways in Assam and eastern Bengal from the Indian rail system, all goods had to be unloaded, taken across the river and reloaded, except at the rail ferries at Tistamukh and Amingaon. The river itself was always changing. Its level varied considerably during the year, and it frequently shifted its bed so that the river ports had not only to be capable of dealing with different levels but often had to be reconstructed, when the river either encroached on or receded from them. Since there was no road access to either Assam or eastern Bengal, all vehicles for these areas had to be taken by rail to the Amingaon–Pandu ferry where there was access to the Assam trunk road, or by rail or sea to Chittagong. The metre gauge railway from Parbatipur to the river port of Amingaon along the foothills of the Himalayas was liable to wash-outs during the annual monsoon.

The capacity of the metre gauge railways in north-east India, Assam and eastern Bengal was not great since they were designed and run to meet the needs of the local tea and agricultural industries. The system was single-line with few crossing places, the number of locomotives and the quantity of rolling stock was small and signalling equipment was of the simplest kind. Traffic density was therefore low and the running of the system not highly efficient. The ferries at Tistamukh and Amingaon were designed solely to meet the average demands throughout the year.

The capacity of the river line of communications to the ports in Assam at Goalpara, Pandu, Silghat, Donaigaon, Neamati and Dibrugarh had been considerably reduced by sending river craft and barges to Iraq.

Throughout 1942 General Headquarters, India, endeavoured to improve communications to Assam and eastern Bengal. The target was to deliver 1,720 tons per day to Dimapur and Ledo (the two railheads) and 250 tons a day to eastern Bengal, exclusive of troop, vehicle and animal trains and civil traffic. The capacity of the ferries at Tistamukh and Amingaon was increased. Additional crossing places on the single-line metre gauge railway were built and the railway telegraph system improved, so that the number of daily train paths could be increased. Work was begun on the Assam access road to Jogighopa to relieve the railways of the carriage of vehicles. The number of metre gauge locomotives and rolling stock on the Bengal and Assam systems was increased by diversion from other metre gauge systems within India, and efforts were made to get supplies of locomotives, trucks and up-to-date signalling equipment etc. from overseas. Roads were built from Golaghat to Dimapur and from Bongaigaon to Jogighopa, and an M.T. ferry installed between Jogighopa and Goalpara; 160 vehicles a day could then be off loaded at Bongaigaon and driven along the Assam trunk road to Dimapur (and so to Imphal) and Ledo, thus relieving rail capacity east of Bongaigaon. A river port capable of handling 700-1,000 tons a day was developed at Neamati (Donaigaon), and the 2 foot gauge rail from Neamati to Furkating was converted to metre gauge. Middle East Command was asked to release river craft from Iraq so that the river route from Calcutta to Dibrugarh could be improved. The port of Chittagong, put out of action in May 1942, was improved in the late summer of 1942 and used to supply the forces in Arakan as far as possible so as to relieve the load on the railways in eastern Bengal.

These efforts to improve the lines of communication were hampered by an exceptionally severe monsoon which caused wash-outs on the metre gauge railway between Lalmanirhat and Amingaon, thus holding up traffic on this section and forcing it to be diverted on to the river route from Tistamukh and Dhubri to Pandu. In addition, the general inefficiency of

APPENDIX 24

the rail system and shortage of locomotives and trucks continually caused traffic congestion, and although the theoretical number of train paths to Amingaon was 11 per day each way, with trains of 40/45 (6 ton load) trucks, it was not till June/July 1943 that the target of 1,720 tons a day (464 tons of petrol and 1,256 tons of stores) was reached. Of this, 52 per cent. was carried by rail and ferry and 25 per cent. by river to Pandu and thence onwards by the Assam railway to the railheads. The remaining 23 per cent. was carried either by river to Dibrugarh or by rail from the Tistamukh–Bahadurabad ferry to Chandranathpur and over the hill section to Lumding, where it joined the main stream from Pandu. In addition to this tonnage, the rail and river routes had to meet the engineer requirements for airfield construction and civil needs, as well as carry both British and American formations and units with their vehicles. The river fleet available was only 27,000 shipping tons. This was used mainly in the upper reaches of the river to shorten the turn-round and to by-pass the bottle-necks on the rail route.

In July 1943, General Auchinleck was planning to deliver to the Assam railheads some 3,400 tons a day by the 1st November 1943. An examination of the problem showed that two train paths daily had to be reserved for British and American troop trains, one for an ambulance train and five for mail, civil goods, coal and railway services. On the eastern Bengal system, served from the Tistamukh rail ferry, four train paths daily had to be reserved for civil needs and three train paths for the maintenance of the troops and air force in the Agartala–Chittagong area (750 tons of stores to Chittagong and 176 tons of petrol). Deliveries to the American and British forces in Assam would have to be:

American—360 tons of petrol and 1,720 tons of stores daily, delivered at Ledo, Chabua, Jorhat and Tinsukia;

British—340 tons of petrol, 1,600 tons of stores and 160 vehicles daily, delivered at Bongaigaon (vehicles), Dimapur and along the L. of C.

This made a grand total of 700 tons of petrol and 3,320 tons of stores daily.

To enable this target to be reached, the following plans were made:

(i) The metre gauge system from Parbatipur to Amingaon and from Pandu to Ledo would be improved to carry a sustained maximum single line traffic of 14 trains of 50/60 wagons daily each way. For this, 16 additional stations and extra loops at other stations would be needed.

(ii) The narrow gauge (tea estate) railway from Jorhat to Mariani would be converted to metre gauge.

(iii) The terminal and transfer capacities would be increased so that:

(a) The broad to metre gauge transhipment facilities at Parbatipur and Santahar could handle 160 motor vehicles, 2,200 tons of stores and 800 tons of oil daily.

(b) The railhead at Bongaigaon could handle 160 vehicles and 250 tons of vehicle stores a day.

(c) The river ports could handle the following tonnages—Goalundo 500, Sirajganj 1,000, Tistamukh 700, Dhubri 1,200 stores and 360 oil, Pandu 1,500 and Neamati 1,200 tons a day.

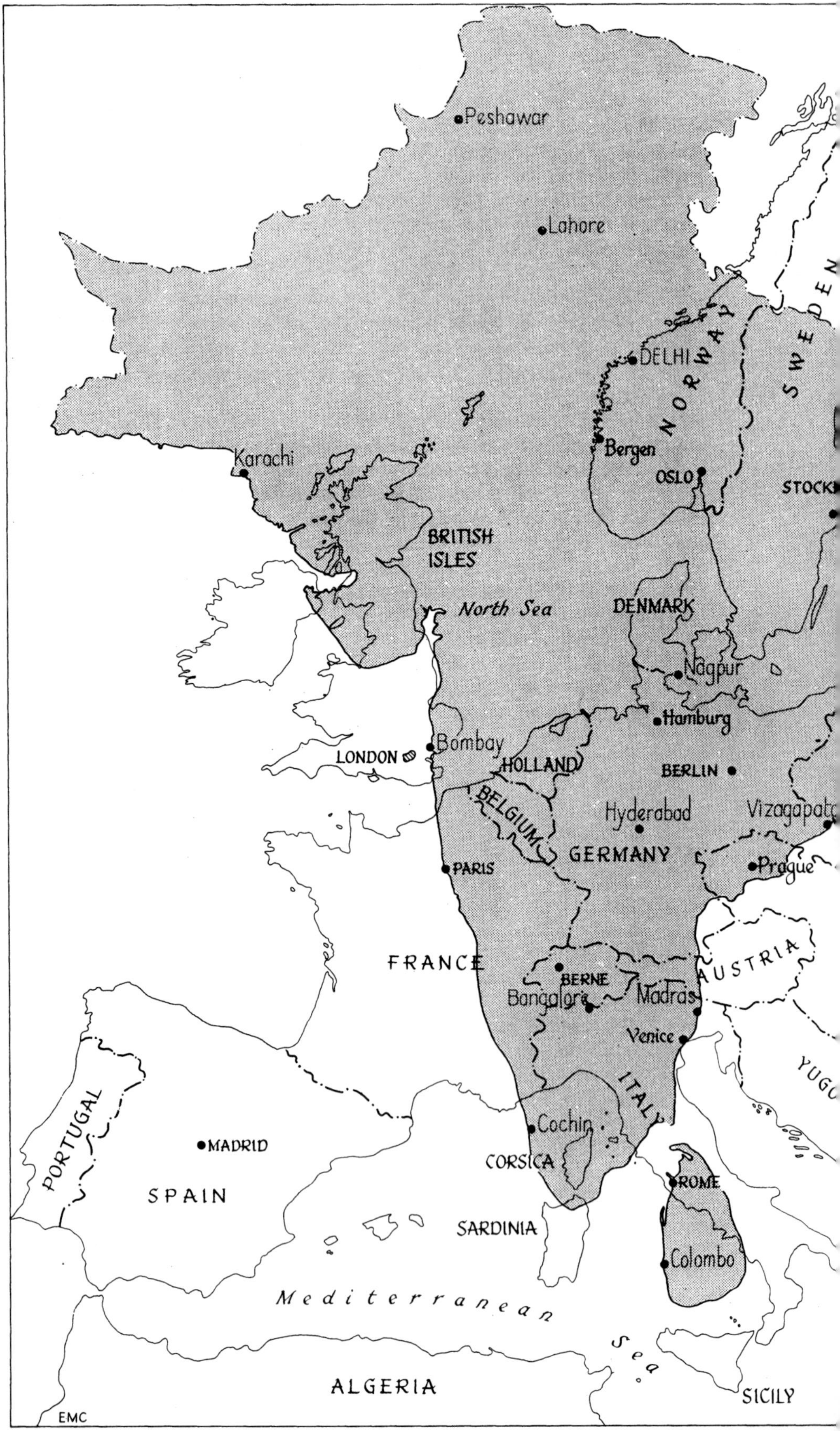

Peshawar
Lahore
DELHI
NORWAY
SWEDEN
Bergen
OSLO
STOCK
Karachi
BRITISH ISLES
North Sea
DENMARK
Nagpur
Hamburg
Bombay
LONDON
HOLLAND
BERLIN
BELGIUM
Hyderabad
Vizagapat
GERMANY
PARIS
Prague
AUSTRIA
FRANCE
BERNE
Bangalore
Madras
Venice
YUGO
PORTUGAL
ITALY
Cochin
MADRID
CORSICA
ROME
SPAIN
SARDINIA
Colombo
Mediterranean Sea
ALGERIA
SICILY
EMC

INDIA SUPERIMPOSED ON EUROPE

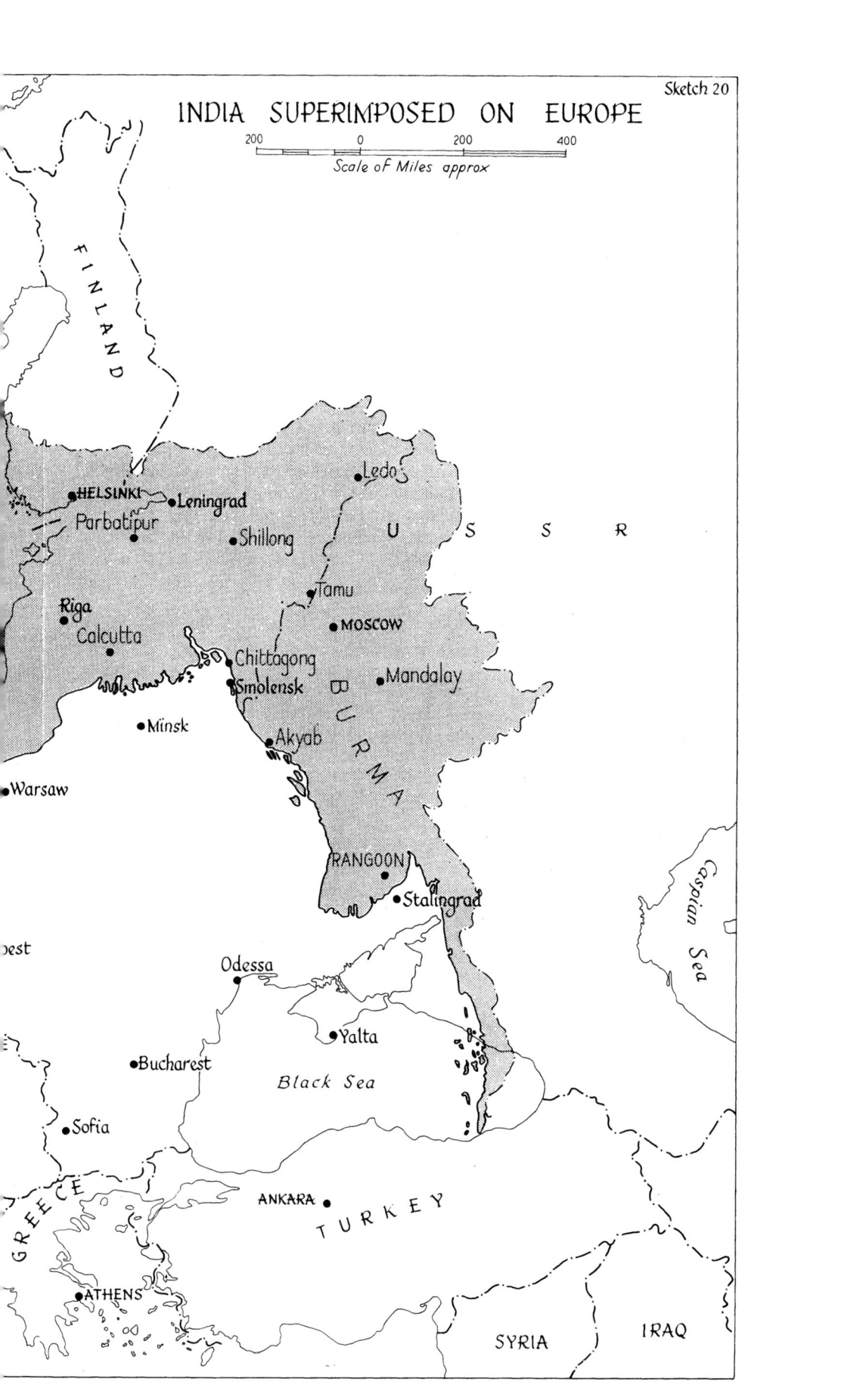

Sketch 20

(iv) Petrol for the airfields in north-eastern Assam, in the Jorhat and Tezpur areas, and for the Ledo area would be routed by rail in bulk containers from Parbatipur to Dhubri and thence by river to Tezpur, Neamati and Dibrugarh. From these ports it would be piped to the airfields and Tinsukia.

(v) Petrol for the Imphal area would be routed either by sea to Chittagong and thence by rail tank wagon to Chandranathpur, or by rail over the Tistamukh ferry to Chandranathpur. From this point it would be piped over the hill section and through Lumding to Dimapur.

(vi) The river fleet available for military purposes would be brought up to an approximate total of 84,000 shipping tons (76,000 for stores and 8,000 for oil).

The transportation and movement plan to meet these requirements is shown in the table at the end of the appendix. There was surplus capacity in many parts of the system, but there were bottle-necks on the rail between Parbatipur and Golakganj and between Lumding and Dimapur which limited the capacity of the whole. It was proposed to double the line in these two sections.

PART III: SUPPLY AHEAD OF THE RAILHEADS IN ASSAM AND EASTERN BENGAL

The line of communication from railhead at Dimapur (Manipur Road) to the frontier was the Imphal Road. In December 1941, for the first 134 miles to Imphal it was an all-weather single-way tarmac road. A roughly metalled and bridged road ran for 28 miles on to Palel; from there a pack track crossed the mountains to Tamu in the Kabaw Valley, 56 miles further on.

From Dimapur the road ran for 10 miles through flat, thickly forested country and then climbed through steep jungle-clad mountains for 36 miles to Kohima (4,400 feet). For the next 21 miles to Mao (4,900 feet), the road traversed the lower slope of the main mountain range, crossing many deep ravines. From there, the road passed through some 39 miles of more open grassland country at an average elevation of 4,000 feet, until it descended to the floor of the Manipur River valley just before Kangpokpi (3,500 feet). It then followed the valley to Kanglatongbi (2,900 feet) beyond which it debouched on to the Imphal plain (2,400 feet). From a point 10 miles south of Dimapur to Mao the road was subject to frequent landslides during the monsoon, the worst point being a few miles on the Dimapur side of Kohima where, for several miles, it traversed a very steep shale slope. In this sector the whole mountainside over stretches of anything from a few yards to a furlong or more would slowly slide downhill for days on end, making it extremely difficult to keep open any sort of track. The normal rock and earthfall type of landslide could usually be cleared in a matter of hours, but the larger shale slides prevented through motor traffic for weeks at a time. The L. of C. to Kohima and Imphal was thus very precarious during the monsoon.

APPENDIX 24

In December 1941, it was planned to make the Imphal Road the main arterial road into Burma by extending it to Tamu and improving it to an all-weather two-way road capable of taking 200 vehicles a day, with bridges to take 10 ton vehicles. With the help of labour from the Indian Tea Association, a fair-weather road from Palel to Tamu was completed by the 28th April 1942, just before the Army in Burma reached the frontier. On the 5th May, Eastern Army took over responsibility for the Manipur Road base at Dimapur from General Headquarters, India. On the 15th, Headquarters IV Corps was established at Imphal and became responsible for the Imphal Road. At that time there were seven General Purpose Transport (G.P.T.) companies and 300 impressed civilian lorries of all types to work the base and carry supplies forward, but mobile workshops and stocks of vehicle spare parts were short.

After the arrival of the Burma Army, it was estimated that 500 tons of stores and supplies would be required daily at or forward of Imphal for maintenance purposes. Plans were made for mixed trains carrying 900 tons to reach Dimapur daily, so that reserves could be built up at the Manipur Road base. During June, traffic had to be diverted to the river because of the wash-outs on the railway, and deliveries to the base fell to 500 tons. On the 18th June the road at Milestone 42 (four miles north of Kohima) slipped, and all stores had to be carried by porter across the gap. The supply of petrol for IV Corps transport was as a result so reduced that troops and animals had to be put on half rations. A temporary repair was made early in July, but under the weight of heavily-loaded supply lorries the road again gradually subsided until the dip was such that no vehicle could make the ascent. Traffic had then to be stopped and the road rebuilt. After each repair, the road could be used for short periods only before it again subsided, since the work was ineffective until a spell of dry weather allowed the ground to dry out.

From the beginning of August, in addition to the stores for the maintenance and re-equipment of 17th Indian Division, the road had to carry reinforcements and returning leave parties, amounting to 27,000 men and 1,800 mules a month. To reduce the load on the transport, a series of staging camps was built at intervals of some fourteen miles along the road in areas as free as possible from malaria so that troops and animals could march. It was soon found necessary, however, to use motor transport to move reinforcements out of the highly malarial area around Dimapur to the Kohima area, and over other malarial stretches of the road.

While the load on the road steadily increased, the carrying capacity along it did not, although one new G.P.T. company arrived every week and theoretically there should have been ample transport. But the drivers were inexperienced and not used to driving on mountain roads in mist and cloud as was normal in the monsoon; the accident rate was therefore very high.[1] Convoys often had to spend the night on the road-

---

[1] Drivers in M.T. training establishments were passed out fit to drive over most difficult obstacle courses. They then went on leave before being posted to units or reinforcement camps, and soon lost their newly-acquired skill. It thus became necessary to institute refresher courses at reinforcement camps.

side where the drivers became infected with malaria and caught chills. Thus casualties from malaria and dysentery among drivers soon became very high in comparison with men of other units in the area and often reached 75 per cent. The supply of drivers could not keep pace, and vehicles frequently were off the road. Eventually newly-raised G.P.T. companies had to be sent to Dimapur without vehicles, and the loss of lift made up by increasing the number of working lorries in the companies already in Assam by 20 per cent.

The maintenance facilities for vehicles on the Imphal Road and within IV Corps were inadequate. The shortage of workshop units, the high rate of sickness, the low standard of skill among workshop fitters, combined with the shortage of spares at the Manipur Road base, resulted in minor damage or breakdowns rapidly developing into second or even third line repairs and the number of vehicles off the road grew steadily. Since the base workshop then under construction for Eastern Army at Jorhat was not in service during 1942, the wastage of vehicles from Assam could not be checked. This in turn added to the strain on the railways, since all replacement vehicles had to be brought forward by rail. By the end of the year, there was a deficiency of 1,600 vehicles in IV Corps area alone, and 1,400 additional vehicles were urgently needed to meet the increasing demands arising from airfield construction.

The effect of all this was that the capacity of the Imphal road was never sufficient to meet the demands. The IV Corps administrative staff had to allot priorities throughout the monsoon. Since the maintenance of the road, including its doubling and improvement, was clearly the first call, high priority had to be given to the provision of transport for engineer stores. The troops had consequently to go on short rations for long periods, and reserves of equipment and ammunition had to be kept back at the base. Even so, engineer stores were in short supply. An engineer war diary of the Chief Engineer (Ops.) IV Corps, responsible for road construction forward of Kanglatongbi, shows that by the 9th August 1942 less than 100 tons of engineer stores had reached him in the previous 11 weeks and that during August only 72 vehicle loads reached Imphal.

Although much work had been done on the road by the end of November 1942, it was still only a one-way all-weather road, with passing places, as far as Palel. In order to increase the tonnage carried, improve the maintenance, reduce the appalling wastage of vehicles and make more vehicles available for stocking forward of Imphal, a new system of operating the traffic on the road was introduced. On the 14th December, a Headquarters Line of Communication Road Transport, under command of Colonel R. J. Holmes and controlled by IV Corps, was formed to take over all the G.P.T. companies operating between Dimapur and Imphal, and organize their running and maintenance on the lines of the system operated in pre-war days by the London General Omnibus Company.[1] The new headquarters became responsible for the technical operation of

---

[1] As a civilian, Colonel Holmes had previously been responsible for the organization of 'help to China' traffic on the Burma Road. See page 36.

transport on the Imphal Road, including collecting from and distributing to depots, and for ensuring that the maximum number of vehicles was loaded and despatched daily to destinations specified by IV Corps.

The features of the system applied to the Imphal Road were:
  (a) Vehicles, but not drivers, were divorced from the G.P.T. units and operated as a pool.
  (b) The road was divided into sections, each of which had its permanent staff of drivers who drove within that section only.
  (c) Vehicles were run through from one terminal to the other, drivers taking over vehicles in their respective sections.
  (d) The officers and men of the G.P.T. companies kept their organization to facilitate administration, and to avoid dislocation if a unit were required for another rôle.
  (e) G.P.T. companies had no responsibility for maintenance of vehicles. This was carried out by a number of service stations manned by officers and men taken from ordnance workshop companies, light aid detachments and ordnance recovery units, all pooled for the purpose.

The advantages and disadvantages of this system were:
  (a) Free, independent and continuous running traffic on a 24-hour basis, but for this the road would have to be two-way.
  (b) No waste of time on shifting loads at intermediate points on the route, and a quick turn-round, provided that the organization at terminal points worked round the clock and there were adequate supervisory staff and labour.
  (c) An even flow along the road, but this demanded efficient traffic and movement control, adequate servicing and recovery arrangements and a reserve pool of vehicles as a buffer between the workshops and those responsible for operating the traffic.
  (d) Sickness would be greatly reduced, since most of the drivers and mechanics could be accommodated in non-malarial areas on the high ground in the vicinity of Kohima and Mao.

Since the road was not fully two-way to Imphal till the 15th February 1943 and to Palel till the early part of March, the system came into being gradually. Much construction work had to be undertaken to provide roads and loading facilities within terminal depots, living accommodation for officers and men in the health belt, accommodation for workshops and parking areas for vehicles. Its control passed from IV Corps to Eastern Army on the 16th March 1943.

On the 1st August, the L.G.O.C. system was modified and renamed the Round the Clock (R.T.C.) system. The change was made because it was found that drivers, divorced from their vehicles, and maintenance personnel in workshops dealing with pooled rather than specified vehicles, had little interest in their proper upkeep, and that the control of the drivers was inadequate. The object of the new system was to ensure that:
  (a) G.P.T. companies and their drivers were made responsible for their vehicles by giving a specific number to each company.

APPENDIX 24

    (b) Workshops were allotted a specific number of vehicles for which they were solely responsible.

    (c) The daily lift would still operate 'round the clock'.

Under the R.T.C. system, each G.P.T. company would hold 90 load-carrying vehicles of which 60 would be operating and 30 at rest or under repair. These 30 would be held by the workshops which serviced the company. The 60 vehicles would operate on specific timings to lift 40 loads (100 tons a day) every 24 hours over a point to point distance of 150 miles (300 miles round trip). Each G.P.T. company would therefore cover 12,000 miles per day or 360,000 miles in a 30-day month, and each of the 60 vehicles 6,000 miles a month. On the 15th and 30th of each month, 30 vehicles would be delivered to the workshops and replaced by 30 from the pool. Hence, after every 30 days of work (6,000 miles) each vehicle would spend 15 days in workshops or at rest, during which time it would be made fit for the next 6,000 miles. Operational casualties would be immediately replaced from the pool. One driver was to remain with each vehicle in the pool to maintain contact between the company and the vehicle. Each workshop would be responsible for approximately 300 vehicles, and for all vehicles breaking down on the section of the road allotted to it.

The statistics for the transport along the Imphal Road are not available before February 1943. The table below gives the figures from February to October 1943.

The figures show that, with the advent of the dry weather, the great efforts put into the improvement and maintenance of the road itself and the organization of the transport operating on it began to bear fruit. From the day he assumed command in Assam, the Commander IV Corps had never been sure what supplies and equipment he would receive by any given time. In October 1943, for the first time, the state of the road and the organization of the transport ensured that he could base his future plans on forecasts of tonnages to be delivered at Imphal which would in all probability be met.

	February	March	April	May[1]	June[1]	July[1]	August[1]	Sept.[1]	Oct.
Average number of load-carrying vehicles	744	873	836	743	754	816	915	1,186	1,323
Average number in workshops	177	315	348	379	373	347	235	459	443
Average number running daily	567	558	488	364	381	469	680	727	880
Average number sent forward daily	245	251	194	144	196	297	207	336	432
Tons delivered a month	18,375	23,343	14,550	11,160	14,175	22,205	15,519	30,204	40,212
Total mileage (millions)	1·8	2·0	1·45	1·1	1·4	2·45	1·6	2·8	3·8
Number of accidents	250	194	103	75	132	176	133	384	313

[1] Monsoon months.

Normal Routing of Stores

	Train paths per day available	Train paths required for troop and ambulance trains	Train paths for mixed civil requirements, Assam	Coal for consumption, Assam	Train paths reserved for military traffic to eastern Bengal	Train paths reserved for civil traffic to eastern Bengal	Total train paths reserved	Balance available for carriage of stores
Parbatipur–Golakganj	14	3	4	–	–	–	7	7
Golakganj–Dhubri	12	–	3	–	–	–	3	9
Golakganj–Bongaigaon	14	3	4	–	–	–	7	7
Bongaigaon–Amingaon	11	3	4	–	–	–	7	4
Amingaon–Pandu	250 wgs	–	80 wgs	–	–	–	80 wgs	170 wgs
Dhubri–Pandu	–	–	–	–	–	–	–	–
Pandu–Lumding	14	3	4	–	–	–	7	7
Santahar–Tistamukh	13	–	1	1	3	4	9	4
Tistamukh–Bahadurabad	200 wgs	–	–	50 wgs	–	80 wgs	130 wgs	70 wgs
Bahadurabad–Akhaura	13	–	1	1	3	4	9	4
Chittagong–Akhaura	11	–	1	–	3	3	7	4
Akhaura–Badarpur	10	–	1	1	–	4	6	4
Badarpur–Lumding	9	–	1	2	–	3	6	3
Lumding–Dimapur	14	3	4	1	–	1	9	5
Dimapur–Mariani	14	2	4	1	–	1	8	6
Calcutta–Neamati and Dibrugarh	–	–	–	–	–	–	–	–
Goalundo–Neamati	–	–	–	–	–	–	–	–
Sirajganj–Neamati	–	–	–	–	–	–	–	–
Tistamukh–Neamati	–	–	–	–	–	–	–	–
Dhubri–Neamati	–	–	–	–	–	–	–	–
Neamati–Jorhat	12	1	3	–	–	–	4	8
Jorhat–Mariani	12	1	3	–	–	–	4	8
Mariani–Tinsukia	14	2	4	1	–	1	8	6
Tinsukia–Ledo	13	3	4	–	–	–	7	6
Tinsukia–Dibrugarh	13	2	4	–	–	–	6	7

Remarks:

Petrol (tons per day):
- Jorhat 180 (A) ⎫
- Chabua 150 (A) ⎬ 360
- Tinsukia 30 (A) ⎭
- Pandu 30 (B) ⎫ 340
- Dimapur 310 (B) ⎭
- Akhaura–Silchar 120·(B)
- Mymensingh 56·(B)
- Local to Ledo 80·(A)

British stores (tons per day):
- Dimapur 1,500 ⎫ 1,600
- Pandu 100 ⎭
- Chittagong (by sea)
  - for eastern Bengal 500
  - for transit 250

American stores (tons per day):
- Ledo 960 ⎫
- Chabua 400 ⎬
- Jorhat 360 ⎭

Petrol to Assam

aximum gons per in after evelop- ment	Wagon loads per day available (tons)	Vehicles per day to Bongaigaon for road to Assam	Balance wagon loads per day available (tons)	Capacity in tons a day available	Petrol	British stores	American stores	Spare capacity	Tonnage of river craft required
60	420	160	260	1,560	360	1,200	–	–	–
60	540	–	–	3,240	330	360	–	2,550	–
60	420	160	260	1,560	30	840	–	690	–
60	240	–	–	1,440	30	840	–	570	–
–	170	–	–	1,020	30	840	–	150	–
–	–	–	–	–	–	360	–	–	4,680
50	350	–	–	2,100	–	1,100	–	1,000	–
60	240	–	–	1,440	–	400	370	670	–
–	70	–	–	420	–	400	–	20	–
60	240	–	–	1,440	56	400	–	984	–
45	180	–	–	1,080	516	250[1]	–	314	–
40	160	–	–	960	460[2]	400	–	100	–
24	72	–	–	432	–	400	–	32	–
50	250	–	–	1,500	–	1,500	–	–	–
50	300	–	–	1,800	30	–	–	1,770	–
–	–	–	–	–	–	–	550[3]	–	34,530
–	–	–	–	–	–	–	300	–	10,500
–	–	–	–	–	–	–	500	–	15,500
–	–	–	–	–	–	–	370	–	10,360
–	–	–	–	–	330	–	–	–	7,920
35	280	–	–	1,680	330	–	1,200	150	–
35	280	–	–	1,680	150	–	840	690	–
50	300	–	–	1,800	180	–	840	780	–
50	300	–	–	1,800	–	80	960	760	–
50	350	–	–	2,100	150	–	520	1,430	–

Total river tonnage:
Stores   75,570
Oil   7,920
         _____
         83,490

Notes:
[1] By sea to Chittagong plus 500 tons for eastern Bengal.
[2] 340 tons to pipe-line, 120 local consumption.
[3] 30 to Neamati and 520 to Dibrugarh.
(A) Petrol for American use.
(B) Petrol for British use.

APPENDIX 25

Supply and Administrative Problems during the First Chindit Expedition

1. Air Supply Organization at Agartala

Once across the Chindwin, the Chindits (77th Brigade) were to be supplied by air at points selected by themselves when and where required.

A small detachment of transport aircraft from 31 Squadron R.A.F. at Tezpur was allotted for this task. It was located at Agartala and varied in size during the expedition, but seldom had more than three Hudson and three D.C.3 aircraft, since the squadron had to supply the detachment at Fort Hertz and the Chin Hills Battalion at Falam. Since the Chindits were to operate in a number of columns which might be widely separated, this threw a very heavy load on it. A base forwarding party under command of the rear headquarters of 77th Brigade, made up of rear parties from the columns and No. 1 Air Supply Company, R.I.A.S.C., and located alongside it, was responsible for the loading of the supply aircraft with the detailed requirements of each Chindit column.

Eastern Army placed 77th Brigade under operational control of IV Corps, but retained responsibility for the administration of the brigade and the air base. This was to prove unsatisfactory in practice.

2. Organization of Supply Drops

The vital factor in the organization was the wireless sets carried by the Chindit columns, since their loss or failure would prevent the column from taking an effective part in the operation or remaining in the chain of supply. Each column was provided with a F.S.6 set for communication within the brigade and a 1082/83 R.A.F. set, converted for pack transport, for communication with the air base. Since the R.A.F. set was bulky and cumbersome and when ready for transport the heaviest part weighed 200/240 lbs., only the biggest mountain artillery mules could be used to carry it.

It was arranged that a column wanting a supply drop would send a warning message in cipher 36/48 hours in advance giving a list of requirements, and the date and approximate locality for the drop. This was to be followed by another, if possible 12 hours before the time of the drop, giving final details of time and place. These demands were to be sent through headquarters of the brigade in the field.

It was assumed that supply drops could be successfully made only on previously reconnoitred flat open spaces, such as ricefields or clearings in the jungle. Since these areas were few in number and were usually near villages and tracks, there was always the risk that the Japanese would forecast the position of the next drop. In practice, it was found that a drop could be made successfully almost anywhere, even in jungle, where it was found that the trees broke the fall of statichutes which opened imperfectly, and those which became entangled in the trees could easily be cut down. Food and equipment were to be dropped by statichute, and fodder for animals by free drop.

After having selected the dropping area, the columns would signal the position by distance and bearing from some definite point which could easily be recognized from the air. When dropping was to take place during the hours of darkness, the selected area would be indicated by a line of fires, or on occasions by Verey lights or Aldis lamps; by day, smoke and ground signals would be used. Standard recognition signals were instituted, and no drops were to take place unless the aircraft received the appropriate signals.

3. Difficulties Encountered in Practice

It was planned that each supply aircraft was to be provided with an escort of two fighters. As the Chindits moved deeper and deeper into Burma, the range became too great for the fighters and they had to refuel at Imphal. This introduced complications. Further, owing to the shortage of fighter aircraft, either the number of supply sorties or the escort had to be reduced. In the latter stages of the operation when drops were very urgent and the range outside that of fighters, the supply aircraft operated without escort. Nevertheless, not a single aircraft was lost throughout the operation.

It was soon found that, owing to the volume of wireless traffic within the brigade, it was not always possible for columns to submit their detailed requirements and arrangements for drops through brigade headquarters, and that they were forced to communicate their drop requirements direct to Agartala. This prevented control of demands in the common interest and tended to squander wireless time. As Agartala had no guidance on priorities, a modest demand meriting priority might have to await the dropping of an excessive demand elsewhere. A solution to the problem was provided by IV Corps taking all supply-dropping messages and relaying items on priorities, as laid down by Wingate, to Agartala.

The division of administrative responsibility between Eastern Army and IV Corps created difficulties. Although IV Corps was responsible for the operations of the Chindits, the detachment at Fort Hertz and the Chin Hills Battalion, Eastern Army controlled the supply organization. With the small number of supply aircraft available, IV Corps, although it had no control over Agartala, had to decide on priorities not only between the Chindits and the other areas for which it was responsible, but often between the columns of the Chindits themselves. These many difficulties were overcome in practice and the organization eventually worked efficiently, but not until IV Corps had in effect taken control over both operations and administration.

4. The Adequacy of the Supplies Delivered

Although the system of air supply was proved and worked as efficiently as could be expected in the circumstances then ruling, it did not follow that the Chindits were adequately fed. The hard scale daily ration laid down was:

Shakapura Biscuit	12 oz.
Cheese	2 oz.
Milk powder	1 oz.
Raisins and almonds	9 oz.
Tea	¾ oz.
Sugar	4 oz.
Acid drops or chocolate	1 oz.
Salt	½ oz.
Cigarettes	2 packets of ten
Matches	1 box

The troops complained that the ration was inadequate. It certainly lacked fats and bulk and needed careful supplementing from local produce, which was often unprocurable. It will be noted that the ration contained nothing which required cooking, except water for tea, since it was expected that the troops would not be able to count on more than twenty minutes for meals. The ration was supplemented at times by drops of such items as tins of corned beef, baked beans.

It was believed that men could keep fit on this ration for three months at a spell. The nature of the operation did not, however, enable columns to organize a supply drop as and when required, and none of them received its full scale in the field. The troops entered Burma in the middle of February and 70 per cent. were back by the first week in June. The average number of rations a man received was approximately 40 in 80 days, or 50 per cent., and the men became emaciated and eventually lost their vigour. This poor result was due partly to the shortage of supply aircraft and partly to the exigencies of the operation. After dispersal, or if wireless communication broke down, the troops had to live on the country, a matter of considerable difficulty when in close contact with the enemy.

5. The Burden and Strain on the Man and the Animal

Each man, when fully equipped, carried about 50 pounds, which increased to 66 pounds when it included the unexpended portions of 7 days' rations. Mules carried the maximum 160 pound load. Thus marching over difficult country under such loads was a great strain on men and animals alike.

The worst feature of the operation was that, in addition to the physical strain on the man, there was the psychological effect of knowing that, if he failed through sickness or wounds, he would have to be left behind to the care of the local population. Next to the shortage of food, this had the biggest effect on morale. After the operation, it was realized that the physical strain would have to be reduced and some method of evacuating sick and wounded by air devised, if long-range penetration groups were to be of any real value in the future.

6. The Suitability of the Columns and Their Equipment

The columns as organized proved suited to the tactical and topographical conditions encountered, but events proved that they were unable to carry out opposed river crossings since they had not the numbers or strength to form and hold a bridgehead. Opposed crossings had therefore to be avoided.

Experience showed that the loads carried by man and animal could be greatly reduced since, as far as supplies were concerned, implicit trust could be placed in the R.A.F. to deliver them as required at any time and almost anywhere, as long as there were adequate numbers of aircraft.

APPENDIX 26

The Composition of 77th Indian Infantry Brigade (The Chindits), February 1943

1. Order of Battle

    13th King's Liverpool Regiment
    3/2nd Gurkha Rifles
    142 Commando Company
    2nd Burma Rifles
    Eight R.A.F. sections
    A mule transport company

2. The Brigade was divided into two groups and seven columns:

    Commander: Brigadier O. C. Wingate

Southern (No. 1) Group
  Headquarters and Nos. 1 and 2 Columns

Commander	Lieut.-Colonel L. A. Alexander[1]
No. 1 Column	Major G. Dunlop
No. 2 Column	Major A. Emmett
142nd Commando Company	Major J. B. Jeffries

Northern (No. 2) Group
  Brigade Headquarters, Group Headquarters and
  Nos. 3, 4, 5, 7 and 8 Columns[2]

Commander	Lieut.-Colonel S. A. Cooke
No. 3 Column	Major J. M. Calvert
No. 4 Column	Major R. B. G. Bromhead
No. 5 Column	Major B. E. Fergusson
No. 7 Column	Major K. D. Gilkes
No. 8 Column	Major W. P. Scott
2nd Burma Rifles	Lieut.-Colonel L. G. Wheeler[1]
Independent Mission	Captain D. C. Herring

Notes

[1] These officers were killed during the operation.

[2] No. 6 (British) Column was broken up to replace casualties during training.

Organization of Columns

Each column was made up of headquarters, an R.A.F. section to maintain wireless touch with Agartala and organize the supply drops, a signal section for communication with brigade headquarters and within the column itself, a medical section, a sabotage group, a Burma Rifles

APPENDIX 26

platoon to provide scouts, guides and interpreters to assist the column in its dealings with the local inhabitants, and the fighting portion of the column. This last consisted of an infantry company and a support group from which battle groups could be formed. The column was supplied with enough mules to carry its weapons, ammunition, equipment and wireless sets and the supplies picked up at the dropping points. The composition was:

	British Officers	Indian or Gurkha Officers	British other ranks	Indian or Gurkha other ranks	Burma Army other ranks	Total
British Columns (Nos. 5, 7 and 8)						
Headquarters	2	–	4	2	–	8
R.A.F. Section	1	–	4	–	–	5
Medical Section	1	–	2	2	–	5
Signallers	–	–	8	3	–	11
Sabotage Group	1	–	18	10	–	29
Burma Rifles Platoon	2	2	–	–	41	45
Infantry Company	5	–	110	–	–	115
Support Group	1	–	30	–	–	31
Second Line Transport	1	1	–	55	–	57
Total	14	3	176	72	41	306
Gurkha Columns (Nos. 1, 2, 3 and 4)						
Headquarters	2	–	–	6	–	8
R.A.F. Section	1	–	4	–	–	5
Medical Section	1	–	–	4	–	5
Signallers	–	–	8	5	–	13
Sabotage Group	1	–	18	10	–	29
Burma Rifles Platoon	2	2	–	–	41	45
Infantry Company	2	4	–	160	–	166
Support Group	–	1	–	40	–	41
Second Line Transport	1	1	–	55	–	57
Total	10	8	30	280	41	369

Each column was equipped with fifteen horses, fifty-one first line and forty-nine second line mules. Each infantry company had four anti-tank rifles and nine light machine-guns, and each support group two three-inch mortars and two heavy machine-guns. The second line transport groups each had two light anti-aircraft machine-guns.

APPENDIX 27

Wingate's Order of the Day, 13th February 1943

Today we stand on the threshold of battle. The time of preparation is over, and we are moving on the enemy to prove ourselves and our methods. At this moment we stand beside the soldiers of the United Nations in the front line trenches throughout the world. It is always a minority that occupies the front line. It is a still smaller minority that accepts with a good heart tasks like this that we have chosen to carry out. We need not, therefore, as we go forward into the conflict, suspect ourselves of selfish or interested motives. We have all had the opportunity of withdrawing and we are here because we have chosen to be here; that is, we have chosen to bear the burden and heat of the day. Men who make this choice are above the average in courage. We need therefore have no fear for the staunchness and guts of our comrades.

The motive which had led each and all of us to devote ourselves to what lies ahead cannot conceivably have been a bad motive. Comfort and security are not sacrificed voluntarily for the sake of others by ill-disposed people. Our motive, therefore, may be taken to be the desire to serve our day and generation in the way that seems nearest to our hand. The battle is not always to the strong nor the race to the swift. Victory in war cannot be counted upon, but what can be counted upon is that we shall go forward determined to do what we can to bring this war to the end which we believe best for our friends and comrades in arms, without boastfulness or forgetting our duty, resolved to do the right so far as we can see the right.

Our aim is to make possible a government of the world in which all men can live at peace and with equal opportunity of service.

Finally, knowing the vanity of man's effort and the confusion of his purpose, let us pray that God may accept our services and direct our endeavours, so that when we shall have done all we shall see the fruit of our labours and be satisfied.

O. C. WINGATE, Commander,
77th Indian Infantry Brigade

APPENDIX 28

The Organization of the Japanese 55th Division for the Counter-offensive in Arakan, March–May 1943

	First and Second Phases	Third Phase	Fourth Phase
Kawashima Column	III/213th Battalion (less one company)	As for first and second phases	As for third phase
Uno Column (Colonel Uno 143rd Infantry Regiment)	143rd Infantry Regiment (less III/143rd Battalion) III/112th Battalion (less one company)	143rd Infantry Regiment (less III/143rd Battalion)	143rd Infantry Regiment (less III/143rd Battalion) II/214th Battalion
Tanahashi Column (Colonel Tanahashi 112th Infantry Regiment)	I/112th Battalion II/213th Battalion 55th Mountain Artillery Regiment	112th Infantry Regiment II/213th Battalion 55th Mountain Artillery Regiment	As for third phase
Miyawaki Column (Colonel Miyawaki 213th Infantry Regiment)	II/112th Battalion One company III/213th Battalion[1] II/33rd Mountain Artillery Regiment (joined for second phase by I/213th Battalion from Kaladan)	I/213th Battalion II/33rd Mountain Artillery Regiment	As for third phase
Kakihara Column		One infantry company and one battalion mountain artillery	
Total	7 battalions	8 battalions	9 battalions

[1] Left to garrison Kaladan valley.

APPENDIX 29

Eastern Army Operation Instruction No. 31

4th April 1943

To: MAJOR-GENERAL C. E. N. LOMAX, C.B.E., D.S.O., M.C.

Comd. 26 Indian Division

1. The following is in confirmation of Directive No. 2 of 3rd April 1943 given to you personally by me.[1] The amplification of paragraph 4 will be noted.

2. The situation West of Mayu Peninsula is not developing unexpectedly. The enemy have established a block about Indin. He has in consequence placed himself in a position not unfavourable to a decisive stroke by us.

Numerically we are in great superiority and provided we do not allow the supply problem to get the better of us complete defeat of the enemy who have penetrated West of the Mayu Peninsula ridge is there for the taking. Progress is being made by 4 Brigade East of the ridge. Steps have also been taken more strongly to secure the position about Gyindaw by placing all troops, there incl, [sic] under command 1/15 Punjab, to whom have also been allotted one Machine-Gun company (less one platoon). The control of this force remains direct under Commander 14 Division, but Commander 1/15 Punjab has been told to get into contact with Commander Hopforce, so as to co-ordinate defence plans.

3. Though not for one moment accepting the fact that the penetration into Indin must cause us to withdraw 6 Brigade from present position, a controlled withdrawal to the Kodingauk position offers the following advantages:

   (a) the position if held by one battalion releases a second battalion as a reserve to 6 Brigade, enabling Commander to dispose two battalions for offensive or counter-offensive action.

   (b) The withdrawal to the Kodingauk position will more securely prevent any further penetration by the enemy from the East towards the Sangan Chaung, the security of the foot track thereto being still in some doubt, though orders have been repeated to 47 Brigade to hold the pass without fail.

   (c) The control of all operations in the Indin area by Commander 6 Brigade will be simplified.

The main disadvantage of the above proposal is the loss of ground.

4. I am prepared to accept the loss of ground as long as all planning for your subsequent operations is directed at inflicting on the Japanese wherever met, a defeat. You will therefore plan as follows in case the Jap penetration into Indin has not been liquidated by the operations now in progress.

---

[1] Directive No. 2 is not published.

APPENDIX 29

(a) 6 Brigade to withdraw in good order to the Kodingauk position thereby releasing a second battalion as a reserve.

(b) 6 Brigade will attack any enemy in the Indin–Kyaukpandu area, clear all road blocks and re-establish the security of the whole Kyaukpandu position.

(c) As soon as this is done 6 Brigade will launch a counter-attack Southwards from its Kodingauk position against any Japs who have followed up the withdrawal from the Donbaik position.

(d) 47 Brigade will continue to hold their ground and ensure the security of the tracks Sinoh–Indin and Auktomaw–Sangan Chaung.

(e) On the 4 Brigade front the advance will continue.

(f) On the 71 Brigade front plans will be made for the capture of high ground known as Pt. 201 (6526) and the continuation of this feature Southwards. The capture of this feature will be a preliminary to any further offensive operations on that front.

5. This Operation Instruction will be read in conjunction with Operation Instruction No. 30 of 4 April 1943 and therefore all offensive operations will be directed on inflicting a defeat and killing Japs rather than capturing ground, the subsequent retention of which may aggravate the problem of monsoon dispositions.

(Sgd.) N. M. S. IRWIN
Lieut.-General
General Officer Commanding-in-Chief
Eastern Army

APPENDIX 30

Order of Battle of 26th Indian Infantry Division, 23rd April 1943

Headquarters 26th Indian Infantry Division
(*Major-General C. E. N. Lomax*)

    99th Field Regiment, R.A.
    130th Field Regiment, R.A.
    23rd Indian Mountain Regiment
    44th Light Anti-Aircraft Regiment
    28th Field Company
    72nd Field Company
    73rd Field Company
    The Sirmoor Field Company
    2/8th Punjab Regiment
    9th Jat M.G. Battalion

4th Indian Infantry Brigade
(*Brigadier A. W. Lowther*)
  in relief of
  Brigadier S. A. H. Hungerford)
    2nd Durham Light Infantry
    3/9th Gurkha Rifles
    7/15th Punjab Regiment
    8/8th Punjab Regiment

6th British Infantry Brigade
(*Colonel B. H. Hopkins*)
    1st Royal Scots
    1st Royal Welch Fusiliers
    1st Royal Berkshire Regiment

36th Indian Infantry Brigade
(*Brigadier L. C. Thomas*)
    1st North Staffordshire Regiment
    8/13th Frontier Force Rifles
    5/16th Punjab Regiment

Mayforce
(*Brigadier A. C. Curtis*)
    1/17th Dogra Regiment
    One company 1/15th Punjab Regiment
    One company 4th Burma Regiment

55th Indian Infantry Brigade
(*Brigadier P. H. Gates* in relief of
  Brigadier J. M. Hunt)
    2/1st Punjab Regiment
    6/11th Sikh Regiment
    1/15th Punjab Regiment (less one company)
    One company 1st Lincolnshire Regiment
    One company 10th Lancashire Fusiliers
    One company Burma Regiment

71st Indian Infantry Brigade
(*Brigadier G. G. C. Bull*)
    1st Lincolnshire Regiment (less one company)
    10th Lancashire Fusiliers (less one company)
    9/15th Punjab Regiment

APPENDIX 31

Administrative Problems during the First Arakan Campaign, September 1942–May 1943

See Maps 11 and 13 and Sketch 15

In September 1942, General Lloyd was faced with a tremendous administrative problem when he was ordered to move 14th Indian Division from the Chittagong area to the general line Maungdaw–Buthidaung in Arakan. The eastern Bengal metre gauge railway ended at Dohazari. There were no road communications between eastern Bengal and Arakan and the only motorable road ran from Chittagong to a point some ten miles south of Dohazari. Beyond that point there was a narrow unmetalled and unbridged track which ran through Ramu and Ukhia towards Maungdaw. Pack transport could use it in dry weather provided the mules swam across the larger chaungs while their loads were ferried in local craft. A road capable of taking motor vehicles from the railhead at Dohazari to Maungdaw was clearly essential, but it would take a long time to build. There was only one all-weather road in Arakan—that from Maungdaw through the Tunnels to Buthidaung. In the immediate neighbourhood of Maungdaw tracks were bridged to take bullock carts for a short distance. The province depended almost entirely on water transport and though there were tracks, passable on foot, from Cox's Bazar to Foul Point, Rathedaung and the Kaladan valley they could not be used for bodies of troops with transport, for bridges were either flimsy bamboo structures or single felled tree trunks. Fords were often only usable at low tide and ferries, where they existed, were primitive. The tracks through the mountain areas were very steep and to make them passable for animals was a major engineering feat, except in one or two cases such as the Kyaukpandu–Atet Nanra and Indin–Atet Nanra tracks. From a few miles south of Alethangyaw to Foul Point, the beach could be used by motor transport for about two to four hours each side of low tide according to the strength and direction of the wind. To the Japanese, operating up the main rivers and plentifully supplied with boats, movement and supply were far simpler problems than to the British whose line of communication ran from the unnavigable upper reaches downwards and who had to traverse long distances through country devoid of anything better than footpaths to get to them.

The sea route from Chittagong to Cox's Bazar (71 miles) and, after it had been occupied, to Maungdaw (144 miles) was limited by the shortage of coastal craft and the very small capacity of the ports. In September 1942 there were only two small coastal steamers (*Nhila* and *Mallard*) with a total carrying capacity of 300 men and 300 tons of cargo and a minimum turn-round on the Chittagong–Cox's Bazar trip of two days. Although a number of 40 and 70 ton sailing vessels (Akyab sloops) were available, they could not be used before the end of the monsoon (end of October–early November). The only other local craft available were paddy (rice) boats, about fifty feet in length propelled by sail and twenty-four oarsmen, capable of carrying some thirty-five tons, and sampans (shallow draft sailing boats) varying in size from ten to thirty feet.

In the spring of 1942 the port of Chittagong had been partially dismantled so as to deny it to the enemy should he invade eastern Bengal; it had therefore to be largely re-equipped. Cox's Bazar had one landing stage but, since the water was shallow, all men and stores brought by the coastal steamers had to be transferred to sampans in a sheltered anchorage some distance from the town. Maungdaw had one jetty with a water depth of seven feet at high tide, and the discharge from deeper draft vessels had to be carried out in mid-stream. During the monsoon coastal vessels could not risk the open sea, so from April to September only river traffic could reach the port. The Naf River was navigable up to Tumbru by vessels drawing seven feet. The Mayu-Kalapanzin River was tidal as far as Goppe Bazar, and was navigable as far as Buthidaung by small river steamers and up to Taung Bazar by large sampans. Between January and May even small sampans could not reach Goppe Bazar when loaded.

Faced with these conditions, Lloyd asked Eastern Army for four 100 ton seaworthy coastal vessels and the necessary air cover to hasten the move of troops to Cox's Bazar. Eastern Army had no vessels nor could they get them from General Headquarters, India, and thus Lloyd was told to make good with what he had. His first move was to send one battalion by sea to Cox's Bazar to make a track from there through Ramu and Ukhia to Tumbru, at the head of the navigable portion of the Naf River, and two field companies to Dohazari to build a road from the railhead to Cox's Bazar and Tumbru. This was to be made fit first for pack mules, then for 15 cwt. and finally for 30 cwt. motor vehicles. The field companies were responsible for bringing the road up to a Class 5 fair-weather road. As each section was completed, it was to be passed over to the Chief Engineer Communications and Works, whose task it was to maintain and improve it to an all-weather Class 12 road. Using mule transport, small supply dumps were meanwhile established some fifteen miles apart between Dohazari and Ramu so that the route could be used by marching troops.

The work on the road to Cox's Bazar was pushed ahead as fast as possible by local coolie labour supervised by the field companies. Progress was slow since there was no local stone for road-making; coal had therefore to be brought from the Calcutta area, and bricks burnt for soling and surfacing this road. Chaungs were bridged with locally cut timber or, if too wide for bridging, made fordable or provided with jetties and ferries. By the 22nd October the road was fit for mule carts and in fair weather for 15 cwt. vehicles, and stocking of a field supply depot in the Cox's Bazar area began. Meanwhile, by road and sea, the leading brigade had been moved forward to the Cox's Bazar–Ramu area with 14 days' supplies and two refills of ammunition. By using locally procured animal transport and porters, the leading battalion had reached Tumbru at the head

APPENDIX 31

of the Naf River by the 21st October. On arrival in the area, the remainder of the brigade was at first employed on turning the track through Ukhia to Tumbru, prepared by the leading battalion, into a road capable of taking 15 cwt. vehicles. Despite delays caused by heavy rains, the divisional second line motor transport was able to take over the maintenance of the leading brigade by the 1st November, and begin to stock a forward supply depot at Nawapara (a few miles short of Tumbru). Towards the end of October a third full company arrived, and was put to work to improve the track from Nawapara to Bawli Bazar.

Early in November heavy and unseasonable rains, accompanied by a minor typhoon, did great damage. Bridges, jetties, sampans, rafts, stocks of timber for bridging and even sections of the new earth road were washed away. Nevertheless, by the end of the month 30 cwt. vehicles could use the roads from Dohazari and Cox's Bazar as far as Tumbru, and it was possible to maintain a brigade of four battalions in the Zeganbyin area, with detachments at Taung Bazar and Teknaf, and a second brigade in the Ramu–Ukhia area. The chain of supply was by sea, supplemented by road, to Cox's Bazar; motor transport to Tumbru; sampans on the Naf River from Tumbru to Bawli Bazar; and pack transport forward of Bawli Bazar and, in the case of Zeganbyin, river transport as well.

To ease the strain on this long and complicated line of communications, Eastern Army reorganized the Sundarbans Flotilla (created early in 1942 for the defence of the Sundarbans[1]) into 2000 Flotilla as a supply or troop-carrying fleet for coastal traffic from Chittagong to Maungdaw, as soon as the latter was captured. Some twenty-five Akyab sloops were requisitioned and included in the flotilla with some small coastal steamers for towing purposes. This flotilla, organized by Captain J. I. Hallett, R.N. (Naval Officer in charge at Chittagong), formed a valuable addition to the line of communications.

On the 17th December Maungdaw and Buthidaung were occupied, and the port of Maungdaw and the motor road through the Tunnels to Buthidaung could be used.[2] The Line of Communication troops had been strengthened early in December by 257th Inland Water Transport Company which was made responsible for all traffic on the Naf River between Tumbru and both Bawli Bazar and Maungdaw.[3] By the end of December, 30 cwt. vehicles could use the road from Tumbru through Bawli Bazar and Zeganbyin to Maungdaw, though a ferry over the Pruma Khal, two miles west of Bawli Bazar, formed a bottle-neck through which only twenty-five vehicles could pass on each tide. In addition, motor transport in small numbers could reach Teknaf through Nhila, except for four hours round high tide, and could be moved from there by raft to Maungdaw. Taung Bazar could be reached from Bawli Bazar by a poor mule track over the Goppe pass and thence by sampan down the Kalapanzin River, or by sampan up the river from Buthidaung. Additional

---

[1] The Sundarbans is the area of the Ganges delta, south of Calcutta.

[2] See page 258.

[3] The journey from Tumbru to Maungdaw could be accomplished in three hours by powered craft and by other craft in one ebb or flood tide.

advanced field depots had been established at Wabyin (the starting point of the track over the Ngakyedauk Pass to Buthidaung and Taung Bazar) and Maungdaw. The capture of Maungdaw did not however greatly relieve the strain on the overland line of communications since, as a result of the change of plan in November[1], six powered vessels from 2000 Flotilla were withdrawn early in December to train 6th Brigade for its proposed short-range amphibious operation from Foul Point on Akyab.

In accordance with the revised plan, 14th Division was ordered early in December to occupy the Mayu peninsula, Rathedaung, and Kanzauk and Apaukwa in the Kaladan valley. South of the Maungdaw–Buthidaung road the line of communication, owing to the topography, branched into three parts: the coastal plain of the Mayu peninsula, the Mayu River basin and across the Arakan Hill Tracts to the Kaladan valley.

One brigade of 14th Division advanced with a battalion on each side of the Mayu range. The battalion on the coastal plain, with the help of two field companies, was required, as it advanced, to improve the track by way of Alethangyaw to Foul Point to take 30 cwt. vehicles. The battalion east of the range was to be maintained by river from Buthidaung until it reached Atet Nanra, after which it was to be supplied by mule transport along the Kyaukpandu–Atet Nanra track as soon as it had been improved to pack standard. By the 31st December 1942, the line Shinkhali–Thitkado had been reached but maintenance difficulties had become acute. The shortage of powered craft on the Chittagong–Maungdaw sea route and of sampans on the Tumbru–Maungdaw river route, coupled with the general shortage of motor vehicles on the long road south of Chittagong, seriously restricted the flow of supplies to Maungdaw. 15 cwt. trucks could reach Alethangyaw with difficulty, since heavy rains had hindered replacement of the flimsy bridges and the beach road had to be used to cross four large chaungs. Beyond this point, except along the beach, only pack mules could be used along the coastal plain and across the range. As a result, both battalions were for a time on half rations and short of ammunition. By the 16th January 1943, the road was fit for 3 ton vehicles up to Gyindaw and by the 4th February up to a point one mile from Donbaik, the furthest point reached by 14th Division. The troops on the peninsula east of the range had still to be supplied by pack transport through Atet Nanra.

The problem of supplying the forward troops east of the Mayu River was equally difficult. Although a track ran from Buthidaung to Taungmaw it was not fit for pack mules and the only route for maintenance was the Mayu River itself. When the Japanese withdrew from Buthidaung on the 16th December, they had destroyed or removed most of the sampans with the result that only a hundred were at first available and these had to suffice for all requirements for the line of communications.[2] Furthermore,

---

[1] See page 257.

[2] On the 21st December a detachment of 257th Inland Water Transport Company was moved to Buthidaung to organize all sampan traffic on the Mayu River. The unit eventually collected a fleet of 250 serviceable sampans and 4 sloops.

vessels using the wide main river flowing through flat country were very vulnerable to air attack. The narrow and winding Ngasanbaw Chaung with its steep and often jungle-covered banks had therefore to be used from Zedidaung to Htizwe, from where there was a usable track to Rathedaung. This chaung was not navigable at low tide and thus the journey from Buthidaung to Htizwe could not be completed in less than two tides, staging at Zedidaung, and the turn-round was some four days. To shorten it, a track for pack mules, later made fit for mule carts and finally for motor vehicles, had to be built from Buthidaung by way of Kindaung and Zedidaung to Htizwe.

For the attack on Rathedaung, sampan convoys were used to bring forward supplies and ammunition during the first week in January to form an advanced depot to contain two days' requirements for the brigade in the Htizwe (Kyauktan) area. The difficulties encountered in concentrating a brigade for the attack are illustrated by the fact that it took five days to move a mountain battery (all pack transport) from Buthidaung to the concentration area, a distance of about forty miles: on the first day the mules, stores and men had to be ferried across the river at Buthidaung; on the second the unit was ferried across the Saingdin Chaung and marched to Kindaung; on the third it marched to Taungmaw; and on the fourth and fifth it went by sampan to Htizwe. During the second and third day five chaungs had to be swum and several mules were drowned.

The track was rapidly improved during the month and motor cycle despatch riders could use it, despite eight ferry crossings, by the 20th January. By the 30th, all the chaungs had been bridged and the brigade's tracked carriers were able to join their units; by the 19th February, 15 cwt. vehicles could reach Thaungdara and jeeps could reach the front line. The ferry at Buthidaung, however, remained the bottle-neck owing to its poor carrying capacity.

When Soutcol (8/10th Baluch) moved from Taung Bazar to the Kaladan valley, it was supplied by sampan from Buthidaung to Taung Bazar and thence by pack mule in five stages across the mountains to Kyauktaw. Later the force was maintained from the Htizwe advanced depot along the Awrama–Kanzauk track. Although shorter, this route was much more exposed to enemy interference from the Rathedaung area. The first effort at supply by air was made when grain for the animals and other stores were free-dropped on Soutcol at Kyauktaw.

By the time that the advance had been brought to a halt on the Donbaik–Rathedaung–Apaukwa line, an advanced base supply depot for 14th Division had been established at Chittagong, field supply depots at Cox's Bazar, Maungdaw and Buthidaung and advanced field depots in the Indin–Kodingauk area and at Htizwe (Kyauktan). The road from Dohazari to Maungdaw was maintained by C.R.E. 13 Works Unit, assisted by 11th Bridging Section, 10th and 17th Engineering Battalions (I.E.) and 336th Forestry Company. Two auxiliary pioneer battalions were also available to provide labour, if required.

The formations at Donbaik drew supplies from Indin and Kodingauk. The brigade on the peninsula east of the Mayu range drew from Indin by animal transport, but the pool of pack mules was sufficient for daily maintenance only and not for building up a reserve; thus, when the track to Atet Nanra became impassable in wet weather, recourse had to be made to emergency rations. Maintenance of this brigade was therefore switched in February to the Htizwe depot and bulk deliveries were made every forty-eight hours by sampan across the Mayu River and up the Kamaungdon Chaung to Sinoh. The turn-round was approximately eighteen hours. At the same time, work was begun on a track from Buthidaung by way of Hparabyin to Atet Nanra. Soutcol was supplied from the Htizwe depot.

Casualties from the coastal strip were evacuated by road from Indin to Maungdaw; those from the Kaladan valley by riding mule or litter and those from Sinoh by sampan to Htizwe. From Htizwe evacuation was by sampan to Buthidaung and onwards by motor ambulance to Maungdaw. From this point the sitting or lying cases were sent by river to Tumbru and then by road to Cox's Bazar. Cases which had to be evacuated to the base were sent on either by coastal vessels to Chittagong or by motor ambulance to railhead at Dohazari. Walking wounded were usually sent by sea direct from Maungdaw to Chittagong.

When the Japanese offensive opened, Soutcol had to be withdrawn from the Kaladan valley to Taung Bazar, for its line of communication to Htizwe had been cut. It was forced to destroy 40 horses and 376 mules to prevent them falling into enemy hands—a very severe loss at that time. When the Japanese occupied Mrawchaung and the hills astride the Awrama track, the Htizwe (Kyauktan) advanced field supply depot was threatened. In these circumstances, 14th Division ordered supplies in the Htizwe depot to be used up and a new supply depot to be opened near Taungmaw.[1] No change was made in the supply route to Sinoh, except that Force 'Z' was ordered to escort all river convoys, and preparations were made to switch to the Indin depot by way of the Atet Nanra track, if the river route to Sinoh were cut. This alternative route had to be brought into use when the Htizwe depot came under artillery fire and the river convoy was molested.[2] Later, when the enemy occupied Atet Nanra and the track up to the crest of the range, the line of communication had to be switched to a hurriedly improved track from Sinoh.

The 4th Brigade, ordered to move south from Buthidaung to prevent the Atet Nanra track being cut, was delayed by the time required to collect its transport mules and by the need to protect a six-mile transport column during the advance.[3] It was thus unable to bring sufficient strength to bear in time. Had air supply been possible, the brigade might well have arrived before the enemy had consolidated his position. When the same brigade was suddenly ordered to move to Gyindaw, leaving one battalion behind, it marched to Buthidaung and then moved in a convoy of one hundred 30 cwt. vehicles to Gyindaw. Its animals, without their loads, moved by road and staged at Buthidaung, Maungdaw and Lambaguna.

---

[1] Later this was moved to Kindaung.
[2] The brigade holding the Htizwe bridgehead was dependent on animal transport for its mobility. The men of the mule companies were unarmed. When the Japanese attacked at Kyauktan on the 14th March, these companies suffered heavy casualties in men and animals and their defence added to the strain on the combatant troops.
[3] See page 340.

APPENDIX 31

The mule leaders changed over at each staging camp, those relieved travelling in motor vehicles to the next camp. The whole move was carried out between the 5th and 7th April.

As 26th Division retired towards its base, no particular administrative problems arose, beyond the backloading of stores from the advanced field depots as they were given up.

The difficulties of maintaining a force some 130 miles south of its main base were great but, complicated though the line of communications was, by February 1943 the forward troops of 14th Division were seldom short of either ammunition or supplies. The early difficulties during November and December 1942 were clearly one of the major causes of the delay which robbed the division of the chance of capturing Foul Point and Rathedaung before the Japanese could reinforce their very meagre forces in Akyab.

The Japanese had three administrative factors in their favour: they controlled river communications, they were far less dependent on their rearward communications and were accustomed to live on the country for considerable periods and could ruthlessly requisition supplies locally. They were thus able to make wide and deep outflanking movements which manoeuvred the British forces out of their defended positions, cut their communications and deprived them of essential supplies.

Among the administrative lessons learnt from this campaign were:

(a) The necessity to arm all administrative units and train them to protect themselves at rest or on the move; and the necessity for all-round defence of divisional and brigade administrative areas by troops especially allotted for the purpose and co-ordinated by a selected commander.

(b) the need for a compact ration on which men could exist for at least a week without loss of efficiency, and for training in jungle lore so that the resources of the country could be used, thus making formations less dependent on their rearward communications.

(c) The great importance of developing an adequate system of air supply so as to provide an answer to the enemy's enveloping tactics, and enable operations to be carried out deep in the enemy's rear which would otherwise be impossible.

APPENDIX 32

Order of Battle of Air Forces, India and Ceylon, June 1943

Air Headquarters, India, New Delhi
Air Headquarters, Bengal, Calcutta

31 (BT) Squadron	Dakota	Kharagpur (with detachments at Agartala and Tezpur)
681 (PR) Squadron	Hurricane Spitfire Mitchell	Dum Dum

221 Group, Calcutta

293 Wing, Calcutta
    136 (F) Squadron — Hurricane — Baigachi
    607 (F) Squadron — Hurricane — Alipore
    615 (F) Squadron — Hurricane — Alipore
    176 (NF) Squadron — Beaufighter — Baigachi
170 Wing, Imphal
    155 (F) Squadron — Mohawk — Imphal
    Det. 28 (FR) Squadron — Hurricane — Imphal
    42 (LB) Squadron — Bisley — Kumbhirgram
175 Wing, Jessore
    99 (MB) Squadron — Wellington — Jessore
    215 (MB) Squadron — Wellington — Jessore
168 Wing, Digri
    Det. 28 (FR) Squadron — Hurricane — Alipore
    159 (HB) Squadron — Liberator — Salbani
    2 (F) Squadron, R.I.A.F.[1] — Hurricane — Ranchi
    5 (F) Squadron[1] — Hurricane — Kharagpur
    45 (LB) Squadron[1] — Vengeance — Digri
    82 (LB) Squadron[1] — Vengeance — Salbani
    110 (LB) Squadron[1] — Vengeance — Digri
    177 (TEF) Squadron[1] — Beaufighter — Amarda Road

224 Group, Chittagong

Det. 28 (FR) Squadron — Hurricane — Cox's Bazar
165 Wing, Comilla
    79 (F) Squadron — Hurricane — Comilla
    146 (F) Squadron — Hurricane — Comilla
166 Wing, Chittagong
    67 (F) Squadron — Hurricane — Chittagong
    261 (F) Squadron — Hurricane — Chittagong

APPENDIX 32

167 Wing, Feni
    11 (LB) Squadron   Blenheim IV   Feni
    113 (LB) Squadron   Bisley   Feni
169 Wing, Agartala
    17 (F) Squadron   Hurricane   Agartala
    27 (TEF) Squadron   Beaufighter   Agartala

222 Group, Colombo

30 (F) Squadron	Hurricane	Colombo
258 (F) Squadron	Hurricane	Dambulla
273 (F) Squadron	Hurricane	China Bay
160 (GR) Squadron	Liberator	Ratmalana
22 (GR) Squadron	Beaufort	Vavuniya
217 (GR) Squadron	Beaufort	Vavuniya
205 (FB) Squadron	Catalina	Koggala
413 (FB) Squadron, R.C.A.F.	Catalina	Koggala
321 (FB) Squadron, Dutch	Catalina	China Bay

225 Group, Bangalore

353 (GR) Squadron	Hudson	Cuttack
212 (FB) Squadron	Catalina	Karachi
191 (FB) Squadron	Catalina	Karachi
240 (FB) Squadron	Catalina	Madras
6 (FR) Squadron, R.I.A.F.[1]	Hurricane	Cholavaram
20 (F) Squadron[1]	Hurricane	Kalyan
135 (F) Squadron	Hurricane	Arkonam
34 (LB) Squadron[1]	Blenheim IV	Madras
60 (LB) Squadron[1]	Blenheim IV	Yellahanka
84 (LB) Squadron[1]	Vengeance	Yellahanka

223 Group, Peshawar

3 (F) Squadron, R.I.A.F.[1]	Hurricane	Kohat
4 (F) Squadron, R.I.A.F.[1]	Hurricane	Kohat
1 (FR) Squadron, R.I.A.F.[1]	Hurricane	Risalpur
7 (LB) Squadron, R.I.A.F.[1]	Vengeance	Phaphamau
8 (LB) Squadron, R.I.A.F.[1]	Vengeance	Phaphamau
62 (Tpt) Squadron[1]	Hudson	Chaklala
194 (Tpt) Squadron[1]	Dakota	Basal

---

[1] Non-operational.

APPENDIX 33

Order of Battle of the Japanese 5th Air Division During the 1943 Monsoon

Headquarters, 5th Air Division, Rangoon

4th Air Brigade, Toungoo
    50th Air Regiment   Fighter   Rangoon, and Singapore
    8th Air Regiment   Reconnaissance and light bomber   Toungoo, and Sungei Patani (Malaya)

7th Air Brigade, Sungei Patani
    64th Air Regiment   Fighter   Rangoon, and Sungei Patani (Malaya)
    12th Air Regiment   Heavy bomber   Medan and Sabang (N.E.I.)
    98th Air Regiment   Heavy bomber   Padang (N.E.I.)
    81st Air Regiment   Reconnaissance   Hlegu, and Sungei Patani (Malaya)

Note

At this period the total strength was about fifty fighters and ninety bombers.

Index

INDEX

Note: Formations and units of the British, Commonwealth and Indian Armies, and of the Burma and Colonial military forces, are indexed under 'Army'. British infantry battalions are in order of regimental seniority.

ABDA Command: 21, 50, 79, 103, 223
Abukuma, Jap, cruiser: 116
Adachi, Lieut.-General: 284, 288
Addu Atoll: 58, 117, 118, 119, 120, 122
Administration, Military (Arakan): 348 fn. 2
Admiralty on 'R' class battleships: 122
Agar, Captain A. W. S., V.C., R.N.: 117, 121
Ainsworth, Rear-Admiral W. L. (U.S.N.): 414, 416
Air-lift, India-China: 113–4; difficulties after loss of Burma, 241–2; China's demands, 305, 366, 380; plans to increase, 307, 367, 368, 381; Chennault's demand, 379; 391, 392, 420, 421, 422
Air losses in first Burma campaign: 210
Air Ministry: estimate Burma's defence requirements, 26; reinforce India, 251
Air operations: *see* R.A.F., Fleet Air Arm, A.V.G., U.S.A.A.F.
Air, Secretary of State for: 85
Air transport: asked for by Burma, 161; in first Burma campaign, 205, 212–3; possibilities of, 214
Air Transport Command (U.S.): 391
Akagi, Jap. aircraft carrier: 230, 231; sunk, 232
Akyab: air attacks on airfield, 150; air attacks on island, 195; island evacuated, 195; occupied by Japanese, 195; plans to recover island, 249–50; advance undertaken, 254–6; new plans, 256–7; preparations for sea-borne attack, 260–1, 331; sea-borne attack cancelled, 333; capture reconsidered, 392, 394, 395, 396, 397; *see also* Arakan operations
Alamo Force (Pacific): formed, 411; operations of, 411
Aleutian Islands: Japanese operations against, 229, 230, 233; recovery of, 409–10
Alexander, General Hon. Sir H.: 82 and fn., 86; assumes command in Burma, 89; his plans for offensive, 89; conducts retreat from Rangoon, 96, 97; plans defence of Central Burma, 147; withdraws to Toungoo-Prome line, 148–9, 150; plans evacuation of Burma, 153, 176–7, 178, 181, 199; on Stilwell's appointment, 154; on command of Chinese armies, 155; reaches agreement with Stilwell, 156; his dispositions round Prome, 157; calls for offensive action, 158, 159; on lack of air support and need of reinforcements, 161; on state of troops, 161; selects new line of resistance, 163; asks for Chinese help, 163, 164; 168; plans withdrawal across Irrawaddy, 178–9; orders withdrawal, 180; 184, 201; his last meeting with Stilwell,

Army—*cont.*
  Alexander—*cont.*
    201; his measures for final withdrawal from Burma, 205, 206–7; relinquishes command, 210
Alexander, Lieut.-Colonel L. A.: 312, 320, 323
All India Congress: initiates civil disobedience, 245, 246
American Volunteer Group (A.V.G.): to Burma, 10; 16, 17 and fn., 18; reinforced, 20; in defence of Rangoon, 24, 25, 26, 48, 84–5; 96
Amery, Mr. L. S. (Secretary of State for India): his proposals for an S.E. Asia Command, 370–1; on subversive influences in Indian Army, 383–4
Amphibious Force, 3rd (Pacific): 413; operations New Georgia Group, 413
'Anakim', Operation (Rangoon): plans for, 236, 237–8; amphibious training for, 248; postponed, 249, 291; 294; approved at Casablanca conference, 297–8; forces required for, 299; affected by shipping available, 302; 361; question of Command, 361–2; risks of seaborne assault, 362; shipping demands reconsidered, 364, 365, 366; preparations delayed, 366, 368; reasons for deferring, 368–9; 390
Andaman Islands: evacuated, 99, 106
Anstice, Brigadier J. H.: arrives Burma, 83; in operations Prome area, 157, 158
Anthony, H.M. destroyer: in 'Ironclad', 136, 139, 140
Arakan: terrain, 253–4; climate, 254; operations in, 254–8, 260–8, 331–4; enemy counter-offensive, 335–45; last phase of campaign, 347–56; retrospect, 356–9; criticisms of failure in, 382–3
Arbuthnot, Vice-Admiral G. F.: in operations off Ceylon, 119, 123
'Arcadia' Conference (Washington): 222
Army:
  Armoured Brigades:
    7th Armoured, R.A.C.: 39, 44, 62, 63, 80, 81; arrives Burma, 83 and fn. 1; 85, 86; in operations N. of Rangoon, 88, 89, 90 fn. 2; in retreat from Rangoon, 96, 98; 147; in operations Prome area, 157, 159; 164; in withdrawal from Minhla-Taungdwingyi line, 166; in Yenangyaung-Pin Chaung operations, 168, 170; 176, 178, 181; in retreat across Irrawaddy, 182, 183; 199, 201; in retreat to Shwegyin, 202, 207; to Iraq, 249

Army—*cont.*
  Armoured Brigades—*cont.*
    50th Army Tank (Indian): 194, 243 and fns. 2, 3, 389, 390
    251st Tank (Indian): 194, 243 and fn. 3, 389, 390
    252nd Armoured (Indian): 243
    254th Tank (Indian): 243 and fn. 3, 389, 390
    255th Armoured (Indian): 243, 389
    267th Armoured (Indian): 243, 389
  Armoured Divisions:
    31st Indian: 47 and fn. 1, 243, 385 fn., 389
    32nd Indian: 47 fn. 2, 243 and fn. 3, 385 fn., 389
    43rd Indian: 243 and fn. 3, 385 fn., 389
    44th Indian: 385 fn., 389, 390
  Armoured Units, R.A.C.:
    7th Hussars: 83 fn. 1, 85; in operations N. of Rangoon, 90 and fn. 1, 92; in retreat from Rangoon, 96; in operations Prome area, 158; in withdrawal from Minhla–Taungdwingyi line, 166; in Yenangyaung–Pin Chaung operations, 173; 177; in retreat across Irrawaddy, 183; at Monywa, 201; in retreat to Shwegyin, 207; in Shwegyin action, 208, 209
    2nd Royal Tank Regiment: 83 and fn. 1, 85; in operations N. of Rangoon, 90 and fn. 2; in retreat from Rangoon, 98; 164 fn. 2; in withdrawal from Minhla–Taungdwingyi line, 166; in Yenangyaung–Pin Chaung operations, 168 fn. 1, 173; in retreat to Shwegyin, 207
    146th Royal Tank Regiment, 243
    149th Royal Tank Regiment, 243
    150th Royal Tank Regiment, 243
  Eastern Army (India): formed, 193; dispositions, 194; 196, 239, 250, 251, 252; plans recovery of Akyab, 255, 256, 260; 310; later dispositions, 389–90
  North-Western Army (India): formed, 193
  Southern Army (India): formed, 193; 194, 390
  Artillery:
    414th Battery, R.H.A.: 83 fn. 1; in operations N. of Rangoon, 90; in operations Prome area, 158; in Yenangyaung–Pin Chaung operations, 168 fn. 1
    455th Light Battery, R.A.: in Madagascar, 133 fn. 1, 136, 137, 139
    9th Field Regiment, R.A.: in Madagascar, 133 fn. 2, 138–9
    99th Field Regiment, R.A.: in Arakan operations, 339, 354
    130th Field Regiment, R.A.: in Arakan operations, 264, 340 fn. 3, 344, 354
    160th Field Regiment, R.A.: in Arakan operations, 353, 354
    2nd Indian Mountain Battery: in

Army—*cont.*
  Artillery—*cont.*
    Yenangyaung–Pin Chaung operations, 170
    5th Indian Mountain Battery: in retreat to Sittang, 70; in Yenangyaung–Pin Chaung operations, 170, 171
    8th Indian Mountain Battery: in Bilin river action, 60; in 'Magforce', 166 fn. 1; in Arakan operations, 264, 354
    12th Indian Mountain Battery: 12 fn., 30 fn.; in defence of Moulmein, 31, 33; in retreat to Sittang, 63, 70
    23rd Indian Mountain Battery: 12 fn.; in Yenangyaung-Pin Chaung operations, 170
    27th Indian Mountain Battery: 38
    28th Indian Mountain Battery: in retreat to Sittang, 70 and fn.
    31st Indian Mountain Battery: in Arakan operations, 340, 348, 354
    1st Indian Field Regiment: arrives Burma, 89; in retreat from Rangoon, 96; in Shwegyin action, 209
    8th Indian Heavy A.A. Regiment: arrives Burma, 25
    3rd Indian Light A.A. Regiment: arrives Burma, 25; 30 fn.; in Shwegyin action, 209
    2nd Indian Anti-Tank Regiment: in retreat to Sittang, 62
    5th Field Battery, Burma Auxiliary Forces: 8 fn. 2
    Rangoon Field Brigade (B.A.F.): in retreat from Rangoon, 96 fn. 3
    1st Heavy A.A. Regiment (B.A.F.): raised, 9; in retreat from Rangoon, 96 fn. 3
  Corps:
    I Australian: destination of, 56; returns from Middle East, 222; in New Guinea, 278
    IV Indian: 194, 195; task on withdrawal from Burma, 196; 197; assists withdrawal from Burma, 204, 206; assumes command of all units from Burma, 210; maintenance problems of, 238; dispositions on eastern frontier, 229, 390; 250, 303, 306, 310, 311, 320
    XV Indian: formed, 194; sends tanks to Arakan, 267; controls Arakan operations, 348; 390
    XXXIII Indian: 390
    'Burcorps': formed in Burma, 148; withdrawal to Prome area, 148–9; operations Prome area, 157–60; withdrawal towards Yin Chaung position, 160–1; on Minhla–Taungdwingyi line, 163–6; Yenangyaung–Pin Chaung operations, 167–8, 170–3; 177, 178, 179; withdrawal to India plan, 181; retreat across Irrawaddy, 182–5, 199; action at Monywa, 200–2;

INDEX

Army—*cont.*
　Burcorps—*cont.*
　　retreat to Shwegyin, 205–8; action at Shwegyin, 208–9; withdrawal to India completed, 210
　Divisions:
　　2nd (British): 130; in India, 235, 243, 249, 390
　　5th (British): allotted to India, 57; 129, 130, 134; in India, 235, 243; for Iraq, 249
　　18th (British): 14, 15
　　70th (British): destination of, 56, 57, 106; arrives India, 110 and fn. 1; 194, 195, 235, 243, 390, 402, 403
　　3rd Australian: in New Guinea operations, 411, 412
　　5th Australian: in New Guinea operations, 411
　　6th Australian: destination of, 56, 57, 106; in New Guinea operations, 279 fn., 286, 288
　　7th Australian: destination of, 56, 57, 81, 83, 84; in New Guinea operations, 278 fn., 286, 287, 288, 411
　　9th Australian: destination of, 56, 57; 222; in New Guinea operations, 411
　　11th Australian: in New Guinea operations, 411
　　4th Indian: 57 fn. 1, 361, 385 fn.
　　5th Indian: 57 and fn., 361, 385 fn., 390
　　6th Indian 47 fn 1, 385 fn
　　7th Indian: 47 and fn. 1, 48, 242, 385 fn.
　　8th Indian: 47 fn. 1, 385 fn.
　　9th Indian: 47 fn. 1, 385 fn.
　　10th Indian: 47 fn. 1, 385 fn.
　　11th Indian: 385 fn.
　　14th Indian: 21, 22, 35, 47, 48, 55, 110, 194, 195, 239, 242, 250, 251; in Arakan operations, 254, 255, 256, 257, 260–8, 331–4, 335–9, 340–8; 385 fn.; converted to training division, 387, 389
　　17th Indian: 14, 15 fn. 1, 16; formed in Burma, 27; in southern Tenasserim operations, 28–9, 30–3; on Salween river line, 37–8, 39, 40; reconstruction of, 38 fn.; condition of, 41, 80, 161; withdrawal to Bilin river line, 42; dispositions, 43, 45, 47, 48; in Bilin river action, 59–63; retreat to Sittang, 63–73; strength, 73; reorganised, 83; change in command, 86; in operations N. of Rangoon, 89–93; in retreat from Rangoon, 96, 97, 98; 147; in withdrawal to Toungoo–Prome, 148; in operations Prome area, 157, 158, 159, 160; in withdrawal from Minhla–Taungdwingy line, 164, 166; in Yenangyaung–Pin Chaung operations, 168, 173; 176, 178, 181; in retreat across the Irrawaddy, 182, 183, 199; at Monywa, 200; in retreat to Shwegyin, 207; in Shwegyin action, 208,

Army—*cont.*
　17th Indian—*cont.*
　　209; arrives in India, 210; 239 and fn. 1, 242, 306, 385 fn., 390, 405
　　19th Indian: 21, 47, 48, 126, 194, 242, 385 fn., 390
　　20th Indian: 47, 194, 242, 385 fn., 390
　　23rd Indian: 55, 110, 182, 194, 239, 242, 306, 313, 385 fn., 390, 405
　　25th Indian: 242, 385 fn., 390
　　Calcutta (26th) Indian: 55, 110, 194 and fn. 1, 195, 243 and fn. 1; in Arakan operations, 348–9, 352–5; 385 fn., 390, 406, 408
　　34th Indian: in Ceylon, 21; 47, 48, 109, 130, 243, 385 fn., 390
　　36th Indian: 248, 385 fn., 389, 390
　　39th Indian: 239 and fn. 2, 242, 385 fn., 387, 390
　Assam: 194
　　1st Burma: formed 12; 83, 85, 89, 147; attacks southward from Nyaunglebin, 148; in withdrawal to Toungoo–Prome, 148, 149; 157, 159, 164; in withdrawal from Minhla–Taungdwingyi line, 165–6; in Yenangyaung–Pin Chaung operations, 167, 168, 170, 171, 172, 173; 176, 178, 181; in retreat across Irrawaddy, 182, 184, 199; at Monywa, 200, 201, 202; in retreat to Shwegyin, 202, 207, 208; reconstituted and renamed, 239 and fn. 2
　　11th East African: 361
　　81st West African: 361, 403
　　82nd West African: 403
　Engineers:
　　14th Field Company R.E.: in operations Prome area, 158
　　38th Field Company R.E. in 'Ironclad', 133 fn. 2
　　236th Field Company R.E.: in 'Ironclad', 133 fn. 2
　　24th Field Company (Royal Bombay Sappers & Miners): in retreat to Sittang, 69
　　60th Field Company (Q.V.O. Madras Sappers & Miners): 30 fn.
　　Malerkotla Field Company (Indian State Forces): at Sittang bridge, 66, 67, 69, 71, 72
　　50th Field Park Company (Q.V.O. Madras Sappers & Miners): 201
　　10th Indian Engineer Regiment: in Arakan operations, 340 fn. 3
　　Burma Sappers & Miners: raised, 9; in retreat from Rangoon, 96 fn. 3
　Infantry Battalions:
　　1st Royal Scots: in Arakan operations, 338 fn. 1, 343, 344, 352
　　1st Lincolnshire Regiment: in Arakan operations, 337, 338, 339, 352, 353
　　1st West Yorkshire Regiment: 34; arrives Burma, 46; 85; in operations N. of Rangoon, 89, 90 and fn. 1, 92; in operations Prome area, 158;

Army—*cont.*
  1st West Yorkshire Regiment—*cont.*
    in Yenangyaung–Pin Chaung operations, 168 fn. 1, 172
  10th Lancashire Fusiliers: arrives India, 240; in Arakan operations, 262, 263, 264, 265, 267, 268, 336, 338, 352
  1st Royal Scots Fusiliers: in 'Ironclad', 133 fn. 2, 137, 139
  2nd Royal Scots Fusiliers: in 'Ironclad', 133 fn. 2, 140
  1st Royal Welch Fusiliers: in Arakan operations, 338 fn. 1, 344
  2nd Royal Welch Fusiliers: in 'Ironclad', 133 fn. 2, 137, 138, 140
  1st Cameronians: 34, 80, 83 fn. 1; in operations N. of Rangoon, 88, 90, 92; in operations Prome area, 158; in withdrawal from Minhla–Taungdwingyi line, 166 fn.; in Yenangyaung–Pin Chaung operations, 170, 171
  1st Royal Inniskilling Fusiliers: arrives Burma, 148, 213; in Yenangyaung–Pin Chaung operations, 171, 172; in Arakan operations, 262, 263, 264, 332, 342, 343
  1st Gloucestershire Regiment: in Burma, 9; 14; in retreat from Rangoon, 96 fn. 3, 97; at Letpadan, 148; in operations Prome area, 157, 158; in Yenangyaung–Pin Chaung operations, 168, 170; at Monywa, 199
  2nd East Lancashire Regiment: in 'Ironclad', 133 fn. 2, 136, 137, 139
  2nd Duke of Wellington's Regiment: 34; arrives Burma, 46; in retreat to Sittang, 62, 65, 66, 68, 69 fn., 70; in operations Prome area, 158; reaches India, 210
  2nd South Lancashire Regiment: in 'Ironclad', 133 fn. 2, 137, 139
  2nd Northamptonshire Regiment: in 'Ironclad', 133 fn. 2
  1st Royal Berkshire Regiment: in Arakan operations, 338 fn. 1, 340 fn. 3, 342, 343, 344 and fn. 2
  2nd King's Own Yorkshire Light Infantry: in Burma, 9; 30, 35, 41; on Bilin river line, 43; in Bilin river action, 59, 60, 61 and fn. 3; in retreat to the Sittang, 73 fn. 1; in retreat from Rangoon, 96; in withdrawal from Minhla–Taungdwingyi line, 166, 167; in Yenangyaung–Pin Chaung operations, 172
  2nd Durham Light Infantry: in Arakan operations, 338 fn. 1, 344
  6th Seaforth Highlanders: in 'Ironclad', 133 fn. 2
  2/1st Punjab Regiment: in Arakan operations, 267, 332, 336, 337, 338
  5/1st Punjab Regiment: 12 fn.; in withdrawal from Minhla–Taungdwingyi line, 166; in Yenangyaung–Pin Chaung operations, 171

Army—*cont.*
  4/5th Mahratta Light Infantry: in first Chindit operation, 311, 312
  8/6th Rajputana Rifles: in Arakan operations, 266, 268, 336
  1/7th Rajput Regiment: in Arakan operations, 261, 262, 263, 264, 266, 267, 332, 341, 342
  2/7th Rajput Regiment: 12 fn.; in Yenangyaung–Pin Chaung operations, 172
  14/7th Rajput Regiment: at Akyab, 110
  2/8th Punjab Regiment: in Arakan operations, 352
  5/8th Punjab Regiment: in Arakan operations, 261, 262, 263, 266, 338
  1/9th Royal Jat Regiment: 13 fn. 1, 28; in Bilin river action, 59; in retreat to Sittang, 64; in retreat from Rangoon, 96 fn. 3; in retreat to Shwegyin, 207; in Shwegyin action, 208, 209
  7/10th Baluch Regiment: 27 fn. 3; in Kuzeik action, 40–1; in retreat to Sittang, 62 and fn., 67, 68, 69 and fn.
  8/10th Baluch Regiment: in Arakan operations, 261, 265, 331, 332
  1/11th Sikh Regiment: 84 fn. 2; in retreat from Rangoon, 97, 98 and fn. 1
  6/11th Sikh Regiment: in Arakan operations, 348
  4/12th Frontier Force Regiment: 13 fn. 1, 30 fn.; in defence of Moulmein, 31, 32, 38; 41; in Bilin river action, 61, 62, 63; in retreat to Sittang, 66, 67, 69 and fn.; in operations Prome area, 158
  2/13th Frontier Force Rifles: 84 fn. 2; in retreat from Rangoon, 97; in operations Prome area, 158
  8/13th Frontier Force Rifles: in Arakan operations, 352, 353 fn. 1
  1/15th Punjab Regiment: in Arakan operations, 255, 256, 262, 264, 265, 267–8, 335, 336, 337, 342
  7/15th Punjab Regiment: in Arakan operations, 349, 352, 353 fn. 1
  9/15th Punjab Regiment: in Arakan operations, 352
  1/17th Dogra Regiment: in Arakan operations, 267, 332, 336, 353, 354
  5/17th Dogra Regiment: 27 fn. 3, 40–1; on Bilin river line, 43; in Bilin river action, 59, 60, 61; 73 fn. 1; in Shwegyin action, 208
  1/18th Royal Garhwal Rifles: 12 fn., 24; in Yenangyaung–Pin Chaung operations, 171
  1/3rd Gurkha Rifles: 36 fn. 1; in Bilin river action, 61 fn. 1; in retreat to Sittang, 64, 67, 69, 70, 72 fn.; in operations N. of Rangoon, 89 fn. 3; in Shwegyin action, 208

INDEX

Army—*cont.*
    5/3rd Gurkha Rifles: in operations N. of Rangoon, 89 fn. 3, 92
    1/4th Gurkha Rifles: 36 fn. 1; in Bilin river action, 60, 61 and fn. 3; in retreat to Sittang, 64, 67, 68; in operations N. of Rangoon, 89 fn. 3, 92; in Shwegyin action, 208; on Tiddim front, 405
    2/5th (Royal) Gurkha Rifles: 36 fn. 1; in Bilin river action, 60, 61, 63; in retreat to Sittang, 67, 69, 70; in operations N. of Rangoon, 89 fn. 3; at Kyaukse, 183; in Shwegyin action, 209; on Tiddim front, 405 and fn. 3
    1/7th Gurkha Rifles: 13 fn. 1, 24, 27; in Kawkareik area, 28, 29 and fn.; on river Salween, 38; in Bilin river action, 59, 60, 61 and fn. 3; in operations N. of Rangoon, 89 fn. 3, 92; at Kyaukse, 183; in Shwegyin action, 208, 209; on Tiddim front, 405
    3/7th Gurkha Rifles: 27 fn. 3; in retreat to Sittang, 70, 73 fn. 1; in operations N. of Rangoon, 89 fn. 3
    1/10th Gurkha Rifles: 84 fn. 2; in retreat from Rangoon, 97, 98, 99
    Assam Rifles; 192, 196, 239
    Patiala Infantry (Indian State Forces): in first Chindit operation, 311, 312
    1st Tripura Rifles (Indian State Forces): 261 fn. 4
    4th Burma Regiment: 348 fn. 2, 349
    1st Burma Rifles: 36
    2nd Burma Rifles: in first Chindit operation, 311, 312, 315, 322, 323
    3rd Burma Rifles: 30 fn.; in defence of Moulmein, 31; 41 and fn. 2; at Sittang bridge, 43, 62 fn., 66, 69 and fn.
    4th Burma Rifles: 28, 29; in retreat to Sittang, 68, 70, 72
    5th Burma Rifles: 36
    6th Burma Rifles: 28
    7th Burma Rifles: 30 fn.; in defence of Moulmein, 31, 32; 43; in withdrawal from Minhla–Taungdwingyi line, 166 and fn.; in Yenangyaung–Pin Chaung operations, 170
    8th Burma Rifles: in defence of Moulmein, 30 fn., 31, 33; in Bilin river action, 59, 60, 61; in retreat to Sittang, 64, 73 fn. 1
    12th Burma Rifles: in retreat from Rangoon, 96 fn. 3; in withdrawal from Minhla–Taungdwingyi line, 166 fn.
    Chin Hills Battalion (Burma Frontier Force): 204
    Kokine Battalion (B.F.F.): 30 fn.
    F.F.1 (B.F.F.): raised, 9
    F.F.2 (B.F.F.): raised 9; raids into Siam, 23; in Bilin river action, 59; in retreat to Sittang, 67, 68 fn.
    F.F.3 (B.F.F.): raised, 9; 36

Army—*cont.*
    F.F.4 (B.F.F.): raised, 9; in retreat from Rangoon, 96 fn. 3
    Infantry Brigades:
    4th (British): 337; in Arakan operations, 338, 340, 341, 343, 344, 347, 348, 349, 354, 355
    6th (British): for seaborne attack on Akyab, 251, 257, 260–1, 262, 266; in Arakan operations, 331, 334, 337, 338, 340, 341, 342, 343, 344, 347, 348, 349, 354, 355
    13th (British): in 'Ironclad', 134, 135, 136, 139; 141
    14th (British): 355
    16th (British): 105, 106, 107; arrives Ceylon, 109
    17th (British): 130, in 'Ironclad', 133 and fn. 2, 136, 138, 139, 140; 141
    29th Independent (British): 130; in 'Ironclad', 133 and fn. 2, 136, 137, 138, 139, 140; 142; in final Madagascar operations, 143, 144; 248, 250, 251, 252, 257
    52nd (British): 387
    53rd (British): 15
    15th Australian: in New Guinea operations, 412
    16th Australian: arrives Ceylon, 109; 129, 130; in New Guinea operations, 287, 288
    17th Australian: arrives Ceylon, 109; 129, 130; in New Guinea operations, 375, 411, 412
    18th Australian: in New Guinea operations, 278, 279, 289
    21st Australian: in New Guinea operations, 278, 279, 288, 289
    25th Australian: in New Guinea operations, 278, 279, 287, 288
    30th Australian: in New Guinea operations, 288
    7th South African: in Madagascar operations, 142, 143
    1st Indian: 110, 182, 194, 206
    3rd Indian: in N.W. Frontier operations, 248
    13th Indian: arrives Burma, 12; 14, 36, 83, 147, 149, 164 and fn. 2; in withdrawal from Minhla–Taungdwingyi line, 165, 166; in Yenangyaung-Pin Chaung operations, 167, 170, 171; 181, 199; at Monywa, 200–2; in retreat to Shwegyin, 202, 207
    16th Indian: arrives Burma, 13; 27, 28; in retreat to Martaban, 29; on Salween river line, 30, 37, 39, 40; 41; on Bilin river line, 43; in Bilin river action, 59, 60, 61 and fn. 3; in retreat to Sittang, 63, 64, 66, 67, 68, 70, 71; 83, 85; in operations N. of Rangoon, 89; in retreat from Rangoon, 97, 98; 147; in operations Prome area, 157, 159; 164; in withdrawal from Minhla–Taung-dwingyi line, 166; in retreat across

INDEX

Army—*cont.*
  16th Indian—*cont.*
    Irrawaddy, 183, 199; at Monywa, 201; in retreat to Shwegyin, 202, 207; 239 fn. 1
  23rd Indian: in Arakan operations, 353, 354, 355
  32nd Indian: 390
  33rd Indian: in N.W. Frontier operations, 248
  36th Indian: in Arakan operations, 348 and fn. 3, 349, 352, 353–4, 354, 355
  44th Indian: 48
  45th Indian: 15, 48
  46th Indian: 21; arrives Burma, 27 and fn. 3; 30, 34, 35; on Salween river line, 37–8, 39, 40, 41; in withdrawal to Bilin river, 42; 43, 48; in Bilin river action, 59; in retreat to Sittang, 63, 65, 66, 67, 68, 70, 71; broken up, 83, 89 fn. 3
  47th Indian: in Arakan operations, 256, 257, 261 and fn. 1, 262 and fn. 2, 263, 264, 266, 331, 332, 334, 340 and fn. 2, 341, 343, 344–5
  48th Indian: 21, 34, 35; arrives Burma, 36 and fn. 1; on Salween river line, 38, 39, 41; 43, 48; in Bilin river action, 59, 60, 61, 62; in retreat to Sittang, 63, 64, 66, 67 and fn., 68 and fn.; 83; in operations N. of Rangoon, 89 and fn. 3, 93; 147; in operations Prome area, 157, 159; 164 and fn. 2; in withdrawal from Minhla–Taungdwingyi line, 165, 166; in retreat across Irrawaddy, 183, 185, 199; at Monywa, 200, 202; in retreat to Shwegyin, 202, 207; in Shwegyin action, 208; reaches India, 210; 239 fn. 1; on Tiddim front, 405
  49th Indian: 194
  55th Indian: in N.W. Frontier operations, 248; 250; in Arakan operations, 256, 266, 267, 331, 332, 333, 337, 338, 348, 349, 352, 353, 354, 355
  63rd Indian: 34, 48, 84 and fn. 2, 85, 86; arrives Burma, 89; in operations N. of Rangoon, 90; in retreat from Rangoon, 97, 98; 147; in operations Prome area, 157, 159; 164, 181; in retreat across Irrawaddy, 182, 183, 184, 185, 199; at Monywa, 200, 201, 202; in retreat to Shwegyin, 202, 207; reaches India, 210; 239 fn. 1; in Tiddim area, 405
  71st Indian: in Arakan operations, 266, 331, 332, 333, 334, 337, 338, 339, 345, 348, 352, 353, 354, 355
  72nd Indian: 389
  73rd Indian (lorried): 243, 389
  77th Indian (L.R.P.): formed, 244; 295, 303, 390, 399, 401, 403; *see also* Chindit operation
  80th Indian: 390

Army—*cont.*
  99th Indian: 390
  100th Indian: 390
  106th Indian: 239 fn. 2
  109th Indian: 110, 195
  111th Indian (L.R.P.): formed, 310, 390; 399, 401, 403
  113th Indian: 239 fn. 2
  123rd Indian: 239; in Arakan operations, 254, 255, 256, 257, 261, 262, 263, 264, 265, 266, 267, 331, 332, 335, 336, 337
  268th Indian (lorried): 243, 389
  North Assam: 239
  Razmak: in N.W. Frontier operations, 248
  1st Burma: formed, 12; 14, 36, 83, 147; attacks southward from Nyaunglebin, 148; in withdrawal to Toungoo–Prome, 149; 159, 164; in withdrawal from Minhla–Taungdwingyi line, 165–6; in Yenangyaung–Pin Chaung operations, 167, 170, 172; 181, 199; at Monywa, 200, 201, 202
  2nd Burma: formed, 12; 14, 27; in defence of Moulmein, 30 and fn. 3, 31–3; on Salween river line, 38; 43; at Sittang bridge, 61, 62 and fn.; 65, 83, 147; attacks southward from Nyaunglebin, 148; in withdrawal to Toungoo–Prome, 149; 159, 161 and fn. 2, 164; in withdrawal from Minhla–Taungdwingyi line, 166–7; in Yenangyaung–Pin Chaung operations, 168; 178, 181; in retreat across Irrawaddy, 182, 184; withdraws to India, 199, 204
  21st East African: arrives Ceylon, 109; 361
  22nd East African: 129; in Madagascar operations, 141, 142, 143, 144

No. 5 Commando: in 'Ironclad', 133, 136, 137
No. 142 Commando: 311
Jat Machine-Gun Battalion: in Arakan operations, 264
50th Indian Parachute Brigade: formed, 244; 390
141st Field Ambulance, R.A.M.C.: in 'Ironclad', 133 fn. 2
Arnold, Lieut.-General H. H. (U.S.A.A.F.): 298, 304, 305
Assam, airfields in: 113; 367 and fn. 2; special construction measures, 367; priority of work, 368
Assam – Burma – China Ferry Command: formed, 113–4; 241–2; renamed, 241 fn.; 307, 391
Assam, Japanese plan to invade: redeployment and reinforcement in Burma, 426–7, 432; political action against India, 427, 431–2; construction of Siam–Burma railway, 427–8; influence of Chindit operations, 428, 430, 434; material required,

Assam, Japanese plan to invade—*cont.*
431 and fn., 432; weakness in the air, 433; final plan, 434, 435
Assam line of communication: 53–4; importance of, 187; difficulties of road transport, 238; monsoon damage to, 238, 239, 394; construction of forward roads, 293, 294; general progress of work, 300–1; creation of G.R.E.F., 367; 368; measures found inadequate, 392–3, 394–5, 396; U.S. assistance for, 397; influence on future operations, 419, 420, 421, 422; decision to amplify, 423
Assam Public Works Department: 53
Astoria, U.S. cruiser: sunk, 274–5
Athelstane, H.M. fleet auxiliary: in operations off Ceylon, 123, 124; sunk, 125
Auchinleck, General Sir C.: 6, 127; becomes C.-in-C. in India, 388 and fn. 1; his problems, 392; reports on Assam line of communication, 393, 395; recommends limitation of offensives, 393–4; suggests postponement of big operations, 396–7, 397–8; on Wingate, 398–9; on L.R.P., 399; criticises Wingate's plans, 402–3, 404; his view of S.E. Asia strategy, 404
Australia, H.M.A. cruiser: 272 fn. 3, 274, 376 fn. 2
Australian coast watchers in Solomons: 272, 273, 373, 413, 414, 417
Australian forces: destination of, 56 and fn. 2, 57–8; offered for Ceylon, 106, 108; arrive Ceylon, 109; return asked for, 129
Ava bridge demolished, 185

Bachaquero, s.s.; 134, 138
Bangkok, air attacks on, 28, 30
Barlow, Brigadier A. E.: in operations Prome area, 159
Bilin river: withdrawal to, 42; actions on, 59–64
Bismarck Sea, Battle of the: 375–6, 377
Bissell, Brigadier-General C. L. (U.S.A.A.F.): 304, 367
Blaker, Brigader E. H.: in Arakan operations, 261, 262, 263, 264
Blamey, General Sir T.: in New Guinea operations, 279, 286, 288
Bond, Major-General R. L.: 191, 391 fn. 4
Bourke, Brigadier A. J. H.: 12; at Moulmein, 30 fn., 31; in withdrawal to India, 204
Boyd, Rear-Admiral D. W.: in naval operations off Ceylon, 116, 121; in 'Ironclad', 136
Brahmaputra river: 50–1, 52, 300, 301
Brereton, Major-General L. H. (U.S.A.A.F.): 113
Brett, Major-General G. H. (U.S.): 16 and fn. 2, 18, 19
British Sergeant, s.s.: 123, 124; sunk, 125
Broad, General Sir C.: 239
Bromhead, Major R. B. G.: 313

Brooke-Popham, Air Chief Marshal Sir R.: C.-in-C. Far East, 7; recommends reinforcement of Burma, 12; his orders for defence of Burma, 13; 14
Broughall, Group Captain S.: 150
Brown, Vice-Admiral W. (U.S.N.): 224
Bruce, Major-General J. G. (204 Mission): 297 fn.
Bruce Scott, Major-General J.: 12, 35; in operations central Burma, 148, 149 fn.; in withdrawal from Minhla–Taungdwingyi line, 165-6; in Yenangyaung–Pin Chaung operations, 167, 170, 171, 172; at Monywa, 201, 202
'Buccaneer', Operation (Andamans): 397
Bull, Brigadier G. G. C.: in Arakan operations, 266
'Bullfrog', Operation (Akyab): 397, 419
'BU' Operation (Jap.): 429
Burma: reason for Japanese invasion, 1; her relation to defence of India, 1; frontiers, 1; terrain and communications, 1–4; climate, 4–5; products, 5; place on Imperial air route, 5; system of government, 5; the revolutionary element, 5–6; temper of population, 6; her place in Far East strategy, 6–7; in Far East Command, 7; transferred to India Command, 8, 14; forces maintained, 8; expansion of forces, 8–9; military deficiencies at outbreak of war, 9; air forces and airfields, 10; naval forces, 10–11; prospect of Chinese assistance, 11; invasion danger considered, 11–12; reinforced from India, 12, 13; defence dispositions, 12, 14; defensive policy, 13–14; Chinese aid for, 16–19; use of lease-lend stores, 19–21; included in ABDA Command, 21; reinforcement policy for, 21–2; transferred to India Command, 81
Burma Auxiliary Force: 8, 9
Burma Frontier Force: 8, 79–80
Burma, Governor of: *see* Dorman Smith
Burma Independent Army: 85 fn.
Burma, invasion and loss of: Japanese plan, 23; first encounter, 23; enemy concentrations, 24; air raids on Rangoon, 24, 25, 26, 84; reinforcements from India, 25, 27, 34–5, 84 and fn. 2; enemy air superiority, 25–6; Hutton's appreciation, 26–7; dispositions in Tenasserim, 28; air operations, 28, 30; defences and loss of Moulmein, 30–3; transportation troubles, 33; entry of Chinese forces, 35; concentration in southern Burma, 35–6; Salween river line, 37–9; Martaban evacuated, 40; action at Kuzeik, 40–1; withdrawal to Bilin river, 42; Bilin river action, 59–64; retreat to Sittang, 63–73; retrospect, 73–7; state of British forces, 79–80, 81–2, 161; operations N. of Rangoon, 85, 87–93, 97–9; evacuation of Rangoon, 95–7; Rangoon retrospect, 100–4; the new situation, 145; Japanese plans, 145–6; strength of Allied forces, 147; Alexander's plans, 147–9; enemy air offensives, 150, 151; loss of Toungoo, 156–7; operations in Prome

Burma, invasion and loss of—*cont.*
  area, 157–60; lack of air support, 161–2; the Minhla–Loikaw line, 163–4; withdrawal, 165–6; Yenangyaung–Pin Chaung operations, 167–8, 170–3; retreat of Chinese armies, 174–6; plans for withdrawal to India and China, 176–7, 178, 181; maintenance difficulties, 181–2; retreat across Irrawaddy, 182–5, 199; loss of Akyab, 195; action at Monywa, 200–2; retreat to Shwegyin, 202, 205–8; action at Shwegyin, 208–9; Burma evacuated, 210; casualties and air losses compared, 210; summary of Allied air operations, 213; battle for central and upper Burma reviewed, 214–8; general retrospect of campaign, 218–20
Burma Military Police: 8
Burma, Puppet Government of: 427
Burma Rifles: quality of, 38 fn., 79–80
Burma Road: cut by Japanese, 185
Burma R.N.V.R.: 10–11; coastal action of, 26, 89 and fn. 2

Cairo conference: 249
Calcutta: air attacks on, 259–60; air defence of, 260
Calcutta conference: 306–7
Caldecot, Sir A.: 108, 109
Callaghan, Rear-Admiral D. J. (U.S.N.): 282; killed, 283
Calvert, Major J. M.: 243 fn., 313, 315, 319, 320, 322, 323
Cameron, Brigadier R. T.: on Tiddim front, 405
Canadian troops in Aleutians expedition: 410
Canberra, H.M.A. cruiser: 273 fn. 3; sunk, 274
Canton Island: garrisoned by U.S., 222
Caroline Islands: Japanese bases in, 221
Casablanca conference: 297–8
Cassells, General Sir R.: 6
Casualties: in 'Ironclad', 140; evacuated from Burma, 205; in first Burma campaign, 210; in New Guinea, 289; in first Chindit operation, 324
Cavendish, Brigadier R. V. C.: in Arakan operations, 338, 343; fate of, 344 and fn. 1
Central Command (India): formed, 193
Ceylon: defence requirements, 55; under India Command, 55 fn. 1; measures to strengthen defence, 57, 105, 106, 107; C.-in-C. appointed, 107; conditions in, 107–9; land and air forces in, 109; air attacks on, 119–20, 123; air defence strengthened, 127; changes in garrison, 129, 130, 390
Ceylon, naval operations off: 115–26
Ceylon War Council: 109
'Champion' ('Trident' decisions): 396
Ch'en Mien Wu, General: 175
Chennault, Brigadier-General C. L. (U.S.A.A.F.): urges claims of C.A.T.F., 297, 298; 304, 307; on air offensive from China, 379; 387

Chetwode, General Sir P.: 6
Chiang Kai-shek: promises aid for defence of Burma, 16; his proposals and conditions, 17; his attitude at Chungking conference, 18–19; his view of lend-lease incidents in Rangoon, 20; 36; his command as Generalissimo, 36 fn. 2; visits India, 38; agrees on disposition of Chinese armies, 44; urges construction of Ledo road, 54; renews promise of co-operation, 86; on command of Chinese armies in Burma, 153; defines Stilwell's status, 154; his orders to Stilwell, 154; favours defensive in Burma, 155; desires unity of command under Alexander, 155–6; hampers chain of command, 156; refuses aid to 'Burcorps', 164, 168; 212; his plans for recovery of Burma, 291; his insistence on naval and air superiority, 293; on broken promises of naval support, 295–6; his refusal to co-operate, 296–7; presses for naval action, 303, 307; receives reassurance, 305; his requirements in aircraft and supplies, 305, 366; favours air offensive from China, 380
Chicago, U.S. cruiser: 272 fn. 3, 274
Chief of the Imperial General Staff (C.I.G.S.): on proposals for evacuation of Burma, 152; sends for Wingate, 398
Chiefs of Staff Committee: on Burma's link with Far East, 6–7; put Burma under India Command, 7–8; give Malaya priority over Burma, 11; call on India to reinforce Burma, 12, 34; divert troops to Malaya, 15; welcome Chiang Kai-shek's offer of aid, 16; transfer Burma to ABDA Command, 21; reinforcement policy for Far East, 21; on Japanese intentions after fall of Singapore, 55; provide for reinforcement of Burma and defence of Ceylon, 57; their plans for Eastern Fleet and Madagascar, 58; on holding Rangoon, 81; transfer Burma to India Command, 81; 105; on military reinforcement of Ceylon, 106, 107; give Ceylon priority over N.E. India, 107, 108; on strength of Eastern Fleet, 107; estimate air forces needed in India, 110 and fn. 3; send air reinforcements, 110–1; increase air forces in Ceylon, 127; forecast Japan's intentions, 128–9; 130; fix date for 'Ironclad', 133; on adverse air situation in Burma, 161; consider 'Anakim', 236, 237, 294; on Command in Burma operations, 292; on Wavell's responsibility for Burma, 294; on troops for 'Anakim', 361; their objections to 'Anakim', 368–9; on expansion of Indian Army, 385; detain assault shipping in Mediterranean, 395; on Assam line of communication, 397; adopt L.R.P. proposals, 401–2; on 'Trident' policy, 404; their proposals for 'Quadrant', 419–21; on formation of S.E. Asia Command, 424; accept Stilwell as Deputy Supreme Commander, 424
Chin levies: 405

INDEX

China: send military missions to Burma and Singapore, 11; British assistance to, 11; promises aid to Burma, 11; Allied policy for assisting, 379–82; *see also* Chiang Kai-shek

China Air Task Force (C.A.T.F.): 297; decision to build up, 298; 305, 391; *see also* Chennault

China, British Ambassador to: 16, 17, 18, 19, 20

Chindit operation, first: approved, 309–10; forward move of brigade, 310; the plan, 310–11; 311 fn.; Southern Group, 312, 314, 317–8, 320, 321, 322–3; Northern Group, 312–4, 315–6, 318, 319–20, 320, 321, 322, 323; enemy reactions, 316–8; casualties, 324; results of, 324–9; effect on Japanese strategy, 328–9, 428, 430, 434

Chindit, origin of name: 244

Chinese Army:
V Army: 17, 18, 27; for Toungoo area, 44; 45, 79, 147, 155, 156; to defend Pyinmana area, 163; in Sittang valley, 174, 176, 178; in retreat across Irrawaddy, 184, 185, 199; 201
VI Army: 17, 18, 19, 27; to defend Burma–Siam frontier, 44; relieves 1st Burma Division, 83; 147, 155, 156; to defend Loikaw area, 163; in Salween valley, 174, 175; in Shan States, 179; retreats into China, 179
LXVI Army: 155; enters Burma, 168, 174; 180, 199
22nd Division: 44, 154, 155, 156, 157 and fn. 1; in Sittang valley, 174, 177, 178; in retreat across Irrawaddy, 183, 184, 185, 199; withdraws to India, 212; trains in India, 245, 390
28th Division: 178, 180, 185
29th Division: 180; at Lashio, 185
30th Division: formed in India, 391
38th Division: 155, 168; in Yenangyaung–Pin Chaung operations, 170, 171, 172–3; 177, 178; in retreat across Irrawaddy, 182, 184, 199; 201, 206, 207; withdraws to India, 212; trains in India, 245, 390
49th Division: 18, 35, 44; in Salween valley, 174; in Shan States, 177, 179
55th Division: condition of, 18; 35, 44, 156; in Salween valley, 175; in Shan States, 179
93rd Division: 16, 18; moves into Burma, 24; 35, 44; in Salween valley, 174, 175; in Shan States, 177, 179
96th Division: 44, 154, 155, 156; in Sittang valley, 174, 177, 178, 180; in retreat across Irrawaddy, 183, 184, 185, 199; retreats into China, 212
200th Division: 44; in Toungoo area, 147 and fn. 3, 149, 154, 155; in action at Toungoo, 156, 157; in Sittang valley, 174; 177; recaptures Taunggyi, 179; retreats into China, 180
1st Regiment: 174, 175
2nd Regiment: 174, 175
3rd Regiment: 174, 175
113th Regiment: 168, 212
1st Reserve Regiment: 156
2nd Reserve Regiment: 156

Chinese forces, difficulties of co-operation with: 36–7, 156

Chinese liaison mission (Burma): 36

Chinthe, The: 244

Chittagong: precautions at, 195–6; policy for, 239–40, 250; air attacks on, 259

Chokai, Jap. cruiser: 116, 274

Christmas Island: garrisoned by U.S., 222

Chungking conferences: on Chinese assistance to Burma, 16–18; on Chinese co-operation in major offensive, 304–5

Churchill, Rt. Hon. W. S. (Prime Minister and Minister of Defence): 8; promises reinforcements for India and Burma, 14; his instructions *re* Chinese lease-lend supplies, 20; asks Australia for troops for Burma, 57; on Alexander to command in Burma, 82; suggests powers for C.-in-C. Ceylon, 108; on defence of southern India and Ceylon, 128; on importance of Diego Suarez, 130; obtains U.S. naval reinforcements for Atlantic, 133; on 'tidying up' Madagascar, 142; advocates southern Burma operation, 235–6; his conditions for launching 'Anakim', 237; at Cairo conference, 249; vote of confidence in, 269; on Chiang-Kai-shek's allegations, 296; 297; on 'Anakim', 368; on alternatives to 'Anakim', 369–70; approves strategy for Far East, 381; criticises Arakan operations, 382; on reduction of Indian Army, 385; on command in S.E. Asia, 387–8; 388; his dissatisfaction at S.E. Asia situation, 398; on Wingate, 398; 399; favours 'Culverin' rather than 'Bullfrog', 419, 420; advocates 'Culverin' at 'Quadrant', 422; on formation of S.E. Asia Command, 424; on Mountbatten, 426

Civil defence: in Rangoon, 13; in Ceylon, 108, 109

Cocanada, air attack on: 126

Colombo, air attack on: 119–20

Combermere, Wellington on: 237

Combined Chiefs of Staff Committee: include Burma in ABDA Command, 21; on command of Chinese forces in Burma, 153–4; on stabilization in Far East, 222–3; control Pacific strategy, 223; their recommendations for Far East strategy, 297–8, 381, 423–4; 422

Combined Operations Directorate (India): 390 fn. 2

Combined Training Centre (India): 390

Committee of Imperial Defence: 6

Coral Sea, Battle of the : 226–8; effect of, 233

Cornwall, H.M. cruiser: in operations off Ceylon, 117, 119, 120; sunk, 121

Cowan, Brigadier D. T.: arrives Burma, 41; 42, 71, 72; commands 17th Division, 86; conducts operations in Prome area, 158, 159, 160; 173; in retreat across Irrawaddy, 183; at Shwegyin action, 208–9

Crace, Rear-Admiral J. G.: 224, 227, 272 fn. 3

Cripps Mission, failure of: 115 and fn. 2, 245
Cripps, Sir S.: 115, 245
Crutchley, Rear-Admiral V. A. C., V.C.: 272 and fn. 3, 274, 376
'Culverin', Operation (Sumatra): 397, 419, 420; rejected at 'Quadrant', 422
Curtin, Rt. Hon. J. (Prime Minister of Australia): refuses troops for Burma, 57-8
Curtis, Brigadier A. C.: arrives Burma, 12; in Arakan operations, 337 and fn., 338

D'Albiac, Air Vice-Marshal J. H.: 109
Darwin reinforced by U.S.: 222
'Death Railway': 428
Deception plan (Chindit): 311, 317
Defence Committees: 7; on policy after fall of Singapore, 55-6
Delhi conferences on an Allied offensive: 291-2, 292, 293-4, 294-5, 299, 302-4
Denial schemes: Rangoon, 34, 94-5; Yenangyaung, 167
Dennys, Major-General L. E. (204 Mission): 11, 16, 17, 18, 20, 21; killed, 297 fn.
d'Entrecasteaux, Vichy sloop: 137
Devonshire, H.M. cruiser: in 'Ironclad', 134, 135, 136, 140, 141
Diego Garcia, defences for: 58
Diego Suarez: 58; *see also* 'Ironclad', Operation
Dill, Field-Marshal Sir J.: 293, 296, 298; at Chungking conference, 304, 305
Dimoline, Brigadier W. A.: in Madagascar operations, 141
Dorman-Smith, Sir R. (Governor of Burma): 6 and fn.; supports transfer of Burma to India Command, 7; his action on lease-lend question, 19-20; reports to Secretary of State, 34; 79; favours evacuation of Rangoon, 86; appeals for transport aircraft, 161
Dorsetshire, H.M. cruiser: in operations off Ceylon, 117, 119, 120; sunk, 121
Dunlop, Major G.: 320, 323

Eastern Fleet: 105; reinforcement of, 107; function of, 107-8; in operations off Ceylon, 115, 116-9, 120-3, 123-5; its limited capacities, 127; reinforces other theatres of war, 127, 129, 134, 282, 296, 389; plans to strengthen, 128, 293; continued weakness of, 295, 296, 303, 389
Eastern Solomons, naval battle of the: 276-7
Eichelberger, Lieut.-General R. L. (U.S.): 288 and fn. 2, 412 and fn.
Ekin, Brigadier R. G.: arrives Burma, 27; at Moulmein, 30-1, 32; on Salween river line, 40; 42; in retreat to Sittang, 66, 68, 70, 72

Emerald, H.M. cruiser: in operations off Ceylon, 118
Enterprise, U.S. aircraft carrier: 224, 225, 229, 230, 231, 232, 272, 276, 277, 281, 282, 283, 376

Far East: British and U.S. commitments defined, 223
Farwell, Brigadier G. A. L.: 12
Fergusson, Major B. E.: 313, 315, 320, 322
Festing, Brigadier (Major-General) F. W.: in 'Ironclad', 133, 134, 138, 139; in India, 248
Fiji reinforced: 222
Fitch, Rear-Admiral A. W. (U.S.N.): 227, 413
Fleet Air Arm:
    788 Squadron: in defence of Colombo, 119-20
    803 Squadron: in defence of Colombo, 119-20
    806 Squadron: in defence of Colombo, 119-20; in 'Ironclad', 137, 138
Fletcher, Rear-Admiral F. J. (U.S.N.): 226, 227, 228, 229, 230, 231, 232, 272, 274, 275
Formidable, H.M. aircraft carrier: in operations off Ceylon, 116
Fort, Rear-Admiral G. H. (U.S.N.): 413
Friendly Isles, U.S. base in: 222

Gaje Ghale, Havildar, V.C.: 406 fn. 3
Gandhi, Mahatma: 245; arrested, 246
Garnons-Williams, Captain G. A., R.N.: 134
General Reserve Engineer Force (India): 367
Ghormley, Admiral R. L. (U.S.N.): 271, 272, 275, 276, 281
Giffard, General Sir G.: 362; commands Eastern Army, 390
Gilkes, Major K. D.: 313
Goddard, Major-General E. N.: 354 fn.
Gough, Brigadier G. H.: 244
Graham, Commodore C. M.: 95
Greater East Asia Co-Prosperity Sphere: 1, 307-8, 426
Grimsdale, Major-General G. E. (204 Mission): 297 and fn.
Griswold, Lieut.-General O. W. (U.S.): 416
Guadalcanal: Japanese landing, 271; U.S. landing 273; struggle for, 272-7, 279-86; Japanese evacuation, 286; comparative naval losses, 290 fn.
Guadalcanal, naval battle of: 283-4
Guerilla companies in China: 11

Halsey, Vice-Admiral W. F. (U.S.N.): 224, 281, 283, 284, 375, 376, 377, 411, 413, 416, 417
Hammond, Brigadier A. V.: in Arakan operations, 262, 264, 267, 268, 333, 335, 336, 337

INDEX

Hartley, General Sir A. E.: C.-in-C. in India, 50; on India's defence requirements, 55; 81; on state of Indian Army, 383
Heemskerk, Dutch cruiser: 117
Heinrich Jensen, s.s.: 95 and fn.
Helena, U.S. cruiser: sunk, 414
Henderson Field (airfield): 273, 275, 277, 280, 283; value of, 373-4
Hermes, H.M. aircraft carrier: in operations off Ceylon, 116, 117, 119, 123; sunk, 124
Hermione, H.M. cruiser: in 'Ironclad', 134, 135, 136, 137, 140, 141
Herring, Captain D. C.: 318 and fn., 319, 323
Herring, Lieut.-General E. F.: conducts New Guinea operations, 288 and fn. 1, 411
Hertz, Fort: garrisoned and supplied by air, 241; activities at, 310 fn. 1; plans to evacuate, 405
Hiei, Jap. battleship: sunk, 283
Hindustan, H.M.I. sloop: 89 fn. 2
Hiryu, Jap. aircraft carrier: 230; sunk, 232
Hobart, H.M.A. cruiser: 272 fn. 3, 376 fn. 2
Hodges, Lieut.-Commander J. M.: 140
Hollyhock, H.M. corvette: in operations off Ceylon, 123, 124; sunk, 125
Holmes, Mr (Colonel) R. J.: 36
'Hopforce': in Arakan operations, 340, 341, 342, 343
Hopkins, Colonel B. H.: in Arakan operations, 340, 344
Horii, Major-General: 278
Hornet, U.S. aircraft carrier: 225, 229, 230, 231, 232, 277; sunk, 281-2
Ho Ying Chin, General: 304-5, 306; on China's part in main Burma offensive, 307
Hugh-Jones, Brigadier N.: arrives Burma, 36 and fn. 1; in Bilin river action, 60; in retreat to Sittang, 64, 65, 69, 71; orders demolition of Sittang bridge, 72; in operations N. of Rangoon, 92
Hump, The: 241
Hungerford, Brigadier S. A. H.: in Arakan, 338
Hunt, Brigadier J. M.: in Arakan operations, 267, 337, 338
Huon Peninsula: *see* New Guinea
Hurricane fighter-bomber: 356 fn. 1
Hurricane fighter: performance of, 260
Hurs, outrages by: 247
Hutton, Captain R. M. S., R.N.: 136
Hutton, Lieut.-General T. J.: to command in Burma, 16, 50; receives directive, 16; his appreciation, 26-7; his dispositions, 27; allows withdrawal in Kawkareik area, 29; orders Moulmein to be held, 30; agrees to evacuation, 32; orders backloading from Rangoon, 33; asks for reinforcements, 34, 45, 79; brings in more Chinese troops, 35; concentrates in southern Burma, 35-6; assists Chinese armies, 36; orders Salween line to be held, 37; asks for warships, 37; his views on withdrawal to Bilin line, 42, 45-6; his dispositions on Sittang, 43; agrees with Chiang Kai-shek on rôle of Chinese armies, 44; reviews situation and envisages loss of Rangoon, 44-5; stands on Bilin

Hutton, Lieut.-General T. J.—*cont.*
line, 60; sanctions withdrawal to Sittang, 62; 65; on prospect of holding Rangoon, 79, 80, 84, 85; his conference on situation, 79-80; begins Rangoon evacuation scheme 80; 82; his measures to cover Rangoon, 83; his preparations for withdrawal, 85; decides to evacuate Rangoon, 86; 88; relinquishes command, 89; 160
Hyakutake, Lieut.-General: 271, 276, 279, 281, 284

Ichiki, Colonel: 276
Iida, Lieut.-General: 31, 38, 39, 87, 93, 145, 146, 163, 199-200, 204, 265
Illustrious, H.M. aircraft carrier: in 'Ironclad', 134, 135, 136, 137; 141
Imamura, General: 284, 286, 375, 414
Imperial General Headquarters (Japan): order capture of Andamans, 100; consider fresh offensive, 226; 229; direct Pacific operations, 271, 273, 279, 280, 284; order defensive in Burma, 308; revert to defensive in Pacific, 374; order central Solomons to be held, 414; decide to withdraw from central Solomons, 417; policy in Burma, 427, 430, 431; order construction of Siam-Burma railway, 427-8; consent to offensive preparations in Burma, 432; 433; *see also* Japan
Inada, General: 430
Independent Western Tribal Legion: 255 and fn. 4, 256
India: concerned with defence of Burma, 6-7, 8, 14; reinforces Burma, 12, 13, 15, 27, 34-5, 36, 46, 48, 89; strength and distribution of air forces, 48-9; airfields, warning system and radar, 49; reorientation of her defences, 49; her administrative problems, 49-50; Assam and Bengal communications, 50-5; defence requirements after fall of Singapore, 55; vulnerability after loss of Rangoon, 106; air reinforcements and reorganization, 110-2, 250-1, 258; airfield construction, 112-3, 191-2, 301, 367; assembly of U.S. air forces, 113; the air-lift to China, 113-4, 366-7, 368, 392; shipping losses off coasts, 126; 'her most dangerous hour', 131; coastal shipping shortage, 187; strain on railways, 187-8, 188-9; increased oil requirements, 189-91; reception of refugees, 192-3; reception of 'Burcorps', 196-7, 238; reception of Chinese troops, 245; internal disturbances, 246-8; enemy air offensive against, 259-60; her responsibilities as a base, 299; work involved, 299-301; shipping requirements, 301-2, 364-6; effect of economic situation, 384, 392; enemy subversive measures against, 383-4, 431-2
Indian Army: expansion of, 47; shortage of weapons and equipment, 47-8; distri-

Indian Army—*cont.*
    bution of, 48; Commanders-in-Chief, 50; frontier dispositions, 110, 194–5, 239–40; weakness in India, 128, 129; raising of guerilla forces, 192; reorganization of Commands, 193; reorganization and training, 242–5, 385–7, 389–90; morale of, 348, 382–4; pay increase, 386 fn.; brigade reorganization, 387
Indian Expeditionary Force: 362
Indian Independence League: 383
Indian National Army: 383, 432
Indian National League: 432
Indian Tea Association: provides labour, 54; aids refugees, 193
Indomitable, H.M. aircraft carrier: 106; in operations off Ceylon, 116, 121; in 'Ironclad', 134, 136, 137, 141
Indus, H.M.I. sloop: 89 fn. 2; 195
Infantry Committee (India): formed, 386; recommendations accepted, 386–7
Inoue, Admiral: 221, 271
Interpreters, Chinese: 149 fn.
'I', Operation (Pacific): 377–8
Ipi, Fakir of: 248
'Ironclad', Operation (Diego Suarez): 127, 129, 130, 131; forces assembled, 133–4; extension of operations considered, 134, 135; concentration, 135; the harbour and coast-line, 135; the plan, 135–6; the landings, 136–7; naval diversion, 137; air attacks, 137; surrender refused, 137; advance from west coast, 137–9, 140; naval landing party, 139–40; surrender, 140; battle casualties, 140
Irrawaddy Flotilla Company: 33, 151, 208
Irwin, Lieut.-General N. M. S.: 182; his dispositions in Assam, 239; commands Eastern Army, 239; controls Arakan operations, 257, 260, 264, 267, 331, 333, 334, 337, 338, 339, 340–1, 341–2, 343, 347, 353, 354 and fn., 355, 390

Japan: her war aims, 1, 115; effect of Tokyo air raid, 225, 226; her achievement (Apr. 1942), 225–6; fosters Indian subversive elements, 383–4; 431–2; decline of her air power, 433–4; *see also* Imperial General Headquarters
Japanese Army:
    Southern Army: directs S.E. Asia offensive, 23, 39, 87, 145; considers invasion of Assam, 308; 427, 428, 430, 431; presses for invasion of India, 432; 433, 434
    Burma Area Army: formed, 426, 427; 430, 431, 432, 434
    8th Area Army (Pacific): 284, 375
    3rd Air Army: formed, 240; 430, 433
    15th Army: occupies Siam and prepares to invade Burma, 23; 25, 26; conducts first Burma campaign, 39, 87, 145–6, 204; conducts Arakan operations, 265, 347; plans invasion of Assam, 308;

Japanese Army—*cont.*
    15th Army—*cont.*
        during first Chindit operation, 316, 317; 329, 426, 427, 428, 429, 430, 434
    17th Army: formed in Pacific, 271; 275, 276, 280, 284
    18th Army: formed in Pacific, 284; 288, 375
    25th Army: 23
Brigades:
    4th Air: in first Burma campaign, 25; 259, 265
    7th Air: in first Burma campaign, 145; 259, 265
    10th Air: 23; in first Burma campaign, 25; to China, 240
    12th Air: in first Burma campaign, 145; 259; to Pacific, 260
    24th Independent Mixed: 432
Divisions:
    3rd Air: 25, 379
    5th Air: in first Burma campaign, 25, 145; 240, 259, 260; in Arakan, 265, 339; 430, 433 and fn. 2
    Imperial Guards: 23
    2nd Infantry: in Pacific, 280, 281; to Malaya, 432
    15th Infantry: 432
    18th Infantry: 100, 146 and fn. 2; in first Burma campaign, 163, 183, 199, 200, 205; 308, 309; during first Chindit operation, 316, 317; 427, 428, 431
    20th Infantry: in Pacific 375 fn. 1
    31st Infantry: 427
    33rd Infantry: 23, 28; in first Burma campaign, 31, 38, 39, 40, 43, 59, 60, 64, 87, 88, 93, 98 and fn. 1, 145, 158, 163, 173, 177, 199, 200, 204–5; in Arakan operations, 265; 308, 309; during first Chindit operation, 316, 317; 427
    38th Infantry: in Pacific, 280, 282
    41st Infantry: in Pacific, 375 fn. 1
    51st Infantry: in Pacific, 375
    54th Infantry: 432
    55th Infantry: 23, 28 and fn. 2; in first Burma campaign, 29, 31–2, 38, 39, 43, 59, 61 fn. 2, 64, 87, 88, 92, 93, 146, 148, 156, 163, 199, 204; in Arakan operations, 265 and fn. 2; 308, 309; during first Chindit operation, 316 and fn. 1; 427
    56th Infantry: in first Burma campaign, 146 and fn. 1, 156, 174, 175, 179, 180, 199, 200, 204; 309; during first Chindit operation, 316, 317; 427, 431
Regiments:
    14th Air: losses at Rangoon, 25; 240; to Pacific, 260
    81st Air: 240
    27th Air: 240
    15th Independent Air Unit: 240
    55th Cavalry: in first Burma campaign, 28 fn. 2, 87
    55th Engineer: in first Burma campaign, 28 fn. 2

INDEX

Japanese Army—*cont.*
Regiments—*cont.*
55th Infantry: in first Burma campaign, 146 fn. 2; during first Chindit operation, 316, 317
56th Infantry: in first Burma campaign, 146 fn. 2; during first Chindit operation, 316, 317
112th Infantry: 24; in first Burma campaign, 28 and fn. 2, 88; in Arakan operations, 245 fn. 2, 337, 347, 355
113th Infantry: in first Burma campaign, 146 fn. 1, 180, 185
114th Infantry: in first Burma campaign, 146 fn. 2; during first Chindit operation, 316
143rd Infantry: in first Burma campaign, 23, 28 and fn. 2, 64, 87, 88, 90, 148, 156; in Arakan operations, 265 fn. 2, 355; 406
146th Infantry: in first Burma campaign, 146 fn. 1, 205; during first Chindit operation, 317
148th Infantry: in first Burma campaign, 146 fn. 1, 180, 185, 205
213th Infantry: in first Burma campaign, 145, 165, 173, 200, 205, 207, 209; in Arakan operations, 255 and fn. 3, 263, 264 fn. 2, 265, 266, 332 fn. 3; 335
214th Infantry: in first Burma campaign, 42, 59, 60 and fn., 64, 88, 98, 99, 158, 159, 165, 167, 173, 200; during first Chindit operation, 316; in Arakan operations, 347
215th Infantry: in first Burma campaign, 38, 40, 42, 59, 60, 64, 88, 99, 158, 159, 165, 173, 200; during first Chindit operation, 316, 317
33rd Mountain Artillery: in first Burma campaign, 165
55th Mountain Artillery: in first Burma campaign, 28 fn. 2
56th Reconnaissance: in first Burma campaign, 205
1st Tank: in first Burma campaign, 146
14th Tank: in first Burma campaign, 146
55th Transport: in first Burma campaign, 28 fn. 2
Kakihara Column: in Arakan operations, 340, 347 fn. 4
Kawaguchi Detachment: in Pacific, 275, 276, 277, 280
Kawashima Detachment: in first Burma campaign, 87, 88, 93, 148
Kawashima Column: in Arakan operations, 335
Ichiki Detachment: in Pacific, 275, 276, 280
Miyawaki Column: in Arakan operations, 335, 336, 339, 347
South Sea Detachment: in Pacific, 221, 271, 275
Tanahashi Column: in Arakan operations, 335, 336, 339, 340, 347, 351

Uno Column: in Arakan operations, 335, 339, 340, 347, 351
Japanese Navy:
Combined Fleet: in Pacific, 226, 229, 279, 281, 374
Southern (2nd) Fleet: raids Ceylon, 115, 127; in Pacific, 230
South-Eastern Area Fleet: in Pacific, 374
1st Air Fleet; attacks Colombo, 115; attacks Trincomalee, 123; in Pacific, 226, 228
11th Air Fleet: in Pacific, 374, 377
4th Fleet: in Pacific, 221, 226, 271
8th Fleet: in Pacific, 271, 374
Malaya Force: attacks shipping, Bay of Bengal, 116, 125, 126
24th Air Flotilla: in Pacific, 221
25th Air Flotilla: in Pacific, 271, 273
3rd Destroyer Flotilla: attacks shipping, Bay of Bengal, 116
4th Submarine Flotilla: attacks at Diego Suarez, 142
3rd Battle Squadron: in attack on Colombo, 116
1st Carrier Squadron: in Pacific, 378
7th Cruiser Squadron: attacks shipping, Bay of Bengal, 116
8th Cruiser Squadron: in attack on Ceylon, 116
9th Special Base Force: occupies Port Blair, 100
12th Special Base Force: occupies Port Blair, 100
Jefferies, Major J. B.: 311, 315 fn.
Jintsu, Jap. cruiser: sunk, 415
Joint Chiefs of Staff (U.S.): 221; their responsibility in Pacific, 223; their directives for offensives, 270, 277, 377; 379; advocate offensive from Assam, 381; approve L.R.P., 421; their policy at 'Quadrant', 421-2; support Stilwell's appointment in S.E. Asia Command, 424
Jones, Brigadier J. K.: 13; his dispositions in Kawkareik area, 28; withdraws, 29; defends Bilin river line, 59-60, 63; in retreat to Sittang, 68, 70, 71, 72
Junyo, Jap. aircraft carrier: 230

Kachin levies: 310 fn. 1
Kaga, Jap. aircraft carrier: 230; sunk, 231
'Kanga force' (New Guinea): 278, 375, 411, 412
Kan Li-chu, Lieut.-General: 44, 175, 179
Kawabe, Lieut.-General M.: 427 and fn. 1, 430
Kenney, Major-General C. C. (U.S.A.A.F.): 286, 376
King, Admiral E. J. (U.S.N.): 223, 270, 282
Kinkaid, Rear-Admiral T. C. (U.S.N.): 281
Kirishima, Jap. battleship: sunk, 283
Kobe, air attack on: 225
Koga, Major-General T.: 265-6, 334-5, 339, 345, 347, 355
Kolombangara, naval action of: 414-6
Kondo, Vice-Admiral: 115, 230, 276
Krueger, Lieut.-General W. (U.S.): 411

Kula Gulf, naval action of: 414, 416
Kunomura, Major-General M.: 429 and fn. 4
Kurita, Admiral: 230, 232
Kusaka, Vice-Admiral: 374, 375, 414
Kuzeik, action at: 40–1

Laforey, H.M. destroyer: in 'Ironclad', 136
Layton, Vice-Admiral Sir G.: appointed C.-in-C. Ceylon, 108; his powers, 108–9; 109, 116, 118, 122
Leander, H.M.N.Z. cruiser: 415
'Leap-frogging' policy in Pacific: 417
Lease-lend supplies: use of in Burma, 16; Rangoon incident, 19–20; 33 fn. 1
Ledo base: 245, 292, 293, 295
Ledo road: projected, 54, 245; construction of, 292, 293, 295, 298; progress of, 300; 303
Lee, Rear-Admiral W. A. (U.S.N.): 283
Lexington, U.S. aircraft carrier: 224; sunk, 228
Lightning, H.M. destroyer: in 'Ironclad', 136, 137
Linlithgow, Marquess of (Viceroy): on defence of Burma, 6; on change of command in Burma, 81–2; on Command in S.E. Asia, 370
Lin Wei, General: 155, 156, 178
Lloyd, Major-General W. L.: 250; conducts Arakan operations, 254–5, 257, 261, 262, 263 and fn. 1, 264, 266, 267, 331, 332, 333, 334, 336, 337, 338, 339, 340, 341
Lo Cho-ying, General: 175, 178, 204
Lomax, Major-General C. E. N.: conducts Arakan operations, 339 and fn. 1, 341, 343, 344, 347–8, 349, 352, 353, 354, 355; 406
Long Range Penetration (L.R.P.): first scheme for, 243; proposals for expanded operations, 398–9; Wingate's plan, 399–401; approved by Chiefs of Staff, 401–2; Auchinleck's criticism, 402–3, 404; Wingate's attitude, 403–4; influence on Chiefs of Staff, 421; discussed at 'Quadrant'; *see also* Chindit operation, first *and* Wingate
Lucia, H.M. submarine depôt ship: 119
Lu Kuo Ch'uan, General: 175
Lyle, Commander K. S., R.N.: 11

MacArthur, General D. (U.S.): his Command and directive, 223; 270, 271; directs New Guinea operations, 278, 279, 288, 289; directs operations in Solomons and New Guinea, 377, 411
'MacArthur's Navy': 286, 376
McLeod, Lieut.-General D. K.: commands in Burma, 7; 13; forecasts scale of invasion, 14; his dispositions, 14; relinquishes command, 16
Madagascar: plan to sieze control, 58 and fn. 2; situation after 'Ironclad', 141; further operations suspended, 141, 142; capitulation refused, 141, 143, 144; operations resumed, 143–4; surrender accepted, 144; battle casualties, 144; *see also* 'Ironclad'
Madras, false alarm at: 126

'Magforce': formed in Burma, 166 and fn. 1; in Yenangyaung-Pin Chaung operations, 167, 168, 170–1, 171
Magruder, Brigadier-General J. (U.S.): 17, 18, 19
Magwe airfield: 149; air attacks from, 149–50; enemy retaliation, 150; aircraft withdrawn from, 150; destruction ordered, 166
Malaria: in Madagascar, 141, 144; in retreat from Burma, 210; in Assam, 238, 239; in Arakan, 348 and fn. 1
Malaya, H.M. battleship: 134
Maldive Islands: 105
Mandalay evacuated: 184
Mansergh, Captain C. A. L., R.N.: 415
Manwaring, Captain P. C. W., R.N.: 117, 121
Marshall, General G. C. (U.S.): 223, 270, 282; on Stilwell's appointment in S.E. Asia Command, 424–5
Martaban: air attacks on, 28, 32, 33, 40; bombarded, 38; evacuated, 40
Maruyama, Lieut.-General: 281
Maughs at Akyab: 195
Mauritius, defences for: 58
'Mayforce': in Arakan operations, 337, 338, 348, and fn. 2, 349, 352, 353, 354
Mergui evacuated: 28–9
Merrill, Colonel F. D. (U.S.): 298, 421 fn.
Merrill, Rear-Admiral A. S. (U.S.N.): 376
'Merrill's Marauders': 421 fn.
Midway, Battle of: 229–33
Midway Island: reinforced, 229; enemy attack on, 230–1
Mikawa, Vice-Admiral: 271, 273, 274, 275
Mineichi Koga, Admiral: 378
Mission, 204 (Chungking): 11 fn., 297 and fn.; *see also* Dennys
Monywa, action at: 200–2
Moran, Commander W. T. A., R.A.N.: 117; lost with ship, 124
Morris, Lieut.-General E. L.: 50
Moulmein: air attacks on, 28, 29; defence and loss of, 30–3
Mountbatten, Vice-Admiral Lord Louis: appointed Supreme Commander S.E. Asia, 426
Mutaguchi, Lieut.-General R.: 146 fn. 2, 329, 427 and fn. 1, 428–9, 430
Myitkyina occupied by Japanese: 205

Nagano, Admiral: 226
Nagoya, air attack on: 225
Nagumo, Vice-Admiral: 115, 116, 118, 123, 125, 226, 229, 230, 231, 276, 377
New Britain, Japanese established in: 221
New Caledonia reinforced by U.S.: 221–2
New Georgia Group, operations against: 411, 413–7
New Guinea: Japanese established in, 221; terrain, 278, 286, 412; operations in, 277–9, 286–9, 375, 411–2; Allied casualties in, 289; reinforced by Japanese, 374, 375; Allied plans for, 375; Japanese air offensive, 377–8; trials of campaigning in, 412
New Guinea Force: 411

INDEX

New Hebrides, U.S. bases in: 222
Nimitz, Admiral C. (U.S.N.): 223, 226, 229, 233, 270, 271 and fn. 1, 375
North Carolina, U.S. battleship: 272, 276, 277
North-West Frontier (India), outbreak on: 248
Noyes, Rear-Admiral L. (U.S.N.): 272

Obata, Lieut.-General H.: 25, 240
Obata, Major-General: 429 and fn. 3
Observer corps (Burma): 9
Oliver, Captain R. D., R.N.: 136
Onslow, Captain R. F. J., R.N.: 117; lost with ship, 124
Oo Kyaw Khine: 195
Orgill, Captain R. C.: 71, 72
Osaka, air attack on: 225
Ozawa, Vice-Admiral: 116, 125, 126

Pacific: Japanese progress southward, 221; U.S. chain of bases, 221–2; demands on shipping, 222–3, 224; Commands and directives, 223; U.S. raids, 224–5; Coral Sea battle, 226–8; the Aleutian islands, 229, 230, 233, 409, 409–10; battle of Midway, 229–33; U.S. plans for offensives, 270–1; Japanese plans, 271; Guadalcanal operations, 272–7, 279–86; action off Savo island, 274–5; battle of the Eastern Solomons, 276–7; New Guinea operations, 277–9, 286–9, 375, 411–2; battle of Santa Cruz, 281–2; naval action in The Slot, 283; naval battle of Guadalcanal, 283–4; naval battle of Tassafaronga, 234; U.S. air superiority, 373–4; Allied plans for offensives, 375, 377, 409; battle of the Bismarck Sea, 375–6; U.S. naval and air strength, 377–8; Japanese air offensive, 377–8; New Georgia operations, 411, 413–7; action of Kula Gulf, 414, 416; action of Kolombangara, 414–6
Pacific Ocean Area Command, sub-divisions of: 223
Pacific War Council: decisions after fall of Singapore, 56–7; composition of, 56 fn. 1; decides to reinforce Ceylon, 105, 106; 295 fn. 3
Palmyra (Pacific) garrisoned by U.S.: 222
Papua: *see* New Guinea
Parkash Singh, Havildar, V.C.: 263 fn. 2
Patch, General A. M. (U.S.): 284, 286
Persia and Iraq Command (PAIC): 249
Philips, Lieut.-Colonel D. C. P.: 348 fn. 2
Phoenix, U.S. cruiser: 376 fn. 2
Pierse, Air Marshal Sir R.: commands air forces in India and Ceylon, 111; urges provision of long-range aircraft, 251; on Akyab operation, 251; 368, 387
Plan 21 (Jap.): 308, 429, 430
Platt, Lieut.-General Sir W.: conducts Madagascar operations, 142 and fn. 1, 143
Port Blair: occupied by Japanese, 100; British air attacks on, 126–7

Port Moresby: threat to, 221; reinforced, 222; Japanese plan to capture, 271 *and see* New Guinea
Pownall, Lieut.-General Sir H.: C.-in-C. Far East, 8; in Ceylon, 109
Prime Minister and Minister of Defence *see* Churchill
Provisional Government of Free India: 423

'Quadrant' Conference: 399, 421–2; decides Far East strategy, 422–3, 424; conclusions of C.C.S., 423; agreement on S.E. Asia command, 424–5
Quincy, U.S. cruiser: sunk, 274

Rabaul: captured by Japanese, 221; importance of, 374
Radar: in Burma, 26, 84; in India, 49; in Ceylon, 108
Ramillies, H.M. battleship: in 'Ironclad', 134, 135, 136, 139, 140; 141
Rangoon: 3; air raid precautions in, 13; importance of, 15, 26; lend-lease supplies incidents, 19–20; air attacks on, 24, 25, 26, 84; preparations for evacuation, 33, 34; air defence priority for, 43; dispersal of civil population, 44, 93; prospects of holding, 79, 80, 81, 82, 84, 86, 89; evacuation measures begun, 80; partial success of denial scheme, 94–5; departure by sea, 95; departure of garrison, 97; entered by Japanese, 99
Ratnagiri, H.M.I. sloop: 89 fn. 2
'R' Class battleships: 116, 117, 118, 122
Refugees from Burma: 44, 192–3, 205, 238
Roome, Major-General H.: 391 fn. 4
Roosevelt, Mr. F. D. (President U.S.A.): 56 fn. 1, 223, 282; on Burma Road, 296; 297; promises build-up of U.S. air forces in China, 307; his policy for assisting China, 380–1; objects to 'Culverin', 422; proposes Stilwell for Deputy Supreme Commander S.E. Asia, 424
Rowell, Lieut.-General F. F.: 278, 288 fn. 1
Royal Air Force: in defence of Rangoon, 24, 25, 26, 84–5; in support of army in Burma campaign, 28, 43, 61, 64, 67, 73 and fn. 3, 149, 149–50, 213; operations following evacuation of Burma, 240–1, 258, 260; operations in Arakan, 261 and fn. 3, 266, 267, 343, 355, 355–6; in support of Chindit operation, 312, 313, 316, 319, 320, 321, 322, 323–4; airfields in Assam, 367 fn. 2; expansion and re-equipment of, 391; operations over Burma and Siam (monsoon 1943); 406 and fn. 2, 408
Royal Air Force:
  Bengal Command: 112, 355–6
  1 (Indian) Group: at Peshawar, 111
  221 Group (Calcutta): 111, 112, 258; monsoon (1943) operations, 406, 408
  222 Group (Colombo): 49, 111
  223 Group (Peshawar): 111

538   INDEX

Royal Air Force—*cont.*
 224 Group (Calcutta): 111, 112, 258; supports Arakan operations, 260, 336, 408
 225 Group (Bangalore): 111
 226 (Maintenance) Group (Karachi): 111
 227 (Training) Group (Lahore): 111
 5 (Fighter) Squadron: 48; operations Burma (Mar-May 1942), 213
 11 (Bomber) Squadron: in defence of Trincomalee, 123
 17 (Fighter) Squadron: in Burma, 26; defends Rangoon, 84–5, 96
 28 (Army Co-operation) Squadron: in Burma, 26; employed as light bombers, 43; 96; in N.W. Frontier operations, 248
 30 (Fighter) Squadron: diverted to Ceylon, 106; defends Colombo, 119–20
 31 (Bomber-Transport) Squadron: 48; transport work in Burma, 212; supply and rescue work, 240–1; supports Chindit operations, 310; monsoon (1943) operations, 408
 34 (Bomber) Squadron: in N.W. Frontier operations, 248; 258
 45 (Bomber) Squadron: in Burma, 26, 96
 60 (Bomber) Squadron: 10; in Burma, 26, 48
 67 (Fighter) Squadron: in Burma, 10, 26, 48; defends Rangoon, 25, 84–5; 96
 99 (Bomber) Squadron: 258
 113 (Bomber) Squadron: in Burma, 26; attacks Bangkok, 28, 30; Burma (Mar.-May 1942) operations, 213
 135 (Fighter) Squadron: in Burma, 26; defends Rangoon, 84–5; 96
 139 (General Reconnaissance) Squadron: in Burma, 96
 146 (Fighter) Squadron: 48
 159 (Bomber) Squadron: 258
 176 (Fighter) Squadron: 260
 205 (Flying Boat) Squadron: 49
 215 (Bomber) Squadron: 244
 258 (Fighter) Squadron: defends Colombo, 119–20
 261 (Fighter) Squadron: diverted to Ceylon, 106
 273 (Torpedo-Bomber) Squadron: 49
 'Akwing': formed at Akyab, 96; moves to Chittagong, 150
 'Burwing': formed at Magwe, 96; moves to Lashio and Loiwing, 150
 X Wing: 96
 170 Wing: monsoon (1943) operations, 406
(Royal) Indian Air Force: in Burma, 26; on N.W. Frontier, 48; morale of, 384; expansion and training, 391; 391 fn. 1
(Royal) Indian Air Force:
 1 (Army Co-operation) Squadron: in Burma, 26; employed as light bombers, 43
(Royal) Indian Air Force V.R.: 48
Royal Indian Navy: 89 fn. 2
Royal Marines: in Burma campaign, 96, 184, 206, 208; in 'Ironclad', 139–40
Royal Ulsterman, s.s.: 137
Russell, Brigadier V. C.: 134

Russell Islands: occupied by U.S. forces, 375
Ryujo, Jap. aircraft carrier: 116, 230; sunk, 276

Sakuma, Colonel: 99
Sakurai, Lieut.-General: 64, 93, 99
Salween river line: dispositions, 37–8, 39; evacuation of Martaban, 40; Kuzeik action, 40–1; withdrawal, 41–2
Samoa garrisoned by U.S.: 221
Santa Cruz, naval battle of: 281–2
Sato, Lieut-General K.: 427
Savige, Major-General S. G.: in New Guinea operations, 412
Savo island, naval action off: 274–5
Scoones, Lieut.-General G. A. P.: to command IV Corps, 239; orders Chindit withdrawal, 321; on Tiddim front, 405
Scott, Major W. P.: 313
'Seabees': 277
Seagrave, Dr. Gordon: 36
Sendai, Jap. cruiser: 116
Seychelles, defences for: 58
Shan States: defence passes to Chinese, 83; operations in, 177, 178, 179, 180; cleared by Japanese, 204–5
Shipping: demands in Pacific, 222–3; India's requirements, 364–5, 366; Allied shortage, 419, 420
Shoho, Jap. aircraft carrier: sunk, 227; 228
Shokaku, Jap. aircraft carrier: 227, 228, 276
Shwegyin, action at: 208–9
Siam-Burma railway: construction of, 427–8; labour force for, 428 and fn. 1
Singapore Conference: 11–12
Sittang bridge: defensive measures at, 43, 61, 62 and fn., 66, 67; description of, 65; action at, 68–9; demolition of, 72
Sittang river, retreat to: 63–73
Situation, General War: March (1942), 105; June (1942), 269; (1942–3), 373
'Skip-bombing': 376
Slim, Lieut.-General W. J.: commands 'Burcorps', 148; orders offensive in Prome area, 158; agrees to rapid retirement, 160; his Yin Chaung position, 160; his dispositions on Minhla-Taungdwingyi line, 164–5; conducts withdrawal, 166; orders Yenangyaung demolitions, 167; conducts Yenangyaung-Pin Chaung operations, 171; 177, 178, 180, 181; in withdrawal across Irrawaddy, 182; orders recapture of Monywa, 200; in retreat to Shwegyin, 207; on tanks in Arakan, 267 fn. 1; controls Arakan operations, 348, 349–50, 352, 353, 354, 355; his plan for a phased withdrawal, in Arakan, 351
'Slot, The': 272; naval action in, 283
Smuts, Field-Marshal J. C.: 134, 141, 142
Smyth, Major-General J. G., V.C.: arrives Burma, 27; his dispositions in Tenasserim, 28, 30; urges evacuation of Moulmein, 32; on Salween line, 37–8, 39; 40; retires to Bilin river, 41–2; his dispositions, 43, 59; conducts Bilin river action, 60, 61; conducts retreat to Sittang, 63, 64, 65, 66, 68, 69, 72; relinquishes his command, 86

INDEX

Solomon Islands: Japanese bases in, 221; situation, terrain and climate, 272; political divisions, 272; coast watching organization in, 272; operations, 272–5, 276–7, 279–86, 289, 373, 376, 377–8, 411, 413–7
Somervell, Lieut.-General B. B. (U.S.): 298
Somerville, Admiral Sir J.: 107; conducts operations off Ceylon, 116–8, 120–3, 125; on limited capacity of Eastern Fleet, 127; covers 'Ironclad', 134; 293; on weakness of Eastern Fleet, 295; 362, 368, 387
Soong, T. V.: 19
Soryu, Jap. aircraft carrier: 230; sunk, 231
'Soutcol' in Arakan operations: 261 and fn. 4, 265 and fn. 1, 266, 331, 332, 333, 336
Souter, Lieut.-Colonel J. H.: 261, 336
South African Air Force in Madagascar: 135
South African armoured cars in Madagascar: 143
South Dakota, U.S. battleship: 281, 282, 283
South-East Asia Command: proposed, 370–1, 387–8; agreed upon, 424–5; Stilwell's appointment, 424–5; pattern of command, 425; Mountbatten's appointment, 426
South-East Pacific Area: 223
South-West Pacific Area: 223; boundary readjusted, 271 fn. 1
Spruance, Rear-Admiral R. A. (U.S.N.): 229, 230, 231, 232
Stevenson, Air Vice-Marshal D. F.: 25, 79; his policy in Burma campaign, 80; 86; redeploys air forces, 96; 150
Stilwell, Lieut.-General J. B. (U.S.): his command in Burma, 147; his appointments in C.-B.-I. theatre, 154; his character, 154; claims independent command in Burma, 154; his plans, 155; reaches agreement with Alexander, 156; conducts Toungoo operations, 156, 157; 168; his operations in Salween and Sittang valleys, 174–5; his operations in Shan States, 177, 179; 180, 184, 185; 201; reaches India, 212; his comment on Burma campaign, 212; 236, 245; on plans for Allied action in Burma, 291–2, 292, 293, 294, 302–3; 304; on importance of land route to China, 379–80; 387; appointed Deputy Supreme Commander, S.E. Asia, 424–5
Stockades (Tiddim front): 405
Strong, U.S. destroyer: sunk, 414 and fn.
Sturges, Major-General R. C.: in 'Ironclad', 133, 135, 139, 140; 142
Subhas Chandra Bose: 432
Sumiyoshi, Major-General: 281
Sundarbans Flotilla: 55 and fn. 2, 195; reorganized as 2000 Flotilla, 256; 261
Sun Li-jen, General: 168 and fn. 3, 172, 173, 206, 212
Syfret, Rear-Admiral E. N.: commands 'Ironclad', 133, 134, 135, 139, 140
Syriam oil refineries: threat to, 89; closed down, 93; demolished, 94

Takagi, Rear-Admiral: 227
Tananarive occupied: 143
Tank action: in Burma, 90, 92, 166, 172, 173, 183; in Arakan, 266, 267 and fn. 1; in New Guinea, 289
Tank tactics: 357 and fn. 2
Tarleton, Brigadier G. W. B.: in 'Ironclad', 133
Tassafaronga, naval battle of: 284
Tavoy, loss of: 28
Tazoe, Lieut.-General N.: 240
Tenedos, H.M. destroyer: sunk, 119
Terauchi, Count: 431
Thakins: 5; at Pauk, 204
Thomas, Brigadier L. C.: 348
Tokyo, air attack on: 225
'Tokyo Express': 277, 280, 284
Tomahawk fighters: 10, 25
Tone, Jap. cruiser: 120
'Torch', Operation (N. Africa): 269, 282, 295 and fn. 2, 296
Toungoo, loss of: 156–7
'Trident' Conference (Washington): 369; C.C.S. recommendations, 381; decision on Far East strategy, 381–2; 390
Trincomalee, air attack on: 123
'Tripforce' in Arakan operations: 261 and fn. 1, 265 and fn. 1, 266, 331, 332, 338
Trobriand Group (Pacific): operations against, 411
Tulagi: occupied by Japanese, 227; 270; recaptured by U.S. forces, 273
Tulsa, s.s.: 19
Turner, Rear-Admiral R. K. (U.S.N.): 272, 274, 275, 282, 283, 413
Tu Yu-ming, Lieut.-General: 44, 163, 174, 177, 204

'U-Go', Operation (Jap.): 434
U Saw: 5; arrested, 6, 24
U.S. Army Air Force, 10th: 113; airlift to China, 113–4; transport work in Burma, 212–3; operations following evacuation of Burma, 213, 259; 236, 251; defence responsibilities, 258; question of Command, 292; airfields needed in Assam, 367 and fn. 2; expansion of, 391; operations over Burma and Siam (monsoon 1943), 406 and fn. 2
U.S. Army Air Force, 14th: 307; proposed build-up, 379; replaces C.A.T.F., 391
U.S. Air Transport Command: 391
U.S. Army:
  I Corps: in Pacific, 416
  XIV Corps: in Pacific, 288
  25th Division: to Guadalcanal, 285
  32nd Division: to Australia, 224, 270; to New Guinea, 286, 288; in Alamo Force, 411
  37th Division: reaches Fiji, 270; in New Georgia, 414
  41st Division: to Australia, 222, 224, 270; in Alamo Force, 411
  43rd Division: in New Georgia, 413
  Americal Division: to New Caledonia, 221–2, 222 fn. 1, 270; to Guadalcanal, 280, 282

540 INDEX

U.S. Army—*cont.*
    126th Regiment: in New Guinea, 287, 288
    127th Regiment: in New Guinea, 288, 289
    128th Regiment: in New Guinea, 279 fn., 288
    162nd Regiment: in New Guinea, 412
    163rd Regiment: in New Guinea, 289
U.S. Marine Corps:
    1st Marine Division: to New Zealand, 270; lands on Guadalcanal and Tulagi, 272–3; withdrawn, 285
    2nd Marine Division: to Guadalcanal, 282, 285
    1st Marine Regiment: 272 fn. 2
    2nd Marine Regiment: 272; in Guadalcanal, 275
    5th Marine Regiment: 272 fn. 2
    6th Marine Regiment: to Guadalcanal, 285
    7th Marine Regiment: in Samoa, 270; 272 and fn. 2; to Guadalcanal, 277
    11th Marine Regiment: 272 fn. 2

Vampire, H.M. destroyer: in operations off Ceylon, 117, 119, 123; sunk, 174
Vandegrift, Major-General A. A. (U.S.): 272, 274, 281, 284
Vella Gulf, naval action off: 416
Vengeance: dive-bomber, 251; light bomber, 356 fn. 1
'V' Force: raised, 192 and fn.; in Assam, 192, 239; in Arakan, 255, 256, 257, 261, 332, 335, 347, 349, 354, 355
Viceroy and Governor-General of India: Wavell succeeds Linlithgow, 388 and fn. 1; to act on behalf of War Cabinet, 425; *see also* Linlithgow, Marquess of
Victorious, H.M. aircraft carrier: 282
Vincennes, U.S. cruiser: sunk, 274
Viper Force: formed, 96; in Prome area, 157; at Monywa, 199
Vizagapatam, air attack on: 126

Wakeley, Major-General A. V. T.: 182
Warburton, Wing Commander J.: 11
War Cabinet: approve Madagascar operation, 143; on expansion of Indian Army, 385; represented by Viceroy of India, 425
Warning systems: Burma, 10, 149, 150, 151; Ceylon, 108, 109; Malaya, 150, 151
Warspite, H.M. battleship: in operations off Ceylon, 116, 117, 118, 123
Washington Treaty: 221
Washington, U.S. battleship: 282, 283
Wasp, U.S. aircraft carrier: 272 and fn. 1, 276; sunk, 277
Watanabe, General: 146 fn. 1, 175
'Watchtower', Operation (Pacific): 270, 271
Water supply in Burma: 164, 166, 170
Wavell, General (Field-Marshal) Sir A. (Viscount): C.-in-C. in India, 6; responsible for defence of Burma, 7; advises reinforcement of Burma, 13; 14–15; visits Burma, 15, 30, 38–9, 86, 159; changes Command

Wavell, General (Field-Marshal) Sir A. (Viscount)—*cont.*
in Burma, 16; his directive to Hutton, 16; visits Chiang Kai-shek, 16, 18, 86; on employment of Chinese armies, 18–19; uses Chinese lease-lend supplies, 20; appointed to ABDA Command, 21, 50; approves of increased Chinese assistance, 35; urges counter-offensive in Burma, 46, 81, 83; reappointed C.-in-C. in India, 50, 86; improves Assam-Burma road communications, 53, 54; presses for Australian troops for Burma, 56; expects Rangoon to be held, 80–1, 82–3, 86; secures change of command in Burma, 82; on spirit of troops, 82; 85; his directive to Alexander, 86; evacuates Andaman islands, 99; on defence of Ceylon, 106, 107; his forecast after loss of Rangoon, 106; presses for air reinforcement of India, 107, 110; sends aircraft to Ceylon, 127; on insecurity of southern India and Ceylon, 127, 129–30; his proposals for withdrawal from Burma, 152, 153; on Stilwell's appointment, 154; plans co-ordination of Command in Burma, 155; on Japanese air superiority, 161; on plan of withdrawal from Burma, 176; reports on Burma situation, 180–1; his measures to assist withdrawal, 182; his administration difficulties in India, 187, 189; organizes guerilla forces, 192; reorganizes Army Commands, 193; his fresh dispositions, 194–5; evacuates Akyab, 195; prepares for reception of 'Burcorps', 196–7, 206; on Alexander's services, 210; his plans for recovering Burma, 235, 236; his note on Combermere, 237; improves organization and training of troops, 242–5; accepts Wingate's services, 243; approves L.R.P. force, 244; 248; on weakness of India's sea and air defences, 249; at Cairo conference, 249; plans to reoccupy Akyab, 249–50, 250, 251, 257; asks for night-fighters, 260; visits Arakan, 264; his plan for concerted action with Chinese, 291, 292; on co-operation with Allies, 293; on maintenance of forces in upper Burma, 293–4, 295; on 'Anakim', 294; on offensive from Yunnan, 295; promoted, 296; on Chiang Kai-shek's attitude, 296; on C.A.T.F., 297; on operations in upper Burma, 303; visits Assam, 305, 309; on British part in a major Burma offensive, 307; on employment of L.R.P. forces, 310; intervenes in Arakan operations, 331, 334; 336, 339, 342; proceeds with 'Anakim' preparations, 361, 361–2; proposes alternative to 'Anakim', 363; on India's shipping requirements, 364–5, 366; on risk of delaying 'Anakim', 366; **agrees to** creation of G.R.E.F., 367; gives priority to China air-lift, 368; 369, 370; his views on a S.E. Asia Command, 371; on Arakan operations, 382–3; on morale of Indian Army, 384; his measures for re-training Indian Army, 385; 387; becomes Viceroy of India, 388 and fn. 1

INDEX

Wedemeyer, Brigadier-General A. C. (U.S.): 298
Wheeler, Lieut.-Colonel L. G.: 322
Wickham, Brigadier J.: 84 fn. 2; in Pegu operations, 89; fate of, 90
Willis, Vice-Admiral A. V.: in operations off Ceylon, 117, 118, 123
Wimberley, Brigadier R. A. A.: in Arakan operations, 340, 341, 342 and fn., 344, 345
Wingate, Lieut.-Colonel O. C.: arrives India, 243; his L.R.P. scheme, 243–4; commands Chindits, 244; his reasons for operations, 309–10; his plans, 310–1; his Orders of the Day, 312, 319; conducts operations, 312, 313 and fn. 1, 314, 315, 316, 317, 318, 319 and fn. 1, 320, 321, 322, 323; his note on L.R.P., 399–401; disagrees with criticisms, 403–4, 404; at 'Quadrant', 421
Winterton, Major-General T. J. W.: 160
Wood, Major-General E.: in Assam, 54
Woolner, Major-General C. G.: 403

Yamamoto, Admiral: 226, 229, 230, 232, 233, 281, 374, 377; death of, 378
Yenangyaung: oilfields denial scheme, 167; action at, 167–8, 170–3
Yorktown, U.S. aircraft carrier: 224, 226, 227, 228, 229, 230, 231; sunk, 232
Yu Fei-peng, General: 19, 20, 21
Yunnan, Chinese offensive from: projected, 291, 292, 294, 295, 296; delay in preparations for, 298–9, 302–3; postponed, 303, 304
Yunnan, defence of: 380
Yura, Jap. cruiser: 116

Zero fighter (Jap.), performance of: 260
'Z', Force: formed 260–1; in Arakan operations, 265, 333, 342–3, 345, 353 and fn. 2
Zuikaku, Jap. aircraft carrier: 227, 228, 276

7643

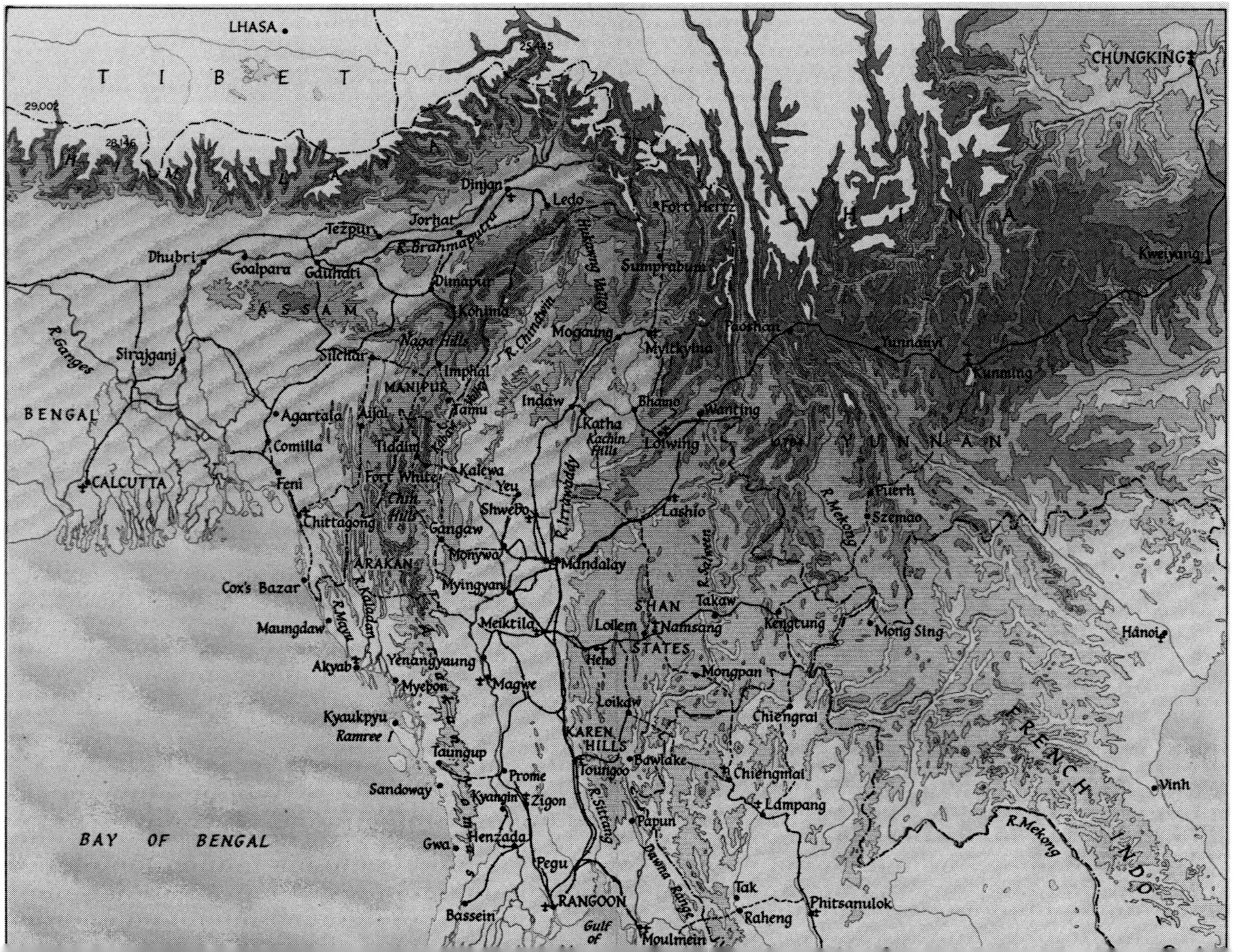

LHASA
TIBET
29,002
28,146
HIMALAYA
CHUNGKING
CHINA
Kweiyang
Dinjan
Ledo
Fort Hertz
Jorhat
Tezpur
R. Brahmaputra
Dhubri
Goalpara
Gauhati
Dimapur
Sumprabum
Hukawng Valley
ASSAM
Kohima
R. Chindwin
Mogaung
Paoshan
Yunnanyi
Kunming
R. Ganges
Sirajganj
Silchar
Naga Hills
Imphal
Myitkyina
MANIPUR
Tamu
Indaw
Bhamo
Wanting
BENGAL
Agartala
Aijal
Katha
Kachin Hills
Loiwing
YUNNAN
Comilla
Tiddim
Kalewa
CALCUTTA
Feni
Fort White
Yeu
R. Mekong
Puerh
Chin Hills
Shwebo
Lashio
Szemao
Chittagong
Gangaw
R. Irrawaddy
Monywa
Mandalay
ARAKAN
R. Salween
Cox's Bazar
R. Kaladan
Myingyan
SHAN
Takaw
R. Mayu
Meiktila
Loilem
Namsang
Kengtung
Mong Sing
Hanoi
Maungdaw
STATES
Heho
Akyab
Yenangyaung
Mongpan
Myebon
Magwe
Loikaw
Chiengrai
Kyaukpyu
Ramree I
KAREN HILLS
FRENCH INDO
Taungup
Bawlake
Prome
Toungoo
Chiengmai
Vinh
Sandoway
Kyangin
Zigon
R. Sittang
Lampang
Papun
R. Mekong
BAY OF BENGAL
Gwa
Henzada
Dawna Range
Pegu
Tak
Phitsanulok
RANGOON
Bassein
Gulf of
Moulmein
Raheng

Strategic Map
BURMA
&
MALAYA

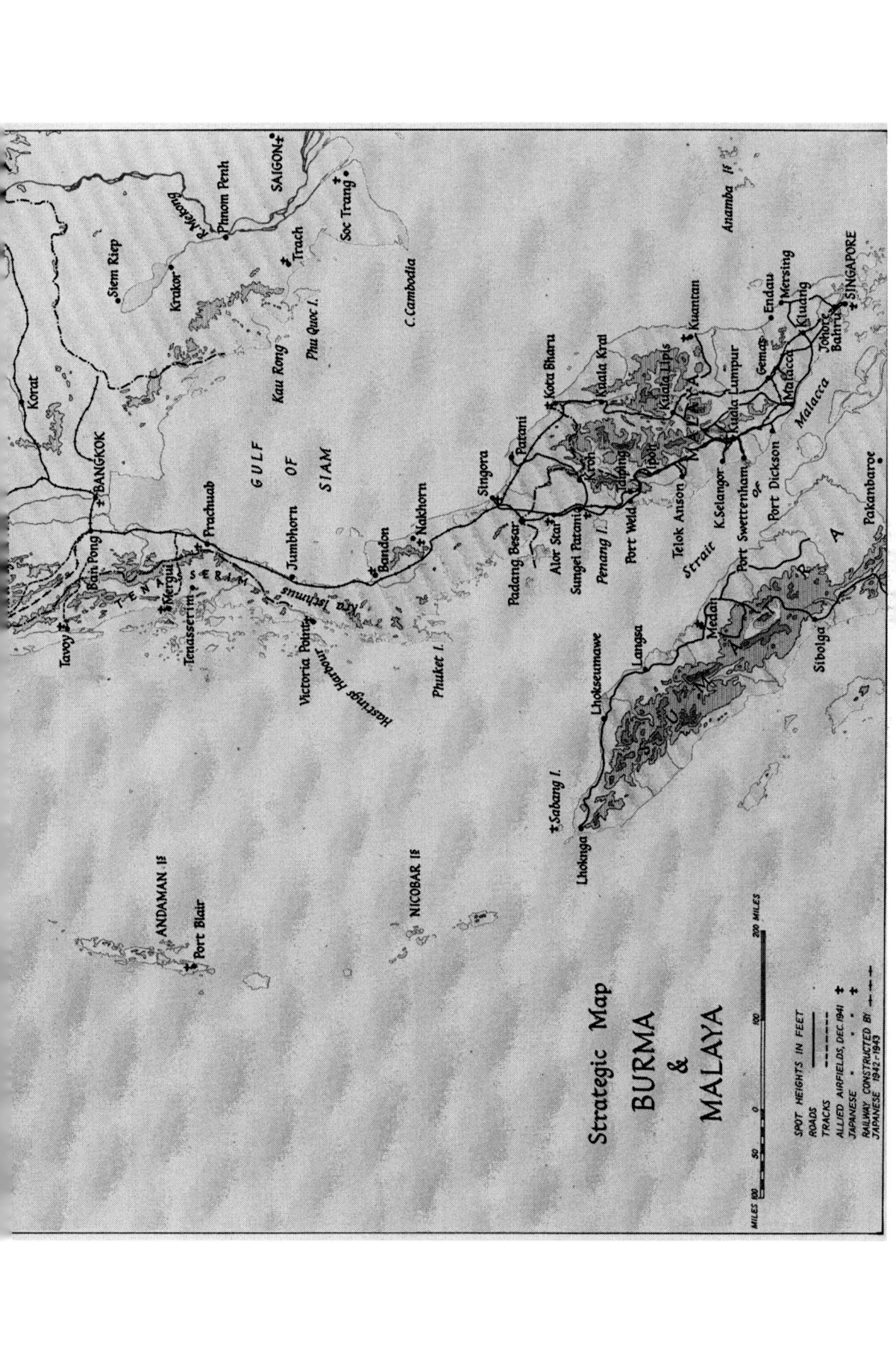

SPOT HEIGHTS IN FEET
ROADS
TRACKS
ALLIED AIRFIELDS, DEC.1941
JAPANESE
RAILWAY CONSTRUCTED BY
JAPANESE 1942-1943

MILES 100   50   0   100   200 MILES

ANDAMAN IS
Port Blair

NICOBAR IS

Korat
R. Mekong
Siem Riep
Pnom Penh
SAIGON
Krakor
Soc Trang
Trach
Phu Quoc I.
Kau Rong
C. Cambodia

BANGKOK
Bán Pong
Prachuab
GULF OF SIAM
Jumbhorn
Tavoy
Mergui
Tenasserim
Victoria Point
Hastings Harbour
Bandon
Nakhorn
Phuket I.

Sabang I.
Lhonga
Lhokseumawe
Langsa
Medan
Sibolga
Pakanbaroe

Singora
Pattani
Padang Besar
Alor Star
Sungei Patani
Penang I.
Port Weld
Taiping
Ipoh
Telok Anson
Port Swettenham
K. Selangor
Kuala Lumpur
Port Dickson
Malacca
Gemas
Johore Bahru
SINGAPORE

Kota Bharu
Kuala Krai
Kuala Lipis
Kuantan
Endau
Mersing
Kluang
Anamba Is

HISTORY OF THE SECOND WORLD WAR
UNITED KINGDOM MILITARY SERIES

Reprinted by the Naval & Military Press in twenty two volumes with the permission of the Controller of HMSO and Queen's Printer for Scotland.

THE DEFENCE OF THE UNITED KINGDOM

Basil Collier

Official history of Britain's home front in the Second World War, from the Phoney War, through the Battle of Britain and the Blitz to victory in Europe.
ISBN: 1845740556
Price £22.00

THE CAMPAIGN IN NORWAY

T. H. Derry

The catastrophic 1940 campaign which caused the downfall of Neville Chamberlain and brought Winston Churchill to power.
ISBN: 1845740572
Price: £22.00

THE WAR IN FRANCE AND FLANDERS 1939-1940

Major L. F. Ellis

The role of the BEF in the fall of France and the retreat to Dunkirk.
ISBN: 1845740564
Price £22.00

VICTORY IN THE WEST
Volume I: The Battle of Normandy

Major L. F. Ellis

The build-up, execution and consequences of D-Day in 1944.
ISBN: 1845740580
Price: £22.00

Volume II: The Defeat of Germany

Major L. F. Ellis

The final stages of the liberation of western Europe in 1944-45.
ISBN: 1845740599
Price £22.00

www.naval-military-press.com

THE MEDITERRANEAN AND MIDDLE EAST

Volume I: The Early Successes against Italy (to May 1941)

Major-General I. S. O. Playfair

Britain defeats Italy on land and sea in Africa and the Mediterranean in 1940.
ISBN: 1845740653
Price: £22.00

Volume II: The Germans Come to the Help of their Ally (1941)

Major-General I. S. O. Playfair

Rommel rides to Italy's rescue, Malta is bombarded, Yugoslavia, Greece and Crete are lost, and Iraq and Syria are secured for the Allies.
ISBN: 1845740661
Price: £22.00

Volume III: (September 1941 to September 1942) British Fortunes reach their Lowest Ebb

Major-General I. S. O. Playfair

Britain's darkest hour in North Africa and the Mediterranean, 1941-42.
ISBN: 184574067X
Price: £22.00

Volume IV: The Destruction of the Axis Forces in Africa

Major-General I. S. O. Playfair

The battle of El Alamein and 'Operation Torch' bring the Allies victory in North Africa, 1942-43.
ISBN: 1845740688
Price: £22.00

Volume V: The Campaign in Sicily 1943 and the Campaign in Italy — 3rd Sepember 1943 to 31st March 1944

Major-General I. S. O. Playfair

The Allies invade Sicily and Italy, but encounter determined German defence in 1943-44.
ISBN: 1845740696
Price: £22.00

Volume VI: Victory in the Mediterranean Part I: 1st April to 4th June 1944

Brigadier C. J. C. Molony

The Allies breach the Gustav, Hitler and Caesar Lines and occupy Rome.
ISBN: 184574070X
Price: £22.00

Volume VI: Victory in the Mediterranean Part II: June to October 1944

General Sir William Jackson

The 1944 Italian summer campaign breaches the Gothic Line but then bogs down again.
ISBN: 1845740718
Price: £22.00

Volume VI: Victory in the Mediterranean Part III: November 1944 to May 1945

General Sir William Jackson

The messy end of the war in Italy, Greece, and Yugoslavia.
ISBN: 1845740726
Price: £22.00

www.naval-military-press.com

THE WAR AGAINST JAPAN

Volume I: The Loss of Singapore

Major-General S. Woodburn Kirby

The fall of Hong Kong, Malaya and Singapore in 1941-42.
ISBN: 1845740602
Price: £22.00

Volume II: India's Most Dangerous Hour

Major-General S. Woodburn Kirby

The loss of Burma and Japan's threat to India in 1941-42.
ISBN: 1845740610
Price: £22.00

Volume III: The Decisive Battles

Major-General S. Woodburn Kirby

Turning the tide in the war against Japan at the battles of Kohima, Imphal and the Chindit campaigns.
ISBN: 1845740629
Price: £22.00

Volume IV: The Reconquest of Burma

Major-General S. Woodburn Kirby

The reconquest of Burma by Bill Slim's 'forgotten' 14th Army.
ISBN: 1845740637
Price: £22.00

Volume V: The Surrender of Japan

Major-General S. Woodburn Kirby

Victory in South-East Asia in 1945 - from Rangoon to Nagasaki.
ISBN: 1845740645
Price: £22.00

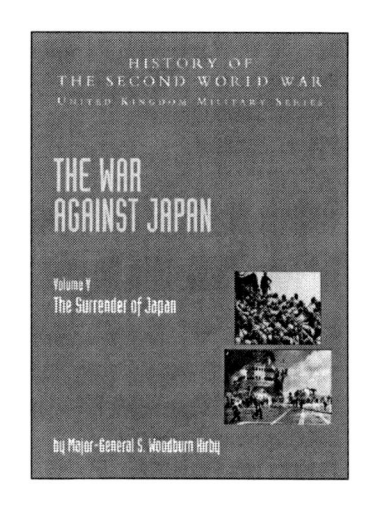

www.naval-military-press.com

THE WAR AT SEA - 1939–1945

Captain Roskill has long been recognised as the leading authority on The Royal Navy's part in the Second World War. His official History is unlikely ever to be superceded. His narrative is highly readable and the analysis is clear. Roskill describes sea battles, convoy actions and the contribution made by technology in the shape of Asdic & Radar.

Volume I: The Defensive

Captain S. W. Roskill, D.S.C., R.N.

2004 N&MP reprint (original pub 1954).
SB. xxii + 664pp with 43 maps and numerous contemporary photos.
ISBN: 1843428032
Price: £32.00

Volume II: The Period of Balance

Captain S. W. Roskill, D.S.C., R.N.

2004 N&MP reprint (original pub 1956).
SB. xvi + 523pp with 42 maps and numerous contemporary photos.
ISBN: 1843428040
Price: £32.00

Volume III: Part I The Offensive
1st June 1943-31 May 1944

Captain S. W. Roskill, D.S.C., R.N.

2004 N&MP reprint (original pub 1960).
SB. xv + 413pp with 21 maps and numerous contemporary photos.
ISBN: 1843428059
Price: £32.00

Volume III: Part 2 The Offensive
1st June 1944-14th August 1945

Captain S. W. Roskill, D.S.C., R.N.

2004 N&MP reprint (original pub 1961).
SB. xvi + 502pp with 46 maps and numerous contemporary photos.
ISBN: 1843428067
Price: £32.00

www.naval-military-press.com

Lightning Source UK Ltd.
Milton Keynes UK
173428UK00001B/5/A